TALES OF
YESTERDAY'S
NEW ENGLAND

Edited by Frank Oppel

CASTLE

CONTENTS

Lime-A Chapter of American Genealogy (1876)

HARPER'S
NEW MONTHLY MAGAZINE.

No. CCCIX.—FEBRUARY, 1876.—Vol. LII.

LYME.
A CHAPTER OF AMERICAN GENEALOGY.

MORRISON R. WAITE.

LYME is a word of four letters; and it brings the cars on the Shore-line Railroad from New York to Boston to a full stop for the space of perhaps a minute at the eastern end of the Connecticut River bridge. That is as far, probably, as your next neighbor, who is descanting learnedly upon the charms of foreign travel, will be able to enlighten you. The car window discloses little save a broad stretch of picturesque scenery, including the natural variations between a fine old sea-beach and rough and ragged undulations piled one upon another half a league inland. Should you suddenly be attacked by the spirit of inquiry, as well as by the notion that, as a native of average intelligence, you are deplorably unfamiliar with the individual features of your own country, you may find yourself, as did the writer on a certain occasion, standing conspicuously alone in apparent possession of the main outpost of this ancient and interesting town.

From Noyes Hill, a few rods north of the station, you obtain your first glimpse of the village, or rather of its roofs and chimneys and spires among the tree-tops; also of Meeting-house Hill beyond, of the salt meadows and Long Island Sound to the right, and of a beautiful river, formerly the harbor for merchant vessels when Lyme was a shipping port, winding lazily to the sea in the foreground. The ferry road crosses a snug New England bridge, and guides you to the Pierrepont House, a new summer hotel, which occupies a commanding position just outside the wealth of shade which shields the town. The name of this hotel hinges upon the romantic. It was given in honor of one of the early ministers of Lyme—Rev. Samuel Pierrepont, a brother of the wife of Rev. Jonathan Edwards—who in 1722 was drowned in crossing the Connecticut on his return from a visit to his lady-love in New Haven.

Lyme itself is the namesake of Lyme-Regis, on the south coast of England, which, with its geographical peculiarities, its history, traditions, and romances, has been so graphically described by Mr. Conway in his "South Coast Saunterings." It covers seven or eight square miles of territory, bounded on the west by the Connecticut River, and on the south by the Sound. It was settled over two centuries ago (in 1666) by an active, sensible, resolute, and blue-blooded people, who gave it a moral and intellectual character which it has never outgrown. Its climate is one of perfect health, and its people live to a great age. The salty, bracing atmosphere tends toward the increase of mental vigor as well as length of years: hence the results which we are about to chronicle. It is a town which has kept pace with the times. It has been near enough

THE WAITE MANSION.

shed where they mend breaks and shoe horses. Signs of business there are none. The scene is one of tranquillity on a broad scale.

One of the first houses which attract attention, through its associations, is a cottage-built, vine-clad, flower-surrounded dwelling, with a body-guard of aged apple-trees. It was the home of the Hon. Henry Matson Waite, Chief Justice of the State of Connecticut, the father of the present Chief Justice of the United States, and where the latter was reared into manhood.

It is only a few months since we witnessed a rare phenomenon, which is fresh in the public memory. An American citizen was elevated to one of the most dignified and important judicial offices in the world without a dissenting voice. When the nomination was announced, a flood of surprise seemed to drown captious politicians and impatient office-seekers. The choice had, singularly enough, fallen outside of their ranks. Ere they came to the surface, Congress had bowed its lofty head to merit, the newspaper press had despairingly confessed its inability to find any fault with the nominee, and the question had rung through the length and breadth of the land, and been satisfactorily answered, "What manner of man is he who is to be henceforth the custodian of the liberties of forty millions of people?"

The office had been entirely unsought. Morrison R. Waite was a lawyer with an immense and valuable practice. He was the acknowledged leader of the Ohio bar, and had been for a long series of years. He was one whose clearness and dexterity of intellect had never failed to bring order out of confusion in the most complicated law cases which had been placed in his hands. He was, moreover, a thorough gentleman, with an acute sense of justice, strong opinions, sound judgment, and a spotless private record. He had meddled little in public affairs, although repeatedly urged to accept a nomination to Congress. He had declined a seat upon the bench of the Su-

the metropolis to partake of its literary culture and many-sided opportunities, and sufficiently remote to escape its dissipating wastes, and it has always maintained a self-respecting inner life. It is exceptionally rich in family reminiscence, occupies in a certain sense historic ground, and possesses elements of national interest. Lyme-Regis is said to have been famous for its physicians. Lyme is, or ought to be, famous for its lawyers, as it has produced more than any other town of its size on this continent, or any other continent, and not only lawyers, "whose trade it is to question every thing, yield nothing, and talk by the hour," but eminent judges, Senators, and Governors, its latest and grandest achievement being a Chief Justice of the United States.

As you proceed from the hotel, "The Street" springs upon you like a new character in a novel. There is no warning of its nearness until you are among its soft shadows. It has a fascinating air of easy old-fashioned elegance, is a mile and a half long, is wide enough to swallow a whole family of New York city streets, is lined with handsome grandfatherly-looking trees, and mansions, some modest, some pretentious, some antique, are planted on either side of it at neighborly distances. Your eye will fall also upon two churches, an academy, a post-office, two or three stores, where groceries, hardware, and dry-goods dwell in harmony together, a milliner's shop with peaches and melons to sell, and a wagon

VIEW OF LYME.

preme Court of Ohio. The few instances in which he had served the government were where the mutual attraction of need and fitness were strikingly apparent. In 1849 he was in the Ohio Legislature; in 1871 he was one of the counsel of the United States at the tribunal of arbitration at Geneva, winning special praise for his labor in the commission; in 1873 he was elected to the Constitutional Convention of Ohio by the unanimous vote of both political parties, and was presiding over that body when he was notified of the action of the administration. He stands out in American history, bright and clear as sunlight, a living refutation of the popular idea that a man must have narrowed and belittled himself with district politics—in short, have gone through the worst possible training for it—before he can receive any national appointment.

Chief Justice Waite is so rounded in character and culture that there are few salient points to seize for purposes of description. He is of medium height, broad physique, square shoulders, large and well-poised head, hair and whiskers slightly flecked with gray, complexion heavy, eyes dark and piercing, and mouth indicative of decision. His general bearing is firm and self-possessed. He was born in Lyme, November 29, 1816. He studied law with his father, after graduating from Yale, but completed his forensic education in the office of the Hon. Samuel M. Young, of Maumee City, Ohio, with whom he subsequently formed a partnership that continued with marked success for nearly a quarter of a century.

He removed his family to Toledo in 1850. The name of Waite is both ancient and honorable. It dates back many centuries. The coat of arms used by the family in both Europe and America was granted in 1512. In the time of Cromwell, Thomas Wayte* was a member of Parliament and one of the judges who signed the death-warrant of Charles I. Shortly after the Restoration the family removed to this country. Thomas Waite, born in Sudbury, Massachusetts, in 1677, settled in Lyme when a young man, and married Mary Bronson, whose mother was the daughter of Matthew and Annah Wolcott Griswold.† He thus became connected with one of the most influential families in the province, and in an age when the distinctions of rank and caste were held in severe respect, even in democratic New England, "where mental and moral cultivation was the first

* From the Waite records it appears that the name anciently was written Wayte, in modern times Waite, and in some instances Wait. It also appears that the names of Thomas, Richard, John, and Joseph, especially the former two, were favorite names in the family. —*History of the Waite Family.* P. 11.

† The Griswolds and Wolcotts were of the old English gentry. Matthew Griswold, the first magistrate of the Saybrook colony, married Annah, the daughter of Henry Wolcott. Matthew Griswold was a descendant of Sir Humphrey Griswold, whose seat was at Malvern Hall. Henry Wolcott was the son and heir of John Wolcott, of Golden Manor. The manor-house is still standing, an immense castle of great antiquity, designed for the purposes of defense against the excesses of a lawless age, as well as for a permanent family residence. It is richly ornamented with carved work, and upon the walls may be seen the motto of the family arms, "*Nullius addictus jurare in verba magistri*" —inclined to swear in the words of no master. It was in keeping with the independent spirit of an English gentleman of the Middle Ages, and with that of a Puritan of a later date, who spurned the dictation of ecclesiastical wisdom. Wolcott sold a portion of his estate before he left England. He was a magistrate in the Connecticut colony, and his descendants in the direct line were magistrates, judges, and Governors for a period of over one hundred and eighty successive years.

"THE LORD'S WILL BE DONE."

Another time the deacon opposed some church measure, which was carried in spite of him. He promptly refused to pay his church taxes, and was sued, and his saddle taken for the debt. He esteemed himself deeply wronged, and rode upon a sheep-skin (wheeled vehicles had as yet hardly appeared in the colonies) forever afterward. And riding upon his sheep-skin one day, he reined his horse up to the cottage door of pretty Betty Lee. It was an old Dutch door, cut in two in the middle. She came and leaned upon the lower half, her blue eyes opened wide, and her dainty hands holding fast to a plate which she was wiping.

"Betty," said he, solemnly, "the Lord sent me here to marry you."

Betty's eyes fell upon the door-step, and so did the plate. The demure maiden, however, rallied instantly.

"The Lord's will be done," she replied.

The deacon nudged his horse and trotted slowly away, and the maiden finished washing her dishes. Betty's father was not friendly to the deacon, and tried to break the engagement. He did not succeed, as appears from the *publishment* which, according to the custom of the times, was posted upon the church door. It was the production of the prospective bridegroom, and ran thus:

"Reynold Marvin and Betty Lee
  Do intend to marry,
And though her dad op-po-sed be,
  They can no longer tarry."

They were married, and lived in peace, and in a small stone house on the west side of "The Street" brought up a large family of children, and in due course of events were gathered to their fathers. On a time-worn head-stone in the Lyme cemetery may be seen the following inscription:

"This Deacon, aged sixty-eight,
  Is freed on Earth from sarving,
May for a crown no longer wait
  Lyme's Captain Reynold Marvin."

essential for access to good society, and honest labor esteemed no shame." He was the father of eleven children. His fourth son, Richard, was twice married; his first wife was Elizabeth Marvin.

I beg pardon for the digression, but I am reminded of a little story. One of the early settlers of Lyme was Reynold Marvin. He was a rich land-holder, a militia captain, and a deacon of the church. He professed to be governed by Divine communications. On one occasion he announced that the Lord had directed him to distribute his cows among the poor. A shiftless fellow who was omitted in the distribution finally went to the deacon and said he too had received a communication from the Lord, who had sent him there for a cow.

"Of course, then, you must have a cow," was the reply. "But what sort of a cow did the Lord say I must give you—a new milch or a farrow?"

"A new milch cow, Sir."

"Indeed! Your communication could not have been from the Lord, for I have no new milch cow."

The baffled beggar departed.

The Marvins were a numerous race, and jurists were thick among them in every generation. They seem to have been native bards also. One Reynold Marvin (not the deacon) closes a letter in 1737 to Judge John Griswold in the following manner:

"Sir, this is yours, at any rate,
To read if you have leisure,
To burn, conceal, communicate,
According to your pleasure."

To return to Richard Waite. He lived on a farm in that part of Lyme known as "Four-mile River." He was a leading man and a justice of the peace, which was more of an honor in those days than we of this generation can comprehend. He had ten children by his Marvin wife, one of whom became the celebrated Judge Marvin Waite, of New London, whose son is the Hon. John Turner Waite, of Norwich. He married secondly Rebecca Higgins, the daughter of Captain Higgins, a large, handsome, imperious woman, who, as the years rolled on, devoted herself with great zeal to the education of her two sons, Remick and Ezra. When the latter graduated from Yale, and then declined to carry out her wishes by studying divinity, she was grievously disappointed; and when he crowned his irreverence by declaring in favor of law, she would have nothing more to do with him. She was severely religious, never allowed cooking or sweeping in her house on the Sabbath, and always entered church at the precise and proper moment. At one time (just prior to the Revolution) both she and her husband withdrew from the communion because of certain charges against their pastor, but finding them untrue, offered to return. Captain Higgins violently opposed such a proceeding. "What!" said he to his daughter, "has our Lyme church become a tavern, where people may go out and come in when they please, without even knocking?" Her son Remick Waite turned his attention to agriculture; but the law in his blood found vent. He was made justice of the peace when quite young, and sustained the office with dignity to the end of a long and useful life. He married Susanna Matson, who was a lady of superior talents and great worth and strength of character. It was her sister who was the mother of Hon. William A. Buckingham, late United States Senator, and the great war Governor of Connecticut, and of Rev. Dr. Samuel G. Buckingham, long a beloved and honored pastor in Springfield, Massachusetts; and she herself was the mother of Chief Justice Henry Matson Waite.

The last-named gentleman deserves honorable mention, not only because he gave direction to and helped to mould the mind which now defines for us the limits of even authority itself, but on account of his own personal excellence and valuable public services in his native State. His career was specially interesting. He graduated from Yale in 1809. The following summer he taught a small select school in New Rochelle, and one of his pupils was William Heathcote De Lancey, afterward Bishop of Western New York. He studied law with Judge Matthew Griswold, of Lyme, assisted by his brother, the accomplished Governor Roger Griswold. One of his classmates was Chief Justice Ebenezer Lane, of Ohio. As soon as he was admitted to the bar he grew steadily in importance. Prior to 1854 he had served several terms in the State Legislature, and had been for twenty years judge of the Supreme and Superior courts. He was then elected by the unanimous vote of both branches of the Legislature to the highest seat on the State bench. A well-known jurist says of him, "He contributed his full share to the character of a court whose decisions are quoted and opinions respected in all the courts of the United States, and in the highest courts of England." He was of stately presence, tall, and yet not tall, with a fair, serious face, keen blue eyes, and light hair. He was highly cultivated by study, chose to use his means for educational and religious purposes, and to help others, rather than in a pretentious mode of living, was social in his tastes, and enjoyed the perfect confidence of the entire community. His wife was of the first order of intellect, and, sympathizing in his pursuits, contributed largely to his professional successes. A fit mother was she, indeed, for her distinguished son.[*] She was Maria Selden, the daughter of Colonel Richard Ely Selden, and granddaughter of Colonel Samuel Selden, a notable officer in the Revolution, who was himself the grandson of Governor Dudley, of Massachusetts, which carries us again into lordly halls across the water, only that we are too intensely republican to need any such background and perspective. We all began on this side.

Chief Justice Morrison R. Waite married his second cousin, Amelia Warner, of Lyme, the great-granddaughter of the distinguished Colonel Selden, of Revolutionary memory. She was a beauty and a belle, a leader in fashion and society, and now, with the

---

* Chief Justice Waite is not the only lawyer son of Hon. Henry M. Waite. Richard Waite has been in active and prosperous law practice in Toledo, Ohio, for some nineteen years. Another son, George C. Waite, who died in his twenty-ninth year, was a promising lawyer in Troy, New York, and an efficient member of the Troy Board of Education. To him that city is mainly indebted for its present free-school system. Hon. Horace F. Waite, of Chicago, a prominent lawyer, member of the Illinois Legislature, etc., is a nephew of the late Hon. Henry M. Waite, and a native of Lyme. Mr. Daniel Chadwick, a leading lawyer, State's attorney, etc., residing in Lyme, is another nephew; and a niece married the accomplished scholar, Rev. Davis Clark Brainard (recently deceased), who for more than a third of a century had been the pastor of the Lyme church.

CONGREGATIONAL CHURCH.

added grace of years, no lady in the land is better fitted by education, culture, and travel for the position in Washington circles which destiny has thrust upon her. She carries good sense, refined taste, and a quiet independence of character to the front, which will prove an invaluable balance-wheel to the great social structure.

Turning north from the Waite mansion, you are confronted by a quaint homestead which seems to be taking life comfortably right in the middle of "The Street." Venerable trees rise above it, and their branches droop over its small-paned windows. Its door-step is foot-worn, its hall of entrance of a pre-Revolutionary pattern, and its whole architecture one-sided; but it has an unmistakable air of gentility. If you enter, you are plunged headlong into an antiquarian mine; paneled walls, curious cornices, enormous fire-places, high mantels, and round tables bring all your forefathers and foremothers round you in their powdered wigs and high-heeled shoes. The chairs and pictures are many of them two hundred years old. You may presume before you get to it that "The Street" ends plump against the little door-yard fence. No; "The Street" is guilty of no such impertinence. It dodges politely around the edifice, and pursues its otherwise unbending course as if accustomed to trifling obstructions.

To the south another mansion has spread itself squarely across the way. It does not, like its *vis-à-vis*, offer the apology of antiquity, but is evidently a freak of modern independence. It is high and broad, the front-door swings in the centre, and it has wings on the side and rear. It is imbedded in

shrubbery, and gay-colored flowers brighten its pretty grounds. The effect of the two houses facing each other half a mile apart is novel in the extreme. They impress you as being active participants in human affairs. They both belong to representatives of the Lord family, who were among the first settlers of Lyme, and who have in all the generations since been lavish in their distribution of doctors, judges, and divines throughout the country.

The Congregational church towers above you, like an anciently bound and well-preserved chapter of ecclesiastical history, on the corner where the ferry road enters "The Street" at right angles. It is an imposing edifice of the Ionic order of architecture, and strikingly ornate. At its right, and under its very droppings, as it were, is a large, square, old-fashioned house half hidden among stately trees, which is the home of a lady of elegant scholarship and rare accomplishments, who has for almost half a century been the educator of the ladies of Lyme, and to whom is due in large measure the credit of having developed the artistic and musical talent for which they are celebrated. Nearly opposite the church is the Mather homestead. It is gambrel-roofed, and was clapboarded before the time of sawing clapboards—when they were rived as staves are split. It has been the home of the Mathers—the ancient and learned family to which Increase and John Cotton Mather belonged—for more than a century. In the palmy days before the Revolution, when Governors drove six horses, and all the consequential families in Lyme owned negro slaves, this house was almost without a rival in the elegance of its appointments.

Side by side with it stands the oldest house in Lyme—a landmark which has been protected with generous care. Like Sydney Smith's ancient green chariot with its new wheels and new springs, it seems to grow younger each year. It is the residence of Hon. Charles Johnson M'Curdy, LL.D., an eminent jurist, who was for many years in the Connecticut Legislature, was Speaker of the House, Lieutenant-Governor of the State, United States minister to Austria, and for a long period judge of the Supreme Court. It was he who, when Lieutenant-Governor of Connecticut, in 1848, originated and carried into effect through the Legislature that great change in the common law by which parties may become witnesses in their own cases—a change which has since been adopted throughout this country and in England.

This antique dwelling has the low ceilings and the bare polished beams of the early part of the last century. Its doors and walls are elaborately carved and paneled. In the south parlor is a curious *buffet*, built with the house, containing a rare col-

CHARLES JOHNSON M'CURDY.

lection of china from ancestral families.* Between the front windows stands an elegant round table, which descended from Governor Matthew and Ursula Wolcott Griswold, and around which have sat from time to time the six Governors of the family—of whom more presently. The whole house is a museum of souvenirs of preceding generations. In the north chamber is a rich and unique chest of drawers, which belonged to the Diodati wife of Rev. Stephen Johnson; also mirrors, tables, pictures, and other relics of great antiquity. This apartment was occupied by Lafayette at two distinct eras in our national history—for several days during the Revolution, when he was entertained by John M'Curdy, while resting his troops in the vicinity; and in 1825, as the guest of Richard M'Curdy and his daughter Sarah, while on his memorable journey to Boston.

The house has historical significance through certain Revolutionary events. It was purchased by John M'Curdy in 1750, a Scotch-Irish gentleman of education and wealth, who was a large shipping merchant. He had no sympathy with the arbitrary measures of the English government, and gloried in the spirit of resistance as it developed in the colonies. (He was the "Irish

* The ancestral families connected with the M'Curdy household are the Wolcotts, Griswolds, Lords, Lyndes, Digbys, Willoughbys, Pitkins, Ogdens, Mitchells (the Scotch family of Mitchells, the same as that of "Ike Marvel"), and the Diodatis. The descent is direct, through the wife of Rev. Stephen Johnson, from Rev. John Diodati (the famous divine and learned writer of Geneva in the time of John of Barneveld), who was from the Italian nobility.

gentleman" mentioned by Gordon and Hollister as "friendly to the cause of liberty.") He was an intimate personal friend of Rev. Stephen Johnson, who was then the pastor of the Lyme church. The two had many conferences upon the subject of a possible independence of the colonies. They grew indignant with the serene composure of Governor Fitch and his associates. The first published article pointing toward unqualified rebellion in case an attempt was made to enforce the Stamp Act was from the pen of Rev. Stephen Johnson, and it was written under this roof. M'Curdy privately secured its insertion in the *Connecticut Gazette.* It was a fiery article, designed to rouse the community to a sense of the public danger. Others of a similar character soon followed; while pamphlets, from no one knew whence, fell, no one knew how, into conspicuous places. Could these walls speak, what tales they might reveal!—two sagacious and audacious men trying to kindle a fire; one feeding it with the chips of genius and strong nervous magnetism, the other fanning it with the contents of his broad purse. The alarm was sounded; organizations of the "Sons of Liberty" were formed in the various colonies; treasonable resolves were handed about with great privacy in New York, but no one had the courage to print them. John M'Curdy, being in the city, asked for them, and with much precaution was permitted to take a copy. He carried them to New England, where they were published and spread far and wide without reserve. This was in September, 1765, and before the end of the same month the famous crusade (which embraced nearly every man in the town of Lyme) moved from New Lon-

TABLE OF THE EX-GOVERNORS.

JUDGE M'CURDY'S HOME.

don and Windham counties against Mr. Ingersoll, the Stamp Commissioner. It was then and thus that the egg of the Revolution may be said to have been hatched.

When Governor Fitch proposed that he and his councilors should be sworn agreeably to the Stamp Act, Colonel Trumbull (afterward Governor) refused to witness the transaction, and left the hall. Others followed his spirited example until only four remained. Ingersoll, as the agent of Connecticut in England, had ably and earnestly opposed the passage of the odious bill; but when all was over, he had been duly qualified to officiate as stamp master. He had scarcely landed in New Haven on his return when a rumor reached him that all was not quiet beyond the Connecticut, and he started at once for Hartford. The same morning five hundred mounted men, carrying eight days' provisions, crossed the Connecticut from the east in two divisions, one at Lyme and the other farther north. Ingersoll and his guard were riding leisurely through the woods near Wethersfield, when they were suddenly met by five horsemen, who turned and joined their party. Ten minutes later they were met by thirty horsemen, who wheeled in like manner. No violence was offered, and not a word spoken. All rode on together with the solemnity and decorum of a funeral procession. Reaching a fork in the road, they were met by the whole five hundred, armed with ponderous white clubs, and led by Captain Durkee in full uniform. The line opened from right to left, and Ingersoll was received with profoundest courtesy. Martial music broke the sombre stillness, and they marched into Wethersfield, halting in the wide street. Captain Durkee then ordered Ingersoll to resign.

The latter expostulated. "Is it fair," he asked, "for two counties to dictate to the rest of the colony?"

"It don't signify to parley," was the prompt reply. "A great many people are waiting, and you must resign."

"I must wait to learn the sense of the government," said Ingersoll.

"Here is the sense of the government, and no man shall exercise your office."

"If I refuse to resign, what will follow?"

"Your fate."

"The cause is not worth dying for," said the prisoner.

A few moments later Ingersoll wrote his name to the formal resignation prepared for him. That was well, but it was not enough. He was required to swear to it in a loud voice, and then shout "Liberty and Property!" three times. This last ceremony he performed, swinging his hat about his head. He was then escorted to Hartford. He rode a white horse. Some one asked him what he was thinking of. "Death on a pale horse and hell following," was his quick retort.

They entered the capital four abreast, and formed in a semicircle about the Court-house, with Ingersoll in a conspicuous position. He was ordered to read his recantation in the hearing of the General Court. He went through the ordeal to the satisfaction of his captors, even to the shouting of "Liberty and Property!" three times again. After which the sovereigns of the soil departed in peace.

Colonel Putnam, who had been one of the instigators of the movement, was prevented by illness from being present. He was shortly summoned before Governor Fitch. In the course of the conversation which followed, the Governor asked, "What shall I do if the stamped paper is sent to me by the king's order?"

"Lock it up until *we* shall visit you."

"What will you do?"

"Demand the key of the room where it is deposited. You may, if you choose, forewarn us upon our peril not to enter the room, and thus screen yourself from blame."

"And then what will you do?"

"Send the key safely back to you."

"But if I refuse admission?"

"Your house will be leveled with the dust in five minutes."

Thus the remarkable interview ended.

Lyme was not without a Tea Party any more than some of the sea-port towns of larger pretensions. On the 16th of March, 1774, a peddler from Martha's Vineyard came into the place on horseback with one hundred pounds of tea in his saddle-bags. He was arrested and examined, and in the evening the "Sons of Liberty" assembled, built a bright fire on "The Street" just above the Congregational church, and committed the peddler's whole stock in trade to the flames, and buried the ashes on the spot.

There are several Noyes houses which it would be pleasant to visit. The first minister of Lyme was the Rev. Moses Noyes, who preached sixty-three years. He was one of the first graduates of Harvard and one of the founders of Yale. He was from a clerical family; his brother was the first minister of Stonington; his father was an eminent divine of Newbury, Massachusetts; and his father's father was a still more eminent divine of England. His wife was the granddaughter of the learned Puritan Elder William Brewster. He was a large land-holder, and owned a number of slaves. His house stood for more than a century on the site of the present residence of Richard Noyes, one of his descendants. Its windows were few, and they were located nearly as high as the top of the door. They were small and square, and leaded over the sash. They must have been painfully inconvenient to the poor Indian when he was seeking a bit of useful information concerning the domestic fireside. The doors were driven full of nails. Ugh! one can

almost catch the glitter of the tomahawk and scalping-knife.

Judge William Noyes, the grandson of the Reverend Moses, flourished a hundred years later. He was a tall, grave man, the terror of Sabbath-breakers. He never allowed a traveler to pass through Lyme on the Lord's Day without some extraordinary excuse. He was strictly conventional. When on horseback with his four grown-up sons, the latter never presumed to ride on a line with him, but always at a respectful distance behind. He inherited the large classical library of the Reverend Moses, also a writing-desk which Elder Brewster brought

BREWSTER'S WRITING-DESK.

to this country in the *Mayflower*, and which is now in the possession of his granddaughter, Mrs. Daniel Chadwick, of Lyme. Judge Noyes built the handsome old house in the northern part of "The Street," now owned by Mr. Schieffelin, of New York, the father-in-law of Rev. Mr. Sabine. By the side of one of the chimneys is a curious hole several feet deep, supposed to have been an invention of the judge to hide liquor from his negroes. Just south of this mansion, in the midst of English-looking grounds, is a great old-fashioned house, with pillars in front, the residence of Captain Robert, the youngest son of Governor Roger Griswold. And a little farther on is the pleasant home of the Huntingtons.

Black Hall is a pleasant drive of three miles from "The Street." You pass the Lyme cemetery, with its kindly shade and its ancient and modern head-stones—itself a history. You pass also a quarry of what seems to be the genuine porphyritic granite, with compact base, spotted with reddish crystals of feldspar; it is hard, and susceptible of a fine polish. The Swedes and Russians have worked a similar variety with success, and pronounce it more durable than any other material for building purposes. A polished specimen, beside one of the Scotch

APPROACH TO BLACK HALL.

granite of which Prince Albert's monument in Hyde Park is made, shows that it is of the same general character, only that the Lyme granite is the handsomer of the two. There is enough here to build a city, and it is significantly within a stone's-throw of the railroad track. Two roads diverge at the foot of Meeting-house Hill, one of which ascends that blustering height (the former site of three successive churches, two of which were burned by lightning), and passes an old burial-ground inclosed by a tumbling stone wall and overgrown by rank weeds, also the original mile-stone which, according to tradition, Franklin planted with his own hands when he was Postmaster-General of the colonies. It was the old stage route from New York to Boston, and most of the illustrious men of the olden time have traveled over it. The lower road passes the Champlin house, which was the scene of the marriage of the famous General Buckner to a daughter of Colonel Kingsbury. He was then a young West Pointer, and was married in his uniform. Just as the final words of the ceremony were being pronounced,

there was an alarm of fire; a neighbor's house was burning. The bridegroom threw off his coat, and, with the minister and others, ran to extinguish the flames; then returned, recoated, kissed his bride, and received the congratulations of his friends.

Black Hall, the seat of the Griswolds, is a cluster of half a dozen houses, in the midst of a thick grove of trees, on the fine segment of land which slopes into the Sound so far that in winter the sun rises and sets over the water. This large property was a fief or feudal grant to the first Matthew Griswold in 1645. He built a log-house—the first house in Lyme — upon the site of the mansion, which you see at the end of the private entrance, and dug a well, which is still in existence. He sent a negro slave to occupy the premises, as the Indians were too hostile for him to venture to remove his family so far from the fort at Saybrook. Tradition says that the log-house was called the "black's hall," which is supposed to have been the origin of the pleasant-sounding name which the place now bears.

The old gubernatorial mansion of Governor Roger Griswold commands a magnificent view of the Sound and its shipping. It is the home of Mr. Matthew Griswold, one of the Governor's sons. It is a well-preserved specimen of antiquity; and one of those dwellings the geography of which can not be read upon the face of it. The rooms seem numberless, and vary in size and shape until the explorer is hopelessly confused. It is full of suggestion, for Governor Roger Griswold was one of our country's ablest statesmen. He was called, at the age of thirty-two, from a valuable law practice into the councils of the nation, and was pronounced one of the most finished scholars in Congress, where he served ten years —during a part of the administration of

GOVERNOR GRISWOLD'S HOUSE.

Washington, the whole of that of Adams, and a portion of that of Jefferson. He was a brilliant talker, and profoundly versed in law. He was the first cousin of Oliver Wolcott, who was at the same time Secretary of the Treasury. He was nominated Secretary of State in 1801, but saw fit to decline. He was subsequently appointed judge of the Superior Court, elected Lieutenant-Governor, and finally Governor of Connecticut, in which office he died, in 1812. He sleeps in the Griswold grave-yard, and his tomb, rising against a background of green, may be seen as you cross Black Hall River. He was the son of Governor Matthew Griswold, who was conspicuous for the energy of his counsels and active measures during the Revolution. Governor Matthew, when a young man, was grave, shy, tall, and somewhat awkward. He courted a young lady in Durham, who put him off, delaying to give an answer in the hope that a doctor, whom she preferred, would propose. He finally tired of his long rides on horseback, and suspecting the state of her mind, pressed for an immediate decision.

"I should like a little more time," reiterated the fair one.

"Madame, *I will give you a lifetime*," was the lover's response; and rising with dignity, he took his leave.

The lady took her lifetime, and died single, as the doctor never came forward. Young Griswold returned to Lyme so deeply mortified with the failure of his suit that he was little disposed to repeat the process of love-making. In course of events his second cousin, Ursula Wolcott, came on a visit to Black Hall. She was a modern edition of her grandmother, the historical Martha Pitkin, bright, beautiful, accomplished, and self-reliant. She was a little older than Matthew. She became assured that his affections were centred upon herself, but he was provokingly reticent. Meeting him on the stairs one day, she asked, "What did you say, Cousin Matthew?"

"I did not say any thing," he replied.

A few days later, meeting him, she asked in the same tone, "What did you say, Cousin Matthew?"

"I did not say any thing," he replied as before.

Finally, meeting him upon the beach one morning, she again asked, "What did you say, Cousin Matthew?"

"I did not say any thing," he still replied.

"It is time you did," she remarked, with emphasis.

Whereupon something was said, the result of which was a wedding, and the brilliant bride had a queenly reign at Black Hall. No lady in American history could introduce you to more Governors among her immediate relations. Her father was Governor Roger Wolcott, her brother was Governor Oliver Wolcott, her nephew was the second Governor Oliver Wolcott, her cousin was Governor Pitkin, her husband was Governor Matthew Griswold, and her son was Governor Roger Griswold.

Black Hall has always been famous for the beauty and spirit of its women. Governor Matthew Griswold had eight dashing sisters, who were known as the "Black Hall boys," from being given to all manner of out-of-door sports; they could ride, leap, row, and swim, and they had withal the gifts and graces which won them distinguished husbands. Phebe married Rev. Jonathan Parsons, the Lyme minister, whose clerical career did not run smoothly, in consequence of his admiration for Rev. George Whitefield. He was a *protégé* of Rev. Jonathan Edwards, and a man of excellent parts. A fair, frank, manly, good-humored face looks down from his portrait. He had a passion for fine clothes, for gold and silver lace, and ruffled shirt fronts, which distressed some of the good Puritans in his church. His wife was given to practical jokes. One evening as he was about to leave the house for the weekly prayer-meeting—after taking a last look in the mirror to satisfy himself that every particular hair was stroked the right way—she playfully threw her arms about his neck, passed one hand over his face, and kissed him. As he entered the church he was nettled by a ripple of smiles which ran through the congregation, and he noticed that some of the brethren were eying him suspiciously. Presently it was whispered in his ear that his face was blackened. On another occasion his fun-loving wife wickedly clipped a leaf from his sermon, and sat in the little square pew before him, quietly fanning herself, and enjoying his embarrassment when he reached the chasm. She was remarkably clever with her pen, and it is said often wrote sermons herself. She was the mother of the celebrated Major Samuel Holden Parsons, and grandmother of Simon Greenleaf, professor of law at Cambridge, author of valuable legal works, etc.*

* In illustration of the statement concerning the remarkable number of lawyers, as well as other brilliant men and women of Lyme origin in different parts of the country, I will mention a few well-known names; but it must not be understood that I am in the garden to cull all the flowers. Chief Justice Ebenezer Lane, of Ohio, was a grandson of Governor Matthew Griswold, and Judge William Lane is a grandson of Governor Roger Griswold. One of the sisters of Governor Matthew married Elijah Backus, of Norwich, from whom descended General John Pope, of the late war. Another sister married Judge Hillhouse, whose descendants are among the prominent families of New Haven. General Joseph G. Perkins, of the late war, also Colonel John Griswold, an accomplished young officer who fell at Antietam, were grandsons of Governor Roger Griswold. Rev. George Griswold, pastor of the East Lyme church for thirty-six years, and Rev. Sylvanus Griswold, of Feeding Hills, were of the same family. Also Nathaniel Lynde Griswold and George Griswold, the great East India importers of New York; the wife of Hon. Frederick Frelinghuysen; the wife of Senator Lanman; the wife of Senator Foster; the wife of John Lyon Gardiner, of Gardiner's Island; the wife of President Tyler; Chief Justice S. T. Hosmer; and Eleanora, the wife of Virginia Cenci, Prince of Vicovaro, present Grand Chamberlain to the King of Italy. The prince is a lineal descendant of the family of Beatrice Cenci, and resides in the ancient Cenci palace. The Seldens have contributed largely to the eminence of our country. Conspicuous among the jurists of the present generation are Judge Samuel Lee Selden and Judge Henry R. Selden, of New York. We may add to the list Hon. Dudley Selden, member of Congress; General M'Dowell, of army notoriety; President Nott; Rev. Dr. Samuel Nott; Professor Eaton, of Yale; A. L. Backus, of Toledo; the wife of Rev. Leonard W. Bacon; Mrs. General Lewis Cass; and Mrs. General Hunt, of Toledo. A daughter of John M'Curdy married the famous and witty ecclesiastic Rev. Nathan Strong, of Hartford; another married Dr. Channing, of Boston. A daughter of Lynde M'Curdy married Hon. John Allen, member of Congress; and their son, Hon. John W. Allen, was also a member of Congress. Robert M'Curdy, the great importing merchant of New York, is a brother of Judge M'Curdy, and the daughter of the latter is the wife of Professor E. E. Salisbury, of New Haven. From the Smiths, Demings, Pecks, Sills, Marvins, Lords, Colts, Elys, Sterlings, Champions, and other Lyme families, the army is legion. Senator Truman Smith; Senator Nathan Smith; Judge Nathaniel Smith; Rev. Matthew Hale Smith; Colonel Henry C. Deming, member of Congress; Rev. Dr. Edward Strong, of Boston; Judge Strong, of St. Louis; Judge Strong, of the United

Two generations farther back we have a curious episode, in which Matthew Griswold the second figured as "Lyme's champion." He was a tall, broad-chested, powerful young athlete, and a justice of the peace. There was a troublesome controversy between New London and Lyme about a tract of land some four miles in width, which both claimed. One summer morning in 1671 a party of Lyme hay-makers went into the controverted meadow to mow the grass, led by Griswold. About the same time a company from New London entered upon the other side. They all pitched in together, and such a scrimmage was never witnessed before nor since in the land of steady habits. It began with words, but quickly came to blows with fists, feet, scythes, rakes, whetstones, and clubs. There were other justices of the peace present besides Griswold, and the belligerents were pretty generally arrested. They went to law, each party indicting the other; twenty-one from New London and fifteen from Lyme. The former were fined £9, the latter £5. The fines were remitted by the General Court of Connecticut, and the land divided between the two towns. But the dividing line was not determined. Then arose another civil or uncivil war. New London kindly offered to take three miles and give one mile to Lyme, and Lyme made a similar disinterested proposition to New London. The wrangling continued for some months. Tradition says "it was finally agreed, since the tract was not worth the expense of further litigation, to settle the question by a *private combat.*" This decision was piously recorded as "*leaving it to the Lord.*" Each town chose two champions, appointed a day, and people gathered in great numbers to see the fight. Matthew Griswold and William Ely fought for Lyme, and so valorously and well that they won the victory, and New London relinquished all claim to the property.

States Supreme Court; Rev. Dr. Stone, of San Francisco; Mrs. Rev. Dr. Hubbell, author of *Shady Side*; Hon. David M. Stone, editor of *Journal of Commerce*; Mrs. Professor Hoppin, of Yale Theological Seminary; Dr. John Peck; Rev. Thomas Ruggles Gold Peck; Judge Seth E. Sill; General Theodore Sill, member of Congress; Miss Sill, of the Rockford Seminary; Judge William Marvin, of Key West, Florida; Judge Richard Marvin, of New York; George Griffin, the famous New York lawyer; Rev. Edward Dorr Griffin, president of Williams College; the inventor of Colt's revolvers; Judge Colt, of the Supreme Court; Judge Colt, of St. Louis; Hon. Alfred Ely, member of Congress, author, etc.; Elias H. Ely, fifty years a member of the New York bar; Abner L. Ely; D. J. Ely; Z. S. Ely, prominent New York merchants; Hon. Ansel Sterling, member of Congress; General Elisha Sterling; Hon. Micah Sterling, member of Congress (all lawyers of eminence); General Epaphroditus Champion, member of Congress; Rev. Henry Champion; Hon. Aristarchus Champion, of Rochester; Chief Justice William L. Storrs; Hon. Henry Storrs, member of Congress; the two wives of Governor Trumbull, and a host of others.

THE GRISWOLD GRAVE-YARD.

A pretty little romance once occurred in this same notable vicinity, which gave the name to "Bride Brook." In the winter of 1646–47 a young couple in Saybrook were to be married. The only magistrate qualified to perform the rite was absent. They sent to New London for John Winthrop, who replied that he would meet them at the river, which was then regarded as the boundary line between Saybrook and New London. It was some six or seven miles east of the Connecticut River, but thither the bridal party proceeded through deep snow-drifts. Arriving on the bank of the specified stream, they found it impassable on account of the ice, which was breaking. Consequently the marriage service was pronounced upon the New London side, and the loving pair promised to love, honor, and obey upon the Saybrook shore, and went their way rejoicing.

Lyme was formerly a part of Saybrook, the settlement of which commenced in 1635. The region was selected for the commencement of empire by Cromwell, Hampden, and several English noblemen who had become dissatisfied with the management of civil and religious affairs under Charles I., and fully determined to remove permanently to the wilds of America. They organized a company, and secured a patent for a large portion of Connecticut, and sent John Winthrop the younger to take possession and build a fort at the mouth of the Connecticut River. It was called Saybrook, in honor of Lord Say and Seal, and Lord Brook, who were foremost in pushing the enterprise. It was located on a peninsula, circular in form, and connected to the main-land by a narrow neck over which the tide sometimes flowed, and was considered safe from any sudden incursion of the Indians. Two great handsome squares were laid out on the rolling land near the fort, designed as a building site for palatial residences.

Colonel George Fenwick was the only one of the original patentees who came to abide in Saybrook. Cromwell and some others actually embarked in the Thames, but were stopped by an order from the king. Colonel Fenwick was accompanied by his young, lovely, golden-haired, sunny-tempered wife, Lady Alice Boteler. She had been reared in the bosom of English luxury and refinement, but could adapt herself to pioneer life, and made her rude home in the quaint fort bright with wild flowers and merry with laughter. She brought with her a "shooting gun," with which she used to practice, to the great diversion of her neighbors, and she had "pet rabbits," and a little garden which grew table delicacies. She was fond of out-of-door exercises, and was often seen cantering over the country on horseback. She had few associates—Mrs. John Winthrop, whose home during that period was on Fisher's Island, Mrs. Lake, a sister of Mrs. Winthrop, Mrs. Annah Wolcott Griswold, and Colonel Fenwick's two sisters (one of whom married Richard Ely), comprised about the whole list. She died after nine years of Saybrook life, and was buried within the embankment walls of the fort. Colonel Fenwick soon after returned to England, where he was one of the judges who tried the unhappy Charles I. He left his private affairs in this country in charge of Matthew Griswold, who erected the monument over Lady Fenwick's grave, which for two and a quarter centuries was an object of sorrowful interest on the treeless, flowerless, desolate bluff which overlooks the flats and shallows at the mouth of the Connecticut River. It is, however, no longer there, but occupies a shady nook in the old Saybrook cemetery. Four years since an enterprising railroad corporation found the world so narrow that it must needs plow directly through this sacred spot, and not only rob us of the last shovelful of earth which our heroic ancestors heaped together, but heartlessly overturn the "quiet couch of clay" upon which Lady Fenwick had so long rested. Her remains were re-interred with imposing ceremonies. Her golden hair was found in a perfect con-

LADY FENWICK'S TOMB.

dition, or nearly so, and a lock of it is preserved in an air-tight box in the Acton Library at Saybrook.

By-the-way, this library, which was dedicated with great enthusiasm on July 4, 1874, will repay a visit. It is an institution which originated with the ladies of Saybrook about twenty years ago, but which remained to take definite shape through the gift of a lot to the trustees by Hon. Thomas C. Acton, the well-known President of the Board of Police Commissioners in New York city in the time of the draft riot. He was also chiefly instrumental in raising funds to erect the handsome building, which, in grateful recognition, was christened the Acton Library. It contains some seventeen hundred volumes already, and the germ of a museum of relics and curiosities. It is situated on one of the principal streets of Saybrook, directly opposite the summer residence and attractive grounds of Mr. Acton.

An attempt was made in 1675 to annex Saybrook and its surrounding territory to New York. Sir Edmund Andros appeared off the coast with an armed fleet, and demanded the surrender of the fort in the name of the Duke of York.

"We will die first," was the reply of Captain Bull, the commander.

The garrison was immediately drawn up and prepared for action. Andros did not wish to incur bloodshed, and sent pacific messages. He finally proposed an interview with the officers, and landed. He was received courteously. But when he ordered the duke's patent and his own commission to be read, Captain Bull, whose messenger, sent in hot haste

to Hartford, had just returned with instructions from the General Court, stepped forward and forbade the reading. The clerk of Andros attempted to go on.

"Silence!" roared Captain Bull; and then with deep sonorous voice he recited the protest of the Hartford authorities. When he had finished, Sir Edmund Andros, pleased with his boldness and soldier-like bearing, asked his name.

"My name is Bull, Sir."

"Bull! It is a pity your horns were not tipped with silver!"

Andros wrote to his royal master after his return to New York that nothing could be done with officers or people in Connecticut, for the existing government was bent upon defending its chartered rights.

Saybrook's historical point, where the lordly palaces of Europe were to have been and are not, was the seat of the first Yale College. The building was one story high and eighty feet long, and, together with the lot, was a donation from Nathaniel Lynde, the great Saybrook land-holder, who was a grandson of the Earl of Digby. The books which formed the college library were donated by the ministers in the vicinity. The scholarly people of Lyme and Saybrook enjoyed the privilege of attending fifteen Commencements, and sixty of the graduates of that period afterward became distinguished in the ministry. When the subject was agitated of removing the institution to New Haven, these two ancient towns at the Connecticut's mouth arrayed themselves in open opposition. But potent influences were working elsewhere. The Governor and his royal council finally visited Saybrook in state—it was in the summer of 1718—and presently a warrant was issued to the sheriff to convey the college library to New Haven. He proceeded to the house where the books were kept, and found resolute men assembled to resist his authority. He summoned aid, entered forcibly, and placed the books

THE ACTON LIBRARY, SAYBROOK.

under a strong guard for the night. In the morning every cart provided for the journey was found broken, and the horses were indulging in the liberty of a free country. Other conveyances were obtained, and the troubled sheriff was escorted out of Saybrook by a company of soldiers. But, alas! the bridges on the road to New Haven were all destroyed. After multiplied delays and vexations the end of the route was reached, when, lo! three hundred of the books were missing, also valuable papers. It was whispered that they had been spirited away and buried.

Saybrook is larger than Lyme, and more given to business. Its streets are broad and beautiful, and well lined with the venerated trees which the first settlers planted. Its homes are mostly surrounded with spacious gardens and grounds. It has a newness hardly in keeping with its length of years, but many houses are standing, nevertheless, which have tasted the salt air for three and four half-centuries, and are full of historic charms and associations. Prominent among them is the Hart mansion. It was built by Captain Elisha Hart, the son of the old minister of Saybrook, and brother of Major-General William Hart, one of the original purchasers of the three and one-half million acres of land in Ohio known as the "Western Reserve." Captain Hart married the daughter of John M'Curdy, of Lyme, and they were the parents of seven of the most beautiful women on this side of the Atlantic. Two of these daughters were courted and wed under this roof by the distinguished naval officers, Commodore Isaac and Commodore Joseph Hull. It was the residence of Commodore Isaac Hull and his family for many years. A third daughter married Hon. Heman Allen, United States minister to South America. A fourth married the celebrated Rev. Dr. Jarvis. The house teems with incident, and many a thrilling romance might be gathered from its silent halls. Saybrook has five miles or more of sea-beach, presided over by Fenwick Hall, a great elegant summer hotel, which draws annually hundreds of visitors.

Lyme and Saybrook are about ten minutes by railroad apart; by carriage and the picturesque old Connecticut River ferry-boat, with its white sail, perhaps an

hour. Lyme embraces a number of small villages scattered over its wide territory, and the intervening drives are exceptionally attractive. The road to North Lyme winds among sharp steeps, wild crags, around glimmering lakes, through weird ravines and darksome gorges, every now and then emerging into the broad sunlight upon the top of some remarkable elevation, where magnificent views may be obtained, stretching for miles up the Connecticut and across the Sound, with the valleys of soft green, the pretty curving creeks reflecting the blue sky, and Lyme half hidden among the leaves below. The variety in the landscape would drive an artist to distraction. It is a singular mixture of the wild and the tame, of the austere and the cheerful.

THE HART MANSION.

Life-Savers on
Old Malabar
(1908)

THE DUNES OF MONOMOY

Life-savers on Old Malabar

BY WILLIAM INGLIS

W ITHIN the memory of men still living, geographies contained this bit of knowledge:

Q. What three capes are on the east coast of Massachusetts?
A. Cape Ann, Cape Cod, and Cape Malabar.

Malabar—how the name rings of fat galleons and hungry pirates!—is the Monomoy of to-day, the lean elbow of Cape Cod thrust boldly out between the Atlantic Ocean and Nantucket Sound. Three life-saving stations on this short strip of sand bear testimony to the dangers of the coast, and it is in the house farthest seaward, the station at Monomoy Point, that Captain Joseph Kelley and his seven rowing-men are sedulously training and waiting for a challenge from the sea. Theirs is a boat-race worth winning—not a struggle for mere dollars or the applause of cheering spectators, but a heart-breaking combat whereof the reward is a handful of human lives dragged back from the edge of the next world. Fifty-two crews saved in the five years since the station was founded is their record.

Upon the sands of Monomoy the sea is always trying its white-edged teeth. The cape is such a shifting ridge of dunes loosely thrown together that he who stands on it must often find himself watching, listening, waiting, with a vague sense of doom, for the one great wave that will surely come and sweep its slack bulk far under the ocean. As the swift currents go racing by, now east, now west, they are ever shearing off part of the land and adding it to the banks and shoals that lie in wait on every hand for lives of men and the bones of stout ships.

Curious old foreign barks with prows quaintly carved, trim Yankee schooners that once looked smart enough to sail themselves, big ships and little, are lying dismembered on the shoals and beaches of this sea graveyard. The skippers lost their way in the fog, they misread the chart, they forgot the meaning of the light, and so staggered to their end. " Dry lead - line," is the epitaph of most of them, for if they cared enough to take frequent soundings all the Atlantic coast is so well charted that they could not go wrong. But no; the wise man has been over the road so often he needs no soundings even in thick weather; so the line lies snug in its coil—and presently a treacherous slant in the current veers the ship toward the trap, and in the twinkling of an eye the roar of breakers under her forefoot is followed by the crash of masts and spars swept by the board, and the deadly crunching of the ship's body on the close-packed sands. If she is a rotten old hulk sent to sea to gather a harvest of insurance, the fate of her company is swift and certain. A few blows of the ponderous waves, a few plunges of her worn old frame down upon the rigid sands, and she is dashed to pieces as swiftly as a house of laths. Four, five, half a dozen cheap sailormen are whirled away in the white spume, trying to swim in a madness of leaping waters where a gull could not live. Not so much as a fragment of clothing is washed up on the beach to tell their fate.

But if the ship is stout she will hold together for hours, and then her crew will be saved beyond doubt. They will be saved according to rule and formula in such cases made and provided by Uncle Sam, carried out precisely, amid the

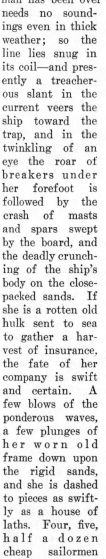

OFF DUTY—A GAME OF "63"

shrieking of the no'theaster and the thundering of the surges, by crews of men who regard the most terrifying displays of ocean's rage with the calm and cheerful impersonal concern that doctors give to an interesting case. Of danger to themselves they do not think. They are simply playing a game with Death. They play it with scrupulous regard to form. Form always wins—at least, almost always wins.

"Give me good gear and a crew that know their business," any life-saving captain will tell you, "and the sea hasn't been kicked up yet that 'll do us any great harm."

All through the night the surfmen are patrolling the beach at Monomoy, as they do from Quoddy Head to Cape Florida, meeting in the little shanty on a sand-dune called Half-way House to tell one another the news of the hour, and to exchange the numbered brass tags by which the captains may know that the watch has gone faithfully to the end of his post. For ten months in the year the vigilance is not relaxed. During June and July the crews are rewarded for their year's labor by the gift of a generous vacation—without pay. They may fish or farm or do what they will for a living. The captains then sit, each one alone, in the life-saving stations, and if any ship is foolish enough to get wrecked at this time, when, according to the rules of Uncle Sam, there should be neither storm nor wreck, the nearest captain picks up a scratch crew of fishermen and other longshore folk and does the best he can to save lives. Storms and wrecks do occur now and then in these periods, but they really should not; and, therefore, Congress in its wisdom refuses to keep the life-savers on duty. From the wisdom of Congress there is no appeal.

Certainly there are more delightful places than the dunes of Monomoy on a raw, darksome March afternoon, when sand-drifts spin through the air, driven by a no'theast gale, stinging like an adder and blinding whom they assail, and the sun is hidden by rushing, ragged, leaden clouds that threaten to discharge at any moment a whirl of icy flakes upon the hissing sea. Yet no place could be more inspiring in its suggestions of heroes ever striving for the greatest prize in the world—the safety of their fellow men. There was no hint of a heroic pose in the homely welcome the cap'n and his hospitable crew gave to the unexpected visitors.

"Come right in and warm ye!" cried the leader. "Must be pretty cold after that walk along the beach. Cup of hot coffee 'll hearten ye up some."

The eight husky men were sitting not too far from the kitchen stove, puffing on pipes of corn-cob and brier, filling the room with strong tobacco smoke and deliberate conversation. Not one of them seemed over one hundred and sixty pounds, but they were of the sort of stuff that would make any rowing coach's heart hunger to train — clear-skinned, deep-chested men, quick and well-balanced, of medium size, but tough as strips of whalebone, bright-eyed and alert; the product of careful selection trained to the minute by right living, good feeding, and lively work in the brisk salt air. Outside, the gale roared and whistled. Now and then a spurt shook the solid wooden house and rattled the thick-framed windows.

The captain led his visitors up the dragging path, ankle-deep in sand, to the top of Gull Point, the very jumping-off place of Monomoy, with the sea grumbling at its foot. One sweeping glance around the horizon showed that the station is perched in the midst of perils, like a crafty spider in the heart of his web. Only, this spider is benevolent in his craft and saves life instead of taking it. Northeast of us the waves were pounding upon Bearse's Shoal; due east lay Pollock Rip, which has cost the lives of scores of ships and many seamen; southeast lurked Stone Horse, Little Round Shoal and Great Round Shoal, well off shore, while close at hand to the south'ard and sou'west'ard were the Shovelful and Handkerchief shoals. And this long spit of shifting sand under our feet afforded the only refuge from all the malices of sea and gale and shoal.

"It's the worst trap I ever saw," said one of the visitors. "I don't understand how your crew can risk their lives in such a place."

"It's a great game—if you like it," the cap'n replied. "Of course you've got to like it or the work would be too hard; and then your gear must be kept in first-class condition, and you've always got to keep cool and use judgment. That's about all you need—judgment and don't get wrought up, no matter how bad things look."

Truly, there must be all the fascination of a game in this serene and skilful contest with raging Death. It cannot be the bait of wages that attracts these heroes to the service. The captains receive $800 a year, and the surfmen $50 a month. During the two months of unpaid vacation they get $3 apiece for each occasion of service. No; there is no money lure in this game. The service

Painting by Harold Matthews Brett

ALL THROUGH THE NIGHT SURFMEN ARE PATROLLING THE BEACH

THEIRS IS A BOAT-RACE WORTH WINNING

requires men of perfect health and strength. Whenever the surgeon discovers surfman or captain to have fallen below perfect condition, he is incontinently put out, no matter how many years he may have spent in life-saving. And there is no pension. Mr. Kimball, the superintendent of the department, has tried again and again to persuade Congress to grant pensions to these men, but Congress in its wisdom has always said no. And from the wisdom of Congress there is no appeal.

A stately procession was marching past Monomoy. One mile to the east'ard we could indistinctly make out, through the gray smother, a great tugboat, followed at long intervals by three huge barges with tall pole rig. This was a coal tow bound from Norfolk to Boston. In spite of the gale, they were making good weather of it; but if the storm should increase, and the heavy tow lurch too savagely upon the hawsers, then one of the barges, or all of them, might break adrift and — sailors' lives are cheap. Coal-towing is the least romantic and most dangerous business that is carried on at sea.

Two deep-laden coal-barges came up on Shovelful Shoal in a blow on March 12, 1902. The *Fitzpatrick* settled on the sands not too far off the beach, about a quarter of a mile south of Gull Point. The *Wadena* struck one-quarter of a mile farther out to sea. When the weather cleared, a few days later, Captain Mack, a stalwart young Ohioan who owned the *Wadena,* determined to do his own salvage work. He chartered two tugs in Boston, and brought over four Portuguese laborers from Marthas Vineyard to shovel off the coal. With the cargo jettisoned, it would be an easy matter for the stout tugs to haul the light barge off the sands. The men worked hard under the spur of the owner's presence, and on March 16 the *Wadena* was almost afloat. The tugs passed hawsers to her and crowded on all steam. She shook and groaned, but the sands still held her fast.

Toward sunset it came on to blow from the southeast. The sea rose. Vague masses of fog came rolling in. The skippers of the tugboats held a consultation, and then hailed the *Wadena* and ordered the hawsers cast off. When these had been properly coiled down, the old-

Painting by Harold Matthews Brett

FIRING THE GUN—SENDING A LINE TO A WRECKED SHIP OFF SHORE

est skipper ran as close to the barge as he dared and shouted a warning to Captain Mack.

"Goin' to be a nasty gale for a couple o' days," he said. "We're goin' over to Hyannis to wait till she blows out. You an' your men come aboard of us."

"No," Captain Mack yelled back. "No, 'twon't amount to much. We're going to stay right here. You fellows 'll be 'round here in the morning again, all right."

The tugs backed carefully away from the big waves that were leaping and growling at the edge of the shoal, set their course to the south'ard, passed safely around Handkerchief Shoals Lightship, and were seen by the bargemen no more.

How the five wreckers passed the night is easily guessed. Seafarers from their youth, they had no fear of an ordinary March storm. The barge, they knew, was new and very stout. What if the ground-swell did lift her now and then and drop her groaning on the flinty sands? She was an able ship built to stand hard knocks, and not one of her seams was started in spite of all the sea's bombardment. So they ate their supper with good relish, smoked contentedly over their cards. and laughed at the foolish captains who had run away from no danger at all. All hands turned in at nine o'clock, and if any one lost sleep it was only the owner, who went on deck at times to see how fared the ship in which he had invested his fortune.

By daybreak the storm had increased. The wind was stronger. A drizzling rain set in. An occasional wall of fog still came rolling in from the southeast. The tide was slack, but would soon begin to ebb against the wind. A heavy ground-swell was running in from the Atlantic in the east. Yet none of these things worried Captain Mack. He knew how far he could depend on his able ship, and he joked with his Portuguese, and ate a big breakfast with them, and offered to bet that they'd all be safe at home within two days. Home!

A sturdy little man they called Manuel ran up to Mack at seven o'clock. His swarthy face had paled to the hue of new-carved meerschaum.

"Ah, Capitano!" he cried, "vaire bad for de sheep. She busta bot' sides an' all gone to de pieces—got two, t'ree feet of water in her. I tell you for sure!"

Mack hurried below and found that Manuel had spoken the truth; there was three feet of water in the hold. He was much cast down. The sea was getting its clutch on the Wadena. If this pounding continued she must soon break up. Disconsolate, he went into the cabin, brought up an American flag, bent it on to the main-rigging, union down, and raised it to the masthead. It was his acknowledgment of defeat by the forces of sea and gale. Whatever might happen now to him and his Portuguese was in the hands of Fate and the life-savers. Soon the barge would be broken apart under their feet.

Marshal Eldredge, keeper of the life-saving station at Monomoy, waded through the sand and dead weeds to Gull Point at eight o'clock that morning. He knew there were five men aboard the Wadena, and the rising gale made him anxious. In a clear interval, between two walls of fog, he made out the signal of distress. He ran to the telephone in the little shelter on the Point and called up his station.

"Hello, Seth," he said. "This is Eldredge. Say, they're in trouble on that Wadena and want to be took ashore. Come on!"

Seth Ellis, the No. 1 man of the crew, wasted no time in explanations as he ran from the telephone to the boat-room.

"Stand by!" he called. And the men dropped their pipes and ran after him to the surf-boat—a long, handsome craft, sharp at each end, like a whale-boat, but much heavier in build. In less than a minute from the time the telephone-bell tinkled, they had launched the boat and were paddling down to the Point.

Cap'n Eldredge was waiting for them on the beach. His practised eye instantly detected a fault—the men had in their haste disobeyed one of the most important rules in the service: they had forgotten to put on their cork life-belts. Should he take them back home? No; the five men out yonder on the barge were in danger, and he could not spare the time. He knew the risk that awaited men who omitted this precaution, but it was too late to go back. Seth Ellis

MEN OF THE CREW SIGNALLING

dropped the steering-oar and clambered up to his station in the bow. Eldredge and No. 6 shoved the boat off the beach and leaped aboard as the men gave way on the long ash sweeps. Eldredge picked up the steering-oar in the stern and kept her head to the sea.

On a windless and glassy day in August you will still find the waves leaping and crashing on the sands of Shovelful Shoal. Imagine, then, with what vehemence they were now pushing heavenward, lashed by the conflict of wind and tide on this March day of storm; how they fell back in boiling white froth upon the maelstrom and raced away in swirling eddies! The tide was ebbing fast in the teeth of the southeast gale, and the easterly

Painting by Harold Matthews Brett

LURID IN THE GLARE OF THE RED SIGNAL LIGHT

ground-swell from the Atlantic, now heavier than ever, was multiplying the fury of the surges.

Eldredge took his boat well outside of the Shovelful Shoal, until he came to the very end whereon the *Wadena* was pounding. Cautiously he manœuvred his craft up in the lee of the barge and fended her off, while the eager Portuguese were hauling in the painter that Seth Ellis hove aboard. Captain Mack was doleful over the loss of his barge; but he was calm, as a good man should be, while he held back his impetuous men, and made them drop gently into the life-boat one by one as the seas swung her up close to the rail. He got in with three of them forward, leaving the cook, a fat Portuguese giant of some three hundred pounds, to take a place in the stern.

As the big fellow perched on the rail, he became frightened and leaped for the boat just as it rose on a wave. He came down feet first upon the after-thwart and went crashing through it. At the same instant Seth Ellis chopped the painter with his hatchet, and the life-boat was swept away on the tide.

The big cook and the three other Portuguese were stunned for a few moments by the crash of the thwart and the tumbling of the waves among which they rode. Just as the life-boat came clear of the shoal one of them leaped up in an agony of fear.

"*Dio mio!*" he cried, "we are all lost! We are all lost!"

"Sit down, you fool, or you *will* be lost," roared Cap'n Eldredge. "Seth, bat him on the head if ye have to, but git him down somehow."

But the cap'n spoke too late. All four of the Portuguese were afoot now, leaping and shrieking in frenzy. The life-savers tried to pull them down. A great sea broke over the gunwale as the boat yawed off her course, and in the twinkling of an eye swamped and capsized her. Not one of the Portuguese rose to the surface. All the Americans came up, swimming in spite of the oilskins and the heavy rubber hip-boots that cumbered them. They struck out for the capsized life-boat, grabbed her keel, and hung on. The sea was cold as ice, but they were still warm from the rowing. Now and then a great wave seized one or another,

tore him away, and tossed him up as easily as if he were a moth, but always hands were reaching for him as he came down and helping him back to the keel. The wind and sea swept the boat toward Monomoy Beach.

Elmer Mayo and Ben Mallows, aboard the barge *Fitzpatrick*, aground on the same shoal, but a quarter of a mile nearer shore, saw the tragedy and were helpless to avert it. No, not quite helpless. Mayo, a gentle-featured, blue-eyed, soft-voiced, big fellow of middle age, ran toward a dory that lay on the deck.

"Don't try it! You can't *do* it, Elmer," cried Ben Mallows. "Your dory wouldn't live a min-nit in that sea, an' look—she hasn't any thole-pins on the sta'b'rd side."

"I'll git 'em, I tell ye," Elmer answered. "Don't you hinder me."

With a calking-mallet he drove a big file into the dory's gunwale for one thole-pin, then plucked out the handle of the mallet, and with the heel of his fist jammed it down into the place of the other missing pin. He tucked a pair of oars under the thwarts, and watching for a lull after three big seas had passed, hurled the dory off the deck into the maelstrom, and jumped. By some miracle he fell into the boat without injuring it, seized the oars, swung her head into the wind, and made for the life-boat.

When the big Portuguese crashed aboard the life-boat he was the thirteenth man in her; when she floated upside down after the capsize only eight were clinging to her keel. There were six left when Elmer Mayo launched his dory; but there were only three when he came near, and only one man was left when he drew alongside. By what process the number was reduced cannot be told here, for Mayo has always refused to talk about the struggles he witnessed that morning.

Well toward the stern of the life-boat, in the after-part of the centreboard trunk, there was a vacant space big enough to contain one hand. Into that space was thrust the right hand of Seth Ellis, No. 1, the biggest, strongest, man of the crew. All the others had vanished beneath the waves. Ellis was almost unconscious when Elmer Mayo dragged him into the dory and rowed him to the beach.

REQUIESCAT

Only once has Elmer spoken of that day's work. A score of men gathered about him in the bereft life-saving station immediately after the rescue, praised him, made much of him, asked him a hundred questions.

"Pretty tired. Cal'late I'll have a cup of coffee," was all they could draw from him. Soon New England raved with his fame. A theatrical manager offered him one hundred dollars a week to go on circuit and be exhibited as the hero of Monomoy. He refused to go; but his brother Ed took up the enterprise and travelled far, enjoying the incense of vicarious adulation and accumulating a tidy bit of money.

The Secretary of the Treasury was so much impressed by the *Wadena* incident that he awarded the Congressional gold medal for exceptional heroism to the rescuer and the rescued. On the day of the presentation the ancient Town Hall of Chatham was crowded with men and women of Cape Cod, who came to pay tribute to their heroes. The Congressman of the district made a speech, a fine speech, recapitulating the horrors of that day, and dwelling upon Mayo's acts. Then he called up Seth Ellis and pinned the gold medal upon his coat. Ellis was thankful. He said so simply and not without eloquence.

Elmer Mayo was called up on the platform. His face was pale, and his eyes were filled with apprehensions. The Congressman told again of his bravery, pinned on his medal, and waited for some reply. Elmer slowly glanced from the Congressman to the people about him, then looked long at Seth Ellis. A sudden sob broke the silence, and Elmer Mayo stumbled blindly from the platform with tears on his cheeks. Since that day Elmer Mayo has never met Seth Ellis face to face.

The Newest and Coziest Hotel in New England

The Brewster

The Brewster

Stairway from Office

Boston has an ideal hotel at last, large enough to offer every modern luxury and comfort, yet small enough to be home-like and cozy, offering to the fastidious public that something so greatly desired—an atmosphere of refinement.

The Brewster is located in the very heart of things, just within a few minutes' walk of Boston's great shopping center and theaters.

You will find here cuisine and service unexcelled, with every attention for your welfare, comfort, and safety.

No pains have been spared to make the Brewster strictly first class in every respect with prices reasonable.

Reservations may be wired to us, if necessary, at our own expense.

Ainslie & Grabow Company

Operating   Hotels Lenox   Tuileries   Empire   Boston, Mass.
New Ocean House, Swampscott, Mass.   Hotel Titchfield, Jamaica, W. I.

A New England
Dairy and Stock Farm
(1878)

HARPER'S
NEW MONTHLY MAGAZINE.

No. CCCXLI.—OCTOBER, 1878.—Vol. LVII.

A NEW ENGLAND DAIRY AND STOCK FARM.

A PERFECT COW.

The stream is dammed and utilized by many mills. One active little town makes thousands of clocks a year, another realizes its wealth from the fabrication of buttons, and the thrifty industry of Connecticut gives abundant traffic to the railway.

We sped northward as the dusk was fading into night, and as the sky, losing the splendors of sunset, made the sterile hills look more sterile and bleak than ever. "It's a queer region for a model farm; there's no climate, and no pasturage to speak of," said the artist, who sat next to me and gazed out disconsolately through the veil of his cigarette smoke. We were obliged to confess that the man who could settle down to agriculture amid such surroundings should be recorded as a hero of uncommon fortitude; and the scantiness of the soil impressed us the more as not many months before we had visited a dairy ranch in the Sierra Nevada, where the grass was unusually luxuriant, and 400 cattle ranged over 6000 green acres.

We alighted at East Litchfield—a dépôt locked in by characteristic hills—and thence a stage-coach carried us four miles to Litchfield village, near which is situated Echo Farm, the objective point of our journey. The air was cold on the uplands, but it bore with it the modest fragrance of the arbutus that was nestling in the damp coverts of the woods. The crests of the hills were lurid against the bleak sky. There were few signs of a good stock-raising or farming country, and we were inclined to convince ourselves that we had made some mistake. As we reached one of the summits, however, the lights of the village became vis-

LEAVING behind us the New Haven Railway, with its shining tracks stretching east and west, we switched off to the north on the Naugatuck, which threads the valley of that name, and penetrates a country whose aspect between the stations conveys with much pathos and no little reminiscence an idea of the valorous endurance of the early settlers. There is some similarity between man and the land he has worked upon every where; his individuality clings to and breathes out of the earth; and particularly true is this of the New England hills, upon which the gray gneiss protruding from the shallow soil testifies to the patient labor and frugal life of the pioneer, and the foliage in and out of the sunshine seems to perpetually fill with the sombreness that environed him. The pastures are scant and the tillage is unprofitable in this little valley of the Naugatuck; but at the stations there are prosperous manufacturing settlements.

VIEW OF ECHO FARM BUILDINGS FROM THE PASTURE.

ible, and the driver pointed to a cluster of buildings near the roadway, which he said was the place we sought. It was true that here amid the rocks of Southwestern New England has sprung up one of those farms called models, which, whether they are pecuniarily advantageous to their proprietors or not, demonstrate the potentialities of the profession by the application of intelligently apprehended formulas, and the substitution of scientific methods for the accidents of empiricism. Why should farming not be scientific? Because the manufacturer labors in a scientific way, his profits are greater and surer than those of the agriculturist who has neither machinery nor system; but it is the unreasonable custom of many to sneer at all innovations, and to look at all methodic variations upon old usages as the fanciful and unprofitable schemes of visionaries with more money than common-sense. It is the people who sneer that are usually most deficient in the latter quality, however; and had they a little more of it they might perceive that careful book-keeping and the adoption of improved methods and implements are as necessary in farming as in any other business.

In a side hollow of that hill from which Litchfield first became visible to us several very distinct echoes can be obtained, and this responsiveness of the "purple glens" gave a name to this farm. It is Echo Farm —a pretty and poetically suggestive name, indeed, which conjures up visions of loveli-

ness, and sets one to dreaming of intertwining vines knitting their pliant tendrils and sweet-scented leaves through the hospitable porch and open lattice; the checkered orchard of fruity abundance; the garrulous brook that never tires of its own monody; the reverberant hills that appease life's turmoil with their easy undulations; lofty barns mossy with age; and clattering mills down in the seclusion of grassy hollows. But, alas! dear reader, model farming is not idyllic or Arcadian; it is inflexibly utilitarian; it keeps all its buildings in a perfect state of repair; it subordinates the picturesque, if it ever recognizes it; it pulls down the old mill because that venerable is in the way of the rectangular new dairy; it diverts the brook from its ferny course into the most common-place of earthen pipes; it tears away the vines that obscure the light, and it looks upon every thing with a pair of the most practical eyes set in a head that weighs, measures, audits, and analyzes with chemical exactness. The proprietor of Echo Farm conducts it as a manufactory. A record is kept of the milk and butter produced by each cow for each day, each month, each year; all the feed is weighed, and the quantity entered upon books, both that purchased and that produced; and a separate account is kept of the yield of each field. Nothing is wasted, nothing done by guessing, and nothing passes unrecorded. The implements are of the latest or most approved model. Three sets of "horse" hay-forks are in use, by which hay is unloaded at the rate of a ton in four forkfuls and in four minutes, including in some instances the carriage of the hay 150 feet. The other machines also embody some novel labor-saving principles. No manure or fertilizers are found necessary, except the 1500 loads made upon the farm and a sort of muck, of which there are several beds.

The history of the farm is interesting. A gentleman of education, intelligence, and

When the fields were being cleared, such large quantities of stones were gathered that some perplexity arose as to where they should be put. Many hundreds of loads were used in the foundations of the build-ings, in the fences, and in filling ravines, but more remained, and these were deposit-ed upon several sterile hillocks of no value, where masses of swamp grass were laid over them, and covered with a light dressing of soil. Grass seed was sown upon the soil,

THE DAIRY.

wealth came to Litchfield some nine years ago in search of a summer home. He had the most superficial knowledge of farming, and entertained no intention of entering that business. But having purchased six-ty-six acres and cleared them, he purchased additional tracts, which became the neucleus of Echo Farm, whose area is now about 400 acres. His interest was enlisted in the rais-ing of choice stock, and beginning with a herd of five, he has gradually increased the number to 100, all the herd being pure Jer-seys, with authentic and valuable pedigrees. The rocky fields were cleared, laid out, and inclosed by massive stone walls. Old and inadequate buildings on the consolidated land were demolished, and new ones of im-proved pattern erected. In 1873 a barn 66 feet by 25 was built; an addition, 100 feet by 40, was made the following year; and in 1875 another addition was made, of 191 by 35 feet. These three buildings form the three sides of the barn-yard. They are built of pine upon massive granite foundations about two feet wide, which are laid in cement. All the wood-work is painted a soft drab color, even the proprietor's residence, and the telegraph poles that line the roadway. A desire for simplicity and durability in preference to ornamentation or showiness is visible every where; there is no litter, and there are no gaps in the fences or walls, which are from eighteen inches to twenty-four in thickness, every crevice being filled like a mosaic with a stone that exactly fits it. Care, thrift, and ingenuity have acted like three charms.

and it took well, soon transforming the bar-ren heaps to verdant knolls, whose blades are remarkably hardy. It was not so much for the sake of the land gained that the stones were thus disposed of, but it was rather to prevent the formation of nurseries for weeds, shrubs, and brambles, which the heaps would have quickly become.

Two and a half acres are planted with beets, which are the only roots fed to the cattle, the crop averaging 1000 bushels an acre, and more than 2000 tons of hay are housed a year.

Before we enter the cow stable let us climb the slope in its rear and observe some of the superficial characteristics of the sur-rounding country. The first thing that im-presses us is the soothing influence of these gray and green hills, over which the wind sweeps in a gentle harmony. Away in the southwest and the south the horizon is formed by the curves of the farthest range; nearer, the houses and steeples of the village project their unimpeachable white from the avenues of elms that embower them, and at one side of the village an extensive lake, bordered by foliage, glances back the fitful sunshine that escapes the clouds on this moist April day. The luxuriance and mel-lowness of more southern regions are absent here, but the low sighing of the breeze, the placid uniformity of the undulations, and the incomparable fragrance of the arbutus, which diffused itself with mild generosity from its dim retreat in the groves of pine that occasionally lent variety to the landscape, gave us to understand the good sense that selected the location of Echo Farm as a resting-place for a wearied business man.

Just at our feet were three springs, which feed a stone reservoir, covered, and connected by iron pipes with the dairy and the barns—for an abundance of constantly flowing water is considered indispensable at such a model farm as Echo—and while these fountains would make a very pretty little glen and a brook if they were left to them-

storage of hay, and a double threshing floor crosses its centre, so that several wagons bringing in hay may enter and discharge their loads at a time. The storage capacity is for more than 150 tons, and each animal (the herd being stalled on the floor below) has its food for one year immediately above its manger. As a safeguard against accidents, there are no trap-doors, the hay being sent down by passages through which a man can not possibly stumble.

CUTTING HAY.

selves, their crystal affluence is hoarded, and carefully distributed through many brass faucets in various parts of the buildings.

The central barn, which includes the cow stable, is built upon a slope, and the main story is approached from the rear by a roadway with granite walls three feet thick laid in cement. The roadway gains a height of twelve feet, and the space between the walls (thirty feet) is filled with stones solidly packed and topped with gravel. It would be difficult to find a more durable, handsomer, or easier approach for any structure. The main floor is used for the

Following the quarter circle of the stone roadway we come to the entrance of the cow stable, and crossing its portals, we are astonished at the extreme cleanliness of the interior, though we have seen enough to make us anticipate much attention to sanitary affairs in a model farm. The air is pure and fresh, the light invades the cornermost rafters, and the horrifying squalor of the ordinary habitation allowed to the bovine is superseded by an ethical economy so admirable that humanitarianism reproaches us and pricks our consciences with the contrast between this shelter for brutes and

MILKING-TIME.

much inferior accommodations for man in the tenements of large cities. The stable is 100 feet long and 40 feet wide; it has stalls for forty-eight cows; the stalls are five feet wide; the mangers are two feet wide; the slanting platforms upon which the animals stand are five and a half feet long, and each cow is allowed 900 cubic feet of air space, or more than double the usual quantity. The two rows of stalls are separated by a longitudinal passage ten feet wide; there is a transverse passage eight feet wide in the centre, and another longitudinal one in the rear of each row of stalls, by which the floor is divided into four sections. The sloping platforms of the stalls end in slightly inclined gutters, from which the manure passes through convenient traps into the cellar for storage. The room is lighted by eighteen large double windows, opening at the top and bottom, and for the early morning milkings fixed lamps with brilliant reflectors are employed. On the north side there is a small apartment with a few chairs or stools, a marble wash-stand, a large mirror, and an amplitude of towel. Whoever looks into the mirror is reminded by an inscription over it, as conspicuous as his own image, that "Handsome is that handsome does." This little room is called "the parlor," and the reader—especially the "practical farmer"—may be disposed to cry out against a parlor in a stable as an absurd piece of Utopian extravagance. It is in reality a dressing-room, and before milking-time each man is required to wash his face and hands and to brush his hair, tidiness of person being insisted upon. We forgot to tell that the floor of the barn is dry and sanded, and that there are no odors to offend the daintiest nostrils. The beds of the animals are changed every day, being formed of dried leaves spread upon the sanded platforms.

Over the entrance to the parlor an unerring clock sedately whispers the seconds, and ten minutes before it marks 5 A.M. and 5 P.M.—the milking-time—any visitors who may be in the barn are excluded; the milkmen (maids are an anachronism) enter the dressing-room, and precisely as the fingers record the hour they re-appear, with hands and faces clean and hair smooth, and sit down to their task. As each cow is milked, its yield is separately weighed and the quantity recorded on a slate, which is passed with the milk to the dairy-maid, who stores the warm, fragrant fluid in shallow pans during winter, and in deep pans surrounded by running water during the summer.

An hour before the milking the animals are fed. In summer they are supplied with nothing besides their grazing, except a sprinkling of dry bran in their mangers; but in winter one peck of beets (the only root supplied) is allowed to each, besides six quarts of wheat bran and oats and corn ground together and moistened with cold

THE PETS.

water. They are also supplied with all the dry hay they can eat. Every thing is of the best obtainable quality; and while Mr. F. R. Starr, the proprietor, believes in giving them all that is necessary, he is opposed to overfeeding. A great difference is noticeable between the deportment of the laborers at Echo Farm and those who are usually employed with cattle. The former are quiet and never blasphemous in the treatment of their animals, and the animals reciprocate

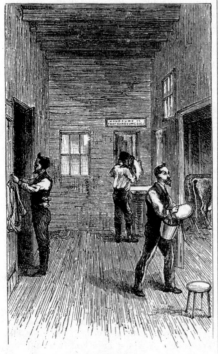

THE STABLE PARLOR.

by evincing confidence, docility, and even affection. In summer the windows are thrown wide open, and in winter the temperature of the stable is kept as nearly as possible at 40°, thermometers being placed where they can be plainly seen. All noises are avoided, and the little wagon that carries the feed from stall to stall has rubber wheels.

Some of our readers, whose knowledge of the agricultural arcana is limited, are inquiring, no doubt, what motive underlies these many excellences of government—this tenderness of care, this cautious observance of sanitary law, and this luxuriance of accommodation. Were cows ever so well ministered to before? Is Mr. Starr a millionaire whose benefactions take effect in ameliorating the condition of the short-horn aristocracy of bovines?

He is simply a business man, and, as a business man, his object is to make money. The stable is light and amply ventilated, the food is of the best quality, and the treatment of the animals is gentle, because he believes that these conditions add to the intrinsic value of the herd, and to the quality of the milk produced. He is so far correct that he has no difficulty in selling his butter at one dollar a pound, which is so much above the market price of other butter that it leaves him a profit large enough to defray the extra cost of his improved system.

The advantage of producing a superior article for the sake of the premium which it commands above the price of ordinary grades has been plainly stated as follows by an experienced Canadian stock-breeder: "Not every one—not many, indeed—can have a choice and large herd of registered Jerseys; but a thorough-bred Jersey bull, or a bull-calf of the best butter strains, is to be had at a price within the reach of all. And if to this a farmer can add a choice heifer-calf, or yearling, costing from $120 to $200, he will be astonished at the rapidity with which he can accumulate a little herd worth thousands of dollars. Should he choose to sell the calves of his heifer as fast as they come, he would find her a far better investment than money put out at fifteen

nadian markets is twenty and twenty-two cents a pound, mine is thirty-five and forty cents, and when it is twenty-eight and thirty cents, mine is fifty cents, for the produce of my dairy is always firm, sweet, and very yellow—qualities that could not be attained without Jersey blood."

JERSEYS.

per cent. A registered heifer-calf, if it is from a good cow, will always bring from $50 to $100 when it is a few weeks old. Then as to butter. Take the price of butter as it is now made by the average farmer, and after deducting all the expenses of production, see how much of this is profit. Only a few cents..... Now if the presence of a little Jersey blood in a man's stable will enable him to command only five cents per pound over the market price, that is clear gain; and five cents per pound above market price is a low calculation, which can be increased according to the skill and experience brought to bear upon the subject. I will give my own experience. I obtained some choice Jerseys and a few grades a year ago. Last winter I printed my butter and sent it all the way from Canada to New York, in a neat, attractive form. I received seventy-two cents per pound for it, and it sold at ninety cents. The expense of sending, including duty and expressage on returned packages, was ten cents per pound. Any surplus that I had was bought up at home. At all times when butter in our Ca-

This brief chapter of actual experience is worthy of the consideration of every farmer.

Personally we like the bovine less than any other of the domestic animals. Its irresponsiveness to caresses, its unsympathetic stolidity, its wide-eyed apathy, and its placid indifference to nearly every thing except its food and any convenient post against which it can rub itself, exclude it from the affection that we gladly bestow upon a horse or the smaller denizens of the barn-yard. But the Jerseys possess these defects in a less degree than any other breed, and they excite our admiration by their external beauties, which are marked and peculiar. In that salubrious island of the English Channel from which they originally came there is a tradition that ascribes their progenitors to some mysterious cross with a deer, and their large, round, lustrous eyes lend credence to the conjecture. Their coats are exquisitely smooth and soft, almost velvety in texture, and their color, varying a little, is always delicate, that of the fawn being the commonest at Echo. As we strolled along the stalls, each of which is

THE CALF STABLE.

ticketed with the name of its occupant and the number of the herd-book register of the American Jersey Cattle Club, the handsome creatures paused in their munching, and quietly permitted us to stroke their heads, as they gazed at us with wide-open, expressive eyes. Here was Vivien, No. 6866; Cedar, No. 1886; Beechnut, No. 3785; Chestnut, No. 1888; and Bessie Allen, No. 3719. These names may have no significance beyond their picturesqueness to the ordinary reader, but to the raiser of choice stock they are celebrated.

On a floor below is the bull stable, in which Litchfield, No. 674, and his son Prince Edward, No. 1442, are stalled—two superb brutes of heroic proportions, and in admirable condition. Litchfield, which took the first special prize at the Centennial Exhibition, is a solid fawn, beautifully dappled, and darker above than below, where he is rather light. His horns are a clear waxy yellow—a sure indication of a good butter stock in all Jerseys—and his body is long. He is patriarch to an incredible number of the herd, and a nobler sire never roared defiance in a pasture. Prince Edward is still better-looking, we fancy, although he portentously thundered remonstrance at us as we neared his stall; but the grand results of stable hygienics are forcibly illustrated in the saturnine majesty and sleek vigor of both animals.

A summary of the most valued qualities in Jersey cattle is given in the following scale of "points" prepared for the guidance of judges at agricultural fairs by the American Club, and adopted by that organization on April 21, 1875:

Points.	Counts.
1. Head small, lean, and rather long	2
2. Face dished, broad between the eyes, and narrow between the horns	1
3. Muzzle dark, and encircled by a light color	1
4. Eyes full and placid	1
5. Horns small, crumpled, and amber-color	3
6. Ears small and thin	1
7. Neck straight, thin, rather long, with clean throat, and not heavy at the shoulders	4
8. Shoulders sloping and lean; withers thin; breast neither deficient nor beefy	3
9. Back level to the setting on of tail, and broad across the loin	4
10. Barrel hooped, broad, and deep at the flank	8
11. Hips wide apart, and fine in the bone; rump long and broad	4
12. Thighs long, thin, and wide apart, with legs standing square, and not to cross in walking.	4
13. Legs short, small below the knees, with small hoofs	3
14. Tail fine, reaching the hocks, with good switch.	3
15. Hide thin and mellow, with fine soft hair	4
16. Color of hide where the hair is white, on udder and inside of ears, yellow	5
17. Fore-udder full in form, and running well forward	8
18. Hind-udder full in form, and well up behind	8
19. Udder free from long hair, and not fleshy	5
20. Teats rather large, wide apart, and squarely placed	6
21. Milk veins prominent	5
22. Escutcheon high and broad, and full on thighs.	8
23. Disposition quiet and good-natured	3
24. General appearance, rather bony than fleshy	6
Perfection	100

In judging heifers, omit Nos. 17, 18, and 21.

The same scale of points shall be used in judging bulls, omitting Nos. 17, 18, 19, and 21, and making moderate allowance for masculinity.

Note.—It is recommended that judges at fairs do not award prizes to animals falling below the following *minimum* standard, viz.: cows, 70 counts; heifers, 55 counts; bulls, 50 counts.

Let us now resume our survey of the buildings. At the eastern end of the cow stable there is a maternity ward and a hospital, clean, light, and airy, like all the other departments, in which a cow of ordinary stock is calmly doing the duty of wet-nurse to a young Jersey, the mothers being separated from their children when the latter are a few days old. Connecting with this is the second floor of one of the lateral barns, which is used for the storage of duplicate implements, and the hay, straw, bedding, etc., of the animals beneath. The manure cellar is continued under the hospital, but the rest of the basement is otherwise occupied. An inclined plane used for the transfer of animals from story to story admits us to the ground-floor of the lateral barn, upon which we find the bull stable previously referred to, and the nursery, where there are twenty miniature stalls, complete in all their appointments. Adjoining these is a storeroom for beets, with a capacity for several thousand bushels, the work-horse stables, a wagon-room, and a harness-room. There is a watchman at night, who inspects every animal and all parts of the buildings hourly. The addition made in 1873 is used for the storage of implements.

The nursery is separated from a paddock by a drive, and the paddock was full at the time of our visit with yearlings, whose confidence and familiarity bespoke, in language

were so aggressively friendly that we had to wave them off several times, one repulse serving only for a few moments, at the end of which they returned, and went to the audacious extent of putting their moist noses into our pockets. Their sagacity also was surprisingly developed, and when they were let into the nursery in the evening, each, except the very tender and inexperienced ones, found and entered his own particular stall.

The dairy is to the westward of the other buildings; it is small, not very well adapted to its purpose, and will soon be substituted by a more commodious structure; but in it soap and water, the scrubbing-brush, and the mop have wrought a whiteness of which a lily might not be ashamed; a whiteness of wall and ceiling microscopically speckless; a whiteness of floor and wainscot such as the elm or ash never confessed before. The dairy-maid apotheosizes herself by miracles of cleanliness. Here there is a dairy-maid, not the degenerate modernization that has superseded the reminiscent milkmaids of the ballads, but a nineteenth-century Perdita, a royal dairy-maid, with a smiling face as round, as smooth, and as rosy as the rosiest pippin, a neat black dress that gloves her comeliness with chaste simplicity, and a

LITCHFIELD AND PRINCE EDWARD.

not the less clear because it was inarticulate, the gentle circumstances of their breeding. Instead of timorously retreating at our approach, they stretched their furry necks toward us, sniffed at us inquisitively, and

snowy front of apron as immaculate as the choicest lawn cried by Autolycus that flows from breast to furbelow. All the work is over as we raise the latchet; it always is over in the dairy before eight o'clock in the morn-

WEIGHING MILK.

nesses of muslin are fastened, like a drum-head, over the end.

The milk stands thirty-six hours before it is skimmed, and after that of the evening has been received, our Perdita, like an excellent clerk, fills out her return for the day. She has printed blanks which give the names of the cows as they stand in the stable. Two columns are ruled for morning's and evening's milk, and the weight of milk given by each cow is recorded as we have said. The disposition made of the whole quantity is then noted, and the dairy is charged with its proportion, when deductions have been made for the house, the families of the men, and the young calves. Such a report is filed daily, and so complete is the system that it takes only a few hours at the end of the year to tabulate a full statement of the 365 days.

The cream is strained or filtered, by which a thorough homogeneousness is secured, and without which it is impossible to obtain all the butter except by a second churning. The strainer in this instance is a cylindrical can divided into two compartments by double bottoms, the upper one having two tube-like sieves with conical mouths, into which two "plungers," worked by a pump-handle, fit. The cream is poured into the upper compartment, and the "plungers" force it through the sieves into the lower compartment, in which it arrives ready for churning. The churning is done twice a week,

ing, and the author of the idyllic neatness, to whom the veriest mote must be a torment, rises to welcome us. An old clock is rhythmically counting the minutes, and the sun floods the room and checkers the floor with shadows of the plants in the window.

When the milking is done, the men deliver the milk to the dairymaid with the record of the quantity on the slate. It is poured from the "strainer" milk pails into a "triple strainer," which is an Echo Farm invention, its spout being a four-inch cylinder with wire-gauze over it inside the pail. A tin hoop fits loosely to the outside of the spout, and by this means two thick-

WORKING THE BUTTER.

in a Blanchard factory churn, and, the temperature being 62°, the butter appears in about forty minutes. The next process is known as "working," which is altogether done by a machine, in quantities of thirty pounds at a time. The machine consists of a turn-table in the form of an exceedingly flat truncated cone and a conical grooved presser. Between the revolving cone and the presser the butter passes, and is crushed and crushed again until all the buttermilk is forced out of it, and discharged into a pail at the outside edge of the turn-table. The crank that causes the revolutions is attended by an assistant, while Perdita herself supervises, dredging in the salt, and taking care that the working is not overdone. The butter is then put up in half-pound prints for shipment, which are of the usual circular form, about one and a half inches high, with a monogram in the centre. Each pat is wrapped in a new muslin napkin, and placed in a dainty pasteboard box, which is inscribed with the exact date of the making, and the following directions: "Please do not keep the butter in this box or napkin, and do not place it near other butter, vegetables, or any article of food. It should be put in a cool, well-aired place, but should not touch any ice."

The shipments are made by express on Tuesdays and Fridays, several dozen of the half-pound boxes being placed in large wooden cases to prevent them from being crushed, and the packages are delivered at the residences of customers on the evenings of those days. Milk also is delivered every morning to customers in Brooklyn and New York. Each can contains two quarts, and is locked; one key is in the possession of the dairy-woman, and another one is in the possession of the consumer, so that a pure article, untouched by middle-men, is assured. About 200 pounds of butter are sold every week.

It is the possibility of bringing producer and consumer together that they create which gives such farms as Echo something more than a commercial or scientific import. The two articles which delicate children and invalids in the cities need most are pure butter and milk, and these are the very things which are ordinarily least obtainable without sophistication. But by the method which Mr. Starr has instituted mischievous and dishonest adulterations can be avoided, and the delicate produce of the dairy may be served in city houses within a few hours of its departure from the farm.

DAIRY TOOLS.

The Howard Watch

There are certain pleasures in life that are worth while—that endure because they are *real*.

The possession of a HOWARD Watch is one of them. It is a satisfaction all the time, whether a man works or plays.

The wider a man's experience of life, the more he appreciates the HOWARD's qualities and comradeship.

There's many a man who would not part with the HOWARD Watch he is carrying if you offered him a thousand dollars and another

HOWARD just as good. He feels the tie of long and intimate association.

Then, too, there are HOWARDS that are heirlooms—handed down from sire or grandsire and priceless because of their memories.

Any way you take it the HOWARD is the best—the most lasting watch investment. It is always worth what you pay for it.

The price of each HOWARD Watch—from the 17-jewel in a fine gold-filled case guaranteed for 25 years) at $35.00; to the 23-jewel in a 14-kt. solid gold case at $150.00—is fixed at the factory, and a printed ticket attached.

Not every jeweler can sell you a HOWARD Watch. Find the HOWARD Jeweler in your town and talk to him. He is a good man to know. Drop us a postal card, Dept. H, and we will send you a HOWARD book of value to the watch buyer.

E. HOWARD WATCH COMPANY
BOSTON, MASS.

The Town of
Brandon, Vermont
(1897)

THE TOWN OF BRANDON, VERMONT.

By Augusta W. Kellogg.

DURING the troublous times when New York, New Hampshire and Massachusetts were contending for possession of the New Hampshire Grants (now the State of Vermont), a settlement was begun there on the northern frontier of a chain of sixteen townships, to which was given the Indian name of Neshobe. There were five young men who, determined to hew homes for themselves out of the primeval forest, spent the summer of 1761 upon the ground; but, as winter approached, four of the pioneers returned to the more comfortable quarters whence they had come. Only one, Amos Cutler, a blacksmith, twenty-four years of age, remained, spending the winter — but for the companionship of his dog — entirely alone. One wonders whether he "stayed by the stuff" in a spirit of bravado or because he had no special ties elsewhere, or if perhaps the solitude were congenial to his temperament. However, with the summer his companions returned, and such progress was made in their work that it was never again necessary to flee from the rigors of the climate. It is said that Jedediah Winslow, a descendant of the Pilgrim, Edward Winslow, erected the first dwelling house.

Little is known of the settlers for the next quarter of a century. There are the usual traditions of incursions by savages, who, carrying off the robust, left the young and weak to perish. One tale, however, ends more happily. It is of Joseph Barker, who was led away captive, leaving a young wife and little child behind him. That night, alone and unfriended, Mrs. Barker gave birth to another baby. Fortunately assistance soon reached her from a neighboring settlement (now Pittsford), where later she was rejoined by her husband, who had feigned illness so successfully in the march northward as to be abandoned at Middlebury by his captors.

The name of Neshobe was changed in 1784 to Brandon, or Burntown, whereby an unusually disastrous fire seems hinted at. The situation that had been chosen for this settlement bespeaks both intelligence and foresight in its founders. There is no better land east of the Rocky Mountains than this watered by the Otter Creek, which runs from Dorset Pond through Addison and Rutland counties to pour itself over the pretty falls at Vergennes before starting on its eight mile course to Lake Champlain.

"Where from the dear incontinent caress
  Of mountains joying in so fair a child,
Slow Otter 'scaped through woody wilderness,
  Illapsed into the lovelorn valley mild
  Of swaying vines, and weeping willows wild,
And many a bloomy grass and many a flower,

With fragrant kiss that the sweet way
   beguiled;
Still in the rath, the late, the middle hour,
To stray through all its banks a bright,
   continuous bower,
Neshobe was; a little lovely spot
You may have dreamed some drowsy
   summer's noon,
But to have seen, has been above your
   lot."

This "long line of intervale receives
annually the best of all top-dressings,
by the gentle overflow of the sluggish
stream, which subsides so quietly as
to leave its rich deposits, brought

mineral wealth." The State reports
describe "the town as situated on an
expanded terrace, or ancient sea-
beach, six hundred feet above the sea,
and, like everything in Brandon,"
they courteously add "this terrace is
well-formed and attractive to the eye."

In the southwest part of the town,
not far from the village, is a frozen
well, which, since 1858, the year of its
accidental discovery, has excited the
interest of such eminent scientists as
Sir Charles Lyell, Professors Agassiz,
Jackson and others who have visited

OTTER CREEK VALLEY.

down from the mountains, more
evenly distributed than could be
effected by any human skill."

Otter Creek receives as the Brandon contribution the Neshobe River,
which, rising at the foot of the Goshen
Mountains, is an outlet for Spring and
Burnell ponds, and in its serpentine
course through a light, sandy soil
drains a district ten miles in length.

According to geologists the town
of Brandon lies not only in "a portion
of one of the richest metalliferous districts of the world, but there is no
other town which furnishes a greater
variety or more extensive deposits of

it. This well lies between two nearly
parallel ridges of limestone, which are
about an eighth of a mile apart. It is
forty feet deep, the water very
clear, with pebbly bed. Ice forms in
the well no later than April, but if not
taken away remains usually through
the summer, while the stones are
coated with ice for four or five feet
above the water, the mercury marking
1° F. above freezing. The phenomenon of this frozen well is thus explained in the latest geological reports:
"The deposit is probably about the
age of moraine terraces, whose peculiarities we have supposed produced

by stranded icebergs, and that the gravel and sand among these were doubtless frozen (formed perhaps by successive layers of ice and gravel) tens of thousands of years ago, but marly clay and pebbles in interstratification is a poor conductor of heat. The conditions are like those of a huge sandstone refrigerator, whose increased and unusual effects beyond those of the ordinary refrigerator are due to the increased and unusual collection of poor conducting materials which form its sides. And more than the non-conducting power of the fragments is the evaporation, which would be large in large fragments. Coating of gravel and clay, twenty feet thick, protected from heat beneath by layer of impervious clay, stratum of pebbles, etc., etc., make, according to Prof. A. D. Hager, 'a perfect, improved refrigerator.'" This peculiar formation, called Hogback (see page 307), is solidly welded gravel in which are embedded larger stone and is a part of the above-mentioned ridges.

As early as 1810 an inexhaustible bed of decomposed brown hematite or bog iron ore was discovered, five or six feet below the surface of the ground, covered by strata of sand and ochre. The first attempt to convert this raw material into manufactured articles was made by Mr. Wait Broughton, who built a furnace with a stack chimney. This failed to "draw." In order to repeat his experiment he would be obliged to expend the remnant of his little fortune; but, encouraged by his wife, he ventured his all, with the result that in 1819-20 the furnace was in successful operation. This new industry, lasting for thirty years, built up a thriving town. The ore-bed teams brought their yellow loads to be weighed

on the village scales before being dumped in the "top-house" for smelting. The ore had been washed by putting it into the upper end of a long box perforated like a strainer and revolving in an inclined position while a stream of water passed through it. The ore rolled over and downwards, of course, falling from the lower extremity into a shallow vat. The blast furnace produced directly from this brown hematite a superior soft gray iron not liable to crack upon exposure to heat, and yielding thus treated fifty per cent pure iron.

Mr. Broughton's daughter married John Conant from Ashburnham, Mass., who, by the purchase of the Neshobe River water power did more than any other one person to advance the material interests of the town. He established grist and saw-mills, and succeeded to his father-in-law's iron business, to which was added in 1825 the manufacture of the first cooking-stoves made in the State of Vermont. It was a great invention for the time and revolutionized the culinary de-

THE PARK AND GROVE STREET.

partment of the New England kitchen. It superseded the old fire-place with its swinging crane of pots and kettles, the hearth-spiders on legs, and tin bakers for roasting before the blazing logs. "The Conant stove" had a fire-box, surmounted with a box-oven, an expanded pannier on each side for heating purposes, with large circular opening in the rear for griddle and wash-boiler, and doors at each end. These stoves went all over New England, and teams carrying them for shipment on Lake Champlain brought

Two hundred men, with machinery, were employed. The blasts, for some reason or other, were supposed to — and probably did — take place at midnight, thus greatly enhancing the mystery of a Dantean scene. It was most impressive to be admitted to the cave-like interior of the furnace, the floor of which was prepared with sand moulds branching on each side of one long, broad centre line. Here men whose children we knew and called by their baptismal names, even with whose own faces too we were more or

PARK STREET.

back the goods sent from New York or Troy via canal, river and lake. The introduction of cooking stoves was soon followed by that of box-stoves, and also of enormous potash kettles, much in use for the making of soft soap from the lye of wood ashes.

Meanwhile a new furnace was started three miles nearer the ore beds, where, in addition to iron, simple and pure, a variety of ornamental articles, like vases, statues and chairs, were manufactured. But the principal output at both furnaces was pig-iron. In 1845 twelve hundred tons were made, also eight hundred stove castings.

less familiar above ground, were, with bared breasts and brawny arms, ladling out from a boiling cauldron vast measures of molten liquid, which, slowly coursing across the black earth, sent out a blinding splendor of glowing flame. It was a weird scene, and those innocent men stand in memory as monsters of a nether-world.

A generation later the wheels for the Car Wheel Company were made in the village furnace. "At a blast lasting one hundred and eighteen days, 14,276 pounds of iron were averaged *per diem.*" This was cast into wheels, and "by a process which hardened the

OLD BRANDON HOUSE.

of "variable quantities ot protoxide and peroxide of iron and of deutoxide of manganese." As a similar paint could be produced in Pennsyl-

flange and surface of the rim covering the rail nearly an inch in depth, and the only part subject to wear, it polished like steel, while the tenacity of the body of the wheel, the part most liable to crack, was not at all diminished."

When the iron ore was washed as described above, there was released an ochre with a mass of decomposed feldspar, which at first went to waste, but later was filtered, fell into vats and, when settled, was shovelled off into drying houses. From this, mixed with oil, a coarsish sort of paint was made, by a company organized in 1864, under the name of the Brandon Paint Company,

NEW BRANDON INN.

vania, nearer to the oil market, this industry was necessarily abandoned.

Another valuable mineral, the existence of which has been known here for upwards of half a century, is kaolin, or paper clay, sometimes called porcelain clay. It is among the best and largest deposits associated with the ochres and ores of iron and manganese. It is described technically thus: "When unadulterated it is snowy white, quite unctuous to the touch, slightly coherent, does not change color by being burned, and is extensively used in the manufacture of stone and earthen ware, porcelain, firebrick, paper and vulcanized India rubber. It is carefully elutriated, and when dried is packed and ready for market. It is applied to paper pulp in an impalpable powder, rendering it opaque and of good body at a much less expense than if white rags alone were used. Firebrick consist largely of kaolin and

with a capital of $300,000 and eighty acres of mineral fields. From five hundred to one thousand tons were made annually, consisting specifically

THE SEMINARY.

arenaceous quartz, and as repeated burnings render the former more serviceable in resisting intense heat, the modus is to mould and burn bricks of it, then pulverize, mix with quartz sand, mould and burn again." The Brandon bed is eighty feet in depth and the bottom not in sight. Sir Charles Lyell thought this clay might eventually be more valuable than the iron.

Lignite exists only in small quantities, but preserves organic remains containing seeds and fruits varying in size from that of a fig to less than that of a barley-corn, and as these fossil seeds and fruit are unlike any vegetation now growing in this country, it is supposed that they have been transferred by water, and that the accumulation took place in an ancient estuary. The form is more or less obliterated, while the parts preserved (of course the hardest) are often botanically of slight value. The species are probably of the same age as the lignites and fruits of Oeningen, Switzerland.

It remains to speak of the marble quarries. The marble from those of the Brandon Italian Marble Company is clouded, and similar in appearance to the imported Italian, but having more character to its clouding. It is

beautiful when finished, and has a degree of hardness and strength of texture which makes it far more durable than the imported Italian for out-door exposure. There is also a pure white marble of great solidity and exquisite firmness but the quarry producing it is not now worked.

Other minerals not found in large quantities are black lead, a variety of psilomelane with implanted crystals of ore of manganese, scarcely differing from the sesqui-oxide of manganese, pyrolusite, copper and iron pyrites, galena, braunite, etc. There is a whole ledge of flux, while jail cell walls have been furnished from solid

ST. THOMAS CHURCH.

blocks of limestone from six to eight inches thick. There are two caves in limestone ledges which have been points of interest since their discovery in 1842. One of these contains a room from sixteen to eighteen feet square.

Vermont is full of pretty villages; and while Brandon may not be the prettiest among them, he would be a

CONGREGATIONAL CHURCH.

bold man who tried to maintain that there is a prettier. From southwest to northeast, its longest diameter, is one mile, cut into nearly equal halves by the Neshobe River. Each half has its pretty park with fountain and trees, whence radiate the broad shaded streets.

"Two undulating lines of hill-top green
  Did hide the rising and the setting sun,
Yet that against the East, excelled, I
  ween."

This "excelling hill-top green" bars on the east the beautiful Park Street with its octuple row of trees embowering the entire length. At its junction with Franklin Street stands the handsome granite Soldiers' Monument, testifying by its long roll of honor that the town bore its full proportion of the loss of the State, which according to its population suffered more than any other in the North. On the one hand is the new Methodist church, on the other the old Congregational church with its mossed steps worn by many feet, now lying under the sod in the graveyard behind it. A charming new hotel built of marble and terra cotta stands on the site so occupied for over a hundred years. Passing a row of shops one comes by an easy descending grade to the bridge, near which are the bank, postoffice and town hall. Turning abruptly to the right is the steep street leading to the building of the old seminary, founded in 1806, and now occupied by a good graded school. The building itself, quite bare of ornament, is by actual measurement almost identical in size with the main building of Solomon's Temple — i. e., about 100 by 30 feet; and while the results attained there may have borne no comparison to the wisdom of the Oriental king, the fact has furnished a standard of interest and reality for Bible classes.

DR. C. A. THOMAS.

REV. W. G. T. SHEDD.

But this apart. Returning to the river and proceeding to a farther ridge, the lovely, gray-towered St. Thomas church is seen, fairly leaning against the green hillside; and just here begins the complement to the star-like arrangement on the other side of the river. The ancient militia ground is included in the breadth of two of the streets. Years ago it was the "chief resort of the trainers at their annual June drill, with their blue coats and white trousers and bell-crowned leather helmets with tall white and red plumes." General Burgoyne had said of the inhabitants of this region in 1777: "They are the most rebellious and warlike race on the continent and hang like a warcloud on my left." This spirit found expression in the "trainings" up to a date not so very far removed from the opening of our Civil War.

The old Baptist church faces this second park, and it is out from its doorway that the road leads to the Pine Hill Cemetery, two miles away. It is to an energetic ladies' association that this cemetery owes its charming rural beauty. An exquisite proportion between nature and art has been maintained, and it would not be easy to find a more attractive spot. From the number of lots belonging to whilom residents it would seem a common enough ambition among such to come back to the shadows of their native hills for their final sleep.

From the top of the Pine Hill itself is a grand panorama of the Lake Champlain valley, with the blue Adirondacks lying away on the horizon. One stone marks the grave of Richard Welch, who served under Wellington in the Peninsular War, receiving his death wound at the battle of Vittoria, June 22, 1813. The bullet lodged in the left leg. When the body was removed from the old to the new cemetery, there was found lying on the bottom of the coffin the fatal bullet flattened to the size and thickness of a large copper cent. The granite receiving tomb, a gift from Mrs. R. V. Marsh, stands near the entrance to the cemetery.

In this part of the town is the good old farm horse which, after drawing hay for twenty summers, was finally taken to Boston "to do depot work." No locomotive astonished him, no whistle affrighted; but one day, seeing a load of hay, he kicked up his heels and ran down Columbus Avenue like a wild creature. It was no part of his policy to betray his rural origin.

Mr. Charles M. Winslow has exerted an intelligent and practical influence upon the breeding of stock not only in the town, but in the state. He has held the position of secretary of the Ayrshire Breeders' Association most successfully for many years. At one time merino sheep raising was a profitable industry. Australian breeders valued this special breed for its extra weight of wool, which sometimes reached thirty-five or forty pounds. They readily brought $500 per head, and not infrequently $1,000

CONANT SQUARE.

blooded stock farm of Mr. H. C. Watson, who is doing much to raise the standard of both race and road horses. Since the days of the exceeding popularity of the Morgan horse, nothing will stir the blood of a Vermonter like the sight of a fine animal. A story is told of a was paid, while now half that sum could not be obtained.

The early rose potato craze too struck Brandon early in its career, and $5 per eye was not considered — by the seller — as exorbitant. Much attention has always been paid to floriculture, and several gardens, notably

THE MAIN STREET.

those of Messrs. John A. and C. W. Conant, Mrs. Button, Mr. Marsh and Mrs. Royal Blake were conspicuous. Drs. Woodward and Dyer continue to cultivate fine wall-fruit as well as flowers. From 1849 to 1856 Colonel David Warren conducted the manufacture of railroad cars in Brandon. Later the manufactory was used by the Howe Scale Company. All kinds of weighing machines were made under a patent issued in 1856 to the young inventors, Messrs. F. M. Strong and Thomas Ross. These scales took — and still bear, for they are now manufactured successfully in Rutland — the name of the purchaser from the patentees, John Howe.

By a coincidence at once singular and common, two young blacksmiths, *employés* at the New Furnace, received a stimulus or inspiration at the same moment, 1834, — the one, Thomas Davenport, thirty years of age, the other, Orange A. Smalley, ten years his junior, — the for-

mer from the fragments of a scientific book, the latter from a lecture given in an adjoining town. By these seemingly accidental means a simultaneous interest in magnetism was excited in these fellow laborers. Davenport heard that there was an

THE NESHOBE.

electro-magnet to be seen at the Penfield Iron Works in Crown Point, N. Y. Thither he betook himself, and found it to consist of a piece of steel bent in the shape of a horse-shoe wound about with copper wire and connected with a galvanic battery. Its weight was but three pounds, and by it 150 pounds of iron could be lifted. It had been used for charging or magnetizing pieces of steel, which were set in a cylinder for "separating" iron ore. Davenport was so happy as to secure this for $18. He carried it home, and experiments were immediately begun, which resulted in obtaining rotary motion by electro-magnetism. There was much excitement over the marvel, and Davenport prophesied that "in a few years steamboats would be propelled by this invisible and mysterious power." Let it be remembered that this was uttered more than a dozen years before the first steam railroad was built in Vermont.

The "Electrical Engineer" of January 7, 1891, thus described the machine. "A permanently magnetized bar was supported at its centre of gravity like a magnetic needle. By placing the pole of an electro-magnet in proximity to the imaginary circle described by the horizontal swing of the bar, and then breaking the circuit by hand at properly-timed intervals, it was found that the bar could be kept in continuous rotation. This proved

STEPHEN A. DOUGLAS.

to be the key to the solution of the problem of the electric motor." The little machine was taken to Middlebury College, and exhibited to Prof. Turner, who declared: "Gentlemen, what you have invented is not a perpetual motion; it is nothing less than a new motive power." Another member of the learned body, Professor Fowler, expressed his belief that the dozen curious bystanders "were then witnessing the first exhibition of what would prove to be one of the greatest inventions of the 19th century." It was not until the invention had reached this stage that Davenport learned —from Stillman's Chemistry — the names of the instruments he had made or of the materials he had used. His wife cut her one silk gown, a wedding gift from her father, into narrow strips, to be used in insulating the helices of the new machine. Davenport and Smalley connected their houses by a wire, on which they transmitted messages by means of electricity, using a battery. This battery they called "cups."

Davenport removed to New York and began the publication of *The Electro-Magnet*, which was printed, as the paper claimed upon its title-page, "by a machine propelled by electro-magnetic force."

Prof. Samuel F. B. Morse, of the New York University, was much interested in electricity, and had often spoken of his intention to experiment.

THE BIRTHPLACE OF STEPHEN A. DOUGLAS.

He was struck with Davenport's machine, and began at once to improve upon it. Davenport's telegraph for the sending of communications over long distance, had twenty-four wires, one for each letter of the alphabet. Professor Morse kept but one, abolishing the other twenty-three. There is but little doubt that Morse borrowed the basis of his invention from Davenport, just as Davenport was indebted to Henry for his initial steps. Morse applied his alphabet to Davenport's discovery. Among his other inventions was a model, two and a half feet in diameter, of a circular railway, embodying every essential element of the modern electric road. He also experimented in driving machines and an electric piano, since so successfully developed. A German baron purchased secretly, from a workman, drawings of some of Davenport's best models, for which the German Diet voted him a reward of $40,000. Thomas Davenport was born in Williamstown in 1802, and died at the age of 49 years. His eldest son, George Davenport, was killed at the Battle of

the Wilderness, and his name leads all the rest on the Soldiers' Monument in the town.

Another native inventor was Patrick Welch, a printer by trade. He produced a type-distributing machine of such merit as to procure him a gold medal from the French Exposition of 1867.

Brandon has given birth to at least one man who has achieved a national reputation in political affairs, viz., Stephen A. Douglas. He was born in 1813, and apprenticed in boyhood to the cabinet-maker's trade. It is said that he originated the saying: "Vermont is a good State to be born in, provided you emigrate early." In accordance with this theory he went West and began, when about twenty years old, the study of law. When in middle life he was elected to the Senate, his power in debate was so marked as to earn him the title of the "Little Giant." Once when abusive language was used towards him, he rose with dignity and said: "What no gentleman should say, no gentleman need answer." In 1858, when Kansas was

AT FOREST PARK FARM.

asking for admission into the Union, the burning question whether she should come in as a slave or a free state was the subject of the famous debate between Douglas and Abraham Lincoln. Douglas insisted that the people of Kansas should be allowed to vote upon their own Constitution and not compelled to accept the fraudulent adoption of the Lecompton Constitution, which fastened slavery upon them. But when the cloud of civil war broke over the land, even before Lincoln had time to issue the proclamation calling for troops, Douglas's offer of support and co-operation was in the President's hands. Peril to the country blinded him to sectionalism, and he exclaimed: "Give me a country where my children can live in peace; then we can have room to settle our political differences." Of secession he said: "There is no justification, nor any pretence of any. If they will remain in the Union I will go as far as the Constitution will permit to maintain their just rights, and I do not doubt but a majority in Congress would do the same. But if the Southern States attempt to

secede from this Union without further cause, I am in favor of their having just so many slaves and just so much slave territory as they can hold at the point of the bayonet and no more."

"Every man must be for the United States or against it; there can be no neutrals in this war —only patriots and traitors."

The birthplace of Douglas remains almost unchanged as it has been in the eighty-seven years and more of its existence. The huge chimney, quaint door and high roof make it an excellent example of early New England architecture.

Brandon can lay claim also to one of the foremost of American Biblical scholars, Thomas Jefferson Conant, born in 1802. He occupied the chair of Hebrew and Biblical criticism in Hamilton University in 1838, and was in the faculty when that institution was removed to Rochester, N. Y. He was prominent among the revisers of the Bible, Genesis, Job and the Psalms coming especially under his hand.

The first newspaper to be printed in the town was *The Vermont Telegraph*, established in 1829, by Orson S. Murray, but was afterwards made an anti-slavery organ by Jedediah Holcomb under the name of *The Voice of Freedom*. Later changes were to the *Vermont Union Whig*, *The Brandon Post*, and *The Brandon Union*, which is at present a very live and attractive sheet. The Rev. Nathan Brown, one of the earliest mission-

JUDGE EZRA JUNE.

aries to India, was for a short time an editor of the *Telegraph.* His experiences abroad were terrible, among them the repeated exhumations of his dead child by the native Indians, for the purpose of despoiling the grave. At last, after vain attempts to secure a permanent resting-place for his little one, the poor father brought the few bones remaining from a feast of jackals to this country for burial. Mr. Brown went later to Japan, where when over sixty years old he learned the Japanese language, into which he translated the New Testament. His poem "The Missionary Call" first printed in Brandon, was sung by Japanese before enthusiastic thousands on the occasion of the National Missionary Meeting at Minneapolis in 1896.

EX-GOV. E. J. ORMSBEE.

The Congregational Church was recently remodelled with good taste. It contains a unique pulpit of flawless white marble, a gift to the society from Mr. Edward D. Selden, now of Saratoga Springs. With no special dissensions, this church has had a large number of pastors, some of them of exceptional ministerial capacity — Rev. Ira Ingraham, Rev. Harvey Curtis, dear to the hearts of children; Rev. Francis B. Wheeler, and the present incumbent, Rev. William Smart. For one short year, 1844-5, this church enjoyed the ministrations of Dr. William G. T. Shedd. Naturally he was called almost immediately to a wider sphere of usefulness, and accepted first a professorship in the Vermont University, and then in the Union Theological Seminary of New York city. He is well known in the literary world as editor of the works of Samuel T. Coleridge.

It is a sad pleasure to recall the men and women who labored here to build up the kingdom of God. Of the former, one of the most eccentric was David M. June, a descendant of one of the first settlers. He was an honest man and shrewd, much opposed to a specially educated ministry. In some of the many interregnums of regular pastorates, he had opportunities to apply his theories, with appalling results of startling personalities and vain repetitions in prayer such as would

BRANDON ITALIAN MARBLE COMPANY'S QUARRY.

organized in 1785 by five men and five women. The first meetings were held in a log cabin. The present house of worship is the fourth, and has been

have convinced a less opinionated man of the error of his ways. He had an inconvenient habit of riding up to his neighbors' doors, and, summoning the busy housewife from her morning duties by a brisk knock with the butt of his whip, calling out: "Do you believe in the Lord Jesus Christ this morning?" A man of very different temperament was one who never dared, when repeating the Lord's Prayer, to leave the phrase, "Thy will be done," without conditions, but immediately added, "measurably, at least, O Lord."

The Baptist church had for its devoted pastors, for forty years, the Rev. C. A. Thomas. He did not belong so much to his society and de-

ENTRANCE TO PINE HILL CEMETERY.

nomination as to the whole town. Both he and his excellent wife were the valued friends of all, young and old. For many years the baptisms took place in the Neshobe River, whose waters, even on Sunday, were heavily tinged with the ochery sediment deposited by the washings of the iron ore. It was not uncommon when women descended into the stream to see their light skirts belly out on the surface of the water as if "making cheeses," and when, as often happened, the gown was familiar under more everyday aspects, the impression upon a childish imagination was peculiar.

The story of Brandon would lose an impressive feature if Judge Ezra June were omitted. He was a factor in the education of successive sets of young girls as they advanced into the ranks of womanhood, especially perhaps, in his Sunday school teaching, but in divers other ways also. His enthusiastic teaching of the Psalms, who that heard him can ever forget? As a bachelor his opinion on the verse, "A good woman is a crown to her husband," had special weight. He appreciated the book of Job, and loved certain Psalms so much that his very intonations in reading them ring in the ears yet, after forty years have passed. Sunday was always a field-day for him, and the inspiration caught from the pulpit or from his own meditations bore fruit in many ways all through the week. On Monday mornings, especially, it was his delight, armed with a favorite book or a new essay, to exact the attention of the young friend selected for instruction. Gradually books of reference were collected, a dictionary here, a pile of cyclopædias there, a history or two were added, and the subject under consideration was thoroughly sifted. Who shall say what help and stimulation lay therein? Judge June cared for nature. An unusual cloud, a wonderful effect of light, would arouse him to a high pitch of enthusiasm. Walking with him once through the little park, when the tree-stems were sharply defined on the snow, he brought his stick down emphatically, and exclaimed: "You never had a collar embroidered like that!" It was an exciting day for the whole village when he went to Boston to hear Jenny Lind's first concert in America. His own excitement was intense, yet subdued by a sense of privilege. Nothing in his experience quite equalled that, though the first coming of the

GRAVEL FORMATION ON HOGBACK.

steam railway train through the still country meadows might almost be compared to it.

That was in 1848. "Brandon had subscribed for more capital stock than any other three towns in the state outside of bids made by contractors," and the interest in the undertaking was enormous. Every town along the route had prepared a collation, and the directors, beginning early in the day, had been feasted from Massachusetts to Vermont. It was no wonder if the stoutest trencher-man began to flag at last, as Bellows Falls, Rutland, Pittsford, and Brandon hospitality was proffered. All this junketing had consumed the day, and it was in the splendid light of the cool autumnal evening that we finally saw the sight for which we had longed. A little group stood reverently on an overlooking ledge where the tangle of bitter-sweet and wild grape-vine sheltered them from the chill night air, while Judge June recited Job's words about the leviathan.

E. J. Ormsbee, who served his State as governor in 1886, resides in Brandon. His honorable war record beginning as second lieutenant in Company G, First Vermont Volunteers, ended as Major in the Third Division of the First Army Corps of the Army of the Potomac. He was Chairman of the Commission to treat with the Pi-Ute Indians in Nevada, and in 1893 went to Samoa as Land Commissioner. The products and curiosities brought by Ex-Governor and Mrs. Ormsbee from Samoa would worthily stock a small museum.

Mr. Frank Knowlton, a scientist connected with the Smithsonian Institute in Washington, D. C., is another citizen of whom Brandon may well be proud. His work in scientific terminology appears in the Century Dictionary.

As to the scenery of Brandon, the views in all directions are fine, in some directions superb. It is always a question whether the creek or the hill road shall be taken to Pittsford, "the best all-round farming town in the United States," but by neither road must the quaint, foreign hamlet of Proctor, three miles beyond, be missed. It is perched on a marble hillside as steep as an Alp. The picturesque Sutherland Falls glint in and out of the wooded country, hanging like a foamy veil before a rugged face. In an opposite direction one sees where Lake Dunmore lies in the lap of solemn Moo-sa-la-moo. Hidden away in the forest are the beautiful Llana Falls, so often painted by their loving friend, Mr. C. W. Sanderson, the Bos-

LLANA FALLS.

LAKE DUNMORE.

Augusta, The Capital of Maine
(1896)

AUGUSTA, THE CAPITAL OF MAINE.

By Ewing W. Hamlen.

THE earliest predecessor of the modern city of Augusta of which history has any record is the Indian trading post which was established near the spot where the capital of Maine now stands, and which was called by the Indian name of Cushnoc. The large tract of land on both sides of the river Kennebec, from Merrymeeting Bay to its source, was occupied by the powerful tribe of Indians named Canibas; and this land was granted by the Council of Plymouth to William Bradford and his associates in 1629. Bradford traded up the Kennebec, more or less, and one of the principal gathering points of the Canibas tribe was Cushnoc.

In 1640 the Kennebec patent was surrendered by Bradford to the New Plymouth Colony; and in that year the council established a trading post at Cushnoc. This post was maintained by the council until 1660, but in that year the patent passed into other hands. Some sort of a post seems to have existed at Cushnoc most of the time, but no attempt was made to erect a settlement here until about a hundred years after the post was given up by the New Plymouth Council. In 1692 the remains of the old trading post were still to be seen; but it was not till 1732 that Governor Belcher contemplated the founding of a settlement and the establishment of a mis-

sion at Cushnoc. This idea was never carried into effect, and when the first settlement actually was founded in 1754 it was on no such peaceful basis as that designed by Governor Belcher.

There was an Augusta in Maine as early as 1714; but it had nothing in common with the present city except the name, and its life was very short. It was a small settlement founded in 1714 by Dr. Oliver Noyes, who was then part owner of the Pejepscot patent, embracing lands near the mouth of the Kennebec; and the remains of the stone fort and fishing settlement which he made on the shores of the Alliquippa harbor at Small Point, and named Augusta, are still to be traced. This Augusta had been deserted when the Plymouth Company in 1754 erected a fort on the eastern bank of the Kennebec River at Cushnoc, which they named Fort Western. This fort was situated close to the river bank, and consisted of a palisade of timber, with a square block house at each of two diagonally opposite corners, and a main building containing the store and dwelling houses. This main building is still standing in good preservation, near the east end of the present Kennebec bridge at Augusta. The fort was garrisoned by twenty men, and four cannon were mounted in it. A road "fit for the passage of wheeled carriages" was built to Fort Halifax, eighteen miles up the river, by order of Governor Shirley, and a series of expresses, by means of whale boats, was arranged between Fort Halifax and Falmouth, calling at Fort Western, the trip up or down the river being made in from twenty to twenty-four hours.

In 1755 the war with the French and Indians broke out; but Fort Western

THE OLD SECOND MEETING HOUSE.

was left in comparative quiet and did not suffer much. In 1760 large grants were made of the land below Cushnoc bordering on the Kennebec, Dr. Sylvester Gardiner and Benjamin Hallowell respectively taking large grants in the towns now bearing their names. In 1762 the first grants were made to the settlers at Cushnoc, and in the following year these grants were extended farther up the river. The peace of 1763, by which France renounced all claim to Canada and other possessions in North America, brought in its train a most favorable change in the condition of things along the Kennebec valley. With the end of the war the colonists settled down to their more peaceful vocations, strengthened their civil organization, and increased their trade.

It was not till after the fall of Quebec, in 1759, that any buildings were erected at Cushnoc outside of Fort Western; but five years later a census showed that there was a population in Gardinerstown and the settlements at Cobbossee, Cushnoc and Fort Halifax of be-

tween two and three hundred whites. The town of Hallowell was incorporated in 1771, and included in its limits the present city of Augusta, the town of Chelsea, and a large portion of the towns of Farmingdale and Manchester. The towns of Vassalborough, Winslow and Winthrop, farther up the river and more inland, were incorporated in the same year.

James Howard may be considered as being the first settler at Cushnoc. He was appointed commander of Fort Western by Governor Shirley when it was built, and after the war he settled down, receiving a large grant on the east side of the Kennebec. This property he increased by purchase from time to time, and on the incorporation of Hallowell he was elected one of the first board of selectmen. The Howard family were the first regular traders in the new settlement; as early as 1763 James Howard was licensed to sell tea and coffee, and in 1765 his son, Samuel Howard, was in command of a trading sloop plying between Cushnoc and Boston.

The rough state of the surrounding country as late as 1776 is shown by the vote passed in that year by the town of Winthrop, that there be paid to Rev. Mr. Shaw "four shillings which he

OLD FORT HOUSE.

paid for a pilot through the woods" when he went there to conduct services.

In the fall of 1775 Benedict Arnold came up to Fort Western on his expedition against Quebec. He established his headquarters at James Howard's, and remained there eight days. Capt. Daniel Morgan of Virginia commanded the riflemen of this expedition; Capt. Henry Dearborn, who was afterwards Secretary of War, commanded a company; and Aaron Burr, then a young man, was a volunteer. The disastrous end of this expedition is told in history, and has nothing to do with Augusta.

While there were undoubtedly a number of Tory sympathizers in the neighborhood at the time of the Revolutionary War, the town of Hallowell took its part in the military organization recommended by the Provisional Congress, and in 1776 sent a draft of men to join the Continental army. In 1777 the town seems to have been in a bad way, for we read that it voted to stop for the time being "the raising of any money for preaching or other uses," but voted to improve its roads by "one day's work laid upon the polls, and eighty days upon the estates."

Among those whose estates were declared forfeit by the law of 1778, as absentee Tories, we find the names of Sylvester Gardiner, Benjamin and Robert Hallowell, and William and John Vassal. These men were among the most important of the first settlers, as is well evidenced by their names

THE WILLIAMS MANSION.

having been given to the towns of Gardiner, Hallowell and Vassalborough. Owing to the law's delay and by the intervention of the signing of the provisional articles of peace at Paris, November 30, 1782, these estates were not actually confiscated, as the sixth article provided that there should be "no future confiscations made"; and as these cases were still pending at that date and this article was held to be a stay to the proceedings, the estates were retained by their owners.

During the twenty years between the Revolutionary War and the separation of Augusta from Hallowell, the settlement prospered. The first meeting-house was erected in 1782, and money was voted from time to time "to procure preaching." In 1784 a census showed the population to be six hundred and eighty-two; but the settlement was still very much in the rough, for of the thirty-eight houses in town, only twenty were reported as being "anyways comfortable or convenient." Among the names of the new settlers during this period we find those of Samuel and Daniel Cony and Seth and Asa Williams, whose families have since that time been foremost in the affairs of the place.

Separation from Massachusetts was a prominent subject of argument at this time; but the establishment of courts at Pownalborough and Hallowell tended to allay the excitement and to render the people of Maine more content with the existing condi-

THE HOME OF JAMES G. BLAINE.

tion of things. At various times the town sent a representative to the General Court at Boston, but sometimes it was too poor to be able to afford this luxury and remained unrepresented.

In 1790 there were two well settled villages in the town of Hallowell, one called "The Fort," around Fort Western, and the other "The Hook," which is the present Hallowell, two miles down the river. In this year also another well known name appears for the first time, when James Bridge was elected town agent. By this time the town had grown to a considerable extent, and two or three ventures were made in the publishing of newspapers, only one of which, the *Kennebec Intelligencer,* lasted more than one year.

The fight between the two villages of "The Fort" and "The Hook" in regard to the building of a bridge across the Kennebec came before the legislature in 1796. Daniel Cony and James Bridge, both of "The

Fort," were then in office as senator and representative respectively, so that "The Hook" was somewhat handicapped at the start. After a bitter contest the legislative committee decided, in view of the fact that "The Fort" was at the head of navigation on the river, that the bridge should be built there, and not at the lower point. Although it is hardly probable that anyone realized it at the time, this decision was the turning point in the fate of the two villages. Owing to the better communication with the rest of the country on the east of the river the village of "The Fort" has grown apace, and has now completely overshadowed "The Hook." The termination of the contest for the bridge brought to a crisis the feeling of "The Hook" against "The Fort"; and the town of Hallowell was in 1797 divided by act of the legislature. The charter of incorporation was granted to the new town February 20, 1797, under the name of Harrington; but the name did not prove acceptable to the townspeople, and in June of the same year, on petition to the legislature, the name was changed to Augusta.

Augusta at its incorporation con-

tained about two-thirds of the territory, about half the population, and about half the valuation of the old town of Hallowell. The building of the bridge was completed in 1797, and from that time the business of the new town steadily increased. Hallowell still held most of the trade with the district to the west, but nearly all the business from the eastern side of the river came to Augusta. The latter town did a considerable shipping business, and during the War of 1812 and for a few years preceding that war, she suffered more than her parent and rival from depression of trade.

The first meeting-house in town was built in 1782, before the incorporation of Augusta.

ing now stands. The old first meeting-house was taken down in 1810, as it had then become an obstruction on Water Street, in which it partly stood, and the materials were used to build a town-house on Winthrop Street. The second meeting-house, of which a view is given, was struck by lightning and burned to the ground in 1864. The present granite church was built on the same site in the following year.

During the years of prosperity at the beginning of the century, besides the

COURT HOUSE.

THE JAIL.

There was a good deal of dispute as to the location of this building, and after considering the matter for two or three years the town voted in 1781 "to reconsider all the votes that ever have been passed in this town in respect to building a meeting-house, and to begin all anew,"—which was certainly comprehensive. The house stood on what is now Market Square in Augusta. It was nothing but a rectangular barn, with a small porch. Early in the present century the town had completely outgrown the accommodations of the old meeting-house, and in 1809 the second building was erected on the edge of the steep hill overhanging the business part of the city, on the site where the third build-

second meeting-house just mentioned, Augusta built her first grammar school, a new court house, and a new stone jail, to replace the old one burned in 1808. The Augusta bank, which was the first established by Augusta capital and under Augusta management, was started in 1814, with Judge James Bridge as president. After his death in 1824, this office was held successively by Daniel Williams, Thomas W. Smith and Samuel Cony, the latter being in office when the bank surrendered its charter in 1864.

The Cony Female Academy was built by Judge Daniel Cony in 1815, and endowed by him for the free instruction of such "orphans and other females under sixteen years of age" as should be found worthy. This academy continued its useful career until 1857, although in 1844 its needs required the purchase of a new building.

THE WATER FRONT.

When the present High School was built a few years ago on the same site, the old building was moved down the hill near to the bridge, and is now used as a cabinet-maker's shop and harness store.

The first Kennebec bridge fell on the morning of Sunday, June 23, 1816, and a second bridge, covered, was built in 1818. This bridge was burned in 1827, when a third bridge, also covered, was erected. The third bridge lasted till half a dozen years ago, when it was removed to make way for the present steel structure.

Upon the separation of Maine from Massachusetts, Daniel Cony, Joshua Gage and James Bridge were elected delegates from Augusta to the convention at Portland to frame a constitution for the new state. This constitution was approved by the people in December, 1819; and by the Act of Congress of March 3, 1820, the state of Maine was admitted to the Union from and after the fifteenth day of that month.

The first number of the *Kennebec Journal* was published on January 8, 1825, the proprietors being Messrs. Eaton & Severance. In 1831 the Democratic newspaper, *The Age,* was

MAINE CENTRAL RAILROAD BRIDGE.

started; and in 1833 the *Journal* was enlarged in order to cope with its rival. Passing through various hands, the *Kennebec Journal* came eventually into the proprietorship of James G. Blaine and John L. Stevens, late minister to Hawaii. Mr. Blaine

HIGH SCHOOL.

gave it up in 1857, and after being owned by several other people the paper was purchased in 1868 by Messrs. Sprague, Owen Nash, who in 1870 successfully issued it as a daily paper. It is now owned by Messrs. Burleigh Flynt, and is one of the best daily papers in the state.

In 1827 the legislature, then meeting in Portland, after a committee (appointed in 1822) had visited and reported upon Portland, Brunswick, Hallowell, Augusta, Waterville, Belfast and Wiscasset, and after years of debate, decided upon Augusta as the seat of government for the state of Maine. In the same year Congress authorized the construction of an arsenal at Augusta, and Kennebec Arsenal was built in the following year. The buildings of the Arsenal are of

granite, and stand to-day as they were originally erected. Major John R. Maginnis, of the U. S. Ordnance Corps, is the present commandant.

The present Court House was built in 1829, of granite, the front having an arcade, the square pillars of which support the more slender columns of the gallery above. The Court House was enlarged a few years ago, to meet the growing needs of the county.

The corner stone of the new State House designed by Charles Bulfinch, the architect of the State House at Boston, was laid in the same year, and the legislature met within its walls for the first time in 1832. The situation of

POST OFFICE.

the capitol was certainly well chosen. It stands on a knoll between the old Hallowell road and the new or river road, facing the east. Situated at the extreme south of the town, it overlooks almost the whole of Augusta. Away to the north stretches the Kennebec, until it is lost not far above the dam behind the bluffs forming the west bank at that point. Covering both banks of the river is the town itself, the houses being for the most part veiled by the magnificent old trees which are

THE BANGS FACTORY.

the new part is in perfect keeping with that of the old, and the addition has much improved the appearance of the building.

Undoubtedly the most important improvement in the history of Augusta was the building of the dam across the Kennebec. The Dam Company was incorporated in 1834, but owing to the unfavorable report of an engineer the scheme languished and came near being abandoned. In January, 1835, however, the corporation took another start, and the four men who then composed it set to work to carry the project through.

plentiful throughout her streets. Directly to the east, across the river, are the Arsenal and the Insane Asylum; and to the south the view extends down the river to Hallowell, Gardiner and the lower Kennebec valley. To the west the capitol is backed by a round and well wooded hill, which in the autumn is one mass of glowing color. In the course of years the State House was found to be too small for the increasing requirements of the legislature, and in 1889 a large addition was made by throwing out a wing to the rear. The architecture of

RESIDENCE OF HON. JOSEPH H. MANLEY.

All the other incorporators had dropped out, and Daniel Williams, Edmund T., James and Horatio Bridge were the energetic men who still held to their intention of erecting the dam. Reuel Williams came in soon after, and a plan was made by the new engineer, Col. William Boardman, of Nashua, N. H. Immediately after the making of this plan, the shares of the company began to go up, and enthusiasm revived. In the same year the construction of the dam was begun, and was

THE KENNEBEC DAM.

continued through 1836 and 1837, with James Bridge as agent. The dam was completed and the lock formally opened, October 12, 1837. Luther Severance, at that time editor of the *Kennebec Journal,* and afterwards the first United States minister to the Sandwich Islands, was one of the first to see the possibility of a dam, and was one of the strongest supporters of the scheme from its very inception. At the banquet given after the

granite, but it was not for several years that granite quarrying was developed to any extent. About 1836, however, many companies were organized, and the granite business continues to this day one of the chief industries of Augusta. The Hallowell granite is well known in the East, and among other large buildings built of it are the Equitable Building, and the new fifteen-story American Surety Company Building, both on Broadway,

LOOKING UP THE KENNEBEC. THE ARSENAL AT THE RIGHT.

completion of the dam, in honor of Colonel Boardman, the engineer, one of the toasts, given by Gen. Rufus C. Vose, was "Old Kennebec, its *perseverance,* its dams, and its *Bridges!*" Up to this time the water power of Augusta had been derived from the little Bond's Brook, on the banks of which the saw, fulling and grist mills of the town were situated.

It was about this time that the first systematic efforts were made to utilize the granite that lay in such profusion around Augusta and Hallowell. The State House was built of Hallowell

New York. The Granite Bank was organized in the year last mentioned, and is the oldest of the banks now doing business in Augusta.

In the spring of 1839 a freshet occurred, which practically ruined those who had put their fortunes into the construction of the dam. During the year which had elapsed since the completion of the work, ten saw mills had been contracted for, and a canal and basin had been built for their accommodation. Some of the mills had also been erected, and prospects were bright. But disaster was at hand.

PUBLIC LIBRARY.

On May 30, 1839, came a freshet of unusual height, and the water made its way through the west wall of the dam, which had been damaged by a freshet in January of the same year, and burst in all its fury into the canal on the west bank of the river. The bank wall of the canal gave way under the strain, carrying with it the newly erected mills. So great was the freshet that the water undermined the bank of the river, and the mansions of Judge Bridge and Edmund T. Bridge fell into the roaring torrent and were washed away. The river had cut out a new channel for itself around the western end of the dam, and in doing so had swept away no less than seven acres of land. When the flood subsided the dam was left high and dry and, with the exception of its western end, practically uninjured.

From this crushing blow the citizens of Augusta rallied nobly, and in 1840 the dam was extended across the river to the new western bank. Saw mills were erected, and in 1845–6 the first cotton mill was built. The population of the town in 1840 was 5,314, and after the starting of the new mills it increased at a still more rapid rate.

Steamers were now running regularly on the Kennebec, and the competition between the rival lines from Augusta to Boston was very keen. At one time as many as five steamers from Boston were lying at the Augusta wharves. The fare to Boston was put down to fifty cents, but, notwithstanding this, one steamer came out at the end of the season of 1845 with a clear profit of nearly ten thousand dollars. The river was dredged between Augusta and Gardiner in order to permit the passage of steamers at any stage of the tide, and for this purpose the town voted to tax itself to the extent of $10,000.

One of the three Presidents of the United States who visited Augusta (the other two being Grant and Harrison) was President Polk, who came there in the summer of 1847. He arrived by the steamer *Huntress* at Hallowell, landing there about one o'clock on the morning of Saturday, July 3, and, together with the committee appointed to receive him, drove to Augusta in carriages. The President's arrival in Hallowell was announced by the firing of a gun, and cannon and the ringing of all the bells in town welcomed him to the capital of the state. The town had been illuminated all the evening, and the appearance of it when the President entered was most festive. A torchlight procession escorted him through the town to the house of Hon. Reuel Williams on Cony Street, where he and several of his friends spent the remainder of the night. In the morning he held an informal reception on the lawn south of Mr. Williams's house, and then drove in an open barouche, escorted by a formal procession, to the State House, where he made a speech from the balcony and afterwards had a great number of the citizens presented to him. Among the gentlemen who accompanied the President on this visit was James Buchanan, then Secretary of State. After midday dinner the President drove to Gardiner, where he stopped for a short time at the house of Robert Hallowell Gardiner, taking the steamer for Portland in the early evening.

In 1849 Augusta became a city, and Gen. Alfred Redington was elected her first mayor. The population in the next year was 8,232, and the valuation of the city was $2,337,138. The Portland & Kennebec Railroad, the con-

ton; her dam provided water power for a large cotton mill, some half a dozen saw mills, a grist mill with six sets of stones, and one or two other mills; her business was in good condition; and her material prosperity was every day increasing.

Immediately upon the declaration of war, the legislature authorized the raising of ten thousand volunteers, and Henry G. Staples was appointed to organize a company in Augusta. This company was fully recruited within two days, and a second company was raised by Moses B. Lakeman in a similarly short time. Six weeks later, on June 5, 1861, these two companies, with the Hallowell company, went to Washington on active service. It is not necessary here to give the history of Augusta during the war. That she acquitted herself with honor may be

THE CAPITOL.

struction of which was begun in 1847, was completed to Augusta by 1851, and great rejoicings greeted the arrival of the first train on the 29th of December of that year. In 1857 a railroad was completed to Skowhegan; and soon after the railroad to Bangor was finished. At the outbreak of the Civil War, the city was connected by railroad with Portland on the one hand, and with Skowhegan and Bangor on the other; she had steamers plying direct between her wharves and Bos-

gathered from the fact that by August, 1862, she had sent out more than four hundred men out of a total of sixteen hundred in her limits between the ages of seventeen and fifty years.

In September, 1865, occurred Augusta's great fire, by which almost the whole of her principal business street was destroyed. Eighty-one buildings were completely burned. The Post Office, two hotels, every bank, lawyer's office, dry goods store, shoe store and clothing store in the city

SOUTH PARISH CHURCH.

UNIVERSALIST CHURCH.

are a large number of houses, the Arsenal and the Insane Hospital. In common parlance, Augusta is divided into four parts, viz., "The Street," "The Hill," "Frenchtown" and "The East Side."

Water Street is undoubtedly one of the finest business streets to be found in a city of the size of Augusta. The solid brick and stone blocks on both sides of the long street are occupied on their lower floors by stores and shops, and in the upper parts by offices, halls, etc. The regularity and substantial nature of these buildings give a well-to-do air and businesslike aspect to the street. At the south end of Water Street are the old *Kennebec Journal* office, the new Masonic Temple, the Post Office and the Opera House. The Masonic Temple was erected a year ago, and has added much to the beauty of the street at that point. It is a handsome red brick block, the first floor of which is occupied by large stores. Half of the second floor is taken up by the Abnaki Club, a flourishing social club which recently came into existence. The

were destroyed, and the total loss was half a million dollars. In the next year most of the burned buildings were replaced, generally by stone or brick structures. The appearance of Water Street, which is the main business street of the city, was greatly improved by the class of buildings erected after the fire, and the character of the street has steadily improved, until at the present time there is but one wooden building in the main part of it, all the others being of brick or stone, and three stories or more in height.

Augusta at the present day has spread out her wings over the steep banks of the Kennebec, and the heart of the city is Water Street, lying parallel with the river, close to the western bank. Several streets, all very steep, lead westward to the upper part of the town, where the majority of the citizens have their houses. To the north, still on the west side of the river, lies the French colony, on the slope of Cushnoc Heights; and across the river on the east bank, scattered over the still steep but more gradually rising hills,

EPISCOPAL CHURCH.

upper floors are devoted to the fine Masonic rooms.

The old Granite Hall, which stood at the corner of Market Square, on the site of the present Opera House, was burned to the ground in the winter of 1890, and the following spring operations were begun on the erection of the present building. The Opera House is one of the best, if not the very best, in Maine; the interior is decorated in white and gold. The Post Office, which stands on the water side of the street, opposite the Opera House, is a

sent out. But one of the principal businesses of Augusta is the publishing of family papers, so called. The late Mr. E. C. Allen was one of the first to take up this business and to introduce it into the city. He was a man of great energy and industry, and by his own exertions created a business in his particular line which was unparalleled. Since his start in business other firms have taken up the family paper, and have also been successful. The principal firms now publishing these papers in Augusta are the Gannett &

COBBOSSEE GREAT POND.

fine structure of granite. It was built during the term of office of Hon. Joseph H. Manley, and is a credit to the town.

A thing to note in connection with the business of the Augusta Post Office is the fact that Augusta stands seventh of the cities in the United States in the amount of mail matter transmitted, being surpassed only by New York, Chicago, St. Louis, Philadelphia, Boston and Cincinnati. It would at first sight appear very strange that a city of twelve thousand inhabitants should take such a high place in the tables of tonnage of mail matter

Morse Concern, and Messrs. Vickery & Hill. There are one or two other smaller publishing firms in the city, but these two do by far the largest share of the business. It is in consequence of the business of these publishing houses that from ten to fourteen tons of second-class mail matter is shipped from Augusta every day. Every morning an empty mail car is put on the siding just below the station, and every night the mail train stops long enough for the engine to run down and pick up the same car, now filled with mail.

This publishing business gives em-

UNITARIAN CHURCH.

ployment to a large number of people, the majority of the hands being girls, who are engaged in folding and preparing the papers for mailing, etc. The Vickery & Hill Company occupies a large building on the hill, and has just put in, in addition to the old presses, a new three-decker press, capable of turning out some five thousand twenty-four page papers per hour. The Gannett & Morse Concern have their place of business on the East Side, near the river. A few months ago they had the misfortune to have one of their buildings burned, but with the enthusiastic help of their employees they were able to get off their publications with only a few hours' delay. A new building was erected within a week, and other and more permanent ones will be put up in the spring.

In the upper floors of the Post Office building is the Pension Department. On the fourth day of each March, June, September and December these offices are crowded to overflowing with veterans, each patiently waiting for his small share of the $750,000 which is paid out at this office every quarter. The sight of these old veterans of the Civil War brings freshly to mind the thought of what they have gone through for their country's sake, and even the most unpatriotic cannot but be affected by the sight. As they throng in and out of the government building, and gather in groups at the banks of the city, or in its shops and stores, the thoughtful of the present generation cannot help experiencing a deep feeling of thankfulness that the lines are cast unto them in pleasanter places than they were to the generation of thirty years ago.

Next to the Post Office is the slope leading down to the Kennebec & Boston Steamboat wharf; and on the other side of Water Street is Market Square, where in the winter the heavy sleds from the surrounding country districts gather with their loads of fir boughs, hay or cord-wood, waiting for customers. In the summer the square is filled every morning with the farmers' wagons, loaded with all the produce of the farms and gardens. Here, too, the travelling fakir takes his stand and discourses to the crowd gathered around him on the all-powerful virtue of the particular balsam which he has for sale, or invites the strong men in the crowd to try their strength of swing with the sledge on his machine with the lofty scale and sliding indicator. On the selfsame spot now occupied by the Italian woman with her little cage of birds, beseeching every passer-by to have his fortune told, stood at the beginning of the century the first meeting-house of Augusta. Those were the days when

NEW CITY HALL.

one had to go to church or run the risk of being publicly reprimanded by the constituted authorities for the neglect, and when our modern fakir might have been ducked as a quack or put in the stocks as an idler; the little Italian woman in still earlier days might have been hanged as a witch.

From Market Square to the bridge is the busiest part of Water Street. Among the many fine buildings, the newest one, which stands out as the handsomest and best, is a commodious block, with a marble and granite

STATE INSANE ASYLUM.

THE NEW BUILDINGS.

pillared front, built recently by Mr. P. O. Vickery. There is an appearance of prosperity about Water Street which is always most encouraging. Even in the bad year of 1893, when the most depressing reports were coming from every part of the country, a look at Water Street cheered one up and seemed to show that here, at least, things were in a prosperous condition. Whether it was from the canny conservatism of the Maine merchants in their methods of doing business, or from some other reason, true it is that Maine generally, and Augusta in particular, suffered less from the bad times than any other part of the country.

From the bridge northward Water Street winds its way toward "Frenchtown," under the bridge carrying the

Maine Central Railroad's main line to Bangor, and passing by the gigantic cotton mills of the Edwards Manufacturing Company. Just before reaching the Edwards Mill a road turns off to the left, and going westward threads the valley of Bond's Brook. It was on this brook that some of the earliest mills were built; and there are still one or two on the lower part of it. This little valley is one of the most picturesque places in the city, and it is hard to say when it is most beautiful,—in the early summer, when the woods covering its sides are in their freshest green; in the fall, when these same trees are ruddy with all the thousand tints of that most lovely season, or in the winter, when the snow covers the ground and the only green things to be seen are the tall fir trees standing in solemn groups around the mill ponds, and when the course of the stream can be traced only by the ice upon it.

Going back to Market Square, and climbing the old Jail Hill, now known as Winthrop Street, we pass the end of the Maine Central passenger station, and at the top of the hill reach State Street, the chief avenue on the plateau lying parallel with the river on the west. At one corner is the new Lithgow Library, recently opened as a public library. The building is of granite, gray, rough hewn, and the roof is of red tile. The combination of color gives the building a striking appearance. In the library have been placed a number of beautiful stained glass windows, commemorative and

SOLDIERS' MONUMENT.

illustrative of prominent incidents in the early history of the town, which are likely to be of permanent value.

On the corner diagonally opposite is the Court House, and next to it stands the jail, both of granite. The latter is one of the best in Maine, and kept in perfect condition within and without. Shutting one's eyes to the heavy iron bars which guard its windows, it looks like anything but a prison, and altogether has a most imposing appearance.

All the churches in the city are grouped on or close to State Street, half a dozen of them being within a stone's throw of the new library. For half a mile up the hill to the west lies a network of streets, bordered with magnificent old trees, on which are the houses of the majority of the citizens of Augusta. All the houses are good; none of them are ostentatious. One of the best features of Augusta society, speaking broadly, is the moral atmosphere pervading it which precludes the idea of the rich vying with each other in outshining their

poorer neighbors. The central idea which may be gathered from the character of the houses of the people is that all should live comfortably and none extravagantly. The cause of this is largely to be found in the direct or indirect influence of the many remaining members of the numerous old families who came here when the settlement was young, and who have lived in the town and for the town ever since. They have modified the stern Puritanism of our forefathers, and have adopted the modern comforts and luxuries, but they have always discountenanced extravagance and empty show. This simplicity tends to make the tone of Augusta society less conventional than that of many other cities of similar size. Augusta's hospitality to the stranger is well known; and one has only to be a stranger and have his lot cast among her people, to find out the reality and warmth of that hospitality.

Away at the south end of State Street is the house of the most distinguished man who ever made his home in Augusta, the late James G. Blaine. The public life of Mr. Blaine need not be touched upon here. In private life he was simplicity itself. Saddened as his last years were by the death of three of his children, in his bereavement he had the sympathy of all his fellow-townsmen. The Blaine house, like most of the houses of the better class in Augusta, is not pretentious in any way. Originally it was a good deal smaller, but the size of his

THE EDWARDS COTTON MILL.

family forced Mr. Blaine to enlarge it by building an addition at the rear. In the garden south of the house Mr. Blaine loved to lounge and walk. In the summer time now his grandchildren may be seen there romping about with a multitude of dogs. The present members of the family are devoted to their canine friends, and when they come to Augusta bring with them everything from a ratting terrier to a mastiff.

Just across the street from the Blaine house is the State House. Every second winter this is the scene of bustle and activity, consequent upon the assembling of the biennial legislature. In legislative winters every hotel in town is crowded to overflowing. Gaieties are continuous in the town, and Augusta people vie with their visitors in hospitality. The halls and lobbies of the capitol are thronged with members of either House, councillors, officers of the state, and the ubiquitous lobbyist. The latter figures most prominently, perhaps, in cases of town division. The state of Maine has not yet resolved herself into her final units, and at every session of the legislature there come up petitions for the division of some town or other and the incorporation of a new one. These battles are the most bitterly fought of the many that are waged each session; for in a town fight there are but two sides, and these are taken and held with a pugnacity and a tenacity characteristic of the Maine people when once fully roused. There is little speaking for effect in the Maine legislature. Most of the members are hard-headed business men, and the business of the state is conducted in a businesslike way. Impassioned oratory makes but little impression, and is somewhat discountenanced when it springs up, although a thoroughly good speech receives the most courteous hearing.

Near the centre of the upper part of the town lies the little park, with the Soldiers' Monument in its centre, a polished granite column, on a triangular plinth, surmounted by a bronze figure of Fame. Descending again to Water Street, the Kennebec bridge is reached. The view, looking up the river, shows, first, the steel bridge of the Maine Central Railroad; farther up the river, on the left, is the Edwards Mill, an immense brick building, a quarter of a mile long; still farther up is the dam, with the lock, now filled up, at the right of it; beside the lock is the pulp mill of the Cushnoc Fibre Company. During the summer months the river is full of floating logs, lumber driving being the principal industry on the Kennebec. The mill of the Augusta Lumber Company, on the east bank below the bridge, is now the only saw mill in Augusta, and save the Millikens' mill at Hallowell, is the lowest on the river. During the open season schooners are always being loaded at their wharf, and it is no uncommon thing in the summer to see ten or a dozen lying at the wharves on the west side of the river loading or discharging cargoes of lumber, granite or coal.

Close by the river bank at the east end of the bridge stands the new City Hall, now in the course of erection. The architect is Mr. John C. Spofford of Boston. The building is being erected by a corporation, from whom the city will lease it with an option of purchase at cost after ten years. In this building all the offices of the city officials will be located, thus bringing all the departments under one roof. One of the features of the new building will be a hall large enough for any state convention, so that in future Augusta can be reckoned as one of the places where large conventions can be conveniently held.

Hardly fifty yards from the new City Hall is the old main house of Fort Western, now degraded to the position of a tenement house of the lower class. The two block-houses and the palisades have long ago disappeared, but the old store and dwelling house, with its twelve-inch timber walls, still stand in good preservation, a memorial of the troublous times of the early settlement.

One of the most interesting houses in Augusta stands on Cony Street, at the top of the hill leading from the bridge. This is the old Williams mansion, which was built in the first years of the century by Col. Arthur Lithgow, then sheriff of Kennebec county, and which was purchased a few years later by Hon. Reuel Williams. The front of the house is toward the south, and the back toward the street. This is said to be owing to a quarrel which the builder had with Judge Cony, who had a brick house on the opposite side of the street, which also stands to the present day. In the Williams house things have been left pretty much as they were when it was first built; and the furniture and wall-papers are the delight of the antiquarian. The south parlor is octagonal, and its walls are still covered with the original paper, which was brought from England at great expense. The design of this paper represents the voyages of the redoubtable Captain Cook, and the figures on it are pictured about half life size. It was in this house that President Polk stayed when he visited Augusta in 1847 and was entertained by Mr. Williams.

Not far from the Reuel Williams mansion stands the present commodious High School building. On a quiet little street close by is the house of Mr. James Bridge, who was one of the prime movers of the Kennebec Dam Company, and in 1836–7 agent for the corporation in the construction of the dam. Mr. Bridge died January 8, 1896, in the ninety-second year of his age, and prior to his death shared with Hon. James W. Bradbury, who is now ninety-three, the distinction of being one of the oldest men now living in Augusta. Mr. Bradbury graduated from Bowdoin College in 1825, and was a classmate of Nathaniel Hawthorne and Henry W. Longfellow. He was United States senator from Maine from 1846 to 1853, having as some of his companions in the Senate such men as Webster, Clay, Calhoun, Douglas and Cass. Opposite Mr. Bridge's house is the old Daniel Williams mansion. Mr. Daniel Williams was a prominent man in the affairs of Augusta in the early part of the century, and his son, Gen. Seth Williams, distinguished himself in the Civil War, becoming Adjutant General under General Grant.

On the road which leads from the bridge to the State Insane Hospital, known as Hospital Street, stands the home of the Hon. Joseph H. Manley, one of the most prominent politicians in Maine. Mr. Manley has twice been postmaster of Augusta. He is at present secretary of the National Republican Committee, and chairman of the Executive Committee.

Just beyond, stretching down to the river, is the United States Arsenal, and still farther on is the Asylum. The main buildings of the latter are of stone, but large brick wings have been added from time to time. The grounds of the Asylum are beautifully laid out, and from them one can get the best general view of the city of Augusta.

Augusta is surely a beautiful city. In the summer, when the trees which line all the streets are in full leaf, it is at its best. Through the hot weather the people take full advantage of the noble river which flows through their midst. The scenery on the Kennebec from Augusta to the sea is very fine, and a sail on the *Kennebec* or *Sagadahoc* is worth taking. At Merrymeeting Bay, where the Androscoggin joins the Kennebec, the sheet of water has the appearance of a lake, and the outlet is hard to find. In the summer, too, many of the inhabitants of Augusta betake themselves to the cottages at Hammond's Grove on Lake Cobbosseecontee, some four miles away. Cobbossee Great Pond, as the lake is sometimes called, is about ten miles long, and affords fine sport for the fisherman. It is surrounded by woods and farms, and dotted with islands. On a number of the islands and at many points around the shores are little camps and cottages, and canoeing is a favorite enjoyment.

The principal industries of Augusta at the present time are the Edwards Cotton Mills, the pulp business of the Cushnoc Fibre Company, the sash and blind factories of Bangs Bros. and of Webber & Gage, the lumber business of the Augusta Lumber Company, the granite paving block business, and the family-paper business of the publishing firms. There are smaller factories and machine shops, all in flourishing condition, and the town is steadily growing in prosperity.

The business spirit of Augusta is not only conservative, but progressive. As the material welfare of the town may be said to have really begun with its separation from Hallowell and the building of the bridge across the Kennebec, so it is argued by the most energetic of Augusta's business men can her prosperity be increased at the present time by still further and better communication with other cities and districts. A scheme is on foot to connect Augusta by railroad with Lewiston on the west and with Camden on the east. The proposed line would connect with the Grand Trunk Railway at Lewiston, and this connection would enable merchants in Augusta to get their freight from the West at a through rate. The continuation of the line to the east would tap a section of the state not now provided with railway facilities, and would bring an increase of business to Augusta. The Board of Trade has this scheme in hand, and it is probable that before another summer has passed the matter will be brought into such shape that the railroad will be an accomplished fact within a very few years. In such ways Augusta is reaching out to make her future fruitful as her past has been.

Noted Inns
of New England
(1904)

Noted Inns of New England

By MARY H. NORTHEND

THE most modern hotels of the present day cannot compare in importance with the ordinaries or inns that were opened in the early settlement of our country, by order of the General Court, in every town under the direct jurisdiction of the minister and the tithing man. These worthies were given authority to enforce the laws that prohibited the inordinate sale of liquors. As the inns were often required by law to be situated next the meeting house, many a pleasant nooning did our ancestors spend before the hospitable fire; for scant comfort did the footstoves of our forefathers' time give during the long church services in the winter months.

The landlords were men of distinction, being often the local magistrates, and the walls of the inn were posted with items of interest, such as notices of town meetings, elections, new laws, bills of sale and auctions. With these exciting topics before them, the men of the town might sit before the great wood fire and sip their toddy while discussing the news.

The tavern in Ipswich was presided over in 1771 by no less a personage than the granddaughter of Governor Endicott, thus showing that some of the best families in New England were represented in this business, also showing that women were appointed innkeepers in many places by the advice of the General Court, so well did they perform their duties.

The business of inn-keeping was not a particularly profitable one, as the sale of liquor was at times prohibited, no games were allowed, and the sale of cakes and buns forbidden. Small wonder that the town of Newbury was fined twice in those early days for inability to secure a person to open an ordinary. These houses were primitive affairs, often having but two rooms and a lean-to. Comfort was not expected, and frequently travelers had difficulty in securing beds. One's dinner cost sixpence by order of the General Court, regardless of quality or quantity of food served, the landlord and his wife always acting as host and hostess at the table.

Among the signs that were ordered placed on conspicuous parts of the houses where was provided "good entertainment for him who passes, horses, men, mares, and asses," was one representing a bust of General Wolfe, surrounded by a wreath of scroll work. It was carved by William Davenport of Newburyport, and was partially destroyed by the great fire that swept through that city in 1811, laying the principal part in ashes. A new sign was then painted by Samuel Cole to replace the original one, and it is still used at the same tavern. In Georgetown also, ten miles from Newburyport, a very ancient sign, bearing a portrait of General Wolfe, is in an excellent state of preservation. The house on which it originally hung was built twenty years after the Pilgrims landed at Plymouth. The original frame of the house still re-

SIGN AT WAYSIDE INN, STOCKBRIDGE, MASS

mains, together with the heavy oak beams and interior panelling. In other respects the building presents a modernized appearance.

Concerning this old sign the following interesting incident is vouched for. Just after the battle of Lexington and Concord, a company of Yankee soldiers were on their way from Ipswich to the seat of war. Passing through Georgetown, they came to the old inn, over the front entrance of which hung the portrait of General Wolfe, swinging in the brisk morning breeze. Up to this time of "unpleasantness" between the mother country and our own, the memory of the brave Wolfe had been revered and loved alike by Englishmen and Americans. But now, in their intense hatred of everything British, the soldiers halted, lifted their old flint locks to their shoulders and riddled with bullets the offending sign. Several passed clean through it, while a few remained imbedded in the wood and are plainly discernible at the present time.

An old tavern at Medford displayed a sign representing two old men shaking hands and bowing, which gave to the place the name of "The Palaver's Tavern." But it proved so offensive to the innkeeper that he substituted another and more appropriate design in the form of a fountain pouring punch into a large bowl. This "Fountain Tavern" had substantial platforms in two large shade trees connected with each other and the house by bridges. In these tree nests the traveler might sit through the long afternoon or in the early twilight, cool and remote among the branches, drinking tea; watching horsemen and cartmen, and sturdy pedestrians come and go, and the dashing mail coach rattle up,—a flash of color and noise and life,—pour out its motley passengers, and speedily roll away with renewed patrons and splendor.

Among the several ancient inns standing at the present time, is one in Byfield, Massachusetts, kept by "Old J. P." as he was familiarly known, from the fact that these initals were stamped on the barrels of rum with which his cellar was filled. This tavern of Jeremiah Pearson's was a lively center on Muster days, and many a yarn was spun across the board in Independence Hall, so christened at a dinner given the returned troops after

COLLECTION OF OLD CHINA, WAYSIDE INN, STOCKBRIDGE, MASS

the Revolutionary War. Hither also, the eccentric Timothy Dexter, often wended his way and drank deep of the flowing bowl,—a habit, no doubt, that enhanced his eccentricities.

Copied from one of the favorite signs of England, "The Bunch of Grapes" formerly hung from the tavern of that name on State Street, Boston. It was made of baked clay and had been brought from England. A portion of this sign can be seen in the Essex Institute, Salem,

spirits of the Ohio Company, called their first meeting. At the expiration of the lease, the old land-mark was torn down and a granite structure erected, and nothing now remains for us but the memory of this by-gone splendor.

The Ames Tavern of Dedham, the original license of which was granted in 1658, was kept by the celebrated almanac maker, Nathaniel Ames in 1735. The sign on this tavern was unique and is said to have portrayed some family history.

WAYSIDE INN, SUDBURY, MASS

while two bunches of the grapes are stored in a steel vault in the Masonic Temple, Boston, for the Masons take every precaution to preserve this old relic of the inn, in which all the meetings of the oldest benevolent association in New England were held in 1767-8. Here also the first President of the United States stayed. The tavern of "The Bunch of Grapes" was moved to Congress Street, and here General Stark came after his victory at Bennington. Here also General Rufus Putnam and Manasseh Cutter, the moving

In the settlement of his son's (Fisher Ames) estate, a suit was brought into court. This so disgusted the inn-proprietor, that, although the suit was decided in his son's favor, he expressed his dislike by causing the whole court to be painted on a sign board for his tavern. So faithfully were each of the judges represented, they could not fail to be recognized. The august court heard of the proceeding and sent a sheriff to seize the sign. Ames was in Boston at the time, and hearing of their intention, rode post haste to Dedham, reaching the tavern first, and in time to save the sign before the sheriff's arrival. What a thriving business would the sign painters of today have, and where should we find space for the signs, if all men showed their disgust of law suits in this manner?

A sign verse which hung in front of "Mother Red Cap Inn," Holway, England, and which was reproduced on ancient signs in America, savors strongly of our dear old Mother Goose, and possibly these old dames were relatives.

"Old Mother Red Cap, according to her tale,
Lived twenty and one hundred years, by drinking this good ale;
It was her meat, it was her drink, and medicine beside;
And if she still had drunk this ale, she never would have died."

As the settlement of New England increased, the demand for pub-lic houses became greater, more attention being paid to the preferences of guests. A public parlor became a necessity for the entertainment of private parties, and gradually the tavern became more like a well-to-do private house, where one could receive the best of care.

Although a few of the original New England taverns still exist, many of those now standing are more recent ones built on the same site and bearing the same name. The house at Stockbridge, Massachusetts first built in 1773, and added to from time to time, was on the stage route between Boston and Albany, and was a large and popular hotel when burnt in 1896. In the public room of the present tavern, which was re-built on the old site, is a collection of old-fashioned furniture, crockery and bric-a-brac, con-

INTERIOR OF WAYSIDE INN, SUDBURY, MASS

BLACK HORSE TAVERN, SALEM, MASS

sidered by collectors of the antique, the best in the country. What better advertisement could any hotel of our day want than the reputation which these inns have won,—that of hospitality, bountiful store and upright management.

"The Wayside Inn" at Sudbury, Massachusetts, made famous by Longfellow's "Tales of a Wayside Inn" was the assembly place of the soldiers after the Battle of Lexington.

"Wright's Tavern" at Concord calls to mind a thrilling scene when Major Pitcairn, the British commander, stirring a glass of brandy with his bloody finger the morning before the Battle of Concord, boasted that he would thus stir the blood of his enemy before night. A great structure once stood on the site of the present Stearns Building, Salem, Massachusetts, known as the "Tavern with many peaks" later on as "The Ship Tavern." Here was formed the Social Library in 1760. The "Salem Coffee House" was kept in a building near the site of St. Peter's church, while "Thomas Beadle's Tavern" stood on Essex Street, nearly opposite its present juncture with Pleasant Street. In this latter house were held the preliminary examinations in witchcraft times.

Many Manchester-by-the-Sea people will tell you of one Elizabeth Crafts, an ancient innkeeper of that town, who went to Boston either by packet or on horseback for her goods. She was an industrious woman and sitting on the deck of the vessel one day, knitting, the sail suddenly veered and Elizabeth was knocked overboard. Tradition, that truth teller, says that she kept on with her knitting and took seven stitches under water before being rescued. This remarkable woman also had a romance. A Scotchman, before leaving his native land, dreamed of a fair-haired American girl with a blue ribbon in her hair. That very night Mrs. Crafts, then a young girl, dreamed that she married a sailor. Not long after the lad's arrival in Boston, he spent the Sabbath in Lynn. Entering the meeting house (this act being the proper thing to do in those days) he saw his dream-girl seated in the choir. He made inquiries, followed her to her home in Manchester, and married her not long afterward. We presume they lived happy ever after, though that was not vouched for.

"Fountain Tavern" at Marblehead was the resort of sea captains and the gentry of the town, and it has

drew rein at the door of the tavern. Sir Harry Faulkland, a young English gentleman who had been sent to superintend the building of the fort and who was also collector of the port of Boston, alighted, and attracted by the maiden's beauty, stopped to speak with her. The acquaintance ripened into a love that pride of race and position prevented from culminating in marriage at

WRIGHT TAVERN, CONCORD, MASS

been rumored that the pirates, who were finally captured in the streets of Marblehead, made this tavern their rendezvous. What better romance could our twentieth century girls have, than that which fell to the lot of Agnes Surriage, a girl of sixteen who was scrubbing the floor of the inn, to be sure, but who was also strikingly handsome. In the autumn of 1742 a coach and four dashed through the streets and

that time. But after long years, through her devotion in saving his life, the thought of class distinction passed away and they were married with the sanction of the Faulkland family. After a brief residence in London, they removed to Boston, where Sir Harry died.

The first temperance inn was opened in Marlboro, New Hampshire, when liquor was of prime importance in all taverns. This innovation was looked upon with disfavor by drivers of stage coaches and loud were their lamentations. Being assured, however, that coffee and tea would be served them, the tavern became one of the most popular in New England, and thus our first coffee house was started many years ago, being heartily recommended by stage drivers.

One of the quaintest and most

make the six-footer duck his head, while the broad fireplaces easily accommodate seven-foot logs. Ancient china, books and prints are here in profusion, and there are canopied bedsteads, claw foot chairs, and two arm chairs once the property of Robert Burns. The paper on the office walls is Shakesperian, old English landscapes are in the hall, while hunting scenes and sports

FERNCROFT INN, DANVERS, MASS

picturesque taverns in all Essex County is "Ferncroft Inn," located on the old Boxford road. The views from the piazzas are unsurpassed in diversity and grandeur. It would indeed puzzle the heads of our modern architects should they attempt to duplicate the architectural designs of this ancient structure that was erected in 1692, with low ceilings and heavy oak cross beams that

of "Merrie England" delight the eye in the dining room. The front of the inn is an exact imitation of the home of Ann Hathaway.

At a bend of the road we come upon a sign used in the beginning of the last century at the old tavern in Topsfield, kept by William Ready. On one side of the sign is a portrait of George Washington, on the other, that of John Quincy Adams.

"The Boynton Tavern" in old Newbury was presided over by a most eccentric man. One of his sons, who was born while the tavern was being torn down, was named Tearing. The second son, coming when an addition to the new inn was under way, received the name of Adding. Mr. Boynton was the inventor of the first silk reel. Groves of mulberry trees were set out in different parts of Byfield, furnishing proper food for the worms. With Tearing and Adding, these groves grew in size and beauty. Several of the trees are in a flourishing condition on a Byfield farm at the present time.

The "West Parish" of Boxford boasted for many years an old tavern that was erected in 1776, where the militia met to be reviewed. The fine country inn, now located in the "East Parish" was refitted from an old tavern, by Deacon Parker Spofford. Here the first post office was kept, mails being brought by the stage coach. The mails were taken to the church and distributed by Mr. Spofford to the people living at a distance. Even in those days the good deacons used drawing cards for church services, it seems.

In the town of Danvers stands the old "Berry Tavern" originally built in 1741. This public house has been maintained continuously from that time, being at the present day a thoroughly equipped hotel. Could

we, for a short time, bring before us pictures of the young farmers on their way to Boston from all parts of New England, on their jumpers, or long sleds, where were heaped the corn, grain, bundles of yarn, homespun cloth, etc., which were to be exchanged for other merchandise; of the severe storms they encountered, making them willing prisoners for a while at these hospitable houses; of the buxom lasses met and oft times made the partner of their joys; and of the merry-makings in the long winter evenings,— would not all this compare favorably with the present mode of enjoyment of our young people, and does it not make us wish for a glimpse of some oldtime inn? for:

"No longer the host hobbles down from his rest
In the porch's cool shadows to welcome his guest
With a smile of delight and a grasp of the hand,
And a glance of the eye that no heart could withstand.

"When the long rains of Autumn set in from the west,
The mirth of the landlord was broadest and best;
And the stranger who paused over night never knew
If the clock on the mantel struck ten or struck two.

"Oh. the songs they would sing and the tales they would spin
As they lounged in the light of the old fashioned inn;
But a day came at last when the stage brought no load
To the gate, as it rolled up the long dusty road."

The Maine Guide and the Maine Camp (1901)

THE MAINE GUIDE AND THE MAINE CAMP

By Herbert L. Jillson

THE Maine guide, in the mind of every sportsman who has "done" Maine properly, is closely associated with memories of pleasant and successful days with the rod on lake and stream, or long tramps through the woods with the rifle. It is his guide, not the sporting camp proprietor or the people he meets, that the sportsman, after return to civilization, remembers most of all. This recollection is almost always tinged with tenderness, for "Charlie" is to the minds of a certain number of sportsmen, not only the best guide in the State, but the staunchest friend in the world; while, on the other hand, Charlie thinks no sportsmen come to Maine except Mr. So-and-So and a few others of his select coterie. All others lack much or little of being up to Charlie's ideal, and he loves to relate, with glowing eyes, in the presence of other guides, the achievements with rod and gun of the mighty Nimrods whom he guides. To the sportsman, on the other hand, all other guides than their own particular are just a bit "off." They talk too much or too little, paddle or walk too slow or too fast, or, possibly, the cooking is uncertain; but their Charlie hasn't a fault. It is a pleasure to converse with him or be in his company, his paddling and gait are just right, and the coffee never fails to be good, the trout cooked to a turn, the bread light, or the flapjacks brown and tender.

Some sportsmen are, indeed, wont to carry their enthusiasm so far as to quarrel about their guides much as children do about their papas, and while Mr. Gun admires Mr. Rod, personally, he cannot for the life of him understand how he can go into the woods with "that blockhead Tommy." Both seem to forget that a guide is much like a wife; what suits one man has no attractions for another. It is the old, old story where people fail to comprehend what there is in the mysterious word—companionship.

The typical Maine guide is just as much a product of the soil as are the mighty forests, and his replica is not to be found elsewhere. They are, of course, all human and differ in temperament. One may be nervous and excitable, another reserved and deliberate; a third, patient and forbearing, and a fourth, quick tempered and unreasonable; but, as a class, good guides are to a man, strong, willing, friendly and ever on the lookout to see that their "sporter" has the best there is to be got. They are good friends and, sometimes, bitter enemies, for their sense of justice is keen and they are ready to retaliate for a just and, sometimes, a fancied grievance. The majority are sober and honest, if one accepts the latter qualification by making allowances for the fairy tales which they are wont to spin for the entertainment of their city guests, and, often, they have told these over and over until they really believe them. Profanity is not a rule among them, although a moderate amount adds zest to their conversation on fitting occasions. With scarcely an exception they know their place and keep it, seldom mistaking kindness for familiarity or imagining that they are the sportsman and the sportsman the guide. They do not expect to be put on a basis of familiarity. They realize that the men they guide come from a world of which they know little, yet they are seldom envious. They only ask to be treated like men, nothing more.

Guiding is a business with them, devoid of all the frills the uninitiated enthusiast might attach, and taken season in and season out, it is about as hard work as one would wish to undertake. To tramp long miles carrying a heavy pack or an eighty-pound canoe over a rough trail, to paddle from morning until night, to be ever at the call of some one who is in the woods for enjoyment, and then to end the day by getting supper, chopping wood for the night, building a lean-to and boughing down the beds is no easy or unimportant task. If ever a class of men earned their money fairly and squarely it is the guides who are working for $2.50 and $3 a day. A good guide gives his employer the benefit of knowledge gained from years of experience in the woods—the art of woodcraft, the habits of fish and game. He does not hesitate, if need be, to risk his life for his employer, and the greatest personal discomfort is a pleasure to him if it only adds to the enjoyment of his party. Who else would sit in a canoe and paddle for hours in a hard rain drenched to the skin? Who else would pack a canoe half a dozen miles without grumbling, simply for the sake of a few hours' fishing? Who else would give up a blanket and sit by the fire that you might be warm, or go without food that you might not go hungry? No one but the guide is the answer of all who have been fortunate enough to be under the care of a good one while in the woods.

The guide does his best work for the man he likes. It adds pleasure to his occupation to have a man who is appreciative, kindly, and patient. The guide likes to be told that the cooking is good, that the day's sport has been satisfactory, and he appreciates any demonstration of personal interest. Above all things he hates a "kicker," and such a man has a hard time in the woods as soon as his failing becomes known. He admires a man who is a good shot or expert with the rod, and will do anything to assist such a one to obtain what he desires, for he feels, and justly, that half the glory of his employer's achievements falls upon him. After taking a man up close to a mammoth moose or big deer and seeing a whole magazine of cartridges fired without effect, or after paddling cautiously up to a fine trout pool and having the water pounded until the fish flee in terror, he gets discouraged, and it is not to be wondered at. He has done his best in every way, and to have grumbling is not pleasant. The guide admires the straightforward

man. He can tolerate anything if he believes one is sincere in it. If a man can neither shoot nor fish he likes to know it, if things are wrong he would feel better to receive a friendly suggestion than to be told something he knew was not true.

First of all the sportsman who wants to enjoy Maine and see the State properly should secure a good guide, for the best fishing is not found on the brooks and lakes close to sporting camps, and the finest hunting is miles distant, even at the wildest and most remote of them. This can be best done by securing information from some old time Maine sportsman who knows such men. A registered guide is not necessarily all right, for there is little opportunity for the fish and game commissioners to investigate and mediocre men get certificates. After securing his guide, the sportsman must treat that guide "white," and there will be no trouble. The guide does not expect you to help paddle the canoe unless you so desire, for the "help" would probably flavor more of hindrance. If you care to "sack" part of the pack over the trail he will be grateful, but he does not expect it. He wants you to get all the pleasure you can and first, last, and always to be reasonable, not to expect more of him than flesh is capable of, to appreciate the good things he brings your way and to make the most of unavoidable discomforts. If you have money and choose to give him $5 or $25 at the end of your stay, as a tip, or a nest egg for the "little 'un," it will further cement his regard for you, for money is scarce in Maine, and people live plainly. If you cannot afford to do this, friendly acts and kindly interest will do just as well. Do whatever the heart prompts and the purse permits, and your guide will ever be your stanchest friend and most ardent admirer. Above all, make no promises of gifts when you "get home," if you are not in earnest. Always keep faith with your guide if you seek his faithful service and respect.

A CABIN INTERIOR.

ATTEAN LAKE—A VIEW FROM THE CABIN PORCH.

THE CAMP

THE Maine sporting camp, as it is in reality, is little understood by those who have not visited it. At the sportsmen's exhibitions, to be sure, one may have seen sample camps, but an impression formed from these imitations would be far from correct; they give a very inadequate idea. Within the past few years, comparatively speaking, sporting camps have been springing up at favorable locations all over northern Maine. The proprietors are generally guides who have seen a possibility to make money through the venture. Each camp has its "preserve," so called. The greater part of the wild lands of northern Maine are owned by men or companies of men, who, on account of their vast lumbering wealth, often will not sell at any price, and the figures set when the lands are on the market, are beyond the reach of any save millionaires. The land owners are willing, however, to lease "sporting privileges," so called, for a term of years at prices varying from $25 to $100 per year. This gives the lessee right to build cabins on the land and to go over it, camping at will, cutting such wood as is necessary for cabins, wharves, rafts, fuel and the like. Others cannot camp upon the land without the consent of the lessee, but the State makes all lands and all water public so far as crossing them is concerned, and one may fish or hunt them at will, so long as he does not build fires or camp upon them. Each sporting camp has from one to five townships, each six miles square, in its preserve. This gives a large territory, numerous ponds and streams for fishing, waters where deer congregate in the summer and forests where big game roams in the autumn. The camp manager opens up this land. There is a "home camp" at a central point and as convenient to the main road as possible, and trails are cut to the best fishing and hunting grounds, where cabins and lean-tos are erected according to the nature of the territory. At the most important of these branch ponds canoes are placed in order to avoid the necessity of carrying them through the woods when guests desire to visit the places. If there is a mountain near at hand, or a place of especial interest, a trail is cut to that and a feature made of it as a tramp.

The ideal location for a sporting camp is at a point where a large mileage through rivers and lakes opens up for canoeing and at the same time a vast country for tramping from the nearby shores. If one can be fortunate in having a railroad close by another card is played, but these ideal locations are few, and the majority of the camps are not so favorably situated. The extent of territory enables the proprietor to handle a large number of people of varying tastes—those who desire the comforts of the home camp continually, others that want a little rougher fare, and the sportsman who desires nothing better than the lean-to or deserted lumber camp. The typical home camps are models in their way and every art and craft known to the backwoods, and much of civilization is used to make them attractive and comfortable. They are located on some river or pond, backed by the forest, and at a central point with a good view of water, forest and mountains. The number of cabins varies from six to twenty, and they are usually of two sorts, single and double.

The single camps are about 16 feet by 22 in size and some 6 feet high to the eaves. The roof is of "splits," shingles made by splitting cedar or pine with a "frow," and the floor is of boards if there is a sawmill near, and if not, of hewn logs. There are single sash windows on either side and the rough logs, chinked with moss, are often concealed from view on the interior, by a lining of splits or birch bark.

The furnishings consist of two wide beds located on either side at the extreme end of the cabin, a table, and comfortable easy chairs, of the folding pattern. Located in a corner at the front of the cabin is either a rustic fireplace made of stones, or a little wood stove. The former method of heating is the most popular, for there are few nights and mornings in Maine, spring, summer or autumn, when a fire is not comfortable and a cheery blaze is always very delightful to chat by, or to watch flicker on the ceiling after one has retired. These furnishings, home made and rustic, together with the cabin lining and the dim light let in by the small, low windows, make the interior of these cabins very unique and artistic. Bright colored curtains at the windows and draperies upon the shelves, together with guns and rods

CAMP AT LONG POND.

hung upon deers' feet and wooden pegs, further delight the artistic senses. There are numerous shelves to hold the many things the visitor needs, hooks for clothes made by nailing up forked sticks cut to the proper length, or driving in rough wooden pegs, and here and there little oddities; a match box of birch bark, an etching on a bit of fungus, and the like. A broad porch springs from the front of the cabin where one may sit or swing in a hammock. It will be seen that a man and his wife or a couple of sportsmen may be very comfortable in this little home, for a long or short stay, making headquarters for such trips as they desire to make from time to time.

The double cabins are much the same, only larger. There is a main living room in the center with the fireplace at the end, and four rooms, each with a bed, on the sides. The porch is larger and the roof higher, thereby letting in more light. These cabins hold four, supposedly, but they may hold eight comfortably, and the single cabins are adapted to four persons who are well acquainted. The dining-room is a large separate cabin joined on to a kitchen which rests at the rear. The rough tables are concealed with clean linen, and plain crockery and knives answer as well as silver and china. The interior of this cabin is lined and there are numerous trophies—mounted heads and fish, outlines of big trout, bits of moss, birds' nests, birds' wings, and the like upon the walls for decoration.

There is usually a separate cabin, or casino, for general assembly, social evenings, entertainments and the like. Here are card tables and chairs invariably, and oftentimes magazines, papers and sometimes a piano. A rustic fireplace is a central feature.

The food is good. In the summer there are toothsome fried trout three times a day if one wishes, and in the autumn plenty of venison. A cow furnishes milk, while a little garden supplies few or many vegetables according to its location. There are delicious berries during the summer. Sparkling spring water is always found.

It will be readily seen that the home camp is entirely "suitable for ladies," and it seems very queer to camp managers

that this question is asked again and again each year, in letters.

The branch or back camps are not so luxuriously fitted out, but even ladies who are fond of roughing it often find their way to them and come back delighted. These camps have supplies, but a guide is necessary to visit them enjoyably. This personage does the cooking, paddles the canoe, shows where the fish and game are, and makes himself valuable as only a guide can. A cook stove helps the cuisine and one forgets that the table dishes are of tin, the dining table covered with oil cloth, the beds of boughs, and that blankets take the place of sheets.

Farther "in" is the lean-to or tent and the meals are cooked by the camp fire, a portable baker being used to bake bread. The farther in one goes the rougher becomes the task and the less the larder affords, but the country is wilder and fish and game abound in astonishing numbers. Here is where the sportsman goes and stays after once tasting the wild life.

It is not strange that year after year Maine is becoming more and more a resort for people who seek rest and recreation as well as sport with fish and game. Rangeley and Moosehead have their hotels, golf links, tennis courts and every luxury to be found at any popular seashore or mountain resort, but the sporting camps seek to cater only to those who love the woods and their solitude, and the magnificent sport which is found all about, together with necessary comforts. For a place to rest and escape the noise of the city or the confusion of the overpopulated summer resort, the camps have no equal.

As long as satisfactory legislation holds in force there can be no doubt about the great future of northern Maine as a resort for all classes of people. The sporting season is from the middle of May until the last of June and from September 1st until December. During July and August the sporting camp is only such in name, and the proprietor strives to fill his cabins with family parties. Each year the numbers who come for weeks and months during this period are increasing. Maine sporting camps as "summer resorts" are as yet little known, but "loving friends" are good advertisers.

Narragansett Pier
(1879)

HARPER'S
NEW MONTHLY MAGAZINE.

No. CCCL.—JULY, 1879.—Vol. LIX.

ON THE BEACH.

NARRAGANSETT PIER.

THE reader who will take the trouble to look at a State or county map of Rhode Island (they come to the same thing) will notice that Narragansett Bay is divided at its mouth by a long, narrow island—Canonicut. At the southern point of the island is the well-known Beaver Tail Light-house, just opposite Newport Harbor. West of the light, on the mainland, a little estuary, Narrow River, or Pettaquamscott Inlet, makes in through the rocks and sand, and then, breaking into a T, sends one arm due north, where it turns into a fresh-water river, and another about two miles southward. Parallel to this branch runs the strip of sandy coast now so well known as Narragansett Beach. At its southern extremity, where the shore breaks up into rock and pebbles, is the village—the "Pier" proper. Between the beach and the inlet the ground swells into a gentle ridge of farm-

NARRAGANSETT BEACH.

ing land, where Senator Sprague has set his villa—a graceful complex of summer architecture, forming one of the most charming residences in the State. Still further inland, west of the inlet, and looking directly down on it, rises the steep bluff of Narragansett Heights, the southern spur of a chain of low hills running far up into the State, and crowned at its southern extremity by Tower Hill Hotel, with its cottages and out-buildings. From the Heights the land slopes still further westward, with open pastures and gentle indentations, till at about three miles inland we come to the more wooded and broken regions of Wakefield Village, Peacedale, and Kingston. South of these settlements runs a chain of ponds, beginning with Silver Lake (fresh-water), and then a string of continuous salt lakes or inlets, opening into the sea just inside Point Judith, where the coast begins to trend sharply to the west. Indeed, the whole region is dappled with just such pretty sheets of water, of greater or smaller magnitude. There is Warden's Pond, and Weston's Pond, and Wash Pond, and Cedar Lake, and Potter Pond, and such a host of others that to say they form a preponderating feature of the scenery, however bad a pun, would be good geographical truth. This pleasant and peaceful country was once the site of an active and wealthy rural community. Relatively, at least, it was far more important in the social economy of the State than now. Old residents can still spin you endless yarns of the busy, genial, comfortable life and people of the olden time. The land is redolent of traditions drawn

from the old Indian and colonial days. Over by Silver Lake is a mound which the farmers declare must have been an Indian barrow. From the Heights one can descry, dim and blue on the northern horizon, the peculiar rounded outline of Mount Hope; and brave, unfortunate King Philip is a favorite figure in local legend.

All through the pleasant country-side the canny Quakers met, trafficked, and hobnobbed with the guileless red man, spinning the socio-commercial copper in that comfortable game which always turned out heads for the Quaker and tails for the savage. Up and down the coast roamed that pirate bold, Captain Kidd, seeking a hiding-place for his unlawful gains. Right at the foot of Tower Hill, too, where in my time sweet Emma K—— and her childish playfellows used to pick blackberries and cull flowers, he is said to have come to his taking off by judicial *sus. per coll.* Far up the coast, toward Bristol, is the sequestered farm-house where the regicide Whaley is supposed to have sheltered himself from the pursuit of Restoration reaction and the minions of Whitehall.

The old post-road from Bristol to New York used to pass through Kingston and Wakefield, and of course supplied the local annals with plentiful sprinkling of murder, robbery, counterfeiting, and other dramatic complication. Boston Neck, the strip of land between the inlet and the shore, was formerly the seat of rather a peculiarly well-to-do and aristocratic community. One or two solid old gambrel-roofed houses on the ridge still speak from their ruins of old-time comfort and geniality. Sitting on the Tower Hill piazza, a shrewd Providence lawyer, who might wear, in Athenian fashion, a Narragansett grasshopper in his hat, so deep-rooted is he in the soil, has told me how long the old-fashioned traditions subsisted in this out-of-the-way community, and how, in his grandmother's family, the pillion on which she used to ride behind her husband on occasional journeys was, almost in his own

sit in the centre of the web, steadily drawing to themselves the main elements of growth.

I would gladly have the reader seat himself with me on the broad shady piazza of the Tower Hill House, and give himself up for a brief space to the sweet influences of the surroundings. The one thing which will seize him at first glance is the sense of vastness and limitless breathing space.

THE ROCKS OF NARRAGANSETT.

time, a familiar bit of furniture. If one needed a proof that the inhabitants were a substantial race who loved their ease and took it, we might glean one from the fact that hereabouts was born Gilbert Stuart, the painter. Later, too, the neighborhood gained a celebrity in national history by the birth of Commodore Oliver Hazard Perry.

But most of these glories have passed away. The centralizing tendency of civilization has gone over the country, curdling the scattered forces of the rural community into ganglia of commercial or social activity. Providence, Bristol, New London, Newport, Wickford, and other pushing young places have spread out their spider lines of economic traction in railways, post-roads, and steamers, and

Nowhere else in all sea-side resorts will he be likely to get so much air and elbow-room. The ocean view, vast as it is, forms but the setting to a foreground of such endless variety, such exquisite delicacy and minuteness, that it takes some days for the stranger to fully comprehend its endless capabilities, and blend them to one coherent picture in his thought. Right beneath us the land slopes sharply eastward from the bluff, through rugged pastures, to the head of the inlet. Just beyond, in the middle distance, lie the rich meadows of the Sprague villa, with its graceful roofs and cupolas peering out above the greenery. Further to the right the Pier spreads out its straggling cluster of hotels and boarding-houses, offering, as they glow and gleam in the afternoon sun,

ANGLING.

more open sea-line, almost down to Montauk Point; and then, farther to the southwest, the land shuts us in, and the view is filled by the varied lines of the Salt Ponds, with their pretty miniature capes and knolls and wooded banks—a perfect mosaic of rich and brilliant tints. But to the minds of most readers the name of "the Pier" carries with it a savor of social rather than of merely æsthetic interest. So in quitting our nature-studies for the moment, we will leave the macrocosm of sunlight and scenery, pack our valises, and go down the hill for a peep at the *microcosm*—the whirl and gayety of "society" at the beach.

Eight or ten years ago there was, in the modern sense at least, no Pier at all. There was a beach and some rocks, a straggling village of the smallest pattern, a dock and breakwater, a few coal and lumber sloops, and two or three plain farmers' houses, where a few quiet summer boarders took shelter for a season's rest, bathing, and fresh air. But somewhere back in the dark ages of 1870—these Argonautic migrations are always a little mythical—some aristocratic Jason, seeking less, perhaps, a new fleece than fleeing from that of the Newport hotels, wandered over to these Colchian shores. He looked upon the land and found it good, and, what is more, he told all his friends. He must have done so, for just at this period we read that the Trimontane and Gothamite Hellas was stirred to its depths. Old and young, grave and gay, beaux and belles, dandies and dandyesses, packed their Saratoga trunks, shouldered their croquet mallets, and came trooping over to the new land of promise, where living was cheap, if not good, and the too-affectionate mosquito a thing of tradition. Straightway, as in a night, the one-time lonely shore blossomed with boarding-houses. Old farm-houses were enlarged, new clapboard and shingle caravansaries hastily run up, sidewalks laid, permanent bathing-houses erected, and due provision made for both spiritual and fleshly wants by the building of two or three chapels at one end of the village and a restaurant and drinking saloon at the other. A lit-

a dazzling mass of light and color, and giving to the picture the light of human interest. Turning farther to the right, we see, breaking the horizon line, the low wooded knoll of the "Haunted Castle," and over the tree-tops, due south, we can make out to-night the gleam of Point Judith Light. Next in order, after a little space of clear sea, come the dim outlines of Block Island, studded, as we can see by morning light, with hotels and fishing villages, and swarming with coasters. Then

tle steamer, a very little steamer—hardly more than a tea-kettle in a coal-box—was set to run between Newport and the Pier. Two or three years after, the growing needs of passenger travel and the Hazard Mills brought about a branch railroad from Kingston, on which in summer a bustling little locomotive with one passenger-carriage comes whistling and fum-

sharp corner by the bathing beach into a group of others, in which the Metatoxet, Elmwood, Delavan, and Seaview are the most prominent. Even in this early period of its socio-municipal history the place is already taking on its class traditions. Each of the houses begins to show a certain specific character and social flavor. The Mount Hope, spacious and

OLD PIER AT NARRAGANSETT.

ing down the valley several times a day from Wakefield. The town seems in the full tide of growth, and no one can well say where it will stop. Just now it looks like a regiment in battle array, with long, shallow, company front, and slight show of reserves or camp equipage in the rear. All along the shore stretches the row of hostelries, beginning at the railway station with Whaley's Cottage, continuing north-bound with the Mount Hope, Continental, Rodman's, Atlantic, Atwood's, Taylor's, and Matthewson, and turning a

well appointed, is crowded, bustling, and showy, the great house of call for transient visitors, and a welcome haven of refuge to belated strangers from Mesopotamia and the parts beyond Jordan. The Continental, similarly large and comfortable, claims aristocratic position for its wealthy New-Yorkers, Southerners, and Philadelphians, of which last there are generally enough to give it a definite local color. Rodman's, a sort of agglutinating, gradual-evolution style of barrack, so far as the building goes, has yet

PETTAQUAMSCOTT RIVER.

gained a reputation for its social good tone, jollity, and swarms of pretty girls. So strongly does the feminine element predominate, and so iron has this law of natural selection become, that its queer little crannies of rooms are regularly handed down, by a sort of anti‑salic law, in the line of female succession, and it has been proposed to set up as a sign‑board the title of the clever little German comediette, *Zehn Mädchen und kein Mann*. The same strictness of inheritance prevails at Taylor's, and to some extent at the Elmwood. Both, in spite of their small, dark, cramped, and inconvenient rooms, have yet acquired a certain social *cachet* which makes a foot-hold there a thing of value. The Matthewson, Metatoxet, Delavan, and others are all comfortable houses, but of less specific character, and more accessible to general patronage.

Exclusive or otherwise, they make altogether a cheery picture on a pleasant afternoon, when the drive along the shore is alive with carriages and promenaders returning from the after-dinner airing. The lawns in front of the houses are dotted with pretty figures in still prettier toilets, intent on croquet, lawn tennis, or battledoor, assisted by an occasional languid dandy, irreproachable in dazzling linen, white flannel, or fashionable tweed. The children are scampering, romping, and squalling in every one's way, yet too pleasant to be dispensed with. The train has just come puffing into the station—a little way down the beach—from which crowds of new arrivals come pouring out, with much effusive hand-shaking, embra-

cing, and eager clamor of welcoming tongues, and the whole is overlooked by the calmer phalanx of philosophic elders on the piazza, who look up from news-papers or knitting to glance over at the sleepy steadfastness of the sea, gently washing in on the pebbles just across the road, and think, no doubt with a trace of hidden heart-ache, how strong the contrast between the awful permanence of the one and the bright, ephemeral gayety of the others. Still prettier is the scene on a fine night, when the moon, rising full over the ocean, floods the Pier front with a tide of strong yet mellow radiance, turning the whole eastern horizon to one sheet of shimmering silver, gleaming white and cold on the long façades of the hotels, blending yet contrasting with the ruddy glare from countless windows and hall doors, and gently touching the soft draperies of the happy groups as they come straying homeward from the evening's social meetings, and fill the balmy night air with girlish merriment and "resounding laughter sweet." And speaking of social gayeties, here may be the place to remark that Narragansett has a specific character among summer resorts. It has not the adventurous solitude of the Adirondacks, nor the frank, gypsy-like abandon of Mount Desert. Equally little has it of the noisy whirl of Saratoga, or the plutocratic grandeur of Newport. There is no Long Branch Corso of jingling "turn-outs" and petroleum splendor, no dazzling ball-room brilliancy of Cape May or New London. The Pier is certainly not shoddy, but equally not athletic. The white umbrella and sketching stool of the

WHERE ARE THE GENTLEMEN?

Conway Meadows would seem as strange here as the rod and gun of Moosehead Lake. If an occasional enthusiast succeeds in catching an exceptionally stupid bass or blue-fish, he is borne in triumph on the shoulders (figuratively speaking) of all his feminine acquaintance, and straightway erected into a mild species of tea-table idol. No one gets—in London street parlance—"outside of a horse," for the elementary reason, probably, that there is no horse to get outside of. No one goes on "tramps," because tramps involve rough coats and boots, some fatigue, and much perspiration, and are radically incongruous with the gauze train and immaculate shirt collar of civilization. No one ventures on the treacherous yachting party, so sure to disturb the equilibrium of toilet, manners, and diaphragmatic action. There was for a season or two a rash and eccentric innovator who roamed the country-side in a blue flannel shirt and trousers, and got helplessly mixed up

WHERE THE GENTLEMEN ARE.

in the Pierian mind with the boatmen at the fish-house or the lads at the lumber-yard. But he was so severely "sat on" by the Narragansett upper classes, and became such a social pariah among all right-feeling people, that his life grew a burden. Even the few friends who clung to him in his degradation inquired anxiously of his health at eventide, as of one recklessly rushing to destruction, blindly throwing away youth, health, and a once unspotted name. No one ever followed his baleful example. No one in this tropic zone ever did or does any thing to seriously interfere with personal appearance or habits. The Pierian world is metropolitan society on a basis of light but graceful *négligé*. Its prominent feature is quiet good tone, with a perceptible shade of exclusiveness which never un-

bends beyond the possibility of recovery at a moment's notice, yields to no enthusiasm which would shake the placid *nil admirari* of the select. A gentle and patronizing approbation of nature claims occasional indulgence, but never beyond the requirements of *crêpes de Chine* and kid boots. Pierians commune with the eternal verities on Sunday afternoons from the rocks below the railway station. Sooth to say, there is a very pleasant Watteauish charm in the scene when the great bowlder-like mass of Indian Rock is studded with its groups of picturesque human barnacles, "camping down" in every phase of comfortable lounging except the ungraceful, the ladies duly fortified with sun-shades and novels, the gentlemen patiently attendant with wraps and mantles, or daintily recumbent in masculine seclusion with the sundry forms of nicotine that comport with feminine neighborhood. It is the social exchange, the pump-room, Kursaal, and Corso of the beach, only second in its easy idleness to the grand event of the day—the morning bath—of which more anon.

You may circulate freely, chatting and exchanging greetings with friends from the different houses, only observing due regard for circumstance and situation. Don't peer too curiously under the shade of that great sun-umbrella as you pass, for the confidential attitude and murmured conversation of the pair it shelters show that one of the "events" of the season— the old, old story—is running its roseate course, and we shall hear more of it next December on Madison Square or at the Rev. Dr. ——'s. Bow to that group of stylish girls, or drop a passing word, if

Gauche Boozy, or Gunnybags Junior may saunter this way at any moment ; far-seeing beauty is armed for conquest in all her terrors, and has no spare fascination for chance or ineligible cavaliers. Do not suppose, however, because the upas shade of Newport fashion stretches over to this quiet coast, that it stupefies all alike. Down in that cool crevice close on the water you will find a little knot of genial women and good fellows in whose company you may light your cigarette, stretch yourself at ease, and talk or be silent, while with the keen enjoyment of a cultivated sympathy you watch the panorama before you. Confess, with me, that it is a lovely spot, a very dreamer's paradise. We are sheltered from the slant rays of the sun by the rock behind us, and the shelf we are lodged on is so fashioned that while the waves foam and dash right

IDLE HOURS.

you choose, but be shy of subsiding under their lee and hinting a design to join the party. They are on the watch for higher game than you, my poor friend. Even the lively little Chicago belle who smiled so confidingly in your eyes last night on the Elmwood piazza will be apt to show an embarrassed chill of manner, as painful as unfathomable to your guileless soul. For does not the *Proserpine*, just from Newport, swing at her anchor in front of the Continental ? Young Crœsus,

below us, within reach of our hands almost, we are safe from any thing worse than an occasional puff of spray. In its wintry rage, however, the surf can do dire work; witness the great schooner taken up bodily and planted on an even keel on the shingle upon the little beach just north of us. Now, as we lie here, they play idly in and out, pouring in miniature cataracts over the little reefs beneath us, and lifting those dark blood-red, weed-draped masses of kelp just below high water with a wet

INDIAN ROCK.

glitter of emerald and ruby which almost dazzles the eye, while the great lazy frondage of bladder-weed "goes to and back, lackeying the varying tide, to rot itself with motion."

Next a little pleasure-boat comes drifting by, her boom swinging free, and the light breeze dead aft. A larger yacht is just firing her pop-gun and rounding to her anchorage in front of the hotels on the beach, and the little *Florence*, on her last trip from Newport, comes sputtering and wheezing toward her wharf down by the railway station. As the sun sinks behind us, and the long streaks of alternate cloud-shadow and light stretch from the sunset in great curved bands of blue and purple and rosy gray toward their converging point on the opposite horizon, the mist banks in the offing begin to blush like the after-glow on Alpine summits, while the sea lies glimmering beneath them cold steely gray by contrast. Overhead the flecked and dappled masses of fleecy cloud gleam in flame - color and gold, setting sharply off against the cool deep azure beyond. The Newport headlands stand out transparent, dusky red, shadowy, yet illuminated in the magical light. The distant sails stud the horizon with spots of pink and crimson, like jewels of amethyst on a ring of purple enamel, varied with the diamond flashes from the Newport casements as one after an-

other catches the sinking rays. It is a picture we might be excused for lingering over, but the lights are beginning to gleam from the cottages on the bluff behind us, and parents and chaperons on the bank are growing impatient. My imagination scents a faint savor of hot biscuit and broiled blue-fish from distant kitchens, and supper is clearly more in order than scenery. So fold the plaids, help the ladies carefully over the steep ledges and slippery bowlders till we can gain the bank. Notice Dr. Houghton's pretty little cottage at the top of the path. They had a garden party there last week, and there was music and dancing on the lawn, and pretty toilets, and "Punch and Judy" for the children, and refreshment table, and much flirtation all along the line. The proceeds went, I believe, to the support of "St. Peter's by the Sea," the pretty little brown-roofed Episcopal chapel back of the Continental. The comfortable plank sidewalk on which we are now sauntering homeward through the huckleberry bushes was paid for from the proceeds of the private dramatic entertainments at the "Academy" (!), in which young Kerbstone and Bella La Mode so dazzled their sympathetic friends just at the close of last season.

Tea over, and the week-day machinery cleared away from the parlors and piazzas in all the houses, the piano is opened, the *Carmina Sacra* got out, and for an hour or two the whole village is vocal with the sober strains of "Hamburg" and "Mear," or the lilting inspiration of "Hold the Fort" and "Pull for the Shore." As music it doesn't touch the highest artistic mark, certainly, but it is soothing and sympathetic. Thoughtless misses and stalwart young swells, who for six days a week know little melody but "Conosci il suol" or *Madame Angot*, feel the gentle infection, and those who came to sneer remain to sing. Quaint, isn't it, to see young Biceps, just arrived with all his blushing Springfield honors thick upon him, roaring away like a sturdy, red-faced, six-foot sucking dove, and rasping his manly larynx with an intractable chromatic, as he looks over the book with sweet Nelly S——, the daintiest little devotee who ever carried a poor fellow's thoughts skyward on the wings of earthly sentiment? But there is nothing like proximity. Biceps won't be the worse for a little vicarious devotion; and if Nelly can make him available in "convertible" (or other) bonds, why shouldn't she? So none of your scoffing, you æsthetic heathen! If you don't like the music, or the spirit of it, light your cigarette and take a stroll down the promenade. By the time you get back the singing will be over, and the crowded piazzas in much the same tide of unsanctified gossip and flirtation as on ordinary evenings.

The culmination of the Narragansett day—if it is not a paradox to put a culmination at the beginning—is the morning bath. The daily dip, in the Pierian economy, takes a most important place. It is so convenient in situation and appurtenance, so pleasant in itself, and so admirably breaks the monotony of the long summer hours, that it has become the great objective point of the situation. From the farthest hotel, the Mount Hope, an easy half-mile walk brings one to the spot, while the guests at the nearer houses have hardly more to do than to step round the corner. The beach is admirably smooth, level, and free from tidal alteration. The influx of sea-weed, which so often leaves the Newport bather in the unpleasant position of a *croûton* in a basin of pea soup, is rare. The deadly chill of the eastern waters gives place here to a tepid, wooing softness which tempts the most delicate to linger, and from a robust exercise of mere hygienic necessity, makes the dip an æsthetic enjoyment. There is but slight under-tow, and the surf is rarely alarming. Life lines and buoys would seem like a satire on our smiling waters, and no case of fatal acci-

dent has ever shocked our careless security. Once, indeed, a few seasons ago, a plucky girl who could float but not swim found, on trying to touch bottom, that she had drifted beyond her depth, but

"ON THE WINGS OF SONG."

with fine presence of mind she recovered her horizontal position, and lay calmly looking skyward awaiting rescue. She was eventually saved by capillary attraction—in plainer English, towed in by the hair of her head, which luckily was not of the patent reversible attachment order so common nowadays. While, therefore, at Mount Desert only a few matutinal fanatics chill their marrow and abrade their cuticle by an early plunge from barnacle-studded rocks, and the languid Newport lounger, like the Turkish pasha with the dancers, would rather pay some one else to do it for him, at Narragansett every one bathes, the doctor permitting.

INDIGENOUS LOUNGERS.

At eleven o'clock the little village square by the "Elmwood" offers a busy scene. Carriages are whirling by in hot haste, or drawing up in front of the post-office, while the inmates chaffer with the fruiterer for the first early peaches from New York, stroll in at the apothecary's for family doses and cream soda, or inquire anxiously of the much-enduring postmaster if "there is any thing for me to-day?" Improvident new arrivals are picking out bathing dresses at the country store, deep in the choice of blue flannel, waist belts, and fancy stockings. The saturnine, good-natured indigenous lounges, piscatorially picturesque, in shirt-sleeved serenity, about the wharf, smoking the philosophic pipe, and watching the queer goings on of "them taown folks," with a lazy, half-amused, half-contemptuous interest. A richer tone and finer *chiar-oscuro* are added to the scene by the funny little darkies—Cupids in ebony or Day and Martin—who swarm from the washer-women's shanties back of the beach, skirmishing about among the carriages, and watching the proceedings with

open-eyed delight. And through and over all the human tide sets steadily down the little back lane to the "Studio" at the head of the beach. Why "the Studio," where art is supposed to give way to nature, no one has ever clearly told. An upper room contains billiard tables and a bar, while the lower floor is devoted to lunch and supper rooms. The long corridor through which we pass to the sands is furnished with a stand for the visitors' register, and a counter loaded with bananas, cake, sweeties, and other concrete forms of indigestion made easy. The front balconies enfilade the beach, and here, on a pleasant forenoon, you will find a fairy phalanx of youth and gayety, of pretty faces, and gauzy toilets, and dainty summer hats, shifting and changing like a kaleidoscope, and enlivened by a cheerful chatter of feminine tongues, like a large opera-box or a Murray Hill reception in morning dress. The same scene is repeated all down the beach, where the great permanent bathing-houses on the sandy ridge, with their sheltered gable ends and benches looking seaward, supply even better ground of observation for the lookers-on.

Nothing could well be prettier. Besides the sober ranks on the benches, groups of peripatetic fair wander along the shore, or sit calmly in the soft sand, careless of starched muslin and kid gloves, ensconced under great sun-umbrellas or extemporized tents, and hedged about by admiring cavaliers, some dry, in the cos-

accuses, as a Frenchman would say, a fine contour of thew and muscle, which would do honor to the Apollo Belvedere, or the Antinous of the Capitol. The ladies have very literally followed suit. Like Pope's Narcissa, they feel that

"One wouldn't, sure, be frightful when one's dead"

—or dipping. So pretty stuffs, abbreviated skirts and trousers, and colored

A RACE ON THE BEACH.

tume of the nineteenth century, others in bathing dress and in varying stages of dampness. The Narragansett bathing costume is, artistically at least, an improvement on the conventional pattern. It is often graceful, almost always compendious. The men have found out that for the swimmer a yard or two of superfluous stuff may advantageously be retrenched at elbows, neck, and ankles. Their dress, with a moderation born of good taste, shrinks from extremities, and the snug *maillot* of the modern haberdasher

stockings have generally replaced the cumbrous proprieties of old. The ancient figure of fun has become a very comely object, wet or dry, and the witch of the pantomime has budded into the Columbine. To meet a party of these joyous young people, in idyllic unfolding, trotting up the beach for a preliminary "breather" before going in, or drying off after coming out, would make a rural precisian faint with dismay.

The stretch of water before the bathing-houses on a fine August morning offers a very cheering spectacle. The little children, golden-haired, blue-eyed, and chubby, in various light and cherubic undress, are paddling in the creamy ripples, screaming with delight as the wavelets

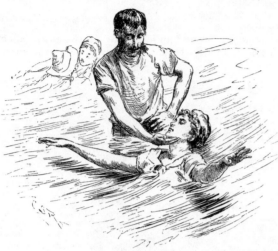

A NATATORY LESSON.

chase them up on the sand, or hanging back and squalling dismally as scolding nurses or papas try to drag them in for a serious dip. Farther out come the compromise ranks of sober matrons or timid youngsters, who stand, or squat rather, mid-leg deep, rising and stooping in solemn cadence, with that queer penguin-like gravity which marks the cockney bather all the world over, or presenting their shoulders to the last ripples of an infant breaker, in the delightful conviction that they are "battling with the surf." Still farther out come the real bathers. The beach is so level and the water in fine weather so quiet that it needs little courage to walk out to one's armpits. At this depth we shall find a fringe of lively people in the very heyday of robust enjoyment. Here a pair of bright-eyed lassies are trying a race, the more skillful showing the other "how to do it," sputtering, screaming, and laughing, but making little headway, while young Biceps stands shoulder-deep beside them, encouraging and criticising their efforts. Next comes the couple we last met under the umbrella, the youth teaching the maiden how to float, keenly relishing the ecstatic familiarity of tapping her soft round chin to make her keep her head back, and the frightened clutch of her convulsive hands

as a roller breaks over her and brings her gasping to her feet.

As we turn, two or three lively girls salute us with a shower of splashes before replying to our morning compliments or plunging into the discussion of a promised picnic. Pretty little Mrs. Tourterelle, a bride from St. Louis, is on her tiptoes and up to her chin, but still sticks fondly to her husband's manly arm, half in pride at the protection, half with the breathless feeling that drowning itself would be bliss at his side. None the less is her heart wrung with anxiety when he quits her tendrils, sends her shoreward, and goes headlong through the clear green crest of a big breaker, which swings him skyward, and flashes round him in a silvery glitter and dazzle of spray, before he settles to his steady swing, and strikes out seaward; for a rod or so out some lads have run in with their cat-boat as far as they dared, and rounded to, for the fun of the more daring swimmers, who are swarming round her, clambering over the sides, dripping, and resting on the cabin deck, or taking "headers" from her stern for the return swim. Don't, if you know what's good for you, imitate Kerbstone and Bella La Mode, who, after their dip, are sauntering up the beach to dry in the sun, dripping but blissful in aquatic intimacy, absorbing salt-water and sentiment at every pore. Go straight to your bathing-house, like a sensible fellow, and then let us join the people in the verandas, clothed and in our right minds. Engaged to Mrs. Coquillage for a *partie fine* over raw clams and lager at the "Studio," are you? Go, then, most absorptive of mortals, while I saunter homeward along the swarming promenade to dinner, deeply pondering on that admirable elasticity of digestion which can assimilate bivalves and beer at 12.30 P.M., yet have room for lamb and blueberry pie less than two hours after.

And so, with bathing and talk and reading and all sorts of pleasant junketing, the summer wears on. We try the resources of the place to the uttermost. We run up mythical "strings" at the bowling-alley back of the beach, where the pins are so very corpulent and "bottly" that they roll over in spasmodic ten-strikes "if Cæsar carelessly but nod on them." We scarify our knuckles and "muddify" our best light trousers boating out with the boys for lilies in the pond at the foot of Sprague's lawn. We go out one nice showery day for perch on Salt Lake, and come back with a longer string of colds than of fish.

Then one golden afternoon we drive down to Point Judith, and clamber up in

And fancy counts the winters gone
　Since, bowed beneath the tempest's hate,
The hapless vessel, drifting on,
　Came groaning, shuddering to her fate,

And gallant lives of stalwart men,
　Borne upward on the raging air,
Went out 'mid terror, night, and pain,
　In one fierce pang of wild despair.

Now while on shore and sea the sun
　Its purple mantle gently lays,
And far-seen islands, one by one,
　Melt in the rosy glimmering haze—

AT THE WRECK.

the little whitewashed tower to see the Fresnel light, and pitch pebbles into the hawse-hole of the old wreck on the beach, and clamber out on her bowsprit, and sit on old timber, and talk pleasant, quiet talk suited to the calm sunset hour and the soft plash of the incoming tide.

And sitting on the topmost rail, leaning against the cat-heads, our poetical member, inspired by the scene and surroundings, takes out pencil and paper and writes the

SONG OF THE WRECK.

High o'er the beach the shattered hulk,
　With storm-wrenched timbers stern and gray,
Mars, with its grim, unsightly bulk,
　The brightness of the golden day;

While tossed on high each gnarlèd beam,
　Clear cut against the amber sky,
Like wrestling giant arms might seem,
　Flung out in helpless agony.

While welling up through breach and seam,
　The sun-tipped wavelets pulsing flow,
Telling the beach their summer dream
　In sea-blown murmurs faint and low—

Fair, gentle girls, with eyes like stars,
　And rippling laughter crisp and sweet,
Cluster around the gray old spars,
　The bright foam dancing to their feet,

Till when the sunset glories fade,
　And twilight deepens into night,
When, keenly flashing through the shade,
　Flames o'er the sea the beacon light,

Their parting voices wane and faint
　To stillness all unknown before,
Save where the night wind moans its plaint
　Round wreck and tower, on wave and shore.

Courage, sad heart! Though dark and chill
　Thy storm-wrecked life in ruins lie,
Though wailing ghosts its chambers fill,
　And strength and hope and impulse die,

Still youth and love some tender gleams,
　Some joy-light, o'er thy gloom shall cast,

AT THE TURNSTILE.

Stirring to transient, happy dreams
  The old sweet yearnings of the past.

And when the darkness falls again,
  Stand, like the watch-tower, strong and sure;
In patience bide thy lonely pain,
  Steadfast, *remember*—and *endure!*

Then, when the twilight deepens and the long lance-like rays from the tower begin to shoot out upon the darkling water, we drive home in the big wagon through the misty moonlight, making the lonely way-side echo with "Up-I-dee," and "Good-night, ladies," and the like good-humored and discordant nonsense, which we should be rather ashamed of in any less frank and gypsyish surroundings. That evening we dress in haste, and go round to the Elmwood for a "hop" in the long pine-floored dining-room, and are profoundly impressed with the gentle shyness of the Pierian youth, who deck their house and bid their guests to a feast, and then set them to capering inside, while they, clever creatures! have the pleasure of watching them *outside* through the long windows of the moon-lit and *spoon-lit* piazza.

And at last, when the days begin to shorten and the gay summer birds are taking wing for the autumnal woods and hills of Plymouth or Gorham, when our state-rooms are engaged, and our trunks are standing packed and ready, we go back for an evening to our old haunts on the Heights. Once more we sit with the new old friends of the season on the broad veranda, and watch the full disk of the harvest-moon rising over the Newport headlands, and throwing out the pretty roofs and towers of Sprague's villa in sharp, jagged silhouette against the silvery glimmer of the sea. And as we talk over the last month's pleasuring, the whole picture—as always when some marked epoch of our lives is drawing to an end—seems to fade into the past. The most recent experiences, the most vivid impressions, grow strangely shadowy and dim, touched with the soft light of a tender and regretful reminiscence. For it has been to us a pleasant and a healthful season. Out in the sweet fresh air, under the influences of rock and sand and breeze and sky and ocean, our bodies and our souls have thriven alike. To the kindred spirits about we have drawn closer in a frank and hearty intimacy. Thoughts and feelings have budded and deepened in this carnival of nature which the closer air of cities would have stifled. Kind words have been said and kind actions done, fine thoughts suggested and sweet emotions brought to utterance, whose traces will be hard to efface. Though we never see each other's faces again, their gentle memory will stand by us in many a time of despondency and trial and bitter need. It has been well for us to live this little space of our lives together, and not for worlds would we forego the having lived it. And so, with many warm hand-clasps and sad, thoughtful faces, we separate for our last night at Narragansett.

When, next morning but one, we come out on the promenade deck of the great steamer, we are gliding down past Black-well's Island, and the clash and hum of the awakening city rise to our ears. Our idyl is over, and work-a-day life is upon us. The August sun is burning hot and bright over the eastern line of the Sound, and as we turn to go in for luggage and wraps we catch ourselves murmuring with the poet:

" Round the cape of a sudden came the sea,
    And the sun looked over the mountain's rim,
    And straight was a path of gold for him,
And the need of a world of men for me!"

Cambridge on
the Charles
(1876)

CAMBRIDGE ON THE CHARLES.

THE WASHINGTON ELM.

advantages save its excellent harbor, had not at that time been fixed upon as the seat of government; and one day in 1630, accordingly, Governor Winthrop and Lieutenant-Governor Dudley jumped on horseback and explored the plains and swamps and forests to the westward in search of a capital. The spot they finally picked out, with the help of some assistant magnates, lay about three miles west of Charlestown, on the banks of the tortuous little river since sung by poets, and already named the Charles by Captain John Smith, who never saw it. The elect location seemed to Winthrop "a fit place for a beautiful town;" and accordingly, on the 29th day of December a goodly number of persons bound themselves to build houses there early in the spring of the following year. The village they named Newtown, and laid out regularly in squares, the streets bearing such simple names as Creek, Wood, and Water, while there were, as lesser ways, Marsh Lane, Back Lane, and Crooked Lane. That was before the days of aristocratic thoroughfares like Brattle and Craigie and Ellery and Fayerweather streets.

THE English colonists, Puritan and Cavalier, who peopled our coast in the early part of the seventeenth century were always shrewd in the selection of sites for their little towns and cities. Commercial or agricultural advantages guided their choice, as a rule; but once in a while they picked out some select location for the express purpose of making it a colonial capital. Something of the sort was the case with the Massachusetts village of Newtown, which has since developed into the American Cambridge. It was not exactly born great, but Governor Winthrop and his associates early tried to thrust greatness upon it. A scholar generally calm and discreet lately declared that the pre-Revolutionary Cambridge was "the first capital of our infant republic, the cradle of our nascent liberty, the hearth of our kindling patriotism." At any rate, this is just what, in a different sense, the Puritans of 1630 wanted it to be. Boston, then a small town with no special

Early in 1631 the houses began to rise, and Governor Winthrop set up the frame of his dwelling on the very spot where he had first pitched his tent. But the people of Boston had been promised by the Governor at the very first that he would never move away any where unless they accompanied him, and of this promise they now reminded him in pretty strenuous terms. Bound by two solemn agreements, and under the necessity of breaking one of them, Winthrop's conscience gave preference to the one first made; and so in the fall of 1631 he disap-

131

GOVERNOR WINTHROP.

pointed his Newtown friends by taking down the frame of his unfinished dwelling and setting it up in Boston. Lieutenant-Governor Dudley's house was completed, meanwhile, and his family installed therein; and he and the rest frigidly let Winthrop return to Boston without offering to accompany him. This affair, as was natural, caused a coolness between Winthrop and Dudley, which was not removed for several years. The Governor's excuse for quitting Newtown was somewhat strengthened in his own mind by the fact that Chickatabut, the chief of the neighboring Indians, had promised to be friendly, so that the necessity of having a fortified settlement in the country, three miles west, was somewhat less urgent. The commercial prospects of Boston, too, had begun to look brighter than Newtown's. Making the best of their opportunities, the remaining settlers proved so thrifty, and courtly too, that they soon began to deserve the praise accorded them by an English writer some years afterward, who warmly described the place as "one of the neatest and best-compacted towns in New England, having many fair structures, with many handsome-contrived streets." "The inhabitants," added this complimentary tourist, "are most of them very rich." In 1632 a number of settlers from Braintree, England, came to Newtown. The quarrel between Winthrop and Dudley continuing, the ministers justified the Lieutenant-Governor by ordering Winthrop to get a clergyman for the town, failing in which he should pay Dudley £20. This sum Winthrop had to render, but the pacified Dudley was magnanimous in his triumph, and returned it with a polite note in which he courteously intimated that he would rather lose £100 than Winthrop's friendship. Their difficulties settled, the two magnates lived on friendly terms thereafter.

By 1634 the Newtown people began to complain of being overcrowded, and loudly talked, some of them, of moving to Connecticut. To that region the original Braintree settlers, to the number of one hundred, accordingly departed two years later, headed by their minister, the Rev. Thomas Hooker, and driving with them 160 cattle. The same year, 1636, this migratory church was replaced in Newtown by a permanent organization under the Rev. Thomas Shepard, a recent arrival from England; and the fortunes of the town were also bettered by the establishment in it of the colony's first school, endowed by the General Court with £400. Nearly all the ministers of the colony happened to be from the University of Cambridge in England, and the most of them, too, from a single one of its colleges, Emanuel. The neighboring Charlestown clergyman, the Rev. John Harvard, a scholarly and gentle graduate of Emanuel, took from the first a hearty interest in the Newtown school; and dying in 1638, he left to it his well-selected library of three hundred volumes and half his fortune. This bequest amounted, it is supposed, to nearly £800, or twice as much as the original gift of the General Court; and such was the effect of so magnificent a gift that the colonists determined to raise the school to the grade of a college, and to give to it the name of its benefactor. The same year, too, the Cambridge graduates concluded to express their esteem for their own university by changing

HARVARD MONUMENT.

the name of the village from Newtown to Cambridge. The scholarly fortunes of the town were also aided by the establishment in it of the first printing-office in America north of Mexico, which was set up in Cambridge in 1639, and the place soon began to be quite a centre of influence both in theology and religion. In 1640 Charlestown Ferry was given to the college, which held it for a hundred

HARVARD COLLEGE, 1720.

dred and fifty years; in 1650 an act of incorporation was granted the president and fellows; in 1652 the first inn was established, one Andrew Belcher being granted liberty "to sell beare and bread ;" in 1660 a bridge was built over Charles River, making the distance to Boston eight miles; and in 1732 a portion of the territory of Cambridge, on the northwest, was set off into a separate town, Newton—a process repeated in subsequent years. The rest of the civic history of Cambridge is dull. It became a city in 1846; and early in the present century its trivial commerce induced the government to make it a port of entry, whence Lechmere's Point, one of the settlements within the town limits, became Cambridgeport.

The history of Harvard College is so closely connected with the literary and architectural annals of Cambridge that it is not worth while to try to dissever them. The Rev. Mr. Harvard, as we have seen, died in 1638, his malady being consumption. Little is known about his personal history, and antiquarian research has not thrown much light upon it. He graduated at Emanuel College in 1631, and came to Charlestown only a year before his death. The graduates of the college built him a plain monument in Charlestown in 1828. His widow married Thomas Allen, her husband's successor in the Charlestown pastorate, in 1639, and the two returned to England some eleven years later. Before this time the college Harvard endowed had become the principal object of interest in Cambridge, and his bequest had led others to follow his example. Who managed the affairs of the college during the first four years of its existence is not known. In 1640, however, there arrived from England the Rev. Henry Dunster, whose qualifications for the office of president seem to have been so apparent that he was elected almost by acclamation. Dunster was poor, and he had not only to look after his

own support, but also to beg for the college and for some of the more needy of his students. Thus he was the prototype of the little army of presidential mendicants who have succeeded him. His administration of affairs was a prosperous one, however, and in 1642 he sent forth his first class of nine members, one of whom became an Oxford D.D., one an Oxford fellow, and one a Leyden M.D. The most illustrious of the nine was George Downing, who became knight, baronet, and minister of Cromwell in Holland, where his success seems to have been great enough to have led to his retention in office by Charles II. A grandson of this Downing was the founder of the youngest of the schools in the English Cambridge, Downing College. Dunster ruled with an iron rod, the students being compelled to stand in hatless silence before their superiors and elders. They had also to talk Latin within the college walls, and, on occasion, to be publicly whipped at prayers. He was a prudent manager of the little chest of the college, and once lent some money just received from England to the General Court, getting something over nine per cent. interest for it. This sum was not repaid until 1713, when interest from 1685 was added to the principal. But all Dunster's thrift, energy, and scholarship did not save him. Long suspected of Baptist, or rather of anti-pedobaptist, opinions, he at length avowed them, and the theological cudgels of the zealous Puritans rang so smartly about his ears that he was compelled to resign, and took up his abode in Scituate. His love for the college did not die out, and on his death his body was buried, at his request, in the graveyard in Cambridge just opposite the college grounds.

Dunster's successor, Charles Chauncy, was also a heretic, but at the other extreme of the pendulum's swing. Chauncy firmly believed in infant baptism, but held that

PRESIDENT QUINCY.

such baptism was invalid unless performed by immersion. Another of his ideas—illustrating a sort of High-Church Puritanism—was that the Lord's Supper ought only to be administered in the evening. If Dunster took away from the creed of the majority of the colonists, Chauncy added to it, and was consequently compelled to endure something of the persecution which surrounded his predecessor. He held his own, however, and died in office in 1672. During

PRESIDENT EVERETT.

his rule the London Society for the Propagation of the Gospel erected a wooden building for the instruction of Indian youth, which stood nearly on the present site of Grays Hall. Only one of the red men ever graduated, the individual who stands in solitary state in the triennial catalogue as "Caleb Cheeshahteaumuck, Indus." He became a Bachelor of Arts in 1665, and promptly died of consumption the next year. Many of the Indian students returned to savage

life, and toward the close of the seventeenth century the Indian college seems to have been used for the printing establishment, Eliot's Indian Bible having perhaps been there struck off. The list of succeeding presidents may be briefly mentioned. From 1672 all of them were graduates of Harvard. Leonard Hoar (1672–75) was very unpopular with the students, and resigning, passed his closing years in melancholy obscurity. His successor, the Rev. Urian

PRESIDENT SPARKS.

Oakes, pastor of the church in Cambridge, was suspected of conspiring for Hoar's seat, but proved to be a useful president until his death, in 1681. John Rogers, Oakes's successor, was the first layman to fill the office. In June, 1685, the celebrated Increase Mather took the chair, but rather neglected the college. "Priest, politician, and president," Mather retained until his death the pastorate of the North Church, Boston, and was once in Europe on a political mission.

PRESIDENT WALKER.

PRESIDENT FELTON.

The colony, after all, was nearer his heart than the college, and to it he gave his more profitable counsels and services. Before his death, however, Harvard received what was then its largest gift, £1000 from Lieutenant-Governor William Stoughton, of the province, a member of the class of 1650. All this time, and for many years after, the college was clerical in its management, and the principal source from which the pulpits of New England were filled. In 1696, out of 121 clergymen in the eleven neighboring counties, 104 were Harvard men. It was still poor, and on one occasion the corporation " voted that six leather chairs be forthwith provided for the use of the library, and six more before the Commencement, in case the treasury will allow of it." This body now determined, warned by Mather's course, to compel the presidents to live in Cambridge. But the Rev. Samuel Willard, their next choice, was minister of the Old South, Boston, and he evaded the new rule by assuming the title of vice-president simply.

Willard's successors were most of them men of industry and faithfulness. John Leverett (1708–24), preacher, lawyer, councilor, judge, politician, and scientist; Benjamin Wadsworth (1725–37), minister of the First Church, Boston; Edward Holyoke (1737–69), minister in Marblehead; Samuel Locke (1770–73), compelled to resign in consequence of immorality; Samuel Langdon (1774–80); Joseph Willard (1781–1804), minister in Beverly; and Samuel Webber (1806–10), mathematician and natural philosopher. In Leverett's time there was a fierce clerical fight over the seats in the corporation—a quarrel repeated in the present century. Wadsworth was annoyed by the attempt of the Episcopal ministers of King's Chapel, Boston, and Christ Church, Cambridge, to claim a place in the Board of Overseers as "teaching elders." Holyoke's

administration embraced the time of Whitefield's bitter attacks upon the New England seminaries, and Harvard in particular, for irreligion—attacks vigorously repelled by the Harvard professors, headed by Edward Wigglesworth, Hollis professor of divinity. In President Langdon's time the affairs of the college were greatly troubled by the Revolution. The buildings were occupied by the provincial troops in 1775–76, the few remaining students were transferred to Concord, and the library and apparatus carted to Concord and Andover. Then, too, John Hancock, treasurer from 1773 to 1777, proved himself a much better patriot than financier, and greatly annoyed the college authorities by carrying their bonds to Philadelphia, and refusing either to give an account or to resign. When the Revolution was over, the nominal property of the college was $100,100, its real property $25,787. About the only gain it received from the war was a few books from the General Court, which that body found among some confiscated Tory property, and gave away, perhaps as a sop to conscience for goods ill-gotten. The other presidents of Harvard have been John Thornton Kirkland (1810–28), who somewhat revived the literary spirit in Cambridge, Josiah Quincy (1829–45), Edward Everett (1846–49), Jared Sparks (1849–53), James Walker (1853–60), C. C. Felton (1860–62), and Thomas Hill (1862–68). President Kirkland was personally a great favorite with his students, and was a man of a good deal of dry wit. The

PRESIDENT ELIOT.

WADSWORTH HOUSE.

famous old tavern on Harvard Square, now the horse-car office, was in his day a great resort of students, whose favorite beverage was "flip," a palatable drink, made more grateful by being stirred with a red-hot poker. Once Kirkland repaired to this tavern and solemnly called for a mug of the beverage, which he drank in silence. Setting down the mug, he remarked to the publican, "I understand the students come here a good deal to drink flip." "Yes, Sir," was the frank reply. "Well," said Kirkland, "I should think they would," and walked away.

By an unexampled experience Presidents Quincy, Everett, Sparks, Walker, and Felton were alive at the same time, and these five heads of the college sit side by side in a portrait hung in the office of their successor, the present occupant of the presidential chair, Charles W. Eliot. President Eliot was inaugurated on May 19, 1869, and was the youngest to sit in Parson Turell's legacy, with the exception of President Locke. A Boston boy, the son of a former treasurer of Harvard, President Eliot graduated from the Boston Latin School in 1849, and from the college in 1853. Before his election he had been tutor and assistant professor in the college, and had also taught in the Institute of Technology in Boston. Probably the event in his pre-presidential life upon which his under-graduates look with most enthusiasm is the fact that he once sat (while a tutor) in a university boat.

The centre of Cambridge is Harvard Square, around which the college buildings cluster so closely that the student, as he takes some country friend into the "yard," finds it hard to divest his descriptions of the guide-book manner. This so-called square is a somnolent triangle, three miles from Boston, whose natural state of calm is vexed only by the bells of the horse-cars that trundle through it, or by the scream of their wheels as they round the curve. Once in a while, too, its dust is stirred by some mortuary procession of cattle on their way to the neighboring *abattoirs*. At the eastern end of the triangle, just where the street begins to widen, stands a generous old gambrel-roofed wooden building, now known as Wadsworth House, which was built in 1726 for the official residence of the presidents of the college. Wadsworth was the first to occupy it, the house having been completed the year after his inauguration. The elms which overtop its venerable roof were set out by President Willard sixty years after the last brick was laid on the chimneys, but they are quite successful in feigning to be coeval with the mansion itself. For a hundred and twenty years the dwelling was occupied by the successive presidents, Wadsworth, Holyoke, Locke, Langdon, Willard, Webber, Kirkland, Quincy, and Everett having dwelt in it. Presidents Sparks and Walker lived in their own houses, and Felton was the first to occupy the new president's house on Quincy Street, at the eastern end of the yard, a modest brick edifice erected a dozen years ago by Peter C. Brooks, of Boston. No building in Cambridge has sheltered so many people of eminence, probably, as Wadsworth House. Washington slept here several times before taking the Vassall House as his permanent

GENERAL VIEW OF THE UNIVERSITY BUILDINGS, CAMBRIDGE.

head-quarters in 1775; and here he was received when he visited Cambridge in 1789. When President Everett, its last occupant, held his final reception, he stood at one door of the generous drawing-room to receive the guests, while the equally courtly Webster welcomed them at the other. In good preservation, the ancient edifice is now used as a dormitory, while the office of the college bursar is in a little brick addition, built in President Webber's time, and lately transferred from the western to the northern side.

Near by, but farther to the west, stands Dane Hall, a rather ugly brick building, built in 1832 for the law school, then just established. Judge Story's lectures attracted so many students that it had subsequently to be enlarged; and in 1870, when the foundations of Matthews Hall were laid, Dane was moved bodily to the southward and denuded of its unpleasing classic portico. Near by stood all the edifices of the First Congregational Church save the present one, a wooden Gothic building on the other side of the street, built the year after Dane Hall was completed. Matthews, mentioned above, was finished in 1872 at the cost of a Boston merchant, whose only condition in giving it was that half the revenues from its rooms should be devoted to the support of students in the college designing to enter the Episcopal ministry. It is built somewhat after the pattern of many of the Oxford colleges, in Elizabethan architecture. North of Matthews and at right angles to the street is Massachusetts Hall, the oldest of the existing buildings. Built in 1720, it originally contained "thirty-two rooms and sixty-four studies," which were occupied as dormitories until 1870, when the four stories were made into two, and the structure began to be used as a reading-room and a place for examinations. The same year a new railing was put upon the roof, which has so caught the spirit of the place that it looks as old as the pile it surmounts. The eastern gable used to contain the college clock, traces of the face of which may still be seen. Tradition accounts for the wooden patch where the clock used to be by averring that the devil, once summoned into Massachusetts Hall by the incantations of students, burst his way out through the attic bricks, and that the hole he made had subsequently to be patched up with wood.

Harvard Hall, just opposite, and also at right angles with the street, was built in 1766 to replace a predecessor of the same name and on the same site, destroyed in 1764. That year the General Court, scared by the small-pox in Boston, came out to Cambridge to sit, occupying this hall for its deliberations; and one cold winter's night, the students being of course absent,

the building caught fire from the legislative stove, and burned to the ground, with the college library and apparatus. President Holyoke delicately hinted that since the hall had been destroyed in the service of the commonwealth, it would be proper for the commonwealth to rebuild it, which was done two years later. But much of the loss was irreparable. This fire not only endangered Massachusetts Hall, but also Hollis Hall, built the previous year, just north. Hollis is in excellent preservation, and is still used as a dormitory for students. In its ancient rooms many an eminent man has lived during his college days, of such occupants being Edward Everett, Ralph Waldo Emerson, Charles Francis Adams, J. G. Palfrey, Prescott, Sumner, Wendell Phillips, Thoreau, and Judge B. R. Curtis. Hollis Hall was struck by lightning in 1768. The shapely old building commemorates a generous family of Baptists in England—Thomas, John, Nathaniel, Timothy, Thomas a nephew, and Thomas his son, all benefactors of the college, which received from them gifts of books, apparatus, and money, and the foundation for professorships of mathematics and divinity. This last endowment caused a fierce theological controversy at the beginning of the present century. The third Thomas Hollis was a man of much eccentricity. He stamped his coat of arms—an owl—on the back of his books, expressing his disapproval of a volume by turning the bird upside down. Several of these condemned works are now contained in the college library. On his death Hollis was buried, by his direction, ten feet deep, in the centre of a field, which was then plowed and sowed with grain.

The next building north of Hollis in the old row is Stoughton Hall, built in 1805 to replace a building of the same name which stood behind Massachusetts and Harvard, and which, having become insecure, was torn down in 1780. This first Stoughton Hall was built in 1699. Stoughton, like Hollis, has had illustrious occupants, rooms within its walls having been occupied by Josiah Quincy, Caleb Cushing, Oliver Wendell Holmes, President Felton, W. H. Furness, E. R. Hoar, Edward E. Hale, and Charles T. Brooks. Everett and Sumner roomed here as well as in Hollis. Between the two halls stands Holden Chapel—a small but beautifully proportioned building, erected in 1744 by the widow and daughters of a London merchant, and originally used as a chapel. Afterward it became in turn a carpenter's shop and a chemical lecture-room, in which latter capacity it was used by Professor John White Webster, the murderer of Parkman.

These various buildings form the west side of the college quadrangle, the northern end of which is filled by Holworthy Hall, built in 1812 from the proceeds of a lottery

EVANGELINUS APOSTOLIDES SOPHOCLES.

losophers, probably, looked less Platonic or Socratic than this their modern expounder.

Turning the corner and passing down the eastern side of what ambitious collegians are already beginning to call the "quad," the first building is Thayer Hall, built in 1870 by Nathaniel Thayer, of Boston, to commemorate his father, old Dr. Thayer, and his brother, John Eliot Thayer. Mr. Thayer will be remembered as the generous patron of Agassiz, who made his Brazilian tour at Mr. Thayer's expense. Next is University Hall, built in 1814, of white Chelmsford granite, and bitterly criticised at the time of its erection. University has a bright and new appearance, and contains the offices of the president, college dean, etc. Weld Hall, just opposite Matthews, was built in 1872 by a Boston merchant in memory of his brother, and, like Matthews, is of English collegiate architecture. The southern end of the triangle is filled by Grays Hall, built in 1863—a modest brick building, which commemorates the gifts of three men of the name of Gray—Francis Calley, John Chip-

authorized by the State. Holworthy has always been a favorite dormitory and the head-quarters of the Senior Class—a precedence which the newer and more elegant buildings have not stolen from it. The Prince of Wales visited room No. 12 in 1860, and left there his autograph and portrait, a process repeated by the Grand Duke Alexis in 1871. In the westernmost room of the second story has lived for many years Evangelinus Apostolides Sophocles, University Professor of Greek. Himself a native of Greece, Sophocles came to the United States under the auspices of the American Board of Commissioners for Foreign Missions, studied for a time in Monson Academy and Amherst College, taught in Hartford, and ultimately settled at Harvard as tutor in Greek. He lives in the simplest manner, his room being furnished with Spartan severity; and the students tell many a story concerning his eccentricities and encyclopedic knowledge. A Harvard professor living in his old age within grim and unadorned bachelor walls, and with frugal economy sending his earnings home to Lycabettus or the banks of the Ilissus, is surely a noticeable person. The scholarly attainments of Professor Sophocles honor his adopted country, and his face, framed in hair and beard as venerable as Bryant's, reminds one of what might have been seen any day in the groves of the Academe. Half of the Greek phi-

GORE HALL.

LOUIS AGASSIZ.

man, and William. The other edifices within the college inclosure—which contains twenty-two acres—are, besides a row of houses on Quincy Street, mostly occupied by members of the faculty, Boylston Hall (1858), a jail-like structure, containing cabinets and chemical laboratories; Gore Hall (1842), the library; and Appleton Chapel (1858). Gore pretends to be a copy of King's College Chapel in the English Cambridge; but it can not be called a very successful rival of that celebrated building. With its tall and meaningless minarets, it not inaptly suggests to others as well as to James Russell Lowell the similitude of a North River steamboat. The building, in fact, is a somewhat melancholy failure. Its towers began to tumble down before they had been built half a dozen years; it contains no officers' rooms, not even one for the librarian; its books suffer from dampness, and its occupants from the stifling heat of a furnace. Appleton Chapel has been about as unlucky. Sixty or seventy thousand dollars were spent when it was built, in 1858, but its acoustic properties proved to be bad, and it was

generally ill heated in winter. A few years ago, however, it was restored throughout, two galleries and some stained-glass windows were put in, and now the students enjoy the unwonted privilege of *hearing* the Gospel within its walls.

The university buildings outside the college yard are College House, a long brick structure occupied as a dormitory in all save its lower story; Holyoke House, built by the corporation in 1871 as a hotel, but now occupied by students; Divinity Hall (1826), an eighth of a mile to the northeast, on a pleasant elm-shaded avenue, the seat of the Unitarian divinity school; the observatory, half a mile west; the herbarium, near by the observatory, in a large botanic garden; Lawrence Hall (1848), just opposite Holworthy, the location of the scientific department, founded by Abbott Lawrence; the medical and dental schools, in Boston; the gymnasium, small and shabby; and the Bussey Institution, an agricultural and horticultural school in West Roxbury. The observatory has been fully described in previous numbers of this Magazine.

Near Divinity Hall, and not far from Norton's Woods (called by the name of Andrews Norton, Unitarian theologian), stands the building of the Museum of Comparative Zoology, so dear to the heart of Agassiz, and densely stored with his priceless collections. As it stands, it is but a single wing of a projected building conceived on so vast a plan that it probably will never be completed. Agassiz dwelt in a house at the corner of Quincy Street and Cambridge Street, now occupied by his son Alexander. Few Cambridge students will soon forget his enthusiastic face and his pleasant voice as he used to expound some favorite theory in the lecture-room of the museum. Agassiz's personal appearance was very fine; he looked well and hearty, and his enthusiasm was contagious. Despite his long residence in Amer-

MUSEUM OF COMPARATIVE ZOOLOGY.

MEMORIAL HALL.

ica, his English pronunciation was quaintly imperfect: thus *laboratory*, a word he must necessarily have pronounced ten thousand times, always came from his lips labo*ra*tory. He was a splendid drill-master for his students and assistants; and his renown was greatly enhanced by the skill with which he utilized their clumsier investigations.

Pretty much the only Harvard building we have thus far omitted to mention is the new Memorial Hall. The *alumni* of the college, when the civil war was over, at once felt a desire to commemorate those who had died in service. After some debate, the erection of a hall was decided on; the triangular plot of ground called the Delta, used by the students as a ball ground, was selected as the site, and the corner-stone was laid in 1870, Judge Hoar delivering the oration, and Phillips Brooks offering the prayer. The building, erected after the designs of two Boston architects, comprehends a large dining hall, a memorial hall with tablets, and an academic theatre for public exercises. The first two are now completed, and the dining hall, adorned with the university's portraits and busts, is used by about five hundred students, organized into a club, which is only indirectly controlled by the corporation. In the memorial hall proper, which is at right angles with the dining hall, is inscribed the name of every graduate or member of the college or professional schools who died in battle or from ailments contracted in the field. The architectural proportions of the building, which has cost over half a million dollars, are, on the whole, pleasing, despite some manifest defects, and its lofty tower is visible for many miles around. The dining hall is a room of im-

posing size, and the sight of a great body of students at commons has become so rare in this country of late years that visitors not infrequently enter the gallery overhead for the sake of watching Harvard eat, or, as the boys themselves express it, to "see the animals feed."

By the middle of the seventeenth century Cambridge had won the reputation of being a favorite abode of courtly as well as scholarly people, not all of whom, by any means, were connected with the college. A hundred years later, curiously enough, the majority of the houses in Old Cambridge were occupied by members of the Church of England, who had little doctrinal, social, or political sympathy with the college authorities, and who were regarded by them, in turn, with considerable suspicion as enemies of the Congregational Church polity, and possible possessors of the hard-won Puritan birthright. Once, as we have seen, an attempt to get seats in the Board of Overseers was made by the Episcopalians, which was repelled by the existing managers with a speed which betrayed their anxiety. Could these worthy men have foreseen that Harvard's increasing catholicity would accept a dormitory from an Episcopalian, and maintain therefrom twelve Episcopal scholarships, their concern would have known no bounds. The Church of England men, most of them persons of considerable wealth, satisfied their social conscience by giving, each of them, an annual entertainment to the president and instructors, while for the rest of the year they confined themselves to their own social clique. The faculty, on their part, considered that they were doing quite enough in the way of Christian charity when they

CHRIST CHURCH.

accepted these stately invitations every twelvemonth. "Church Row" was the name popularly applied to the homes of these polite citizens, loyal to their king and their Church, most of whom lived on Brattle Street. Their ecclesiastical home, Christ Church, was built in 1761, just opposite the common, its architect being Peter Harrison, who had designed King's Chapel, Boston, seven years before. Its organ was made in London by the renowned Snetzler, and during the Revolution some of its pipes were melted into bullets. Between Christ Church and the Unitarian church lies the old village cemetery, celebrated in the verse of Longfellow and Holmes, in which are buried Presidents Dunster, Chauncy, Leverett, Wadsworth, Holyoke, Willard, and Webber; Andrew Belcher, Cambridge's first inn-keeper; Stephen Day and Samuel Green, the first printers; Thomas Shepard, the first minister; and many another man of the elder day. The first rector of Christ Church was the Rev. East Apthorp, a native of Boston, who wanted, the Congregationalists thought, to be appointed Bishop of New England. Apthorp built a large and beautiful house on Main Street, just opposite the present Gore Hall, which is still called the Bishop's Palace. He was disappointed in his aspirations for the rochet, and was so sensitive to the coldness and the somewhat persecuting antagonism of his theological opponents that he resigned and moved to England in 1764. In his house General Burgoyne was imprisoned after his capture. Subsequently a new proprietor built a third story, for the accommodation, it is supposed, of his household slaves.

Christ Church presents its ancient and shapely front toward Cambridge Common, over which a chime of bells, placed in the tower in 1860, pleasantly rings every Sunday. The common contains some twenty acres, and will always be remembered as the place where the American troops mustered and encamped in 1775. Every morning there started from this now peaceful inclosure the guards for Lechmere's Point, Winter Hill, and the other posts, and here the roughly equipped and poorly drilled provincial troops prepared to lay siege to Boston, held by ten thousand experienced and well-prepared soldiers. At the western end stands the elm under which Washington on July 3, 1775, formally assumed his position as general-in-chief of the Continental army. This venerable tree is, it is thought, of an age far greater than a hundred years. It is surrounded by a simple iron fence, and a plain granite slab tersely records the fact that "Under this tree Washington first took command of the American army, July 3, 1775." Just behind stands the new granite edifice of the Shepard Congregational Church, the pulpit in whose chapel is partly made of wood from a branch of the elm necessarily removed. In the middle of the common, facing the college buildings, is a costly but very ugly monument erected to commemorate the men of Cambridge who fell in the rebellion.

North of the common stands a gambrel-roofed old house, near where the sign of the Red Lion Inn used to swing, which was the home of Abiel Holmes, the annalist of New England, and the birth-place of his more famous son, Oliver Wendell Holmes. To the readers of the doctor's books the house and its surroundings are not unfamiliar. About a hundred and fifty years old, it had among its proprietors before Dr. Abiel, Jabez Fox, tailor, of Boston, Jonathan Hastings, farmer, and Jonathan, his son, college steward. During the ownership of the latter the building was occupied by the Committee of Safety, who established themselves in it in 1775, and formed plans for the collection and management of the provincial forces. In one of the ground rooms Benedict Arnold received his commission as colonel; and here, probably, were the headquarters of General Ward. Washington dwelt in it for three days. It is now owned by the college, and occupied by William Everett, a son of Edward. When Dr. Holmes lived in it the house was in the heyday of its architectural glory, and although it proved a few years ago to be somewhat decayed, recent repairs have pretty much restored it to its old strength. Although the eminent author of the *Autocrat* has always lived in Boston, he has never lost patriotism for his birth-place, in which he seems to consider himself fortunate to have been born. The foundations of his literary reputation were laid here; for in 1829, the year of his gradu-

OLIVER WENDELL HOLMES.

ation, when he was but twenty years old, he sat in one of its attic rooms and scribbled in pencil his poem on the threatened destruction of the frigate *Constitution*, or "Old Ironsides:"

" And one who listened to the tale of shame,
    Whose heart still answered to that sacred name,
    Whose eye still followed o'er his country's tides
    Thy glorious flag, our brave Old Ironsides!
    From yon lone attic, on a summer's morn,
    Thus mocked the spoilers with his school-boy scorn."

HOLMES'S HOUSE.

HENRY WADSWORTH LONGFELLOW.

Brattle Street, which begins at the University Press and extends in a westerly direction, is one of the most venerable of American thoroughfares. The winding course of the street was caused by the necessary avoidance on the part of the Puritan road-makers of the worst parts of the marsh which used to cover this portion of the town. Nearest the university printing establishment is the Brattle House, formerly owned by Thomas Brattle, a Boston merchant, who founded the Brattle Street or "Manifesto" Church in that city. It was the head-quarters of General Mifflin, quartermaster of the colonial troops. In later times Margaret Fuller lived in it, and in her optimistic philosophy "accepted the universe." Judge Story's residence, in which dwelt, too, his son William, the sculptor and poet, is near by. Farther down the street, on the southern side, is one of the most venerable mansions in the country, certainly built during the reign of Queen Anne. Before 1720 it was the home of the Belcher family, one of whom, Jonathan, was Lieutenant-Governor of Massachusetts Bay from 1730 to 1741, and then Governor of New Jersey until his death, in 1757. Its present owner retains, at the age of ninety-one, his physical vigor and his literary tastes, and spends much of his time in his large and choice library. Nearly opposite this ancient mansion, which stands in generous grounds, are the three new buildings of the Episcopal Theological School, established in 1867 by Benjamin T. Reed, of Boston. The pretty St. John's Chapel, pertaining to the school, was built by Robert M. Mason, of the same city, in memory of several members of his family, of whom his father, Jeremiah, of the New Hampshire bar, was the most distinguished.

Few private houses in the United States are so well known as the residence of Henry Wadsworth Longfellow, so often has it been described by affectionate antiquarians and enthusiastic pilgrims. It is not only the

LONGFELLOW'S RESIDENCE.

LONGFELLOW IN HIS STUDY.

home of our most celebrated poet, it also surpasses in historic interest any building in New England, with the sole exception of Faneuil Hall. Its age, as compared with that of other Cambridge houses, is not great. It was built in 1759 by Colonel John Vassall, a firm loyalist, who fled to England in 1775, his property in Cambridge and Boston having been confiscated. Its next occupant was Colonel John Glover, a bold little Marblehead soldier, who quartered some of his troops in the spacious structure. When Washington rode into Cambridge on Sunday, June 2, 1775, he was greatly pleased with the appearance of the house, and having had it cleaned, he established himself therein during the same month. Martha Washington arrived at the house in December, and Washington remained in it until April of the following year. The southeast room on the first floor Washington took for his study, in which the councils of war were all held during the stay of the commander-in-chief in Cambridge. He slept just overhead, always retiring at nine o'clock. The spacious room behind the study, which Mr. Longfellow now uses for his library, was occupied by Washington's military family, as a rule a pretty large one. A general's "military family," in English parlance, comprised his whole staff. Washington was not averse to a certain amount of official splendor, and was luckily rich enough to carry out his whim in the matter of making his assistants a part of his ordinary household. Trumbull, the artist, complained rather sarcastically that he, for one, could not keep his head up in the magnificent society of the house. "I now found myself," he averred, "in the family of one of the most distinguished men of the age, surrounded at his table by the principal officers of the army, and in constant intercourse with them. It was further my duty to receive company and do the honors of the house to many of the first people of the country." But Washington was thrifty and frugal personally; and his generous maintenance at his own cost of a sort of court was of great service to the colonial cause.

JAMES RUSSELL LOWELL.

The owners of the house after the Revolution were Nathaniel Tracy (whom Washington visited for an hour in 1789), Thomas Russell, and Dr. Andrew Craigie. Talleyrand and Lafayette slept in it, and in 1833 Jared Sparks commenced to keep house within its historic rooms. Everett, and Worcester the lexicographer, also occupied it for a time, and Mr. Longfellow took up his abode in it in 1837. At first he merely rented a room, establishing himself in Washington's southeast bed-chamber. Here he wrote "Hyperion" and "Voices of the Night." In the dwelling, in one room and another, almost all his books, save the two which date from his Bowdoin professorship, have been produced. Longfellow had not long been an occupant of the house before he bought it. Its timbers are perfectly sound. The lawn in front is neatly kept; and across the street there stretches a green meadow as far as the banks of the Charles, bought by the poet to preserve his view. Mr. Longfellow himself, as he draws near seventy, is a fine picture of beautiful manhood. It has been remarked by his friends that his health has much improved since he delivered his poem, "Morituri Salutamus," at the fiftieth anniversary of his graduation. And all Cambridge, down to coal-heavers and hod-carriers, reveres him for his benignity, and remembers him not only as a poet, but as a kind and gentle man.

The Lechmere House, on the same Brattle Street, used to bear a certain resemblance to Mr. Longfellow's. It was built in 1760, or thereabouts, by Richard Lechmere, who sold it to Jonathan Sewall. Both of them were royalists. Baron and Baroness Riedesel had their quarters here as prisoners, and one of them wrote an autograph on a window-pane, which the baron's biographer claims as his, but which is generally supposed to be that of the baroness. West of this Lechmere mansion, lately repaired and raised a story, stands what is probably the oldest house in Cambridge, a building generally supposed to date from the days of Charles II. Its foundations are cemented, like those of the Belcher House, with clay mixed with pulverized oyster shells, since mortar was unknown at the time of its erection.

Quitting this shady and venerable thoroughfare, one sees between Brattle and Mount Auburn streets what is, on the whole, about the most attractive of all the residences of American authors—Elmwood, the home of James Russell Lowell. Save the porter's lodge, an entire square is occupied by the wide grounds surrounding the old house, which is of wood, nearly square, and three stories high. It was built about 1760 by Thomas Oliver, the last Lieutenant-Governor of the province. Four thousand patriots mobbed the house in 1774, and demanded Oliver's resignation; and he, fearing for the safety of his family, handed them back a paper signed thus: "My house at Cambridge being surrounded by four thousand people, in compliance with their demands I sign my name, Thomas Oliver." He went to England in 1776, and died there in 1815. Elbridge Gerry succeeded him as occupant some years later, and in 1817 the Rev. Charles Lowell, father of the poet, bought it of Mrs. Gerry, the Vice-President's widow. Mr. Lowell was pastor of the West Church, Boston, a Unitarian organization, which in these days, under Dr. Bartol, has become a headquarters of the Free Religious wing of that denomination. Mr. Lowell, however, was hardly so radical in his views, and never permitted himself to be called a Unitarian. He preached in the old edifice for the great space of fifty years. James Russell Lowell was born in the house on Washington's birthday, 1819, only two years after his father occupied it, and he has had the somewhat rare good fortune, for this country, of living all his life in his birth-place. He graduated at Harvard in 1838, in the class with Nathan Hale, W. W. Story, Dr. Rufus Ellis, of Boston, Dr. E. A. Washburn, of New York, and Professor Eustis, of the Lawrence Scientific School. R. H. Dana, Jun., and Henry D. Thoreau were in the class before him, and Edward E. Hale in the succeeding one.

Few remember that Oliver Wendell Holmes began life as a law student, and not many more care to know that Lowell did the same thing, and was actually admitted to the bar and opened an office in Boston. Whether his legal duties were arduous or not, he soon relinquished them, and four or five years after his graduation entered the field of periodical literature as editor, with Robert Carter, at present also a resident of Cambridge, of *The Pioneer*, a very æsthetic magazine, for which Poe and Hawthorne wrote, and which went to the tomb after the publication of three numbers. In this magazine William W. Story, then a Boston lawyer, made his first essays in art in the shape of some outlines in the Flaxman manner. Lowell's early volumes were almost all published at Cambridge. Mr. John Owen, who first issued them, and also Longfellow's "Voices of the Night," "Ballads," "Poems on Slavery," and "The Belfry of Bruges," is still alive, and as he walks around Cambridge, with long white hair and venerable beard, is one of the most noticeable of its citizens. One of Mr. Lowell's first books was dedicated to William Page, the artist, in language of the most extravagant sentimentalism. Those were the days of sentimental friendships; but Page, Lowell, and Mr. Charles F. Briggs, who then formed a triad of kindred minds, still retain their mutual esteem. In 1853 died Mr. Lowell's wife, Maria White, of Watertown, herself a poet; and the next year Longfellow commemorated the event by publishing in Mr. Briggs's magazine "The Two Angels," one of his best poems. From his Elmwood windows Mr. Lowell can look across the flats stretching toward Boston, four miles away, while on the other side lies Mount Auburn. The grounds are not adorned with any modern landscape gardening, but stand in simple beauty, while the tall trees to the westward are almost sombre when the night-breeze blows through them. The old yellow house is a poet's home, and thither bards, as well as birds, seem naturally to fly. When the owner was in Europe lately for a couple of years he gave his keys, for occupancy of the house, to Mr. Thomas Bailey Aldrich, whose dainty verse was written meanwhile to the crooning of the Elmwood chimneys mentioned somewhere by the elder poet. Mr. Lowell himself is now in the full vigor of middle life. His hair and beard are tinged with auburn and streaked with gray; but he is a muscular bard, in perfect health, and of uniform courtesy and good nature. In his personal appearance, as in the management of his affairs, there is nothing of the traditional heedlessness of the poet. The

ELMWOOD.

poetical nature, he thinks, is akin to order, and in his own case certainly the opinion is true.

Many of the old houses in Cambridge have been torn down or moved away, and not a few have been turned over to Celtic occupants. Of the former the most celebrated is the Inman House, in Cambridgeport, Putnam's head-quarters, now standing on a strange street, and so transformed as to be scarcely recognizable. But of dwellings built in the present century which have already acquired some little interest there are not a few. Thus, Dr. A. P. Peabody, preacher to the university, and well known as an orthodox Unitarian theologian, occupies the large house on the corner of Quincy and Harvard streets, within the college inclosure. It was once used as an observatory, the late George P. Bond having thus occupied it while professor in the college. Dr. Peabody's predecessor in his official chair, Dr. Huntington, now Bishop of Central New York, also preceded him as occupant of this house. Without great age, it presents a stately and dignified appearance well befitting the home of a professor of Christian morals. The town, too, seems to-day quite as attractive as of yore to men of letters, several of its present residents being of our younger authors, not graduates of Harvard, but drawn hither by their literary tastes, and readily domesticated in the old haunts. The most eminent of these newer settlers is William D. Howells. Mr. Howells is an Ohio man, who never went to college, but acquired his education at the compositor's case and the country editor's desk. President Lincoln sent him to Venice, where the duties of a somewhat unimportant consu-

WILLIAM D. HOWELLS.

was an author as well as a printer, having written a couple of books on punctuation and several treatises in defense of the religious faith he professed.

We have thus traced the records of an old New England town from its foundation in struggle and poverty to its calm and modest prosperity of to-day. In a country none too rich in historic landmarks it has something to remind one of a creditable past. Perhaps Sir Charles Dilke was not unduly enthusiastic when he wrote of it: "Our English universities have not about them the classic repose, the air of study, which belong to Cambridge, Massachusetts......Even the English Cambridge has a breathing street or two, and a weekly market-day; while Cambridge in New England is one great academic grove, buried in a philosophic calm which our universities can not rival as long as men resort to them for other purposes than work."

late left him ample opportunity for study and thought amidst specially attractive and romantic surroundings. He likes, we imagine, his poetry better than his prose, but the public chooses to rank him as one of our best masters of style, and most delicately witty tellers of tales. A man of medium height, of a temperament so happy as almost to seem jovial, he lives in his own house on Concord Avenue, under wide-spreading trees, and not far from the Washington Elm and the historic common. Toward the town Mr. Howells has proved a most dutiful adopted son, his *Suburban Sketches* having celebrated anew, in agreeable prose, many of her old and new features.

Cambridge contains some cabinet organ, glass, and other factories; but, curiously enough, the only industries by which it is known to the outside world are its printing establishments. The first press in the colonies was set up here in 1639, and the University Press of to-day claims to be the direct successor of Stephen Day's office. The late Charles Folsom made an attempt to organize an establishment which should be after the pattern of the University Press at Cambridge, England, and the Clarendon Press at Oxford, but he failed; and the present University Press is such only in name, not even printing all the college catalogues. There are two other printing houses, the Riverside Press, occupying handsome brick buildings on the banks of the Charles, and John Wilson and Sons', domiciled in an old wooden structure on Dunster Street. The late Mr. Wilson, a Scotchman,

The Armory
at Springfield
(1852)

GENERAL VIEW.

THE ARMORY AT SPRINGFIELD
BY JACOB ABBOTT

SPRINGFIELD

THE Connecticut river flows through the State of Massachusetts, from north to south, on a line about half way between the middle of the State and its western boundary. The valley through which the river flows, which perhaps the stream itself has formed, is broad and fertile, and it presents, in the summer months of the year, one widely extended scene of inexpressible verdure and beauty. The river meanders through a region of broad and luxuriant meadows which are overflowed and enriched by an annual inundation. These meadows extend sometimes for miles on either side of the stream, and are adorned here and there with rural villages, built wherever there is a little elevation of land—sufficient to render human habitations secure. The broad and beautiful valley is bounded on either hand by an elevated and undulating country, with streams, mills, farms, villages, forests, and now and then a towering mountain, to vary and embellish the landscape. In some cases a sort of spur or projection from the upland country projects into the valley, forming a mountain summit there, from which the most magnificent

views are obtained of the beauty and fertility of the surrounding scene.

There are three principal towns upon the banks of the Connecticut within the Massachusetts lines · Greenfield on the north—where the river enters into Massachusetts from between New Hampshire and Vermont—Northampton at the centre, and Springfield on the south. These towns are all built at points where the upland approaches near to the river. Thus at Springfield the land rises by a gentle ascent from near the bank of the stream to a spacious and beautiful plain which overlooks the valley. The town is built upon this declivity. It is so enveloped in trees that from a distance it appears simply like a grove with cupolas and spires rising above the masses of forest foliage ; but to one within it, it presents every where most enchanting pictures of rural elegance and beauty. The streets are avenues of trees. The houses are surrounded by gardens, and so enveloped in shrubbery that in many cases they reveal themselves to the passer-by only by the glimpse that he obtains of a colonnade or a piazza, through some little vista which opens for a moment and then closes again as he passes along. At one point, in ascending from the river to the plain above, the tourist stops involuntarily to admire the view which opens on either side, along a winding and beautiful street which here crosses his way. It is called Chestnut-street on the right hand, and Maple-street on the left—the two portions receiving their several names from the trees with which they are respectively adorned. The branches of the trees meet in a dense and unbroken mass of foliage over the middle of the street, and the sidewalk presents very precisely the appearance and expression of an alley in the gardens of Versailles.

THE ARMORY GROUNDS.

On reaching the summit of the ascent, the visitor finds himself upon an extended plain, with streets of beautiful rural residences on every hand, and in the centre a vast public square occupied and surrounded by the buildings of the Armory. These buildings are spacious and elegant in their construction, and are arranged in a very picturesque and symmetrical manner within the square, and along the streets that surround it. The grounds are shaded with trees; the dwellings are adorned with gardens and shrubbery. Broad and neatly-kept walks, some graveled, others paved, extend across the green or along the line of the buildings, opening charming vistas in every direction. All is quiet and still. Here and there a solitary pedestrian is seen moving at a distance upon the sidewalk, or disappearing among the trees at the end of an avenue; and perhaps the carriage of some party of strangers stands waiting at a gate. The visitor who comes upon this scene on a calm summer morning, is enchanted by the rural beauty that surrounds him, and by the air of silence and repose which reigns over it all. He hears the distant barking of a dog, the voices of children at play, or the subdued thundering of the railway-train crossing the river over its wooden viaduct, far down the valley—and other similar rural sounds coming from a distance through the calm morning air—but all around him and near him is still. Can it be possible, he asks, that such a scene of tranquillity and loveliness can be the outward form and embodiment of a vast machinery incessantly employed in the production of engines of carnage and death?

It is, however, after all, perhaps scarcely proper to call the arms that are manufactured by the American government, and stored in their various arsenals, as engines of carnage and destruction. They ought, perhaps, to be considered rather as instruments of security and peace; for their destination is, as it would seem, not to be employed in active service in the performance of the function for which they are so carefully prepared; but to be consigned, when once finished, to eternal quiescence and repose. They protect by their existence, and not by their action; but in order that this, their simple existence, should be efficient as protection, it is necessary that the instruments themselves should be fitted for their work in the surest and most perfect manner. And thus we have the very singular and extraordinary operation going on, of manufacturing with the greatest care, and with the highest pos-

sible degree of scientific and mechanical skill, a vast system of machinery, which, when completed, all parties concerned most sincerely hope and believe will, in a great majority of cases, remain in their depositories undisturbed forever. They fulfill their vast function by their simple existence—and thus, though in the highest degree useful, are never to be used.

THE BUILDINGS.

The general appearance of the buildings of the Armory is represented in the engraving placed at the head of this article. The point from which the view is taken, is on the eastern side of the square—that is, the side most remote from the town. The level and extended landscape seen in the distance, over the tops of the buildings, is the Connecticut valley—the town of Springfield lying concealed on the slope of the hill, between the buildings and the river. The river itself, too, is concealed from view at this point by the masses of foliage which clothe its banks, and by the configuration of the land.

The middle building in the foreground, marked by the cupola upon the top of it, is called the Office. It contains the various counting-rooms necessary for transacting the general business of the Armory, and is, as it were, the seat and centre of the power by which the whole machinery of the establishment is regulated. North and south of it, and in a line with it, are two shops, called the North and South Filing Shops, where, in the several stories, long ranges of workmen are found, each at his own bench, and before his own window, at work upon the special operation, whatever it may be, which is assigned to him. On the left of the picture is a building with the end toward the observer, two stories high in one part, and one story in the other part. The higher portion—which in the view is the portion nearest the observer—forms the Stocking Shop, as it is called; that is the shop where the stocks are made for the muskets, and fitted to the locks and barrels. The lower portion is the Blacksmith's Shop. The Blacksmith's Shop is filled with small forges, at which the parts of the lock are forged. Beyond the Blacksmith's Shop, and in a line with it, and forming, together with the Stocking Shop and the Blacksmith's Shop, the northern side of the square, are several dwelling-houses, occupied as the quarters of certain officers of the Armory. The residence of the Commanding Officer, however, is not among them. His house stands on the west side of the square, opposite to the end of the avenue which is seen opening directly before the observer in the view. It occupies a very delightful and commanding situation on the brow of the hill, having a view of the Armory buildings and grounds upon one side, and overlooking the town and the valley of the Connecticut on the other.

A little to the south of the entrance to the Commanding Officer's house, stands a large edifice, called the New Arsenal. It is the building with the large square tower—seen in the view in the middle distance, and near the centre of the picture. This building is used for the storage of the muskets during the interval that elapses from the finishing of them to the time when they are sent away to the various permanent arsenals established by government in different parts of the country, or issued to the troops. Besides this new edifice there are two or three other buildings which are used for the storage of finished muskets, called the Old Arsenals. They stand in a line on the south side of the square, and may be seen on the left hand, in the view. These buildings, all together, will contain about five hundred thousand muskets. The New Arsenal, alone, is intended to contain three hundred thousand.

THE WATER SHOPS.

Such is the general arrangement of the Arsenal buildings, " on the hill." But it is only the lighter work that is done here. The heavy operations, such as rolling, welding, grinding, &c., are all performed by water-power. The stream which the Ordnance Department of the United States has pressed into its service to do this work, is a rivulet that meanders through a winding and romantic valley, about half a mile south of the town. On this stream are three falls, situated at a distance perhaps of half a mile from each other. At each of these falls there is a dam, a bridge, and a group of shops. They are called respectively the Upper, Middle, and Low-

THE MIDDLE WATER SHOPS.

er Water Shops. The valley in which these establishments are situated is extremely verdant and beautiful. The banks of the stream are adorned sometimes with green, grassy slopes, and sometimes with masses of shrubbery and foliage, descending to the water. The road winds gracefully from one point of view to another, opening at every turn some new and attractive prospect. The shops and all the hydraulic works are very neatly and very substantially constructed, and are kept in the most perfect order: so that the scene, as it presents itself to the party of visitors, as they ride slowly up or down the road in their carriage, or saunter along upon the banks of the stream on foot, forms a very attractive picture.

THE MUSKET BARREL.

The fundamental, and altogether the most important operation in the manufacture of the musket, is the formation of the barrel; for it is obvious, that on the strength and perfection of the barrel, the whole value and efficiency of the weapon when completed depends. One would suppose, that the fabrication of so simple a thing

as a plain and smooth hollow tube of iron, would be a very easy process; but the fact is, that so numerous are the obstacles and difficulties that are in the way, and so various are the faults, latent and open, into which the workman may allow his work to run, that the forming of the barrel is not only the most important, but by far the most difficult of the operations at the Armory— one which requires the most constant vigilance and attention on the part of the workman, during the process of fabrication, and the application of multiplied tests to prove the accuracy and correctness of the work at every step of the progress of it, from beginning to end.

The barrels are made from plates of iron, of suitable form and size, called *scalps* or barrel plates. These scalps are a little more than two feet long, and about three inches wide. The barrel when completed, is about three feet six inches long, the additional length being gained by the elongating of the scalp under the hammer during the process of welding. The scalps are heated, and then rolled up over an iron rod, and the edges being lapped are welded together, so as to form a tube of the requisite dimensions—the solid rod serving to preserve the cavity within of the proper form. This welding of the barrels is performed at a building among the Middle Water Shops. A range of tilt hammers extend up and down the room, with forges in the centre of the room, one opposite to each

THE WELDING ROOM

hammer, for heating the iron. The tilt hammers are driven by immense water-wheels, placed beneath the building—there being an arrangement of machinery by which each hammer may be connected with its moving power, or disconnected from it, at any moment, at the pleasure of the workman. Underneath the hammer is an anvil. This anvil contains a die, the upper surface of which, as well as the under surface of a similar die inserted in the hammer, is formed with a semi-cylindrical groove, so that when the two surfaces come together a complete cylindrical cavity is formed, which is of the proper size to receive the barrel that is to be forged. The workman heats a small portion of his work in his forge, and then standing directly before the hammer, he places the barrel in its bed upon the anvil, and sets his hammer in motion, turning the barrel round and round continually under the blows. Only a small portion of the seam is closed at one heat, *eleven* heats being required to complete the work. To effect by this operation a perfect junction of the iron, in the overlapping portions, so that the substance of iron shall be continuous and homogeneous throughout, the same at the junction as in every other part, without any, the least, flaw, or seam, or crevice, open or concealed, requires not only great experience and skill, but also most unremitting and constant attention during the performance of the work. Should there be any such flaw, however deeply it may be concealed, and however completely all indications of it may be smoothed over and covered up by a superficial finishing, it is sure to be

exposed at last, to the mortification and loss of the workman, in the form of a great gaping rent, which is brought out from it under the inexorable severity of the test to which the work has finally to be subjected.

RESPONSIBILITY OF THE WORKMEN.

We say to the *loss* as well as to the mortification of the workman, for it is a principle that pervades the whole administration of this establishment, though for special reasons the principle is somewhat modified in its application to the welder, as will hereafter be explained, that each workman bears the whole loss that is occasioned by the failure of his work to stand its trial, from whatever cause the failure may arise. As a general rule each workman stamps every piece of work that passes through his hands with his own mark—a mark made indelible too—so that even after the musket is finished, the history of its construction can be precisely traced, and every operation performed upon it, of whatever kind, can be carried home to the identical workman who performed it. The various parts thus marked are subject to very close inspection, and to very rigid tests, at different periods, and whenever any failure occurs, the person who is found to be responsible for it is charged with the loss. He loses not only his own pay for the work which he performed upon the piece in question, but for the whole value of the piece at the time that the defect is discovered. That is, he has not only to lose his own labor, but he must also pay for all the other labor expended upon the piece, which through the fault of his work becomes useless. For example, in the case of the barrel, there is a certain amount of labor expended upon the iron, to form it into scalps, before it comes into the welder's hands. Then after it is welded it must be bored and turned, and subjected to some other minor operations before the strength of the welding can be proved. If now, under the test that is applied to prove this strength—a test which will be explained fully in the sequel—the work gives way, and if, on examination of the rent, it proves to have been caused by imperfection in the welding, and not by any original defect in the iron, the welder, according to the general principle which governs in this respect all the operations of the establishment, would have to lose not only the value of his own labor, in welding the barrel, but that of all the other operations which had been performed upon it, and which were rendered worthless by his agency. It is immaterial whether the misfortune in such cases is occasioned by accident, or carelessness, or want of skill. In either case the workman is responsible. This rule is somewhat relaxed in the case of the welder, on whom it would, perhaps, if rigidly enforced, bear somewhat too heavily. In fact many persons might regard it as a somewhat severe and rigid rule in any case—and it would, perhaps, very properly be so considered, were it not that this responsibility is taken into the account in fixing the rate of wages; and the workmen being abundantly able to sustain such a responsibility do not complain of it. The system operates on the whole in the most salutary manner, introducing, as it does, into every department of the Armory, a spirit of attention, skill, and fidelity, which marks even the countenances and manners of the workmen, and is often noticed and spoken of by visitors. In fact none but workmen of a very high character for intelligence, capacity, and skill could gain admission to the Armory—or if admitted could long maintain a footing there.

The welders are charged one dollar for every barrel lost through the fault of their work. They earn, by welding, twelve cents for each barrel; so that by spoiling one, they lose the labor which they expend upon eight. Being thus rigidly accountable for the perfection of their work, they find that their undivided attention is required while they are performing it; and, fortunately perhaps for them, there is nothing that can well divert their attention while they are engaged at their forges, for such is the incessant and intolerable clangor and din produced by the eighteen tilt hammers, which are continually breaking out in all parts of the room, into their sudden paroxysms of activity, that every thing like conversation in the apartment is almost utterly excluded. The blows of the hammers, when the white-hot iron is first passed under them and the pull of the lever sets them in motion, are inconceivably rapid, and the deafening noise which they make, and the showers of sparks which they scatter in every direction around, produce a scene which quite appalls many a lady visitor when she first enters upon it, and makes her shrink back at the door, as if she were coming into some imminent danger. The hammers strike more than six hundred blows in a minute, that is more than *ten in every second;* and the noise produced is a sort of rattling thunder, so overpowering when any of the hammers are in operation near to the observer, that the loudest vociferation uttered close to the ear, is wholly inaudible. Some visitors linger long in the apartment, pleased with the splendor and impressiveness of the scene. Others consider it frightful, and hasten away.

FINISHING OPERATIONS.—BORING.

From the Middle Water Shops, where this welding is done, the barrels are conveyed to the Upper Shops, where the operations of turning, boring and grinding are performed. Of course the barrel when first welded is left much larger in its outer circumference, and smaller in its bore, than it is intended to be when finished, in order to allow for the loss of metal in the various finishing operations. When it comes from the welder the barrel weighs over seven pounds: when completely finished it weighs but about four and a half pounds, so that nearly one half of the metal originally used, is cut away by the subsequent processes.

The first of these processes is the boring out of the interior. The boring is performed in certain machines called boring banks. They consist of square and very solid frames of iron, in which, as in a bed, the barrel is fixed, and there is bored out by a succession of operations performed by means of certain tools which are called augers, though they bear very little resemblance to the carpenter's instrument so named. These augers are short square bars of steel, highly polished, and sharp at the edges—and placed at the ends of long iron rods, so that they may pass entirely through the barrel to be bored by them, from end to end. The boring parts of these instruments, though they are in appearance only plain bars of steel with straight and parallel sides, are really somewhat smaller at the outer than at the inner end, so that, speaking mathematically, they are truncated pyramids, of four sides, though differing very slightly in the diameters of the lower and upper sections.

The barrels being fixed in the boring bank, as above described, the end of the shank of the auger is inserted into the centre of a wheel placed at one end of the bank, where, by means of machinery, a slow rotary motion is given to the auger, and a still slower progressive motion at the same time. By this means the auger gradually enters the hollow of the barrel, boring its way, or rather enlarging its way by its boring, as it advances. After it has passed through it is withdrawn, and another auger, a very little larger than the first is substituted in its place; and thus the calibre of the barrel is gradually enlarged, *almost* to the required dimensions.

Almost, but not quite; for in the course of the various operations which are subsequent to the boring, the form of the interior of the work is liable to be slightly disturbed, and this makes it necessary to reserve a portion of the surplus metal within, for a final operation. In fact the borings to which the barrel are subject, alternate in more instances than one with other operations, the whole forming a system far too nice and complicated to be described fully within the limits to which we are necessarily confined in such an article as this. It is a general principle however that the inside work is kept always in advance of the outside, as it is the custom with all machinists and turners to adopt the rule that is so indispensable and excellent in morals, namely, to make all right first within, and then to attend to the exterior. Thus in the case of the musket barrel the bore is first made correct. Then the outer surface of the work is turned and ground down to a correspondence with it The reverse of this process, that is first shaping the outside of it, and then boring it out within, so as to make the inner and outer surfaces to correspond, and the metal every where to be of equal thickness, would be all but impossible.

TURNING.

After the boring, then, of the barrel, comes the turning of the outside of it. The piece is supported in the lathe by means of mandrels inserted into the two ends of it, and there it slowly revolves, bringing all parts of its surface successively under the action of a tool fixed firmly in the right position for cutting the work to its proper form. Of course the barrel has a slow progressive as well as rotary motion during this process, and the tool itself, with the rest in which it is firmly screwed, advances or recedes very regularly and gradually, in respect to the work, as the process goes on, in order to form the proper taper of the barrel in proceeding from the breech to the muzzle. The main work however in this turning process is performed by the rotation of the barrel. The workman thus treats his material and his tools with strict impartiality. In the *boring*, the piece remains at rest, and the tool does its work by revolving. In the *turning*, on the other hand, the *piece* must take its part in active duty, being required to revolve against the tool, while the tool itself remains fixed in its position in the rest.

Among the readers of this article there will probably be many thousands who have never had the opportunity to witness the process of turning or boring iron, and to them it may seem surprising that any tool can be made with an edge sufficiently enduring to stand in such a service. And it is indeed true that a cutting edge destined to maintain itself against iron must be of very excellent temper, and moreover it must have a peculiar construction and form, such that when set in its proper position for service, the cutting part shall be well supported, so to speak, in entering the metal, by the mass of the steel behind it. It is necessary, too, to keep the work cool by a small stream of water constantly falling upon the point of action. The piece to be turned, moreover, when of iron, must revolve very slowly; the process will not go on successfully at a rapid rate; though in the case of wood the higher the speed at which the machinery works, within certain limits, the more perfect the operation. In all these points the process of turning iron requires a very nice adjustment; but when the conditions necessary to success are all properly fulfilled, the work goes on in the most perfect manner, and the observer who is unaccustomed to witness the process is surprised to see the curling and continuous shaving of iron issuing from the point where the tool is applied, being cut out there as smoothly and apparently as easily as if the material were lead.

THE STRAIGHTENING.

One of the most interesting and curious parts of the process of the manufacture of the barrel, is the straightening of it. We ought, perhaps, rather to say the straightenings, for it is found necessary that the operation should be several times performed. For example, the barrel must be straightened before it is turned, and then, inasmuch as in the process of turning it generally gets more or less *sprung*, it must be straightened again afterward. In fact, every important operation performed upon the barrel is likely to cause some deflection in it, which requires to be subsequently corrected, so that the process must be repeated several times. The actual work of straightening, that is the mechanical act that is performed, is very simple—consisting as it does of merely striking a blow. The whole difficulty lies in determining when and where the correction is required. In other words, the *making straight* is very easily and quickly done; the thing attended with difficulty is to find out when and where the work is crooked; for the deflections which it is thus required to remedy, are so extremely slight, that all ordinary modes of examination would fail wholly to detect them; while yet they are sufficiently great to disturb very essentially the range and direction of the ball which should issue from the barrel, affected by them.

STRAIGHTENING THE BARRELS.

The above engraving represents the workman in the act of examining the interior of a barrel with a view to ascertaining whether it be straight. On the floor, in the direction toward which the barrel is pointed, is a small mirror, in which the workman sees, through the tube, a reflection of a certain pane of glass in the window. The pane in question is marked by a diagonal line, which may be seen upon it, in the view, passing from one corner to the other. This diagonal line now is reflected by the mirror into the bore of the barrel, and then it is reflected again to the eye of the observer; for the surface of the iron on the inside of the barrel is left in a most brilliantly polished condition, by the boring and the operations connected therewith. Now the workman, in some mysterious way or other, detects the slightest deviation from straightness in the barrel, by the appearance which this reflection presents to his eye, as he looks through the bore in the manner represented in the drawing. He is always ready to explain very politely to his visitor exactly how this is done, and to allow the lady to look through the tube and see for herself. All that she is able to see, however, in such cases is a very resplendent congeries of concentric rings, forming a spectacle of very dazzling brilliancy, which pleases and delights her, though the mystery of the reflected line generally remains as profound a mystery after the observation as before. This is, in fact, the result which might have been expected, since it is generally found that all demonstrations and explanations relating to the science of optics and light, addressed to the uninitiated, end in plunging them into greater darkness than ever.

The only object which the mirror upon the floor serves, in the operation, is to save the workman from the fatigue of holding up the barrel, which it would be necessary for him to do at each observation, if he were to look at the window pane directly. By having a reflecting surface at the floor he can point the barrel downward, when he wishes to look through it, and this greatly facilitates the manipulation. There is a rest, too, provided for the barrel, to support it while the operator is looking through. He plants the end of the tube in this rest, with a peculiar grace and dexterity, and then, turning it round and round, in order to bring every part of the inner surface to the test of the reflection, he accomplishes the object of his scrutiny in a moment, and then recovering the barrel, he lays it across a sort of anvil which stands by his side, and strikes a gentle blow upon it wherever a correction was found to be required. Thus the operation, though it often seems a very difficult one for the visitor to understand, proves a very easy one for the workman to perform.

OLD MODE OF STRAIGHTENING.

In former times a mode altogether different from this was adopted to test the interior rectitude of the barrel. A very slender line, formed of a hair or some similar substance, was passed through the barrel—*dropped* through, in fact, by means of a small weight attached to the end of it. This line was then drawn tight, and the workman looking through, turned the barrel round so as to bring the line into coincidence successively with every portion of the inner surface. If now there existed any concavity in any part of this surface, the line would show it by the distance which would there appear between the line itself and its reflection in the metal. The present method, however, which has now been in use about thirty years, is found to be far superior to the old one; so much so in fact that all the muskets manufactured before that period have since been condemned as unfit for use, on account mainly of the crookedness of the barrels. When we consider, however, that the calculation is that in ordinary engagements less than one out of every hundred of the balls that are discharged take effect; that is, that ninety-nine out of every hundred go wide of the mark for which they are intended, from causes that must be wholly independent of any want of accuracy in the aiming, it would seem to those who know little of such subjects, that to condemn muskets for deviating from perfect straightness by less than a hair, must be quite an unnecessary nicety. The truth is, however, that all concerned in the establishment at Springfield, seem to be animated by a common determination, that whatever may be the use that is ultimately to be made of their work, the instrument itself, as it comes from their hands, shall be absolutely perfect; and whoever looks at the result, as they now attain it, will admit that they carry out their determination in a very successful manner.

CINDER HOLES.

Various other improvements have been made from time to time in the mode of manufacturing and finishing the musket, which have led to the condemnation or alteration of those made before the improvements were introduced. A striking illustration of this is afforded by the case of what are called *cinder holes*. A cinder hole is a small cavity left in the iron at the time of the manufacture of it—the effect, doubtless, of some small development of gas forming a bubble in the substance of the iron. If the bubble is near the inner surface of the barrel when it is welded, the process of boring and finishing brings it into view, in the form of a small blemish seen in the side of the bore. At a former period in the history of the Armory, defects of this kind were not considered essential, so long as they were so small as not to weaken the barrel. It was found, however, at length that such cavities, by retaining the moisture and other products of combustion resulting from the discharge of the piece, were subject to corrosion, and gradual enlargement, so as finally to weaken the barrel in a fatal manner. It was decided therefore that the existence of cinder holes in a barrel should thenceforth be a sufficient cause for its rejection, and all the muskets manufactured before that time have since been condemned and sold; the design of the department being to retain in the public arsenals only arms of the most perfect and unexceptionable character.

At the present time, in the process of manufacturing the barrels, it is not always found necessary to reject a barrel absolutely in every case where a cinder hole appears. Sometimes the iron may be forced in, by a blow upon the outside, sufficiently to enable the workman to bore the cinder hole out entirely. This course is always adopted where the thickness of the iron will allow it, and in such cases the barrel is saved. Where this can not be done, the part affected is sometimes cut off, and a short barrel is made, for an arm called a musketoon.

THE GRINDING.

After the barrel is turned to nearly its proper size it is next to be ground, for the purpose of removing the marks left by the tool in turning, and of still further perfecting its form. For this operation immense grindstones, carried by ma-

chinery, are used, as seen in the engraving These stones, when in use, are made to revolve

GRINDING.

with great rapidity—usually about *four hundred times in a minute*—and as a constant stream of water is kept pouring upon the part where the barrel is applied in the grinding, it is necessary to cover them entirely with a wooden case, as seen in the engraving, to catch and confine the water, which would otherwise be thrown with great force about the room. The direct action therefore of the stone upon the barrel in the process of grinding is concealed from view.

The workman has an iron rod with a sort of crank-like handle at the end of it, and this rod he inserts into the bore of the barrel which he has in hand. The rod fits into the barrel closely, and is held firmly by the friction, so that by means of the handle to the rod, the workman can turn the barrel round and round continually while he is grinding it, and thus bring the action of the stone to bear equally upon every part, and so finish the work in a true cylindrical form. One of these rods, with its handle, may be seen lying free upon the stand on the right of the picture. The workman is also provided with guages which he applies frequently to the barrel at different points along its length, as the work goes on, in order to form it to the true size and to the proper taper. In the act of grinding he inserts the barrel into a small hole in the case, in front of the stone, and then presses it hard against the surface of the stone by means of the iron lever behind him. By leaning against this lever with greater or less exertion he can regulate the pressure of the barrel against the stone at pleasure. In order to increase his power over this lever he stands upon a plate of iron which is placed upon the floor beneath him, with projections cast upon it to hold his feet by their friction; the moment that he ceases to lean against

the lever, the inner end of it is drawn back by the action of the weight seen hanging down by the side of it, and the barrel is immediately released.

The workman *turns* the barrel continually, during the process of grinding, by means of the handle, as seen in the drawing, and as the stone itself is revolving all the time with prodigious velocity, the work is very rapidly, and at the same time very smoothly and correctly performed.

DANGER.

It would seem too, at first thought, that this operation of grinding must be a very safe as well as a simple one; but it is far otherwise. This grinding room is the dangerous room—the only dangerous room, in fact, in the whole establishment. In the first place, the work itself is often very injurious to the health. The premises are always drenched with water, and this makes the atmosphere damp and unwholesome. Then there is a fine powder, which, notwithstanding every precaution, will escape from the stone, and contaminate the air, producing very serious tendencies to disease in the lungs of persons who breathe it for any long period. In former times it was customary to grind bayonets as well as barrels; and this required that the face of the stone should be fluted, that is cut into grooves of a form suitable to receive the bayonet. This fluting of the stone, which of course it was necessary continually to renew, was found to be an exceedingly unhealthy operation, and in the process of grinding, moreover, in the case of bayonets, the workman was much more exposed than in grinding barrels, as it was necessary that a portion of the stone should be open before him and that he should apply the piece in hand directly to the surface of it. From these causes it resulted, under the old system, that bayonets, whatever might have been their destination in respect to actual service against an enemy on the field, were pretty sure to be the death of all who were concerned in making them.

The system, however, so far as relates to the bayonet is now changed. Bayonets are now "milled," instead of being ground; that is, they are finished by means of cutters formed upon the circumference of a wheel, and so arranged that by the revolution of the wheel, and by the motion of the bayonet in passing slowly under it, secured in a very solid manner to a solid bed, the superfluous metal is cut away and the piece fashioned at once to its proper form, or at least brought so near to it by the machine, as to require afterward only a very little finishing. This operation is cheaper than the other, and also more perfect in its result; while at the same time it is entirely free from danger to the workman.

No mode, however, has yet been devised for dispensing with the operation of grinding in the case of the barrel; though the injury to the health is much less in this case than in the other.

BURSTING OF GRINDSTONES.

There is another very formidable danger connected with the process of grinding besides the insalubrity of the work; and that is the danger of the bursting of the stones in consequence of their enormous weight and the immense velocity with which they are made to revolve. Some years since a new method of clamping the stone, that is of attaching it and securing it to its axis, was adopted, by means of which the danger of bursting is much diminished. But by the mode formerly practiced—the mode which in fact still prevails in many manufacturing establishments where large grindstones are employed—the danger was very great, and the most frightful accidents often occurred. In securing the stone to its axis it was customary to cut a square hole through the centre of the stone, and then after passing the iron axis through this opening, to fix the stone upon the axis by wedging it up firmly with wooden wedges. Now it is well known that an enormous force may be exerted by the driving of a wedge, and probably in many cases where this method is resorted to, the stone is strained to its utmost tension, so as to be on the point of splitting open, before it is put in rotation at all. The water is then let on, and the stone becomes saturated with it—which greatly increases the danger. There are three ways by which the water tends to promote the bursting of the stone. It makes it very much heavier, and thus adds to the momentum of its motion, and consequently to the centrifugal force. It also makes it weaker, for the water penetrates the stone in every part, and operates to soften, as it were, its texture. Then finally it swells the wedges, and thus greatly increases the force of the outward strain which they exert at the centre of the stone. When under these circumstances the enormous mass is put in motion, at the rate perhaps of five or six revolutions in a

second, it bursts, and some enormous fragment, a quarter or a third of the whole, flies up through the flooring above, or out through a wall, according to the position of the part thrown off, at the time of the fracture. An accident of this kind occurred at the Armory some years since. One fragment of the stone struck the wall of the building, which was two or three feet thick, and broke it through. The other passing upward, struck and fractured a heavy beam forming a part of the floor above, and upset a work-bench in a room over it, where several men were working. The men were thrown down, though fortunately they were not injured. The workman who had been grinding at the stone left his station for a minute or two, just before the catastrophe, and thus his life too was saved.

POLISHING.

We have said that the grinding room is the *only* dangerous room in such an establishment as this. There is one other process than grinding which was formerly considered as extremely unhealthy, and that is the process of polishing. The polishing of steel is performed by means of what are called *emery wheels*, which are wheels bound on their circumference by a band of leather, to which a coating of emery, very finely pulverized, is applied, by means of a sizing of glue. These wheels, a large number of which are placed side by side in the same room, are made to revolve by means of machinery, with an inconceivable velocity, while the workmen who have the polishing to do, taking their stations, each at his own wheel, on seats placed there for the purpose, and holding the piece of work on which the operation is to be performed, in their hands, apply it to the revolving circumference before them. The surface of the steel thus applied, receives immediately a very high polish—a stream of sparks being elicited by the friction, and flying off from the wheel opposite to the workman.

Now although in these cases the workman was always accustomed to take his position at the wheel in such a manner as to be exposed as little as possible to the effects of it, yet the air of the apartment, it was found, soon became fully impregnated with the fine emery dust, and the influence of it upon the lungs proved very deleterious. There is, however, now in operation a contrivance by means of which the evil is almost entirely remedied. A large air-trunk is laid beneath the floor, from which the air is drawn out continually by means of a sort of fan machinery connected with the engine. Opposite to each wheel, and in the direction to which the sparks and the emery dust are thrown, are openings connected with this air-trunk. By means of this arrangement all that is noxious in the air of the room is drawn out through the openings into the air-trunk, and so conveyed away.

The sparks produced in such operations as this, as in the case of the collision of flint and steel, consist of small globules of melted metal, cut off from the main mass by the force of the friction, and heated to the melting point at the same time. These metallic scintillations were not supposed to be the cause of the injury that was produced by the operation of polishing, as formerly practiced. It was the dust of the emery that produced the effect, just as in the case of the grinding it was the powder of the stone, and not the fine particles of iron.

The emery which is used in these polishing operations, as well as for a great many similar purposes in the arts, is obtained by pulverizing an exceedingly hard mineral that is found in several of the islands of the Grecian Archipelago, in the Mediterranean. In its native state it appears in the form of shapeless masses, of a blackish or bluish gray color, and it is prepared for use by being pulverized in iron mortars. When pulverized it is washed and sorted into five or six different degrees of fineness, according to the work for which it is wanted. It is used by lapidaries for cutting and polishing stones, by cutlers for iron and steel instruments, and by opticians for grinding lenses. It is ordinarily used in the manner above described, by being applied to the circumference of a leathern covered wheel, by means of oil or of glue. Ladies use bags filled with it, for brightening their needles.

Emery is procured in Spain, and also in Great Britain, as well as in the Islands of the Mediterranean.

PROVING.

When the barrels are brought pretty nearly to their finished condition, they are to be *proved*, that is to be subjected to the test of actual trial with gunpowder. For this proving they are taken to a very strong building that is constructed for the purpose, and which stands behind the Stocking Shop. Its place is on the right in the general view of the Armory buildings, and near the foreground—though that view does not extend far enough in that direction to bring it in. The exterior appearance of this building is rep-

THE PROVING HOUSE.

resented in the above engraving. It is made very strong, being constructed wholly of timber, in order to enable it to resist the force of the explosions within. There are spacious openings in lattice work, in the roof and under the eaves of the building, to allow of the escape of the smoke with which it is filled at each discharge; for it is customary to prove a large number of barrels at a time. The barrels are loaded with a very heavy charge, so as to subject them to much greater strain than they can ever be exposed to in actual service. The building on the left, in the engraving, is used for loading the barrels, and for cleaning and drying them after they are proved. The shed attached to the main building, on the right hand, contains a bank of clay, placed there to receive the bullets, with which the barrels are charged.

The arrangement of the interior of this building, as well as the manner in which the proving is performed, will be very clearly understood by reference to the engraving below.

INTERIOR OF THE PROVING HOUSE.

On the right hand end of the building, and extending quite across it from side to side, is a sort of platform, the upper surface of which is formed of cast-iron, and contains grooves in which the muskets are placed when loaded, side by side. A train of gunpowder is laid along the back side of this platform, so as to form a communication with each barrel. The train passes out through a hole in the side of the building near the door. The bank of clay may be seen sloping down from within its shed into the room on the left. The artist has represented the scene as it appears when all is ready for the discharge. The barrels are placed, the train is laid, and the proof-master is just retiring and closing the door. A moment more and there will be a loud and rattling explosion; then the doors will be opened, and as soon as the smoke has cleared away the workman will enter and ascertain the result. About one in sixty of the barrels are found to burst under the trial.

The pieces that fail are all carefully examined with a view to ascertain whether the giving way was owing to a defect in the welding, or to some flaw, or other bad quality, in the iron. The appearance of the rent made by the bursting will always determine this point. The loss of those that failed on account of bad welding is then charged to the respective operatives by whom the work was done, at a dollar for each one so failing. The name of the maker of each is known by the stamp which he put upon it at the time when it passed through his hands.

The barrels that stand this first test are afterward subjected to a second one in order to make it sure that they sustained no partial and imperceptible injury at the first explosion. This done they are stamped with the mark of approval, and so sent to the proper departments to be mounted and finished.

The bayonets, and all the other parts of which the musket is composed are subjected to tests, different in character indeed, but equally strict and rigid in respect to the qualities which they are intended to prove, with that applied to the barrel. The bayonet is very carefully gauged and meas-

TESTING THE BAYONETS.

ured in every part, in order to make sure that it is of precisely the proper form and dimensions. A weight is hung to the point of it to try its temper, and it is sprung by the strength of the inspector, with the point of it set into the floor, to prove its elasticity. If it is found to be tempered too high it breaks; if too low it bends. In either case it is condemned, and the workman through whose fault the failure has resulted is charged with the loss.

THE FORGING.

The number of pieces which are used in making up a musket is forty-nine, each of which has to be formed and finished separately. Of these there are only two—viz., the sight and what is called the *cone-seat*, a sort of process connected with the barrel—that are permanently attached to any other part; so that the musket can at any time be separated into *forty-seven* parts, by simply turning screws, and opening springs, and then put together again as before. Most of these parts are such that they are formed in the first instance by being forged or rather *swedged*, and are afterward trimmed and finished in lathes, and milling engines, or by means of files. *Swedging*, as it is called, is the forming of irregular shapes in iron by means of dies of a certain kind, called swedges, one of which is inserted in the anvil, in a cavity made for the purpose, and the other is placed above it. Cavities are cut in the faces of the swedges, so that when they are brought together, with the end of the iron rod out of which the article to be formed between them, the iron is made to assume the form of the cavities by means of blows of the hammer upon the upper swedge. In this way shapes are easily and rapidly fashioned, which it would be impossible to produce by blows directed immediately upon the iron

The shop where this swedging work is done at the Armory contains a great number of forges, one only of which however is fully represented

THE BLACKSMITH'S SHOP.

in the engraving. The apparatus connected with these forges, differing in each according to the particular operation for which each is intended, is far too complicated to be described in this connection. It can only be fully understood when seen in actual operation under the hands of the workman. The visitor however who has the opportunity to see it thus, lingers long before each separate forge, pleased with the ingenuity of the contrivances which he witnesses, and admiring the wonderful dexterity of the workman. There is no appearance of bellows at any of these works. The air is supplied to the fires by pipes ascending through the floor from a *fan blower*, as it is called, worked by machinery arranged for the purpose below.

THE STOCKING SHOP.

The Stocking Shop, so called, is the department in which the *stocks* to which the barrel and the lock are to be attached, are formed and finished. The wood used for gun stocks in this country is the black walnut, and as this wood requires to be seasoned some years before it is used, an immense store of it is kept on hand at the Armory—sufficient in fact for four years' consumption. The building in which this material is stored may be seen on the right hand side in the general view placed at the head of this article. It stands off from the square, and behind the other buildings. The operations conducted in the stocking shop are exceedingly attractive to all who visit the establishment. In fact it happens here as it often does in similar cases, that that which is most interesting to witness is the least interesting to be described. The reason is that the charm in these processes consists in the high perfection and finish of the machines, in the smoothness, grace, and rapidity of their motions, and in the seemingly miraculous character of the performances which they execute. Of such things no mere description can convey any adequate idea. They must be seen to be at all appreciated.

A gun stock, with all the innumerable cavities, grooves, perforations, and recesses necessary to be made in it, to receive the barrel, the lock, the bands, the ramrod, and the numerous pins and screws, all of which require a separate and peculiar modification of its form, is perhaps as irregular a shape as the ingenuity of man could devise—and as well calculated as any shape could possibly be to bid defiance to every attempt at applying machinery to the work of fashioning it. The difficulties however in the way of such an attempt, insurmountable as they would at first sight seem, have all been overcome, and every part of the stock is formed, and every perforation, groove, cavity, and socket is cut in it by machines that do their work with a beauty, a grace, and a perfection, which awaken in all who witness the process, a feeling of astonishment and delight.

The general principle on which this machinery operates, in doing its work, may perhaps be made intelligible to the reader by description. The action is regulated by what are called *patterns*. These patterns are models in iron of the various surfaces of the stock which it is intended to form. Let us suppose, for example, that the large cavity intended to receive the lock is to be cut. The stock on which the operation is to be performed is placed in its bed in the machine, and over it, pendant from a certain movable frame-work of polished steel above, is the cutting tool, a sort of bit or borer, which is to do the work. This borer is made to revolve with immense velocity, and is at the same time susceptible of various other motions at the pleasure of the workman. It may be brought down upon the work, and moved there from side to side, so as to cut out a cavity of any required shape; and such is the mechanism of the machine that these vertical and lateral motions may be made very freely without at all interfering with the swift rotation on which the cutting power of the tool depends. This is effected by causing the tool to revolve by means of small machinery within its frame, while the frame and all within it moves together, in the vertical and lateral motions.

Now if this were all, it is plain that the cutting of the cavity in the stock would depend upon the action of the workman, and the form given to it would be determined by the manner in which he should guide the tool in its lateral motions, and by the depth to which he should depress it. But this is not all. At a little distance from the cutter, and parallel to it is another descending rod, which is called the guide; and this guide is so connected with the cutting tool, by means of a very complicated and ingenious machinery, that the latter is governed rigidly and exactly in all its movements by the motion of the former. Now there is placed immediately beneath the guide, what is called the pattern, that is a cavity in a block of iron of precisely the form and size which it is intended to give to the cavity in the wooden stock. All that the workman has to do therefore, when the machine is put in motion is to bring the guide down into the pattern and move it about the circumference and through the centre of it. The cutting tool imitating precisely the motions of the guide, enters the wood, and cutting its way in the most perfect manner and with incredible rapidity, forms an exact duplicate of the cavity in the pattern. The theory of this operation is sufficiently curious and striking—but the wonder excited by it is infinitely enhanced by seeing the work done It is on this principle substantially that all the machines of the Stocking Shop are constructed ; every separate recess, perforation, or groove of the piece requiring of course its own separate mechanism. The stocks are passed from one of these engines to another in rapid succession, and come out at last, each one the perfect fac-simile of its fellow.

DIVISION OF LABOR.

We have said that the number of separate parts which go to compose a musket is forty-nine ; but this by no means denotes the number of distinct operations required in the manufacture of it—for almost every one of these forty-nine parts is subject to many distinct operations, each of which has its own name, is assigned to its own separate workman, and is paid for distinctly and by itself, according to the price put upon it in the general tariff of wages. The number of operations thus separately named, catalogued and priced, is *three hundred and ninety-six.*

These operations are entirely distinct from one another—each constituting, as it were, in some sense a distinct trade, so that it might be quite possible that no one man in the whole establishment should know how to perform any two of them. It is quite certain, in fact, that no man can perform any considerable number of them. They are of very various grades in respect to character and price—from the welding of the barrel which is in some points of view the highest and most responsible of all, down to the cutting out of pins and screws of the most insignificant character. They are all however regularly rated, and the work that is performed upon them is paid for by the piece.

ASSEMBLING THE MUSKET.

When the several parts are all finished, the operation of putting them together so as to make up the musket from them complete, is called "assembling the musket." The workman who performs this function has all the various parts before him at his bench, arranged in boxes and compartments, in regular order, and taking one component from this place, and another from that, he proceeds to put the com-

ASSEMBLING THE MUSKET

plicated piece of mechanism together. His bench is fitted up expressly for the work which he is to perform upon it, with a vice to hold without marring, and rests to support without confining, and every other convenience and facility which experience and ingenuity can suggest. With these helps, and by means of the dexterity which continued practice gives him, he performs the work in a manner so adroit and rapid, as to excite the wonder of every beholder. In fact it is always a pleasure to see any thing done that is done with grace and dexterity, and this is a pleasure which the visitor to the Armory has an opportunity to enjoy at almost every turn.

The component parts of the musket are all made according to one precise pattern, and thus when taken up at random they are sure to come properly together. There is no individual fitting required in each particular case. Any barrel will fit into any stock, and a screw designed for a particular plate or band, will enter the proper hole in any plate or band of a hundred thousand. There are many advantages which result from this precise conformity to an established pattern in the components of the musket. In the first place the work of manufacturing it is more easily performed in this way. It is always the tendency of machinery to produce similarity in its results, and thus although where only two things are to be made it is very difficult to get them alike, the case is very different where there is a call for two hundred thousand. In this last case it is far easier and cheaper to have them alike than to have them different; for in manufacturing on such a scale a machinery is employed, which results in fashioning

every one of its products on the precise model to which the inventor adapted the construction of it. Then, besides, a great convenience and economy results from this identity of form in the component parts of the musket, when the arms are employed in service. Spare screws, locks, bands, springs, &c., can be furnished in quantities, and sent to any remote part of the country wherever they are required; so that when any part of a soldier's gun becomes injured or broken, its place can be immediately supplied by a new piece, which is sure to fit as perfectly into the vacancy as the original occupant. Even after a battle there is nothing to prevent the surviving soldiers from making up themselves, out of a hundred broken and dismantled muskets, fifty good ones as complete and sound as ever, by rejecting what is damaged, and assembling the uninjured parts anew.

To facilitate such operations as these the mechanism by which the various parts of the musket are attached to each other and secured in their places, is studiously contrived with a view to facilitating in the highest degree the taking of them apart, and putting them together. Each soldier to whom a musket is served is provided with a little tool, which, though very simple in its construction, consists of several parts and is adapted to the performance of several functions. With the assistance of this tool the soldier sitting on the bank by the roadside, at a pause in the middle of his march, if the regulations of the service would allow him to do so, might separate his gun into its forty-seven components, and spread the parts out upon the grass around him. Then if any part was doubtful he could examine it. If any was broken he could replace it—and after having finished his inspection he could reconstruct the mechanism, and march on as before.

It results from this system that to make any change, however slight, in the pattern of the musket or in the form of any of the parts of it, is attended with great difficulty and expense. The fashion and form of every one of the component portions of the arm, are very exactly and rigidly determined by the machinery that is employed in making it, and any alteration, however apparently insignificant, would require a change in this machinery. It becomes necessary, therefore, that the precise pattern both of the whole musket and of all of its parts, once fixed, should remain permanently the same.

The most costly of the parts which lie before the workman in assembling the musket is the barrel. The value of it complete is three dollars. From the barrel we go down by a gradually descending scale to the piece of smallest value, which is a little wire called the ramrod spring wire—the value of which is only one mill; that is the workman is paid only one dollar a thousand for the manufacture of it. The time expended in assembling a musket is about ten minutes, and the price paid for the work is four cents.

THE ARSENAL.

The New Arsenal, which has already been alluded to in the description of the general view of the Arsenal grounds, is a very stately edifice. It is two hundred feet long, seventy feet wide, and fifty feet high. It is divided into three

THE NEW ARSENAL.

stories, each of which is calculated to contain one hundred thousand muskets, making three hundred thousand in all. The muskets when stored in this arsenal are arranged in racks set up for the purpose along the immense halls, where they stand upright in rows, with the glittering bayonets shooting up, as it were, above. The visitors who go into the arsenal walk up and down the aisles which separate the ranges of racks, admiring the symmetry and splendor of the display.

The Arsenal has another charm for visitors besides the beauty of the spectacle which the interior presents—and that is the magnificent panorama of the surrounding country, which is seen from the summit of the tower. This tower, which occupies the centre of the building, is about ninety feet high—and as it is about thirty feet square, the deck at the top furnishes space for a large party of visitors to stand and survey the surrounding country. Nothing can be imagined more enchanting than the view presented from this position in the month of June. The Armory grounds upon one side, and the streets of the town upon the other lie, as it were, at the feet of the spectator, while in the distance the broad and luxuriant valley of the Connecticut is spread out to view, with its villages, its fields, its groves, its bridges, its winding railways, and its serpentine and beautiful streams.

THE ADMINISTRATION OF THE ARMORY.

The manufacture of muskets being a work that pertains in some sense to the operations of the army, should be, for that reason, under *military* rule. On the other hand, inasmuch as it is wholly a work of mechanical and peaceful industry, a *civil* administration would seem to be most appropriate for it. There is, in fact, a standing dispute on this subject both in relation to the Armory at Springfield and to that at Harper's Ferry, among those interested in the establishments, and it is a dispute which, perhaps, will never be finally settled. The Springfield Armory is at this time under military rule—the

QUARTERS OF THE COMMANDING OFFICER.

present commanding officer, Colonel Ripley, having been put in charge of it about ten years ago, previous to which time it was under civil superintendence. At the time of Col. Ripley's appointment the works, as is universally acknowledged, were in a very imperfect condition, compared with their present state. On entering upon the duties of his office, the new incumbent engaged in the work of improvement with great resolution and energy, and after contending for several years with the usual obstacles and difficulties which men have to encounter in efforts at progress and reform, he succeeded in bringing the establishment up to a state of very high perfection ; and now the order, the system, the neatness, the almost military exactness and decorum which pervade every department of the works are the theme of universal admiration. The grounds are kept in the most perfect condition—the shops are bright and cheerful, the walls and floors are every where neat and clean, the machinery and tools are perfect, and are all symmetrically and admirably arranged, while the workmen are well dressed, and are characterized by an air of manliness, intelligence, and thrift, that suggests to the mind of the visitor the idea of amateur mechanics, working with beautiful tools, for pleasure.

And yet the men at first complained, sometimes, of the stringency of rules and regulations required to produce these results. These rules are still in force, though now they are very generally acquiesced in. No newspapers of any kind can be taken into the shops, no tobacco or intoxicating drinks can be used there, no unnecessary conversation is allowed, and the regulations in respect to hours of attendance, and to responsibility for damaged work are very definite and strict. But even if the workmen should be disposed in any case to complain of the stringency of these requirements, they can not but be proud of the result ; for they take a very evident pleasure in the gratification which every visitor manifests in witnessing the system, the order, the neatness, and the precision that every where prevail.

Nothing can be more admirably planned, or more completely and precisely executed than the system of accounts kept at the offices, by which not only every pecuniary transaction, but also, as would seem, almost every mechanical operation or act that takes place throughout the establishment is made a matter of record. Thus every thing is checked and regulated. No piece, large or small, can be lost from among its hundreds of fellows without being missed somewhere in some column of figures—and the whole history of every workman's doings, and of every piece of work done, is to be found recorded. Ask the master-armorer any questions whatever about the workings of the establishment, whether relating to the minutest detail, or to most comprehensive and general results, and he takes down a book and shows you the answer in some column or table.

After all, however, this neatness, precision, and elegance in the appearance and in the daily workings of an establishment like this though very agreeable to the eye of the observer, constitute a test of only secondary importance in respect to the actual character of the administration that governs it. To judge properly on this point, the thing to be looked at is the actual and substantial results that are obtained. The manufacture of muskets is the great function of the Armory, and not the exhibition of beautiful workshops, and curious processes in mechanics for the entertainment of visitors. When we in-

quire, however, into the present arrangement of this establishment, in this point of view, the conclusion seems to be still more decidedly in its favor than in the other. The cost of manufacturing each musket immediately before the commencement of the term of the present commander was about seventeen dollars and a half. During the past year it has been eight dollars and three quarters, and yet the men are paid better wages now per day, or, rather, they are paid at such rates for their work, that they can earn more now per day, than then. The saving has thus not been at all made from the pay of the workmen, but wholly from the introduction of new and improved modes of manufacture, better machines, a superior degree of order, system, and economy in every department, and other similar causes. How far the improvements which have thus been made are due to the intrinsic qualities of military government, and how far to the personal efficiency of the officer in this case intrusted with the administration of it, it might be somewhat difficult to decide.

In fact, when judging of the advancement made during a period of ten years, in an establishment of this kind, at the present age of the world, some considerable portion of the improvement that is manifested is due, doubtless, to the operation of those causes which are producing a general progress in all the arts and functions of social life. The tendency of every thing is onward. Every where, and for all purposes, machinery is improving, materials are more and more easily procured, new facilities are discovered and new inventions are made. the results of which inure to the common benefit of all mankind. It is only so far as an establishment like the Armory advances at a more rapid rate than that of the general progress of the age, that any special credit is due to those who administer its affairs. It always seems, however, to strangers visiting the Armory and observing its condition, that these general causes will account for but a small portion of the results which have been attained in the management of it, during the past ten years.

CONCLUSION.

As was stated at the commencement of the article, it is only a small part of the hundreds of thousands of muskets manufactured, that are destined ever to be used. Some portion of the whole number are served out to the army, and are employed in Indian warfare, others are destined to arm garrisons in various fortresses and military posts, where they are never called to any other service than to figure in peaceful drillings and parades. Far the greater portion, however, are sent away to various parts of the country, to be stored in the national arsenals, where they lie, and are to lie, as we hope, forever, undisturbed, in the midst of scenes of rural beauty and continued peace. The flowers bloom and the birds sing unmolested around the silent and solitary depositories, where these terrible instruments of carnage and destruction unconsciously and forever repose.

New England Fences
(1880)

NEW ENGLAND FENCES.

POST AND RAIL FENCE.

A QUESTION of the future, that troubles the mind of the farmer more than almost any other is, What are we to do for fences? The wood-hungry iron horse is eating away the forests greedily and rapidly, and our people are ready to feed him to his fill for a paltry present fee, apparently learning no wisdom from the follies of our forest-destroying ancestors, but carrying on the same old, senseless, and indiscriminate warfare against trees wherever found, and seldom planting any except fruit-trees and a few shade-trees.

And, alas! no just retribution seems to overtake these evil-doers, except that most speculating deforesters go to the bad pecuniarily, but the curse descends on the sorrowing lovers of trees, and will fall on our children and our children's children,—the curse of a withered and wasted land, of hills made barren, of dried-up springs and shrunken streams.

It seems probable that a generation not far removed from this will see the last of the rail fences, those time-honored barriers of New England fields, too generous of timber to be kept up in a land barren of forests. The board fence will endure longer, but will pass away at last, and after it, what? Where stone walls are, they may continue to be, and where there are stones enough there may be more stone walls, but all New England is not so bountifully supplied in this respect as parts of it that I have heard of, where if one buys an acre of land, he must buy another to pile the stones of the first acre on. In some of our alluvial lands it is hard to find stones enough for the corner supports of rail fences. The hedge, except for ornamentation in a small way, does not, somehow, seem to take kindly to us, or we to it; at least, I have never seen one of any great length, nor one flourishing much, that was intended to be a barrier against stock. If ever so thrifty for a while, is it not likely that the pestiferous field-mice, which are becoming plentier every year, as their enemies, the foxes, skunks, hawks, owls and crows grow fewer, would destroy them in the first winter of deep snow? Great hopes were entertained of the wire fence at one time, but it has proved to be a delusion and indeed a snare. Some are temporizing with fate, or barely surrendering, by taking away the fences where grain fields or meadows border the highway. To me it is not pleasant to have the ancient boundaries of the road removed, over which kindly-spared trees have so long stood guard, and along whose sides black-raspberry bushes have sprung up and looped their inverted festoons of wine-colored stems and green leaves with silver linings, bearing racemes of fruit that the sauntering school-boy lingers to gather. And far from pleasant is it to drive cattle or sheep along such unfenced

stared a little at first at Ridgeway's Ready Restorative, but never took any.

However, it is not my purpose to speculate concerning the fences of the future, nor to devise means for impounding the fields of posterity, but rather to make some record of such fences as we now have, and some that have already passed away.

The old settlers, when they had brought a patch of the earth face to face with the

BRUSH FENCE.

ways, which they are certain to stray from, and exhaust the breath and patience of him who drives them and endeavors to keep them within the unmarked bounds; moreover, it gives the country a common look in more than one sense, as if nothing were worth keeping in or out. It will be a sad day for the advertiser of patent nostrums, when the road fence of broad, brush-inviting boards ceases to exist, and if we did not know that his evil genius would be certain to devise some blazoning of his balms, liniments, and bitters, quite as odious as this, we should be almost ready to say, away with this temptation. That was a happy device of one of our farmers, who turned the tables on the impudent advertiser, by knocking the boards off and then nailing them on again with the letters facing the field. The cattle

sun, and had sown their scanty seed therein, fenced it about with poles, a flimsy-looking barricade in the shadow of the lofty palisade of ancient trees that walled the "betterments," but sufficient to keep the few woodranging cattle out of the field whose green of springing grain was dotted and blotched with blackened stumps and log-heaps. The pole fence was laid after the same fashion of a rail fence, only the poles were longer than rail-cuts. There were also cross-staked pole fences, in which the fence was laid straight, each pole being upheld by two stakes crossing the one beneath, their lower ends being driven into the ground. This and the brush fence, though the earliest of our fences, have not yet passed away. That the last has not, one may find to his sorrow, when, coming to its lengthwise-laid abatis in the

SNAKE OR VIRGINIA FENCE.

woodland, he attempts to cross it. If he achieve it with a whole skin and unrent garments, he is a fortunate man, and if with an unruffled temper, he is certainly a good-natured one. According to an unwritten law, it is said that a lawful brush fence must be a rod wide, with no specification as to its height. You will think a less width enough, when you have made the passage of one. Coming to it, you are likely to start from its shelter a hare who has made his form there; or a ruffed grouse hurtles away from beside it, where she has been dusting her feathers in the powdery remains of an old log; or you may catch glimpses of a brown wood wren silently exploring the maze of prostrate branches. These are the fence viewers of the wood lot.

To build or pile a brush fence, such small trees as stand along its line are lopped down, but not severed from the stump, and made to fall lengthwise of the fence; enough more trees are brought to it to give it the width and height required. Many of the lopped ones live and, their wounds healing, they grow to be vigorous trees, their fantastic forms marking the course of the old brush fence long after it has passed from the memory of man. I remember a noted one which stood by the roadside till an ambitious owner of a city lot bought it and had it removed to his urban patch, where it soon died. It was a lusty white oak, a foot or so in diameter at the ground, three feet above which the main trunk turned at a right angle and grew

horizontally for about ten feet, and along this part were thrown up, at regular intervals, five perfect smaller trunks, each branching into a symmetrical head. It was the finest tree of such a strange growth that I ever saw, and if it had grown in a congenial human atmosphere, doubtless would have flourished for a hundred years or more, and likely enough, have become world-renowned. It was sold for five dollars! No wonder it died!

The log fence was a structure of more substance than either the pole or the brush fence, but belonged to the same period of plentifulness, even cumbersomeness, of timber. The great logs, generally pine, were laid straight, overlapping a little at the ends, on which were placed horizontally the short cross-pieces, which upheld the logs next above. These fences were usually built three logs high and formed a very solid wooden wall, but at a lavish expense of material, for one of the logs sawn into boards would have fenced several times the length of the three. I remember but one, or rather the remains of one, for it was only a reddish and gray line of moldering logs when I first knew it, with here and there a sturdy trunk still bravely holding out against decay, gray with the weather beating of fifty years, and adorned with a coral-like moss bearing scarlet spores.

From behind the log and brush fences, the prowling Indian ambushed the backwoodsman as he tilled his field, or reconnoitered the lonely cabin before he fell upon its defenseless inmates. Through or over these old-time fences, the bear pushed or clambered to his feast of "corn in the milk" or perhaps to his death, if he blundered against a harmless-looking bark string and pulled the trigger of a spring-gun, whose heavy charge of ball and buck-shot put an end to his predatory career.

After these early fences came the rail fence, as it is known in New England, or the snake fence, as it is sometimes called from the slight resemblance of its zig-zag line to the course of a serpent, or the Virginia fence, perhaps because the Old Dominion was the mother of it as of presidents, but more likely for no better reason than that the common deer is named the Virginia deer, or that no end of quadrupeds and birds and plants, having their home as much in the United States as in the British Provinces, bear the title of *Cana-*

sheen of a whole fence of such freshly riven material. Some one has called the rail fence ugly or hideous. Truly, it must be confessed, the newly laid rail fence is not a thing of beauty, any more than is any other new thing that is fashioned by man and intended to stand out-of-doors. The most tastefully modeled house looks out of place in the landscape till it has gained the perfect fellowship of its natural surroundings, has steeped itself in sunshine and storm, and became saturated with nature, is weather-stained, and has flecks of moss and lichen on its shingles and its underpinning, and can stand not altogether shamefaced in the presence of the old trees and world-old rocks and earth about it. So our fence

LOG FENCE.

densis. But rail, snake or Virginia, at any rate it is truly American, and probably has enclosed and does yet enclose more acres of our land than any other fence. But one seldom sees nowadays a new rail fence, or rather a fence of new rails, and we shall never have another wise and kindly rail-splitter to rule over us; and no more new pine rails, shining like gold in the sun, and spicing the air with their terebinthine perfume. The noble pine has become too rare and valuable to be put to such base use. One may catch the white gleam of a new ash rail, or short-lived bass-wood, among the gray of the original fence, a patch of new stuff in the old garment, but not often the

must have settled to its place, its bottom rails have become almost one with the earth and all its others, its stakes and caps cemented together with mosses and enwrapped with vines, and so weather-beaten and crated with lichens that not a sliver can be taken from it and not be missed. Then is it beautiful, and looks as much a part of nature as the trees that shadow it, and the berry bushes and weeds that grow along it, and the stones that were pitched into its corners thirty years ago, to be gotten out of the way. Then the chipmunk takes the hollow rails for his house and stores his food therein, robins build their nests in the jutting corners and the wary crow is not afraid to light on it. What sheltering arms half inclose its angles, where storm-blown autumn leaves find their rest, and molder to the dust of earth, covering the seeds of berries that the birds have dropped there— seeds which quicken and grow and border the fence with a thicket of berry bushes. Seeds of maples and birch and basswood, driven here by the winds of winters long past, have lodged and sprouted, and have been

to complete it. Then they are so easy to climb and so pleasant to sit upon, when there is a flat top-rail; and when a bird's nest is found, it can be looked into so easily; and it is such jolly fun to chase a red squirrel and see him go tacking along the top rails; and there are such chances for berry-picking beside it. In winter, there are no snow-drifts so good to play on as those that form in regular waves along the rail fence, their crests

BOARD FENCE.

kindly nursed till they have grown from tender shoots to storm-defying trees; there are clumps of sumacs also, with their fuzzy twigs and fern-like leaves and "bobs" of dusky crimson. Here violets bloom, and wind-flowers toss on their slender stems in the breath of May; and in summer the pink spikes of the willow herb overtop the upper rails, and the mass of the golden rod's bloom lies like a drift of gold along the edge of the field. The children who have not had a rail fence to play beside have been deprived of one abundant source of happiness, for every corner is a play-house, only needing a roof, which half a dozen bits of board will furnish,

running at right angles from the out-corners, their troughs from the inner ones. I am sorry for those children of the future who will have no rail fences to play about.

The board fence is quite as ugly as the rail fence when new, perhaps more so, for it is more prim and more glaring, as there is no alternation of light and shade in its straight line. But age improves its appearance also, and when the kindly touch of nature has been laid upon it, and has slanted a post here and warped a board there, and given it her weather-mark, and sealed it with her broad seal of gray-green and black lichens, by which time weeds and bushes have grown in its shelter, it is very picturesque. Its prevailing gray has a multitude of shades; the varied weather-stains of the wood, the lichens, the shags of moss and their shadows, and some touches of more decided color, as the yellowish-green mold that gathers on

The fence which is half wall and half board has a homely, rural look, as has the low wall topped with rails, resting on cross-stakes slanted athwart the wall, or the ends resting in rough mortises cut in posts that

OLD HALF-WALL FENCE.

some of the boards, the brown knots and rust-streaks from nail-heads, patches of green moss on the tops of posts, and here and there the half—or less—of a circle, chafed by a swaying weed or branch to the color of the unstained wood.

The wood-pecker drills the decaying posts, and blue-bird and wren make their nests in the hollow ones. There is often a ditch beside it, in which cowslips grow, and cat-tails and pussy-willows, akin only in name; on its edge horse-tails and wild grass, and higher up on the bank a tangle of hazel, wild mulberry, gooseberry and raspberry bushes, with a lesser undergrowth of ferns and poison ivy. The field and song sparrows hide their nests in its slope, and if the ditch is constantly and sufficiently supplied with water, sometimes the musk-rat burrows there, and you may see his clumsy tracks in the mud and the cleanly cut bits of the wild grass roots he has fed upon. Here, too, the hylas holds his earliest spring concerts.

All this applies only to the plain, unpretending fence, built simply for the division of fields, without any attempt at ornament. Nature has as slow and painful a labor to bring to her companionship the painted crib that encloses the skimpy door-yard of a staring, white, new—or modernized—farm-house, as she has to subdue the glare of the house itself; but she will accomplish it in her own good time,—the sooner if aided by a little wholesome unthrift of an owner who allows his paint-brushes to dry in their pots.

are built into the wall, which is as much of a "post and rail" fence as we often find in northern New England. A new fence of either kind is rarely seen nowadays in our part of the country, and both may be classed among those which are passing away.

Of all fences, the most enduring and the most satisfying to the eye is the stone wall. If its foundation is well laid, it may last as long as the world,—which, indeed, it may slowly sink into; or the accumulating layers of earth may in years cover it; but it will still be a wall—a grassy ridge with a core of stone. A wall soon gets rid of its new look. It is not propped up on the earth, but has its foundations in it; mosses and lichens take quickly and kindly to it, and grass and weeds grow out of its lower crevices, mullein and brakes and the bulby stalks of golden-rod spring up beside it. Black raspberry bushes loop along it, over it, and stretch out from it, clumps of sweet elders shade its sides, and their broad cymes of blossoms, and later, clusters of blackberries, beloved of robins and school-boys, bend over it. When the stones of which it is built are gathered from the fields, as they generally are, they are of infinite variety, brought from the far north by glaciers, washed up by the waves of ancient seas, and tumbled down to the lower lands from the overhanging ledges. Lumps of gray granite and gneiss, and dull-red blocks of sandstone, fragments of blue limestone, and only a geologist knows how many others, mostly with smooth-worn sides and rounded corners and edges. All together, they make a line of beautifully variegated color and of light and shade. One old wall that I know of has been a rich mine for a brood of callow geologists, who have pecked it and overhauled it and looked and talked most wisely over its stones, and called them names hard enough to break their stony hearts.

At the building of the wall, what bending and straining of stalwart backs and muscles; what shouting to oxen—for it would seem the ox can be driven only by sheer strength of lungs; what rude engineering to span the rivulet; what roaring of blasts, when stones were too large to be moved in whole, and the boys had the noise and smoke and excitement of a Fourth-of-July celebration without a penny's expense, but alas! with no gingerbread nor spruce beer. Then, too, what republics were convulsed when the great stones, underneath which a multitude of ants had founded their commonwealth, were pried up, and what hermits were disturbed when the newts were made to face the daylight, and earwigs and beetles forced to scurry away to new hiding-places! But when the wall was fairly built, the commonwealths and hermitages were re-established beneath it, more secure and undisturbed than ever.

make a breach in his stronghold through which the dogs can reach him, or throw him a "slip-a-noose" into which he hooks his long teeth and is hauled forth to death. The weasel frequents a wall of this kind, and there is hardly a fissure in its whole length through which his lithe, snake-like body cannot pass. You may now perhaps see his eyes peering out of a hole in the wall, so bright you might mistake them for dew-drops on a spider's web, or see him stealing to his lair with a field mouse in his mouth. In spring, summer and fall, nature clothes this little hunter in russet, but in winter he has a furry coat almost as white as snow, with only a black tip to his tail by which to know himself in the wintry waste. The chipmunk, too, haunts the wall, and the red squirrel finds in it handy hiding-places into which to retreat, when from the topmost stone he has jeered and snickered at the passer-by beyond all patience.

Long after our people had begun to tire of mowing and plowing about the great pine stumps, whose pitchy roots nothing but fire would destroy, and when the land had become too valuable to be cumbered by them, some timely genius arose and invented the stump puller and the stump fence. This fence with-

OVER THE STUMP FENCE.

The woodchuck takes the stone wall for his castle, and through its loopholes whistles defiance to the dogs who beseige him, but woe be to him if the boys join in the assault. They

stands the tooth of time as long as the red-cedar posts, of which the boy said he knew they would last a hundred years, for his father had tried 'em lots of times; and now many fields of our old pine-bearing lands are bounded by these stumps, like barricades of mighty antlers. These old roots have a hold on the past, for in their day they have spread themselves in the unsunned mold of the primeval forest, whereon no man trod but the wild Abnaki, nor any tamed thing; have had in turn for their owners swarthy sagamores, sceptred kings and rude backwoodsmen. Would they had life enough left in them to tell their story!

There is variety enough in the writhed and fantastic forms of the roots, but they are slow to don any covering of moss and lichens over their whity-gray, and so they have a bald, almost skeleton-like appearance. But when creeping plants— the woodbine, the wild grape and the clematis—grow over the stump fence, it is very beautiful. The woodbine suits it best, and in summer converts it into a wall of dark green, in autumn into one of crimson, and in winter drapes it gracefully with its slender vines.

This fence has plenty of nooks for berry bushes, milk-weeds, golden rods and asters to grow in, which they speedily do and, as a return, help to hide its nakedness. Nor does it lack tenants, for the robin builds on it, and the blue-bird makes its nest in its hollow prongs, as the wrens used to, before they so unaccountably deserted us. The chipmunk finds snug cells in the stumps, woodchucks and skunks burrow beneath it, and it harbors multitudes of field mice.

In the neighborhood of saw-mills, fencing a bit of the road and the sawyer's garden patch, but seldom elsewhere, is seen a fence made of slabs from the mill, one end of each slab resting on the ground, the other upheld by cross stakes. It is not an enduring fence, and always looks too new to be as picturesque in color as it is in form. The common name of this fence is quite suggestive of the perils that threaten whoever tries to clamber over it, and he who has tried it once will skirt it a furlong rather than try it again. The sawyer's melons and apples would be safe enough inside it if there were no boys,—but what fence is boy-proof?

SAWYER'S FENCE.

Of all fences, none is so simple as the water fence, only a pole spanning the stream, perhaps fastened at the larger end by a stout link and staple to a great water-maple, ash or buttonwood-tree, a mooring to hold it from going adrift when the floods sweep down. If the stream is shallow, it has a central support, a big stone that happens to be in the right place, or lacking this, a pier made like a great bench; if deep, the middle of the pole sags into the water and the upper current ripples over it. On it the turtle basks; here the wood-duck sits and sleeps or preens his handsome feathers in the sun, and the kingfisher watches

the same chance getting perhaps as many as they lose.

I have seen a very peculiar fence in the slate region of Vermont, made of slabs of slate, set in the earth like a continuous row of closely planted headstones. It might

A WATER FENCE.

for his fare of minnows, and the lithe mink and the clumsy muskrat rest upon it. Neighbors' cattle bathe in and sip the common stream, and lazily fight their common enemies, the fly and the musquito, and for all we know compare the merits of their owners and respective pastures.

The fences of interval lands cannot be called water fences, although during spring and fall freshets they divide only wastes of water, across which they show merely as streaks of gray, or, as they are too apt to do, go drifting piecemeal down stream with the strong current. Then the owners go cruising over the flooded fields in quest of their rails and boards, finding some stranded on shores a long way from their proper place, some lodged in the lower branches and crotches of trees and in thickets of button-bushes, and some afloat,—losing many that go to the gain of some riparian freeholder further down the stream, but by

give a nervous person a shudder, as if the stones were waiting for him to lie down in their lee for the final, inevitable sleep, with nothing left to be done but the stone-cutter to come and lie on the other side the fence.

The least of fences, excepting the toy fences that impound the make-believe herds of country children, are the little pickets of slivers that guard the melon and cucumber hills from the claws of chanticleer and partlet. These are as certain signs of the sure establishment of spring as the cry of the upland plover. They maintain their post until early summer, when, if they have held their own against bugs, the vines have grown strong enough to take care of themselves, and begin to wander, and the yellow blossoms meet the bumble-bee half way.

The "line fence," of whatever material,

may generally be known by the trees left growing along it, living landmarks, safer to be trusted than stones and dead wood, and showing that, as little as our people value trees, they have more faith in them than in each other. The burning and fall of the "corner hemlock," on which was carved in 1762 the numbers of four lots, brought dismay to four land-owners. The old corner has lost its mooring, and has drifted a rod or two away.

What heart-burnings and contentions have there not been concerning line fences, feuds lasting through generations, engendered by their divergence a few feet to the right or left, or by the question as to whom belonged the keeping up of this part or that! When the heads of some rural households were at pitchforks' points, a son and daughter were like enough to fall into the old way, namely, love, and Juliet Brown steals forth in the moonlight to meet Romeo Jones, and they bill and coo across the parents' bone of contention, in the shadow of the guardian trees. If I were to write the story of their love, it should turn at length into smooth courses, and have no sorrowful ending—no departure of the lover, nor pining away of the lass, but at last their bridal bells should say:

> "Life is sweeter, love is dearer,
> For the trial and delay;"

and the two farms should become one, and nothing remain of the old fence but the trees where the lovers met, and under which their children and their children's children should play.

The ways through and over our fences are few and simple. The bar-way (in Yankeeland "a pair of bars") seems to belong to the stone wall, rail and stump fences; though the balanced gate, with its long top bar pivoted on a post and loaded with a big stone at one end, the other dropping into a notch in the other post for a fastening, is often used to bar the roadways through them. The more pretending board fence has its more carefully made gate, swinging on iron hinges and fastened with a hook. Sometimes its posts are connected high overhead by a cross beam,—a "gallows gate,"—past which one would think the murderer must steal with terror as he skulks along in the gloaming.

The sound of letting down the bars is a familiar one to New England ears, and after the five or six resonant wooden clangs, one listens to hear the cow-boy lift up his voice, or the farmer call his sheep. The rail fence is a stile all along its length, and so is a stone wall, though a stone or so is apt to tumble down if you clamber over it in an unaccustomed place. The footpath runs right over the rail fence, as easy to be seen in the polishing of the top rail as in the trodden sward. On some much frequented ways "across lots" as to a spring, a slanted plank on either side the fence affords a comfortable passage, and down their pleasant incline a boy can no more walk than his marbles could. Let no one feel too proud to crawl through a stump fence, but be humbly thankful if he can find a hole that will give him passage. A bird can go over one very comfortably, and likewise over a brush fence, and this last nothing without wings can do; man and every beast larger than a squirrel must wade through it, unless they have the luck to come to a pole-barway in it.

A chapter might be written of fence breakers and leapers; of wickedly wise cows who unhook gates and toss off rails almost as handily as if they were human; of sheep who find holes that escape the eyes of their owners, and go through them with a flourish of trumpets like a victorious army that has breached the walls of a city; of horses who, in spite of pokes, take fences like trained steeple-chasers, and another chapter of fence walkers, too,—for the rail fence and stone wall are convenient highways for the squirrel whereon to pass from nut-tree and corn-field to store-house and home, and for puss to pick her dainty way, dry-footed, to and from her mousing and bird-peaching in the fields; the coon walks there, and Reynard makes them a link in the chain of his subtle devices.

One cannot help thinking of the possibility that, by and by, high farming may become universal, and soiling may become the common practice of farmers, and that then the building and keeping up of fences will end with the need of them, and the boundaries of farms be marked only by iron posts or stone pillars; then the old landmarks of gray fences, with their trees and shrubs and flowering weeds, will have passed away and no herds of kine or flocks of sheep dot the fields; and then, besides men and teams, there will be no living thing larger than a bird in the wide landscape. The prospect of such a time goes, with many other things, to reconcile one to the thought, that before that day his eyes will be closed in a sleep which such changed scenes will not trouble.

The City of Elms
(1858)

HARPER'S
NEW MONTHLY MAGAZINE.

No. XCVII.—JUNE, 1858.—Vol. XVII.

"THE GREEN," NEW HAVEN.

THE CITY OF ELMS.

I.

A WINTER day of 1636, and London is foggy and chilly. Within a low counting-room in "the city," before a glowing fire, sit three middle-aged gentlemen, solemnly still, toasting their toes, and semi-occasionally sipping good ale from huge silver flagons. So dark is the day that the bright fire-light has no great task to drive the gray daylight out through the small, smudgy window; then it has all to itself the little low room, and it flickers and flashes on wainscot and carving, makes three uncertain, huge shadows along and over the dark back wall, gilds the bright silver of the jolly old ale-flagons, reddens the faces of the three solemn sitters, and seems—so still are they—the only life in the room.

"I will go!" breaks the silence, coming from Hopkins, the youngest; and he seizes his flagon and drains the last pint, as if in relief at the birth of the long gestated purpose.

"Thank God!" exclaims Davenport, piously, and thirstily seeks relief also.

Eaton, the eldest, seizes his flagon and drinks long and deep, saying a gusty and hearty "Amen," when he finishes. The word echoes hollowly within the cavity of the empty utensil, and the lid falls *clack!* and signals the end of the ale and the meeting. They have been waiting only for Hopkins's tardy consent to the plan; that gained, the solemn triumvirate breaks up its dim session, content for the present with this first step from tyranny at home toward freedom in the wilderness.

The weakest of the brethren may not impute

his own inclinations, which led him to London and commercial prosperity. Getting rich in the "east-country trade"—along the shores of the Baltic—he was chosen deputy-governor of the mercantile company to which he belonged, visited the northern countries of Europe, and was the agent of the King of England at the court of Denmark. When a boy at school in Coventry, he became an intimate friend of John Davenport, son of the Mayor; and when John came to preach at St. Stephen's, Theophilus became one of his parishioners.

Although married to a daughter of the Bishop of Chester, and, according to Mather, "arrived unto a fair estate, and a merchant of great credit and fashion," he easily became, under the influence of his old friend John, a zealous and active Puritan. He, as well as Davenport, was one of the patentees of Massachusetts, and early in the history of the emigration, formed plans to join the adventurous Pilgrims.

Edward Hopkins, the youngest of the three, was a native of Shrewsbury, and born about the year 1600. He was step-son to Eaton, like him was "a merchant of credit and fashion," and may be pardoned if, on account of his youth and his position, he was the last to say "I will go." Yet he also was deeply imbued with the feelings and principles of the Puritans, and the sacrifice he made of fortune and station was not less hearty and sincere than that of his relative Eaton.

These three, whom we have seen to have been gentlemen of rank and wealth, were the founders of a colony which sailed from England early in the spring of 1637 for Massachusetts Bay. They embarked in two ships, taking with them a large amount of property, and a number of persons in the capacity of servants. Their voyage was favorable, and they arrived at Boston on the 3d of June, 1637.

II.

Another picture.

It is mid-April, in 1638. The south wind—hazy and perfumed, blowing warm from San

it for a sin against the Puritans that they drank beer; it was a custom of the times, and they, at least, did not observe it with excess. Blame not the lips through which they drank "gude ayle," nor the noses through which they sang unharmonious psalms. They thought they did God service; and so they did, in their queer but conscientious ways of living and doing. Laugh, if you please, at the peculiarities of the Puritans; but acknowledge that they were bold, true men, God-fearing, self-denying, Christian heroes, for all that.

John Davenport, son of the Mayor of Coventry, was Master of Arts and Bachelor of Divinity by Oxford authority, and had preached in St. Stephen's, at London, for some years, before he began to favor the doctrines of the Puritans. When his convictions resulted in actions, Laud, that zealous hater of Puritanism, made England an unpleasant place of abode for him; so he went over to Holland, lived there three years, corresponding and planning, and then came back to London to meet his friend Eaton, and perfect their great project of removing to America. He was not a ranter; he was a gentleman, a scholar, and a Christian, grown hopeless at length of reform in the State Church, and hopeful of Christian liberty for himself and his friends only in the free wilderness of the New World.

Theophilus Eaton, whose counting-room the three have just left, was older than Davenport by a few years, having been born in Oxfordshire in 1590, where his father, says Mather, was "a faithful and famous minister." Disappointing his parents, who were desirous that he should follow the profession of his father, he followed

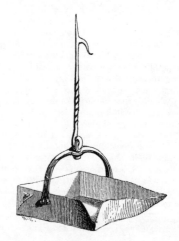

Salvador, along that mystic thermal ocean-current which flows northward from the dreamy, glowing islands of the Western Indies — has kissed new life into the outermost buds of the grand forest trees; the maples are flushed with faint green, the elm-boughs thicken hourly, the oak-buds are swollen almost to the birth of life; along the southward-facing banks the flowers and grasses dance to the music of the breeze and sunlight; the meadows, which level away toward the bay, have already grown brightly green; the wavelets beyond are playing with each other, half merrily, half lazily; farther away in the distance a bright blue reach of waters meets the horizon, with a fringe of dim, low-lying shore.

Under this great oak are assembled the members of the London colony. Here at last they have raised their altar, and, in "a temple not made with hands," whose arches of meeting boughs let through the smiles of heaven on this their first Sabbath in the wilderness, they gather around John Davenport, their loved pastor and guide, and join in singing praises to the God of Israel—to Him who has led them, as of old He led the Hebrews, across the sea, to the Canaan of their hopes.

From their ships—which you may see through the lower branches, swinging with the tide in the bay—they have toilsomely brought the huge iron-bound chests and the heavy oaken furniture which lie scattered under the trees. Clumsy farming-tools of the times, silver-chased muskets and pistols, kitchen utensils, rich outer-garments of silk, cut and embroidered in the showy fashion of two centuries ago; these lie in chance places, heaped or singly, among the rocks and trees.

With some show of order the Pilgrims have arranged themselves to listen to this first sermon; and yet, knowing that it will be a long one—two hours long at the shortest—they have chosen convenient positions. Some recline on the fresh grass; some lean against rocks, or the more accommodating gnarlings of the old trees; husbands support their wives, and mothers gath-

er children—who may be restless, and will be sleepy—within the folds of their full dresses. A few of the stiffest of the men stand piously erect, or lean upon their stout muskets. Steel-clad soldiers, the servants of the company, tread solemnly and slowly on guard around the borders of the group; the Quinnipiacs are friendly, but the Puritans trust in Providence *and* powder.

Davenport preaches from the text, "Then was Jesus led up of the Spirit into the wilderness, to be tempted of the devil;" and he warns his attentive hearers that even here temptations are to be encountered, and that the fight with Satan has not ended, though they have changed the battle-ground from London to "the wilderness."

The April Sabbath sun has set, and the *new haven* has been consecrated as the new home of our London Puritans and Pilgrims.

The colony arrived at Boston, from England, on the 26th of July, 1637. The fame of Mr. Davenport, and the reputation and good estates of the principal gentlemen of this company, made a warm and hearty welcome for them with the

WEST ROCK, AND PART OF WESTVILLE.

good people of "the Bay." Not only the leading men of the several towns, but also "the General Court," made advantageous offers to them to settle in their midst. Charlestown made liberal proposals; Newbury (port) offered to give up the whole town to them; and the Court invited them to settle at any place they should choose.

But they had determined to form a distinct colony, as far as possible beyond the reach of the long arm of Laud, who was even then stretching his powers to interfere with the disagreeable independence of the exiles. Our friends had planned, even from the beginning, the founding of a commonwealth in the regulation of which they might be compelled to recognize no human authority foreign to themselves.

By the pursuit of the Pequots, the Bay settlers had become acquainted with the pleasant shores of what is now called "the Sound." The land was represented as fruitful, and the harbors were known to be large and accessible; "wherefore the land seemed favorable for commerce," to which the founders of the colony had originally determined, if possible, to devote themselves.

In the fall of 1637, therefore, Mr. Eaton—who from the first and till his death was the leader of the colony, both on account of his wealth and character—started on an expedition of exploration along the coast. On arriving at Quinnipiac, he was satisfied. The place was remote from "the Bay" on the one hand, and not too near "the Manhadoes" on the other. The

harbor was commercially inviting, the meadows and forests agriculturally attractive, the Indians friendly; deer abounded in the woods, fish in the waters; the climate was milder than that endured by his brethren at the North. In short, he was content, and thankful that Providence had provided so goodly an heritage for his company. So he left a few men to guard the claim through the winter and returned to Boston.

As soon as spring came, the colony re-embarked, and, sailing around the Cape, coasted along the shore until they came in sight of "Red Rock"—as the Dutch, sailing eastward, had already named the bold headland which stands sentinel over the harbor—and landed at the *new haven* about the middle of April; the precise date is unknown.

The planters of Quinnipiac, determined to maintain peace and friendship with the Indians, began from the first to treat them kindly, and by gifts, fair purchases, and amicable treaties, conciliated the good-will of the small and feeble tribe which held the territory. By the Pequots on the east and the Mohawks on the west, the Quinnipiacs were often "unseasonably assaulted and terrified," and it seems they were not at all unwilling to receive the powerful English as neighbors and friends. In the November after their arrival we find from the records that Momauguin, sole sachem of the Quinnipiacs, on the one hand, and Theophilus Eaton and John Davenport on the other, entered into a covenant, in which it was stipulated that, in consideration of promises of protection and "twelve

EAST ROCK, FROM WHITNEYVILLE ROAD.

coats of English cloth, twelve alchymy spoons (pewter, probably), twelve hatchets, twelve hoes, two dozen of knives, twelve porringers, and four cases of French knives and scissors," he, Momauguin, sole sachem, etc., yielded up all his right, title, and interest to all lands, rivers, ponds, and trees, with all the liberties and appurtenances belonging to the same, to said Theophilus and said John, their heirs and assigns, forever. It was covenanted, also, that the Indians should always have land for planting corn on the east side of the harbor and river toward Saybrook.

The treaty was a fair one on both sides. The Indians regarded it as such; and by this act, and by subsequent fair dealings and kindnesses, the colonists made firm friends of their neighbors, by whom they never were seriously molested.

Another purchase was made in the December following from Montowise, sachem of another tribe, claiming lands to the north of Quinnipiac. This tract was ten miles long and thirteen broad, and seemed then large enough for all the wants of the colony.

In the ancient records of New Haven the original agreements are still preserved, signed by the contracting parties, the rude delineations of bows, arrows, and hatchets still telling of the unaccustomed grasp of pen of "Momauguin, Sugcogisin, Quosaquash, Carroughood, Woosauruck, and Shaumpishuh," and of "Montowise and Sawsounck," of whom the second purchase was made.

During the first year there appears to have been no act of civil, ecclesiastical, or military authority. The settlers were busy in providing homes and food for their families, under the acknowledged authority of Eaton and Davenport. The colony was wealthy—by far the richest in men and means of the companies which came to New England—and there is no appearance from the record or letters that they were ever straitened for bread, as the other colonies were.

Their first settlement was made in George Street (now called) and on the opposite hill; but within a short time, in keeping with the design of the founders to plant a capital colony, they laid out their town in squares. In the centre was a large and beautiful square, left unoccupied, and this was "compassed" with others, making nine in all. These remain to this day unaltered in boundaries. The town has spread in all directions, but the original plan has been adhered to, and most of the broad and shaded streets of the modern city cross each other rectangularly.

For the first fourteen months the new settlers acted under what they called a "plantation covenant," in which they solemnly pledged themselves to each other and to God that they would be governed in all things "by those rules which the Scripture holds forth." An attempt is made at the present day to maintain the same principles, but with a success by no means commensurate with that of our ancestors.

During the hurry and bustle of this first year

EAST ROCK, SOUTH VIEW.

the ten or twelve leading men were praying, fasting, inquiring, and debating over the great work of laying the foundations of Church and State. The breadth of Scripture rules was ample, but too indefinitely bounded. Rulers and magistrates were needed, and some form of government: and so—quotation is made from their own records:

"The 4th day of the 4th moneth called June 1639, all the free planters assembled together in a general meetinge to consult about settling ciuill Gouernm^t according to God, and about the nominatiō of persons thatt might be founde by consent of all, fittest in all respects for the foundacō worke of a church which was intend to be gathered in Quinipieck."

Within the rough walls of "Mr. Newman's barn" a civil compact was agreed upon, and signed, after most solemn deliberation, the like of which may not be any where found in modern history. Not the laws of England, for from them they had just fled as unjust and tyrannical; not the Roman civil law, for that was foreign to the spirit of Englishmen, and to the spirit of civil and religious freedom which animated the Puritans; not the wiser and juster laws of Solon, or Lycurgus, or King Alfred; but simply and only the laws of Moses, a copy of which was in every man's hand, and which were familiar to every subject of the jurisdiction. These were the laws adopted by the one hundred and eleven "free planters of Quinipieck."

Objections have been made to some of the peculiarities of the government thus inaugurated—objections, some of which are not entirely unreasonable—but it has been generally con-

ceded that the leaders of the new commonwealth were wise and just and liberal for their times, and for the circumstances amidst which they acted.

In this article, which must be brief, and which should be mainly descriptive, there is neither space nor place for a discussion of the principles and results of the renowned compact of the Quinnipiac colonists. The reader who desires to examine the subject more thoroughly is referred to the discourses of Kingsley, Bacon, and Dutton, wherein the actions of their ancestors are ably defended.

Let us turn over a few of the pages of the old colonial records of matters which came before "the General Court." We may thus learn how the state prospered under the laws of Moses; may see how they lived and labored, watched and prayed. It must be remembered, however, in justice to the colonists, that a large number of them were servants, hired in England—more or less intelligently devoted to the principles of Puritanism, it is true, yet in many cases ignorant and careless:

"October 25th. 1639.

"—— the worde of God shall be the onely rule to be attended vnto in ordering the affayres of gouernment in this plantatiō."

"Nouember 3d.

"Itt is ordered thatt Mr. Hopkins have two hogsheads of lime for his vse, and as much more as will finnish his house as he now intends itt, he thinking thatt two hogsheads more will serve."

It may be significant of a curious chapter in the secret history of the settlement, this single mention of the name of Mr. Hopkins. The

WEST ROCK.

reader may remember him as one of the original three, the step-son of Eaton, the merchant of wealth and fashion in London. It is certain that he came with the colony, and here we have the record of his building a plastered house, one of the few first; but his name does not appear among the one hundred and eleven, nor is it mentioned again in the records. It is said that he shortly removed to Hartford, but the usual leave to depart does not appear to have been voted to him. We may only guess at the causes of the disaffection of this, one of the leading men of the colony, for the rest were wise enough to leave no record of the affair.

"December 4th 1639.

"*Roger Duhurst and James Stewart are injoined to make double restitution to John Cockerill for five pound, seaventeene shillings, w*ch *they stole out of his chist on the Lords day in the meetinge time, and they being servants to the said Cockerill, for w*ch *aggravation they were whipped allso.*"

This dispensation of justice is decidedly Mosaic.

"Jan: 4th 1639.

"*Itt is ordered thatt those thatt kill wolves and foxes shall have for every wolfe head 15s and for every foxe head 2s 6d.*"

"Febr: 5th 1639.

"*Isaiah, Captaine Turners man, fined 5l for being druncke on the Lords day.*

"*John Jenner accused for being drunke w*th *strong waters was acquitted, itt appearing to be of infirmyty & occasioned by the extremyty of the colde.*" (!)

"1t of the 7th moneth 1640.

"*Itt is ordered that eu*ry *man that is appoynt-* ed to watch whether M*rs *or servants, shall come every Lords day to the meetinge compleatly armed, and all others shall bring their swords, no man exempted save Mr. Eaton, o*r *pasto*r*, Mr. James, Mr. Samuell Eaton and the 2 deacons.*"

"*This towne now named Newhaven.*"

"25th of 12th mon: 1641.

"*Itt is ordered that a free schoole shall be sett vp in this towne.*"

Was not this the first "free schoole" of New England? Can any other "towne" in the Union boast of having enjoyed the benefits of free education for two hundred and sixteen years?

"Ezechiell Cheevers" was the master of this school, and the first of the famous race of "Connecticut school-masters."

"Novemb: 1644.

"*The propositiō for the releife of poor schollars att the colledge att Cambridg* [Harvard] *was fully approved off, and thereupon itt was ordered thatt Josuah Attwater and William Davis shall receive of every one in this plantatiō whose hart is willing to contribute thereunto, a peck of wheat or the vallue of itt.*"

III.

"Take counsel, execute judgment; make thy shadow as the night in the midst of the noonday; hide the outcasts; bewray not him that wandereth. Let mine outcasts dwell with thee, Moab; be thou a covert to them from the face of the spoiler."—ISAIAH, xvi. 3, 4.

From this text Mr. Davenport preached when the emissaries of the King were in New Haven in pursuit of "the Judges," Goff, Whalley, and Dixwell. The pursuit was energetic and the escapes narrow, but "Moab" hid the "outcasts," and the soldiers of Governor Andross searched in vain.

THE JUDGES CAVE.

Sir Edmund himself, who was by no means popular as a man or a magistrate, when resting at New Haven over the Sabbath, during one of his tours through the colony of Connecticut, was insulted, as he thought, at meeting, where the deacon gave out the 52d Psalm, of Sternhold and Hopkins's version, commencing—

"Why dost thou, tyrant, boast abroad,
    Thy wicked works to praise?
Dost thou not know there is a God,
    Whose mercies last always?"

On reprehending the deacon, the "tyrant" received, as an excuse, that it was the usage to sing the Psalms in course, "and so was obliged to put up with it;" but although this might have been the usual custom, it is not unlikely that this Moabitish deacon selected the psalm for Sir Edmund's particular contemplation.

There are numerous traditions of the aid and comfort given by the people to the objects of the King's hatred and pursuit.

When it became unsafe for them to remain in the town, they resorted to the Rocks, on one of which, in a cave called still the "Judges' Cave," they lived for weeks together. This spot, which is on West Rock, about two miles and a half from the city, is a favorite resort of excursionists, and the gray rocks are covered with ambitious initials. Far up on the side of

TOMBSTONES OF THE REGICIDES.

one of the huge boulders which form the cave appears the ancient inscription,

> " Refiſtance to Tyrants is
> obedience to God."

On one occasion, when the pursuers were on the track of the fugitives, they escaped from the city and hastened toward one of their "coverts" upon East Rock; but the soldiers were so close upon them that they had scarcely time to conceal themselves under "Neck Bridge" (seen in the engraving) when the horsemen clattered over the bridge, on their way to Hartford. Tradition has it that, if the soldiers had thought of examining the bridge they would have needed bright eyes to discover their prey, for only the three noses of them were above water.

The lives of "the Judges" were romances, their deaths and burials romantically mysterious. They feared, with reason, as the result proved, that even the sanctity of their graves might not be left inviolate. Dixwell lived seventeen of his twenty-nine years of exile in New Haven, under the name of James Davids, Esquire, enjoying the esteem of the few who held his secret. When he died, at a good old age, he requested that no monument should be erected at his grave giving an account of his person, name, and character, alleging as a reason, "lest his enemies might dishonor his ashes." His friends yielded to his last wishes, and a plain stone, of which we give a sketch, was the only memorial of the regicide.

"Often," says President Stiles, in his "History of the Judges"—"often have we heard the Crown officers aspersing and vilifying them; and some, so late as 1775, visited and treated the graves with marks of indignity too indecent to be mentioned."

One of the Dixwells of Boston, a descendant of Colonel Dixwell, has, within a few years, erected a noble and beautiful monument to the memory of his ancestor, of which the accompanying sketch is a good representation. On one face of the stone is cut the Dixwell coat of arms. The crest is a hand clutching firmly the talon and fluttering wing of an eagle; the motto is,

DIXWELL'S MONUMENT.

"*Esse quam videri*"—To be, rather than to seem.

Whalley was cousin to Cromwell, and fought valiantly at Naseby, charging, "with a psalm," the squadrons of Langdale and Prince Rupert, victorious over both. Goff aided in "purging the Parliament," at the head of musketeers, and was called to the Protector's House of Lords. Dixwell was a colonel in Cromwell's army, and a member of his Parliament in 1654. They crowned their heroism in the Puritan cause by acting with the thirty judges who condemned and beheaded King Charles the First; and then, at the Restoration, the drama was ended. Pursued and almost taken, hiding and almost discovered, fearful yet always trusting in God, the judges spent the remainder of their lives in New England, and were summoned at last to meet the Judge of all. Awaiting the great decision, they sleep in peaceful, honored graves.

Let us fill up, somewhat, this imperfect sketch of the main outlines of the first half-century with a few chiaroscuro touches of the home life of our ancestors.

The colonists of New Haven, as has been noticed, founded their civil polity upon the laws of Moses; Sunday, consequently, was observed with the greatest reverence and strictness. At three o'clock on Saturday afternoon they ended the week's labors, and spent the rest of the day as "the preparation." All youths under twenty-one were catechised publicly in the meeting-house, the Westminster Catechism being the text-book. Seated in the front seats of the gallery, each rose in turn to answer the question propounded by the minister. This exercise was unpopular with the young folks, who looked forward to the attainment of freedom with eager anticipation; but governmental and parental authority was stronger then than now, and they were obliged to submit.

Saturday night, after sundown, was regarded as part of "holy time," and to this day, in many parts of New England, the law is observed—"From even to even shall ye celebrate your Sabbaths." On "the Lord's Day" no one was excused from attending "meetinge," except upon the plea of sickness. Non-attendance was punished by fines, and sometimes by whipping, as we see in the following quotation from the record of 1647:

"*William Blayden was publicly and severely whipped for not attending meeting, although he plead that all the clothes he had were unfit to wear, being all wet through the preceding Saturday, as he had been abroad after cattle in the woods in a violent rain, and on the Sunday had kept his bed.*"

Meeting-time was announced by beating a drum or blowing a conch-shell.

> "The time we tell,
>   When there to come,
>   By beat of drum
>   Or sounding shell."

When gathered within the meeting-house, the

men and women occupied seats on opposite sides of the broad aisle, the young people sitting in the galleries, in full view of their watchful parents and guardians. In their services they evidently endeavored to differ as much as possible from the forms of the English Church. They stood, instead of kneeling, during prayer, and sat while singing. They made it a matter of conscience to stand motionless during the longest prayers. At the present day, in the meeting-house which succeeds the original framed building, the degenerate posterity of the Puritans indulge in various "unseemly" postures during prayer: the majority compromise between kneeling and sitting, a very few of the older men stand during the whole or a part of the exercise, while many, especially the younger part of the *audience*, sit at ease and gaze around them.

Imagine the look of old John Davenport, were he to rise from his grave some Sunday morning and walk up the broad aisle of the "Centre Church" during "the long prayer!" Not more astonished would he be at marble pulpit, frescoed walls, cushioned seats, and gilded organ-pipes, than at the slothful and independent, not to say irreverent, positions of the congregation. Manners and men have changed "considerably" (using that word in Jeremy Taylor's sense) since "the good old colony times."

Social intercourse was very formal. Every man received his title: ministers and magistrates were called Mister, and few addressed them uncovered; church members were saluted as brethren and sisters; and the commonalty, who were not in church fellowship, were simply "goodman" and "goodwife." Besides these the records abound with military titles, sergeants and corporals, even, receiving the lawful handle to their names.

Especial pains were taken that there should be no disorderly conduct between "young men and maidens." The following law is copied from Eaton's code:

"*Whosoever shall inveigle or draw the affections of any maide or maide-servant, either for himself or others, without first gaining the consent of her parents or guardians, besides all damages the parents may sustain, shall pay to the plantation* 40s. *for the first offense, and for the second towards the same party,* £4; *for the third, shall be fined, imprisoned, or corporeally punished, as the plantation court shall direct.*"

Under this law, as appears by the New Haven records, at a court held in May, 1660, Jacobeth Murline and Sarah Tuttle were prosecuted "*for setting down on a chest together, his arme about her waiste and her arme upon his shoulder or about his neck, and continuing in yt. sinfull posture about half an hour, in which time he kyssed her and she kyssed him, or they kyssed one another, as ye witnesses testified.*" Each of them was sentenced to pay 20s. to the treasurer. It was lucky for them that they escaped being "corporeally punished," for there seems to have

been a remarkable fondness for this method of punishing offenders of all kinds.

During the first half-century, and even later, it was the custom to cut the hair "round by a cap," a trencher or bowl often serving the purpose of marking the track of the shears. Wigs were afterward in fashion, and were worn even by boys. After the wigs were out of fashion it became the mode to dress the hair by cueing or clubbing it behind, the cue being worn in silk bags, adorned with large black rosettes by the rich, and in eel-skins by the common people. Dress coats were made with long, full skirts, stiffened with buckram to make them stand out; the sleeves were short and full, and bars of lead were sewn in the lining to make the cuffs hang down when the arm was raised. Vests were worn with immense pocket-flaps, reaching nearly to the knees. Knee-breeches were worn by old and young, the pantaloon being a modern invention. Many of the ancient silver shoe-buckles are still preserved in old families.

The dress of women varied often then, as now, but at first was remarkable for simplicity. Striped linen short-gowns and petticoats, in summer, were worn in public, and in winter, garments of linsey-woolsey cloth, of home manufacture. When calico was first introduced, it was sold at about a dollar a yard, and she was dressed in the first fashion who wore a calico gown. In later times the well-known open-fronted gowns were worn, displaying the worked "stomacher" and quilted petticoat. Hoops had their day, and gowns with trails—"sweep-streets," as they were called, the end of the trail being carried on the arm of the wearer, unless she were a personage of rank and wealth enough to have a waiter to carry it for her. Dress shoes were made of cloth, with high, wooden heels; and it was thought no great impropriety for the ladies to display these, or even the "clocks" on their stockings. Black velvet masks were worn by some in winter, to shield the face from the cold; they were kept on by a silver mouth-piece, held between the teeth. Green masks were worn in summer. Parasols, as well as umbrellas, were unknown; the ladies used, instead, large paper fans, to shield their faces from the sun. As for bonnets, we have not space to describe their varieties; it is enough to say that they were generally *very* small in the crown and *very* large in the brim, beneath which the hair was dressed in bushy curls or "rolled over" a cushion, and stiffened up with pomatum to twice the height of the forehead. "Against the wind," the modern hat would be preferable.

Had we space we should delight to describe the solid old houses and their heavy old furniture; to tell how they lived in the home-spinning, home-brewing days of 1700 and thereabout; to sketch the glittering corner-cupboards, where goodwives displayed their "chaney" and silver, or the immense "chists" of home-made linen, kept carefully in the "spare-room;" but we must pass on to the next era in the history of New Haven.

YALE COLLEGE.

IV.

In 1700 ten clergymen met at Branford, each bringing a few books under his arm. Placing these on the table in Parson Russell's study, each said, solemnly, "I give these books for the founding a college in this colony." A century and a half has gone by, and Yale College counts her books and her graduates by thousands.

As early in the history of the New Haven colony as 1652, or within thirteen years after the first settlement at Quinnipiac, the project of establishing a college was started by Davenport and favored by the people. The well-founded remonstrances of the people of Massachusetts, who very justly observed that the whole population of New England was scarcely sufficient for the support of the single institution at Cambridge, prevented the prosecution of the noble plan. It may have been noticed among our quotations from the colonial records, that the people of New Haven contributed to the support of Harvard in "wheat, or the vallue of itt," thus sacrificing their own wishes for the general good.

The "Collegiate School," which, at first, struggled for existence, became afterward the principal attraction of the town; indeed no just history or description of New Haven can be written which omits mention of "the College." "Old Yale" is so well known and so well loved and respected throughout the land that even the general reader will not be uninterested, it is hoped, in a short account of the olden times of the venerable institution; while, among the thousands of *Harper's* readers, many an *alumnus* will be pleased, not only to see the elm-shaded sanctuary within which four happy years of his life were passed, but also to read again a few of the annals of "*Alma mater* Yale."

The Revolution, which divides the history of the college into two nearly equal parts, effected great alterations in college life and manners, and broke up many traditionary English usages, which had been adhered to from the foundation. It reads strangely nowadays, this extract from the manuscript laws of the college: "Every student shall be called by his sir-name except he be the son of a nobleman, or a knight's eldest son;" yet this distinction between noblemen and commoners existed down to 1768, until which time the name of the student highest in rank headed the list of his class. The only relic of titular distinction at the present time is noticed at "Presentation Day," when one of the college officers presents the Seniors to the president, in a formal Latin address, naming each member of the class as "Dominus" Jenkins or Jones.

In those days the president was a being of majestic dignity: no undergraduate was per-

YALE COLLEGE LIBRARY.

mitted to wear his hat within ten rods of that august person. The professors might not be approached uncovered within eight rods, and even a tutor, *then*, received obeisance by law, within twenty-seven and a half yards. The Freshman, poor fellow! whenever he spoke to a superior, which included all above him, even the Sophomores, or was spoken to by one, was obliged "to keep his hat off until bidden to put it on."

It will amuse modern collegians to read the following quotations from the college laws, printed in 1764, and in force long after:

"A Freshman shall not play with any members of an upper class, without being asked; nor is he permitted to use any acts of familiarity with them even in study-time.

"In case of personal insult, a Junior may call up a Freshman and reprehend (?) him. A Sophomore in like case must obtain leave from a Senior, and then he may discipline (?) a Freshman, not detaining him more than five minutes.

"Freshmen are obliged to perform all reasonable errands for any superior, always returning an account of the same to the person who sent them. When called, they shall attend and give a respectful answer; and when attending on their superior, they are not to depart until regularly dismissed.

"When a Freshman is near a gate or door belonging to college or college-yard, he shall look around and observe whether any of his superiors are coming to the same; and if any are coming within three rods, he shall not enter without a signal to proceed."

Humble as they were, it may be imagined that puny Sophomores sometimes found "five minutes" quite too short a time in which to "discipline" the pluckiest of the Freshmen; and as for the "errands," the "superiors" were occasionally outwitted, as witness the following:

A Senior once gave a Freshman a dollar, and bade him go to the most distant store from the college and purchase pipes and tobacco. The Freshman departed, with becoming humility, and soon returned with ninety-nine cents' worth of pipes and one cent's worth of tobacco. Whether he was thereupon "disciplined" tradition saith not.

Referring to this servitude of the Freshmen, President Woolsey remarks, in his "Historical Discourse," delivered to the graduates in 1850: "All this was very gravely meant, and continued long in use. The Seniors considered it as a part of the system to initiate the ignorant striplings into the college usages, and they performed their duties with the decorum of dancing masters."

Even as late as 1800, it was required of the "ignorant striplings" that they should run errands for resident graduates and for the two upper classes, any where within the limits of one mile. The poor fellows were formally exempted from such duty in 1804, but even now they are the butts of college ridicule, and the victims, occasionally, of various practical jokes, although these are becoming rarer every year.

Up to the time of the Revolution, the system of instruction was very limited, compared with the present course. The graduates were expected, for the most part, to choose the clerical profession; indeed, the college was founded as a nursery of the Church; on which account the study of Hebrew was thoroughly pursued, and the New Testament diligently read by all classes; and this was the only Greek studied. The mathematical sciences received but little attention; rhetoric was almost unknown as a study until 1770; and the physical sciences were unheard of until a much later period. What would the students of the present day say, were they "weekly called to recite, *memoriter*, the Assembly's Catechism in Latin?"

"Commencements," a hundred years ago, differed, in some respects, from the mild affairs of nowadays. Then they were occasions of such noisy mirth and even of riot, that the corporation was obliged to exert itself, by stringent laws, to control the exuberance of the departing Seniors. Cannons were fired, and it was usual for the graduating class to provide a pipe of wine, free to all comers. This, in 1760, took the place of the "barrel of metheglin," which, by a law of 1746, "the Seniors may provide and give away, and nothing more;" and when the authorities, compelled by the disturbances and confusions which flowed from the pipe of wine, undertook to break up the custom of the general "treat," the Seniors rebelled, brought large quantities of rum into college, and "carried on" to that degree that the Commencement exercises were suspended. "Similar scenes are not known to have occurred afterward, although for a long time that anniversary wore as much the aspect of a training day as of a literary festival."

During the Revolution the students were enthusiastic rebels. The news of the first battles echoed loudly, we may well believe, in the quiet cloisters of the college. The young patriots joined eagerly with the citizens in celebrating the great event of the first blow struck for liberty. Studies were abandoned, and military drills took their place. It was found almost impossible to keep up the regular exercises of the classes; and during almost the whole war the college was in a state of confusion which endangered its continued existence. At the inauguration of the Rev. Ezra Stiles as President, the students, who had been scattered in several of the neighboring towns, were reassembled, and under his energetic administration the college began the career of prosperity which has distinguished it from that time to the present.

It is unnecessary to speak of Yale College as it stands to-day. Its name and fame are as wide-spread as the Union. Its past is written in the history of the country; its present prosperity is indicated by its annual catalogues. Six hundred students are gathered within its walls to-day; its two lower classes number, respectively, one hundred and twenty-eight, and one hundred and thirty-four; and its corps of instructors are not inferior, either in numbers or reputation, to that of any similar institution on this side of the Atlantic.

"*Semper floreat, alma mater, Yale!*"

ARNOLD'S RESIDENCE.

When the news of the battle of Lexington arrived, by express, at New Haven, Captain Benedict Arnold, who was at that time commander of the "Governor's Guard," immediately called out his company, and the next morning about forty of them started with him for the seat of war. At Pomfret, on their way, they were joined by General Putnam. On their arrival at head-quarters at Cambridge, the company proved to be the only one which was complete in its uniform and equipments, and as such was selected to deliver the body of a British officer who had been taken prisoner at Lexington and had died of his wounds. Upon this occasion, one of the British officers, appointed to receive the body from the Guards, expressed his surprise at seeing an American company appearing so well, and remarked that "they were not excelled by any of his Majesty's troops."

While at Cambridge, Arnold was sent, with a thousand men, on the memorable expedition into Canada. About a dozen of his men accompanied him; the remainder of the company shortly returned to New Haven. "The Governor's Guard" still flourishes, and is justly proud of its history. Arnold "kept store" in New Haven for many years, and his sign is still preserved as a relic. He was in easy circumstances, as his house, still standing, gives evidence; and although maintaining a good position among his fellow-citizens, was yet regarded by many of them as a shrewd, selfish, unprincipled man. When the news arrived of his treachery at West Point, not a few who knew him declared that it was nothing more than might have been expected of him.

During "the war," while the enemy held possession of New York, the towns on the seaboard were continually liable to attack. In the campaign of 1779, the British seem to have aimed at little more than to plunder, distress, and consume. The attack on this town took place on Monday, July 5, 1779. The fleet, consisting of two men-of-war, with tenders, transports, etc., anchored off the West Haven shore. The forces on board numbered 3000 troops, under the command of the infamous

General Tryon. Of these, about 1500 landed at West Haven, and a smaller detachment at South End, on the eastern side of the harbor.

The inhabitants of the city were entirely unprepared to offer resistance to such a force, but a few of the boldest men sallied out to meet the enemy, with the intention of harassing them and giving time for the removal of women and children to places of safety. These, carrying a few of their most portable valuables, hurried away, in carts, and wagons, and on horseback, to the woods beyond and behind West Rock, and from the summit of that eminence many of them watched the advance of the enemy and the smoke of the fire which their husbands and fathers were pouring at them from behind the trees and fences.

The writer, when a boy, has often listened to his grandmother, with breathless attention, as she narrated the events of that flight, or how, from "the top of the Rock," she watched "the red-coats" defiling along "the Allen-town road." The bridge over West River was so well defended by our militia that the enemy chose to make a circuit of nine miles in order to enter town by the Derby road. This course brought them almost to the very foot of West Rock, and the sight of their brilliant uniforms and glittering muskets, as it appeared to the women and children on the height above, was one never to be forgotten.

Meanwhile the other divisions, which had landed on the other side of the harbor some time after the landing of the main body, had marched toward the city, meeting with little resistance, and entered the town nearly at the same time with the larger force. Notwithstanding the proclamation in which General Tryon announced that the persons and property of the unresisting should be spared, the town was delivered up to promiscuous plunder; "in which," says the record published at the time, "besides robbing the inhabitants of their watches, money, plate, buckles, clothing, bedding, and provisions, they broke and destroyed their household furniture to a very great amount. Some families lost every thing their houses contained; many have now neither food nor clothes to shift.

"Although in this expedition it must be confessed, to the credit of the Britons, that they have not done all the mischief in their power, yet the brutal ravishment of women; the wanton and malicious destruction of property; the burning of the stores upon the wharf, and eight houses in East Haven; the beating, stabbing, and insulting of the Rev. Dr. Dagget (Professor of Divinity in the College) after he was made prisoner; the mortally wounding of Mr. Beers in his own door; the murdering the aged and helpless Mr. English in his own house; and the beating, and finally cutting out the tongue of, and then killing, *a distracted man*, are sufficient proofs that they were *really Britons*."

Twenty-five of the inhabitants were killed during the skirmishing on the road and the sacking of the town, and between thirty and forty were carried off prisoners. By the next morning the militia of the neighboring towns had collected in such numbers that the "Britons" thought it prudent to retire. So they retreated on board their fleet and set sail to the westward.

Thus ended the attack on New Haven—one of the most cruel and savage of the whole war.

The detachment which marched up along the East Haven shore received a check at "Black Rock," where there was a rudely-constructed fort, in which were nineteen men and three field-pieces. During the war of 1812 a larger fort was built there, and named "Fort Hale," in honor of Nathan Hale, the martyr spy. This noble young man entered the army under General Washington, immediately after his graduation at Yale College. He was well known

NEW HAVEN FROM "THE FORT."

here, and his memory is still cherished with pride for his brave self-devotion, and grief for his sad martyrdom. The fort is now in ruins.

Sailing from that enchanted island, the abode of semi-translated Puritans, which superstitious skippers of fog-enveloped mackerel-smacks assert to be floating mysteriously along the indefinite shores of "Away Down East"—sailing thence in high-pooped pinnace, were good old Theophilus Eaton to enter our harbor in the twilight of some summer evening, he would have no difficulty in recognizing the spot on which he founded a city nearly two centuries and a quarter ago. East and West Rocks—

"Twin giants, guarding sea and land"—

still stand on duty, scarred veterans though they be. Between them, and spreading its verdure to the very shore of the bay, stands a forest, as thick and green as that which attracted his primeval admiration; and the tall spires which pierce the trees would be almost the only signs of the changes which had taken place during his long absence. Not till he had sailed well up the harbor would he notice, with surprise, the masts and steeples and numerous white houses of old "Dragon," where his men caught innocent seals, and called them by that fearful name, so long ago; which ancient fishing-place has changed into a prosperous village, and grown famous for "Fair Haven oysters" and fast yachts. Coming nearer, he might wonder at the long arm which Trade extends to beckon Commerce in,—"Long Wharf," in prosier phrase, grasping its great handful of sugar-laden West Indiamen, and telling him of the realization of his old commercial hopes and plans. Looking in that direction, toward the glowing west, a roaring, screaming train of cars might cause him a justifiable exclamation of surprise; or he might port his helm, in sudden terror, to escape destruction at the huge

wheels of the incoming steamboat. Not, however, until he had moored his venerable bark securely among "the oyster-stakes," and had entered the shaded streets of the modern city, would he realize the changes which two hundred years have made.

Hurry back to your pinnace, old patriarch! The boys don't touch their hats to governors even, nowadays; a disrespectful crowd is gathering around you; for

"Your old three-cornered hat,
And your breeches, and all that,
Are so queer."

"The City of Elms" owes a great part of its reputation to its beautiful trees. Its streets are lined with grand old elms or luxuriant maples, and its public squares are thick-shaded groves. The streets present long vistas of arched verdure; and one of these, a view of which is given by the wood-cut on the next page, is the admiration of strangers and the pride of the native-born. The meeting branches of the magnificent elms which border the long aisle form a Gothic archway of perfect symmetry and beauty. For these old trees, and for the taste which leads to the planting of others, the city is mainly indebted to the late Hon. James Hillhouse, who, about the year 1800, inclosed "the Green" and set out the noble rows of elms which are, and will long remain, most beautiful memorials of his taste and public spirit. The citizens should honor his memory with some more enduring monument; yet, till the last shadow falls from the oldest elm, his name will be gratefully mentioned by all who enjoy the summer shade or winter sheen of the grand old trees he planted.

A pleasing peculiarity of New Haven is that its dwellings have so generally the appearance of *homes.* The houses are mostly built in the cottage or villa style of architecture, and each embowers itself in shade and shrubbery, through which are given glimpses of gardens and grape-

TEMPLE STREET.

arbors. The people are famous horticulturists, and fruits and flowers abound in their seasons; nor is the enjoyment of these confined to the wealthy; for *every* house has its garden, and every man seems to live beneath his own "vine and fig-tree." Indeed the stranger will find it difficult to fancy himself within a thrifty commercial city of thirty thousand inhabitants; or, at least, will hesitate in deciding whether New Haven is *rus in urbe*, or *urbs in rure*. The cloisters of College, though in the heart of the city, are yet undisturbed by the rush of trade, while even the New Yorker will not miss the rattle of Russ and "cobble" pavements.

"The Green," as the principal public square is rurally named by the New Haveners, is unequaled by any similar park in the country. Its attraction consists not so much in the beauty of the public buildings situated within its inclosure as in its hundreds of large elms, each in its prime of age and symmetry. Most of these monarch elms are omitted from the sketch given on page 1, lest a stranger might imagine that "The Green" were only a grove of trees. Beyond the churches is seen the State House—an edifice of pure Doric architecture; and farther beyond appears the front of the College Chapel.

The College, also, is almost hidden by thick elms, many of which are sacrificed in the engraving. The row of plain brick buildings which form the factory-like façade of "old

Yale" is certainly more venerable than beautiful; but the Library and the new Alumni Hall are specimens of the more fitting structures which the sons of Alma Mater are beginning to provide for the old lady's future residence.

From the settlement of the town until 1796 that part of the Green upon which stand the Centre Church and the State House was used as a burial-ground; but the land being deemed more appropriate for a park, a new burial-place was opened in the northern part of the town. The old graves, however, were left unmolested until 1821, when the stones were removed to the new cemetery. The only monuments left were those of the Judges, and the few which are covered by the Centre Church. The new cemetery is very beautifully inclosed and laid out; and here may be seen the monuments of Governor Eaton, of several presidents of the College—among which those of President Stiles and President Dwight will attract the notice of every scholar and patriot; of Colonel Humphreys, the aid-de-camp of Washington, a soldier, historian, and poet; of Noah Webster; of Roger Sherman, one of the purest patriots among the signers of the Declaration; of Eli Whitney, the inventor of the cotton-gin, and of many others renowned in the history of the State and country. The remains of Colonel Trumbull, the companion of Washington and the painter-patriot of the Revolution, rest beneath the walls

HILLHOUSE AVENUE.

of "Trumbull Gallery," on the College grounds. Here are collected his numerous works, illustrating the great events in many of which he was *magna pars*—an actor in the scenes which he depicted. The collection is particularly rich in portraits of the heroes of the Revolution. There are in this room *two hundred and fifty* portraits of distinguished men of that period, painted *from life*. Many of these are grouped in eight historical paintings, in which the accuracy of drawing, the admirable coloring, the va-riety of figures introduced, the force of expression displayed in attitudes and countenances, have determined for them a place among the first productions of American art.

Since the days of Ezekiel Cheever, the first of the race of Connecticut schoolmasters, whom, by-the-way, we may fancy as not dissimilar in appearance to the "Ichabod Crane" of Irving and Darley, New Haven has been celebrated for its schools. Among those which are now particularly worthy of mention are the "Hopkins Grammar School," which was founded, in 1664, by the liberality of Governor Hopkins, who left a large bequest "for the breeding up of hopeful youths," and which has flourished from that day to this; the "Collegiate and Commercial Institute" of Dr. Russell, which has long been justly celebrated for the unusual advantages it offers for a thorough education; the young ladies' "seminaries" of Miss Dutton and Professor Roberti; and several very excellent public schools, which are not surpassed, in any respect, by similar institutions in the country. At the Reading Rooms of the

PERCIVAL'S HOUSE.

THE PAVILION.

"Young Men's Institute" may be found the leading journals of the Union; its library and evening classes, and its annual course of lectures, are sources of profit and enjoyment to the young mechanics and business men of the city.

In closing this brief and imperfect sketch of New Haven as it is, it should, perhaps, be remarked that much has been omitted. Statisticians are referred to gazetteers and guidebooks for the numerals expressing the population and wealth of the city; yet it may be said, in general terms, that New Haven is a Yankee city, and may boast, with equal right, of its Mechanics and its Masters of Arts.

The sketches scattered along the pages of the article may need a word of explanation:

The quaint-looking structure on page 17 was erected for the residence of the poet Percival. The house was built in accordance with his hermit tastes; the only entrance is at the back of the building, and the largest room is the library, the large windows of which would have opened on the front. It was never occupied, and has recently passed from the hands of the poet's executors.

The venerable chair represented on page 2 was the property of Rev. Abram Pierson, the first President of Yale, and did duty on state occasions as early as 1701. It is carefully preserved in the Library of the College.

The rusty sword, on page 3, might tell an eventful history. Its blade was forged in 1666, and it *flourished* in the early Indian wars of the colony, in "the old French War," and in the war of the Revolution. Captain Nathaniel Turner, one of the original settlers of New Haven, first wielded it, and in the hands of his descendants it played an important part on many a bloody field. It rests now, in well-earned repose, in the rooms of the Historical Society, at Hartford.

The lamp and boot, on pages 2 and 3, are from the same collection. The age of the former is not known; but the stout boot stubbed over the rough roads of Connecticut in 1675. The lamp is decidedly primitive. It is of iron, and is now rusty and black; but, hung from the lofty "mantle-piece," its two wicks floating in abundant grease and projecting from the lips at the corners, it must have lighted up the beams and rafters of some grand old kitchen of "the good old colony times."

The clock, on page 3, keeps time yet, as it has done these hundred years and more—keeps time and shows the phases of the moon with never-questioned truth. It traces its descent through the family of one of the leaders of the colony, and has never disgraced its ancestry.

NEW HAVEN HOUSE.

The White and Franconia Mountains (1885)

THE WHITE AND FRANCONIA MOUNTAINS.

By Fred Myron Colby.

WHITE MOUNTAIN RANGE FROM MILAN.

What would the world be without mountains? Geographically, one vast monotony of unchanging surface ; geologically, a desert waste. Mountains are the rib-bones of the great skeleton of nature, and they hold together the gorgeous outline of river, valley, lake, and savannah that gives the earth all its varied beauty. Beautiful and grand as they are, they are as useful as ornamental, and serve a momentous necessity in mundane affairs. They are grand landmarks of the Almighty's power and mercy and goodness, and historically occupy a *high* position in the lives of nations.

The seers and saints of the old time speak of the strength of the hills as if they were the special gifts of the Creator to his favored people for their defence. The history of later nations has shown us that they have found more in the strength of the hills than defences against the attacks of outside enemies ; that they have drawn from them a moral vigor of character, a keenness and activity of intellect, and a love of country, which has produced the most enduring and elevated patriotism. And, indeed, we must bless God for mountains ; those who live near them are larger, better, nobler than the denizens of the plains. " Flee to the mountains," cried the angel to Lot. Ah ! there was meaning in the command. Men stagnate upon the plain; they grow indolent, sensual, mediocre there, and are only vivified as they seek the great alphabet of nature, as they pulsate with her in her wondrous heart-beats. It has been the mountain men who have ruled the world.

New Hampshire is a land of mountains. She is indeed throned among the hills, and well deserves the title of the " Switzerland of America." Her cloud-capped peaks, even in mid-summer, glisten with frosts and snows of winter, and they stand watchful sentinels over the liberties of her children. Our Alps are the White Mountains, and they hold no mean place beside their rivals in the old world. Their lofty elevation, their geological formation, the wild and romantic scenery in their vicinity, and their legends of white and red men, all concur to render them peculiarly interesting.

The White Mountain range is located in Coos, Grafton, and Carroll Counties, covering an area of about two thousand square miles, or nearly a third of the northern section of the State. Four of the largest rivers of New England receive tributaries from its streams, and one has its principal source in this region. The peaks cluster in two groups, the eastern or White Mountain group proper, and the Franconia group, separated from each other by a table-land varying from ten to twenty miles in breadth. These mountains differ from

OWL'S HEAD AND MOOSILAUKE, WARREN, N. H.

most others in being purely of a primitive origin. They are probably the most ancient mountains in the world; not even the organic remains of the transition period have ever been discovered near them; and they are essentially of granitic formation. Underneath these coherent and indurate ledges the most valuble ores exist, but coal and fossils are searched for in vain. Many a change during the geological periods have these granite mountains looked upon. They have seen fire and water successively sweep over the surface of our globe. Devastating epochs passed, continents sunk

"OLD MAN OF THE MOUNTAINS."

and rose, and mountains were piled on mountains in the dread chaos, but these stood firm and undaunted, though scarred and seamed by glaciers, and washed by the billows of a primeval sea, presenting nearly the same contour that they do to-day. They are the Methuselahs among mountains.

The Indians generally called these mountains Agiocochook, though one of the eastern tribes bestowed upon them the name of Waumbek Ketmetha, which signifies White Mountains. A mythic

obscurity shadows the whole historical life of this region till the advent of the white men. The red man held the mountains in reverence and awe. What Olympus and Ida were to the ancient Greeks, what Ararat and Sinai were to the Jews, what Popocatapetl and Orizaba were to the Aztecs, so were the summits of the White Mountains to the simple natives of this section. An ancient tradition prevailed among them that a deluge once overspread the land and destroyed every human being but a

PEABODY RIVER AND MOUNT WASHINGTON.

propogated many marvelous stories of what they alleged could there be seen. Among other things, they gave accounts of immense carbuncles seen far up the steep and inaccessible sides, which shone in the darkness of night with the most brilliant and dazzling splendor.

The first white men who visited these mountains, were Messrs. Neal, Jocelyn, and Field, who explored the region carefully in the year 1632. They were incited partly, no doubt, by curiosity, but more probably by the hope of finding mineral treasure. They were disappointed in finding gold, however, but they gave a glowing account of their adventures, and of the extent and grandeur of the mountains, which they single powwow and his wife, who fled for safety to these elevated regions, and thus preserved the race from extermination. Their fancy peopled the mountains with invisible beings, who indicated their presence and manifested their power by storms and tempests, which they were believed to control with absolute authority. The savages, therefore, never attempted to ascend the summits, deeming the undertaking perilous, and success impossible. But, though thus cherishing a superstitious respect for their utmost elevations, they still frequented the environs and mountain defiles, and

THE BOURNE MONUMENT.

called Crystal Hills. A few years later, Captain Richard Vines and others were attracted there by the reports they heard. They remained some time in their vicinity, but returned without anything more than a knowledge of their romantic scenery and the fine facilities they afforded for game. Since then, they have been frequented by hunters and men of science, and within a number of years they have become one of the most fashionable places of summer resort in the United States.

thousand feet above the plain, these mountains rise presenting every variety of mountain scenery, slopes, ravines, precipices, towering cliffs, and overhanging summits.

To the south of the mountains and nestling among the foot hills, lies Lake Winnipiseogee — "Pleasant Water in a High Place," or "The Smile of the Great Spirit," as the aborigines termed it, with its surface broken by hundreds of islands : one, they say, for every day of the calendar year ; and its shores the de-

FRANCONIA MOUNTAINS, FROM THORNTON.

The White Mountain plateau is approached by travellers from four directions, namely : from the east by the Grand Trunk, Eastern, and Ogdensburg Railroads ; from the south by Lake Winnipiseogee and the Pemigewassett rivers ; from the south-west by way of Connecticut River and White Mountain Railroad at Littleton, and from the north by the Grand Trunk at Northumberland. The approach is grand from all sides, and the mountain combinations picturesque and beautiful. From five to six

light of artists in search of the picturesque, as well as of the sojourner after pleasure. Its waters smile eternally pleasant, and the visitor will not find the fountain of perpetual youth of the swart old navigator a fable ; for here he will regain lost youth and strength in the contemplation of scenes as beautiful as poets' dreams. O ! Lake Winnipiseogee, we recall the sails across thy bright waters with delight, and long to see thy rippling tide once more murmuring beneath the keel of our boat.

What haunts form a magic chain along the verdant shores of this charming lake! The Wiers, Wolfborough, Alton Bay, Centre Harbor, each a name that moves the heart to thrill it. A voyage across the lake will be remembered a life-time. Says Edward Everett, commenting upon a sail from Wiers up the lake: "I have been something of a traveller in my own country, though far less than I could wish — and in

GEORGIANA FALLS.

Europe have seen all that is most attractive, but my eye has yet to rest upon a lovelier scene." A climb to the summit of Red Hill, at Centre Harbor, Starr King's favorite haunt, well repays for the labor. The lake presents a charming picture from its crest. Across its waters can be seen the domes of Belknap and more distant Kearsage and Monadnock. In the east are the Ossipee Mountains and bold Mount Chocorua. Toward the north is a throng of lofty mountains overtopped on a clear day by distant Mount Washington, which towers king-like over all his neighbors. In the west one has a view of Squam Lake, with its many islands bordered by beaches of white sand, the little village of Centre Harbor, Meredith, and that popular lakeside resort, the Weirs.

At the Weirs, which is a way-station of the Boston and Montreal Road, on the borders of the lake, is a cottage city. Here in front of each domicile is built the miniature wharf off which is moored the row boat or yacht, dancing feather like on the waves. Lofty trees with dense foliage grow to the water's edge, affording grateful shade. Within the grove is an auditorium in one of nature's amphitheatres where the weary people, assembled from their homes in the dusty city, listen to words of eloquence or exhortation while fanned by lake breezes. On the sides of the hill the veterans of the Grand Army have erected barracks, and there they annually assemble, build their camp fires, recount old scenes, fight mimic battles, and close up their ranks thinned by time. The approach to their camp is guarded by cannon, used to salute some honored comrade, and overlooked by an observatory on which stands no sentinel.

We had made up our minds " to do " the White Mountains, Molly, Fritz and I, the latter being an indefinite person, and we calculated on going prepared. We had spent a fortnight reading Starr King's " White Hills," studying hand-books and Hitchcock's Geology of New Hampshire. Then it took us a week to

Fritz, " but I had rather have been born there."

Following up the valley by the river-road through the towns of Campton, Thornton, and Woodstock, one sees himself surrounded on either hand by towering mountains and the most exquisite rural scenery. Another road following the Indian trail from Canada to the coast, over which the weary feet of many a captive passed in the old time, driven ruthlessly from their homes to the wilderness by their savage captors, passes through Rumney and Wentworth to Warren summit, the lowest land in the " divide " between the Connecticut

WHITE MOUNTAIN RANGE, FROM JEFFERSON.

do the packing. One bright summer day we started ; night found us at Plymouth on the banks of the Pemigewasset, at the very gate-way of the mountains. We slept at the Pemigewasset House, where we were shown the room in which Hawthorne died twenty years ago, while on an excursion for health with his friend Franklin Pierce. That will be what Plymouth will be famous for one hundred years hence — the place where Hawthorne died. " It is a pleasant place at which to die," said

and Merrimack valleys, yet a thousand feet above the ocean. Moosilauke, the ancient Moosehillock, here stands sentry, almost five thousand feet above the sea level. It is the western outpost of the mountain region and deserves a visit. A good carriage road leads from the station to Breezy Point House, at its base, where buck-boards are chartered for the ascent. At first the road leads through rocky pastures, thence into primeval woods in which the way becomes more and more precipitous ;

and as we go up the trees become dwarfed to bushes, until as one emerges to the open space on the shoulder of the mountain a most impressive scene breaks upon him. An immense gulf lies beneath him, while before him towers the lofty summit.

The morning or evening view from Moosilauke is grand in the extreme. The valley of the Connecticut for many miles is in view, through which winds the "long river" like a blue ribbon. Over in Vermont are the Green

which Mounts Washington and Lafayette are monarchs. To the north lies the Gardner range, and in the valley near at hand the sheltered community incorporated by the name of Benton and overlooked by Mount Kinsman.

As the sun sinks below the western mountains, one stands in brilliant daylight, while the valleys below him are shrouded in the gloom of night; when the sun has disappeared, darkness has come. One can well spend a night on the summit if only to behold the glori-

ADAMS AND MADISON, FROM GLEN PATH.

Mountains, commanded by Mount Mansfield, while across the State and over Lake Champlain one catches a glimpse of the distant Adirondacks. In the south can be seen Ascutney and the mountains and lakes of central New Hampshire, while a distant peak beyond Monadnock may be Mount Wachuset in Massachusetts. To the eastward is massed an ocean of mountains, of

ous sunrise in the morning. Before the dawn comes, one is on an island in an ocean of foam. The sun springs gladly from behind the hills on the eastern horizon, and scatters the early mists as by an enchanter's wand. As a matter of course there is a Tip Top House on Moosilauke, and a genial landlord.

Owl's Head the traveller passes on the right as he leaves Warren summit. Be-

CASTELLATER RIDGE OF MOUNT JEFFERSON.

declared Molly. " I like the modern way best ; besides we get our money's worth Why ! any one of these views is worth, oh,— ' ever so much,' which includes hotel bills and all," laughed the cynical Fritz.

At Wells River a very high bridge spans the Connecticut. Here the waters of the tumbling Ammonoosuc, the wildest and most rapid stream in New Hampshire, joins the Connecticut in its

tween Owl's Head and Moosilauke there is a deep valley through which winds a road leading from Warren to Benton and Dansville, affording a lonely but pleasant route through the mountains.

"That road," said Molly, "looks as if it might be haunted by Claude Duval and his ilk ; I suppose there are robbers among the mountains."

Fritz smiled. "We find them at the hotels now and then, and they wear diamond studs generally," he said. "Our modern highwaymen do not haunt lonesome defiles and cry 'Stand and Deliver.' That style is obsolete ; nor are there any romantic stories told of their dancing on the green with the victims they have plundered. They are not gallant enough for that."

"I don't care,"

journey to the sea. The highlands of Bath repay attention as we journey northward. Littleton is a thriving village, which controls the business of this section, and promises to be a northern metropolis.

A few miles from Littleton is Bethlehem, a regular mountain village, with an altitude higher than that of any other village east of the Mississippi. This is one of the most charming resorts in the

RAVINE IN MOUNT ADAMS, FROM RANDOLPH HILL.

White Mountain region. The long, main street of the town runs along the side of Mount Agassiz, and its elevation is such as to banish hay fever and all kindred complaints.

After we had dined, Fritz, Molly, and I, proceeded to investigate the place by carriage. The day was warm, but Bethlehem has the luxury of admirably-shaded streets; and although tropic heat may flood the outer world, they

lage are palatial, and compare favorably with the best in much older communities. Their accommodations are fully appreciated by the army of health and pleasure seekers who annually visit them.

This village has lately been directly connected with the outside world by a narrow-gauge road, which runs parallel with the street and joins the main line at Bethlehem Junction. In laying the track very little attention was paid to

VIEW ACROSS THE SUMMIT OF THE RAVINE.

lie temptingly cool beneath the great boughs; delightful breezes sweeping from the mountains, so that a ride is always enjoyable. There are regulation drives, and there are other drives, for one can take a different route every day for a month, and each drive will seem to surpass the other. In fact, the drives, walks, and woodland paths about this village, rival those of Central Park in New York City. The hotels of the vil-

the grade, and the train follows the undulating surface. The train after leaving the junction seems fairly to climb to the upper level.

Southerly from Bethlehem Junction a narrow-gauge railway extends into the heart of the Franconia Notch, having its terminus at the celebrated Profile House, which is a considerable village in itself. At the end of the route the road skirts the shores of Echo Lake, a gem of water surrounded by lofty mountains, a fit home for nymphs and naiads.

"I should like to read 'Manfred' here," said Molly one morning (Byron was one of her favorites). "It is just the place, mountains, forests and all, and who knows — the wizzard."

"There is the Old Man of the Mountain; perhaps he would volunteer," suggested Fritz.

"I thought it was a witch," observed the indefinite person.

"Well, it matters not which it was,"

SILVER CASCADE IN THE NOTCH.

said Molly, seeing that we were attempting to badger her. "Here is the hour and the scene."

"But the *man*, O, where is he?" cried Fritz.

"The truth is, we cannot appreciate Byron till we come here," pursued Molly. "If we could only have a tempest now. Ah, I can imagine those mountain Alps. How beautiful and grand it is. Within this wide domain romance, science, and nature, murmur an eternal anthem, which wooes for every soul that finds itself herein a new aspiration, and a realization that, after all our study and care, we have appreciated creation so lightly!"

That afternoon Molly had her wished-for tempest. The heat had been sultry, but by five o'clock a heavy wind began to blow and hugh billows of clouds began to appear above the tops of the mountains. The sky grew blacker every moment. By and by a mighty river of clouds began to pour itself down over the peaks into the valley below; one by one each haughty crest disappeared beneath the flood. In a few moments every ravine was filled with rolling masses of clouds and the rain was falling in sheets. We could trace its rapid flight over the space between the hotel and the distant mountains. A gentleman who has been at the Profile House for several summers said that he had never seen so grand a storm-cloud as the one just described. When the storm was past and the clouds began to melt away, it was natural enough that we should call to mind the following passage from "Lucile:"

GIANT'S STAIRS, BARTLETT.

Meanwhile,
The sun in his setting, sent up the last smile
Of his power, to baffle the storm. And, behold
O 'er the mountains embattled, his armies, all gold,
Rose and rested; while far up the dim airy crags,
Its artillery silenced, its banners in rags,
The rear of the tempest its sullen retreat
Drew off slowly, receding in silence, to meet
The powers of the night, which, now gathering afar,
Had already sent forward one bright signal star.

A whole host of natural beauties and attractive scenes lie at hand near this great mountain caravansary. Turn in any and all directions, at every point a view greets the vision which rivals the touches of an almost divine brush on Oriental canvas. Avenues lead through a perfect labyrinth of forests in all directions, and many are the famous sights

to be seen. Profile Lake lies close by at the base of Cannon or Profile Mountain and Mount Lafayette. From its shore can be seen that inspiring curiosity known the world over as the " Old Man of the Mountain," about which much good prose and passable poetry has been written. The profile is produced by the peculiar combination of the surfaces and angles of five huge granite blocks, and when viewed from one spot the resemblance is perfect. Colossal as it is in its proportions, being seventy feet from chin to forehead, the lines are softened by distance, and the sphinx itself is not carved more justly. There it stands, calm, grand, majestic, wearing from age to age the same undisturbed expression of sovereign and hoary dignity — the guardian spirit of the region. No wonder the simple red man, as he roamed these wilds, should pause as he caught sight of this great stone face gazing off through the mountain openings into the distant valley, and worship it as the countenance of his Manitou. All are impressed with it, and its influence is magnetic.

To climb Mount Lafayette will be scarcely less interesting than the ascent of Mount Washington, though it is more tedious, as it has to be made wholly on foot. But the charming views from its sides and summit will repay the labor of the tourist. A fine view of the Franconia Mountains can be obtained from the summit of Bald Mountain, to the top of which a carriage road has been constructed.

Following down the outlet of Profile Lake, the head-waters of the Pemigewasset, one may visit with profit and pleasure Walker's Falls, the Basin, the Cascades, and the Flume. The Flume is one of those rifts in the solid rock caused by some titanic force in ages long since. For many years there hung

Franconia is a fairyland of wonderful fascination; and the weary of body and mind, or the despondent and languid invalid, and no less the strong and healthy, will find their physical faculties invigorated, and the mind and soul elevated by a sojourn among the attractions of that lovely town. It was with the deepest regret that we turned from those delightful regions.

WHITE MOUNTAINS, FROM THE GLEN.

suspended far up above the path a huge granite boulder. In 1883 a sudden mountain storm caused a torrent to dash through the chasm, and the boulder became a subject for history. It disappeared, thus partially explaining how it was originally lodged in its former resting place. A short distance below the Flume are the Georgiana Falls, where the water descends for more than a hundred feet over a sheer precipice.

Our time was not lost, for as we pant and struggle in "life's ceaseless toil and endeavor," a thousand memories come to cheer us from those sojourns in this romantic and magnificent mountain land.

Again at Bethlehem Junction we follow the main thoroughfare through the mountains to the great chain of hotels of world-wide fame known as the Twin Mountain House, Fabyan's, and the

Crawford House. Up the valley of the Ammonoosuc to the Twin Mountain House, which takes its name from two prominent peaks of the Franconia range, is a delightful ride. We are now in the midst of the mountain region, the White Mountain plateau. Here nature, *en dishabille*, with locks unkempt and loosened zone, reclines at ease in her most secret chamber, beyond the reach of intrusion, and neither thinking of, nor

in Indian myth blew the breeze from the Land of Souls."

" Do you remember the other time we were here, Molly? " asked Fritz, "and the beautiful moonlight evenings we enjoyed? "

" Oh, yes. How many nights we sat here or promenaded among the trees. It was in September and the moon was full. As she arose over the eastern hills and threw her light upon the valley be-

SQUAM LAKE AND MOUNT CHOCORUA.

caring for, the critical philosophy of the outside world ; an emerald-crowned Cleopatra, revelling in the midst of her great vassals.

The Twin Mountain House, like Fabyan's and the Crawford House, is a post-office. It is a hostelry, also, that is not surpassed in its management, cuisine or in magnificence by any in the chain.

" It is good to be here," said Molly, lying back in her chair on the long piazza, " while the wind blows fair, as

neath, I never saw her more majestic. The soft, mellow radiance of the queen of night filled every nook and crevice with light. The trees waved their branches, and beckoned the woodland nymphs forth to a dance on the green. Surely, it seems as if Shakespeare must have had just such evenings in his mind when he wrote " Midsummer Night's Dream."

" Ah, that was a 'Lover's Pilgrimage,'" observed Fritz, grimly, "now it is a pilgrimage for — "

MOUNT MADISON, IN GORHAM.

"What?"

"You interrupted me; we will call it an æsthetic pilgrimage."

What days those were we passed in the upland region. Fabyan's is situated in the very heart of the White Hills and is the objective point for all tourists. From the verandas of this spacious hotel, one obtains an uninterrupted view of the whole Presidential Range, and can watch the course of the train of cars as it creeps slowly up the precipitous sides of Mount Washington.

Taking the train at Fabyan's, one glides rapidly up the steepest practical grade to the Base station, where he leaves the ordinary passenger coach and takes his seat in a car designed to be pushed up the Mount Washington Railroad. After the warning whistle the train starts slowly on its journey — the grandest sensation of the whole trip to the ordinary traveller. The most magnificent scenery is soon spread before the tourist. No other three miles of railway in the world affords such a succession of wild and startling views as the passenger has on his mountain ride on this iron line up the steep inclination of this mighty summit of the great northern range. We get glimpses of the wide valley below, the bold landscape ever changing, yet always filled with grand and startling outlines. Up and up we go. We pass Gulf station, Naumbet station, Jacob's Ladder, and the monument of stones which marks the spot where, in 1855, Miss Lizzie Bourne of Maine died from exposure. At last we are at the summit, in front of the hospitable looking Tip Top House. We are standing at an altitude of over six thousand feet above the sea, or to be exact, 6,293 feet, according to Professor Guyot, on the highest point of land with one exception east of the Rocky Mountains.

"Isn't the thought inspiring," I remarked to my companions, "that we are on the highest land for which our fathers fought a century ago?"

"And is it not the theme the *ultima*

MOUNT MORIAH, IN GORHAM.

1784, Mount Washington received its name?" asked Fritz. "Well it was, and eight years later Captain Eleazar Rossbrook penetrated into the heart of the mountains and made a clearing where the Fabyan House now stands. His son-in-law, Abel Crawford, the patriarch of the mountains, settled the next season in the Notch, in the vicinity of Bemis station. Captain Rossbrook built the first house for the reception of visitors in 1803. Ethan Allen Crawford, son of Abel Crawford, took Captain Rossbrook's house in 1817, and

thule of grandeur in an artist's pilgrimage?" said Molly. "What a prospect! The plains of Canada, the forests of Maine, the mountains of New York, and I really believe the sea, if I mistake not that faint blue line in the far distance over the billowy land! What a grand spectacle a sunrise or a sunset would be, viewed from this height!"

The next morning we saw the sun start from its bed in the Orient, swathed in radiant clouds and vapors, and rise up behind the eastern range of hills; we had never seen anything so beautiful and striking before, and the scene is one which neither pen can describe nor pencil portray. Our memory will not fail to cherish it as the choicest revelation to be seen in a life time.

"Do you know it was just one hundred years ago this very year,

ECHO LAKE.

two years later opened the first foot-path to the summit of this mountain, where he soon after built a stone cabin. There, I give all that information to you *gratis*."

"Very kind of you, I am sure," said Molly, "but who will vouch for its authenticity?" you used to be a terrible story-teller."

"Clio does not lie; this is history."

"You would have us believe the staid muse very modest," said Molly. "But I remember some one has said history is a great liar."

"A libel, a *positive* libel! Shall we believe nothing?"

"Only absolute truth. Do you believe in the Trojan war? Do you believe that Marshal Ney said at Waterloo, 'Up guards and at them?'"

"Do you believe there is a Mt. Washington? Your iconoclasts would destroy everything. There are White Mountain legends, of course, but there is also White Mountain history, and the time is not so remote but that the data can be relied upon."

"No one can argue with you, Fritz," answered Molly. "I accept your data in this case. You are welcome to wear the wreath of victory."

A night spent at the White Mountain House, one of the old-fashioned hostelries, cheery, hospitable, and with an excellent cuisine, cool, airy chambers, where one is made to feel at home by the urbane landlord, Mr. R. D. Roun-

send, and we turned from this section.

The Crawford House, four miles below Fabyan's, is one of the finest in its plans of the mountain houses, its wide piazzas extending the entire length of the buildings. It is magnificently situated upon a little plateau, just north of the gate of the White Mountain, or Crawford Notch. The Saco River has its source not far from the house, its birthplace being a picturesque little

LEDGES ON MOUNT HAYES, IN GORHAM.

lake. At the right hand Mount Willard rears its shapely mass, from whose summit a glorious view can be obtained. The ascent is easily accomplished by carriage, and the prospect, though not so grand and wild as that from Mount Washington, exceeds it in picturesque beauty. The whole valley of the Saco, river of the oak and elm, lies spread before the vision. The grand outlines of the gorge, the winding road through the whole extent, the leaping cascades flashing in the sunshine, all appear before the eye as in a picture. One feels like exclaiming with Cowper :

GIANT'S GRAVE, NEAR CRAWFORD HOUSE.

" Heavens! what a goodly prospect spreads around,
Of hills, and dales, and woods, and lawns, and spires,
And glittering towers and gilded streams,
The stretching landscape into smoke till all decays.

One of the beauties of the Notch is the Flume, a brook that goes leaping through its curious zigzag channel of rock on the side of Mount Webster, hastening on its way to join the deeper current of the Saco. Then here is " Silver Cascade," which is above the Flume, a series of leaping, dashing, turning waterfalls, descending now in a broad sheet of whitened foam, then separating into several streams, and again narrowing to a swift current through the rocky confined channel. The visitor will pause by its whitened torrent, loth to depart from the scene.

The White Mountain Notch, after Mount Washington, is the great natural feature of the range. For three miles the road follows the bottom of a chasm between overhanging cliffs, in some places two thousand feet in height, and at others not more than twenty-five feet apart. This is the great thoroughfare of travel, from the northern towns on the Connecticut to Conway and the Saco valley, and *vice versa ;* and through it pass the headwaters of the Saco, which afterwards broadens out into a great river, and flows with rapid course through the loveliest of valleys to the sea. Much of the natural wildness and grandeur of the pass has been destroyed by laying the line of the Portland and Ogdensburg Railroad, which has been graded through the ravine. Railroads serve a great utilitarian purpose, but they have their defects; it seems out of place to ride across Egypt or the Holy Land behind a locomotive ; a prancing steed or a camel with tinkling bells seems the most fitting motive power. There is nothing sentimental about a railroad, but after all who would care to return to the old methods of locomotion?

The Willey House, famous in story, stands upon the Notch road nestling under the steep acclivity of Mount Willey, which rises some two thousand feet behind the house.

" Why don't some of our authors use more of the historical material of this region in story writing than they do?" asked Fritz.

" The material is so romantic that romance can add nothing to it," answered Molly. " But you forget Hawthorne. His Ambitious Guest has imparted a weird interest to the event. He makes a young man, travelling through the Notch, partake of the hospitality of the family on the fatal night. At the fireside they fall to talking of their individual plans, the guest expressing himself as desirious of achieving fame. It seemed a terrible thing to him to die and to be forgotten, to leave no name behind and no monument to mark his resting place. In the midst of the conversation the ruin came, and the ambitious guest, flying with the family, found his burial with the others. The story will live in Hawthorne long after the true facts have been forgotten; or they will live because Hawthorne's narrative will have conferred immortality upon them."

This memorable event happened on the night of Monday, the twenty-eighth of August, 1826. A terrible storm of wind and rain prevailed, the mountain branches of the Saco and the Ammonoosuc speedily overfilled their rocky channels, and the steep sides of hills loosened by the rain swept down upon the valleys, destroying many an ancient landmark. One of these slides swept down toward the Willey House, then occupied by Samuel Willey, his wife, and family. The frightened inmates, seeking safety by flight from the impending ruin, were overwhelmed by the avalanche and perished, while the house remained untouched. The bodies of two sons and one daughter were never found; the rest of the Willey household lie buried in a small cemetery enclosure near the mansion house of Willey Farm at North Conway.

A most charming ride is that down the line of the Saco river to North Conway, whether by rail or stage. The beauty and boldness of the scenery on either side alternately enchants and awes.

"It reminds me of Switzerland," said Fritz, who had travelled on the continent, "only there are more rocks and

VIEW FROM BRIDGE IN BERLIN.

ledges visible. The lower Alps are clothed in green and the upper ones in perennial snow. The Simplon Pass is not nearly so rugged as the Notch. Only in the West among the Rockies is there anything to compare with this. But below, a few miles, we have a view as pleasant as Christian and Hopeful saw from the Delectable Mountains."

"And do we have to pass Doubting castle, as they did?" asked Molly. "I don't think I should care for their experience with giants and giantesses."

were seen only at a distance. Glimpses were caught now and then of charming vistas, with the waters of the Saco gleaming brightly between the trees. No fairer valley can be found in our land than that of the Saco; and as for skies and sunsets, stop at North Conway and see what cannot be matched in Italy or the Orient.

That is what we did. A broad, level plain, five miles long by three wide, is the site of the village, which is a quiet and picturesque rural hamlet of the

MOUNT CARTER, FROM GORHAM.

"Here are castles and strongholds, but the giants, if there are any, are as helpless as Giant Pope was, who could only sit in the sun and gnaw his finger nails."

The towering cliffs on either side smile like the walls of a prison. We felt a relief when once they were passed, and we found ourselves in the broader valley below, stretching wide and green and beautiful in the summer sunshine — the famous meadows of the Saco. All of the savage aspects disappeared or

average size of country towns. Far in the north towers the lofty Presidential Range, in full sight, the distance softening all harsh and rugged outlines into beautiful curves and combinations, Mount Washington wearing a snowy forehead often through the entire heated term. The swelling summit of Mount Pequakett rises at the northeast of the village, a lone sentinel, guarding the gateway of the mountains with bold and unchanging brow. On the western side extends a long range of rocky hills, with the single spire-like summit of Chocorua far beyond, piercing the blue vault of heaven.

Sitting on the cheerful piazzas of any of the many hotels, one can breath the mountain air as freely as if they sat under the tower of Fabyan's or the French roof of the Twin Mountain House, but much of the grandeur of course is missed. The mountains do not seem to frown down upon you ; they smile rather, and seem to beckon and wave as if desiring to gain your closer acquaintance. To know the mountains you must visit them, press their scarred, rocky sides, feel their cool breezes on your forehead, then you will love them, reverence them. And this privilege is free to every one. Great railroads penetrate into the very heart of the hilly region, and the cost of travel is reduced to such a minimum that the poorest man can once in a while take

his family for a pleasant sojourn among the mountains. One can start from Boston in the morning, take a dinner at the Pemigewasset House, Plymouth, and at night eat his supper at Fabyan's. And even a short visit is so refreshing, so invigorating to mind and body, that it repays when even the sight is not a novel one.

Glorious, grand, old mountain, lifting thy brow among the eternal snows ; thou needst not the presence of Jove, nor the voice of a Homer to consecrate thee ; and although Greeks and Trojans have never battled at thy base, still to us art thou dearer than Ida's wooded height where the gods sat enthroned to witness that divinely-recorded combat. Thy hoary peaks bear the names of chiefs and heroes who are not myths, and in the hearts of the people they are an everlasting memory.

WHITE MOUNTAIN NOTCH.

Hall's Vegetable Sicilian Hair Renewer

Brings the old color back; no more faded or gray hair.
Makes growth more rapid; short hair becomes long hair.
Holds the hair firmly in place; the hair stops falling out.
Completely removes dandruff; baldness is prevented.
Feeds the hair bulbs; new hair grows on bald heads.

Old Deerfield
(1892)

"A quiet street overarched by mighty elms."

OLD DEERFIELD.

By Mary E. Allen.

Door of Williams House.

REEN meadows stretched in the sunlight, with the horizon of the gently curving hills; a quiet street overarched by mighty elms— the rows of stately trunks and the branches meeting overhead, like the pillars and arches of a cathedral aisle ; a path below in green shadow, with splashes of yellow light,—this is old Deerfield. Though snow and rain come here as elsewhere, we think of Deerfield as always lying in the summer sunshine. On either side the ancestral homes, too much a part of the street to suggest the idea of conscious building, seem rather to have grown with the trees. An atmosphere of perfect quiet reigns, — the only hint of labor, a farmer's cart rumbling slowly down to the fields, its meditative driver with his elbows on his knees, the reins hanging loosely from his idle hands. Nowhere a sign of hurry or of worry.

This venerable town, and mother of towns, is passing a serene and beautiful old age. Her natural force is not abated, her faculties are unimpaired, but the strenuous season of youth is past. The time for rest and reminiscence is come.

A stranger to old Deerfield once said that in his mental picture of the place, wild Indians were always whooping through the streets, brandishing tomahawks. The picture his fancy painted is symbolically true, though time has softened the fierce aspect of the savage. His spirit haunts the village streets, in peaceful companionship with the shades of our ancestors. We harbor no feeling of resentment toward the red man. He gives a touch of color to the past. George William Curtis said, after a stroll through the old burying-ground, that he, as well as the forefathers of the hamlet, was "captivated by ye salvadges." The haze of those far-off

Old Deerfield Academy, now Memorial Hall.

Indian summers still hangs on the town.

The first tales of adventure which we who are Deerfield children heard were the stories our grandfathers lived. I remember lying on the floor, before the open Franklin stove, and reading by the firelight a worn copy of Hoyt's "Antiquarian Researches." The book opened of its own accord to the account of the slaying of my own great-great-grandfather by the Indians. The touch of the bloody tomahawk conferred knighthood and renown on its victim. The honors which I tried to bear with modesty are borne by many Deerfield children. Boys at play read history as they run. They gather chestnuts on the low resting-places of the martyrs, and crack the burrs

Spinet in Memorial Hall.
From Dr. Willard's Family.

on the mossy stone tables, sacred to their memory. They watch the ploughshare turn up arrow-heads, broken pieces of pottery, and even bits of charcoal from some old wigwam fire. Every bright boy has his private collection of such antiquities.

Many of the homes in "the street" have continued in the same families for generations, so favoring the accumulation of family relics, family traditions and, let us not hesitate to say, family pride.

The Pocumtuc Valley Memorial Association is both a result and a cause of this distinctive flavor of the town. Its annual meetings on the anniversary of the sacking of the town in 1703 – 4 keep the memory of our fathers fresh. No one is in danger of forgetting the adventurous men from Dedham, who came to make a home in this fertile valley, in 1670, or the catastrophe at Bloody Brook, in 1675, and the abandonment of the settlement, or the quick renewal of the attempt to plant an outpost here by men too brave to be discouraged by the constant attacks, or even by the overwhelming disaster of 1704.

The story of that fearful February night has been sung almost as fully as the Siege of Troy. The Helen of this war, the bell of St. Regis, which long had the credit, or discredit, of bringing destruction on the town, has, like that other Helen, been condemned as a myth by our iconoclastic historian, but it still rings in our ears.

Prof. James K. Hosmer, in a witty letter written at the time of the "Indian Door" celebration, professed to have discovered a journal corroborating the legend, and says:

"There need be no question about the beautiful old traditions. . . . It was really a bell which made the trouble, a bell made for the Canadian missions, taken by a privateer, and brought into Boston, bought by the commissioners of Deerfield, set up in the steeple, then fought over and carried off to the banks of the St. Lawrence, through the woods, and down the streams. Hertel de Rouville did really have his half-breeds and Indians run over the crust, then halt for a moment, then run again, when they were coming on through the north meadows, that the advance of his force might be taken for the rush of the rising wind."

These legends are true at any rate in spirit, if they are not in letter, and they ought not to be forgotten; although as matter of fact there is evidence that the expedition against Deerfield was planned by the French, merely to gratify the Abenaki Indians and prevent any possibility of a truce between them and the English.

The best-known account of the attack is the quaint narrative of the "Redeemed Captive," Rev. John Williams, the minister of Deerfield at the time. We can see through his eyes how "the enemy came in like a flood" over the palisades on the drifted snow, in that darkest hour before the dawn, waking their sleeping victims by breaking in doors and windows, and pouring into their bedrooms "with painted faces and hideous acclamations," before the terrified people could realize what was happening.

But one house within the stockade was successfully defended. A few persons escaped to a stockaded house south of the "Great Fort," which was unmolested, and one or two ran, half clad, over the snow to Hatfield, fifteen miles away, "coming of with frozen feet."

The savages did their work quickly, fearing reinforcements from Hadley. "About sun an hour up," the plunder was collected and put in packs, and one hundred and eleven captives were distributed among their masters ready for the return march of three hundred miles to Canada, through snow knee-deep and thawing. The last of the marauders hurried out of the north gate just as the expected aid came galloping in from the south, too late to rescue their friends.

Mr. Williams describes the sorrowful march day by day. His wife was ill, but he was not allowed to walk with her to help her on the way. On the second day, the whole party was obliged to wade a small river "above knee-deep and very swift," and then to climb a mountain. Mr. Williams sank down exhausted when he reached the top, and looked back for his wife.

"I entreated my master to let me go down and

help my wife, but he refused. I asked each of the prisoners, as they passed by me, after her, and learned that, passing through the above-said river, she fell down and was plunged over head and ears in the water, after which she travelled

The "Indian Door."

not far, for at the foot of that mountain the cruel and bloodthirsty savage who took her slew her with his hatchet at one stroke, the tidings of which were very awful."

A party of neighbors following the trail of the captives found Mrs. Williams's body and brought it back for burial. The Pocumtuc Valley Memorial Association has placed a monument on the spot where she was killed.

The handful of men and women who escaped death and captivity that night wavered. What wonder that the comparative safety of older settlements tempted them to leave this twice desolated outpost! The Connecticut colonies saw the wisdom of keeping the frontier line as far to the north as possible, and sent help and encouragement, and the brave men rallied and held the fort. A large proportion of the captives were, in course

The old Kitchen in Memorial Hall.

of time, ransomed or exchanged. Some perished on the march. Some children were adopted by the French or Indians, and through a change of name were lost sight of, until Miss Alice Baker, by the aid of old baptismal and marriage records, traced the history of several and found their descendants, still bearing the old Gallicized English names.

It is fitting that the home of the Pocumtuc Valley Memorial Association, Memorial Hall, should be the first noticeable building a stranger sees, on coming down Academy Lane from the station on the hill. It is chiefly due to Mr. George Sheldon, the head and front of that society, that so many valuable antiquities have been here collected and classified. The Indian room is filled with the weapons, tools, and various belongings of the red man. In the middle of the room is the "Indian door," saved from the wreck of the "Old Indian House," when it was torn down forty or fifty years ago. This sturdy old garrison house escaped the flames of 1704, and defied time for a century and a half afterwards. It was built, about 1686, by Ensign John Sheldon, an ancestor of our own Mr. Sheldon. It was then the largest and finest house in the village. The walls were filled with brick to turn back the bullets of the enemy. The upper story projected over the lower one three or four feet and had loop-holes command-

ing all approaches to the front door or windows. Its strength did not save its inmates. Entrance was made through a back door, and by an irony of fate this house, which was looked to as a refuge in time of danger, was used as a depot for the captives before the march began. The hole through the heavy nail-studded door, now worn smooth by curious hands, was cut by Indian hatchets. A leaden bullet which was fired through the opening and imbedded itself in the ceiling, hangs on the door-post; it is said to be the very one which cut short the sorrows of poor sick Mrs. Sheldon, as she sat up in bed, startled from sleep by the furious blows. Two heavy brackets which supported the projecting upper story, and some ornamental pieces of woodwork, are placed over the door. One wonders how those men found time or heart for carving, in their hand-to-hand fight for existence.

The room opposite gives an idea of an ancient kitchen, with its high-backed settles drawn up to the fireplace, and dresser laden with shining pewter. The ever ready gun hangs over the mantel. Another room contains all the apparatus for spinning and weaving; another, memorial tablets and portraits. The library is an interesting medley of past and present. It can show many rare old books and papers and MS. letters and journals dear to the heart of the antiquary. The upper hall is full of beautiful old china and furniture, and a thousand and one treasures.

The building itself is a relic. It is the old home of Deerfield Academy, which for years made Deerfield one of the chief educational centres of western Massachusetts. Many well-known men and women look back to the days spent in the shadow of the elms, as the beginning of a broader life. Those were the days when academies "prepared young men for life instead of for examinations." The older part of the building was dedicated on New Year's Day, 1799. There is on record a code of by-laws of thirty-six articles, for the government of the school, passed by the trustees, with that propensity for governing others which the makers of Independence Day sometimes showed. Absence from meeting, walking on Saturday night or Sunday, playing cards, checkers, or backgammon, at any time, were to be punished by a fine of one dollar. Pupils of different sexes were forbidden to meet upon the grounds, or within the walls of the Academy, except at meal times or prayers, or to walk or ride together, under the same penalty of one dollar. A high board fence was finally built across the yard to keep the boys and girls apart; but who doubts that there were knot-holes through which Pyramus and Thisbe could gaze into each other's eyes without forfeiting their whole allowance?

One of the first "preceptors" was

South End of the Street.

Hosea Hildreth, father of the historian Richard Hildreth, who was born in the Willard house. Edward Hitchcock studied and taught here. While teaching, he made the apparatus for the necessary astronomical observations, and for several successive years computed an almanac, an unusual feat for a country schoolmaster. The volumes are arranged after the plan of the common farmer's almanac, weather predictions and all. The

The Frary House before the Restoration.

predictions and nuggets of wisdom appear on opposite pages in the spaces

The Willard House.

unoccupied by the moon's phases, tides, etc., as for instance, August, 1818:

The Mexicans salute their new-born infants in this manner. "Child! thou art come into the world to suffer: Endure and hold thy peace."	Relaxing weather succeeded by much thunder. Some foggy nights particularly near rivers that run to the south. Cool and clear. Rainy and moulding weather. Sudden change.

President Hitchcock's later work in deciphering the secret of the Connecticut Valley red sandstone foundations is too well known to need our comment.

The memory of another principal, Mr. Luther B. Lincoln, is revered by all who came under the influence of his gentle spirit. Those of his pupils who are left are now gray-haired men and women. Such teachers as these kept the school for fifty years in the rank of our smaller coleges; and its influence can still be seen.

Passing down Academy Lane, by the modern Town Hall and White Church, we come to the gambrel-roofed house Godfrey Nims built, early in the seventeen hundreds, on the ruins of the home the Indians burned and over the ashes of three of his children who had hidden in the cellar.

Next is the Old Tavern or Frary House — our oldest inhabitant. After years of neglect it has fallen into appreciative hands, and has been restored to more than its original beauty, while its individuality has still been preserved. In Revolutionary days, Major Barnard kept tavern here. Every other tavern in New England may have sheltered that restless traveller, George Washington. This claims a rarer fame. Benedict Arnold stopped here in 1775 while on his way to reduce Ticonderoga. He had just received his promotion as colonel. His fame was as untarnished as his new military trappings. People expected much of him, and he expected more of himself. His business here was to engage Colonel Thomas Wells Dickinson to furnish beef for his force of four hundred men. The bargain was made in the north front room, then the bar-room. Colonel Dickinson and his fourteen years old brother, Consider, whom we shall hear of again as "Uncle Sid," drove the cattle through the long stretch of Vermont, up hill and down, following the hungry four hundred. Somewhere in Rutland County they met men return-

The Rear of the Willard House.

ing from the already captured fort. Impetuous Ethan Allen and his Green Mountain boys, "in the name of the Great Jehovah and the Continental Congress," had snatched the glory Arnold considered already his own. This was one of the first of a series of wounds to Arnold's pride, which ended in his giving up the cause of the colonies. Colonel Wells was at the camp at West Point in September, 1780, and, to quote Mr. Sheldon's excellent account, heard read

added interest to the house as a relic had not added to its comfort as a home. Mr. Hoyt, I think, offered the building to the town, if the town would move it away. Strange to say, no one made a move in its behalf, and it was torn down to make room for the present house. Its oaken timbers were still sound. It is said that the old elm which appears in all the pictures of this house, and still bears its unnumbered years with vigor and grace, was in its youth the "whip-

The Williams House.

on parade, perhaps from the very orderly book now owned by the Pocumtuc Valley Memorial Association, the startling announcement that "*Treason of the blackest die was yesterday discovered !!!*"

Just north of this old tavern the street widens. The houses stand in an irregular circle around the common and soldiers' monument, as their predecessors used to stand around the meeting-house and within the stockade which encircled "Meeting-house Hill."

The Old Indian House stood until 1848, a little west of the present Brick Church. Its history attracted a constant train of visitors. They flocked from every stage that stopped to change horses, considering this one of the curiosities of the place which must not be missed. The Hoyt family grew weary with the burden of fame. The years which had

ping-tree," its slender trunk used as a whipping-post in the days when slaves and white sinners were thus publicly taught the error of their ways.

Only one other house now standing shares with the Frary house the honor of having been present, in embryo, at the memorable massacre. The Willard house, since grown to grander proportions, is one of our most interesting landmarks. Its history has been charmingly told by its present owner, Mrs. Yale, in "The Story of the Willard House." The northeast wing, with jutting eaves, was, in 1704, the home of Samuel Carter. His wife and six children were among the captives taken to Canada. Soon after he sold the desolate home and moved away. His successor was Samuel Allen, grandfather of Ethan Allen. Ethan's father was born here.

The main part of the present house was built in pre-revolutionary days. It is said that the builder was thirteen years in selecting the timber, so careful was he that every stick should be free from knot or flaw. The beautiful carving and panelling, unharmed by time, show that the workmen were faithful to the master's high ideal.

In the long list of occupants, Dr. Willard seems to have been the one to fix his name and character on the house. He came here in the early years of the liberal movement headed by Channing.

Dickinson High School.

His opinions were too radical and too honestly expressed to be accepted by the council; but the people recognized the strength of the man and called him. The time was probably ripe for his teaching. The conservatives seceded and founded a new society, and the First Congregational Church was henceforth Unitarian. For fifty years Dr. Willard was a trusted guide in matters spiritual and practical. His wisdom is still cited. A faded picture of his benign face

people, his son-in-law, Mr. Lincoln, the principal and patron saint of the Academy.

The son and grandson of these two men, Mr. Luther J. B. Lincoln, is now making Deerfield a gathering place for writers and readers and all sorts of interesting and interested people, by his Summer School of History and Romance, which holds its sessions in Dickinson Hall, on the other side of the Common. During the month of July there are almost daily meetings for lectures, readings, or discussions, on various subjects, usually having some bearing, near or remote, on the growth of American literature, with such men as Mr. Stedman, Mr. Cable, Charles Dudley Warner, and Robert Collyer to lead in the talks.

One of the old houses which used to stand in the circle facing the Common has been moved west, down Hitchcock Lane, to make way for the High School building, and it was somewhat mutilated during the removal. It was built, in 1707, by the town — town and church were one in those days — for its minister, Rev. John Williams, when he came back to begin life over again, with a new wife, in the brave way those old survivors had. It was repaired in 1756, but the building is probably substantially as it was first built. It was a typical early colonial house, finished with beautiful woodwork, carved and fitted by hand. The front rooms are still partly panelled. The windows are high and narrow, with deep window seats. Corner cupboards with curved shelves and ornamental tops, delicately fluted like a shell, were built into

The Hitchcock House.

is treasured in all the older families, along with Willard's Hymns, and Channing's Life and Works in nine volumes. He had but one rival in the hearts of his

the walls. The hall stairway is quite imposing, with its wide landing and carved railing. The front doorway is finished in a peculiarly elaborate design. The house had the secret chamber without which no colonial house seemed to be complete. It was on the second floor, and had no connection with other rooms on that floor, but by an arrangement of trap-doors and secret stairs could be reached both from the cellar and the attic. It contained a fireplace and a closet. What possible use could good Parson Williams have had for such a room — unless he desired a secluded spot to write his sermons, secure from interruptions from his ten children, those that were left of his sixteen. These secret rooms are usually explained as places of refuge "when the Indians came"; but as the Indians usually burned the houses they came to, the concealment could have been little protection.

Parson Williams died suddenly in 1729. It was a "grievous dispensation of Providence" to his people. He was laid in the old burying-ground, beside his "Vertuos and desirable Confort," who "fell by the rage of ye Barbarous enemy, March 1, 1703¾." Their headstones are alike, with grinning death's heads at the top and intricate scroll work around the inscriptions. His second wife "lyes" the other side. Her headstone is of a later fashion. It is ornamented by a clock-face, one hand at twelve, with a shovel and pickaxe, and crossbones below.

Rev. John's grandson, "Esquire John," sold the house, in 1789, to "Uncle Sid" Dickinson, who spent in it a long life of money-getting and money-saving. These two men have similar claims to the gratitude of the youth of Deerfield. Esq. John was instrumental in establishing the

old academy and left the bulk of his property to its fund. Half a century or more later, Uncle Sid's property founded the Dickinson High School and a free library and reading-room. The two corporations are now united, and Dickinson Academy stands on the site of the old homestead.

Uncle Sid was a queer old fellow. He is remembered equally as a teller of funny stories and as a subject for such. His remark on hearing of the suicide of an eccentric neighbor, "What *will* that man

The Old Burying-Ground.

do next?" has become classic. He was a shrewd, careful, hard-working man, who knew from experience the amount of time and strength a dollar represented. His wealth made him a target for divers demands in the name of charity. These he was apt to refuse, and so gained the reputation of being "close." Those who knew him best say his crabbed manner hid a kindlier heart than he would have cared to acknowledge. Perhaps he heeded Sancho Panza's warning proverb: "Make yourself honey and the flies will eat you." His first wife died long before he did. His love for her and hers is touchingly shown by two slabs in the old burying-ground to the memory of her parents. A foot note tells the passer-by: "These stones were gratuitously erected by their son-in-law, Consider Dickinson." Uncle Sid left his large property to his second wife without restriction, though there was a tacit understanding as to its final use. She carried out his wishes faith-

The Sheldon House.

fully. So completely did she identify herself with him that she was known as "Aunt Sid." She was for twenty years a trusty guardian of his money, spending no more of it than was absolutely necessary to support life. She died in 1875, just one hundred years after the boy "Sid" took the long tramp after Benedict Arnold's cattle. It would be hard to measure the good the money they saved is doing for the boys and girls of Deerfield.

Across the way from the Williams house is a little brown cottage, its doorway nearly hidden by lilacs. We like to call it the birthplace of Edward Hitchcock — though our historian says he was, in fact, born next door. This was, however, the home of his ancestors. It has recently been transformed into a studio.

A little farther down the lane is the old burying-ground. The dead of 1704 are supposed to lie together in one corner of the yard. It was the new burying-ground then. The oldest stone is that of Joseph Barnard, killed by the Indians at Indian Bridge in 1695. "Ye salvadge foe" helped to fill many another grave, as the frequent inscriptions, "captivated by ye salvadges," "slain by yᵉ ennemy,"

show. The last victims of that enemy were those who fell in the Bars Fight in 1745. The Widow Amsden's two boys lie in a wide grave together. Samuel Allen's stone bears this inscription :

> "Liſten to me ye Mortal men, Bewareᵉ
> That you engage no more in direfull
> War. By means of War my Soul from
> Earth is fled — My Body Logᵈ in
> Mansions of the Dead."

No shadow of those old tragedies darkens the sunshine now. Daisies and golden-rod make every day Memorial Day. The ground is cared for sufficiently to show respect, without being trimmed too closely, a thing more fatal than neglect. In our memory this spot always lies in the warm haze of a fall afternoon. Crickets are always chirping in the dry grass ; the soft shadows are growing long on the meadows below ; the mountains in the west are blue and indistinct ; and the low murmur of the river pervades all.

The grass-grown lane that runs past, down to the old ford, was once the beginning of the highway "To Albany," so the signboard said. All military expeditions for the north or west started here, after being fitted out by Major Williams, son of Rev. John, at the old

"Corner Store," which stood, until the building of Dickinson Academy, on the corner next the common. Sergeant John Hanks started here on snowshoes, in the winter of 1747–8, with but one companion, to go through the wilderness to Canada to exchange a French prisoner for two captive boys. Ensign John Sheldon had made the same journey, for a similar purpose, three times, long before. The place where those travellers crossed the river is " mowing land " now.

Doorway of the Sheldon House.

perforce have been an antiquary. His home is over one hundred and fifty years old. The home-lot has descended to him in a direct line from father to son, back to Ensign John Sheldon, who bought it after his home in the old Indian house was so rudely broken up. Still farther back, the Indians had their wigwams here, if one may judge from the relics brought to light. The back-yard was evidently a burial - place. The bones from several graves, with the heads,

The river is continually pilfering from the farmers on one side and bestowing the spoils upon the town land on the opposite side. It used to flow much nearer the burying-ground than it does now. An old lady who belonged to that geologic and theologic age used to tell this story :

"I remember, when I was a child, hearing people say the river was wearing away the burying-ground down by the ford. I used to lie awake nights, thinking how dreadful it would be to ride across the ford and see the bones of the dead lying under the water. After a while the current turned away, and I thought the Lord changed the course of the river to save the burying-ground."

We rejoice that this God's Acre was spared, and mourn that a still older burial-ground of the Indians, which lay west of it, could not also have been saved. It was a convenient gravel - pit and has been carried away bodily, load by load.

There are several more fine old houses in the street left in their primitive state, besides many that have been more or less modernized. The stately gambrel-roofed Stebbins house stands much as it did when Colonel Joseph Stebbins left his wife and babies to go to fight Burgoyne.

If a man's birthplace can determine his natural tendencies, Mr. Sheldon must

ornaments, and utensils buried with them, have been placed in Memorial Hall. Mr. Sheldon's life has been in harmony with his surroundings. His exhaustive studies of Indian life and customs and of colonial life in the valley have made him an authority. His history of Deerfield, his genealogies, and his numerous papers on disputed points in history are invaluable to the student of that epoch.

Another old house is the summer home of J. W. Champney, the artist. It has been in Mrs. Champney's family nearly a century. It used to stand close to the street, under the shadow of a gigantic elm, a tree so noble that the "Autocrat

Home of J. W. Champney.

of the Breakfast Table" mentioned it in his list of mighty elms. Mrs. Champney laid the scene of one of her stories in the old home. The legend which she wove into the tale,—

"When falls one, then fall all three,
    Tree and house and family,"—

happily did not hold true. A winter storm overthrew the giant tree a few years ago. The house has been moved back from the street and partly restored, partly remodelled.

Old Deerfield is built on a narrow strip of land, somewhat higher than the surrounding meadows. The south end of the street, like the north end, terminates abruptly in a terrace, skirted by a row of elms, whose trunks and drooping branches make a dark frame for the sunny picture beyond. This happy valley is protected on the east by a range of red sandstone hills, ending in the distance with Sugar Loaf and King Philip's Seat.

The road divides here, turning sharply to the right and left. The right, the Meadow Road, leads to the Bars, the home of George Fuller, whose name is

George Fuller.

Deerfield's pride and glory. Mr. Fuller's house stands on the edge of a terrace overlooking meadow and river toward Old Deerfield Street, two miles away to the north, and toward Stillwater and the Hoosac Hills on the west. In the farther distance are Arthur's Seat and the hills of Shelburne and Leyden. The old house across the way was for the last few years of his life, his studio. But little of his later work remains here, though there is in the house and the studio an extremely interesting and valuable collection of family portraits and sketches and records of his work before he became famous. The house he used as a studio was built, in 1739, by Samuel Allen, who a few years later was slain on the meadow close by " while bravely defending his own life and his children's "—as his headstone says — from a swarm of Indians who poured down from the hills above Stillwater.

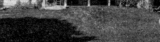

Home of George Fuller.

One more bloody field claims notice, though it is not within the limits of Old Deerfield. This meadow-road is the one Captain Lathrop and his young men, "culled from the towns of the county of Essex," took in the early morning of September 18, 1675, having under their protection a train of carts loaded with grain to feed the Hadley garrison. We will follow their footsteps afar off — up Bars Long Hill and across an upland plain to Bloody Brook, three miles below. Their journey ended here. There is no need of retelling the sorrows of that day. A flat stone marks the spot where "sixty persons were buried in one dreadful grave." A monument with appropriate inscriptions stands on the battlefield.

A Corner of George Fuller's Studio.

streets that day declared that not even a dog was left at home. I have two accounts of this memorable day, both written by eyewitnesses, which are interesting as showing the different way different persons see the same thing, and as indicating the way in which Old Deerfield must be looked at to be seen at all.

Harriet Martineau was then making her tour of America, and chanced to be present. Her critic's eye found the scene amusing. She was greatly diverted by the bland manners of the militia, the efforts of the amateur band, the posing and gesticulating of the orator. She

In the old Burying-Ground.

Its corner stone was originally laid September 18, 1836, with imposing ceremonies. Edward Everett, the orator of the day, gave one of his eloquent and dramatic addresses. All the people from the towns about flocked to hear him. A stranger who rode through Deerfield

Bloody Brook Monument.

could not understand the spirit of the celebration or its purpose. She wrote :

"This (massacre) was a piteous incident in the history of the settlement, but it is not easy to

George Fuller's Studio.

see why it should be made an occasion of commemoration in preference to many others which have a stronger moral interest. . . . No virtue was here to be had in remembrance, nothing but mere misery. The contemplation of mere misery is painful and hurtful. The only salutary influence that I could perceive to rise from the occasion was the far-fetched and dubious one — thankfulness that the Indians are not now at hand to molest the white inhabitants."

Harriet Martineau was not born in Deerfield !

There was in the audience another hearer, a childish idealist, who from her seat on her mother's knees saw and heard everything. Under the spell of the orator, "the march of that fated band through the forest on that other 18th of September became a living reality." One page of history became a personal experience. Heroism and self-sacrifice became living virtues. She saw that it was not alone the piteous death of the "flower of Essex" which was commemorated, but their brave, self-denying lives spent where such a death was always near. So deep an impression did the day make on the child, that the woman now cites the occasion as an example of the possibilities for education in the fit celebration of such anniversaries. All towns with a past like Old Deerfield's hold this power of education. They are pictures on the pages of History, which bring the past before us more vividly than words can do it, if we look at them with understanding eyes.

Deerfield River.

In the Ossipee Glens
(1892)

IN THE OSSIPEE GLENS.

By Lucy Larcom.

Winnepesaukee — From the Ossipee Mountain Park.

PLACES are like persons, in many ways. They have their franknesses and their reserves, and in regions of both landscape and character supposed to be well known, or not worth knowing, we often come upon unexpected revelations of beauty, subtle clews to inexhaustible delight. And perhaps the most desirable daily companionship of either kind is that which does not offer us too much of the surface attraction obvious to the whole gazing world, but which beckons the seeker elusively from behind apparently commonplace barriers.

Everybody goes to Niagara, to the White Mountains, to Mount Desert, to the Adirondacks; pictures of their prominent points of interest are in all the guide-books; but not very many dream of the lovely nooks that they fly past with the crowd on their way to the popular resort. And it is well that they do not; for an invasion of tourists often involves the destruction of a landscape's peculiar charm — certainly of its freshness.

Anyone who thinks of it for a moment must, for instance, be aware that there are innumerable delightful hide-away places in the hill-country of New Hampshire, fairy nooks and corners of which the railway-travelling world has not the remotest guess. This has been found true of the green heights of the Ossipees, thirty miles or so south of the Presidential group, rarely thought of except as a threshold or stepping-stone to the loftier peaks. That shaggy bulk hides dells and gorges in its bosom, fragrant with breezy bloom, and musical with the laughter of rivulet and waterfall. Picturesque homes, inhabited and deserted, are hidden in its glens; and half-obliterated histories are written on its gray ledges. Homely enough, in some aspects, are those rugged crags; but the rose-breath of friendship haunts with undying sweetness many a recess that they shelter; and over that mountain-wall the heart of more than one pilgrim gives response to scattered fellow-pilgrims, "And I, too, have dwelt in Arcady!"

243

The Ossipee range is made up of closely-piled green summits, rounded or conical, interspersed with easy slopes and almost level ridges. The sharp peak of Chocorua, and the grand pyramidal shapes of Passaconaway and Whiteface of the Sandwich range, neighbor it so closely that to the passing glance it might seem an inferior group — as in height it is, though not in romantic interest. At least one remarkable lake is hidden in its heart, — a mountain tarn that reflects the loftiest of the Ossipee summits in its unfathomed deep, sunk like a well in a hollow wilderness of hills, and unvisited except by an occasional guest — usually some stray woodsman or fisherman.

Several beautiful streams run down these secluded mountain-slopes, one or two of which are styled rivers; but the most fascinating among them are the nameless brooks, such as would have delighted the soul of a Wordsworth, and would have made him murmur beside them

"A music sweeter than their own."

This range, fortunate in being accounted uninteresting by the common traveller, has not been without its merited poetic appreciation. Sweet songs from our truest New England poet flow down its sides in lovely blending with the melody of brook and cascade. Whittier writes:

"The years are many since at first,
For dreamed-of wonders all athirst,
I saw on Winnepesaukee fall
The shadow of the mountain-wall."

And scarcely another mountain-poem of his has more subtle tenderness of suggestion than that "Mystery," in which he doubtless gives us a glimpse of his first vision of the Bearcamp and Chocorua:

"The river hemmed with leaning trees
Wound through its meadows green;
A low blue line of mountains showed
The open pines between.

"One sharp, tall peak above them all
Clear into sunlight sprang:
I saw the river of my dreams,
The mountains that I sang!"

For the poet had told how "Chocorua's horn of shadow pierced the water," long before he had seen for himself the marvellous reflection of that savage summit in its own lake-mirror. Hardly less perfect is "Sunset on the Bearcamp," a noble picture-poem, the result of a later visit. "The Seeking of the Waterfall" is another fine inspiration drawn from this locality, — the region about West Ossipee and the Bearcamp River House, for many years a favorite summer resort of our poet. The site of that old-fashioned hostelry is now but a desolate mound, the buildings having been destroyed by fire a few years since. But the lonely spot is peopled with delightful memories, clustering about this one honored figure, whose presence heightened the natural charm of the place, always the centre of some group of friends he had won hither, intermingled with whom were transient housemates, at once cordially received as

"I saw on Winnepesaukee fall
The shadow of the mountain-wall."

friends. The rare merriment, the genial good fellowship that were shared around that blazing parlor wood fire, must yet be felt as a warmth at the heart by scores of regretful mountain sojourners.

Out-door associations with the same beloved and revered name, are not less abundant. His initial has been written in light on the hillside. Not many Septembers since, there was an encampment of young men and maidens, mostly neighbors or friends of the poet, on the high slope of the Ossipees near the inn — Camp Whittier — with its emblematic "W" blazoned in Chinese lanterns through the evening gloom on the wondering gaze of farm-folk and hotel-tarriers. None who saw it will be likely to forget the strange illumination of that distant camp-fire, danced about by a fly-

perhaps the most impressively beautiful in outline of any mountain range in New England. Beyond its broken horizon-line dimly loom Kearsarge and the summit of Mount Washington.

The little river, rippling down its valley-vista from somewhere among the solemn gorges far off underneath Sandwich Dome, reveals itself here and there in a blue gleam of sinuous light that wins your eye, as the road winding along be-

The Park Buildings.

ing circle of silhouette-shapes that seemed witch-like in the gloaming, — a weirdly brilliant spectacle.

The "Whittier Maple" is a tree of enormous girth a few rods down the highway, to the unusual dimensions of which the poet first called his fellow-travellers' attention; and the boldest summit of the Ossipee range on the pleasant westward valley-road fitly bears his name — "Whittier Peak."

The view from the old inn on the Bearcamp was — and of course the viewpoint remains unchanged — one of quiet, idyllic loveliness. The stream clings so closely to the bases of the two hills directly in front of the now deserted hotel site, it seems as if they ought to be named for it, — Bearcamp Crest and Bearcamp Spur. They are easy heights to climb, and command a noble prospect — Ossipee Lake and its sister-ponds, Chocorua, — and the long, undulating stretch of the Sandwich Chain, which is

side it is likely soon to win yourself. It is a delightful drive, for ten miles or so, between the two ranges, with a continually changing outlook mountainward, right and left.

The massiveness of the nameless interlocked heights of the Ossipees — covering an area of sixty square miles — emphasizes itself along this road. Nameless we almost wish the early settlers had left them all. That dark olive-green cone which rises as a landmark from the corner of the range, — what a shame that it should be known by the libellous cognomen of "Black Snout!" Let us beg this sentinel hill not to bristle his sombre shagginess in objection, while we travellers re-christen him "Spruce Cap," and pass on.

On the western side, towards Centre Harbor, the Ossipee Mountains are built up like a continuous rampart, with gradual slopes, showing open rocky uplands and cultivated fields more than half way

Lake Winnepesaukee from the Lawn.

to their summits. There is a glimpse of blue water as you skirt the Sandwich hamlets — Bearcamp Pond — and through this pretty basin one branch of the familiar stream bearing the same name finds its way around the curve of the hills to Ossipee Lake.

The road gets a little steeper; sunny pasture-lands, cornfields, and orchards become more and more closely interknit with forest glooms as you ascend; and presently, if you are intent to know what those overhanging wilderness heights may hide, you stop before a closed gate, opposite a typical New Hampshire cottage, one of those which almost seem indigenous to the soil. The sign-board at the gateway points upwards. You open the gate and shut it again as you are bidden, and are on your way to Ossipee Mountain Park.

Some majestic old oaks greet you near the entrance; clumps of sweetbrier nod gracefully from among the wayside shrubbery; the excellence of the winding mountain road — although, being a private one, it is labelled "dangerous," — wins your admiring wonder; a beautiful panorama opens before you as you emerge from the forest and approach the, gateway of a smooth green lawn which seems uplifted from the lower world, shelved above rocks and woodlands, like the high summer pastures where Alpine shepherds tend their flocks.

The house and its surroundings have a sunshiny, hospitable look, which corresponds to the welcome within; and seated on the spacious crescent-shaped verandah, you may take a long, full breath, for a world of immeasured horizons is before you. Lake Winnepesaukee is at your feet, apparently, although several miles away, mingling its vivid blue waters and green islands with the mistiness of mountain distances. You are seven hundred and fifty feet above the lake, and more than twelve hundred feet above the sea-level.

The southern Kearsarge is the central object in the expanse before you, dim with distance, but not so dim as Monadnock, which is yet visible, in pale outline, farther south. The twin-headed Belknap rises on the left, and Cardigan lifts his humped shoulders to look across on the right. Countless inferior summits and ranges intervene. Looking for human associations, your eye rests upon scattered white dots, which represent the villages at the Weirs and at Centre Harbor. More than ten miles across, you can distinguish the pencilled outline of a tall pine-tree, which, if not Whittier's "Wood Giant," is its near neighbor, "The Sentinel." Eighteen miles away toward the sunsetting, are Shepard Hill and the Asquam House, which have often exchanged sun-signals with the Park, when friends have been sheltered under the two far-separated roofs.

The dark mass of Red Hill on the right, and the slopes of "Crow's Nest" and "The Steep" that skirt the lawn on the left, give to the whole grand view the harmony of a perfectly-balanced picture. You gaze and dream, with the feeling one might have suspended on the edge of a cloud: there is the earth below you, and you are of it, but not in it, having risen to the green threshold of a rural heaven.

The dazzle of the lake may drive you from your enchanted dreams around to the north porch, where a verdurous semi-

John Greenleaf Whittier.

lief you drop your eyes to the broad, green carpet at your feet, murmuring to yourself, perhaps, the words of our poet of the hills, —

> "Touched by a light that hath no name,
> A glory never sung,
> Aloft on sky and mountain-wall
> Are God's great pictures hung."

But here again you have human reminders. There is a weather-worn farmhouse behind the stone wall across the way, and the creak of its antiquated well-sweep will bring you to a consciousness of neighbors, if the gray parrot, Joe, has not already startled you thereto, with some sudden guttural ejaculations from his perch above you, or by his unnaturally natural whistle to the good dog "Snyder," whose big, handsome bulk is lying in protective concealment under the bench where you sit.

Joe, by the way, is a regular habitué of these heights, coming up with the family every season; and a very independent character he is, not without a cynical tone in his human-like utterances, at times. New-comers can scarcely escape his sharp-eyed criticism, although he usually reserves the expression of his judgment until just as they are leaving.

A group of picnickers had gathered around him one day, and were trying in vain to make him respond to their wearisome iteration of "Poor Polly!" "Polly want a cracker?" in the usual irritatingly patronizing tones.

"He can't talk! That kind of a par-

circle of mountains seems to enclose you, as in the Happy Valley of Rasselas. The contrast with what you have just beheld is complete. You have the same sense of separation from the lower world, but now you look up instead of down. If it is October, and the hillsides have taken on their autumnal splendor, you might imagine yourself in an immense tapestried room, gorgeous with embroideries of every tint and shade and color. For re-

The Lawn and Crow's Nest.

rot never does talk," broke in oracularly from the lips of one of the unfamiliar crowd.   Joe turned his head slowly and inquiringly in the direction of the speaker, and, with great gravity and deliberation, enunciated the words "What do you *soy* ?" then backed around towards the landscape, not condescending to utter another syllable.   It was like the story

likely to follow their flight or question their title-deeds, any more than they would the claims of the blue-jay or the eagle.

Up the road and across the brook a little way, is a cluster of old cellars, the remains of what must have been a small hamlet.   This has been a school-district within the memory of living men.   Chil-

Pee-Wee's Pool.

of "Who stuffed that white owl?" where the meditative bird suddenly moves his head upon its living pivot and confronts his critics with a wide-staring revelation of his "true inwardness."

There are plain tokens of an early settlement that flourished at this elevation, but has died out, leaving only a few farmers and their families, who have but a slight hold on the past, by memory or by inheritance.   People have lived and died here, but little trace is left of them, how they came or when they went.   A few of the present occupants of the soil can trace their ancestry back to Revolutionary times.   Their grandfathers came up here from the seacoasts of Massachusetts or Maine, and perched among these rocks ; if you ask why, the answer given is "Poverty, poverty !   The land was cheap."   And in those days nobody was

dren climbed the mountain side from below, to study their spelling-book and multiplication table by the light of lake and hillside sunshine.   What inspirations were possible to childhood under such influences, though barefoot and scantily fed !   But the ruins of the old schoolhouse have been removed, and only these cellar - excavations remain, haunted by the pathos which always clings about the deserted habitations of human beings.   The homely vestiges of the pioneer's cabin breathe out the same spirit of desolation that exhales from the crumbling walls of a palace of the Cæsars.

" All houses wherein men have lived and died
      Are haunted houses : "

And so are all places where men's houses have stood, — the foundation only left, like the chair from which the aged

The Deserted House.

tenant rose and shuffled to his grave. It is strange what trifles can thrill us with that touch which "makes the whole world kin." Close to one of these cellars — perhaps the very oldest — is a small ring of stones piled one upon another, the upper sides overgrown with lichens, while beneath they are bare and clean as on the day they were laid there. It is doubtless a play-time relic left by pre-Revolutionary children of the mountain side ; a sort of miniature Druid-circle, perhaps a juvenile mock - fortification against an imaginary attack of the red Indians. It is not improbable that the make-believe garrison was hurriedly forsaken on account of a real alarm of savage invasion; for the war-path of bloodthirsty hordes was not far away, and their camp-smokes must have been visible from this height. Whatever it was, the oldest dwellers on the mountain side remember this small stonehenge looking mossy - gray with age in their childhood, as it does now, without any tradition of the adjoining cabin's original tenants. Few of the solid ancestral edifices of New England have outlasted this little enclosure of loose stones. Half in

Benjamin F. Shaw, the Developer of Ossipee Mountain Park.

irony, half in tender sentiment, Time overturns the results of man's painful labor, but leaves the careless work of childish fingers untouched.

Many of the cellars are of more recent date ; and wherever the tenant of a removed house is known, the proprietor of the Park has placed a tablet, with name inscribed, on its site. One of these perpetuates the memory of a personage familiarly known as Charley Brown, recalled on the mountain side as rollicking and powerfully built, and an excellent fiddler. He had tales to tell of war times, having been an eye-witness of the fray known as the " Boston Massacre," on the 5th of March, 1770.

Another slab records the name of Theodore Evans, who was in the battle of Plattsburg, in 1813.

The few remaining inhabitants have led uneventful lives, startled only by such incidents as the unceremonious irruption of a hedge-hog into a cottager's kitchen at breakfast-time, or the sliding of a cow off a steep precipice to premature death, or the capture of a bear that had manifested too persistent a fondness for fresh lamb.

Once a house far from neighbors on the mountain side was burned down in the night. The children — there were nine of them — had been playing with flax in the unfinished loft, and a lighted candle had come too near. The family fought the flames without help and in vain. They left their home in ruins, and appeared in the early dawn, a woful pro-

who "live down on the ground." "Folks that belong down on the ground had better stay down on the ground," has sometimes been the remark made concerning those who have sought to scale their heights. And who shall say that this reveals an unnatural trait? The habit of isolation breeds a self-sufficient haughtiness in human nature, equally fostered by

Mary's Arch.

cession, at the door of a farmhouse a mile or two away.

A stone set up in a cleared field tells of a more tragical occurrence, indicating the spot where Ebenezer Horne perished in a snowstorm only a few feet from his own threshold, as he returned from an errand to the settlements below, on a bitter night in the year 1813.

Little as these few mountaineers have had to break the monotony of their existence, they have not altogether relished the advent of new neighbors. They have had a way of speaking of the inhabitants of the world below them, as people

the solitude of wildernesses or of castle walls. Certainly the proprietors of so grand a domain as this — though only vaguely conscious of its splendors — may well be pardoned for resenting intrusion. Something of the awe that pervades these lonely hill-presences has crept into their expressions, as when they say of the sound that rushes down through the high forests before a storm, "The mountain is roaring"; or of the strange echoes that steal up from under the frozen floor of Winnepesaukee in midwinter, "Hear the lake groan!"

It is an illusion of the city-reared and

Bridal Veil Falls.

academy-bred, that they have a monopoly of literary taste—that rustics can have no true appreciation of the beautiful or grand, at least in books. But there are thinkers and sages and seers everywhere. They who doubt it should hear a son of this mountain, who was born on one of its loneliest slopes and has lived in its shadow well-nigh three-score years, referring in his conversation to Homer, quoting Emerson with genuine admiration, repeating snatches of Whittier's songs, and reciting passages of Isaiah, as in his opinion the noblest poet of all.

The impressiveness of his tones as he looked across the lake into the crimson sunset — he had come up the mountain in search of a pair of steers, and was attired suitably for the pursuit, — will never fade from the memory of one listener, at least; nor the admiring reverence with which he repeated the verses containing the prophecy, "Thy sun shall no more go down; neither shall thy moon withdraw itself; for the Lord shall be thine everlasting light." It was like the voice of the shaggy hills themselves uttering benediction.

"There has been a good deal of praying up here; we used to have meetings very often," he said; and the mountain airs seemed sweeter for having borne heavenward the aspirations of these hardy children of the hills.

A sister of this man is a Druid priestess in massiveness of figure, and in eloquence of scriptural quotation a Miriam the Prophetess. Her whole language is Biblical. There was something weird in the echo of her powerful tones, floating up to a group who sat, one summer's evening, an involuntary audience, on the bench at "The Steep," several hundred feet above her on the hillside. At that altitude, the sound of her voice was just indistinct enough to be construed into blessing or malediction, according to the listener's mood. The notes of the hermit-thrush and the whippoorwill filled in

termination. You have come suddenly to the brink of a precipice, and are gazing over wide reaches of woodland below you, with the sensation a bird might have, looking down into forest-tops across which he is premeditating a flight toward the hills and waters beyond. The feeling is peculiar, — almost as if you were to be disembodied. Wordsworth must have strayed to some such cliff as this when he breathed the enraptured lines:

" O, what a joy it were, in vigorous health,
    To have a body, — this our vital frame
    With shrinking sensibility endued,—
    And to the elements surrender it
    As if it were a spirit! How divine
    The liberty for frail, for mortal man
    To roam at large among the unpeopled glens,
    . . . and, reckless of the storm
    That keeps the raven quiet in her nest,
    Be as a presence or a motion — one
    Among the many there!"

Returning from The Steep, an easy

View from Mount Shaw.

the pauses, like hymns between exhortations at a prayer-meeting; the solemnity of twilight was falling upon the lake and the hills; and the effect of the whole was far from inharmonious, — not without a touch of supernatural suggestion.

"The Steep," is one of the noblest view-points at the park. You come to it by a long, downward-winding wood-path, which seems as if made only for its own sweet sake, but unexpectedly you find that there was a purpose in its plan and

stairway of rock leads you up to the Crow's Nest, an elevation from which you have a bird's-eye-view of the park in its prominent features and surroundings. There is the cheerful, double-verandahed mansion on its sunny lawn, the lodge, the barn, the windmill, and the pathetic little graveyard, where the scattered mountaineers have an inalienable right, whoever owns the estate. The two or three inhabited cottages are almost

Twin Falls.

more pathetic in their unneighbored loneliness; and the deserted "Witham" house, far out on the mountain slope, which raccoons and hedge-hogs have made an undesirable home for other tenants, has a solitary expression all its own.

That darkest gorge in the hills is the North Wind Ravine. It is a curious weather phenomenon, that, whatever way the wind may have blown through the day, in nine nights out of ten it sweeps down towards the lake out of this ravine. Therefore, summer nights at the Park are invariably cool.

Mount Shaw, the highest peak of the range, named for the owner of the Park, is nearly east of you, and the observatory on its summit is about three thousand feet above the sea. It does not, however, assert its height from this point, retreating and losing itself behind its lower companions. It has three distinct elevations, one of which corresponds so nearly in shape and color to the conical height at the northern end of the range as to have formerly unfortunately shared with it the barbarous characterization of "Black Snout"; but it is now more euphoniously spoken of as "Melvin Peak," or the "East Knoll."

A picturesque glimpse of Melvin village is revealed from the outreaching lowlands near the Lake, its white walls and spires scattered among meadow and orchard greenery, in idyllic contrast with blue water and the outlines of hills hitherto unseen, — Dopple - Crown — or Mount Caryl — and the low ranges about Alton Bay.[1]

Somewhere near that pleasant hamlet crumbles the mysterious skeleton that inspired Whittier's poem, "The Grave by the Lake."

> "Ringed about with smooth gray stones,
> Rests the giant's mighty bones. —
>
> "Who that Titan cromlech fills?
> Forest-Kaiser, lord o' the hills?
> Knight who on the birchen tree
> Carved his savage heraldry?
> Priest o' the pine-wood temples dim,
> Prophet, sage, or wizard grim? —
>
> "Wordless moans the ancient pine;
> Lake and mountain give no sign."

And the villagers seem to know nothing of this traditional cairn. Perhaps its

[1] "On the shore of the lake, at the mouth of Melvin River, a gigantic skeleton was found (early in the present century) buried in a sandy soil, apparently that of a man more than seven feet high — the jaw bones easily passing over the face of a large man. A tumulus has been discovered on a piece of newly-cleared land, of the length and appearance of a human grave, and handsomely rounded with small stones not found in this part of the country."—*Hayward's New England Gazetteer.*

rocks have been taken to build stone-walls with, for farm boundaries, and perhaps the grave itself has been ploughed over into a potato field. Our proverbial Yankee disregard of antiquity is not incapable of such vandalism. It would scarcely have spared the rude tumulus from the path of its ploughshare, had it indicated the burial-place of Passacona-way, the last and greatest of the mountain Bashabas.

That southern side of the Ossipee range was a favorite resort of the savage tribes, traces of them being found all along the shores of the lake. Their usual choice of picturesque spots for an encampment will be recognized on sailing about Melvin Bay, or in approaching by the road the abrupt mountain-wall

Chocorua Mountain and Lake.

straw-color of the evening primrose, a sumach waving its crimson pennons close at hand, while the grand horizon stretches far around the Lake, from Moosilauke in the north to the dreamy hint of Monadnock in the south, your thoughts easily wander back to aboriginal associations that haunt the scenery. This height, with the steep below, may well have been a look-out for scouting parties on either side, during the French and Indian wars, and it is known that this mixed soldiery

Chocorua Peak.

chose the route through the country that lies before you, for their incursions.

Along the southeastern border of the lake, captives were dragged through the pathless wilderness as early as the year 1686, after the destruction of Cocheco (Dover, N. H.) by the Saco Indians. Among them was a woman, Sarah Gerrish, of whom an early chronicler writes:

"The fell salvages led her a terrible march through the thick woods and a thousand other miseries, till they came to the Norway Plains. (Now Rochester, N. H.) From thence they made her go to the end of Winnopeseag Lake, and from thence to the Eastward, through horrid swamps where sometimes they must scramble over huge trees fallen by storm or age, for a vast way together, and sometimes they must climb up long, steep, tiresome and almost inaccessible mountains."

This poor woman was taken to Canada,

behind the farm-lands of Melvin village. The precipitous face of Bald Peak, the southernmost important summit of the Ossipees, forms a grand background to a very lovely landscape.

Sitting, on an Indian-summerish afternoon, under the umbrella-shaped shelter erected at the top of Crow's Nest, with a wind-harp sending out a wild strain now and then from somewhere in the roof above you, the sky-tints of the harebell at your feet contrasted with the delicate

where she remained for sixteen months, part of the time the unhappy slave of a brutal aboriginal master, who required of her the most menial drudgery. She found shelter in a nunnery after awhile, and was eventually restored to her friends.

It was a very unsafe region to live in,

The Falls of Song.

but the fascinations of pioneer life seem to have been irresistible to those first-settlers. Fortifications for their protection were here and there erected; traces of them are left at the lower end of Lake Winnesquam, and at some other points. The native tribes near Lake Winnepesaukee, the Ossipees, the Pemigewassets,

and others, seem to have been peaceable and friendly, but they gradually disappeared as the white men began to settle themselves around the Winnepesaukee basin, about the year 1760.

The name of Lovewell, the captain of the famous Pequawket fight in 1725, lingers among these hill-fastnesses yet.

Lovewell's River, — which perpetuates his name — is the principal stream that flows through the Ossipee mountains towards the east, and some remains of this ill-starred leader's fortified retreat are still to be seen near the outlet of the river, at Ossipee Lake. Traditions of a skirmish between some of his men and the Indians of this region linger only a little way from us down the mountain side.

But the wildest reminiscence of border history associated with the scenery upon which we gaze relates to Rogers' Rangers, who, having penetrated the Canadian wilderness and sacked the Indian village of St. Francis, despoiling the little Roman Catholic church of its treasures, in the autumn of the year 1765, lost their way on their return, having been led astray by the Indian guide, whom they might have expected would betray them. Strange stories are told of their wanderings, laden with the silver image and candlesticks they had sacrilegiously taken, — of weird visions which chased them down the black gorges of Moosilauke, when the delirium of starvation was upon them; of their bleaching bones scattered far and wide amid unknown forest-desolations. Relics of their flight are now and then found among these islands and along these shores; but no one can guess in what lonely valley, or upon which of the hundreds of isles that dot the azure surface of Squam Lake and Winnepesaukee, lies buried the silver image stolen from the shrine of St. Francis.

Ah! what ghosts might be conjured

up from the smiling expanse upon which we gaze! But it is not worth while to dwell upon the painful pages of the blood stained past.

Before descending from our Crow's Nest perch, a few steps down the brow of the hill will bring us to Pilhannaw's Crag, a precipice of shattered rock which contrasts well with the wooded and grassy smoothness about us: for the charm of the scenery here is not so much that of sublimity as it is of grand expanses and beautiful detail. The quaint name is a historical one. A traveller who was here in 1672 speaks of "a very Princely Bird nearly as large as an ostrich, called the *Pilhannaw*. She Ayries in the Woods upon the high hills of *Ossapy*, and is very rarely or seldome seen." If Pilhannaw were, as is conjectured, only the blue heron, she must have been a picturesque object, "ayried" on such a crag as this.

There are winding paths down the hillside leading to many an exquisite surprise of the landscape. But we return nearly as we came, and, pausing amid the wild shrubbery that fringes the home-plateau, it may be well to announce that hitherto we have only been in the outer court, the vestibule of the woodland sanctuary. The soul of the region has yet to be unveiled to us.

A turnstile — and then a footpath. To what will it lead us? It has sufficient excuse for itself in its own pleasantness. We dreamily follow its mazy turnings, through a thick intergrowth of witch-hazel and alder, of birches, beeches, and maples, watching the sun glintings on the brown sod at our feet, and on the cool border-mat of glossy gold-thread and arbutus leaves, spotted here and there with the clear scarlet of bunch-berries and partridge-berries; or we stop to guess at the lineage of a stray bird hopping from bough to bough in the greenery. But gradually we are made aware of something beside ourselves in the woods — something more than leaf or bird stirring and whispering near us. There is a lisp of waters,— a gleam of spray; a little brook is running along with us, keeping always close to our path. Here is a rustic bridge, and under it a cascade lulling itself in a tiny pool which reflects two slender white birches with a clump of brakes at their roots — a picture that captures the artist-eye at once, with its unconscious woodland grace. We are entering Glen Ossipee, the Glen of the Beautiful Brook.

The water wins us on with a picture and a song at every turn, — narrowing itself between miniature precipices, with an attempt at masculine bass in its baby-voice, that blends softly with an undertone of fairy-laughter as it slips along, spreading and crinkling and shining like the silvery tresses on a young gray head. With every few steps it pauses at a pool, and we may be inclined to pause, as it does, for reflection where the pewees come to dip their tiny beaks, and, glancing down into the pellucid shimmer of crystal over a bed of tinted pebbles, lose ourselves and our thoughts in the enchantment of this brook's many-toned cadences.

And, indeed, what a poet this little mountain wanderer is! Not even sweet-voiced Keats could sing so melodiously, though he could make his verse repeat that—

"Little noiseless noise among the leaves,
    Born of the very sigh that silence heaves;"

nor Wordsworth himself, though he listened among the wayward rivulets until he became the interpreter of their

"Beauty, born of murmuring sound."

The human voice could scarcely add anything of spiritual suggestion to the liquid harmonies that surround us; subduing, soothing, yet beckoning us onward. This Undine has already found her soul.

For a mile this bright presence descends the rocky glen, filling it with every various mood of a brook's life, from rivulet to waterfall. This next crossing we might call the Bridge of the Seven Cascades; for the stream which just now seemed so narrow has parted itself into that number of distinct little falls. We can almost distinguish the different keys upon which their songs are pitched, as we recline upon the bench beyond, leaning against the supporting trunks of poplar and pine, the hemlock-boughs behind tapping our shoulders with graceful fingers.

The rustic bridges that span the brook are laid across it so lightly that they often seem scarcely more than a net-work of overhanging branches. All has been planned with a lover-like care for the preservation of the rare natural beauty ot the place.

This evergreen arbor — we shall pass it without heeding, unless we look for it — is but a group of young trees buttressed by some fallen ones behind. The pines have carpeted it with their own brown needles, and the trailing arbutus is trying to creep in. Listen! We may hear the voices of other summers blending with the murmur of running waters; for here, when we once passed, a poet and his friends sat reading and talking of the country "Beyond the Gates"; wondering, doubtless, whether any lovlier seclusion than Glen Ossipee were ever pictured upon the visions of romancer or saint.

Just below this spot we come to the most exquisite nook on the stream — Mary's Arch — a combination of grotto and cascade, leaning bough and waving blossom and dripping moss and tinkling chime of crystal upon crystal, in which Nature seems to have turned artist, and almost to have outdone her own expectations. It is a perfect, living picture, one that we can get into the heart of, taking with us — but forgetting on the way — all our childhood's dreams of elf-land. Hither came the minstrel to whom allusion has just been made, the rightly-crowned laureate of all this lake and mountain region, — and would go no further, having a wise regard, doubtless, for "the charm of not too much."

But the brook herself has something more to do than merely to be as beautiful to look at as possible. She moves on more quietly for a time, disturbed by fewer falls; still wimpling and curling with many a pretty turn, and winning us to rest with her at some pool which the mosses of the rock underneath have tinted with vivid emerald, or to drink from some cool spring at her side. Her way has become more sombre now. She steals under the shadow of darkening cliffs, as if to avoid the grotesque shapes, suggestive of wild beasts and reptiles, that form themselves out of the jagged bowlders she must pass. And a little shiver, as of something impending, thrills us as we follow her slower course along the lonesome stretch that we feel inclined to call "The Spook's Walk."

Something does await us both; — our charming brook cannot escape the crisis of her fate. We lose sight of her for a few moments; then, as we go forward to meet her, she reappears, a vision of bridal whiteness, veiling the rocks that make a stairway for her descent with a hundred spreading rills of translucent light, — the "Veil Falls," as the cataract is appropriately named. She is a modest little cataract, however, trying to hide herself among her sheltering trees, while she concentrates her energies for another and a final effort. It is a quick, silent rush between almost meeting barriers of adamant, a flying leap, and a song ·of triumph — that last blending of many musical cascades, which they call "The Falls of Song." She has done all that a brook could do to express her own delight in being, and to make her life a gladness to the world into which she was born, and thereafter she moves on, staid and gentle, through levels that broaden to the completion of her destiny.

And her destiny is the lake. She is coming in sight of it now, lying beyond there like a great, silent, unsatisfied soul, which has received the tribute of hundreds of hearts like hers from leagues of surrounding hills, and is yet hungry for more, to send on by the messenger-rivers to the all-absorbing sea.

Dear little Brook! If she could have foreseen through what dingy canals her pure drops must run, what weary wheels of labor they must by and by turn, would she not have paused yet longer before making this last fatal plunge? But mountain brooks and mountain maidens must leave their lovely dreams behind, and give of their sweetness to refresh the fever of the work-a-day world, and help forward its complicated endeavors. By and by our forest-sprite may reappear in a mist-wreath from the ocean, then glide as a cloud to some far off hill-top, and, joining unknown rills, sing her old song over again, with new and richer intonations.

Statistically told, Glen Ossipee Brook (sometimes called Welahka) descends two hundred and fifty feet in one mile. The lower fall — of nearly fifty feet — plunges at an angle of eighty degrees into a narrow, flume-like chasm. Above and below there are traces of pre-historic convulsions. The little stream must once have been a furious torrent. An enormous loose bowlder, as large as a good-sized dwelling-house, has been discovered near the bed of the brook at a little distance below the Falls.

There are indications that the savages used a cavernous hollow below the cataract as a hiding-place from their enemies. It is well known that the Ossipees, and other native tribes, lived in constant deadly fear of Mohawk invasions. And there is a tradition that Lieutenant Chamberlain, one of Lovewell's officers in the Pequawket battle, was once pursued by an Indian to a point just above the falls, where he leaped the chasm, eighteen feet wide, and escaped. His pursuer attempted to follow, but fell from the precipice, and was instantly killed. A white arrow marks the spot where the lieutenant performed his well-nigh miraculous feat.

We have by no means exhausted the secret of our brook's loveliness. As satisfying in its way, and as suggestive of more than itself as true friendship, — anything so living as this limpid, silver-tongued presence must be lived with, to be really known. And it is wonderful how nearly an unconscious development of nature, like this, can symbolize the inspirations and the sympathies we receive from a full and friendly human heart. The world of nature and the world of spirit are indeed inseparably linked.

The usual way of visiting Glen Ossipee Brook and Falls is to go down the hill-path through the pines, coming out at the two cataracts, and then to follow the stream up to its issuing place among the alders. Whether you do so or not depends upon the question with which you seek its companionship — "Whence come you?" or "Whither go you?" We have preferred to have the second question answered first; and now we return as we came, knowing that we shall be as delightfully met as we were accompanied. The visible source of the brook is far up the hillside, in a circular spring hidden by enclosing woods, a sort of fairy-fountain, with ice-cold water perennially bubbling up through clear sands. Its real, unseen sources lie deep within the mountain's heart.

Coming out of the dim woodland-glen into the wide home-opening of breezy slope and lawn, we have a sudden feeling of being in another world, although under the same canopy of sky. How large it looks! What almost infinite distances are hinted by that pale mountain-horizon beyond the lake! And can we say whether this beloved earth of ours is more to us in its releasing immensities, or in its befriending seclusions? It is not well for us to try to do without either, so let us be grateful for both.

In this mountain-park of several hundred acres there are exploring grounds herein unsuggested, idyllic vistas, and old, overgrown highways, health-giving springs, and space-unfolding summits. We can talk them over at our leisure by and by, as a background for legends of pioneers and aborigines, sitting on the wide crescent of the verandah, between sunset and moonrise. Perhaps the good fairies, wearing gossamer caps, will bring their tea-trays out to us there, as they did once, and we shall sup by moonlight under the cloudless roof of heaven, with the blue and green mosaic of the lake as a floor below us. If it is cool, we shall finish our stories around the blazing hearth within. Curfew will warn us when it is time to retire to the world of dreams. Our slumbers will perhaps be lightly stirred from within by the imaginary chant of Indian maidens blended with tinkling waters and Æolian melodies, and it will be no surprise to us to be awakened at dawn by a chime of silver bells. And if, hereafter, any un-disillusionized child shall come to us with the artless question, "Is there, really and truly, such a place as Fairy Land?" we shall answer "There is; we have been there. It is hidden away on the mountain shores of Lake Winnepesaukee, in the beautiful Ossipee Glens."

The City of Chicopee
(1898)

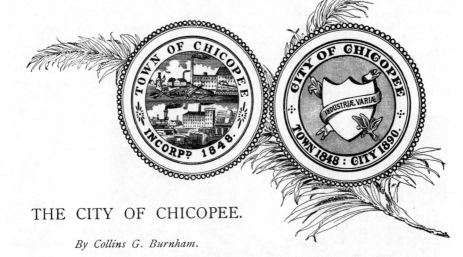

THE CITY OF CHICOPEE.

By Collins G. Burnham.

THE settlement of this fair city on the "river of elms," — whence its name, — dates back into the seventeenth century. It is connected with that of Springfield, of whose territory Chicopee was a part for over two hundred years. If less quick to sever home ties than other daughters of Springfield, this one had attained greater maturity and was better equipped than the others to set up an independent establishment.

The early doings of this child are somewhat indistinct in the family records. When and where was the first settlement within our limits? Who first ventured away from the protection of the fortified houses at Springfield to brave the perils of a more exposed region? There were two points of early settlement, one at "Skeepmuch," and the other at "Chikkuppy river's mouth," both on the south side of the river. Dr. Holland, in his History of Western Massachusetts, writes: "The first settlement of its territory occurred very early, on what is known as Chicopee street, probably within four years from the date of the first settlement at Springfield in 1636." The Chicopee street section, including the islands in the river and extending "up the great river northward to the brook

called Wullamansep," was granted, in 1654, to John Pynchon, "for a farme," and a committee was appointed by the town to view "the farme" and report its boundaries. The early records of land grants, as far as they are preserved, hardly substantiate the claim of such an early settlement of Chicopee as 1640 or 1641. It is some years later than Dr. Holland's supposed date that the records begin to give evidence of land grants for "home lotts" in Chicopee.

At the Skipmuck point of settlement, above Chicopee Falls, Symon Beamon received an allotment of land in 1656, "provided he remaine in town 5 years," a provision frequently made in connection with land grants. He remained, and in 1661 a home lot was given him. John Pynchon, who seemed to own land about everywhere in the valley, had a grant of a farm with Mr. Holyoke, "betwixt y^m" at Skipmuck. James Warriner, Jeremy Horton, John Horton, Abel Wright, John Crowfoot, Nathaniel Ely and Daniel Cooley are some of the names appearing earliest in connection with various parts of Chicopee. Rowland Thomas received a grant of land on the south side of the river in 1659, and built upon it. The town bestowed land upon Henry Chapin adjoining Thomas' land in 1660, and "liberty is granted to build on his land" at a town meeting the next year. Japhet Chapin lived at the head of Chicopee street. The cellar hole of his house existed in the younger days of some who now live on that street. The first location of the Chapin brothers was on

These brothers were the sons of Deacon Samuel Chapin of Springfield, who is the progenitor of this family in America, a friend of the Pynchons, father and son, a deacon of the First Church, a man of high character; the fine statue, modeled by St. Gaudens, erected to his memory in Springfield, is a deserved tribute to a worthy and distinguished pioneer. He is the grandfather of Chicopee, for whatever doubt may exist as to whom belongs the credit of first settling our town there is no question that the Cha-

the south side of the river. Under date of January 5, 1665, is the following: "Japhet Chapin hath granted to him by ye Plantation to him & his Heirs and Assigns forever four acres of land adjoining to that Lot his House stood on formerly on this Side or South side of Chickobee River." Two deeds given in June, 1679, now on record at Springfield, of property on the south side of the river, make mention of Japhet Chapin's house as a boundary. Henry Chapin's house "stood by a little brook" on the south side of the river, near, it is supposed, the junction of Exchange and West streets.

CHICOPEE FALLS AND CABOTVILLE IN 1838.
Redrawn from old prints.

pins populated it. Japhet and Henry Chapin were the fathers of eight sons who grew to manhood. Japhet's grandchildren numbered sixty-five, and Henry's twenty-three. Sons predominated in these patriarchal families. Many of these grandchildren settled in Chicopee; but as the genealogist of the family says, "The spirit of emigration seized early upon the descendants of Japhet and Henry. But mind ye, they did not emigrate to the

CHICOPEE FALLS IN 1857.

CHICOPEE IN 1856.

263

state of New York, nor to the rich lands of the then unknown West, but they went as far as Wilbraham, Ludlow, South Hadley, Granby, and one grandson of Deacon Samuel Chapin ventured as far as Cold Spring, now Belchertown." Notwithstanding this drain upon the family by emigration to adjoining towns, the Chapin name became a conspicuous one in all lists and catalogues in Springfield and Chicopee. The Chapin family and those related to them comprised for a long time about the entire population of the present territory of our city.

Relics of the Indians are found here. They planted in the meadows and fished in the river. One of the Indian wading places across the Chicopee was the ford by which Chicopee street people crossed the river until the first bridge was completed in 1783, with funds raised in part by a lottery. The settlers sometimes came into conflict with the red men. Japhet Chapin was in the fight at Turner's Falls. There was written on an old account book of his, now lost, these words: "I went

INDIAN RELICS FOUND IN CHICOPEE.

the los of 37 men and Captin Turner, and came home the 20th of May."

The fear of the Indians was upon the settlers. When Hannah Chapin was making a dress before her marriage to John Sheldon, Jr., of Deerfield, her mother advised her to make it strong enough to wear into captivity; but whether or not she thought to put it on before she leaped from her chamber window with her husband while the war whoop was waking Deerfield, records do not tell. She was taken to Canada and was redeemed by the elder John Sheldon, who made various journeys thither to recover captives. The house of Lieut. Wright at Skipmuck was attacked and several persons

FROM THE OLD CHURCH.

out Volunteare against ingens the 17th of May, 1676, and we ingaged batel the 19th of May in the morning about sunrise and made great spoil upon the enemy and came off the same day with

IN THE OLD CEMETERY.

killed in the summer of 1708. In a diary kept by Deacon Edward Chapin of Chicopee is frequent mention of encounters between the settlers and the Indians, and evidence of the fear that the enemy would break through the frontiers and descend upon this part of the valley. He wrote one day in May, 1747: "This day I was called upon to bear arms, there being a great alarm. Husoock was beset by Indians on Monday last." A later entry: "About this time the scalpers come in,

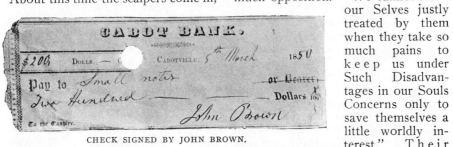

CHECK SIGNED BY JOHN BROWN.

having been out about a month." A house that stood just north of the present church on Chicopee street, as some recall who have seen it, had its door thickly studded with nails to give it greater resistance to Indian hatchets.

A minor feature of early life was slavery. The first slave in town was, perhaps, Roco. We learn this because Colonel Pynchon desired a grant of more land at Skipmuck, where, we read, "he is settling Roco, his negro." The earliest list of the First Church, 1753, bears the name Pompe. It is a tax list for church expenses, and Pompe, like his master, is taxed a sixpence. Recently a catalogue of thirty abolition books, an annex to the Sunday School library, has come to light, and we know what strong abolition doctrine was taught in 1839. Some years later some Chicopee citizens purchased the freedom of a fugitive slave who was living in town, that his master might not claim him again.

The relation of church and state in early New England makes the formation of a parish an important event in our history. The people north of the

river were the ones most interested in the movement for a parish. There was no bridge across the Chicopee river, and the journey to church was a hard one. They felt able also to settle a minister among themselves. The Springfield parish, interested in building a new meeting house, objected to any separation. In their petition to the General Court, Chicopee people esteem it "extreeme hard" that their fellow parishioners should make so much opposition. "We cannot think our Selves justly treated by them when they take so much pains to keep us under Such Disadvantages in our Souls Concerns only to save themselves a little worldly interest." Their petition was granted, June 30, 1751; the first parish meeting was held July 30 following, and in September, 1752, the first minister, Rev. John McKinstry, was settled.

The parish bounds extended over the Connecticut, including a part of

GEORGE S. TAYLOR.
First Mayor of Chicopee.

West Springfield and all of Holyoke. This part of the parish was assessed to settle the minister, but not to build the meeting house. Deacon Chapin, in his diary, gives us a pleasant view of the interest in building the first meeting house. On New Year's day, (1751), the people "with united voices declared for cutting timbers" for it. Two days later, "about 40 men advanced into the woods," and the next day half that number finished cutting the timber. How merrily the axes rang, wielded by those stout arms! Then they wait for snow. Five days pass; then "thers snow eno, O we are very glad;" but when the snow is "almost gone as twere," they are sad. The midwinter month passes and no sledding; but with the new month comes a "week of Comfortable proper winter weather and pretty sledding" and the "Chicopee MH Timber got Home very successfully." On June 5 the record is: "This Day thro ye Indulgence of Heaven we had our Meeting House Raised with great Safety and Joy." Remembering the abundant

THE BLUFFS.

supply of liquors furnished on such occasions, the entry, "with great Safety," is significant. Not all raisings had such happy issue.

The dimensions of this meeting house were 43x33 feet. It stood north of the present meeting house on Chicopee street. Though raised so safely and joyfully, it was not wholly finished until 1765; but it was occupied when the minister came, and to the call of the drum the people assembled and took the seats assigned them by the committee for "seating the meeting house," on the principle that "age be esteemed Equivalent to Four pounds of estate." Our ancestors

CHICOPEE FALLS.

frowned upon "gold rings," and had no "respect to him that weareth gay clothing"; but they did have a code of procedure for seating the meeting house that was not altogether unworldly, or scriptural. The "unseated pew" in this plain house was for "the use of Girls yt are under sixteen years of Age"; and the negro pew was in the gallery.

By means of the parish Chicopee obtained ecclesiastical independence.

The act of incorporation was signed by the governor, April 29, 1848.

Chicopee came into the family of towns well equipped. The assessed valuation was $2,476,210.00. The population was 7,861. She had highways, newspapers, schools, churches, well-developed water power turning the wheels of established industries, and, above all, industrious, intelligent, and public-spirited citizens.

City life began with a charter of the

POINTS NEAR THE FALLS.

The next step was municipal independence. For fifty years Chicopee has been walking the paths of the municipal world by herself. A move on the mother's part to form a city establishment aroused the daughter to gain municipal separation. She thought the proposed change would not benefit her, and did not relish an extra tax for a city house while living in the country. So when the mother began to set her cap for a mayor, the daughter decided to live by herself.

usual pattern, but recently we have adopted some new municipal fashions. The first venture in municipal ownership was made in 1892. The legislature had granted authority to purchase the property and privileges of the existing water companies, and to enlarge their capacity by the use of new sources of water supply. The city now owns a system of water supply, including pumping station, standpipes and other necessary equipment, of the estimated value of about $400,000,

THE CHICOPEE RIVER, THE AMES WORKS AND DWIGHT MILLS.

THE CHICOPEE RIVER, SHOWING ELECTRIC LIGHT PLANT AND HIGH SCHOOL.

capable of furnishing 2,800,000 gallons of water daily. The net income of the water department from March 1, 1893, to December 1, 1897, was $32,382.32; that is, the department pays its running expenses and the interest on its bonded debt and has returned the sum named to the treasury of the city. A board of three commissioners has charge of this department, employing a superintendent.

The city embarked in the electric light business in May, 1896. Previous to that date there was, as usual, the purchase of a franchise, formerly granted "without money and without price," for a good round price, and the erection of a new station and its equipment with high-grade apparatus. This property is now valued at $89,543.22, after the five per cent depreciation charge required by state law has been made. The department has had but a brief space in which to show results; but the report of its work for the first full year is promising:

Total income from street lights, $9,650.00; total manufacturing expense of street lights, $9,242.17; total income from incandescent lights, $5,877.92; total manufacturing expense of incandescent lights, $2,-892.95; profit on lights, $3,392.14.

The profit on street lights seems small; but we quote from the superintendent's report: "The street lighting system has made a creditable showing, inasmuch as the amount of light furnished has been increased sixty per cent over the amount previously supplied the city, and at a manufacturing cost inside the prices formerly paid by the city." This means to the public that the lamps burn longer nights, and that the almanac is not consulted so frequently to learn if the man in the moon, who formerly possessed great power in extinguishing street lights, is expected to show his face. The service to private houses is in its infancy, but as the demand for this service increases the profits of the light department will grow larger. Chicopee is well satisfied with its experiments in municipal ownership.

Our new charter, which went into operation this year, gives us a mayor and a legislative department, consisting of one alderman from each of the seven wards and ten at large. The mayor, clerk, treasurer, aldermen and school committee are elected by the voters; the auditor, collector and messenger by the aldermen; the solicitor, marshal, superintendent of streets, overseers of the poor and water com-

HON. GEORGE D. ROBINSON.

missioners are appointed by the mayor. The distinctive features of the charter are a single legislative board and the separation of the legislative and administrative departments. No member of the board of aldermen has anything to do with the expenditure of money, or with the appointment or election of any officer who expends money. T h e mayor has no vote. The principle of minority representation is adopted. Each voter ballots for only three of the five aldermen annually elected.

Chicopee soldiers have been in many campaigns. The early settlers went out "against ingens." They defended their homes at the frontiers. Chicopee men lost their life in the campaign against Louisburg in 1745. In the cemetery on Chicopee street, on Decoration Day, flags wave over the graves of Revolutionary soldiers.

The militia served as a safe means for the gratification of military ardor after peace came; and of more than one olden time citizen it could be said, as of John Gilpin:

"A train-band captain eke was he."

No poet has sung the praises of our militia-men; but of one his biographer writes: "He had quite a military genius, but no opportunity to display it, except in the militia." The Cabot Guards was the military organization of fifty years ago in Chicopee. The name of the first captain, Jones S. Davis, heads the list of those who signed the by-laws of the company. The Guards in their flourishing days mustered about sixty men. They led the usual life of a militia company in times of peace — drilling, attending musters, doing escort duty, arrayed in all the glory of their blue uniforms with the buff trimmings, gilt buttons and gold lace. The company disbanded long ago. An organization of survivors was formed in 1880; but now only four are left of the four score and more whose names are on its records. At some funeral of late years one or two of the survivors may have been seen

GOVERNOR ROBINSON'S HOME.

with crape upon the arm and a ribbon on the breast marked: *Cabot Guards, Co. F, Tenth Regiment, M. V. M., 1844.* The dead and the living were comrades in the days of old lang syne.

Our citizens rendered noble service in the war of the rebellion. Hundreds of men were busy in the shops forging instruments of war, and other hundreds bravely used them on many a battlefield. The Tenth Massachusetts regiment marched away with   38

HON. GEORGE M. STEARNS.

son, and gives silent testimonial to his diligence and fidelity, and also to the love he bore to those whose service and patriotism he recorded. This manuscript volume contains the names, as far as the compiler could obtain them, of all citizens of Chicopee who served in the army and navy, of those who were assigned to the town by the state, and of non-residents who enlisted as a part of the town's quota. His regiment, the period of his service, a list of the engagements in which he took part and in every case where the necessary information could be gained, a brief sketch also of each man's life, are given. The list contains the names of

Chicopee men in its ranks, and the Seventy-seventh with 62 men. The First Massachusetts regiment of cavalry had 57 Chicopee names on its roll, while the Forty-sixth had 105. The town furnished its quota for the call of nine months' men by enlistment. An entire company composed of and officered by Chicopee men went into the first camp of the Thirty-seventh regiment. In the care of the city clerk is a record book of which our citizens may well be proud. It is in the handwriting chiefly of George D. Robin-

MR. STEARNS'S HOME.

529 residents of Chicopee who served in the army, and of 38 who were in the navy, with the name of the ship in which each served. This volume was compiled under the direction of the city. It is a story of camp and march and battle, of hospital and prison, of suffering and death, a glorious record of devotion and heroism, from the war's sad beginning to its end, of our citizens, who left the farm, the store, the loom, the lathe and the forge, to defend the Union.

Two tablets at the entrance of the city hall bear the names of seventy-two soldiers whose lives were given for the life of the nation. The decreasing number of the survivors are gathered into the Otis Chapman G. A. R.

THE STEARNS MEMORIAL GATE, FAIRVIEW CEMETERY.

EDWARD BELLAMY.

Post, a name commemorating a citizen and officer of the town who was active in filling its quota and won the hearts of the boys by his kindly interest in them.

Chicopee is a manufacturing centre. Our seal bears the motto, *Industriae Variae*. We are a community of skilled workmen. Our rich men have for the most part made their money in the industries that have made our name so widely known. Manufacturing began at the Falls 110 years ago, when James Byers and William Smith erected a furnace and made hollow iron ware from ore dug in the vicinity. We are told that "the furnace was considered a work of no small magnitude in those days." As we study the historical strata we discover the fossil remains of extinct species of industry. The pots and kettles of the blast furnace are in the lower strata. Paper was made here long before our neighbor, the Paper City, existed. Leather cuttings for boots

and shoes were made here, we find, in the past. Some claim the invention of lucifer matches for Chicopee. Some grant it to us; but the more conservative, considering that other places claim the honor, judge the invention to be a case of spontaneous combustion simultaneously at several points. At any rate, matches were made here, and Chicopee smokers could light home-grown tobacco with home-made matches. Somewhere are to be found relics of ship building. "This Day met at South Hadley a number of Gentlemen And entering into articles concluded on Building a Schooner at Chickapee." So wrote Deacon Edward Chapin 150 years ago. There is an extinct water traffic awaiting resurrection by the potent voice of Congress. Mention is made in the old Springfield records of a place where "Capt Gerson first made rosin at Chicopee river." One of the oldest industries not extinct is brick making. Deacon Chapin made bricks as early at least as 1751.

The leading industry to-day is cotton. It employs more people than any other single industry. A small mill equipped with two carding machines and two spinning frames of 48 spindles each was in operation here for a while over ninety years ago. The

MR. BELLAMY'S HOME.

CHICOPEE CHURCHES.

yarn was sent out to families to be woven on hand looms. The real cotton business began in 1825 at the Falls. Our two corporations are the successors of earlier ones. The Dwight is an early instance of combination, absorbing the Perkins and Cabot mills and uniting their factories to its own by building in between them, till now their mill presents a frontage but a few feet less than a third of a mile. One of the beautiful sights from the north side of the river is this long mill with its thousands of lights shining in the darkness. Mill No. 1 of the Chicopee Manufacturing Company, built in 1875 upon modern principles of mill construction, is one of the finest in the country. The products of these whirling spindles and flying shuttles seek the usual markets open to American cotton goods. The Dwight is trying the experiment of operating a mill in the South.

Fifty years ago mechanics and operatives in the mills worked twelve hours a day; and the average of men's wages was about $1.08 cents per day, and of women, $1.75 per week, exclusive of board. It cost as much to board a man as a woman received per week, while the women paid $1.37 1-2 on the average for their board.

Important to our city as is a business employing 2,700 or 2,800 people, our manufacturing body is not a monarchy ruled by King Cotton, but a republic in which other industrial interests have voice and power; and our fame as a manufacturing centre rests upon the many other products of our skilled labor. The Ames Manufacturing Company, founded by Nathan P. Ames in 1834, has given a great name in the manufacturing world to Chicopee. The list of its products is a long one. Before and during the Rebellion, implements of war were made, — swords, bayonets, cannon and projectiles. Tools for the manufacture of guns were produced and sent abroad. The British Board of Ordnance and the Royal Artillery Department of Spain received Chicopee products. And when the Chicopee boys went to battle for the nation's life, there were sabres made at home and purchased by the states of Virginia, Mississippi, Maryland and Georgia, as late as 1860, in the hands of Southern cavalry, to oppose them. Uncle Sam has sent to Chicopee when there was some dark spot on his coasts to be lighted and he needed a light-house, or when he needed a crane to lift some ponderous thing in a navy yard; and the Ames works have loyally responded. Were a thousand men to parade in the glory of the regalia of some mystic brotherhood, the Ames Sword Company could furnish all their outfit of plumed chapeaux and glittering sash and belt and gloves and gauntlets and streaming banners, a n d arm each one, if desired, with a sword of distinct pattern, but of finest metal and unsurpassed workmanship.

Our bronze work has a national fame. The equestrian statue of Washington on the Boston Public Garden is one of several pieces at the state's capital cast here. What citizen of the Bay State, or of the country, does not have a thrill of pride, when he recalls the story of the Crawford doors at the nation's capital? The models were first sent abroad to a Munich firm, which, in the dark days of the Rebellion, demanded the deposit of the contract price. The government would not discredit its ability to pay by complying with such a demand, and ordered the models returned. They came back so shattered that it took a long time to repair them. The Ames Company undertook the work, and cast the doors, to the glory of Yankee patriotism and Yankee skill.

The man who successfully demonstrated that bronze work of a high character could be done in America was Mr. Silas Mosman, who superintended this department of the Ames works for many years. Bronze work is also done by Mr. Melzar Mosman, who was associated with his father. The largest piece sent from his work-

THE CITY HALL.

shop is the equestrian statue of General Grant in Lincoln Park, Chicago. He does work from the conception of the model as an artist to its reproduction in metal.

The lover of the bicycle is familiar with the name of Chicopee. The Overman, the Lamb, the Ames, and the Chicopee Falls are our four manufacturers of bicycles. The Overman Wheel Company and the Lamb Manufacturing Company have a world-wide

FRENCH CANADIAN BOARDING HOUSES.

Nineteen hundred miles of travel over mountain ranges, through mud, water and sand and over rocks thoroughly tested the virtues of the new Chicopee warhorse.

Peace has her victories; and the plows of the Belcher & Taylor Agricultural Tool Company turn furrows in many fair fields in our own and foreign lands, — and its other agricultural implements have a like wide use. The knitting machines which one Chicopee firm makes another fits with their curiously crooked latch needles. Sportsmen shoot with the Stevens Arms Company's single-shot rifles in all climes, and some of the finest shooting with pistols has been done with Chicopee made weapons. Chicopee sporting goods are gaining a wide reputation. Englishmen and Scotchmen play golf with Chicopee equipment.

reputation for their wheels. Frank Lenz, the first to attempt a trip across Asia on a bicycle, rode a Victor. He found no bicycle paths in China or India or Turkestan or Armenia. He was murdered when his remarkable journey was nearly completed.

The 25th United States Infantry Bicycle Corps, under Lieutenant James A. Moss, mounted Spalding military bicycles, and, carrying their arms, ammunition, rations, tents and other necessary equipment, rode from Fort Missoula, Montana, to St. Louis, to test the practicability of the bicycle as a machine for military purposes.

We turn from the factory to the greenhouse and recall the work of

A CORNER OF THE SQUARE.

Dexter Snow, who was the second florist in western Massachusetts and the first in Chicopee. He was known as the "Verbena man." He cultivated this flower, beginning in

SOME OF CHICOPEE'S INDUSTRIES.

1855, till he had one of the finest collections of it in the world. He also had a rare collection of ferns. Mr. Snow was a pioneer in sending plants by mail, and his verbenas, wrapped in oil of silk and packed in old cigar boxes, went by mail all over the country. An honorable and distinguished part in the history of Chicopee was borne by Hon. George M. Stearns and ex-Governor George D. Robinson. Against their names now

"The fatal asterisk of death is set."

Each in his profession, the law, gained a high position, each filled a large place in the municipal life of the town as legal adviser and in other services, and a larger place in the affec-

tions of his fellow citizens. Besides these gifts to the bar, our city contributed to the judiciary of the Commonwealth an eminent member, the late Judge John Wells; and to the social discussions of the day her offerings are "Looking Backward" and "Equality," by Edward Bellamy.

Mr. Stearns came to Chicopee to study law. His sign still indicates his office over the Center post-office, but citizens miss the familiar sight of him descending the stairs with letters in his hand for the mail. His home was on the Hill. Governor Robinson lived opposite. Mr. Stearns was a genial host, a delightful conversationalist, and possessed a large fund of stories and a keen sense of humor. He held few public offices. He served in both branches of the state legislature, but nominations to Congress were declined. He found recreation in driving and in reading. He loved a horse and liked a novel.

Governor Robinson early in his life

was called to Chicopee to teach, and for nine years was the successful principal of the Center high school. His interest in the schools continued through life. He planned engagements to admit attendance upon the reunions of the high school alumni. He left the school for the law office. He entered political life as representative to the legislature from Chicopee. When congressional and gubernatorial honors came, he never missed the town meeting, of which he was frequently moderator. Chicopee was fortunate in having such prominent citizens as Mr. Stearns and Governor Robinson interested in municipal matters. These two men, differing in many points of character, as well as in politics, had in common a great love of home. They equally loved Chicopee, and Chicopee equally loved them.

Edward Bellamy was born in Chicopee, and most of his life has been spent here. His home, an attractive place to the friends admitted to its intimacy, has been at the Falls. He was admitted to the bar of Hampden County, but his strong literary tastes drew him to other work. "A Nantucket Idyl" and "Dr. Heidenhoff's Process" are not forgotten, although overshadowed by the popularity of his later works on social questions.

A national bank and two savings banks are our financial institutions. The First National came into existence under state law as the Cabot Bank, beginning business May 21, 1845. Several officers of this bank have checks with John Brown's name upon them. The Chicopee Savings Bank began business in 1854. It has had in these forty-four years but one treasurer, Mr. Henry A. Harris, whose continuous service is a record that has few parallels.

What school privileges were given the boys and girls of Chicopee in the days of its first settlement we do not know. Springfield made a grant in 1714 "to the farmers of Chicopee and Skipmuch" for schools, and in 1716 three precincts for schools were established, "Upper Chickopee," "Lower Chickopee," and "Skipmuch." From this date regular appropriations were made. In 1761 a two-storied school house was built on Chicopee street. It had a great fireplace. The seats in the lower room were arranged around three of its sides, on one side in three rows, on the others in two rows, each row one step higher than that in front of it. The town has made liberal appropriations for its schools, which have attained a high standard.

The City Library had its origin in Cabot Institute, a literary and social organization of long ago. The Chicopee papers of the time report the meetings and the questions for debate, among which is the following: "Will the increase of the manufacturing interests in New England tend to depress the condition of the laboring class?" The books, 900 in number, which the institute gathered, were transferred in 1853 to the town, and became the nucleus of the present library, which numbers 18,000 volumes. The library has had three homes, and needs another. The teachers, the scholars, the college girls, the clergymen and the general reading public are finding the library a source of increasing profit as they come to it with their varying needs.

Over twenty houses of worship open their doors in Chicopee, and eight denominational names tell our creedal diversities. A feature of the Grace Episcopal church is its parish house work. The equipment of this house includes accommodation for the ordinary social work of the parish and a gymnasium, baths, reading-room, pool tables and various games for men and boys. Girls also are using the gymnasium. Out-of-door sports receive attention—canoeing, foot-ball and base-ball. At Temperance Hall, the St. Joseph Total Abstinence and Benevolent Society, a Roman Catholic organization connected with the Church of the Holy Name, has its quarters, with an assembly room, parlors, reading and game rooms, a gymnasium, bath room and bowling alley.

In early days, the stage-coach, the ferries and the toll-bridge were features in Chicopee's means of travel. The locomotive engine began his race up and down the valley in 1845. Now we have the electric cars. The first street railway line was built in 1888, from Springfield *via* the Centre to Chicopee Falls. With the opening of the bridge at Willimansett (1892) the zeal for street railways waxed fervid. Men, women and children signed petitions to companies to build a line past their houses. Streets, avenues, and boulevards were marked out on the vast sandy plains. A forest of stakes shows where one speculator bought acres of land and divided it into house lots "far from the maddening crowd." Now we have three lines to Holyoke and as many to Springfield from various sections of the city.

The present population of Chicopee is about 18,000. Our valuation is a little over $9,000,000. The last considerable addition to our heterogeneous population are the Poles. They form a numerous part of the Babel chorus of tongues one hears on our streets. If their social status generally is not high, they are industrious and thrifty. Many read and write in their own language, and some of them have aspirations. They come to work in the cotton mills, and form a large per cent of their operatives. Their tenements are overcrowded. A Polish house is sure to be full. On the north side of the river at the Centre they are burrowing into the side-hills. They are gaining property; they are building homes and churches and establishing parochial schools, and some children

GEORGE D. ELDREDGE.
The present mayor of Chicopee.

are in the public schools. They are becoming voters, and the influences of their new surroundings will mould them, as they have other nationalities who have left the old world for the new.

The development of Chicopee has been in sections. The Centre, the Falls, Willimansett, Chicopee Street, Fairview, Aldenville are names of localities still presenting some distinct features and interests. Our letters come to four post-offices; our friends are confused by the various railway stations; our rogues have three lock-ups awaiting them. Yet we are growing together and attaining a stronger feeling of municipal unity.

The sections whose growth has been most noticeable of late are Willimansett, Fairview and Aldenville. At Aldenville we have a creation of recent years. Its growth is interesting as an illustration of home-making for working people. This section was opened in 1891. The building lots are of good size, varying in price from $50 upwards. The first dwellings consisted (chiefly) of an outside; the inside came because the frame was boarded and shingled. The interior finishings were meagre in most cases, the aim being to keep the first cost of the house small. Payment was made by monthly installments of $10 or more. These houses have had a development — cellars, interior finishings, paint, perhaps a piazza — till the original is scarcely recognized in the trim and comfortable home of to-day. The electric cars, the school and the church have also come.

Our city is situated in one of the most beautiful sections of the Connecticut Valley. From many points we have views of Tom and Holyoke on the north, and to the west the hills of western Hampden, while perhaps from the same spot the sweep of the majestic river may be seen with glimpses of Wilbraham hills on the east. We have facilities for the manufacturer and the skilled workman. We also have a fair city for their home, and easy communication with the larger cities and the great world beyond.

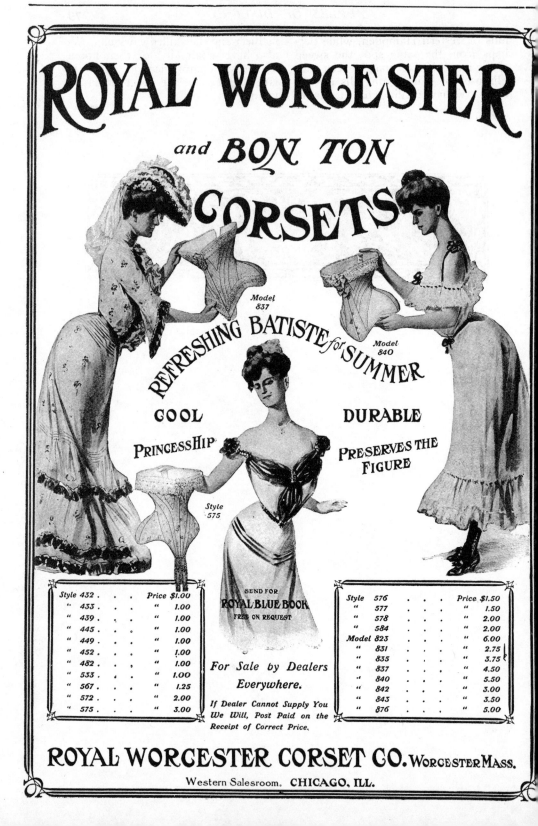

Heroism in the Lighthouse Service (1897)

HEROISM IN THE LIGHTHOUSE SERVICE.

A DESCRIPTION OF LIFE ON MATINICUS ROCK.

WITH PICTURES BY W. TABER.

N two articles of mine which have appeared in THE CENTURY — «Life on the South Shoals Light-ship» and «Life on a Lighthouse (Minot's Ledge)»—I have given instances of heroism displayed in the United States lighthouse service. The Nantucket light-ship, as the South Shoals is now called, has been moored even farther out than when I was aboard her. Her crew displays that quality of heroism which appeals most forcibly to the heart and the imagination, the unconscious, every-day heroism of those who serve on the deep; for mere service on this light-station, the most exposed in the world, imposes a strain upon the mental, moral, and physical stamina of the men which even a long and dangerous voyage does not involve. But their heroism is not passive. Though not obliged,—in fact, though cautioned against running any risk to save life, for fear their own ship might be left short-handed in case of disaster to themselves,—they have never

hesitated to lower away and hasten to the rescue of the shipwrecked.

The most noted instance of heroism in the lighthouse service was, however, the devotion to duty of the two assistant keepers of the first Minot's Ledge lighthouse, which was destroyed in the great storm of April, 1851. These men—one a German, the other a «Portugee»—«kept a good light» until it was extinguished by the rising sea, in which they themselves soon after lost their lives.

When the Sharp's Island light in Chesapeake Bay was carried away by ice, the keepers, though they could have abandoned it and made sure of their own safety, tended the light to the last, and clung to the structure, so that when they were rescued, after many hours of peril, they were able to report that they had saved a large portion of the valuable apparatus.

Some of the most picturesque light-stations in the United States lighthouse establishment are on the rocks and islands off the coast of Maine. The ever-surging ocean; the fissured granite, seaweed-stained and tidemarked; the overhanging pines, gnarled and wind-whipped into fantastic shapes, impart a wild beauty to these sites. The towers which stand thereon are among our oldest coast lights, are built of granite the hard gray of which has been softly darkened by age, and are of the old-fashioned type which the lover of the sea always associates with the idea of the school which she had been attending at Ragged Island. It was characteristic of the life these people lead—this girl's returning to the rock from school in midwinter, in an open boat across a long reach of ugly sea.

When the *Iris* lay to off the rock we cast

ENGRAVED BY M. HAIDER.

A SOUTHEAST GALE.

a lighthouse. Rising with an antique grace from among their picturesque environs, they seem peculiarly fitted to shed their light like a benediction upon the waves.

About a lighthouse which even among these is conspicuous for its beauty—that on Matinicus Rock—cluster a number of incidents which give it peculiar interest. Life there is, as it has been for many years, a constant struggle of human nature against the elements which seek to wear it out. When the lighthouse tender was off Matinicus Island, six miles north of the rock, we spied, about half-way across the reach, a dory laboring in the waves. Our mate, a typical old sea-dog who had braved danger in pretty nearly every part of the Western ocean, remarked, «That fellow has cheek, to be out here in a dory in such a sea!»

As we approached the dory we discovered that one of the assistant keepers of Matinicus Rock was at the oars, while in the bottom sat a girl, warmly wrapped, and utilizing one of the seats as a back-rest. Having taken the dory in tow, we learned that the keeper was bringing his daughter home to the rock from loose the dory, and the assistant keeper, having safely landed his daughter, returned with Keeper Grant. There were now stowed in the little craft, besides myself, two of the keeper's nephews. They had passed their boyhood on the rock, and had made use of this chance to revisit their old home. There were thus five people in the dory, besides some baggage.

The landing was sheltered by a rocky ledge which jutted out in such a manner that in order to get behind it the dory was obliged to turn broadside on to the sea. This morning the breakers were executing what was nothing less than a grand flank movement around the southwestern end of the rock, and rushing in upon a ledge a little to the left of the landing. We made the passage safely to the point where it was necessary to turn. For a while we lay stern to the breakers, riding them safely. Then, at what seemed a favorable moment, we turned the little craft. We had, however, pulled only a few strokes when we saw a series of huge breakers flanking the rock and rushing toward us. In vain we tried to slue the dory around to meet them head on. It was too heavily loaded to respond quickly enough. We saw the crest of a breaker towering above us, there was the rush and roar of a deluge, and a moment later the dory was careening over on top of the ledge abreast of which we had been, and we were spilled into the icy water between it and the rock. Had the dory been hurled against the ledge instead of lifted on top of it, the consequences might have been most serious. In fact, it was one of those narrow escapes which are very pleasant to look back upon, but which one would rather not have repeated. As an actual experience of one of the dangers to which the dwellers upon Matinicus Rock are exposed, it was, however, a brilliant success. Keeper Grant's nephews said it made them feel at home again, it was so much like old times. The father of the boys had been an assistant keeper of these lights, while their grandfather on their father's side, and their great-grandfather on their mother's, had been keepers.

The Matinicus Rock light-station stands upon a huge granite rock off the southeastern entrance to Penobscot Bay, Maine, about twenty-two miles out at sea. The rock is some thirty-two acres in size, oblong-shaped, and presents its high southeastern front to the ocean, sloping away toward the northwest. Boulders, strewn in fantastic confusion over its surface, are believed to have been loosened from its front by the destructive force of the sea applied for countless centuries, then lifted during some frenzied outburst, and deposited on top of this cliff-wall, to be gradually moved down the opposite slope when the sea, as not infrequently happens during wintry storms, makes a clean breach over the rock. Not far from the northwestern end is a boulder, the weight of which has been calculated by a stone-cutter to be about a hundred tons, which has been moved twelve feet within the memory of the present keeper, and has been moved nearly a hundred feet if appearances can be trusted. Its pointed top rises high above the surrounding boulders, and after a snow-storm resembles a miniature snow-capped mountain-peak. Where the sea sweeps around the northeastern point

it has formed along the low edge a sea-wall of small, smooth-worn rocks.

The original Matinicus Rock light-station, erected in 1827, was a cobblestone dwelling with a wooden tower at each end. In 1847 these towers were removed, and a granite dwelling with semicircular towers was built. Since then it has developed into an establishment of considerable dimensions, requiring the services of a keeper and three assistants. The granite dwelling still stands, but the present station has two gray granite towers one hundred and eighty feet apart, and connected by a low covered passage; for in high winter storms it would be a hard scramble for the keepers to make their way from tower to tower in the open, not only on account of the wind, which often blows a hurricane, but also because of the heavy seas which break over the rock. Then there are the keepers' dwellings, a brick house with engines for operating two fog-whistles (one held in reserve, in case of accident to that in use), and, as a further precaution, a fog-bell swung from a wooden pyramidal skeleton stand, a brick storehouse for oil, and the boat-house with a timber-way slanting into the water, up which the boats are hoisted by a winch. The towers are ninety-five feet above the sea. The lights, classed as of the third

A BIT OF THE SHORE.

order, are seen fifteen miles away. The rock where the towers stand is fifty feet above the sea, and presents what seems a precipitous front to the ocean. Yet the waves have beaten a sluiceway out of the granite, up which the seas rush, bursting among the boulders, and hurling tons of spray in all directions, or making a clean breach over the rock, the water pouring like a cataract down the northwestern slope, now losing itself among the rocks that are strewn in all directions, now striking one of them, and spouting high into the air, now streaming through some granite trough toward the reach of breakers. The sea has indulged in some curious pranks during these larks. The occupants of a room in the second story of one of the dwellings were awakened one night by a crash of window-glass and a flood of icy water pouring in upon them, and were obliged to flee for safety. The windows had been broken by spray from a wave that had burst among the boulders. A favorite amusement of the ocean was to bowl down the whistle-house, as if intent upon diminishing in some way the efficiency of the station. The old whistle-house stood a little farther forward from the eastern tower than the present structure. That little was just too much. Two buildings on that spot were lifted off their foundations and strewn among the rocks, the boiler being rolled more than a hundred feet. The old foundations, considerably strengthened by a breakwater, now form a guard for the new whistle-house.

Several of the violent storms that have whirled over Matinicus Rock have tried the fortitude of the little band of faithful watchers upon it. One of these watchers, Abby Burgess, has become famous in our light-house annals, not only for long service, but also for bravery displayed on various occasions. Her father was keeper of the rock from 1853 to 1861. In January, 1856, when she was seventeen years old, he left her in charge of the lights while he crossed to Matinicus Island. His wife was an invalid, his son was away on a cruise, and his other four children were little girls. The following day it began to « breeze up »; the wind increased to a gale, and soon developed into a storm almost as furious as that which carried away the tower on Minot's Ledge in 1851. Before long the seas were sweeping over the rock. Down among the boulders was a chicken-coop which Abby feared might be carried away. On a lonely ocean outpost like Matinicus Rock a chicken is regarded with affectionate interest, and Abby, solicitous for the safety of the inmates of the little coop, waited her chance, and when the seas fell off a little rushed knee-deep through the swirling water, and rescued all but one of the chickens. She had hardly closed the door of the dwelling behind her when a sea, breaking over the rock, brought down the old cobblestone house with a crash. While the storm was at its height the waves threatened the granite dwelling, so that the family had to take refuge in the towers for safety; and here they remained, with no sound to greet them from without but the roaring of the

THE BREAKWATER.

ENGRAVED BY J. TINKEY.

ABBY SAVES THE CHICKENS.

wind around the lanterns, and no sight but the sea sheeting over the rock. Yet through it all the lamps were trimmed and lighted. Even after the storm abated, the reach between the rock and Matinicus Island was so rough that Captain Burgess could not return until four weeks later.

During a subsequent winter there was so long a spell of rough weather that provisions ran low, and Captain Burgess was obliged to utilize the first chance of putting off for Matinicus Island, although there was no telling how soon the sea might roughen up again. In point of fact, a heavy storm broke over the coast before he could return, and before long there was danger of famine on the rock. In this strait Captain Burgess's son, who happened to be at home, decided to brave the storm in a skiff rigged with a spritsail. A small group of anxious watchers followed the little sail with straining eyes until the storm-scud hid it from sight. Twenty-one days passed before he and his father returned—days of hope alternating with fear, and the hardship of meager fare through all, the daily allowance dwindling to an egg and a cup of corn-meal each, with danger of that short ration giving out if the storm did not abate. During all this time Abby was obliged not only to care for the lights, but also to tend an invalid mother and cheer up the little family in its desolate state.

In 1861 Captain Burgess retired from Ma-

A JIG IN THE KEEPER'S PARLOR.

ENGRAVED BY PETER AITKEN.

Grant proved a very apt pupil—so apt that he was soon able not only to take care of the lights, but also to persuade his instructress to let him take care of her. She became his wife and his helpmate in a double sense, for not long after their marriage she was appointed an assistant keeper. When she was married she had lived on the rock eight years, and she remained there until 1875, when her husband was appointed keeper, and she assistant keeper, of the light on White Head, an island separated from Spruce Head only by a narrow channel. Matinicus Rock, twenty-two miles out at sea, with the grand sweep of the ocean, the rough shores of Ragged Island and Matinicus Island on the west, the dim outlines of Vinal Haven to the north, and in the background the dark, towering forms of the Camden Mountains—this rock, with its wilderness of boulders, its wind, snow, and fog, its shrieking whistle and clanging bell, its loneliness and perils, had been her home for twenty-two years. There

tinicus, Captain Grant and his family succeeding him. And now the grim old wave-rent rock became the scene of as pretty a romance as could be devised. A son of Captain Grant had been appointed assistant to his father, and Captain Burgess had left Abby on the rock to instruct the newcomers in the care of the lights. Young she had performed the triple duties of wife, mother, and lighthouse-keeper. The transfer to White Head brought some change from the old accustomed surroundings; but the duties, requiring such faithful performance, were the same. The Grants remained fifteen years in charge of White Head. In May, 1890, they removed to Middleborough in Plymouth

County, Massachusetts, expecting to pass the remainder of their lives out of hearing of the turmoil of the sea. Yet life away from it seemed strange and unattractive, and two years later found them again on the coast of Maine, this time at Portland, where the husband had reëntered the lighthouse establishment, working in the Engineers' Department of the First Lighthouse District. With them lives Captain Grant, who in the fall of 1890, at the age of eighty-five, retired from the position of keeper of Matinicus Rock, which he had held for twenty-nine years.

Shortly before leaving White Head Mrs. Grant wrote to a friend:

Sometimes I think the time is not far distant when I shall climb these lighthouse stairs no more. It has almost seemed to me that the light was a part of myself. When we had care of the old lard-oil lamps on Matinicus Rock, they were more difficult to tend than these lamps are, and sometimes they would not burn so well when first lighted, especially in cold weather when the oil got cool. Then, some nights, I could not sleep a wink all night, though I knew the keeper himself was watching. And many nights I have watched the lights my part of the night, and then could not sleep the rest of the night, thinking nervously what might happen should the light fail.

In all these years I always put the lamps in order in the morning and I lit them at sunset. Those old lamps—as they were when my father lived on Matinicus Rock—are so thoroughly impressed on my memory that even now I often dream of them. There were fourteen lamps and fourteen reflectors. When I dream of them it always seems to me that I have been away a long while, and I am trying to get back in time to light the lamps. Then I am half-way between Matinicus and White Head, and hurrying toward the rock to light the lamps there before sunset. Sometimes I walk on the water, sometimes I am in a boat, and sometimes I seem going in the air—I must always see the lights burning in both places before I wake. I always go through the same scenes in cleaning the lamps and lighting them, and I feel a great deal more worried in my dreams than when I am awake.

I wonder if the care of the lighthouse will follow my soul after it has left this worn-out body! If I ever have a gravestone, I would like it to be in the form of a lighthouse or beacon.

Before Captain Grant retired from the rock three of his sons had served under him as assistants, and one of them succeeded him as keeper. But the old rock still has such attractions for the old keeper that he visits it at intervals. The summer he was eighty-seven years old he went mackerel-fishing from the rock, and returned with the largest individual catch to his credit.

His grandchildren, the nephews of the present keeper, who went out with me on the *Iris*, loved every inch of the rock. «Few children who are brought up on the mainland,» said one of them, «have such good times as we had.»

Along the edge of their rocky home, and among the boulders, these boys had roamed so often that what to a casual observer would seem nothing more than reaches of fissured granite and a confused heap of jagged rock had assumed for them that variety of form and feature which we would look for in a highly diversified landscape. Every little indentation became a cove, every little pool among the rocks a pond, and for these miniature topographical features they had names like Spear Point, Western Guzzle, Devil's Gulch, Fort George, Canoe Pond; while a mass of boulders became the Rocky Mountains of this thirty-two acres of granite.

On Canoe Pond they built a miniature fishing-village, with all its accessories. Besides the dwelling they erected four little wharves, «flakes» (the long tables on which fish are cleaned and split), and fish-houses—all, of course, on a Lilliputian scale. On the pond they had various typical little craft—the dories so characteristic of the New England coast, smacks, lobster-sloops with club-sails, and even a steamer that had clockwork for an engine, and transported fish from the village to a port at the opposite end of Canoe Pond. On a point at the entrance to the village harbor they erected a miniature lighthouse; the shallows in the harbor were buoyed, and on one ledge they set a cage-spindle as a day-mark. The lobster-boats had the regulation lobster-pots, and there were reels for drying the nets, for which latter mosquito-netting was utilized. The boys split and salted minnows at the flakes, packed them in little barrels, and shipped them by steamer to the trading-port across Canoe Pond. Trade was facilitated by money from the Matinicus Rock mint, which issued copper for gold and tin for silver, while cigar-box stamps served as greenbacks. The fame of this fishing-village spread all over Penobscot Bay, fishermen often putting in at Matinicus Rock for a look at it.

Gulls and ducks by the thousands circle about the rock. The gulls make their nests among the broken rocks at the northern end, and the boys found no end of amusement hunting for eggs. They constructed two gunning-stands on the sea-wall, building two sides of loose stones, and roofing them with driftwood, and thus had many a shot at the

A FUNERAL.

end of the rock are filled with a soil so rich that it has been sent for from Matinicus Island, and, even from the mainland, for flower-potting. The elder Grant had an old sailor's love of flowers, and he scraped together enough soil from the crevices to make a little patch of ground, and there he planted a flower-garden the beauty of which was noted far and near. The steamers which ply between Boston and St. John, New Brunswick, pass the rock several times a week, but in the night, on their regular trips. Extra trips, however, may bring a steamer of this line to the rock during the day. Of course there is a bond of sympathy between the seafarer and the lighthouse-keeper; and in summer, when it was possible on these extra trips to do so, the captain of the steamer would lay her to abreast of the rock long enough for Captain Grant to put off in a dory with a large bouquet from his garden, and the captain of the steamer would reciprocate with a bundle of newspapers.

When I was on Matinicus Rock it had eight inhabitants: the keeper, who is a bachelor; his housekeeper; and the three assistant keepers, one of whom had a family of three girls living on the rock. It was the eldest of these that we met in the dory half-way across from Ragged Island, on her return from school. The second girl had charge of the chickens, but she had not yet been obliged

ducks as they swam in to feed on the mussels that had been washed up on the ledges. Often the ducks were so numerous that the sportsmen desisted, because gunning would simply have been slaughter.

The little family was not without its sorrow. A sister who had been born on the rock died there, and was buried in a fissure of the granite, the open end of which was walled up with brick. This little soul had never been off the rock. The thirty-two acres of granite about which the sea was ever beating formed her world, and there she now lies at rest.

Some of the crevices near the southern

to imperil her life in rescuing them, as Abby Burgess once did. The coop stands picturesquely among the rocks on the southwestern end, a stony path winding in and out among the boulders descending to it. The wind howls about the coop, and the chickens, as they wander over the rocks, can see the spray dashing over the ledges. These chickens are a thoughtful-looking lot. Though well fed, they seem moved to melancholy by the constant surging of the sea about their little world. Even the rooster, who need fear no rival from a neighboring barn-yard, does not strut about with the pride of a bespurred cavalier, and his crowing is saddened by a pathetic overtone.

The ducks—there is a flock of tame ones on the rock—are more in their element. But in winter they, like the chickens, are often storm-bound in their coop several days at a time; and as conversation under such circumstances is apt to flag, they, no doubt, fall to meditating, which probably accounts for their serious air and their disinclination to quack except at infrequent intervals. Perhaps while out of the coop in fair weather they are making mental notes for debate during the next blizzard. The surroundings of their coop are such as to cause even a very dull duck to reflect. It stands with its back to an old boat-house, and is fenced in with lobster-pots and half of an old wherry.

It is said that in desolate stations like that on the rock keepers will sometimes pass days without exchanging a word, not because of any ill will between them, but because they are talked out. I am sure, however, that this never happens on Matinicus Rock. The keeper is one of those kindly souls who always have a pleasant word, and his assistants have caught his spirit. He is a well-read man. Like many of the more intelligent keepers in the service, he manages to make time that would otherwise hang heavy on his hands pass pleasantly by utilizing the little library which the Lighthouse Board supplies, the library being changed from time to time. He has been for some years a subscriber to THE CENTURY, having been first attracted to it by the Lincoln biography and the Siberian articles; and about the time it is due he endeavors, no matter what the weather, to pull across to Matinicus Island for the mail. He performs his duties in a cheerful spirit, and he loves Matinicus Rock. Before coming there he sailed with his father. During the war the Confederate cruiser *Tallahassee* approached the rock. The Grants thought she would shell the towers, but they remained at their posts. They saw her destroy a number of small fishing-vessels, and this so incensed the younger Grant that he forthwith transferred his services to the United States navy. After the war he sailed on the lakes, but he

FLOWERS FOR THE STEAMBOAT.

ENGRAVED BY R. C. COLLINS.

WATCHING THE «TALLAHASSEE» DESTROYING FISHING-BOATS.

missed the smell of salt, and returned to the rock. Like every intelligent seafarer, he appreciates the grandeur of the ocean. «Sometimes after a storm,» he told me, «when I watch the waves bursting over the ledges, I just have to shout to express my feelings.» Another time he said: «I should think the sea would get worn out beating against this old rock.» We were then standing at the northeastern end of the rock, and looking along its high face, with its deep rents and jagged points, and its rough black ledges thrown out like a vanguard to meet the first onslaught of the sea. As the great waves rushed in they burst over these ledges, and sent their spray, now in one huge white mass that, falling back into the fissures, was shattered into myriads of glistening particles, to be blown in nebulous showers before the wind, now whipped into fantastic shapes, now taking the ledges at a leap and landing high upon the rock. Over all blew a fine spray that half veiled the gray towers at the extreme end of the vista. Not far behind us

was the huge boulder which the sea had moved from its original point of rest. We could not see it as we looked at the ocean; but we felt its nearness, so that coupled with the grand scene before us was the sense of the vast power vested in the ocean when it vents its wrath.

The keeper owns the only quadruped on the rock—a cow. This valuable beast is named Daisy. Like the chickens and ducks, Daisy is sensibly affected by her environment. The very method of her landing upon the rocks was enough to cause her to lose faith in human nature during the rest of her existence. She was brought over from Matinicus Island in a small boat, and when within a short distance of the rock the boat was tipped over so far to one side that Daisy lost her balance and fell into the water, where she was left to swim ashore. Although she is an object of affectionate regard to the little community on Matinicus Rock, she does not seem to have forgotten her involuntary plunge. Often I have seen her standing upon that mass of barren granite, the only living thing in view, the wind furrowing up her hide. She would gaze out upon the wild waste of waters with a driven, lonely look, the pathos of which was almost human. The patches of soil on the rock yield about grass enough to last her during the summer. In winter the sear aspect of these patches adds to the desolate appearance of this treeless, shrubless ocean home. Often the cow looks across the reach in the direction of Matinicus Island, and moos pathetically, as if longing to wander over the distant pastures. She formerly found some companionship in a rabbit, with which she was accustomed to play at dusk; but the rabbit died. The cow's existence was again brightened by the birth of a calf. It became necessary, however, to kill the little cow baby, and the mother's grief over the taking off of her offspring was so intense that she refused food for three days.

There are usually several dogs on the rock that are trained to retrieve ducks. At present, however, the cow is the only pet. The keeper once captured a young seal which had been washed up among the ledges, and succeeded in taming it to such a degree that it would drag itself along after him, and whinny when it could not follow him. Attached to the boat-house is a bird-cote, where for several seasons a family of martins has made its home.

One Sunday we had what the keeper called « a regular old grayback of a snow-storm.» During the morning the keeper told me that

Captain Grant had usually conducted a short service while keeper of the lights, and had done so again during his visits to the rock. I offered to read aloud from the Bible and lead in singing a few hymns for as many as would care to join. He was delighted with the suggestion, and in the evening every member of the little community was in the keeper's dwelling, and we had some Bible-reading, chiefly from the Psalms, with the Sermon on the Mount as a substitute for a discourse, interspersed with hymns like « Pull for the Shore,» which, because of the nautical surroundings, I judged would most appeal to the congregation on Matinicus Rock. I do not know that anything has touched me more than the simple earnestness of these worshipers as they lifted their voices above the roaring of the wind and the detonation of the breakers. Life on Matinicus Rock may have its hours of loneliness, but it does not deaden the finer emotions. The ever-surging, ever-sounding sea allows no dweller upon its shores to become a dullard.

The spirit which pervades the personnel of our lighthouse service is well illustrated by an experience of Keeper Grant. The wherry which now forms part of the duck-coop was not always put to such base use. It has known the touch of the sea. Keeper Grant, while an assistant to his father, started in it from the rock one stormy winter day to row over to Matinicus Island. Out in the reach the storm increased, and finally a sea filled the wherry. Its occupant's only safety lay in

ENGRAVED BY A. NEGRI.

AN UNCOMFORTABLE POSITION.

FROM A TINTYPE.

FREDERICK T. HATCH, THE ONLY RECIPIENT
OF THE GOLD BAR FOR HEROISM.

ver medal for rescuing two men from drowning while he was keeper at White Head; and Keeper Marcus A. Hanna, of the Cape Elizabeth light-station, Maine, received the gold medal for the daring rescue of two sailors from a wreck during a severe winter storm.

When the recipient of the gold medal again distinguishes himself by an act of heroism, he is awarded a gold bar, the highest honor the government can bestow. It has been awarded only once, and to a lighthouse-keeper, Frederick T. Hatch, keeper of the Cleveland Breakwater light-station, Cleveland, Ohio. The medal Mr. Hatch received for services performed while a member of the life-saving crew at Cleveland, which rescued twenty-nine persons from two vessels on two successive days during a terrific gale. The gold bar was awarded in February, 1891. A wreck occurred just outside the breakwater at night during a heavy gale and sea. The eight people aboard the wreck, among them the captain's wife, succeeded in reaching the breakwater pier; but the heavy seas swept several of them back, one of them losing his life.

Pulling to the pier in a small boat, Keeper Hatch succeeded in taking off the captain's wife; but she was hardly in the boat before it was swamped and capsized. At the risk of his life, Hatch now seized her. She was utterly exhausted and almost a dead weight; but though nearly overcome himself, he maintained his hold upon her until he could reach a line thrown from the light-station, with which he and his helpless burden were drawn to the lighthouse steps.

overturning it and climbing upon the bottom. He had saved an oar, and might easily have made a signal of distress; but he reflected that if his father came off after him, as he would undoubtedly do, and any accident happened to him, only one man, and he elderly, would be left in charge of the lights. Therefore, he simply clung to the bottom of the boat, though he was in peril of being blown out to sea or perishing through exposure in the wintry storm. By a lucky chance the wherry was blown upon Wooden Ball Island, which lies between the rock and Vinal Haven, and he found shelter in the solitary house there.

Keepers in the lighthouse service have, however, done more than display heroism within the duties required of them. A number of them hold life-saving medals from the United States government for feats of heroism performed under the impulse of a higher duty. Keeper Grant's brother, Isaac H. Grant, who married Abby Burgess, holds a sil-

Ida Lewis Wilson, whose name is almost as familiar as Grace Darling's, is keeper of the Lime Rock lighthouse in Newport harbor. She received the gold medal for the rescue of two soldiers who had broken through the ice near Lime Rock. In making the award, the government also considered the fact that she had previously rescued at least thirteen persons from drowning.

Gustav Kobbé.

ENGRAVED BY J. F. JUNGLING.

A GRAVE.

Grand Manan
and Quoddy Bay
(1878)

EEL BROOK POINT.

GRAND MANAN AND 'QUODDY BAY.

ILLUSTRATED BY BRICHER.

I HAD some thoughts of entitling this article "Fog and Fundy." For what nature has joined together, literature should not put asunder. Passamaquoddy Bay is an appurtenance of the Bay of Fundy, as is also the island of Grand Manan,* but to describe the Bay of Fundy without mention of the fogs that harbor in it would be as grave a short-coming as to write a scientific treatise on fog without analysis of the article as found in the Bay of Fundy. Fogs, we may say, are never missed in the Bay of Fundy, though *mist* is a feeble word to denote them. To *see* the Bay of Fundy, in fact, in some weathers one might about as well look on the map, and go no further.

There is another conspicuous feature of the Bay of Fundy, namely, its swollen and tumultuous tides, which sweep with unexampled volume and swiftness in from the Atlantic, and up its harbors and rivers, rising to an audacious height, and, when retiring, uncovering an impressively wide expanse of rock-bound and weed-matted shore. At low tide in the Bay of Fundy the shores look as if the sea had receded never to return. At high tide it looks as if the deep was rising to overwhelm the land. To stem the resulting currents even under steam is sometimes difficult; under sail or with the oar, it is often impossible.

"Does the Gulf Stream have any thing to do with forcing these tides in here?" I innocently asked of a landsman on Grand Manan as we were discussing the phenomenon.

GRAVE OF WRECKED FISHERMAN.

"No," was his emphatic reply; "it's more likely the tides has suthin' to do with pushin' the Gulf Stream off."

The Bay of Fundy, which may be regarded as the out-doors of the secluded precincts we are now to explore, might be called the American Bay of Biscay, except that its waters are a little less exposed to the powerful winds which sweep the open sea. It may be described to the eye as a short stout *left hand* of the Atlantic thrust up in a northeasterly direction between Nova Scotia and New Brunswick, and terminating only in a thumb and little finger. The *little finger* sinuously penetrates New Brunswick very nearly to Northumberland Strait, beyond which lies Prince Edward Island, and with which it is proposed to make a connection by means of a canal, so cutting off Nova Scotia into an immense island. The *thumb*, entering Nova Scotia and bending to the east and south,

---

* I adopt that spelling of this name which prevails on the island itself and in the British Provinces. Menan seems to be an American variation.

broadens into the Basin of Minas, which gives to the great promontory almost an inland sea. Here,

"on the shores of the Basin of Minas,
Distant, secluded, still, the little village of Grand-Pré
Lay in the fruitful valley. Vast meadows stretched
to the eastward,
Giving the village its name, and pasture to flocks
without number.
Dikes, that the hands of the farmers had raised with
labor incessant,
Shut out the turbulent tides; but at stated seasons
the flood-gates
Opened, and welcomed the sea to wander at will o'er
the meadows.
West and south there were fields of flax, and orchards
and corn fields,
Spreading afar and unfenced o'er the plain; and away
to the northward
Blomidon rose, and the forests old, and aloft on the
mountains
Sea-fogs pitched their tents, and mists from the
mighty Atlantic
Looked on the happy valley, but ne'er from their
station descended.
There, in the midst of its farms, reposed the Acadian
village."*

It is into this Basin of Minas and up along its influent Windsor River that the Fundy's tides pour with their greatest volume and

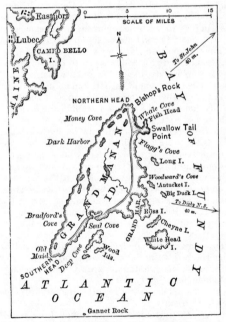

MAP OF GRAND MANAN, BAY OF FUNDY.

force, rising, it is affirmed, to an occasional height of sixty feet, and with such sudden velocity as now and then to surprise and overwhelm cattle feeding on the marsh lands by the shore. In the Windsor River, steamers, it is said, have to dodge the tides. The extreme length of the Bay of Fundy

* Longfellow's *Evangeline*.

is about one hundred and seventy miles; its width ranges from thirty to fifty miles; its depth is generally great. Its shores are for the most part bold and rocky, sometimes grandly precipitous. It is a capacious ocean pocket, filled and emptied twice in the twenty-four hours. With its tides, fogs, winds, and "iron-bound" shores, it is any thing but an inviting water to mariners, and has been the scene of some of the direst tragedies of the sea, while not without attractions of the strongest sort for the artist, the tourist, and the sportsman.

Even as I write, the daily paper brings this dispatch from the scene:

"EASTPORT, MAINE, *July* 23.—The brig *Olga*, of Scotland, has just been towed in here. She went ashore on Thursday on Murre Ledges, Grand Manan, in a fog. She was loaded with deals, and was from St. John for Ireland. She will discharge and hold a survey."

This, or much worse, is the story over and over again.

At the upper (northwestern) angle of its base the Bay of Fundy bulges into a kind of inner pocket, which receives the outflow of the St. Croix River. This river constitutes the boundary between Maine and New Brunswick, and so in part between the United States and the territory of Great Britain. This inner pocket is Passamaquoddy Bay. Just how to mark it off from the Bay of Fundy might be something of a geographical problem, inasmuch as the waters of the two mingle upon an invisible line; but the natural demarkation is furnished by a chain of islands of which Campobello and Deer Island are chief, and M'Master's, Pendleton's, and Indian islands, and the Wolves, subordinate; while the really grand island of Grand Manan lies as a solitary outpost well out upon the border of the Atlantic, content with its own sublimity.

All these islands are British territory—sentinels, as it were, upon the line.

It was on a fine July morning that from the deck of the good steamer *New York*, bound from Boston to St. John *via* Portland and Eastport, our little party first caught sight through the lifting fog of the western face of Grand Manan. "Face," I say, not *shore*, because the western front of Grand Manan, along its entire length of twenty miles or more, rises cliff-like almost perpendicularly from the water to a height ranging from two hundred to four hundred feet, presenting at a distance of a dozen miles an appearance not unlike that of the Palisades upon the Hudson River above New York. As we ran on toward Quoddy Head, close in under the wild Maine shore, the island lay off to our right, looming loftily and formidably through the dissolving mists, heavy with the shadows of the morning's sun, and massive as might be the hand-laid wall of

" ROW, BROTHERS, ROW. "

as she dropped down from Eastport, past Lubec again, and out by Quoddy Head upon the dancing, sparkling waters of the bay, provokingly died out when we were not half-way to our destination, and left us to toss about in a chop of the sea, with nothing for Skipper Sullivan to do but to muster in three of his passengers as crew for a four hours' toilsome row to Northern Head. Shall I pause here to pay tribute to the manly young sailor, just back from a long voyage, and bound now to his home at the Southern Head of Grand Manan, or to the gentlemanly young student-associate of the Boston Society of Natural History, both of whom with their strong arms served us in such good stead in this miniature extremity? or to administer a chastising word to the lazy passenger who would not row a stroke, because, as he said, it "hurt him across here" (pointing to his chest), and to the disagreeable passenger who would neither row nor offer any excuse, even a lame one, for his indolence? Is not human nature human nature in the Bay of Fundy as elsewhere? and do we not find the evil and the good "whene'er we take our walks abroad," and on whatsoever seas we sail?

The island of Grand Manan has a length variously estimated at from sixteen to twenty miles, and a width ranging from three to five. From the lofty brow of its nearly straight western face its surface slopes evenly and gently away to the eastern shore, which has an irregularly convex outline, and is for the greater part low and level. The Northern and Southern heads are connected by a well-kept road, which skirts this eastern shore, and on which, at points where it touches the most important coves, are gathered the little hamlets of the island. This habited edging is somewhat cultivated, but the sea hereabouts yields better revenues than the land; and such farms as there are have to share the coast with the forest, which in the interior and close up to the western cliffs has the island all to itself. Some twenty small fresh-water lakes dot this inland solitude, and one or two brooks find their way from these or other sources down the hill-sides to the

a giant's fortress. The outline of the island as gathered in from this point is exceedingly imposing. At that distance there is nothing to soften the apparent perpendicularity of the cliffs, which yet trend gently and gracefully away on either hand, the successive headlands showing in fine perspective as they recede. As we rounded Quoddy Head, and made our way up the narrow, tortuous, and weir-marked channel between the Maine shore and Campobello Island, past dilapidated Lubec, toward Eastport, the island temporarily disappeared; but closer acquaintance was quickly to follow.

The means of access to Grand Manan are both regular and irregular. Twice in the week during the summer season the steamer *William Stroud*, enlarged and elevated to the responsibilities and dignities of a passenger and freight traffic, runs down to the island from Eastport and the harbor and river ports above, returning the following day. She carries the mails, and is the island's only regular connection with the main-land. Reaching Eastport as we did on a Saturday, we concluded not to wait two precious days for the *Stroud*, but, as being both more expeditious and romantic, to charter a sail-boat, and so make the little voyage on "our own bottom," as it were. "Romantic" this method proved to be; but it barely escaped being not much more expeditious, for the good breeze with which the *Annie S.* was favored

ocean coves. The highway above alluded to is fairly well settled along its entire length, but the chief clustering of houses is at Flagg's Cove and Woodward's Cove, at Centreville (called also Sinclairville), between these two, at Grand Harbor, and at private conveyance must be had, by land or water.

It was just as the afternoon was blending with the evening that the *Annie S.* reached an anchorage in Whale Cove. This picturesque nook, whose beauties are derived from

FISHING SMACKS OFF NORTHERN HEAD.

Seal Cove. At Flagg's Cove, Woodward's Cove, and Seal Cove there are post-offices, the first-named being a money-order office. Flagg's Cove and Woodward's Cove are the points directly served by the *William Stroud.* To the more southern portions of the island both sea and shore, is a circular bit of pebbly beach snuggled in between the wild rocks and scraggy firs of Fish Head on the east and the beetling Eel Brook Point on the west. A sailor's snug harbor it would seem to be but for the memory of that ter-

OLD BOAT-HOUSE ON THE ROAD TO SOUTH HEAD.

rible winter night, twenty-six years ago, when the *Lord Ashburton* was wrecked on the point. On the present occasion the scene wore an aspect of secure shelter and supreme repose. The waters infolded within the cove's protecting arms lay hushed and still. The faintest ripple enlivened and only a single sail illumined the distant bay beyond. Under the hills to the left nestled a cottage or two. Behind them the sun had already sunk, and long shadows were fast gathering with the advancing tide upon the beach. The tinkling of a cow-bell and the bleating of a yew sheep in a neighboring pasture were the only sounds to be heard.

Making our landing and shouldering our luggage, we slowly ascended the ribbed and rugged neck which joins Fish Head and Swallow-tail Point to the body of the island, and which had to be surmounted before we could reach our expected shelter at Flagg's Cove. A five minutes' climb brought us to the summit, and to a view that embraced the cove before us, the trending shore to the southward, the islands and the bay beyond. Five minutes more of descent brought us to our home for the time being, with its grateful supper and still more grateful beds. It had been a rare and fortunate day and hour for the approach. How different proved the circumstances of our departure!

Accommodations for the public at Grand Manan are not as yet very ample. In fact, the public has hardly yet learned that there is a Grand Manan. Until recently visitors have had to depend on such chance hospitality as the plain homes of the islanders could afford. Two small public-houses have now been opened at Flagg's Cove. They provide comfortable accommodations and a fair table at reasonable prices. The fine view from this point when there is no fog they can not monopolize.

Our first full day upon the island being the Sabbath, we put a restraint upon our curiosity. The Grand Mananites—or should we say the Grand Mananers?—are emphatically a Sabbath-keeping people, and we could not well have done otherwise than respect their customs toward the day, even had we been so inclined. "The heft of 'em are Baptists," was one good man's reply to my inquiry as to the denominational divisions of the inhabitants. To this fact the four Free-will Baptist churches on the island would clearly testify. There is also an Episcopal church at Grand Harbor, and a small band of Latter-day Saints, who own a "temple," as they rather loftily designate their lowly meeting-house. The Saints established themselves here half a dozen years ago or so, but have never numbered more than twenty-five. They are disciples not of Brigham Young, but of Joe Smith, and do not practice polygamy. For indulging in that social luxury their former leader, Sheppey, was expelled from the fold. Their present shepherd, Elder Joseph Lakeman, was formerly a Baptist, and is commonly reputed as "a model-living man." His flock, too, are well spoken of. As a whole the churches are well supported, considering the circumstances. The minister of the most prosperous of the Baptist churches gets a salary of $400 a year, with as many Sundays "off" to preach in other pulpits, apparently, as he desires. The Church of England minister is a missionary, and gets $100 from his parish, to which $600 is added from the diocesan fund.

There being no service easily accessible to us in the morning, we went apart by ourselves over upon Swallow-tail Point, which is perhaps the most romantic and picturesque precinct of Grand Manan. The bold and rugged promontory is crowned with a light-house, and adjacent is Pettes's Cove, the very perfection of a fisherman's abode— a little bit of circular beach flanked by the frowning Swallow-tail on the one hand, and backed with a row of fish-houses and cottages, and with a fleet of boats for a foreground; the whole so retired, and approached by such a sudden turn of the road, that it bursts upon the eye without a premonition

ing us into the tower on that day. Reenforced by a trio of ladies, we paid a second visit to it on a subsequent evening, when the lantern, rising nearly fifty feet above the cliff, and nearly one hundred and fifty feet above the water, was lighted, and was

SWALLOW-TAIL LIGHT.

of what is coming, and adds to the charm of absolute quaintness that of surprise. The whole scene looks like a picture by some old master turned into a reality. In the course of our ramble we made a quiet call on Mr. J. W. Kent, the keeper of the lighthouse, who, true to the principles of the island, politely excused himself from show-

shedding its far-reaching beams around. The path of access is steep and difficult. At points it winds dizzily near the brink of the precipice. In one place it crosses an ugly chasm by means of a slender bridge, the passage of which requires a steady foot and a strong hand. This particular night, moreover, was pitchy dark. The fog was dense, and was blown by a strong wind directly in our faces, while below us the tide beat tumultuously. We could not hear each other's voices, and could scarcely see each other's forms, as we ascended and descended in single file. Such an adventure has its charm, nevertheless, though it is one not to be commended, except to persons of good courage and steady nerves. By daylight, in good weather, the promontory can be gained without the slightest peril, and proves a place of singular power and beauty. It holds one forth, as it were, in the midst of the waves, and gives him new sense of the majesty of the ocean, of the firmness of the earth, and of the feebleness of man in presence of the wilder elements of nature.

Strolling on the afternoon of the same Sabbath in another direction, we came upon an old burial-ground a short distance to the southward of the landing-place at Flagg's Cove. Here, among other more correctly wrought inscriptions to the memory of the departed, we found one which read as follows:

> The race appointed i halve run
> The combats o'er the prise is won
> And now my witness is on high
> And now my records in the skie
>
> I leve the world without a tear
> Save for the friends i hold so dear
> To heal their sorrows Lord descend
> And to the friendless prove a friend.

The stone which bears this rude lettering is of recent erection, and is the acknowledged handiwork of a firm of St. John "artists." Perhaps the stone-cutter only "followed copy."

A deeply interesting and truly pathetic spot in this same burial-ground is the last resting-place of the crew of the ill-fated ship *Lord Ashburton*, which was wrecked on Eel Brook Point in 1851. The only mark of the spot is a small wooden paling inclosing the common grave, bearing on the side toward the road a rude sign-board, on which these words are painted in black letters:

IN THE MEMORY

OF 21 Seamen Drowned on the 19 oF January 1851 Belonging to The Ship 𝕃𝕆ℝ𝔻 Ash Burton Wreck on The Northern Head of GRAND MANAN.

Curiously the paint which forms the lettering has preserved the wood under it while the rest of the surface has been worn away by the storms, thus leaving the inscription in a sort of relief. A more striking monument to the memory of these men is Eel Brook Point itself. The savage headland is in full view from the burial-ground, half a mile away. Nobody passes it without speaking of the *Lord Ashburton*, whose wreck seems to have been the most memorable the island has ever known. Standing by this lonely grave under the soughing pines, and looking across to the point, now washed by a gentle sea, it is easy to make the melancholy event with which it is associated a vivid reality.

Hard by the burial-ground there now lives one of the few survivors of that dreadful night—Mr. James Lawton. Learning of this fact a day or two afterward, some of us called upon him, and heard from his own lips the oft-repeated tale.

"The good ship *Ashburton*," said Mr. Lawton, "sailed from Toulon, France, for St. John, November 17, 1850. She was a merchantman of a thousand tons. On the 17th of January we were in sight of St. John. This was Saturday. A thick snow-storm set in and shut out all sight of land. All the next day, Sunday, we were driven about in the bay. At midnight that night we wore ship. We had just sounded, and found sixty or seventy fathoms of water. It was my watch, and I was on deck. The storm was still on, and it was so thick we could see nothing. We supposed we had plenty of water. All of a sudden the look-out saw something a little blacker than ordinary looming up in the darkness just ahead. His first thought was that it was a cloud, but before we had time to make it out we had struck, head on. It was Eel Brook Point. It was about one o'clock Monday morning when we struck. In half an hour the ship was all to pieces. There was no chance to get out the boats. Every man had to shift for himself. There were twenty-nine of us, all told. Ten of us got ashore, but two of them perished afterward by freezing. It was bitter cold. We staid under the cliff till daybreak. Three of us then managed to climb up the cliff. I worked my way over to the point where the fog-whistle now is. There was a barn there then. I crept into that, and lay there, half frozen, till afternoon, when I was found almost dead. Fifteen bodies were found Tuesday, and six afterward, including the captain's."

"Was this your first voyage?" I asked.

"Oh no," replied Mr. Lawton; "I'd eaten a good many hard biscuit before that time. I was out at St. John too, once before."

"Every bitter winter night now," he continued, "the people on the island remember that wreck, and say, '*Lord Ashburton!*'"

"And here you are settled for life?"

"Oh yes; I love Grand Manan. I shall never leave here again. The captain's brothers came for his body and carried it away, so that now there are only twenty buried up yonder, and not twenty-one. I shall lay my bones in place of the captain's by-and-by, and so make up the number."

Sabbath evening opportunity was afforded to join an island congregation in its customary worship. The hour appointed was seven o'clock, but it was nearly half past seven before the doors of the old wooden meeting-house near Flagg's Cove were opened by the tardy sexton, and the handful of people who had gathered on the door-steps, including the minister, were let in to the enjoyment of their usual religious privileges. Not all the men and boys, however, had courage to enter at once by the open door. A good proportion of these lingered without until the services were fairly begun, and then slipped sheepishly in by twos and fours behind the tittering girls, the two sexes being marked off from each other pretty much as effectively as if a rule prevailed. While the minister, an itinerant stranger, mounted the

"THE OLD MAID" AND SEA-GULL CLIFF, AT SOUTHERN HEAD.

pulpit and fumbled for his places in Bible and hymn-book, the keeper of the keys proceeded with a leisurely bearing to light his lamps. These being of the class known as kerosene, and requiring some trimming as he went along, the process was a slow one. When it was at last completed, the waiting choir, consisting of one woman at the "cabinet organ" and two men singers, struck up an "opening piece," and the service proceeded. During the long prayer the preacher, who seemed to combine the more striking qualities of both the Baptist and the Methodist styles, managed to get up considerable steam, and the sermon which followed was a prodigious one, so far at least as noise was concerned. The congregation appeared attentive, and I supposed the discourse must have taken effect as a masterpiece of pulpit eloquence, until, on the way home, I overheard a discriminating young woman say, "I never heerd sech a hollerin' sence the day I was born."

At the close of the meeting a collection was taken up for the laborer "worthy of his hire." I asked one of the pillars of the church how much he probably got. He said he "guessed a dollar or two." The probable truthfulness of this estimate had a substantiation in the jingling of pennies which attended the passing of the boxes—a sound unrelieved by any thing like the rustling of currency or bills.

Despite any possible rudeness in their religious privileges, the Grand Mananers are plainly a religious and virtuous people. They are reverent in the observance of the Sabbath day. No fishing is allowed by the laws of the Province between six o'clock Saturday evening and six o'clock Monday morning; and, so far as I could learn by inquiry, a statute so easily evaded is honestly obeyed. I saw no dram-drinking on the island, nor any public facilities for it; nor did I hear profaneness or vulgarity of speech. The people are courteous, hospitable, and kind, sober and industrious, fond of music, and with tastes generally above their advantages. There is little that is peculiar in their costumes. They measure time, to some extent, by the trips of the boat, e. g., such a thing happened "boat before last;" such a man will be at home about "boat after next." In the case of some funerals the burial takes place first, and the funeral service follows. The Provincial currency is reckoned in dollars and cents, and American money passes at a very slight discount, often, when small sums are concerned, with no discount at all. Book accounts are kept in American terms.

The population of Grand Manan is now not far from 2000, and is said to be steadily increasing. The men of course are chiefly followers of the sea. The fisheries in the surrounding waters are very productive, herring, hake, cod, and pollock being the varieties most largely taken. The herring fishery is carried on by means both of seines and weirs, the weirs being immense pens of brush-wood built in shallow water for the entrapping of the fish at high tide. The weir privileges are not free, but are rented annually by the government under the direction of the fish-wardens. The herring are cured in smoke-houses in great quantities, and then packed away to the markets of the world. The extracting of fish-oil is also an important industry. The numerous fish-houses which dot the shores, and the ancient and fish-like smell which pervades the atmosphere in many localities, combine with other signs in unmistakable evidence of the sea-faring habits of the people. A hardy and courageous race is the result—men whose brawny arms and weather-beaten cheeks tell of buffeting waves and winds; women to whom fogs and storms bring anxieties and sorrows which their sisters of different lives know little of; children who take to the water as a natural element, and who can handle an oar or sail a boat at a surprisingly tender age.

The inhabitants of Grand Manan are without a government of their own. In fact, they require very little government of any description. Their sea-girt territory forms a parish by itself in the county of Charlotte, New Brunswick, whose shire town is St. Andrews, at the head of Passamaquoddy Bay. The county is incorporated, and holds a semi-annual council for the management of its internal affairs, to which Grand Manan sends two councillors elected by its own citizens. There is, of course, a Provincial Legislature, which transacts general business much after the manner and in the forms prevailing in our State bodies corresponding, though with some differences of expression.

Almost the only public expenses of the island are for the maintenance of roads and schools. The schools are several in number, but are not graded higher than into

primary and advanced departments. The young Grand Mananer who wishes to pursue his education beyond this point must repair to the Methodist College at Sackville,

TEMPLE OF THE LATTER-DAY SAINTS.

or to the Normal School or the University at Fredericton, New Brunswick. The schools are governed by a board of three trustees chosen by the residents. The government of the Province subsidizes both the schools and the roads, the islanders meeting the remainder of the cost by a self-imposed tax. For the maintenance of the roads every male adult having a family is annually taxed three days' labor, or its equivalent in money at $1 50 a day, with one day's tax additional for every hundred pounds of property he may own. The aged are exempted, except from the property tax. The accompanying surveyor's notice was copied *verbatim et literatim* as found tacked to a fish-house door in one of the island districts, names alone being omitted. Appended was a list of taxable citizens, with the number of days' labor exacted from each.

Notis is her by given to all persons libel to preform stated labor on the Roads in —— Destrict to met at the —— Cove with tules Suted to preform the labor on Monday morning the 9 of July 1877. —— —— Survyor.

The Grand Manan produce market, if neither abundant nor varied, is reasonable as to prices. Eggs sell for twelve cents a dozen, lamb for nine and ten cents a pound, beef for fifteen. Butter is as high as thirty cents, and milk does not get lower than six. Wild berries are plentiful in their season. A novelty among these is that known as the "baked-apple." The "baked-apple" closely resembles a blackberry in structure, but is sharply distinguished from it in color, which is almost precisely that of the larger cooked fruit whose name it has appropriated. The children of Grand Manan go "baked-appling," as their main-land mates go strawberrying and blueberrying. And the "baked-apple" is said to be a peer among berries.

None of the some twenty ponds which are scattered about upon the island are very large, but they and the brooks which flow from them afford some trout-fishing, and the woods around are haunted by a variety of game, which, with the fowl of the air, make up quite an assemblage of animal life. There are a few deer roaming wild, one of which now and then attempts a swim to the main-land. There are foxes, too. Of sea-fowl the variety is large, including gulls and gannets, of course, the lesser bittern, the little auk, the little ice-bird, the sea-pigeon, sea-swallow, and gray plover, while the woods inland contribute both the American and Canada owls, woodpeckers, yellow-hammers, and other more common members of the feathered tribe.

The finer scenery of Grand Manan is to be found at the Northern and Southern Heads, and, looking from the sea, along the western face. Bishop's Rock, Eel Brook Point, Fish Head, and Swallow-tail Point, all at the Northern Head, are imposing examples of bold and rugged coast of rock, and at Southern Head the cliffs rise even more markedly out of the beating waves. Wild estimates have passed current as to the height of these lofty and lengthened walls, which are highest at Money Cove. But even there, as our keen-eyed skipper said, "after you get up 400 feet, you wouldn't find much left." Seven hundred feet is the elevation to which some imaginations have soared. The Sea-gull Cliffs at Southern Head do not exceed 350 feet, but they are sharply perpendicular from the water's edge, their base being worn away smooth by the beating waves of the Atlantic. These features of the island have long made it a favorite resort of artists, who have found in its various aspects a source of unfailing inspiration. Church, I am informed, was the first to be attracted to the spot, somewhere about 1851 or 1852. He was followed by Bradford, who took many sketches of the shore scenery. In one cliff near Deep Cove he found a profile which furnished quite a striking resemblance to the countenance of Wilkes, the English statesman, and it was duly christened with his name. After Bradford came Gifford; and among others of the profession whose names have come to be associated with the spot are De Haas, J. G. Brown, Harry Brown, Griggs, Gall, Burns, and W. E. Norton. Mr. Norton, indeed, did not content himself with brush-work; he carried off one of the island belles as his wife.

Besides the localities already mentioned, there are others which should not escape the visitor's attention. A good pedestrian would greatly enjoy an afternoon's tramp from Flagg's Cove by a backwoods road across the island to the fog-whistle near Bishop's Rock. In a somewhat nearly corresponding position at Southern Head is Bradford's Cove. The pond over the brow of the cliff at this point supplies a small stream which falls down into the sea, at which sailors make a call when in quest of fresh-water. No other water-works, I think, are found on Grand Manan.

Of course we devoted one day to a drive down the eastern shore of the island from Head to Head. There is no stated conveyance; but Mr. Kendrick, keeper of the modest livery-stable at Flagg's Cove, harnessed up for us his comfortable old one-horse carry-all, and out of the excursion down and back, with him for driver and guide, we made a day of pleasure. We studied with new delight the majestic sweep of Flagg's Cove, as we followed its outlines and rude embellishments to and through Centreville. We admired the neat and attractive school-houses; we praised the men whom we found specimens of the birds of the island, prepared by a resident taxidermist; and there, in addition, made a street acquaintance with the buxom wife of the hard-working rector of the English church at Grand Harbor.

BISHOP'S ROCK.

attempting to make good roads better; we chaffed the children on their way with baskets and pails after "baked-apples." We drove through long reaches of woods, enriched with the graceful hackmatack, and fragrant with a hundred odors. We snuffed with zest the salt-laden air as it rolled up with the rising mists from beach and headland. In the woods between Centreville and Woodward's Cove we paused before the lowly temple of the Latter-day Saints, and listened to an amusing story from our conductor of the capture of a burglar-tramp who had once taken refuge with his booty in its vacant belfry. At Woodward's Cove we called on Dr. Cameron, the village druggist and physician, to see his fine collection of stuffed

Further on we smiled at the odd coincidence of passing a house where Isaac Newton lives and a grave-yard where Walter Scott is buried, nearly side by side. We watched with curious interest the habit our vehicle had of passing other travellers to the left, as is the English custom, instead of to the right, as is the custom in "the States." And at last we drew up at Mr. W.

HEAD HARBOR LIGHT.

B. M'Laughlin's, near to Deep Cove, where we found rest, a welcome, and probably the best dinner to be had on Grand Manan.

Mr. M'Laughlin has belonged to the island all his life, and knows it "like a book." Born and bred to the light-house business, he is now the keeper (by deputy) of the lonely Gannet Rock Light, eight miles off in the bay. This desolate ledge of conglomerate, seen at this distance, presents something of the appearance of a ship under full sail. In Mr. M'Laughlin's album we found these lines associated with the spot:

" On a wrinkled rock in a distant sea
  Three white gannets sat in the sun.
  They shook the brine from their feathers fine,
  And lazily, one by one,
  They sunnily slept while the tempest crept.

" In a painted boat on the distant sea
  Three fowlers sailed merrily on;
  They each took aim as they came near the game,
  And the gannets fell one by one,
  And fluttered and died, while the tempest sighed.

" There came a cloud on the distant sea,
  And a darkness came over the sun,
  And a storm wind smote on the painted boat,
  And the fowlers sank one by one,
  Down, down, with their craft, while the tempest laughed."

The portion of the Bay of Fundy seen from Mr. M'Laughlin's is full of the most dangerous ledges, of which the Gannet Rock is only one. Among them are the Machias Seal Islands, the Murre Ledges, the Roaring Bull, the Old Proprietor, and others whose names are in divers ways suggestive of their character.

Grand Manan was visited by Champlain in 1605. His mention of it, under the names of Manthane and Manasue, is believed to be the first in history. He anchored off Southern Head. In 1842 Mr. M'Laughlin found on the beach at this point the remains of an old anchor, which he reasons must have been left by Champlain. The shank of this anchor was eleven feet long, and one part of the shank seven inches in diameter—dimensions which would give it an original weight of at least fourteen hundred-weight. But at the time of discovery it weighed less than three hundred pounds, and for such a reduction of bulk by the action of the elements a period of at least two hundred years is argued.

A characteristic fog, unhappily, was beginning to lessen the enjoyment of the day. It had made its appearance in the early morning, and was now settling down so thickly as to cut us off from all visible connection with the world around. The attractive views which the region of Southern Head commands were no longer to be had. These fogs must ever remain a serious obstacle to the development of Grand Manan as a pleasure resort for the multitude. They come in with the southerly winds, and lie oppressively and gloomily over the bay and all that it contains until there is a change of wind to the northerly quarter. The island is thus sometimes curtained off and roofed in for a week or ten days, and even more. No sun for all this time, no sights; nothing but the cool, gray, penetrating drift of dampness. The fogs are thicker and more frequent at the southern part of the island than at the northern. Naturally, too, they are more prevalent in wet seasons than in dry. And there may come days and even weeks of clear sunshine and fresh breezes and delightful air. The visitor must take his chances; he can hardly calculate the probabilities.

Of the Bay of Fundy in what may be called its glory we had a vivid experience on the day of our departure. At an unseasonably early hour the gruff and impatient whistle of the *Stroud* announced her arrival off our landing. The wind was blowing a gale, and the fog drifted by in dense masses. The tide was too low for the steamer to approach the wharf. She accordingly cast anchor in the roadstead and sent her boat ashore. With difficulty, though scarcely with danger, we were taken aboard the tossing packet; and lo! almost instantly the shore was buried from our sight. The anchor was weighed, the gig was swung up by the davits, the screw started, the bow swung around, the whistle took up its monotonous signaling, and we were off into the thickness of grayness which extended impenetrably in every direction. Once or twice we caught sight of "a lone fisherman" in his skiff at work thus early upon his seine or trawls, and for a while we passed along close in under the bold cliffs of Northern Head, getting a light-house's friendly greeting from Mr. Kent as we rounded Swallow-tail Point on the way. But presently our course was laid for Campobello, and our plucky little steamer struck out through the mists and winds and waves across the open bay. A rough hour or two we had of it, though it could not be said that there was any storm; and the peculiarity of the situation was heightened by the reflection that fairly on shore, twenty miles away, all was probably sunshine and peace.

And so we bade good-by to Grand Manan.

At certain states of the tide and in foggy weather the channel between Campobello Island and the Maine shore below Eastport is not easily navigable by either large vessels or small. It was so on this occasion, and our passage up around the northern head of Campobello would have afforded us, had the fog not been so thick, delightful views of this island's ragged shores, and of Eastport, as seen when approaching from the Bay of Fundy. This entire locality, in clear weather, abounds with charming scenes, which are constantly blending one with another as you advance among them. The confines of the two intermingling bays are studded with islands, between which long vistas are opening in every direction, disclosing new reaches of water and mountains in the distance. In all this succession of the sublime and the picturesque there is perhaps no spot which will more quickly arrest attention than Head Harbor and its light, at the extreme northeastern point of Campobello. A deep indentation of the sea is here guarded by a natural breakwater of ragged rock. On the very extremity of it stands the light-house, kept by a brother of the Mr. M'Laughlin whose acquaintance we made at the Southern Head of Grand Manan.

Looking north from the wharves at Eastport, one has another pleasant view of Indian, Plum, and Cherry islands a mile away, and of the hither end of Deer Island beyond. The waters off the near point of Deer Island are distinguished by the presence of powerful whirlpools, occasioned by the conflicting currents as they sweep round and about the irritating headland. An hour or two before and after the tide reaches its flood these whirlpools become positively dangerous to small boats, which sometimes, venturing too near, have been caught and overwhelmed. Several cases are on record in which row-boats, and even two-sail boats, have been swallowed down in this miniature maelstrom, and a number of lives have been lost in this way. Prudent boatmen give the spot a wide berth. Our smart little river steamer, the *Belle Brown*, running between Eastport and the landings on the St. Croix, cut her way directly across this death-hole in the bay, as if to defy its power, and at the same time illustrate it. She is a long steamer and a stanch one, and the moment of her passage happened to be a couple of hours before the whirlpools would

STERN REALITIES.

be at their height; but she no sooner touched the writhing currents with her bow than she trembled and recoiled, careened and swung well over, in spite of helm and helmsman, making it easy to see how helpless any small craft would be that should recklessly follow in her course.

Eastport is said to be a pleasant place for a summer sojourn, and is provided with a large hotel, which has a good reputation among travellers. We preferred, however, to seek more original quarters somewhere up the bay, and counted it a kindly providence that directed us to St. Andrews.

The *Belle Brown*, running in connection with the steamers between Boston and St. John, makes one round trip a day between

Eastport and Calais, touching at Robbinston, on the Maine shore, and at St. Andrews and St. Stephens, on the way. The sail up

AT THE POST-OFFICE, ST. ANDREWS.

the bay from Eastport to the mouth of the St. Croix occupies about one hour, and is in every sense delightful. The only possible drawback is a chance fog. The rough waters of the Bay of Fundy are left behind, for it is only in the late autumn and the winter that the generally peaceful Passamaquoddy gives any trouble to the traveller. All the way along one has for company the wooded hill-sides and rocky edges of Deer Island, and farther in the distance on the left the more refined slopes of Perry and adjoining towns of Maine. As the boat draws in sight of St. Andrews the bay opens and deepens to the northward. Big and Little Letete*—passages opening between islands into the Bay of Fundy—came in sight upon the right, and then with growing distinctness the islands themselves, among them Pendleton's and M'Master's, each with some peculiarity which has a beauty of its own. A western headland of M'Master's Island is brilliant with the coloring of metallic soil and rock. It is pre-eminently a subject for a painter. I commend it to the attention of any artist who is prospecting through this region. No pencil sketch can give any idea of its richness and splendor when lighted up by an afternoon sun.

The town of St. Andrews lies on a tongue of land a mile wide and two or three miles long, jutting out into the bay. The mouth of the St. Croix River adjoins it on the southwest. It is more than beautiful for situation, being favorable for commerce as well. Fifty years ago the largest ships, and plenty of them, lay at its wharves. It was then almost, if not quite, the commercial metropolis of New Brunswick, with half a century or more of honorable and prosperous history already. Its merchants had accumulated wealth, and an atmosphere of culture and refinement was beginning to gather around them. Then a change set in. Commerce deserted to rival ports. Trade took itself elsewhere. And now St. Andrews is "a Sunday town," as one of its residents described it, with nothing doing. The stranger sees this quickly. The broad streets remain, but they are going to grass. The warehouses still stand, but they are either shut up and empty, or abandoned to petty business. The massive wharves are daily washed by the tides, but few are the ships that load or unload beside them. The New Brunswick and Canada Railroad has a terminal station here, but shows only the signs of an indolent and indigent road, and can hardly give any life to the town or get any from it. Just now St. Andrews rests

A CITIZEN OF ST. ANDREWS.

its hopes for the future on the extension of this road to a connection with Montreal, which would make it Montreal's nearest sea-port by several score of miles, and so restore it, perhaps, to a relation of importance to all the Canadas. At present almost the only sign of animation which the town

* The spelling of this word is derived from the natives. I am not sure of its correctness, nor can I discover the origin or meaning of the term. On the one hand it is said to be of Indian derivation; but may it not be, on the other, some corruption of the French?

LOW TIDE, ST. ANDREWS.

OLD STONE HOUSE
St ANDREWS.

presents is at evening, while the daily mail is being opened; during which period of suspense the street in front of the office is occupied with an impatient throng of citizens.

But a far likelier fulfillment of its destiny would seem to be the development of its resources as a summer resort. For this it is admirably adapted. Remote and yet easily accessible, roomy and generous in its topography and architecture, commanding at once the finest facilities for recreation both on the water and on the land, environed with varied and impressive scenery, and a convenient point of departure for at least half a dozen places of exceptional interest, it has certainly rare endowments for the purpose named. Its un-American aspect would increase the charm for Americans. Already, indeed, capital and enterprise have realized the opportunity which St. Andrews presents for an investment in this direction, and have erected an immense hotel near the extremity of the point. The projectors became embarrassed, however, and the building has stood unfinished for several years. With this hotel completed, St. Andrews could present attractions of the first order. As it is, there are one or two boarding-houses in the town and a comfortable tavern.

Persons of quiet tastes, who like to get into scenes the reverse of Newport and Saratoga and Narragansett Pier, would never tire of sauntering about the desolate streets and the deserted wharves of this old border town of the Provinces. There is a fine English church, with a courtly canon-rector and a daily service. The old burial-ground pertaining to this church is a pleasant place in which to spend an hour.

A curious old church is the Scotch Kirk, called also the Greenock Church, and bearing on the front face of its tower an image in relief of a huge oak-tree, painted green, with the inscription, "Finished June 1824." There is a curious history connected with this house of prayer. It was begun by the congregation, who found themselves unable to finish. A rich eccentric old gentleman helped them out. Presently he quarrelled with them, locked up the church, and went away. In time he relented, returned to St. Andrews, bearing a dove as an emblem of peace, mounted the dove over the pulpit, and restored the congregation to their former occupancy. The dove, holding an olive-branch in its mouth, remains to this day. The pulpit is fearfully and wonderfully made—a regular double-decker. What governs the minister in his selection between the two stories I am unable to say. When he occupies the upper, I can testify to the loftiness of his eloquence.

On the crown of the hill just back of the town are the ruins of Fort Tipperary—a now deserted military post, once of importance, when British apprehensions found it necessary to guard the border—and a mile or two beyond, still to the north, rises Chamcook Mountain. The summit of Chamcook is easily gained, and commands a magnificent view for miles in all directions, including in clear weather not only the St. Croix River, the Maine and New Brunswick background, and Passamaquoddy Bay, but the Bay of Fundy, the headlands of Grand Manan, and, with a good glass, even the low line of the Nova Scotia shore. A romantic excursion may be made from St. Andrews to St. George, "up Magaguadavick* way," among the mountains which flank the northern shores of Passamaquoddy Bay—one that may be accomplished either by land or water. Here is a village of a few hundred inhabitants of the true Provincial type, a fine water-fall on the Magaguadavick River, a Lake Utopia, and a valuable deposit of red

---

* Pronounced Makadavick.

granite. A wheezy little tug-boat makes the trip several times a week between St. Andrews and St. George.

Two practical remarks, in conclusion, to any reader who may be tempted by these pages to a jaunt toward Grand Manan and Passamaquoddy Bay:

1. Dress warmly, in semi-winter under-clothing, with thick and serviceable outer garments, and carry a heavy overcoat.

2. Bring your own table napkins, unless you are willing to use one that "belongs to the house" and to the public generally. The hotels of New Brunswick have not, all of them, learned to be tidily accommodating in this vital matter of prandial comfort.

THE WRECK.

A Vacation in Vermont
(1883)

A VACATION IN VERMONT.

OF the Green Mountains one might probably say, paraphrasing Montesquieu's famous prediction about the *spirit of laws*, that they are more generally admired than visited. Poets sing without seeing them. They have furnished ready and familiar figures to orators who could hardly point them out on the map. That they stimulate the virtues of the patriot, and grow a stalwart race of men, is one of those axioms which one meets over and over again in the pages of writers who have never felt their rugged breezes, or measured the sons of Vermont in their own homes. Nor is this service which the State renders to rhetoric shared in anything like an equal degree by other States, which also have mountains, loftier perhaps and grander than its own. Even the White Mountains seem to be less frequently used, while the Alleghanies, the Rocky Mountains, and other noble chains throughout the country are almost unknown in literature and oratory. Only one thing is therefore wanting to complete the singular pre-eminence of Vermont. If her mountains and valleys were more often traversed and better known, if her children were studied through personal contact and acquaintance, the phrases of enthusiasm and admiration would not perhaps be subdued, but they would be well informed, just, rational, more serviceable to their authors, and not less complimentary to their objects.

The present article can, of course, repair this neglect only in part. To describe the whole State, or even all its leading beauties, would require a dozen volumes instead of as many pages; or if attempted on a small scale would be little more than a catalogue of natural objects, without those minute details which could alone justify them to the critical eye. We shall therefore take for description two favorite points in the Vermont landscape, and then invite the reader with their aid to complete the picture. One of these shall be the highest peak in the State; the other, one of the lowest valleys. The former is in the northeast, and stands guard over the Connecticut; the latter is in the southwest, and opens out into Champlain and the Hudson. Mount Mansfield will illustrate the grandeur and majesty of the Green Mountains themselves. Otter Creek irrigates a narrow vale between the mountains, and supplies the power for one of the leading industries of the State. Both regions, too, are somewhat frequented by tourists, and one of them is on the direct line of a railway.

Mount Mansfield is accessible either from the east or from the west. If from the west, the last railway station is Underhill, where there is a popular summer hotel, and whence carriages can ascend as far as the Half-way House. For the rest of the distance the tour is only for pedestrians, but there is a good foot-path, and a succession of views, as one ascends, affords a pleasant diversion, relieves the labor, and prepares for the final panorama which is revealed from the summit. The favorite route is, however, by way of Stowe, which lies southeast of the mountain. It is reached by stage from Morrisville, eight miles distant on the St. Johnsbury and Lake Champlain Railroad, or from the better known and more convenient station of Waterbury, ten miles distant, on the Central Vermont Railroad. This great thoroughfare furnishes the means of easy access from New York and Boston, and connects with the more important lines of communication in all directions.

The tourist who like myself chooses the last described course finds at Waterbury the final traces of a corrupt urban civilization. Beyond here all is primitive, idyllic, Arcadian; at Waterbury the contentious hackman still survives. But it is a mild form of contention, sobered apparently and rendered decorous by the clear air, or the solemn mountains, or the grave religious tone of a Vermont village. We had missed the stage, and the runners for several livery-stables offered to provide special transportation. Their rivalry, though really keen, was suppressed into a sympathetic desire to furnish the traveller the most comfortable, the swiftest, and safest conveyance; and from this desire every low, mercenary consideration was sternly banished. "Don't take that other fellow's team," said one of them, in a sad tone; "the last time he went over, a wheel run off, and he nearly killed his party." "That man," retorted the other, brushing a kindly tear out of his eye, "lost his way last week, and was five hours on the road." Then a third began, in a mild, expostulating voice: "Ladies and gentlemen, I wouldn't go with either of them men. If you *really* want to go, I have a team," etc. Thus the strife of these benevolent gentlemen went on. We finally decided to wait for the stage, and the three rivals walked off together with an air of pious resignation, humming in chorus one of Moody and Sankey's hymns. In some other parts of the world, I suppose, a writer who wished to show that the inherent friendship of these men could survive all brief professional differences would say that they repaired to the nearest bar and took a drink together. At Waterbury the evening prayer-meeting would seem to be a more fitting place for the fraternal reconciliation.

The stage is ready at last, and the two hours' drive, especially if one has an outside seat, is no unpleasant experience on a July evening. It is the very heart of the Green Mountains. The road is good; the hills are neither too prolonged nor too abrupt. Enticing trout streams shoot across the way or ripple along its side. Mount Mansfield and Camel's Hump are seen, now on one hand, now on the other, as we pursue our sinuous course. The farms are neat, orderly, and apparently prosperous, although the oats and wheat seem to have a hard battle for life with the rocks and the sand. The people are plain, but cheerful, civil, and obliging. One observes little of that outward sullenness by which in some other parts of the country

the poorer farmers take revenge on society for inequalities that are really due to their own idleness and improvidence. The Vermont farmer works, saves, keeps clear of mortgages, and—is polite.

At a little village where we stopped to water the horses a Green Mountain boy of some seventy summers, wrinkled and browned, but with flexible muscles in his gaunt frame and a smart twinkle in his eyes, entertained the passengers with some conversation.

"Goin' up to Stowe?"

"Yes."

"Ever been there?"

"No."

"Wa'al, our girls about these parts they've all gone to the White Mountains."

"Indeed! That's surprising. There's such fine scenery right here at home, why do they go to the White Mountains?"

"Why do they go to the White Mountains? Wa'al, they go there because they git three dollars a week."

"Oh!" rejoined the coach, hastily, with some embarrassment; "we had not thought of it in that light."

"Yes, sir," added the veteran, clinching his argument—"yes, sir, one of my girls gits three dollars a week, and don't have nothing to do but wash tumblers." And he bowed kindly as the stage moved away.

It seemed fitting to one of our party, a cynical person, to remark afterward that even washing tumblers day after day might become monotonous, and exclude the opportunities for that æsthetic culture now so much needed by domestic servants. "Still," he added, "if the newspapers may be trusted, they have the society of Dartmouth students in the busy season."

Let us respect honest toil. Not all Vermont girls are drawn to the White Mountains even by the liberal conditions which are there offered. Enough of them at least remain to do the service of the Mount Mansfield House, and to do it well. Neat, quick, intelligent, obliging, they lose no caste by earning their way; in winter they are the belles of "society." Brawny young farmers will find them the best of wives, and if another war should afflict the country, their sons will rush to arms not less promptly than did their fathers and brothers twenty years ago.

Stowe is a typical Vermont village of some one thousand inhabitants. The houses are nearly all white, and the white houses nearly all have green shutters,

MOUNT MANSFIELD FROM STOWE.

though slight differences in the styles of architecture and a modest discrimination in the choice of flowers and the arrangement of flower beds afford a partial satisfaction to the eye. There is a small white church, and its spire, or "steeple," as the parishioners call it, shoots ambitiously upward into the clear blue air. There is a hotel, the Mount Mansfield House, built in 1864, and for some time in charge of a veteran Boston journalist—a spacious building, with broad verandas and long halls, with vast *salons,* where the waltz may safely be attempted, and well-disposed lawns, across which the croquet balls bound from morning till night, and the harmless missiles of tennis make their abrupt flights. From "Sunset Hill," a sharp elevation back of the hotel, the village resembles a flock of geese on the wing, the two main streets diverging toward the east and the west, while the apex, where the leader may be imagined, points timidly toward Waterbury on the south. Many other things may also be seen from Sunset Hill.

In the rear is the Worcester range; south, Camel's Hump; west, Mount Mansfield itself; and in the intervals, especially toward the northwest, the green valley with its silver streams, its well-stocked farms, its neat farm-houses, with their barns and other buildings grouped in little colonies about them. This is, too, a good point from which to begin the work of seeing a man's face in the profile of Mount Mansfield. The illustration provides all the materials of the problem. The features are all there in bold relief—forehead, nose, mouth, lips, chin—and the reader who fails to catch the resemblance will never understand why the mountain was called "Mans-field." He will be reduced to the false theory that its namesake was a famous English judge.

The distance from Stowe to the summit of the mountain is about nine miles. For five miles the route follows the ordinary country road through a pleasant valley; then it breaks off into the mountain, and winds about by easy grades to the top.

The carriage road has now been open several years, and the ascent can be made in any vehicle with the greatest comfort.

The way is thickly wooded—along the lower part with beech, maple, birch, and even oak, which, however, gradually disappear, until the evergreen varieties alone remain, and these seem ill satisfied with their existence. Shade is therefore abundant, and the sun's rays are little felt. But this is at the cost of another form of enjoyment. Short of the summit itself no satisfactory view is obtained, with perhaps a partial exception in favor of the Half-way House. This seems once to have been a habitable house, at least for horses; though, thanks to the fretful por-

cupine, it now offers hospitality neither to quadrupeds nor to bipeds. The hedgehogs have attacked the stalls and floor with ferocity and persistence, and have created vast intervals in the most solid partitions. The little animals are abundant all over the mountain, and many wild stories are told of their exploits. A horse belonging to the hotel was attacked by one, said John, the driver, and they afterward pulled seven hundred quills out of the poor beast; and if John had been coining a story he would not have been so recklessly exact.

Half a mile before the summit is reached the woods open, and the carriage climbs a stiff rocky ledge for the rest of the way. The Nose towers up directly above us, and the other features stretch away in the distance, massive, solemn, forbidding.

The description of the mountain and its views may properly be prefaced by a few useful facts and figures. The highest point, the Chin, is 4359 feet above sea-level, and 3670 above the village of Stowe. The Nose, the next peak, is 340 feet lower; the Forehead, 160 feet below the Nose.

THE NOSE AND SMUGGLER'S NOTCH.

THE MOUNTAIN ROAD.

From the Nose to the Chin—the extreme points of ordinary exploration—the distance is about one and a half miles. The mountain has long been accessible to adventurous tourists, but it is only within the last twenty years, or since the opening of the Mount Mansfield House, that they have come in any number or regularly. The completion of the carriage road to the summit brought, of course, a large increase of both transient and permanent guests.

We can now examine the face of the giant as calmly and fearlessly as the Lilliputians walked about over the prostrate Gulliver.

To reach the point of the Nose involves a sharp though short climb, facilitated by a flight of rude steps which have been formed by the ledges of the rock. The old Latin line must be reversed before it can be applied to the Nose. The ascent is safe and not difficult, but the descent—*hic labor, hoc opus est.* The stone is as smooth and slippery as ice; and a single false step would precipitate one two hundred feet or more to the bottom. This is

on the west. The northern side is nearly perpendicular; and although the process which shaped it began thousands of years ago, it has not yet ceased. From time to time immense masses of rock detach themselves and plunge into the abyss below, where they still lie heaped upon one another in wild disorder. One of these terrible bowlders was formerly poised on the very end of the Nose, almost without visible means of support. It was supposed that it could be pried loose by hand, but repeated attempts led only to disappointment. One day in 1859, however, it started voluntarily, and rolled down the precipice, shaking the mountain like an earthquake, and at the bottom bursting into a thousand fragments. A party of men and women had been on the rock but half an hour before it fell, and others had been strolling about the foot of the cliff where it lodged.

The Summit House is situated at the foot of the Nose, on the eastward slope of the ridge. It is a frame building of two stories, with ample balconies, comfortable rooms, and a satisfactory cuisine. Its

MOUNT WASHINGTON FROM MOUNT MANSFIELD.

manager at the time of our visit was Demis, a French Canadian, who had been
so long on the mountain that he could
hardly walk on level ground. He was,
of course, well stocked with stories, most
of them based on personal experience.
Thunder-storms on the summit are not
infrequent, but Demis remembered one
in particular which broke forth without
any warning on a bright sunny day. He
was sitting in the "parlor," when he saw
a flash, and before he knew it the room
was full of lightning, and he was up to
his knees in the electric fluid. "I was
half stunted to death," added the veteran
Gaul, somewhat obscurely. And in proof
of his story he showed us where the same
bolt had struck the end of the Nose, leaving a long scar, brightly polished as by
some mechanical instrument. Demis's
only permanent companions on the mountain were five cats, a few chickens, and
Dolly the cow. Dolly had lived nine years
in this lofty region. Her predecessor was
there seventeen years. An artificial grass-
plot, built up much as the peasants on the
Rhine create soil for vineyards, was her

only pasture, except such browsing as she
might get among the evergreens and ferns;
but she seemed happy, and in the winter,
when brought down to the village, she returned invariably to the summit as often
as she could escape.

For the walk to the Chin some little
time is necessary, though the rise is gradual and not troublesome. The ridge of
the mountain is narrow and nearly bare,
a few dwarfish cedars, and a carpet of
moss softer and richer than the finest
tapestry of Smyrna, being the only forms
of vegetable life. By a brisk walk the
visitor can in fifteen minutes reach the
Lips. These are mere accumulations of
great bowlders, deposited there by volcan-
ic or glacial movements, and not specially
interesting, except, perhaps, the so-called
"Rock of Terror," which, poised precari-
ously on its apex, seems ready on slight
provocation to roll down, and the caves,
which are formed by series of overlying
bowlders, though one of them is of considerable depth. Geologists have found evidence for the glacial theory in scars or
scratches made on the surface of the rocks

here and there in a direction pretty consistently from the northwest to the southeast. But the eye of the layman will not readily find or recognize them.

From the Chin the spectator has one of the most comprehensive, variegated, and cludes the spires and towers of Montreal, one hundred miles distant. Directly beneath, and between the first and second chins, lies the Lake of the Clouds; lower down, the dark recesses of the Smuggler's Notch; and across this, the Sterling Mountains. Moving to the east, the eye falls first upon a succession of dark and heavy ridges, thickly wooded, giving and receiving shadows in

OLD WOMAN OF THE MOUNTAINS.

ROCK OF TERROR.

beautiful views to be found in all New England. Toward the west, the eye, starting from the base of the mountain, runs over the Winooski Valley, threaded by roads and streams, and dotted with countless white villages; takes in Lake Champlain, which on a clear day can be seen for nearly its entire length; and is arrested only by the Adirondacks in the remote horizon. On the north, the outlook is even more extensive, and at rare intervals, under peculiarly favorable conditions, even in-

endless variety; farther away, the valley of the Connecticut; and beyond, the White Mountains. Mount Washington itself can sometimes be seen, though indistinctly. The picture is completed by Stowe and its neighbors, nestling in the rich valley, and directly south the rival peak of Camel's Hump and the main chain of the Green Mountains. Such is, in general, the scope of the view afforded from the summit of Mount Mansfield. The countless details which give it grace, picturesqueness, and value can not even be enumerated, but must be left with the assurance that not one which the imagination could crave will be found wanting by the most exacting lover of nature.

The neighborhood of Stowe affords a multitude of other charming resorts, some of which must be at least mentioned. One of these is the Smuggler's Notch, a narrow pass between Mount Mansfield and the Sterling Mountain. It is supposed to have been used in former times by smugglers, as it is an easy and convenient connection between western and eastern Vermont, and a link in the chain of communication between Montreal and Boston, once an important thoroughfare for contraband traffic. At the summit of the pass there is a deserted inn, the Notch House. The local guide-book says it affords accommodation for man and beast; and this is true, for if the visitor brings with him sandwiches for the man and oats for the beast, they can be eaten in the ruins of the edifice. Otherwise a common famine will be the result. A good road following the course of a noble trout stream ends only at the Notch House, and the source of the stream, the "Mammoth Spring," which is not improperly named. Beyond the house a foot-path leads through a succession of mighty bowlders which have fallen from the cliffs above, under abrupt precipices which stretch up on either side to appalling heights, through damp ravines where the ferns grow in fantastic luxuriance and beauty, finally issues at the western mouth of the pass, and then descends swiftly to the valley. It is customary in visiting the Notch to include also Bingham's Falls, named after an eminent citizen of Stowe, who has done much to make the region accessible and agreeable to tourists. They are composed of a series of chasms worn in the solid rock.

Other attractions are Moss Glen Cascade, only four miles from Stowe, in Worcester Mountains; Gold Brook, a favorite drive; Morrisville Falls and Johnson Falls, somewhat more distant; and various other choice rural nooks which will well repay a visit. The roads are, for mountain roads, uniformly good, and ladies unaccompanied ride in confidence and safety all over the country.

For loftiness, grandeur, and majesty,

Mount Mansfield is, of course, inferior to Mount Washington. Its charms are of a more modest nature. But it has, nevertheless, peculiar advantages of its own, which will not escape the eye of discerning visitors, and which to a large class of persons will recommend it even above the White Mountains. One of these is the singular extent and freedom of the view which may be had from its summit. Instead of being only one of a vast army of peaks, and distinguished from its comrades merely by a slight superiority in height, it is more like an isolated structure rising out of a surrounding plain. In at least two directions, east and west, the landscape is unobstructed for a hundred miles. The country lies spread out in a vast plateau, beginning at the very base of the mountain, and enlivened by every element which belongs to a complete picture. The landscape itself is therefore an ample reward for the toil and expense of the visit. But there is a further felicity in the exemption of the real lover of nature from the intrusion of unsympathetic Philistines. Unfortunately no part of the world in these days of rapid and cheap travel is absolutely free from the shoddyite, the cockney, and the snob; but Mount Mansfield as a resort is in this respect at least comparatively favored. It is little frequented by "fashionable" people, and even less so by that still lower class who pursue and imitate fashionable people. Serious, thoughtful, and appreciative persons form the larger part of its summer patrons. They who spend there one season generally spend also the next and the next; acquaintances are renewed from year to year; and in this way Mount Mansfield is gradually enrolling a considerable band of faithful, zealous, and devout disciples.

The scene changes now abruptly to another part of Vermont, and to other elements of interest and attraction. Our route lies diagonally across the State, from the Alps to the Apennines; from Mont Blanc to Carrara; from a region newly settled and still full of a wild beauty and vigor to a region rich in colonial and Revolutionary traditions, and throbbing with a varied and active industry.

The history of southwestern Vermont goes back to a time when, strictly speaking, there was no Vermont; when there was a New Hampshire and a New York, but when it was uncertain to which of

SMUGGLER'S NOTCH.

the two the valley of Otter Creek belonged. The settlers in the disputed tract hat-
ed, indeed, the "Yorkers." The bailiffs
of the western tyrant found no little difficulty in performing their duties; and if
the local chronicles are veracious, the
sturdy villagers now and then tied one of
them to a tree and, whip in hand, taught
him the error of his ways. Incidents in
this border warfare are given in Miss He-
menway's excellent *Vermont Gazetteer*,
and in various productions, poetical and
unpoetical, of home talent. Not even the
outbreak of the Revolution wholly allay-
ed this fierce hostility. There exists, for
instance, the record of a meeting of delegates from "the towns on the west side of
the Green Mountains," held September 25,

1776, in Dorset, at the house of Deacon Cephas Kent, a leading patriot, and ancestor of many eminent men, Chancellor Kent being one. There were present Colonel Seth Warner, the Revolutionary hero, several Allens, and representatives of the Chittendens, Morgans, Fays, Saffords, Robinsons, and Marshes, all historic families of Vermont. The tone of the assembly may be learned from the resolutions which were adopted. They affirm that the people of that section were tired of the "tyranny of New York toward the New Hampshire Grants"; that, for geographical reasons, they could not well co-operate with New York in the war of Independence; and that they were determined, in their participation in the common cause, to recognize only the superiority of the Continental Congress. In virtue of this, and a still higher authority, Ethan Allen demanded and obtained the surrender of Fort Ticonderoga. On this basis the Vermonters fought the battle of Bennington, and thus prepared the way for the surrender of Burgoyne himself. Every town and hamlet throughout the region has its own proud Revolutionary legends, its own noble list of martyrs, its own heroes. Take Dorset again. The champion of Revolutionary Dorset is a valiant citizen who, aided by one ally, captured at Bennington seven prisoners, one of them a colonel, and brought them safely off the field. It is evident that such a people would not submit to the authority even of New York if it were unjust and distasteful. By their efforts they won, in fact, a double independence—first their independence, with the other colonies, from England, and then their independence as a State in the Union of States.

In the neighborhood of Dorset arise two streams, which, after this single early meeting, turn their backs rudely upon each other, and thenceforth flow in opposite directions. The Battenkill bears southward for twenty miles or more, then strikes westward through the mountains, and onward to the Hudson. Otter Creek is true throughout to its Vermont allegiance. Its course is north, and it finally empties into Lake Champlain, at Vergennes. The valley through which the two flow is narrowest about the point where the Battenkill leaves it; obtains its most striking natural characteristics near Manchester and Dorset, and then, pro-

ceeding northward, gradually widens out into a spacious and fertile plain, lying between the main line of the Green Mountains and Lake Champlain.

The first of the towns just named, Manchester, is, in respect to outward beauty and to popularity as a summer resort, easily superior to all the others. It lies on a high plateau formed by a long, low spur of Mount Equinox; has one broad street, luxuriantly shaded; is calm, decorous, and soothing; and being well provided with hotels, is favorably known to the annual fugitives from New York and Boston. The ascent of Equinox is easily made, and the vicinity affords an abundance of delightful excursions.

One of these is, for example, to Dorset Mountain. It should first be explained, however, that the term Green Mountains is applied only to the range east of the valley, that on the west being known as the Taconic Mountains. Between the two chains there are also some striking differences. The Taconic Mountains are higher, bolder, and more imposing. The water which flows down from them is much harder than that from the east. They are also much richer in natural deposits, yielding marble, slate, and a superior quality of the ordinary building limestone. Mount Equinox is one of the peaks in the Taconic range. Dorset Mountain, five miles farther north, is another, and the one at which Otter Valley properly begins.

I have adhered to the older name, Dorset Mountain, although an attempt has been made to provide another, more ambitious, more sonorous, but not more honorable or dignified. This upstart term is Mount Æolus, and the author of the unhappy innovation is Professor Charles H. Hitchcock, who in 1861 visited the region with a class of students from Amherst College. Dr. Hitchcock gave the following explanation of the phenomenal absence of snow in Dorset Valley: "Æolus, the god of the winds, fled from fallen Greece, and took up his abode in the caves and marble halls of this mountain. When this god calls home Boreas, driving before him snow and hail, there comes also Auster, with warm breath and weeping showers, and the frost-work volute and scroll soon disappear." The ceremony of christening was performed. Standing on a natural platform near the mouth of the cave, the party broke a bottle of water over the mountain, the chorus of the winds furnished music, and when this had subsided a poem was read, of which the following stanza is a sample:

> " Then blow, ye winds, ye breezes all,
>   Obey your king's command ;
> He sits in this grand marble hall ;
>   Ye are his servant band."

six wide, and it is said that explorers have penetrated forty or fifty rods without finding any end.

If Dorset Mountain is little favored by snow, it has plenty of snowy marble. Viewed from the east, the whole hill-side seems to be ridged and furrowed with quarries, and the vast accumu-

SKETCHES NEAR STOWE.

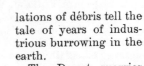

Thus Dorset Mountain became Mount Æolus; for the new term has obtained some little currency, and has the authority even of print.

The cave to which allusion has been made is no insignificant affair. It is composed of a succession of rooms, one of which is eighty-six feet long and thirty-

lations of débris tell the tale of years of industrious burrowing in the earth.

The Dorset quarries were the earliest to be discovered and worked in Vermont, and their products are still, in respect to quality, among the best. The first quarry was opened in 1785, six years before the State was admitted into the Union, and it is still owned by the descendants of the original proprietors. This discovery was the great sensation of the day. People came hundreds of miles to get the crude slabs for fire-place stones and other domestic uses, and a brisk traffic in the new commodity soon sprang up. In 1808 a second quarry was opened, and subsequently many others, following in rapid succession. All but two of these are still in operation. The channelling process, now familiar to mining engineers, was introduced in 1841; the first derrick for hoisting the blocks in 1848; the first tunnelling in 1859. In 1818 the first attempt at sawing marble was made, but it was many years before the experiment proved successful. For a long time after these works were opened they had little competition, and the demand for their products far exceeded the supply; but the trade was subsequently injured by the introduction of Italian marbles, and the discovery of other Vermont quarries, especially those near Rutland.

Of this town, Rutland, some patriarch who should die now might say that he found it brick or frame and left it marble. The chaste, cold, glossy stone is almost oppressively plenty in this smart and thriving village, and meets the eye in a multitude of forms and uses—buildings, pavements, walls, besides interior decoration and finishing. Rutland is in fact the best advertisement of its own leading industry. To use the language of the exchange, its principal capitalists are already "in marble" before their death, and without the aid of the sculptor. Concerns like the Vermont Marble Company, Sheldon and Slason, Flint Brothers, Ripley and Sons, Gilson and Woodfin, and others, with their fifteen or twenty quarries, give an idea of the extent to which the marble interest engrosses the capacity and the resources of this neighborhood.

The more important quarries and works are situated north and west of the town itself, at Centre Rutland, West Rutland, Sutherland Falls, and lesser points in the vicinity. The Vermont Marble Company is, in fact, domiciled at all three of these places. It has finishing-works at Centre Rutland, quarries at West Rutland, and both quarries and mills at Sutherland Falls. At the first-named point no marble is excavated, but there is a splendid water-power, which naturally is not neglected,

and here one can observe every stage in the process except the quarrying itself. The marble is brought to the mills in massive cubes, is sawed, turned, chiselled, polished, mounted, and emerges as tombstones, capitals, cornices, columns, mantelpieces, and table-tops. Much of this work, especially the hand-work, can, of course, be studied in every place where people die and have monuments set up by the local stone-cutter over their graves, but the heavier preliminary labor is best to be seen near the quarries themselves.

The marble is delivered at the mills in elongated cubes—parallelopipeds, I suppose Euclid would say—from ten to fifteen feet long and three to five feet square, and placed on the frames for sawing. An expert will then decide as to the manner of reduction, that is, the thickness and number of the slabs, according to the quality, the shape and size of the block, or the special nature of the orders to be filled. In outward appearance a "gang," as a set of saws is called, resembles the old-fashioned upright saw-mill, except that the vertical frame contains not one but many saws, arranged at different intervals, corresponding to the desired thickness of the cuts. One process, therefore, divides an entire block into slabs. The saw has, it should be added, no teeth. The cutting is the joint effect of the hard edge of the steel blade and the wet sand which is fed into the opening, and thus produces an incisive friction. The ordinary progress is about two and a half inches an hour, and the gangs work night and day. The polishing of small pieces is done on a revolving iron disk some twelve feet in diameter. The marble is thrown upon this, and caught by fixed wooden strips like the radii of a circle, while the motion of the wheel, which is supplied with sand and water, furnishes the attrition. It takes two or three hours to polish a surface down one inch. Heavy pieces are smoothed by hand, with the aid of pumice-stone. Marble is turned into circular shapes in a lathe, exactly like iron, and is bored with an ordinary dry drill.

The West Rutland quarries are not, like those of Dorset, in the side of a great mountain, but seem to form the bed of a low hill or ridge rising very little above a level. The excavations follow, therefore, nearly vertical lines directly into the earth; and the cuts themselves, which are shaped to the seams of the stone, have at the sur-

A MARBLE QUARRY.

face an eastward inclination of about forty degrees, then of sixty, and again of twenty, until in some places they are almost perpendicular. The cuts are marked off from fifty to seventy feet long, twelve to sixteen feet wide, and about four feet deep, and are afterward subdivided into desired or convenient sizes. Some of this work, under ledges and in close quarters, is still necessarily done by hand; but the substitution of machinery for manual labor is nowhere more strikingly illustrated than in a Vermont marble quarry. Three of the machines thus used may be described. For the diamond borer or drill the power is steam, and the work is done by two drills terminating in diamond points about one foot apart. By going frequently over the course a close line of holes is formed, not unlike the perforated division between postage stamps, and as the instrument works with great rapidity, it makes a cut one foot deep and seventy-five feet long in one day. It can be adjusted to any angle near the perpendicular, and is used for upright drilling. Another machine, the Wardwell, for vertical work, is a spe- cies of locomotive on a track, along which it moves backward and forward, and makes complete cuts by means of systems of chisels acting on the trip-hammer principle. There are two of these, four or five feet apart, and both sides of a block are therefore cut at once. The horizontal cut is made by the Ingersoll drill. It is a small instrument hanging and movable on a fixed cylinder, and adjustable there to an angle either above or below the horizontal. The power is supplied in the form of steam in rubber pipes. Besides

SUTHERLAND FALLS.

these three leading varieties there are other machines, differing in slight details, all of use for special kinds of work, but difficult to describe in the language of a layman.

The final rupture between a block and its ancient bed is an interesting process. Let us suppose the two cuts to be made, one nearly vertical, and the other, or horizontal one, at right angles to it, and both one or two feet deep. A series of wedges is then inserted into the openings, and a man with a heavy hammer goes along tapping them lightly one after another. As they are driven in, the men listen sharply for the effect, the crack gradually widens, the great mass of stone begins to heave and swell under the strain, the quick ear of the experts detects the critical moment, and a simultaneous blow on all the wedges throws the monster loose. Now and then, of course, a failure is made, and a block splits in two. But the judgment of the workmen is singularly correct, and the block is generally thrown out in its full integrity.

At West Rutland there are half a dozen or more quarries belonging to as many different firms; and others are strewn along the hill-sides throughout the region, especially between Rutland and Sutherland Falls, and north as far as Brandon. One of the finest quarries in respect to quality, connected with one of the most extensive mills, is that at Sutherland Falls. The common laborers are nearly all foreigners — French Canadians, Irish, and Swedes—but they are temperate and orderly; strikes are rare; and here, as in the other marble districts, the proprietors have shown themselves the friends of their employés by building neat little cottages, founding libraries and reading-rooms, and endowing churches. For the Green Mountain State likes to boast of its men as well as of its mountains.

Moose in the
Maine Woods
(1899)

MOOSE IN THE MAINE WOODS.

BY C. BAILEY.

A HUNT in the Maine woods; limit of time, two weeks; sole object, a moose.

By the end of October the leaves have fallen, the undergrowth has become comparatively clear, and the moose have left the lakes and streams and sought shelter in the more thickly wooded hills and ranges. The rutting season is over, and all fight has left the bull, who busies himself in selecting a "yard," some well-protected hillside, where the tender tops of the moose-wood and maple will furnish him food during the heavy snows.

The sportsman in quest of moose in Maine arrives at the little station nearest the hunting region, puts up at the country hotel, listens to stories of the many heads carried out of the woods, is assured by his guide of the plentifulness of game, and *if* a snow will only fall, and *if* luck is only with him, and *if* other things combine, everything will turn out satisfactorily.

Thus, regaled with yarns, he imagines in the warmth of the hotel smoking-room that killing a moose is such an easy matter that it is a wonder more sportsmen do not try it. In fact, he is most anxious to get started lest some man may have gone in the woods ahead of him and, perhaps, gotten the very moose that would have fallen to his own rifle.

So, by the rising of the morrow's sun, the Nimrod finds himself rigged in soft knee-breeches, sweater, numerous heavy woolen socks, and oil-tanned moccasins, and seated in a heavily-laden buck-board pulled by four scrawny horses over a rough, muddy road, such as only Maine horses can stand. Ten, fifteen or twenty miles through a dense forest of spruce, pine and hemlock brings him to a little cluster of log cabins. He is at his camp, situated usually in a hollow near some swift-running brook, and entirely shut in by the tall trees and thick undergrowth in the neighborhood.

Thus passes the first day.

The second day gives the guide an opportunity to test the endurance of the sportsman, who is taken over hills and through swamps with only the possibility of happening suddenly on the object of his hunt. His chances are poor, for the dry leaves crack under his feet, and the breaking of every twig sends a noise through the silent woods as of the tramping of an ox.

The third and fourth days are perhaps as fruitless. Not a sign of moose. The snort of a deer or two as they bound through the young hemlock, or perhaps the glimpse of a white flag, may give the hunter a momentary thrill of excitement ; but, if he must have a moose it behooves him not to shoot at other game. For, once started, the moose will leave that particular locality and not stop short of many miles running. So back to camp as darkness comes on, tired and weary, perhaps discouraged, certainly hungry.

The next morning—what joy! The ground is covered with snow, soft and velvety, four or five inches. Just the right depth, not too much for fast traveling, yet just enough to cushion the leaves and deaden one's footfalls.

The hunter, with whatever rifle he fancies, and the guide with his pack make an early start. Three or four miles over one range, with here and there a view of a distant lake, or a glimpse of a long stretch of crimson and blue hills, down into a swamp, across treacherous brooks, when lo! a moose-track. Immediately the hunter's spirits mount high, his strength is doubled, and every sense is on the alert.

The guide examines the track critically and fears that it is of a cow. However, it might be a young bull. At any rate, it will probably lead to a yard or to other three or four moose, so for the next three or four hours the trail is followed through bogs, over fallen tree-tops, and under overhanging boughs, which the guide scrutinizes closely. No bark is knocked off. There is very little hope of its being a bull. The "going" grows tiresome, and when the tracks lead from the top of some high hill to the foot and it is then found that the quarry has turned and gone up again, perhaps not

a hundred yards from the old trail, the time is observed and lunch decided upon.

Being refreshed, they resume the trail, and after crossing more hills and working their way through more swamps, find the distance between the tracks to grow shorter and here and there a freshly nipped twig. The moose has slowed down and is beginning to feed. Another quarter of a mile of slow and careful trailing ; then, on reaching the edge of a more open growth, it is seen, quietly browsing amongst the saplings some two hundred yards away. The rifle is cocked, and both hunter and guide crane their necks to try to discover whether it is a cow or a bull. In vain they look for horns ; peer as they will the horns are not there. There is nothing to be done. The law forbids the killing of cow moose, so they can only withdraw and try not to disturb her.

It is getting late, and six or seven miles separate the wearied trampers from their camp. By carefully selecting a route over certain well-known hills, and by constant reference to the compass, the welcome lights of the huts appear just as darkness has settled down.

The fifth day has gone, and with it what encouragement the beginning of it brought forth. By the time all hands are in their bunks the unwelcome patter of drops of rain is heard on the roof, and soon there is a steady downpour.

Sapristi ! What miserable luck ! Tomorrow the snow will freeze, and with a thin crust it is absolutely useless to try to hunt anything. And so it is. A few hours tramping is enough to convince even a tyro that stalking is out of the question. So the day is spent in the vicinity of the camp after partridges. A bag of half a dozen is not an unusual one. The absence of their heads is pointed to with pride as a proof of good marksmanship.

Thus the sixth day and also the seventh and eighth pass. Six days more —only five hunting days, for one day must be spent getting out of the woods. Impatience seizes upon the sportsman as he counts the days and figures on his probabilities. In his dreams he kills the biggest moose ever carried out of the woods, spread of horns six feet, twenty points on one horn and nineteen on the other. Then again, the questions his friends will ask : "What!

killed nothing?" "Two weeks in the woods?" serve to make the day long and his waking hours restless and uncomfortable.

So, with a rabbit foot in his vest pocket, or carrying some other article that his superstition tells him will prove efficacious, he again sets forth, more determined than ever, and quite prepared to stand whatever exertion he may be called upon to undergo. There is still a crust on the snow, but the "going" is not quite so noisy. Hour after hour is spent in trudging through the snow, the thermometer down to ten below zero, moccasins leaky, and feet tired and sore. A lunch of sandwiches and coffee, and on again, stepping to one side to examine a bear-track, or again to look at an unusually big deer-track, until at last the guide's quick eye discovers moose-sign.

A peeled sapling, broken twigs, and finally the tracks of two moose, one large and one small track, evidently a bull and a cow. Again we are on the alert, and the trail is taken up with the eagerness of a hound in full cry. A mile of fast, quick work, when, on stopping a second to listen, there is heard, growing fainter each instant, the heavy, crashing sound made by the monarch of the forest as he bounds down the valley. Too late. He is off. We were too anxious. And then the blanked crust. There is no use following immediately, and, as it is nearly sunset, it is decided to camp on his trail. So some forked sticks are set up, poles laid on them, these covered with long strips of birch-bark, boughs cut and laid for a bed, a blanket spread, and everything made as comfortable as possible for the night.

Daylight breaks on the morning of the tenth day and ends a restless night spent in rolling over and turning about in the endeavor to keep warm. As the sun sheds its first glow over the hill-tops the pursuers are off. Mile after mile is covered with no indication of a slacking of speed on the part of the moose. Noon, one, two, and three o'clock pass, and not a turn in the trail. The moose are leaving the country and must be given up.

Disheartened and wearied, hunter and guide set a course for camp and wend their way through tangled undergrowth, over slippery logs, across brooks and streams into which they not infrequently slip, until they are at last before a cheery fire in camp, recounting the trials of the preceding days.

The next day dawns bright and clear, with a soft melting of snow. A few miles from camp, when again moose-sign is discovered. Bark freshly peeled from young trees, bushes bent over, and fresh tracks which the guide decides were made during the early morning. There are three in the herd, big tracks, and from the bark scraped off the trees, there is evidently a bull amongst them. The trails cross and wander about aimlessly. The beasts are possibly in the near neighborhood. Now great caution must be observed. A finger is wetted and held up to find the exact direction of the wind. Taking note of the general appearance of the surrounding hills and valleys, the guide leads the sportsman circuitously to leeward of a certain narrow little valley, where they again discover the trail, which, fortunately, leads up the valley and against the wind.

Creeping, half crawling, they cautiously select a place for each step. The signs grow fresher every minute, and the hunters grow more alert and careful. Just as they reach the top of a little rise, a black object is seen to move amongst the growth some hundred yards distant. Crouch low and be ready! A moment later the object turns, and presents a broadside showing a fine pair of horns. Now quick, but take a careful aim. Bang! once, twice. Shoot again as he runs—three, four—yea, more times if necessary. The old bull stops and weakens, then, staggering, falls heavily to the ground, dead.

A moment to realize that he has actually killed his moose, and then the triumphant hunter produces a flask that he and his guide may drink to their success, and to each other's health—and to everybody else's good health. They then fill their pipes and sit down to enjoy a little of that calm contentment that follows the complete and successful accomplishment of one's most cherished desires.

The next day is spent in "blazing" and "swamping out" a way by which the moose may be hauled out. And on the thirteenth, after much labor and difficult driving, he is hauled into camp on a sled.

Aboard a
Sperm-Whaler
(1854)

ABOARD A SPERM-WHALER.

WE dare say the reader is sufficiently familiar with the many-times-told story of the Greenland whale-fishery, but we may be permitted to doubt whether he knows much about the sperm-whale, and its capture in the far-off South Seas. We therefore invite him to accompany us on board a whaler, on its cruising station—and to do this he need not quit his cushioned arm-chair by the parlor fire—and we will show him the whole art and mystery of capturing the sperm or cachalot whale.

But before stepping on board, it may be as well to say a few words about the South-sea whalers and their equipment. These vessels are not old double-sided tubs like the Greenlandmen, but smart, well-formed, thoroughly rigged ships and barques of 300 to 400 tons, manned by a crew of which at least three-fourths are prime A. Bs. These ships make voyages which frequently occupy three years, and which call into exercise the utmost degree of nautical skill, both scientific and practical. During this prolonged voyage, the mariners generally make the acquaintance of foreign people of all colors and all degrees of civilization, in the South Sea Isles, the coast of South America, the Indian Archipelago, &c., and find abundant exercise for every manly virtue—courage, endurance, patience, and energy, all being absolutely requisite, together with no small amount of real talent on the part of the commanding-officers. The South-seaman surpasses all merchant vessels in the very romantic nature of its service. It roves round the globe; and in the vast Pacific Ocean sails to and fro, and from island to island, for years at a spell. The crew employed in such a service, if they only possess the ordinary intelligence of seamen, can not fail to have their powers of observation sharpened, their reasoning faculties called into exercise, and their whole mental development stimulated. Accordingly, sperm-whalers are remarkably shrewd intelligent men; close observers of the phenomena of nature so liberally exhibited in their ocean pathways; and altogether noble specimens of seamen.

On the deck of a sperm-whaler, there is a platform to receive the portions of the whale taken on board, and at the mainmast-head are strong pulleys, called the cutting blocks and falls, which are used to hoist the blubber, &c., on board by aid of the windlass. There is also on deck a square brick erection, a little abaft the foremast, made to support a couple of great iron caldrons, called *try-pots*, in which the blubber is boiled. Adjoining them is a copper cooler; and every possible precaution is adopted to guard against accidents from fire. The number of casks carried by a South-seaman is very great, and the sizes vary up to nearly 350 gallons. The crew generally have abundance of fresh water till the cargo is nearly full; and besides the casks, there are four large iron tanks. Indeed, we have been informed that recently the South-seamen have been entirely fitted with iron tanks for the oil, and carry no more barrels than are requisite for the supply of fresh water, which in some instances is also kept in iron tanks.

On a somewhat similar system to that adopted in the Greenland trade, the officers and crew of South-seamen are paid for their services, not in fixed wages, but in a certain percentage on the cargo—thus stimulating them to obtain as large a freight in as short a period as possible, and insuring the best exertion of their energies for mutual advantage. The *lay*, or share of the captain, is, on the average, about one-thirteenth of the value of the cargo; and an able seaman gets about the one-hundred-and-sixtieth part for his portion. The entire crew, including master, mates, surgeon, harpooners, &c., amount to from thirty to forty men. A supply of provisions for three years and upward is taken out; and the arrangements now made for the preservation of health are so judicious, that scurvy is of very rare occurrence. South-seamen are remarkably *clean* ships—the reverse of the popular notion concerning whalers; within a few hours after the capture of a whale, the vessel and crew exhibit no signs of the temporary disorder the cutting-up necessarily occasions.

A South-seaman usually carries five swift boats, thirty feet in length, built of light materials, and shaped both ends alike, in order that they may with greater readiness be *backed* from the vicinity of a dangerous whale; they are steered with a long oar, which gives a much greater and more decided command over a boat than a rudder. Five long oars propel each boat, the rowlocks in which they play being muffled, in order to approach the destined victim without noise. Sockets in the floor of the boat receive the oars when apeak. As these whale-boats are thin in the timbers, for the sake of buoyancy and speed, they very frequently get shattered by blows from the fins, flukes, and tail of the whale attacked; and consequently their crews would inevitably perish, were it not for a contrivance which we think can not be too generally known to all who go a-boating either on business or pleasure. Life-lines are fixed at the gunwales of the boat; and when an accident causes her to fill, the oars are lashed athwart by aid of these lines, and although she may be quite submerged, still she will not sink, but bear up her crew until rescue arrives. We are sure that were this simple expedient known and adopted by merchant seamen and others, many hundreds of lives would be saved every year; for it is rarely that a boat is swamped so rapidly that there is not time to lash the oars athwart her gunwale.

And now, reader, please to step on board the sperm-whaler. We are cruising somewhere in the great Pacific Ocean. Our ship is clean from stem to stern—from try-works to cutting-falls; our boats are hanging ready to be launched at a moment's notice; keen eyes are sweeping the horizon in every direction, and sharp ears are anxiously listening for the anticipated cry of "There she spouts!"—for we are sailing along the edge of a current, and sperm-whales are known to be in the vicinity. It is early morning, with a fine working-breeze; and if you will take your station with us on the cross-trees—or, if that is too lofty an elevation, on the foretop beneath them—we will point out to you the well-known indications of sperm-whales being hereabouts. First of all, you probably glance, with a sort of wondering smile, at the queer-looking machine at the cross-trees overhead. Well, that is the *crow's-nest*; but its tenant is not a feathered creature, but a tarry, oily, old Salt, who is the look-out man for the nonce, and whose keen gray eye, even while he refills his cheek with a fresh plug, is fixed with absorbing attention on yonder tract of water, where he seems to expect every instant to see a whale rise and spout. The crow's-nest, as you perceive, is composed of a framework in the shape of a cask, covered with canvas, and furnished with a bit of seat and other little conveniences, to accommodate the look-out, and, when necessary, shelter him in some measure from the weather, as he frequently has to remain long aloft at a time. We believe, however, that South-seamen do not use, nor require, the crow's-nest so much as the Greenlandmen.

Now, look around, and mark what vast fields there are of the Sally-man, and of Medusæ of all kinds, and observe the numerous fragments of cuttle-fish floating about, remnants of the recent meals of the cachalot; and, above all, see the great smooth tracts of oily water, which show that a party of whales has passed over this portion of the ocean's surface not very long ago. Ah! you admire the countless flocks of birds hovering close by the ship. Yes, they are in unusual numbers, for they know by instinct that they will soon obtain abundance of food. But for one bird in the air, there are a thousand fish just beneath the surface. See! for hundreds of yards on every side of the ship, the water is literally blackened with albacores. They have attended us for many weeks, and will not be got rid of, unless a strong wind drives the ship along at a very rapid rate. They swim sociably along with us from one cruising-ground to another, and can be captured by hook and line with the greatest ease. They are fine fellows, averaging some four feet in length, and are of excel-

lent quality for the table. Watch them frightening the poor little flying-fish into the air! The latter are soon snapped up by the hovering birds, or are seized and devoured by the voracious albacores, the moment their feeble powers of flight are exhausted, and they drop helpless into the sea again. The albacores, too, have a very terrible enemy in turn—nothing less than the sword-fish, many of which corsairs make a rush, from time to time, through the dense droves of albacores, and transfix them, one or two together, with their long projecting swords, off which the slain albacores are then shaken and devoured by their ruthless enemy. It sometimes happens that the sword-fish misses his aim, and drives his weapon into, and even through a ship's side, to the great danger of the vessel.

Ha! our old look-out man sees a sign! Now he hails the deck. "There she blows! there she spouts!" What lungs the old fellow has! Hark to what follows. "Where away?" sharply cries the officer on deck. "A school of whales broad off the lee-bow, sir!" "Main-yard aback! &c. Out boats!" "There she blows again! There she flukes!" "How far off?" "Three miles, sir! There she breaches." "Be lively, men! Lower away!" "All clear, sir! Lower away it is!" "Cast off falls!—unhook!—out oars! —give way, men!"

You will please to bear in mind, worthy companion, that you and we are now seated somewhere in the boat, as it pulls away, "With measured strokes, most beautiful!" and that we shall consequently see whatever takes place. Meanwhile, let us take advantage of the interval which must intervene ere the whale we pursue is within harpoon's reach, to enlighten you a little about sperm-whales generally. The cachalot or sperm-whale is one of the largest of all the cetacean tribe, not unfrequently attaining the length of 60 feet: there is an authenticated instance of a sperm-whale 76 feet in length, and 38 feet in girth—a leviathan among leviathans! The female cachalot does not attain much more than half the size of the male, and yet gives birth to young ones 14 feet in length, and of proportionate girth. The average yield of oil is about eighty barrels for a full-grown male, and twenty-five for a female. The cachalot is black in color, but is occasionally spotted with white toward the tail. The head is one-third the entire length of the creature, and is of a square form, with a very blunt snout. The body is round, or nearly so, and tapers much toward the tail. The fins are triangular shaped, and very small; but the tail is of immense size, very flexible, and of tremendous power. When the animal strikes it flatly on the water, the report is like that of a small cannon. When used in propulsion, the tail is bent back beneath the body, and then sprung out again; when aiming at a boat or other object, it is bent sharply, and strikes the object by its recoil. The eyes are placed far back in the head, and well protected by integuments. They do not measure more than two inches in length by one in breadth, and have small power of gazing in an oblique direction. The tongue is small, and can not be protruded; but the gullet or throat is quite in proportion to the bulk of the animal, so that it could easily swallow a man; and this fact clearly disposes of the skeptical objection to the Scripture narrative of the prophet Jonah. The expansion of a pair of jaws nearly a score of feet in length must be a startling sight! The lower jaw appears slender in comparison with the vast bulk of the upper one.

The greater part of the head of the sperm-whale is composed of soft parts, called junk and case. The junk is oily fat; and the case is a delicate fluid, yielding spermaceti in large proportion. The teeth of the cachalot appear mainly on the lower jaw, projecting about two inches through the gum, and they are solid ivory, but without enamel. The black skin of this whale is destitute of hair, and possesses such a peculiar alkaline property, that seamen use it in lieu of soap. The lard or blubber beneath it varies from four to fourteen inches in thickness, and is perfectly white and inodorous. What whalers term schools are assemblages of female cachalots in large numbers—from twenty to a hundred, together with their young, called calves, and piloted by one or more adult males, called bulls. The females are called cows. As a general rule, full-grown males either head the schools or roam singly; sometimes a number of males assemble in what is called a drove.

And now let us revert to the chase we are engaged in. See! the school has taken the alarm, and is off at the rate of eight miles or more an hour. Is it not a beautiful and exciting spectacle to watch these huge monsters tearing along on the surface of the water, spouting vapor from their spiracles like steam from the valve of a steamboat, and leaving a creamy wake behind them, almost equal to that of a ship. Their movement is easy and majestic, their heads being carried high out of the water, as though they were conscious of being the monarchs of old Ocean. See, again! there is a sperm of the largest size, which has just leaped so as to show its entire bulk in the air—almost like a ship in size. What a crash and whirl of foam as it falls into its native element! But we gain on one fine fellow, which our headsman is steering for. Ay, now we are within fair striking distance, and a harpoon is hurled by the brawny arm of the harpooner in the bows, and pierces deep into the cachalot's side. A second follows; and the wounded animal gives a convulsive plunge, and then starts off along the surface at astonishing speed, dragging our boat along with it. You observe that the whale-line runs through a groove lined with lead, and is secured round a logger-head. The 200 fathoms of line will soon be all out, for the whale is preparing to *sound*, or dive deep beneath the surface. There he sounds; and the practiced harpooner has already bent on a second line to the end of the first. Well, he can not possibly remain above an hour beneath the surface, and probably will reappear very soon. Just as we thought; and now we must

haul gently alongside, the officer in command standing with his formidable lance poised ready to dart on the first opportunity. That blow is well planted; more succeed, and already the victim is in its last *flurry*. Our watchful rowers back water, to be beyond reach of a blow from the expiring monster's tail or flukes. He now spins round, spouting his life-blood, and crimsoning the sea far and near; now he turns over on his side, and the cheers of the men proclaim their easy victory.

While preparations are making to tow the dead cachalot to the ship, permit us to impart a little further information concerning the chase and capture of the sperm-whale. You have beheld a very easy capture; but not unfrequently the cachalot makes a most determined resistance, and with every appearance of being actuated by revenge, as well as by the instinct of self-preservation, attempts to seize and destroy a boat with its jaws. In this it frequently succeeds. At other times, it sweeps its tail rapidly through the air, and suddenly bringing it down on a boat, cuts the latter asunder, and kills some of the crew, or whirls them to a great distance. Occasionally, so far from fleeing from approaching boats, as the Greenland whale almost invariably does, the terrible cachalot will boldly advance to attack them, rushing open-mouthed, and making every effort to crush or stave them. Often will the cachalot turn on its side or back, and project its long lower jaw right over a boat, so that the terrified crew have to leap overboard, oars in hand. Sometimes it rushes head-on at the boat, splintering it beyond repair, or overturning it with all on board. But what shall we say to a cachalot attacking the ship itself, and actually coming off victor? An enormous cachalot rushed head-on, and twice struck the American sperm-whale ship *Essex*, so as to stave in the bows, and the ship was lost, the crew barely having time to escape in the boats! We refer the reader who desires to know more of the peculiar habits of the sperm-whale, to the books of Herman Melville, the American sailor-author, and of Mr. Bennett. We may say a few words more, however, on the subject of the dangers incident to the capture of the cachalot. The harpooner, especially, is liable to be entangled in coils of the line as it runs out after a whale is struck, and to be then dragged beneath the surface; and even although the line is severed at the moment by the ax kept in readiness, the man is usually gone. Yet more appalling is the calamity which occasionally befalls an entire crew, when the struck whale is diving perpendicularly. It has happened repeatedly on such an occasion, that the line has whirled round the loggerhead, or other fixture of the boat; and that in the twinkling of an eye, almost ere a prayer or ejaculation could be uttered, the boat, crew, and all, have been dragged down into the depths of ocean! Such, too, is the pressure of the water upon a boat when it descends to a certain depth, that on being drawn to the surface again, it will not float, owing to the fluid being forced into the pores of the planks, not only by the m⸺ ⸺lensity of the ocean, but also by the rapid rate at which the whale has dragged it. It has happened many a time, that a boat at a distance from the ship has been seen to disappear suddenly, pulled bodily down by a harpooned whale, not a vestige of boat or crew being ever seen on the surface again! If we regard whaling merely as a manly *hunt* or chase, quite apart from its commercial aspects, we think it is far more exciting, and requires more nerve and more practiced skill, and calls into exertion more energy, more endurance, more stout-heartedness, than the capture of any other creature—not even excepting the lion, tiger, or elephant.

But let us return to our own captured cachalot. You perceive that the men on board the ship are preparing to receive it. They have placed some short spars outside the vessel to facilitate operations, and have removed a dozen feet of the bulwark in front of the platform to which we before directed attention. The cutting-falls are also all ready, and the ship itself is hove-to. We will anticipate what ensues, and describe it for you. The dead whale floats buoyantly—although in some rare instances it will sink—alongside the ship, where it is well secured, and a stage is slung over the vessel's side, from which the officers overlook and direct operations, &c. The blubber between the eye and pectoral fin is cut through with the spade, which is a triangular-shaped instrument, as sharp as a razor, attached to a long shaft or handle. A man now gets upon the whale—his boots being spiked to prevent slipping—and fixes the hook of the falls to it. The windlass is then manned, and lifts up the detached blubber, the spades cutting away and the whale slowly turning over at the same time. The strip of blubber thus in course of separation is about four feet in breadth, and is called a blanket-piece. It is cut in a spiral direction, and lowered on deck when it reaches up to the head of the cutting-falls. Fresh hold is then taken, and the operation is continued until the whale is entirely flenshed. If the whale is a small one, the whole of the head is at once cut off, and hoisted bodily on deck; but if a large one, its important parts are separately secured. Finally, the skeleton is cut adrift, to float or sink, as may happen. The entire operation occupies at least ten hours, if the whale is very large.

During this cutting-up affair, the water far and near is red with blood, and great flocks of petrels, albatrosses, &c., hover about to pick up the floating morsels. Swarms of sharks also never fail to attend; and so voracious are these creatures, that the men have to strike at them with their spades, to prevent them from devouring the whale piecemeal, ere its remains are abandoned to fish and fowl as their legitimate prey. Although the whalers generally kill many sharks on such occasions, it is said that if a man slips from the carcass of the whale into the midst of these devourers, they seldom attempt to injure him. Personally, however, we can not say that we should like to put the generosity of Messieurs Sharks to such a test.

The blubber is carefully separated from the bits of flesh which may adhere to it preparatory to boiling, an operation first undergone by the head matter, which is kept distinct from the body matter—the former yielding spermaceti, the latter sperm-oil. The scraps, or refuse matter from the oil, themselves supply the furnace with fuel, burning clearly, and emitting intense heat. This operation is called trying-out, and is only dangerous when proper precaution is not used to prevent water from falling into the boiling oil, or by carelessly throwing in wet blubber; in which cases the caldrons may overflow very suddenly, and every thing be in flames together. From the try-works the oil is conveyed to the coolers, and thence to the casks; and a good-sized whale, in favorable weather, may be cut up and converted into oil, &c., within a couple of days.

The spectacle of trying-out on a dark night is exceedingly impressive. There is the ship, slowly sailing along over the pathless ocean, the furnace roaring and producing lurid flames that illumine the surrounding waves, the men passing busily to and fro, and dense volumes of black smoke continually rising in the air and drifting to leeward. Trying-out in a gloomy midnight has a touch even of sublimity about it; and we can conceive the feelings of awe and terror it would inspire in a spectator beholding the ghastly show for the first time from the deck of another ship. We think it is Herman Melville who compared the crew of a sperm-whaler, on such an occasion, to a party of demons busily engaged in the celebration of some unhallowed rite; nor is this fancy at all outrageous, to our thinking. What a picture might a painter of genius make of the scene!

And now, reader, we hope you do not begrudge the time spent with us aboard a sperm-whaler? But we crave the favor of your company, or rather, in Shakspearian language, we say, "lend us your ear" yet a little longer. Certain announcements appeared recently in the papers concerning improved methods of killing the leviathans of the deep. First in order was a simple and presumably effective plan for projecting the harpoon into the body of the whale. A small cannon or swivel was fixed in the bow of the boat, so as to be capable of being raised or depressed, and to turn on its pivot in any required direction. The harpoon was fired from this gun at the object—with a few fathoms of small chain attached, so that no injury would result to the whale-line itself in the act of firing. This scheme appears to have been well received for its apparent feasibility; but whether it has, on fair practical trial, been found to fall short of what was expected from it, we are unable to state. Its advantages were expected to be the following :— The harpoon could be fired from such a distance, that there would not be any necessity of approaching dangerously near the animal at the outset; and the force of its projection would be such, that the harpoon would be certain to be firmly planted, and very probably might penetrate a vital part, and nearly kill the whale at a blow.

A yet more important and extraordinary innovation is that which was proposed some two years ago, and is now again attracting new attention—being nothing less than whaling by electricity. The electricity is conveyed to the body of the whale from an electro-galvanic battery contained in the boat, by means of a metallic wire attached to the harpoon, and so arranged as to re-conduct the electric current from the whale through the sea to the machine. This machine is stated to be capable of throwing into the body of the whale such strokes of electricity as would paralyze in an instant its muscles, and deprive it of all power of motion, if not actually of life.

Should all we are told about this whaling by electricity be true, a marvelous change will take place in the fishery. The danger of attacking and killing the cachalot will be reduced to its minimum; few or no whales which have once received the fatal galvanic shock will escape; the time consumed in their capture will probably not average the tenth of what it does at present; and the duration of the ship's voyage will be materially shortened, for there will be no limit to the success of the chase, and the rapidity with which the cargo will be made up, except the time which now, as always, will be absolutely necessary to boil down the blubber. But how long will the supply of cachalots be sufficient, under the new system, to yield remunerative freights? We know that the sperm-whale has already been seriously thinned in some localities, and that a certain time—perhaps much longer than whalers and naturalists reckon—is necessary for whales to grow to a profitable size. Now, the electric battery, according to our authorities, being so deadly in its application, we should suppose that when a whaler falls in with a large school of cachalots, and sends out all his boats, each armed with a battery, they will be able to kill perhaps thrice the present maximum number (five), which can be secured at one chase and attack, and in one-fifth of the usual time. If they do this, it matters little whether they can secure all the dead whales for cutting up—the animal is at any rate destroyed, and years must elapse ere another will have grown to take its place in the ocean. To drop this speculation, however, we may at least reasonably conclude, that the capture of sperm-whales will become a matter of more certainty and greater expedition than it is at present; and if the number does *not* rapidly diminish year by year—although we seriously anticipate that it will—the price of sperm-oil, and the other commercial products of the fishery, may be expected to become materially lower. That this would cause an increased demand for these products, there can be no doubt, for at present the limited supply, and the large quantity of sperm-oil used for lubricating delicate machinery keep up the price.

Let us now conclude with a few words on the commercial products of the cachalot. The most important is the sperm-oil, used for lamps and for lubricating machinery. It is more pure than any other animal oil. Spermaceti is a transparent fluid when first extracted from the whale, but it becomes concrete when exposed to a cold temperature, or placed in water. It is found in all parts of the whale, but chiefly in the head and the dorsal hump. After being prepared, it is cast in moulds for sale in the shops, and is chiefly used for making candles. Formerly, as Shakspeare tells us, it was considered to possess curative properties—

The sovereign'st thing on earth
Is spermaceti for an inward bruise.

The teeth yield ivory, which always sells at a remunerative price. Lastly, there is the rare and mysterious substance called ambergris—the origin of which was long a problem, which even the learned could not solve. It is now known to be a kind of morbid excrescence produced in the intestines of the cachalot, and in no other species of whale. It is sold as a perfume, fetching five dollars an ounce when pure, and rare in the market even at that price. When found floating on the sea, it has undoubtedly been voided by the cachalot, or has drifted from it when the body became decomposed after death.

A Pilgrimage
to Plymouth
(1853)

A PILGRIMAGE TO PLYMOUTH.

BY CALVIN W. PHILLEO.

TWO hundred years ago the colony of Plymouth was one of the most important on the North American continent. Its chief town was the equal in rank with New Amsterdam and Boston. Its governors and magistrates were statesmen whose names are immortal. The acts of its Council, the wars in which it was engaged, the famines and pestilences it endured, and every event that affected its welfare and prosperity, are matters of which we read in the histories of the nation. The classic names of Athens, of Sparta, and even of Rome itself are not more familiar to the memory than is that of·Plymouth ; and in the time to come there is no spot upon the earth that will possess in the hearts of men an interest more universal and enduring than the Rock at which ended the long and weary voyage of the passengers of the May-flower. And yet, though we have all heard and read of Plymouth since we began to remember, though we know its early history by heart, and the very mention of its name sounds in our ears like the keynote of a national anthem of liberty, though five millions of us claim to have descended from its early colonists, and pride ourselves accordingly, though there is hardly a day in all the year in which we do not hear or utter an allusion to Plymouth or the Pilgrim Fathers, —either in sermon, oration, speech, or conversation, though we boast of the religion of the Puritans as if we hoped to be saved by the merits of our ancestors, and daily assert—what no one can deny—that the Pilgrim Fathers shaped the model which has given the form to our free institutions and government, though, in fine, we acknowledge the town of Plymouth to have been the birth-place of our nation, great already, and with a destiny of unexampled greatness, there are scarcely fifty thousand of the five million descendants of the Puritan exiles, outside of the ancient county of Plymouth, that could answer correctly the probable questions of an intelligent foreigner, curious to know the present state and condition of a town so celebrated in the history of the country, and of the world as is the town of Plymouth.

A few school-children, fresh from their recitations in geography, might be able to repeat the brief paragraph of " fine print" in their class-book, which informs them of the pleasant situation of Plymouth upon the bay of the same name, about forty miles from Boston; that it was here that the Pilgrims landed in 1620, and commenced the first settlement of New England; that the present town has considerable coasting and some foreign trade, and is largely engaged in the fisheries, and that its population in 1850 was 6026.

We start on our Pilgrimage to Plymouth, from Boston, in the early afternoon of a bright August day. Thrice has our carriage been obliged to halt during the short ride between the hotel and the railroad station, in consequence of a choking up of the narrow and crooked streets. Nevertheless, we have a good ten minutes before the starting of the train, when we draw up at the door of a handsome brick edifice, built in the Italian style, with brown stone cornices and window caps. This is the front of the Old Colony Railroad Terminus.

But we are bound to Plymouth, and have no time to spare for the improvements made in the rival colony of Massachusetts Bay. Let us enter the station-house. Do not be dismayed at learning that your baggage must be consigned to the tender mercies of a man who says that he is the baggage-master, but who, nevertheless, may be an impostor for all that one can tell, inasmuch as he is too much of a republican to wear a badge, and refuses to give us checks for our trunks. There is doubtless an occult method in their system of management on this road, with respect to baggage. Let us have faith, then, in the baggage-master's curt prophecy, that we shall find our trunks " all right" when we shall have arrived at Plymouth.

But what a long train! Seven—eight first-class cars, besides second-class and baggage-cars —and all nearly filled with people. Plymouth Rock, one would think from these indications, must be what it should be—the Mecca of American pilgrims. But the truth is, that there are scarcely twenty passengers in the whole train that are going through with us. We shall arrive at Plymouth with only one first-class car. Of the others, some will have been switched off at the Braintree Junction, and some at the

Bridgewater Junction, and one will have been left at this station and another at that station. The Old Colony Road is a trunk from which diverge several branches, some of which, indeed, are of more importance than itself. Traveling upon this road is much like the journey of life. One starts with a host, but at the end of the course but few remain who have traveled with him all the way. So, although there are several drawbridges to cross, we must take the foremost car, the only one of its class that goes through. We will sit on the left-hand side. The sun comes in the other way, and, besides, there is more to see in this direction.

It is a sterile-looking country we are passing through. There is scarcely enough of the thin soil to cover half the rock with a scanty green mantle, and so great ledges lie bare above ground, and barberry-bushes, loaded with unripe fruit, and sometimes stunted firs, grow from the crevices. But there are some good farms, nevertheless, and fields where heavy crops will be gathered. But such farms and fields have cost much labor and money to make them fertile.

The people have grown rich hereabouts, in spite of the niggardly soil. There is a look about the houses that betokens the thrift of the dwellers in them. The little crowds at the station-houses are composed of well-dressed people. The cattle in the pastures are sleek, well-fed, and well-cared for, and people drive good bits of horse-flesh in easy, handsome carriages.

We are losing cars from our long train at almost every station, as I foretold, and the speed of those that remain is increased.

Kingston Station is the last this side of Plymouth. Here it was that Daniel Webster left the hurry and bustle of the world behind him, as he descended from the cars for the last time in his life. Marshfield lies about seven miles northeast from here.

We are nearing our journey's end. Yonder is the round, smooth summit of Captain's Hill, in Duxbury, that overlooks the whole of Plymouth Bay, and forms a prominent land-mark for vessels. It rises some two hundred and fifty feet above the level of the sea at its base. It was named after Captain Myles Standish, who, for many of the later years of his life, lived near the foot of it.

And now the train rounds a curve, the wheels ringing as they grind against the rails. A moment more—look now—the cool sea-breeze fans your cheek again, as you gaze for the first time upon the wide and beautiful Bay of Plymouth. It is high water—that is to say, it is full tide, or nearly so—and the extensive flats left bare at low ebb, exposing to view ugly sand-banks and unseemly patches of eel-grass, are now hidden beneath the surface of as handsome a sheet of blue water as ever sparkled in the rays of an afternoon sun. The bay is, you perceive, almost landlocked; and viewing it from this point one might almost imagine it to be a lake instead of

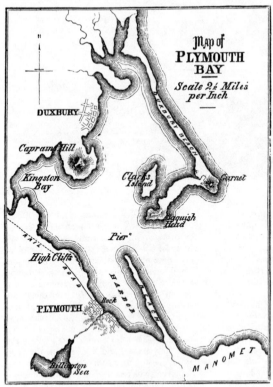

MAP OF PLYMOUTH BAY.

of the bay;" and although upon its western slope there are no trees, except a few solitary and flat-crowned cedars — more ancient, probably, than the settlement of Plymouth—the tops of groves and orchards growing upon the eastern side are visible far above the undulating summit-ridge, with here and there the tapering forms of Lombardy poplars shooting up above the surrounding foliage, like steeples towering aloft among the house-tops of a city.

A few minutes more, and we have reached a point from which we can look straight out to sea. But half-way across the channel —the inlet to the bay, which has grown wider and wider with each instant of our advance toward it— runs a narrow spit of land, upon the extreme point of which stands a small black beacon. This is Plymouth Beach; and the part of the bay inclosed within its sweep, forms the shallow harbor of the town. The dark object in the water, apparently at a little distance from the beacon, is a square pier of granite rocks, erected upon a shoal that is oftentimes bare at very low water. Into the channel, upon the left, extends a small cape with a large, solitary tree grow-

an arm of the sea. On our left, Captain's Hill rears its bald crown between us and the village of Duxbury, which lies concealed behind it, straggling along the shore for miles. Far away to the north, beyond those distant hills ruddy with fields of buckwheat-stubble, is Marshfield and the grave of Daniel Webster. From thence the shore sweeps with a gentle curve to the southward, the hills diminishing in height, until it becomes a low sandy beach, with here and there a clump of cedars crowning a knoll, and dark copses of stunted plum-bushes fringing and tufting the white and sparkling sides of the sand-hills. This is Duxbury Beach—a strip of land, that, averaging scarcely twenty rods in width above high-water mark, stretches from the main-land miles to the southward, interposing its narrow barrier of drifting sand between the thundering surges of the stormy Atlantic and the haven within its protecting embrace.

Half-way between us and the beach lies an island, a mile in length, with an oval outline rising with a gentle slope from the extremities toward the centre; near which stands a large gray rock, that one might, from its size, well mistake for a house, but that its irregular form shows plainly in the rays of the western sun shining straight upon it. The round surface of this island is green to the very brink of the gravelly bluff, against which dash the "waves

ing near the edge of its bluff point, and a single weather-beaten house, nestling under its western slope as if striving to gain a lee from the cold northeasters, that so often blow here fiercely, for days at a time. This is Saquish Head, the termination of Duxbury Beach, and the few acres of tillable upland and the little wood-colored house, already mentioned, form the homestead of a family of hardy fishermen.

Beyond Saquish and rapidly opening from it, as we glide to the eastward, we observe a high promontory stretching boldly forth into the sea. The two white twin towers standing up on its highest point, in full relief, against the dark blue eastern sky, with flashing lanterns reflecting the dazzling rays of the sun, I need not tell you are light-houses. The promontory is called the Gurnet, and the light-houses the Gurnet Lights. Besides the light-keeper's white dwelling, there is only one habitation upon the lonely cliff. But of the Gurnet more anon, when we make it a visit.

Almost in front of us, forming the southern portal of the entrance to the bay, rises a lofty cape, four hundred feet in height, extending for miles from the mainland into the ocean. The air is so clear to-day that the blue haze of distance is hardly noticeable; and the play of the rosy light upon the heavily wooded sides of the frowning promontory, the different shades of green of the thick foliage, the ruddy tints of

GURNET.

the leaves where autumn has prematurely laid her hand, and the glitter of the sand upon the shore at the foot of the cliff, are distinctly visible, notwithstanding the miles that intervene. Manomet, as this cape is called, forms a magnificent back-ground to the lovely picture upon which we gaze. Beyond it lie the unknown regions of Cape Cod.

The southern shore of the bay and harbor is formed by a range of hills, gradually increasing in height as it extends to the eastward. Upon the northern slope of this range stands Plymouth. Yes, yonder village of old-fashioned, square-roofed houses, built upon the hill-sides and in the valleys between, of queer-looking stores and warehouses, and ropewalks huddled together at the water's edge, with the long ruinous-looking wharf, built upon piles, projecting into the harbor in front, with the square gray turret, and two or three steeples and cupolas just visible above the glaring shingled roofs, is Plymouth—the Old Colony, the home of the Pilgrims, the most ancient town in New England. We hardly have a fair look at it, for we are on the wrong side of the car; but never mind, this is not its best point of view, and tomorrow we will see it from the beach yonder; nay, perhaps this very night, by moonlight, from the bay.

At last the abbreviated train, with ringing bell and sounding whistle, rattles into the station-house. The groaning brakes perform their office. The train stops. Our journey is ended. We follow the few remaining passengers, and descend from the cars. The crabbed baggage-master's prediction has proved true. Our trunks are safe. Nobody but ourselves claims them. They are delivered to us upon demand. Pray, what need is there of checks, then?

A carriage is in waiting to convey us to the Samoset House; but we prefer to walk. The distance is but a few rods. Let the driver have our baggage while we go afoot. The soil is holy, albeit a trifle sandy.

We did not come to Plymouth to talk about hotels; so let us dismiss the Samoset House with a word, while we are on the way to it, and mention it no more. You will find it a very

well-kept hotel—quiet, roomy, cool, and pleasant. You will see few gentlemen there, except on Saturday evening and Sunday. There will be plenty of ladies, however (if of ladies there can ever be a plenty)—the wives and daughters of "solid men of Boston," and lots of happy children. The view of the bay from the long piazzas on the northeastern front of the house is very fine, and in hot weather the cool sea-breeze that plays there during the afternoon, is delightful. A prettier place in which to sit and smoke, and weave after-dinner fancies, read the morning newspaper, and take nice little naps, can rarely be found. Moreover, mine host of the Samoset gives one a good dinner, his wines are fair, and his bills are by no means extortionate. So much for the Samoset.

We have two hours before tea. Let us wash the dust from our mouths, and then commence our rambles immediately. The street that leads southeastwardly from the hotel toward the centre of the village is called Court-street. The houses on each side of the way are generally wooden, two-story, square-roofed dwellings, painted dingy white, with faded green blinds, and with scanty little front door-yards, full of dusty shrubbery. A few steps bring us opposite a structure standing a short distance in the rear of the line of houses, on the left-hand side of the street. It is built in the style of a Grecian temple, of rough granite, with a wooden front, and a colonnade of wooden Doric columns, painted in imitation of wrought granite. This edifice is Pilgrim Hall. The corner-stone was laid, with appropriate ceremonies, on the 1st of September, 1824. It is seventy feet long by forty feet in width; and contains a dining-room in the basement, where the Pilgrim Society and their fortunate guests are wont to eat capital dinners, on appropriate occasions, in commemoration of the famines experienced by their forefathers. Truly a most pleasant custom. The hall above is a spacious apartment, fitted up plainly for the reception and preservation of interesting memorials of the Pilgrim Fathers and the ancient times of the Old Colony. All these will we see—but not now—for I am desirous that you have a look at Plymouth

PILGRIM'S HALL.

and its bay, from the summit of Burying Hill, before sunset, and while it is yet high-water. But although we will not at this time enter Pilgrim Hall, let us pause awhile before it. Approach with me to the iron railing within the yard, inclosing a small elliptical space. You behold a large fragment of a huge granite boulder, split in twain, and the crevice filled with cement, and upon which somebody has painted, in great black figures, "1620." Fear no imposture; you behold a genuine, authentic fragment of the upper surface of the Forefather's Rock.

FRAGMENT OF PILGRIM ROCK.

The portion of this celebrated rock which here reposes, and which will here remain for a thousand years after we, who now gaze upon it, shall have crumbled into dust, was removed from its original position at the water's edge, to the Town Square, by some zealous whigs, in the year 1774. It was the intention of these worthy patriots to remove the entire rock, but, in the attempt, it split asunder. An ardent whig, with great presence of mind, seized upon this untoward occurrence, and pronounced it to be a most favorable omen, indicating the speedy, final separation of the colonies from the mother-country. It was finally concluded, however, to lower the base of the rock into its original bed, where it now remains, as we shall see it, just visible above the surface of the ground. The other portion was drawn by twenty yoke of oxen to the Town Square, and a liberty-pole erected over it. Here it remained until the 4th of July, 1834, when it was again removed to this spot, and inclosed within this iron-railing, which is, you perceive, composed of alternate harpoons and boat-hooks, and inscribed with the names of the illustrious forty-one who subscribed the compact on board the Mayflower, at Cape-Cod harbor, November 11th, 1620.* This compact

---

* This celebrated compact, which was, probably, the first written instrument of the kind in the world, was as follows:

"In the name of God, Amen. We, whose names are under written, the Loyal Subjects of our dread Sovereign

was drawn up and signed, as well-authenticated tradition reports, upon the lid of the sea-chest of Brewster. This chest, together with the iron pot of stout Myles Standish, are now in the possession of the Connecticut Historical Society at Hartford.

BREWSTER'S CHEST AND STANDISH'S POT.

On our way down the street we pass, upon the right, the Court House—a well-built brick edifice, painted white, with a shady green inclosure in front of it, called, in former times, Training Green, and in these latter days, Court House Square. A few rods further on, we en-

ter Main-street. This avenue may evidently lay a well-founded claim to the distinction of a business street. On the right-hand corner, a showy lantern of stained-glass indicates an oyster and ice-cream saloon of no mean pretensions. Upon the opposite corner a three-story hotel rejoices in the title of the Mansion House. The houses are generally built close upon the side-walks, and the lower stories are occupied as shops and stores. We discover two dry-goods stores, with chintz and calicoes hanging about the doors; an apothecary's shop, with a rusty-looking gilt mortar for its sign; a bookstore; several grocers' shops; a news-room; a daguerreotype saloon, and a barber's pole. One well-built house, moreover, bears upon its front the signs of two banks and an insurance company. There are two printing offices in this street, at each of which is published a weekly newspaper. The Old Colony Memorial is the organ of the Plymouth County Whigs; while its younger neighbor, the Plymouth Rock, rejoices in the publication of the laws and treaties of the United States, "by authority." Of course the "Rock" is Democratic in its politics. From Main-street we turn into Leyden-street. This

Lord, King James, by the Grace of God, of Great Britain, France, and Ireland, King, Defender of the Faith, &c., having undertaken, for the Glory of God and advancement of the Christian Faith and Honor of our King and Country, a Voyage to plant the first Colony in the Northern Parts of Virginia; Do, by these Presents, solemnly and mutually, in the Presence of God and one another, Covenant and Combine ourselves together into a Civil body Politic, for our better Ordering and Preservation, and Furtherance of the ends aforesaid, ; and by Virtue hereof, to enact, constitute, and frame such just and equal laws, Ordinances, Acts, Constitutions, and Offices, from Time to Time, as

shall be thought most meet and convenient for the General Good of the Colony; unto which we Promise all due Submission and Obedience.

"In witness whereof, we have hereunto subscribed our Names, at Cape Cod, the 11th of November, in the year of the Reign of our Sovereign Lord, King James, of England, France, and Ireland, the Eighteenth, and of Scotland, the Fifty-fourth. Anno Domini, 1620."

The following are fac-similes of the Handwriting of the Pilgrims, some of whose names were subscribed to the compact; they were copied by Mr. Russell, from ancient documents:

William Bradford   *Tho: Prence*

Edw: Winslow   *Nathaniell Morton*

Willm Brewster   *Thomas Cushman*

Myles Standish   *John Winslow*

Isaac Allerton   *Constant Southworth*

John Bradford   *Tho: Southworth*

is the oldest street in the town. Lots were laid out upon it as early as the 28th of December, 1620, but a week after the landing. In a letter found in the archives of the Hague by J. Romeyn Brodhead, Esq., written by one Isaack De Rasieres, of the colony of NewNetherlands, who visited Plymouth, on an embassy, in the year 1627, the following description is given of Leyden-street: "New Plymouth lies on the slope of a hill stretching east toward the sea-coast, with a broad street about a cannon-shot of 800 [yards] long leading down the hill; with a [street] crossing in the middle northward to the rivulet, and southward to the land. The houses are constructed of hewn planks, with gardens, also inclosed behind, and at the sides with hewn planks; so that their houses and court-yards are arranged in very good order, with a stockade against a sudden attack; and at the ends of the streets there are three wooden gates. In the centre, on the cross-street, stands the Governor's House, before which is a square inclosure, upon which four patereros [steen-stucken] are mounted, so as to flank along the streets." With respect to the length of Leyden-street, the worthy Dutchman must have been mistaken, or else the yard of Holland was not of the same extent as the Yankee measure of that name is now; for the ancient street could not have been more than four hundred yards in length.

Let us go to the left as we turn from Main-street, and walk a few paces down Leyden-street toward the water-side. At the brow of the hill the road forks—one path descending the declivity, and the other keeping upon the edge of the bank, and following its curve. We will choose the latter. At the corner stands the Universalist Church, upon foundations that are higher than even the chimneys of the houses hard by in the next street below. Upon its site, in 1826, stood a house, at that time the oldest in town, but which was, in that year, pulled down to give place to the church. It was known by the name of the Allyn House, and was the birth-place of the mother of James

THE ALLYN HOUSE.

Otis, who was the grand-daughter of Edward Dotey, a Pilgrim of the Mayflower. At the time of its demolition it was at least one hundred and fifty years old; and if it had remained, would now have been fast verging toward its third century. Although the Universalist Church is very respectable in its appearance, we can not help wishing that its place was still occupied by the ancient house that for so many years survived the ravages of time and the elements, and the "march of improvement."

Beyond the church we come upon an open level space, or square, upon the summit of the hill. The green-sward is intersected by irregular foot-paths, leading across it to flights of steps that afford the means of descent to the level of Water-street. The western side is formed by a row of dwellings facing the bay. On the right, we overlook the roofs and chimneys of the houses built upon the water side, peering up above the edge of the walled cliff. Beyond is the bay, and before us, in the distance, we catch a glimpse of Captain's Hill.

Here, in this square, were buried those who died in the years 1620 and 1621. Here was buried Governor John Carver, and, six weeks afterward, his gentle wife, who could not survive the loss of "so gracious an husband," was laid by his side. Here stood, beside the graves of their wives, dug in the frozen earth, Myles

Standish, Edward Winslow, and Isaac Allerton. Here lie the ashes of fifty of the passengers of the Mayflower, who died of the hardships and the "sore sickness" of that first dreary winter. Fifty out of one hundred and one ! So many that their graves were smoothed, that the Indians might not count the number. And here stood the wasted band of survivors, and saw the homeward-bound Mayflower lift her anchor, spread her sails, and put to sea, leaving them, of their own free-will, alone in the wilderness with their dead.

When we have turned to retrace our steps we perceive, standing directly before us, on the southern side of Leyden-street, just where the steep descent of the hill commences, a plain square-roofed, two-story wooden house. It is

HOUSE ON SITE OF THE COMMON HOUSE.

the residence of Captain Samuel D. Holmes, and stands upon the former site of the Common House—the first substantial building erected in New England. It was a frame-building, twenty feet square. In the year 1801, some men, who were digging a cellar in this spot, found sev-

eral tools and a plate of iron, seven feet below the surface of the ground. These interesting relics were carefully preserved.

The site of the first parsonage house is on the northern side of the street, near the fork of the roads. It is at this time occupied by the residence of Mr. James Bartlett. The present parsonage of the First Church stands on this street, further west. The land upon which it was built was given to the church in 1664. It is at the present time the residence of Dr. Kendall, the venerable senior pastor of the church, an octogenarian, having been settled in the ministry in the year 1800.

The grocer's shop at the northwest corner of Main and Leyden streets stands upon the ground formerly included within the fortified square inclosure in front of Governor Bradford's house, mentioned in the letter of Isaack De Rasieres. The site of the Governor's mansion is occupied by the next house on Leyden-street, standing opposite the foot of the street, which turns to the left. This building, the lower story of which is used as the Post-Office, is a long, low, wooden house, and is undoubtedly very ancient, but whether it was the immedia'e successor of Governor Bradford's fortified mansion, even the oldest inhabitant can not tell.

Market-street turns to the north, and leads down the hill and across the town brook, the finding of which in this place probably determined the exploring party sent out from the Mayflower, to select the site which they did for the location of the town. Herrings were formerly taken in this brook by the colonists in such vast numbers that they were used as a manure for the soil ; but the dams of the numerous mills, rope-walks, and other manufacturing

POST-OFFICE BUILDING, ON THE SITE OF BRADFORD'S MANSION.

establishments located on the stream, have long since caused it to be forsaken by the shoals of fish that formerly frequented it for the purpose of spawning. It has its rise in a small lake or pond lying in the woods some two miles southwest of the village. This beautiful sheet of water was discovered on the 8th of January, 1621, from the top of a high tree, by honest Francis Billington, who supposed it to be the great western ocean; and a week afterward, with the master's-mate of the ship, actually made a tour of exploration to its shores. These circumstances have given it the name of Billington Sea.

Standing on the corner of Market and Leyden streets, and looking westwardly, the Town Square lies before us. The branches of a grove of noble elms (planted in the year 1783, by the late Thomas Davis, Esq.) meet each other in mid-air, and form with their dense foliage a canopy of green leaves that completely excludes the glare of the sunlight from every part of the square. A prettier spot can not be imagined. On the right, is the ancient house, now occupied as the Post-Office, which, as I have already told you, stands in the place of the Governor Bradford house. West of this building, a little in the rear, is the Church of the Pilgrimage, a plain wooden structure, painted brown, with a low tower. On our left, nearly opposite us as we look across Market-street, is the Town House, formerly the County Court House, an ancient building, erected in 1749, and at that time esteemed one of the finest models of architecture. In front of us, upon higher ground, commanding a view of the whole length of Leyden-street, stands the house of worship of the old First Church, the lineal descendant (so to speak) of the meeting-house in which the Pilgrim Fathers assembled for prayer and praise. It is a handsome edifice, built of wood, in the Gothic style, with a large, square buttressed tower, lifting its four sharp pinnacles above the sun-gilded crowns of the elm trees that surround it.

It is probable that previous to 1622 public worship was held in the Common House. In that year a fort was erected on Burying Hill, a glimpse of which you catch between the two churches, rising steeply behind them. This fort was constructed in such a manner as to combine the means

of defense with accommodations for public worship. This curious edifice is described in the letter of Isaack De Rasieres, a part of which I have already quoted: "Upon the hill," says he, "they have a large, square house, with a flat roof, made of thick sawn planks, stayed with oak beams, upon the top of which they have six cannons, which shoot iron balls of four and five pounds, and command the surrounding country. The lower part they use for their church, where they preach on Sundays and the usual holidays. They assemble by beat of drum, each with his musket or firelock, in front of the captain's door; they have their cloaks on, and place themselves in order, three abreast, and are led by a sergeant without beat of drum. Behind comes the Governor, in a long robe; beside him, on the right hand, comes the preacher with his cloak on, and on the left hand the captain with his sidearms and cloak on, and with a small cane in his hand—and so they march in good order, and each sets his arms down near him. Thus they are on their guard night and day."

Fancy this quaint procession assembled before Captain Myles Standish's door, pausing at the

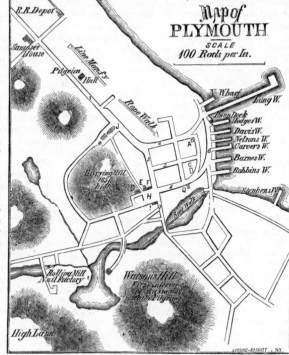

A. *Joanna Davis House—Cole's Hill.*
B. *Plymouth Rock and Wells's Store.*
C. *Universalist Church.*
D. *First Church.*
E. *Church of the Pilgrimage.*
F. *Post-Office—Site of Gov. Bradford's House.*
G. *Saml. D. Holmes's House—Site of Common House.*
H. *Town Square.*
I. *Town House.*
J. *Court-House Square.*

1. *Court-street.*
2. *North-street.*
3. *Middle-street.*
4. *Leyden-street.*
5. *Main-street.*
6. *Water-street.*
7. *Market-street.*

gate of the Governor's mansion to receive the worshipful Chief Magistrate, and then marching solemnly through this very square before us, and up the hill yonder, to the embattled meeting-house.

The present church is the fourth that has stood upon this site. The first meeting-house was erected in 1637, and taken down in 1683, when the second was built in its place, and stood until 1744, in which year it was removed, in its turn, and a third meeting-house erected, which remained until the present modern church was built.

But let us hasten to the top of Burying Hill before the sun shall have declined too far. We will stay there to see him set, and there receive his parting rays. You remember, of course, the verse of Pierpont's Ode:

> " The Pilgrim Fathers are at rest:
>   When Summer 's throned on high,
> And the world's warm breast is in verdure dressed,
>   Go stand on the hill where they lie :
> The earliest ray of the golden day
>   On that hallowed spot is cast,
> And the evening sun, as he leaves the world,
>   Looks kindly on that spot last."

Crossing Town Square diagonally, we pass through a gateway at the corner of the fence that surrounds the hill, about midway between the two meeting-houses, and commence the steep ascent. Upon the side that we are climbing, near the summit, stood the building mentioned in the letter of De Rasieres, partly fort, and partly meeting-house. Here, from time to time, were erected other fortifications, and a watch-tower, until the death of King Philip, in 1676, relieved the colonists from any further apprehensions with respect to Indian aggressions, when they were sold and removed, or suffered to fall into decay. In those days, therefore, the hill very naturally received, and for a while retained, the appellation of Fort Hill. Let us remember how many dreary nights has the lonely sentinel gazed forth from the tower which formerly stood here, watching and listening intently, lest the stealthy advance of the crafty foe should surprise the sleeping town below, and the little spark of civilization and Christianity, shining with a steady but feeble lustre upon the border of the immense wilderness of barbarism and heathendom, be extinguished in blood. Strive to realize the difference between now and then. You behold at your feet a well built and populous town—yet one that has, in these respects, a thousand equals in the country. The sentinel in 1622 kept watch over a hamlet of a score of rude huts ; yet, withal, the only homes of civilized men in all New England. You carry in your mind the idea of Boston, the dust of whose busy streets still cleaves to your shoes ; of New York, with its seven hundred thousand inhabitants, where you may sleep to-morrow night, if you will, borne thither on cushioned sofas in swift and gilded cars ; of the other great cities of the Union, of the hundreds of smaller cities, the thousands of large towns and villages, and the tens and hundreds of thousands of civilized

dwellings in more isolated situations, scattered thickly over the land. You know that if some great calamity should to-night befall the town before you—a sweeping conflagration, or (if in these days such a thing may be supposed) a sudden invasion of an enemy, before the setting of to-morrow's sun the tidings would be spread throughout the Union, and millions of countrymen would be sympathizing with the sufferers in their distress, or, if need be, promptly devising and providing the means of relief or defense. From the Puritan sentinel, New Amsterdam, Jamestown, and Saint Augustine, the only other Christian settlements on the continent, lay at a distance so vaguely remote—so far beyond unknown seas and trackless forests—that they seemed scarcely nearer than Europe itself. Even the colonists of these settlements were unfriendly to him. New Amsterdam was a Dutch colony. St. Augustine was peopled by Spaniards and Papists ; and the Cavaliers of Jamestown, though Englishmen, bore him a hatred more bitter than that of a alien. He and his fellows were alone, without human aid to help them in their weary struggle for existence. When you turn your glance inland, you look toward a country, lying beyond the chain of hills that forms the western horizon, with which you are familiar. Your notions with respect to its form, extent, character, condition, and other circumstances are distinct, well-defined, and correct. You have a map of it in your pocket, which you consult only for its minutiæ. It is a land full of countrymen, kinsmen, and friends. It is your country, your native land, your home. When he directed his anxious, watchful gaze toward the western hills, he beheld, skirting the narrow belt of cultivated fields, the borders of a wilderness, dense, vast, untrodden, of unknown extent, the covert where fierce and dangerous beasts roamed in savage freedom, and built their lairs, and bred their young ; and the congenial home of hordes of crafty and treacherous enemies, more cruel than the beasts of prey. Horrible as were the realities that surrounded him, his imagination peopled the wilderness with terrors still more frightful. Dragons, and monstrous beasts with scaly, impenetrable hides, and forked tongues, and breaths of sulphurous and poisonous flame, were supposed to lurk in the depths of the forest ; and it was shudderingly whispered that demons of extraordinary ferocity and wickedness were the familiar spirits of the Indian magicians, and attended upon the powwows and pagan incantations, celebrated with human sacrifices and revolting ceremonies, in the dark and gloomy swamps and recesses of the solemn woods. The blue expanse of ocean that you behold is covered with the white-winged messengers of commerce. Its coasts, shoals, rocks, and currents are all known, and marked upon a thousand charts. Beyond the horizon, hence only some ten days' sail, is Europe. The great highway of nations that lies between is a crowded thoroughfare. Indeed, a collision with another ship is the peril most to be dreaded by the traveler, who, borne over the yielding waves in a floating palace, gorgeously furnished and decorated, has scarcely time to weary of his voyage before it is concluded. The stormy ocean that met the Pilgrim's gaze, as he turned from the dismal forest toward merry England, was a trackless waste of dreary waters, a hundred weary days in width. Indeed, there is now no country on earth that lies beyond so broad and dangerous a sea as that which then separated the exiled colonists from the land of their birth. The thought of venturing forth from the sight and knowledge of men into the awful solitude of such an ocean, floating upon a bark so frail as were the slender, ill-built shallops that were then called ships, might well dismay the stoutest heart, and chill the warmest blood.

The place where we stand is indeed holy ground; for the hallowed dust of the Fathers forms the soil upon which we tread. Though Cole's Hill was the ground where the passengers of the Mayflower buried their numerous dead, the loftier elevation upon which we stand was probably used for purposes of interment as early as 1622. There are fewer ancient gravestones bearing very early dates than one would suppose. But, alas! there were in those dismal times so many graves to dig, and the survivors were obliged to struggle so hard to live, that there was little leisure in which to erect durable monuments over those that died. The white marble monument upon the brow of the hill covers the ashes of Governor William Bradford, but you perceive it is in the modern style, having been erected but a few years since by some of his descendants. His widow, the lovely and celebrated Alice Bradford, and two of their sons, both worthy of their parentage, are buried near this spot. The graves of several others of the early colonists are identified. Those of John Howland and his wife, pilgrims of the Mayflower, are marked by a handsome headstone, erected a few years since by their descendant in the fifth generation, the Hon. John Howland, of Providence. Near the graves of William Crowe, Elder Thomas Cushman, Elder Thomas Faunce, and others, beside the ancient and almost illegible headstones, have been placed white boards, with the names, dates, and ages in black paint. It is to be hoped that ere long each one of these hallowed and venerable graves will be distinguished by a handsome and durable monument, so that the knowledge of where sleeps the sacred dust of the early Pilgrims, that has been preserved to the present time, may be transmitted to future generations and perpetuated. Here, also, not unworthy of a grave among the Pilgrims, repose the remains of the noble-hearted pioneer missionary, Dr. Adoniram Judson.

It is almost sunset, and we must hasten. But, before we go, stand with me awhile by the side of the monument of the stout old Puritan Governor, and look about you beyond the hill upon which we stand. Views finer than that which is visible from this point are but few in number. Looking to the right, over the roofs and chim-

neys of houses, shops, mills, and manufactories standing in the deep and narrow valley through which the hard-working town brook struggles to escape from its numerous task-masters, and gain a brief repose with the quiet waters of the bay ere it seeks the wild freedom of the restless ocean, we see the round, smooth, green summit of a neighboring hill, crowned by a wind-mill of the most picturesque Dutch style. At the foot of its western slope lies, in deep shadow, a little lake, formed by damming the town brook, and behind it rises one of the chain of wooded hills that forms the background of the landscape in the rear of the town.

This is Watson's Hill, that whilome bore the pleasant title of Strawberry Hill, where, on the 22d of March, 1621, the great Sagamore Massasoit appeared, with a retinue of sixty painted warriors, on the friendly errand of negotiating a treaty of peace with the Pilgrims. Yonder stood the band of wondering savages, and in the street below were collected the stern and solemn-visaged exiles, preparing to make as imposing a display before the eyes of their visitors as their limited resources would allow. Each party distrusted the other. " We," says an eye-witness of the scene, "were unwilling to send our Governor to them, and they were unwilling to come to us." So the brave Edward Winslow went alone to the Indians as a hostage, and Massasoit, being met at the town brook by Captain Myles Standish and an escort of six musketeers, was conducted to an unfinished house, furnished for the occasion with a green rug and three or four cushions. Thither presently came the Governor, in great state, with a guard of musketeers, and followed by a drum and trumpet. The two chieftains saluted and kissed each other, and the Indian was regaled with a draught of strong waters, "that," says the eye-witness historian, "caused him to sweat all the while after." A treaty of peace and alliance was afterward concluded between Massasoit and the colony, and the interview came to an end.

Between this memorable hill and the bay, the village and its suburbs extend for a mile along the bending shore. On the extreme right Manomet, still glowing ruddily in the slanting sunbeams, looms grandly up against the darkening eastern sky, and beyond its farthest point, stretching out into the sea, marking the line where sky and water meet, appear a range of white, sparkling points, the tops of the highest sand cliffs of Cape Cod. On the left Captain's Hill heaves its bare summit high in the air, concealing with its huge bulk a large portion of the gorgeously-tinted sunset clouds, and casting a deepening shadow upon the villages of Kingston and Duxbury and the placid waters of the inner bay. Before us, at our feet, lies the town, sloping toward the waterside, and so showing every one of its hundred gleaming roofs, with here and there among them a steeple with its glittering vane, or the great, round, green crown of an elm, towering aloft above the house-tops.

The breeze has died away, and the surface of the harbor before the town is as smooth as glass. The small craft and boats, with idle sails, float motionless above their pictured shadows in the water, and even the roadstead is disturbed only by the long, regular heaving of the ground swell, that does not break or raise a crest until it suddenly tumbles in upon the shelving beach, with a weltering wash, the sound of which we can hear through the still evening air, even at this distance. Directly before us, beyond the point of the beach, the regular, mound-like form of Clark's Island rises from the middle of the bay, with its green fields and pleasant groves mirrored in the quiet waters that surround its shores. In the far distance, beyond the narrow white ribbon that marks the sweeping curve of the sandy beach, the ocean forms the northern horizon, a narrow verge of the deepest blue, with the sails of vessels upon it here and there visible, some gleaming brightly in the sun, and others, on a different tack, showing dim and gray, and fading into the sky, like ghosts. Even the bleak sand hills of Saquish are clothed with beauty by the magic of the hour, and the western slope of the bold headland of the Gurnet reflects the parting beams of the setting sun, and glows like an emerald flashing in the light. But while we gaze a change comes over the brilliant scene. The rosy light begins to fade from the landscape. The gleaming roofs in the town below us turn pale, and the sparkling windows are suddenly extinguished. A shadow falls upon the bay as the sun sinks below the horizon, and when, a few moments afterward, we again turn from the faded west toward the sea, we behold the lanterns of the twin towers on the Gurnet beginning to twinkle faintly, and to cast two long, flickering wakes of wavy light across the dull, leaden-gray waters of the roadstead.

Thank the propitious gods! (if such a heathenish expression may properly be used within a mile of Plymouth Rock.) The vaticinations of the lady in the cars, who yesterday predicted a northeast storm for to-day's weather, have signally failed. To-day beginneth not the annual August storm, as the lady falsely prophesied; for a brighter, balmier morning never shone on Plymouth Bay. It will be a little hazy in the afternoon, possibly, for the reign of the dog-star is not yet over; but as we stand upon the piazza of the Samoset, and inhale the fresh sea-breeze, we say to each other, over and over again, that it is a fine morning, and a very fine morning, and a very fine morning indeed. When a salt-water bath and an excellent breakfast have prepared us for the heat and fatigues of the day, we resume our explorations among the memorials of the Forefathers. We will first direct our steps toward Pilgrim Hall. Upon entering the vestibule of this building, we turn to the left, and in the ante-room we find the attentive and obliging janitor, Mr. Holmes, of whom, if we are wise, after inscribing our names in the register, we shall buy a little volume that he has for sale, entitled "Pilgrim Memorials and Guide

for Visitors to Plymouth Village." The author is William S. Russell, Esq., a resident of Plymouth, Recording Secretary of the Pilgrim Society, and an enthusiastic and reliable antiquarian. The book contains, you perceive, besides other interesting matter, a catalogue of the antique curiosities deposited in Pilgrim Hall. It will be a better and less obtrusive guide than I can be. Let me, however, point out a few of the most interesting relics of which this place is full. Upon the wall yonder is an ancient deed, bearing the signature of Myles Standish. The faded sampler in another frame was wrought by the fair fingers of his daughter, Mistress Lorea Standish. Let us read the legend embroidered upon it:

> "Lorea Standish is my na ie.
> Lord, guide my hart that I may doe thy will:
> Also fill my hands with such convenient skill
> As may conduce to virtue void of shame;
> And I will give the glory to thy name."

A winsome young lady and a pious was Mistress Lorea Standish, and "conveniently skillful" with the needle withal, if the sampler is taken as evidence.

Another deed, framed and glazed, bears the signature of John Alden, who, saith tradition, went a-wooing for the gallant Captain Standish, and won the lady for himself. There is a bond signed Peregrine White, the first native Yankee, having been born in November, 1620, while the Mayflower lay at Cape Cod; and another ancient instrument, the receipt of the heirs of Governor Thomas Prince, containing the signatures of Governor Josiah Winslow and others. The tall clock, decorated with faded gilding and lacquering, which, notwithstanding its great age, still keeps good time, though not itself a memorial of the Pilgrims, is worthy of a place here. It formerly belonged to Governor John Hancock, and was a whig refugee during the occupation of Boston by the British army in the war of the Revolution, having been removed with other valuables from the city-house of its owner to a place of safety in West Bridgewater. The ancient leathern sofa, the form of which is less unfashionable now than it was twenty years ago, also came from the parlor of the same stout-hearted rebel. Adams and Otis have sat together upon its broad cushion and talked treason with Hancock and Warren many a night, I warrant you, until the sound of yonder clock, striking the hour of twelve, warned the trio of visitors to depart.

Upon entering the principal apartment, our attention is at once attracted to the large historical painting of the Landing of the Pilgrims which hangs upon the opposite wall. The scene represented is the disembarkation of the passengers of the Mayflower at Plymouth Rock. A dull, gray, cheerless light filters through a stormy sky of heavy, lowering clouds, and falls upon a wintry sea and a rocky shore covered with ice and snow. In the distance is seen the weather-worn Mayflower, lying with furled sails at anchor. The foreground of the picture is almost

LANDING OF THE PILGRIMS, FROM SARGENT'S PAINTING.

entirely filled by a group of figures of the size of life. In the centre stands the stately form of Governor Carver, sword in hand, in the act of replying to the greeting of an Indian chief (Samoset), who is advancing in an attitude of humility to bid a welcome to the exiles. His wife, shrinking back as the Indian approaches, clings to her husband's side (without whom she could not live, poor lady), and leans trustingly on his shoulder, while at the feet of the father their children, trembling with cold and fear, gaze upward with tearful eyes in wonder and alarm at the savage chieftain. Immediately behind Carver stands Governor William Bradford, over whose left shoulder we catch a glimpse of John Alden's face, that Mistress Priscilla Mullins thought so handsome; and, indeed, it is not a matter of amazement that the discreet and modest, though somewhat frank and adventuresome damsel should have preferred this well-favored youth above the middle-aged widower, Captain Myles Standish, whose sharp features appear in the picture beneath the shadow of a slouching, broad-brimmed hat, his keen eye vigilantly watching the approach of the Indian warrior, and his stout hand grasping the staff of his trusty pike. Near the left of the picture William White is seen bearing in his arms his new-born son, Peregrine (who was to live to see the House of Stuart twice dethroned), and turning as if to speak encouragingly to Elder William Brewster, whose aged limbs seem to totter with the exertion of climbing the steep and slippery bank. On the extreme left, Isaac Allerton stands in an attitude of devotion, and

at his side kneels his wife with clasped hands, offering to God her thanks for having safely preserved them through the dangers of the long and perilous voyage. The upturned face is one of singular beauty, and redeems many of the faults of the picture. The principal figures on the extreme right are those of Governor Edward Winslow and his wife. Near them the face of Rose Standish is partly visible, with a sweet but sad expression, as if she foreboded her impending doom; and, standing in advance of her husband, the wife of Stephen Hopkins recoils upon him with terror at the approach of Samoset, who is, indeed, the object toward whom the eyes of nearly all the group of English are directed.

There is no intermixture of myths and uncertain traditions with the well-authenticated facts of the history of Plymouth Colony. So that it is surprising that a painting, professing to depict one of the most remarkable events of this well-known history, and relying upon no aid that might be derived from allegory, should contain such an error as the introduction of Samoset as one of the most prominent figures upon the canvas. The absence of Mary Chilton from the picture is hardly pardonable; for that sprightly damsel, to say the least, has a fair claim to the honor of having imprinted the first footstep upon the rock that day made so famous, which should not be so entirely overlooked. That Mary Chilton certainly was present at the Landing of the Pilgrims, and that Samoset as certainly was not, one can not help remembering. The picture, which however is a work of considerable merit, is a gift from the clever and generous artist, Henry Sargent, to the Pilgrim Society. Its size is 13 by 16 feet, and it hangs in a handsome frame and in a bad light upon the eastern wall, so as to face the visitor as he enters the Hall.

In the recesses of the windows, between which this picture is suspended, are placed two ancient chairs, both of which, undoubtedly, came over in

CARVER'S CHAIR.

the Mayflower. The one upon the right belonged to Governor Carver, and the other to Elder William Brewster. Each of these sacred relics had suffered from the pilferings of whittling tourists; and, worse still, a commission to Governor

BREWSTER'S CHAIR.

Edward Winslow, dated April, 1654, hanging, in a frame over the Hancock sofa, which formerly bore the signature of Oliver Cromwell, has been despoiled of the autograph that gave it its chief value, by some graceless rogue, whose ears richly deserve to be slit by his own infamous jack-knife.

In a glass-case in a corner of the room are contained a large number of curiosities, a careful enumeration and description of which are given in Mr. Russell's Guide-Book. There is the spoon of Elder Thomas Cushman, affording the strongest circumstantial evidence of the great capacity of that worthy Puritan's mouth; a cabinet, formerly belonging to Peregrine White,

PEREGRINE WHITE'S CABINET.

inlaid with pearl; a Bible, brought over in the Mayflower by John Alden, imprinted in the old English type in the year 1620, at London, bought undoubtedly by the pious youth just previous to the embarkation; the corsets, against which was wont to heave the gentle bosom of sweet Mistress Alice Bradford; the good sword of Captain Myles Standish, and a pewter dish and an iron pot, both brought over in the Mayflower by the same gallant soldier. Here, also, is the gun-barrel from which sped the ball that pierced the brave, despairing heart of King Philip; and, scattered about in different parts of the room, are other relics, duly labeled, so that he who wanders near them may read, and be enlightened and informed. I pray you look for yourself, until you are wearied, if it please you.

Several portraits grace the walls, among which are one of Governor Edward Winslow, and another of Governor Josiah Winslow, the first native governor of the colony; both copies by C. A. Foster, from the originals, painted in London in 1651. The originals are the property of Isaac Winslow, Esq., of Boston, and are now in the rooms of the Massachusetts Historical Society in that city.

In an adjoining apartment are deposited a part of the library belonging to the Pilgrim Society, and a collection of marine, Indian, and South-Sea Island curiosities. Among the most noticeable things in the room is a copy of the Indian Bible, translated by the "Apostle to the Indians," John Eliot.

Before we leave this spot, let me not fail to inform you concerning a most pious and praiseworthy custom among the staid Plymotheans. On the evening of each Forefather's Day, as the 22d of December is styled throughout the Old Colony, a ball is held in the large apartment of Pilgrim Hall, and the just-risen generation of the descendants of the Pilgrims are wont to dance quadrilles and polkas, and whirl around the hall in the giddy mazes of waltzes and schottishes, in honor of the memory of their Puritan ancestors. Meanwhile the elders, full of good things devoured and imbibed in the dining-room beneath the springing floor, look on complacently, and call to mind the good old times when they themselves were light of foot as well as of heart, and used to figure bravely in Hull's Victory, Moneymusk, Virginia Reel, and other sprightly country dances, now, alas, fallen into desuetude!

Let us now, instead of proceeding further along Main-street, as we did yesterday, turn to the left and go down toward the water-side, through the shady avenue of North-street. At the declivity of the hill, as in Leyden-street, the road forks in twain—one path leading to the open space upon the brow of Cole's Hill, which we visited yesterday, and the other rapidly descending to the water. The old-fashioned gable-roofed dwelling that stands upon the curve of the upper path, is called the Joanna Davis House, taking its name from that of a former proprietor and resident. Besides the picturesqueness

JOANNA DAVIS HOUSE.

of its elevated situation, it is remarkable in consequence of the fact that it stands near the centre of the ground where were buried the dead of the winter of 1620. Its foundations were laid among the forgotten graves, and it marks the spot in the stead of the monument that should soon replace it.

Proceeding down the hill, we find ourselves at the head of Long Wharf—a pier of wooden piles, built for the accommodation of the steamboats that formerly visited Plymouth, but now fallen into a state of ruinous decay—and turn to the right around a corner formed by a range of low-roofed shops, as quaint in outward appearance as any thing ever seen in a picture. Pipes and tobacco, sheath-knives and belts, fishhooks and lines, fly-specked pastry and confectionery, coarse woolen socks and striped shirts, shriveled onions in strings, and plump new potatoes in their native dirt, seem to be the principal commodities exposed for sale. Groups of shaggy-looking men stand in the

doors, clad in canvas-trowsers, soiled beyond description and the efficacy of soap and water, and Guernsey frocks, or coarse red flannel shirts. Judging from the peculiar odor prevalent in the atmosphere that surrounds these worthies, it is safe to affirm them to be fishermen just landed from a voyage to the Grand Banks of Newfoundland.

Passing a few rods along the dingy street, we arrive opposite a large store-house, painted of a pale yellow tint, that stands at the head of a well-built and busy wharf. This building, as you perceive by the signs it bears upon it, is occupied as a flour and grain-store. Let us go a few paces down the wharf, the name of which is Hedge's Wharf. That is a good-looking schooner yonder discharging her cargo of corn; and the yacht lying in front of her bows is a handsome little craft. Stop here, and face about! See yonder group of people. They are gathered around Plymouth Rock as it lies in the very place where the Pilgrims landed upon it in 1620,

PLYMOUTH ROCK.

It is proposed to clear away the unsightly buildings that encumber this space, covering an area of about half an acre, to lay it out as a public square, inclosing it with a handsome iron fence, and to erect upon the spot where the rock now lies, a monument that shall be worthy of the memory of the Pilgrim Fathers, and of the mighty nation which they founded. The town of Plymouth has already subscribed for this object the sum of seven thousand dollars. There is scarcely a town in the Union that does not, as well as Plymouth, contain descendants of the Puritan settlers of New England. Let each of these towns contribute but one-tenth part of its fair proportion, taking the offering of Plymouth as a standard, and a fund would be raised sufficient to make the Monument of the Pilgrims the proudest structure in the land.

But, although we have stood upon Plymouth Rock, we must not consider our pilgrimage finished until we have visited Clark's Island, which lies beyond the mouth of the harbor, on the northern side of the bay, about four miles from the village. Selecting the handsomest of half a dozen neat little sail-boats, kept in the neighborhood for hire, and dispensing with the services of the boatman, we take a short cut through the ruins of Long Wharf, where the waves are poppling merrily among the barnacled piles, hoist our sail to the fresh western breeze, and stand across toward the beach, on our first tack. We have a fine view of the town from the harbor. Yonder are the two towers of the First Church and the Church of the Pilgrimage, rising out of and above the elm-tree tops that grow in the Town Square. Behind them is the steep ascent of Burying Hill, dotted with grave-stones and monuments. Beyond the hill is the High-School, from which the shady North-street seems to lead to the head of Long Wharf. A little to the right is the Court House; and further still, the Samoset House and the Railroad Station. The Universalist Church stands between the First Church and the water, overlooking Hedge's Wharf and the Rock. Immediately to the left is the valley of the town brook, beyond which is Watson's Hill and its wind-mill. There—put your helm down—we will go about. The next tack, I reckon, we shall fetch the point of the beach. As I told you—now keep her for the square pier yonder.

just even with the surface of the ground—so that just now you walked upon it, unconsciously, the soil having been filled in around it when the wharf was constructed. Here for scores of years it has remained a part of the pavement of the street, trodden under foot of man and beast. Often and again, when the mention of its name in the eloquent speech of the orator has been received with acclamations and thunders of applause, it has been lying here, covered with the mud and mire of this obscure street. And let us not ascribe to the people of Plymouth more than their share of this fault. Already they have removed a portion of the rock to a place of safety, inclosed it, and taken measures for its preservation. Fortunately, however, the larger portion was suffered to remain in its original position, where it still marks the spot so distinguished in the history of the nation. Payment for the property in this land, and for the injuries occasioned to private rights and interests by closing these streets and wharves, would require a larger sum of money than a small, and by no means wealthy town, like Plymouth, is able to expend for such a purpose. This sacred soil ought to belong to the American people; and the citizens of each State should contribute its share for the purpose of purchasing this spot, laying it out, and beautifying it as a public ground, and erecting here a noble monument, which, for centuries to come, shall lift its head to the skies above the hallowed spot where first the Pilgrims trod. The Pilgrim Society have taken the first step toward the performance of this pious national duty. It has secured the refusal of the property lying between Leyden and North streets, bordered on the west by the brow of Cole's Hill, including Hedge's Wharf and the Rock, at the price of $26,000, for a limited time.

We are in the Horse-Market, as it is called —a place where three tides meet, from Plymouth, Kingston, and Duxbury. Though it is tolerably smooth now, sometimes, when the wind is against the tide, there is a very rough sea here. Look out to seaward at the grand view we have of the mouth of the bay, with the Gurnet and Manomet frowning at each other from the opposite sides. Do you see

PLYMOUTH, FROM THE BEACH.

that long line of breakers between? Hark! you may hear their continuous roar above the screaming of the gulls that hover over them in great flocks. They mark a dangerous shoal, of considerable extent, where, two hundred years ago, there was an island with heavy woods growing upon its upland. The settlers gave it the name of Brown's Island, which the shoal, though it is completely submerged at high-water, still retains. It has been the occasion and the scene of several terrible shipwrecks.

At length, Saquish Head gradually shuts by the Gurnet, and we are slowly creeping up the channel against the strong ebb-tide toward the island. Let me take the helm, or we may get aground, and be obliged to wait on the flats until the flood. Now we go through a space of clear water, with the quick current rippling against our bows, where you may look over the gunwale and see the horse-shoes, crabs, and star-fish crawling on the white sandy bottom, and the next moment we encounter a patch of eel-grass, waving and twisting with the tide like myriads of serpents, through which we force our way with a low, hissing sound, like snow drifting against the window-pane. We shall land in yonder cove that indents the southeastern shore of the island, where the little stone pier projects into the deeper water and the boats are at anchor.

There—stand by to lower the foresail—very well indeed. Fend off her bow from the stones of the pier—that's it—and now, here we are ashore.

We follow the path that ascends the gentle acclivity between two rows of ancient balm of Gilead trees, leading to the venerable mansion which was for many years the only dwelling on the island. There is now another house, nearer the centre of the island, where reside the widow and family of the lately deceased brother of Mr. Edward Watson, whose own hereditary mansion stands before us. This island has been in the possession of the Watson family for nearly two hundred years. The father of the present proprietor, the late John Watson, Esq., was one of the founders of the Old Colony Club, in 1769, and was President of the Pilgrim Society after the year 1820 until his death in 1826. Yonder is his worthy successor advancing to meet us. Prepare yourself for a hearty greeting and a warm welcome.

Now, after dinner, as we sit in the cool piazza, shaded from the sun that vainly strives to send his rays through the dense foliage of the chestnuts and the balm of Gilead trees, while we listen to the chirping of the grasshoppers in the open fields hard by, the humming of bees in the garden before us, and the lazy quacking of ducks in the poultry-yard—talking in their naps—and watch, between the boles of the trees, the soft tint of the cloudless sky blending with the deep blue of the ocean; and catch, at times, the breath of the wakening sea-breeze, bringing with it a low, whispering murmur of the surf upon the distant beach, like the sound heard in a sea-shell. Now, while we sit with tilted chairs and unbuttoned waistcoats,

WATSON'S HOUSE, CLARK'S ISLAND.

smoking fragrant Havanas, while our host prepares to accompany us in the projected ramble over his little dominions, let me tell you why Clark's Island is memorable.

On the 6th of December, 1620, O.S. (corresponding to December 16th, N.S.), ten of the pilgrims, among whom were Carver, Bradford, Standish, and Winslow the master's mate of the ship, Mr. Clark the gunner, and several seamen set out in the shallop from Cape Cod, where the Mayflower then lay, on a voyage of exploration. Having coasted Cape Cod Bay for a distance of fifteen leagues, on the afternoon of Friday, the 8th of December, they found themselves at the mouth of Plymouth Bay. A storm of snow and rain begins. The wind and sea rise, and the rudder of the shallop breaks, so that two men are required to steer it with oars. The pilot, however, encourages them, and bids them be of good cheer, saying that he knows the harbor they are approaching. The light of the brief winter's day begins to fade from the lowering sky, and with the darkness the violence of the gale increases. Still, they forbear to shorten sail, desirous to gain the shelter of the harbor while they can yet see. The pitiless storm drenches them to the skin. Wet, hungry, and shivering, they cower under the lee of the gunwale. Their sole earthly dependence is the pilot, who stands in the bows, peering anxiously through the driving snow and rain at the barren, inhospitable shores, dimly visible. Suddenly, a terrific blast comes howling from the north—it strikes them! the boat heels violently—the mast breaks, and with the sail falls overboard. The flood-tide, however, bore them toward the land, until the pilot, in a fright, exclaimed that he had mistaken the place for another,

and that he knew not where he was. The officers were about to run the boat ashore in the cove yonder, between Gurnet and Saquish, among the breakers; but a sailor at one of the steering-oars bade the rowers to put her about; which was done; and after hard labor they weathered Saquish, and came up with the tide, under the lee of this island. The fury of the storm overcame their dread of Indians. So they landed, and with great difficulty kindled a fire; at which they dried and warmed themselves; and here they rested safely through the night. The next morning they found the place to be an island; and having discovered, near the highest land, a large rock, commanding a view of the whole extent of the island and of the approaches to its shores, thus enabling them to prevent being surprised by the Indians, they resolved to stay and keep the Sabbath here.

But here comes our host. He will lead us to this other Plymouth Rock, from whence as-

GREAT ROCK, CLARK'S ISLAND.

cended the first praises to God ever offered "on the wild New England shore." After crossing the orchard we come in sight of it, situated near the ridge on the eastern slope of the island. Its highest point on the down-hill side is at least twelve feet from the ground. This and the southern sides are precipitous, and are partly hidden by a cluster of sumachs. The western side slopes gradually toward the rising ground, thus affording an easy access to the broad summit, from which are visible the bay and its surrounding shores, the island lying in the midst, Gurnet and Manomet and the ocean beyond, and sometimes the far-distant cliffs of Cape Cod. Here was the sentinel stationed, while the remainder of the party, shielded from the cold northerly and easterly winds by the rock, and on the west by the rise of the hill, lay safely under the warm southern lee. So this gray rock was the first shelter the New World gave the Pilgrims. Here they kept the first Christian Sabbath of New England. Here they prayed and exhorted each other to good works; here they sang and

". . . . shook the depths of the desert's gloom
With their hymns of lofty cheer."

I must admit that this place has a greater interest for me than any even in the village of Plymouth.

Our boat, which for a space at dinner-time was left aground by the ebbing tide, is once more afloat. We bid adieu to Clark's Island and its hospitable owner, and with a smart sea-breeze filling our sails stem the coming tide down the channel to Saquish Point. We are bound to the Gurnet. We round the Point, and coast along the shores of the cove where the shallop of the Pilgrims so narrowly escaped shipwreck. A fleet of boats are out to-day fishing for mackerel and perch, and as the breeze freshens they pitch and splash in the growing sea, and pull at their anchors like a young colt at the halter. On we go, the bold headland before us seeming to rise higher and higher from the water, and the white towers upon the cliff growing farther and farther apart. Are you in a mood for marvelous stories of the past, sailing over the bay that the brave Smith and the villainous Hunt explored; the bay plowed by the keel of the Mayflower, with Plymouth in sight astern, and the dim shores of Cape Cod in the distance ahead, where so much of the treasure of the pirate Kidd lies hid? Listen, then:

Once upon a time, nearly a thousand years ago, a man named Thorwald Ericsson, an Icelandic Northman, sailed from Ericsford, in Greenland, a colony of Icelandmen, on a voyage of exploration to a country called Vinland. This country had been discovered a few years before by one Biarni Heriulfson, who, in a voyage from Iceland to Greenland, had been driven from the usual course a great many days' sail to the southwest. Lief, the brother of Thorwald, had also visited this strange shore, sailing south and west from Greenland to find it; had given to it the name of Vinland, and built upon the shores of

a land-locked bay a house, which he named Lief's-booths. Some people, who have given much attention to the subject, think it by no means unreasonable to suppose that Lief's-bay is now known by the name of Mount Hope Bay. Thorwald easily found Lief's-booths, and wintered there two seasons. The second summer of his sojourn in Vinland, he sailed to explore the coasts that lay to the eastward from his habitation. After several days, a violent storm drove his ship upon a promontory extending far into the sea, and its keel was broken. From this unlucky circumstance, and also, as some think, from the peculiar form of this promontory, he gave it the name of Kialarness, or Keel Cape.

Sailing from thence, westwardly across a broad bay, Thorwald and his company discovered another high promontory, covered with forest trees, situated at the entrance of a deep bay. They anchored here, and landed. Then said Thorwald, "This spot is beautiful; here should I like to build myself a habitation." Soon afterward, having wantonly killed several of the natives, they were attacked by a vast number of canoes, filled with warriors armed with bows and arrows, and forced to flee to their ship. In the battle which ensued Thorwald was mortally wounded. While dying, he commanded his followers to bury him upon the promontory, to erect crosses at the head and foot of his grave, and to call the place Krossaness, or Cross Cape; saying, "It may be that I have spoken true, in saying that I should like to dwell yonder." Thorwald died, and was buried as he had commanded. And now many very learned antiquarians pretend to be perfectly certain that Krossaness is no other than the Gurnet, where we shall shortly land. Whether these worthy gentlemen are correct or not, I can not say.

When we have landed, the light-keeper gives us the more modern history of the Gurnet. It has long been a light-house station. The first structure of this kind was erected here by the Province of Massachusetts Bay in 1768, and was consumed by fire in 1801. Two years afterward the United States Government built two towers upon the spot, and ever since, "soon as the evening shades prevail," the Gurnet sends forth the gleam of its twin stars far out upon the sea. During the last war with Great Britain a small redoubt was erected upon the highest part of the bluff, the remains of which are still visible, and a small garrison was set to watch the movements of the British fleet that so constantly hovered near the shores of New England during a greater part of the war.

At our departure, the friendly light-keeper accompanies us to our boat, ceasing not his entreaties to partake still further of his hospitalities, and stay to tea; but if we mean to take advantage of the flood-tide we must be off at once. Again we spread our little sail to the favoring breeze, and ninety minutes afterward we disembark as near to Plymouth Rock as Hedge's Wharf will permit.

Wellesley College
(1876)

HARPER'S
NEW MONTHLY MAGAZINE.

No. CCCXV.—AUGUST, 1876.—Vol. LIII.

WELLESLEY COLLEGE.
By EDWARD ABBOTT.

WELLESLEY COLLEGE.

WHAT would "Dorothy Dudley" have said had she been entered as a "Freshman" at Wellesley College! That

> "Fair maiden, whom a hundred summers keep
> Forever seventeen,"

would have told us a very different story of female education from that which can be related by the less mythical Dorothys and Dudleys of to-day. At the time to which the first entry of her "Diary" introduces us, when nine British redcoats stopped at Bradish Tavern, in Cambridge, for dinner, and then galloped on toward Lexington with suspected design of seizing John Hancock and Samuel Adams, there was no female seminary or young ladies' boarding-school in all the colonies, and no college to which a girl might go. Our nineteenth-century ideas of education were largely nebulous matter. The now rising project of the co-education of the sexes was very far below the horizon. Not even at William and Mary College was there any place except for the Williams. The Marys were left to shift for themselves. Their facilities for the acquisition of knowledge were few, the obstacles in their way were many. A view of such an institution as Wellesley College becomes, therefore, an important part of the general inspection we are all now so much interested in making for the measurement of the century's progress. And it is doubtful if at any point the contrast between the two extremities of the hundred years be more striking than at this of the education of young women.

Half an hour's ride by a swift train due west from Boston, over the Boston and Albany Railroad, brings one to Wellesley, fifteen miles away. A tasteful church, one or two stores of the common country kind, a junction of several roads, and a few dwelling-houses, scattered rather than clustered, give only the slightest emphasis to the spot selected by the railroad for its station, while of the whereabouts of the distant college building there is no hint except to those who know exactly where to look. Neither is there any intimation to one alighting at this station of the beautiful rolling country that stretches away to the southward. Through that country pleasantly wind the upper waters of the Charles River. In its

nadnock still farther in the other. If the college has a soul—and one may sometimes think it must have—it may daily study the grace and beauty of its form in the mirroring waters of Lake Waban, which stretch away at its very base, a most lovely sheet for beauty, and a most admirable one for use.

Years ago Dr. Bowditch instituted careful research to ascertain the most healthful town in Massachusetts, and to this was accorded the honor.

We may reach, by a short walk or drive along the South Natick road, the pretty lodge which marks the main and commonly used entrance to the college grounds. These grounds comprise about three hundred acres,

PORTER'S LODGE.

midst lies the historic village of South Natick—the "Oldtown" whose "Folks" Mrs. Stowe has so pleasantly delineated—sacred with the associations of John Eliot, apostle to the Indians, and containing a monument to his memory. Around are the rural towns of Grantville, beautiful for situation; Weston, wooded and retired; Natick, once the home and now the burial-place of the lamented Henry Wilson—busy and noisy with the plying of a great and useful industry.

Over all of this wide and varied prospect the eye can rove from the heights of Wellesley College, and, clear air permitting, can mark the blue hills of Milton far in one direction, and the dim outline of Mount Mo-

beautifully diversified. It does not seem as if the most accomplished landscape gardener, with fifty years of time and unlimited supplies of money, could have created the like out of any material. Nature, one would almost think, must have anticipated the want, and striven by long and patient process to meet it. The estate was kept as a gentleman's country-seat for many years, and the old forest trees are carefully preserved. The surface rises occasionally into picturesque summits, and as often sinks away into wild and retired dells. Miniature forests dispute with carefully nourished lawns for the supremacy. Established evergreens and ancient oaks join with the flowering shrub and the young tree fresh from the nursery in contributing to the foliage that screens the soil. Yet nowhere is there an appearance of rawness and immaturity. The scars of engineering surgery are mostly healed. It is a delightful drive, after you leave the lodge, for three-fourths of a mile along the wide, smooth avenue, under the shade, if it be summer, and following easily the varying contour of the grounds. At one point on the left a glimpse is to be had of the farm-houses and accompanying buildings, of which a spacious greenhouse is one. The en-

One is not long upon the avenue approaching it before the building bursts upon the view. At no point probably do its qualities of size, proportion, and style more impressively present themselves to the eye. So far as such an inanimate structure may be pictured as having a countenance, the expression which this wears is one in which dignity, grace, and repose predominate. There is, moreover, a certain feminine delicacy to its aspect befitting its character, but with nothing of weakness blended. It is evident that the architect

GENERAL VIEW OF THE COLLEGE BUILDING.

graving presented of this, however, is taken from another point of view, the beholder in this instance being supposed to stand in the town road outside the college grounds. The pretty effect of the inclosing trees, through and beyond which the greenhouse is here seen, is only one of countless little touches upon the landscape which on every side delight the eye.

The farm, it should be understood, is a very important adjunct of the institution, though space will not allow more than this passing reference to it.

was an artist. Mr. Billings—Hammatt Billings—did indeed consider it his chiefest work. From our side of Providence, it seems a thing to be deplored that he could not have lived to witness its completion, and so to have had his share in the enjoyment over its occupancy.

Architecturally described, the building is in the form of a double Latin cross, designed in a style of the Renaissance, crowned with a Mansard-roof, and set off at various points with towers, bays, porches, pavilions, and spires, the whole producing an irregu-

THE GREENHOUSE.

lar but harmonious exterior, which is ornate without a touch of the finical, and substantial without being unwieldy. The combination of such masses in a form so light and airy must be set down as a rare achievement of architectural skill. The extreme length of the building is four hundred and seventy-five feet; the extreme width at the wings about one hundred and fifty. There are, in the main, four stories, though at points these expand into five. The material is brick, laid in black mortar, with plain trimmings of brown freestone. The outside walls are of unusual thickness, and to a considerable extent the minor partition walls throughout the building are of brick, with fire-proof floors at exposed points. The interior wood finish is of Western ash. The best of materials and the most thorough workmanship were every where made a first consideration in building; all was done under a scrutinizing supervision that spared no expense and no effort to have the utmost possible degree of excellence.

The building is approached upon its northern side. The generous and inviting entrance, sheltered by a spacious *porte cochère*, opens into an imposing hall which occupies the entire length and breadth and height of the central section. The centre of this hall is appropriated to an immense marble basin planted with palm-trees and other tropical growths, whose size and curious beauty seem worthy of such an uncommon setting. Standing by one of the polished granite pillars, two rows of which flank the court, and by means of arches support the ceiling above, one looks up through the great opening to the very glass-capped roof, story rising above story, column ranging upon column, balustrade crowning balustrade. The general plan of each floor comprises broad corridors running from this central court to each distant extremity, with rooms opening therefrom on either side. Arched doorways, occasional wainscotings, hard-wood floors, bits of fret-work and touches of fresco, contribute to the prevailing elegance, which, however, is always chaste and subdued. Easy stairways at the rear angles of the central hall and of the two main transepts afford communication between the different floors. The taste with which these stairways are treated is well illustrated in the accompanying view.

Having entered the building, and paused in the noble central hall long enough to take in its general plan, the visitor may turn to the left into its eastern half. Here, upon this same ground-floor, is, first, the reception parlor, a stately apartment, its walls of hard-wood wainscot and Pompeian red hung with pictures, including autographed portraits of Longfellow, Bryant, and Tennyson, each of which has a history. Opening out of this is the president's room, fitted with a safe and the other appurtenances of a business office, which it is. A short walk along the corridor brings one to the east transept, whose northern arm, that which faced the visitor as he approached the college, constitutes the library. This library, all things considered, must be accounted the gem of the building. It is arranged in alcoves, and superbly finished throughout in solid black-walnut. It is the very ideal of a library for young ladies, with cozy nooks and corners, where a book is twice a book; with sunny windows, some of them thrown out into deep bays; with galleries, reached by winding stairs, where the girls seem to have a keen delight in coiling themselves away in such mysterious fashion that you can only see above the balustrade a curly head bending over some book, doubtless found more fascinating than it could be if simply spread out on the table below. There is shelf-room for one hundred and twenty thousand volumes.

Compared with its capacity, the contents of the library at present seem inconsiderable, but, taken by itself, a collection of ten or twelve thousand volumes is a very respectable one. Already the library is rich and valuable for its size. It is quite complete in standard English works and in Greek, Latin, French, German, and Italian classics, while possessing also some rare old folios, many choice editions, and not a few precious memorials of the great and good whose names are imperishable in literature.

Opposite the library is the reading-room, a sunny room, as it should be, well supplied with the periodical literature of the day. The teachers and students of this college are to have not only abundant access to the intellectual treasures of the past, but every means of following the progress of modern thought in all its currents. Besides the most valuable of European and American reviews, scientific journals, and magazines, which come regularly to the tables of the library, the reading-room is provided with leading papers, daily and weekly, secular and religious. A unique and interesting feature of the reading-room is the "Gertrude Library," a collection of about one thousand commentaries and other helps to Biblical study, the gift of a gentleman in memory of a deceased daughter who bore that name.

Directly over the library is the chapel, occupying all the remaining portion of this northern half of the east transept. This too is a gem in its way, a spacious and lofty apartment, conveniently adapted to its purpose, and handsomely furnished. The prominent window of the deep bay is one of impressive design in painted glass, executed in Munich, and presented by ex-Governor Claflin, of Massachusetts, in memory of a deceased daughter.

Retracing now our steps, and exploring in like manner the western half of the building, we find on this same floor, in the transept corresponding to that which contains the library,

A NEAR VIEW—NORTHERN SIDE.

the dining-room, where, three times a day, the three hundred students and their instructors gather to their meals. Here we are brought suddenly face to face with the college life, and at a very interesting point of it too. The domestic labor of the students is an incidental only of their daily routine. and, measured by the time it takes,

The domestic offices of the establishment, among which we are now lingering, are all clustered at this extreme western end of the building. They are a sight by themselves, as has already been hinted, though it is not every visitor who has the privilege of looking into them. The domestic hall, linking the dining-room and the kitchen, is fitted with soap-stone sinks and hot closets, and adjoined by an immense china closet. The kitchen, which is separated into a wing at the northwest angle, is furnished with huge ranges, and steam-boilers for soup and vegetables. Beneath these apartments are to be found the laundry, which includes a large steam-drying room, and also the bakery and the larder. In the upper story of the kitchen wing are the sleeping-rooms of the Swedish laundresses and the few other house servants. In this same direction, too, at a safe remove from the main building, are located the boilers whose steam sup-

A STAIRWAY.

rather an unimportant one; but so unique, so essentially important, and of such relation to the internal economy of the college, and of such value in the training of the students, as to require careful notice. The young ladies of the institution do the lighter portion of the "house-work" which it occasions. Of their own rooms they take care, of course. They divide between them the care of those public portions of the building which are shared in common. They do all the table-work in the dining-room, setting the tables, serving them, clearing them, and washing the dishes. They do not do any cooking or kitchen-work, the kitchen being so furnished with modern scientific apparatus that two or three men-servants, under the direction of a professional cook, can easily prepare the food. The experience thus acquired by the students is priceless, and they fully appreciate its value. Indeed, the domestic work is decidedly a popular feature among the students. Division of the labor distributes it evenly to all, and makes little for any one. One hour only is given by each student to her share.

plies the heat for the building by the indirect method, the same being distributed into every part of the structure by not less than fourteen miles of piping. Hard by are the gas-works, for the building is lighted with gas; and water for its various uses is carried over it by pumping from the Artesian well, which furnishes a pure and inexhaustible supply. Over the kitchen is the gymnasium, and over the domestic hall the hospital. This hospital, with its open fire-places, cheerful wood fires, and adjoining rooms for visiting mothers of the sick, the whole carefully sheltered from the bustle of the building proper, and occupying its sunniest and brightest corner, is one of the most pleasing precincts of all.

With this survey of the physical basis of the life which goes on at Wellesley College, the reader may be supposed to be quite ready for introduction to its social and intellectual aspects. Viewed as a huge dormitory, the unit of the structure is, of course, the student's room, into which all will wish to take a peep. The plan provides a suit of two rooms for each two students—a parlor for common use and a bed-chamber for common

THE LIBRARY.

use, the latter, however, being provided with two single beds, two bureaus, and other articles of furniture in duplicate. The furniture is of uniform pattern throughout, being made of black-walnut after artistic designs in tasteful but simple styles. The rooms are carpeted, and present, without exception, a very cheerful and inviting appearance. Occasionally two suits have been combined in one for the accommodation of four students. Commonly a single suit occupies a space of about fourteen feet by twenty. For the professors equally suitable quarters have been provided, the rooms of the president of the faculty being in the extreme part of the east wing, and those of her associates conveniently distributed about in other parts of the building, so as to keep the whole of it under a proper degree of supervision. Special provision is made for the social wants of the professors by their private parlors, while for general uses there is a stately drawing-room, about fifty feet square, looking out upon the lake. The arrangement of the building is such, with its bold projections and many angles, and the living-rooms have been so located, that with few exceptions all have the sunshine during some portion of the day. All are finely lighted and most effectually ventilated. All command pleasant views, while from some, those especially along the southern front, the prospect is one that for breadth, variety, and loveliness is not often to be enjoyed. Nothing that can contribute to the cheerfulness of the rooms or to the sanitary condition of the establishment has been neglected. The natural advantages of the situation and the soil have been supplemented by the most careful attention to scientific principles, and the most thorough application of the best modern methods. While pure air is constantly being supplied to the interior, the impure air is as constantly being withdrawn. A resident physician gives personal attention to hygienic discipline, as well as to the wants of the sick; and it is safe to believe that whatever physical evils may have crept into systems of female education as commonly administered, all such will to a great extent be avoided here.

THE CHAPEL.

After all that has thus been written in attempted description of this building, the reader can have but a faint idea of its vast dimensions, its fine proportions, the symmetry of its lines, the harmony of its forms and colors, the response of the interior to the expectations awakened by the exterior, its excellent general plan, the convenience of its arrangements, the refined nicety of all its details, the solidity and delicacy which are seen blended at every point, the mingled sumptuousness and simplicity which characterize it throughout. We are fully justified in the statement that there is no finer building of its kind in the world.

And now is all this a mere shell? Within this magnificent body is there a living soul to correspond? Such a building is properly only a means to an end. Grand as the means is, the end ought to be grander.

The plan of work at Wellesley College is the fruit of the years of observation and experience of the distinguished college presidents and professors who constitute so large a proportion of the Board of Trustees. It is the intention to graduate from Wellesley students who shall be fully on a par in scholarship with the graduates of Harvard and Yale. The curriculum of study will, of course, differ somewhat from that of these and other colleges for men, but the very highest standard of culture is to be maintained.

The greatest practical difficulty to be overcome at the outset in the execution of this important design is that students present themselves with such irregular and imperfect preparation. They come from all parts of the country—from Maine to Texas, and from Georgia to Colorado—trained in differing studies by different methods, from all grades of private and public schools. It has been impossible to arrange all of them

Emerging from these more retired portions of the building, set apart to the private uses of the students, we enter those public precincts devoted to the college work proper. There are sixteen recitation-rooms scattered about upon the several floors, averaging about twenty feet square. These rooms are all as finely finished as any, and many of them are fitted with appropriate photographic views, maps, charts, and other illustrations relating to the studies pursued. A laboratory, replete with every convenience, adjoins the chemical lecture-room, and facilitates the study of applied chemistry. A natural history room, one hundred feet by fifty, contains already three hundred and seventy feet of cases for the display of specimens, and, by means of a gallery encircling the apartment, can be made available for three times that amount. There is a large art gallery, occupying the upper story of the west wing, and in the same quarter a lecture-room and laboratories for the use of the professors of physics and natural history. There are also a large number of music-rooms for piano practice.

at once into regular and fully graded classes. Hence has arisen the necessity of a preparatory department alongside of the college proper. This preparatory department is more than a feeder to the college. It provides classes of different grades for making up deficiencies on the part of candidates for the college. Students are examined as they enter, and instead of being sent home if unfitted, are placed in proper course of training for the Freshman Class.

The college proper is intended only for those young women who wish to become scholars in the very highest acceptation of the word. The trustees resolved at the outset on thus establishing the very highest standard, and on providing facilities for advanced study in every department. They have provided especially for those scholars who desire to become teachers. The daughters of the wealthy are not forbidden to come to Wellesley, but it is easy to see that none will stay who do not seek to become learned women. The low price, the high requirements for admission, the extended course of study, the simple style of dress, the methods of instruction and discipline, all point to the fact that life at this college is work and not play.

It is really remarkable how quickly the new college has shaped itself in accordance with these principles, and established its character as a place for thorough study. The *esprit de corps* in this respect is already very high. It has become the fashion to study. An honorable ambition for the best scholarship is the rule, and not the exception.

The reader may be interested to know in particular of the conditions of admission. For the preparatory department these are very moderate. Candidates therefor must be over fifteen years of age, and must pass

STUDENT'S PARLOR.

satisfactory examinations in reading, writing, spelling, English grammar, modern geography, arithmetic, history of the United States, Latin grammar and reader. In the case of those who are sixteen years or older, a thorough knowledge of French or German and of the elements of algebra is accepted in place of Latin. The course of preparatory study covers two years of thorough training in Latin grammar and Latin prose composition, Cæsar, Virgil, Cicero, the elementary part of Olney's University Algebra, geometry, German or French, geography of the Roman Empire, and outlines of its history to the Augustan age, English grammar, analysis and composition, physical geography, elocution, English literature, and drawing. Those who intend to elect Greek in the college course also commence the study of it in the preparatory department.

While the college is confined to its present building, bringing the students of the two departments under the same roof and similar regulations, it is the plan of the trustees that the preference should be given to those candidates for admission who are fitted to enter the college proper, since they must reap the greater benefit from the advantages provided. At the same time many of the finest college students must be those who have enjoyed the exceptional training furnished in the preparatory department. It is, therefore, hoped that the Christian public, as it becomes interested in this seat of learning, will in some way provide funds for erecting another building in the ample grounds of the college, when the important preparatory department can be separated to a still higher usefulness. The instant success of the college warrants this extension of its resources. There were so many applications at the opening in September, 1875, that between two and three hundred were refused of necessity, and if there were other buildings on the grounds equal to the first, they would doubtless be as readily filled.

The requirements for admission to the collegiate department in September, 1876, have been established by the trustees to meet the comparatively low standard of preparation among young women; but they are to be increased year by year, until the full standard adopted in the leading colleges for young men shall be reached. Candidates must be at least sixteen years old, and are required to pass examinations in ancient and modern geography; physical geography; arithmetic; algebra through involution, evolution, radicals, and quadratic equations; geometry through five books of Loomis's Geometry or their equivalent; Latin grammar; and four books of Cæsar, four books of Virgil, and four Orations of Cicero. An equivalent amount of reading in other Latin authors is accepted. Candidates are further

advised to be prepared for examination in French and German. No Greek is positively required, being, in fact, an elective throughout the entire course; but a preparatory study of Greek is most strongly urged upon those who intend to fit for the college, and it will probably soon be made a requisite for admission.

We can not give space to a detailed account of the studies of the four years' college course, for which those who desire it are referred to the published circulars. It must be enough for the general reader to state that elaborate courses are laid out in all the branches of learning commonly pursued in our highest institutions. No doubt will be entertained by those who examine the courses of study that this is to be a college of the highest standard of culture. The studies are mostly elective, and the students can pursue any in which they may desire to become specialists as far as they can be pursued in most colleges for young men. The course in modern languages which has already been arranged and announced is very comprehensive and thorough; but with the next college year it will be supplemented by an extended special course, which shall carry students to the highest degree of proficiency and culture, and remedy some of the many deficiencies which mark the common methods. The students receive general instruction in vocal music, and also in drawing, unless already practiced in that useful accomplishment; while for those who intend special and advanced study of either art the best facilities are at hand. The art gallery is furnished with an extensive array of casts and models, selected in Europe by Walter Smith, Esq., the distinguished State Director of Art Study in Massachusetts; and the certain prospective demand for competent teachers of drawing makes this department one of great importance. In general, class-room instruction is supplemented at every point by lectures, to the delivery of which specialists in art, science, and literature are summoned; while Friday evening is usually appropriated to a concert or a more popular lecture in the chapel.

There are many things about the Wellesley methods of study which are new and interesting, for which we have no space. We wish, however, to notice the chemical department. The instruction in chemistry is confined almost exclusively to actual work in the laboratory. This is fitted up with every convenience for a class of ninety-six students, divided into four sections of twenty-four each. Every one of the ninety-six has her own drawer and cupboard. There is no committing of text-books to memory, no waste of time in witnessing sensational experiments by the teacher. The students work out their own experiments.

In addition to the regular college classes,

non-resident students in chemistry are received. They can spend all their time in the laboratory, and thus qualify themselves as teachers for that instruction in chemistry with laboratory practice which is now considered so essential.

At the opening of the second year of the college, in September, 1876, it is the intention to receive, to a limited degree, non-resident students in other advanced studies, the desire being to give to teachers, who wish to qualify themselves for higher situations, opportunities for becoming specialists. This privilege is given to teachers only. They will be "special students," not connected in any other manner with the college.

But the intellectual life is not made the sole object of pursuit at Wellesley College. The place which Biblical study receives in the curriculum indicates the importance which is attached to it here. Christianity is accepted as a great fact to be studied. And more, it is esteemed as an experience which is to be individualized. The cross which is carved into the key-stone of the arch which spans the entrance door, and which rises above the highest pinnacle of the noble pile, is emblem and pledge of the sacred aim which has inspired all.

To the bracing tone of the Wellesley atmosphere and the wholesome effect of Wellesley ideas the students themselves are the best witnesses. Three hundred healthier, happier, more blooming girls it would be hard to find in company together. They are not cumbered with much serving; they are not hampered by many rules. They appreciate their privileges, and are worthy of them. To a large degree they are their own governors. Never had young women finer opportunities for study in the midst of surroundings more attractive. If in their beautiful rooms they ever grow weary, all the beautiful grounds without are before them. They ramble at will through all the broad domain. The lake is their skating park in winter, the scene of their boating exploits

ON THE GROUNDS.

in summer. When Mr. Longfellow visited them last autumn, it was a delightful row they gave him in an eight-oared barge, called the *Evangeline;* and after a season or two of practice, it would be a fine crew which they could doubtless send to compete, in grace and skill, if not in strength, with their brothers of Harvard and Yale.

Who ever heard of a fire-brigade manned exclusively by women? There is one at Wellesley, for it is there believed that, however incombustible the college building may be, the students should be taught how to put out fires in their own homes, and be trained to presence of mind, to familiarity with the thought of what is to be done in case of fire, and to a full realization of the most important fact that any fire can be put out at the beginning. Twenty hand-pumps are distributed throughout the building, each supplemented by six pails filled with water. Every pump has its captain and company of six girls, one of whom is lieutenant; and all the companies are drilled at convenient opportunities in handling the pumps, in forming lines, and in passing the pails. The whole organization is officered by a superintendent and secretary. Hose companies for the operating of the great steam fire-pump are organized in a similar manner.

The property of the college and its administration are vested in a Board of Trustees, chartered as a perpetual legal corporation, under the name of Wellesley College. President Porter, of Yale College, is president of the Board of Trustees, and Dr. Howard Crosby, chancellor of New York University, is the vice-president. The trustees represent the Congregational, Presbyterian, Episcopal, Methodist, and Baptist churches; several universities, colleges, and theological seminaries; the leading foreign missionary society of the country; both sexes; and the laity as well as the clergy. The evident design is to keep the college in close affiliation with the great academic centres, and under the eye of experienced educators, at the same time securing for it the special confidence of all those Christian denominations known as evangelical, the knowledge of affairs possessed only by business men in active life, and indispensable counsel from woman herself.

Wellesley College needs the generous remembrance of the rich. What institution presents a stronger appeal for endowment than this? At present there is no endowment. The price of board and tuition has been fixed as low as $250 a year, in order to bring its choice privileges within the reach of many who deserve them, but would otherwise be debarred from them. But at that price it can hardly be expected that the college will pay its own current expenses. The benevolent here see a grand foundation already laid to their hand, and, by the creation of an endowment, may communicate an immediate and immense impulse to the usefulness of the institution. The many vacant shelves of the library likewise invite contributions. One hundred thousand dollars could be at once most profitably expended in supplying them with those costly works which are such a boon to both student and teacher. There is great need of an observatory. And then, how much good could be effected by the creation of scholarships! Our colleges for young men are beginning to be liberally provided with them; but there is even more need for them in a college for young women, whose means are just as likely to be moderate, and whose opportunities for self-support are more likely to be restricted.

VIEW OF WELLESLEY COLLEGE FROM THE OPPOSITE SIDE OF THE LAKE.

Exeter and it's Academy (1894)

EXETER AND ITS ACADEMY.

By S. Alice Ranlett.

The Old Tower House

OWHERE is England more truly Old England than in Devon; though the world's people gather for a summer holiday at the gay little watering-places on the south shore, and though the locomotive rushes many times daily through wild, romantic Dartmoor, the land of Lorna Doone, there are still secluded nooks upon the sea-beaten northern shore, and beautiful quiet glens among the forests and hills of the interior; there are lonely farmhouses and cottages, and quaint, old-time parish churches, and lovely Devonshire lanes, winding between the tall hedgerows, in springtime gay and fragrant with the hawthorn, and in summer starred with the pale pink blossom of the English bramble entangled with the glossy masses of ivy;

the country people speak in a strange, uncouth dialect wellnigh unintelligible to the stranger, and still place faith unlimited in the Black Witch, who sends misfortune and disease, and in the White Witch, whose kindly power wards off ill and exercises healing even to mending broken bones.

Hard by one of the slipping, shining Devonshire streams, the Exe, there sits upon a hill a city of unknown antiquity; Caer-Isc, the old Britons called it; the Romans named it Isca Damnoniorum, and, making an important settlement there, left behind them many traces of their life; for to this day are found occasionally coins, bronze statues, and the remains of richly tessellated pavement. So important was this town in Roman days that Antoninus and Ptolemy mention it. The West Saxons had here a strongly fortified enclosure, and in Rougemont Castle, whose ruins crown an adjacent hill, lived the warrior kings; Exan-cester (the castle or camp on the Exe) it was

THE CATHEDRAL, EXETER, ENGLAND.

in the days of good King Alfred, when the Danes surprised the garrison.

The furious waves of war beat often upon the town. William the Norman captured it during his conquering career, and rebuilt the ruined walls of Rougemont. In the Civil Wars, Exeter espoused the royal cause, and was taken by the parliamentarians, but retaken by Prince Maurice, and made the headquarters of the royalists and the residence of Charles's queen; in 1646, after a trying siege, it was surrendered to Fairfax.

The modern Exeter, its grand country residences, its tiny villas, each with a

saint, opens upon the vista of the nave whose clustered columns rise heavenward ; in the rosy and amethystine light of the windows are seen the tombs and memorials of men whose names are honored and reverenced in two continents and in the isles of the sea. The Norman towers, pierced with graceful window-openings, contain, the one the Great Bell of Exeter, weighing 12,500 pounds, and the other the eleven sweet chiming bells which daily send out their melodious summons and ring in a delirium of joy when they join all the other bells in welcoming the judges; for in Exeter is still preserved the old custom, born in the

HIGH STREET.

pocket-handkerchief bit of lawn, and a gay bed of scarlet geraniums surrounded by a wall on which is the legend, Rose Villa, Laburnum Lodge, Woodbine Cottage, or Holly House, as the case may be, its quaint, many-storied old townhouses and its thirty parish churches, with sweet-voiced bells, — all these form the setting to the priceless gem, the Cathedral, which for nearly eight hundred years has stood showing forth in its outward form of beauty the unseen inward beauty of the Church of God. The great door in the western front, beneath a marvellous design of many a sculptured king and

days when the rights of the people were scanty, of ringing a joyous peal when " the judges come to town."

In the green turf of the close shine the tiny English daisies, descendants, in the many-eth generation, of the flowers which bloomed there two hundred and fifty years ago; in those summer days when men were leaving the old homes in the shadow of Cathedral walls to establish themselves in the wilderness beyond the ocean. Devonshire men found their way to Maine and to New Hampshire, and the same family name is engraved on the knightly tomb in an English church and on the bramble-overgrown stone in a lonely storm-beaten nook of the New England seashore; and it may well be that among the men who in 1638 signed John Wheelwright's "combination," there were some who in childhood had picked the Exeter daisies, and in manhood had half unconsciously learned to love the gray towers and the chiming bells of Exeter Cathedral, and who therefore gave to the new home the old English name.

To Wheelwright and his companions is attributed the establishment of the settlement at Exeter, New Hampshire, although there is a tradition of former settlers on the site of the town. The founder of Exeter was an Independent among Independents. A Lincolnshire man and a Cambridge graduate, he was for some years a clergyman of the English Church in Alford; when displaced by Archbishop Laud, he emigrated to Boston and was made a "pastor" in Braintree; he soon became a sharer in the religious views of Mrs. Anne Hutchinson, his sister-in-law, and differences of opinion led to difficulties between him and Mr. Wilson, the Boston pastor. The General Court of

THE SQUAMSCOTT HOUSE, FORMERLY GORHAM HALL.

1636–37 appointed a day of fasting, with a hope that these dissensions might be healed; but Mr. Wheelwright's sermon preached on this occasion did not prove a conciliatory production, and he was pronounced by the Court guilty of sedition and contempt, and, some months later, was banished from the colony. He had previously purchased from Passaconaway, the famous chief of the Penacook Indians, a tract of land in the southeastern part of New Hampshire, where the snowy peaks of the White Mountains slope away into low hill-ridges, and the dancing mountain brooks, sobered by lowland life, wind silently through green meadows or salt marshes; to this district he now withdrew, and in 1638 a town was legally organized. Wheelwright drew up a form of government for the little colony, since as yet New Hampshire had no laws, and caused it to be signed by the heads of families; this agreement was called a "combination," and was readopted in 1640. The original document, in the handwriting of Wheelwright, has been preserved and is in the town clerk's office in Exeter.

EXETER TOWN HALL.

The little frontier settlement did not spring at once into prosperity; many a day of anxiety and anguish befell the settlers in the wilderness; the Indian and his cruelties were always with them, and for years Exeter suffered much from the depredations of the red man; some citizens were killed, and others were led into captivity, and in 1697 a plot was formed for the destruction of the town;

THE OLD GARRISON HOUSE.

the savages were already lying in ambush near the settlement when the reports of guns alarmed them and caused them to retreat hastily, killing a few persons as they fled. To protect the townspeople from the Indians, a garrison house was built, and this relic of the frontier settlement, adapted in modern times to the peaceful and prosaic purposes of trade and residence, has been proudly cherished by the Exeter people.

A spirit of independence worthy of the founder has from early times character-

THE CASS HOUSE.

ized the men of Exeter. A thrill of sympathy excited them, when in 1683 a dozen armed horsemen, with the avowed intention of overthrowing the government, passed through the town, on their way to Hampton, where the Provincial Assembly was in session. At another time, a marshal and his deputy, sent by the tyrannical Governor Cranfield to collect unlawfully levied taxes, were treated in Exeter with so slight consideration that they were only too glad to make their escape. In 1734, Lieutenant-Governor Dunbar, suspecting that the lumbermen of Exeter were felling trees which were the property of the Crown, despatched from Portsmouth a barge manned by ten men, who had directions to seize and carry away the suspected timber; on their arrival the men were most vigorously handled, and their boat was unfitted for use, so that they were obliged to return to Portsmouth without the king's trees.

The Revolutionary crisis roused the patriotic zeal of Exeter, and at a town meeting in January, 1774, the citizens "almost unanimously" adopted the resolution, "That we are ready on all necessary occasions to risk our lives and fortunes in defence of our rights and liberties." Soon after they joined in the plot for seizing the ammunition in Fort William and Mary, at the entrance of Portsmouth Harbor, and thus took a leading part in the early armed resistance to Great Britain. When the news of the march of the British to Lexington came, a company of one hundred and eight men was immediately formed and marched, arriving at Cambridge on the following day. When the Declaration of Independence reached Exeter, fourteen days from Philadelphia, the Committee of Safety was in session, and the Declaration was most impressively read aloud by John Taylor Gilman, who had devoted his unusual abilities to the service of his country. He had been one of those who marched to Cambridge, and he afterward served in the Federal Congress, and was governor of New Hampshire for fourteen years. The stately mansion which was the home of his later years still stands beneath the Exeter elms, and is rich in many a memory of the past. The visitor is impressed by the grand hall and stately stairway, and the "landscape chamber," which contains a large panel, bearing upon it a picture painted nearly a hundred years ago by an English artist.

On the morning of Nov. 4, 1789, the Exeter people were early astir, for on that day they were to welcome with all loving honors the nation's chieftain, Gen. Washington. When the General arrived, soon after sunrise, the cavalcade which was to perform escort duty was unmounted, but the people were in the streets, and the Exeter artillery fired a salute of thir-

FIRST CHURCH.

teen rounds. Col. Nicholas Gilman, who had been a staff officer of Washington's, and many prominent citizens did the honors of the occasion, and entertained the famous guest at a breakfast at Folsom's Inn. Washington in his diary noted of his visit to Exeter: "This is considered the second town in New Hampshire, and stands at the head of the tide-water of the Piscataqua River, but ships of three hundred and four hundred tons are built at it. Above are considerable falls which supply several gristmills, a slitting mill, and a snuff mill. It is a place of some consequence, but does not contain more than one thousand inhabitants. A jealousy subsists between this town, where the Legislature alternately sits, and Portsmouth, which, had I known of it in time, would have made it necessary to have accepted an invitation to a public dinner; but my arrangements having been otherwise made, I could

THE COUNTY HOUSE.

not." So Exeter missed the glory of giving a dinner to the Father of his Country!

On Sept. 20, 1786, the town was disturbed by the Paper Money Riot. An armed mob of several hundred men arrived in Exeter, intending to compel the Legislature, in session there, to authorize

JOHN PHILLIPS.

FOUNDER OF PHILLIPS EXETER ACADEMY. FROM A PAINTING IN THE ACADEMY HALL.

the issue of paper money; but Exeter maintained its dignity, put the mob to flight, and captured the leaders.

When the English fleet arrived off Portsmouth in 1814, and the rumor spread that the British would attempt a landing, the heart of Exeter beat fast; the alarm bells were rung, and a company of one hundred and twenty men was quickly raised and marched to Portsmouth, under the command of the young Capt. Nathaniel of the ever-patriotic family of Gilman.

Again, in 1861, the patriotism of the town came to the rescue of the country,

and gifts of money and wise thought were bestowed upon her, while the women wrought well in sanitary work, and three hundred strong men, as sailors or soldiers, entered the national service.

One of the first measures adopted by Wheelwright, in 1638, was the establishment of a religious society, of which he was the pastor. The first house of worship was small and primitive, and was replaced by a second building during the pastorate of Samuel Dudley, who succeeded Wheelwright in 1650. Still another house was built before the arrival of John Clark, who was ordained on Sept. 21, 1698. On the Sunday before his ordination a covenant was signed by the members of the "First Church" in Exeter, whose organization and title have since been maintained. A fourth meeting-house was built in 1731, which lasted until the erection of the present edifice in 1798. This stands near the Town Hall on a small hill rising from the river-bank, and, though the successor of so many buildings, bears numerous marks of the old times and customs; in its tower is the town bell, which nightly rings the curfew.

In 1743, forty-one members of the original parish withdrew, were organized as the "Second Church," and erected a meeting-house. Hon. John Phillips was invited to become the pastor, but declined because of his many duties.

Among the more modern and graceful houses of worship which raise their spires skyward and join with silvery bell-voices in the Sunday chorus, these two stand with quiet dignity and modest pride of age and association.

Exeter lays claim to being the first town in the state which established schools; for among the colonists who came thither in 1638 was one Philemon Pormont, doubtless a man of learning,

THE OLD ACADEMY, DESTROYED BY FIRE IN 1871.

whose vocation was that of "teaching and nurturing children"; and though no urchin who sat beneath his frowns and smiles has left us a diary, it is supposed that the said Philemon did indulge in pedagogic frowns and smiles. A century later, we must believe that the youthful twigs of the town were most wisely inclined, for John Phillips, the founder of the Academy, was the master of the public school. In early Revolutionary days a grammar school was maintained at the town's expense.

If Exeter is proud of her early steps in pursuit of wisdom, still more does she rejoice in her Phillips Academy, the noble

THE PRESENT ACADEMY BUILDINGS.

institution which for more than a hundred years has flourished in her borders.

Among the followers of Winthrop who landed at Salem, in 1630, and part of whom settled at Watertown, were Sir Richard Saltonstall and his friend and

DR. BENJAMIN ABBOT.

FROM A PAINTING BY CHESTER HARDING.

pastor, George Phillips. These pilgrims on the good ship "Arbella" brought with them their children and their schools; and while the little vessel was ploughing through the stormy Atlantic, they "taught and catechised," and five years after they landed in the New England wilderness, that wilderness began to smile with the promise of the future; for in 1635, free schools were established, and soon after the college at Newtowne, afterward called Cambridge, from the college home of George Phillips, and so many of the scholars of the colony in England. Then followed the need of preparatory schools,—and Dummer Academy was established; and to this school there came, a hundred years later, an earnest, thoughtful boy, Samuel Phillips, fifth in descent from George Phillips, the pilgrim of the "Arbella," and direct ancestor of the man whom Massachusetts loves to honor,

her son and lamented shepherd, Phillips Brooks.

To this boy, slow in learning but sure in remembering, belongs the honor of originating the New England academy system. Young Phillips, leaving Harvard at the age of nineteen, plunged at once into the struggle for independence, and became a member of the Provincial Congress, and later lieutenant-governor of Massachusetts. When Putnam cried, "Ye gods, give us powder!" Phillips galloped home, summoned his neighbors, told them that upon them hung the fate of the young nation, then set to work himself,—and the result was powder, and the evacuation of Boston. This generous young man urged his father and his uncle John to use in founding an academy the wealth which would come to him as their heir. The elder men, both Harvard graduates, cordially entered into Samuel's plans and indorsed the constitution which he, aided by a friend, drew up; and the result was Phillips Academy at Andover, which probably inspired one of its founders with the purpose which,

DR. GIDEON LANE SOULE.

six months later, in 1781, resulted in the incorporation of Phillips Exeter Academy.

John Phillips, the uncle of Samuel, and the founder of this Academy, was born in 1719, in Andover, and as a boy was a true lover of learning. He entered Harvard at the age of eleven, and, after graduation, studied theology with his father and taught in Andover for a time, then opened a classical school in Exeter. Having been made ruling elder in the "New Parish," he began to preach, and was called a "zealous, pathetic, and animated" preacher; but after hearing the fiery language of Whitefield, he distrusted his own powers of eloquence and, abandoning preaching, turned his attention to business, in which he became most successful, thanks to his habits of economy and regularity, his native good sense, and his liberal education. In the Phillips mansion the backlogs were soaked in water to burn the longer, and the candle was extinguished during the long evening prayer; in these and similar ways were saved the pennies which rolled into the pounds of the Academy foundation. Dame Phillips, sharing in these close economies, aided her husband in his great work; and not only this, but she freely relinquished all rights of dower in his estate, reserving for her own subsistence only the barest pittance, but winning a better inheritance in the honor which she deserves. John Phillips was a rigorous Puritan and a man of severe, old-time dignity; he reverenced authority, and was faithful to the rule of the mother country; though disapproving the Revolution, he did not resist it. Before the Declaration of Independence, he received many important offices under

FACULTY OF PHILLIPS EXETER ACADEMY.

W. A. STONE.	W. A. FRANCIS.	B. L. CILLEY.
G. R. WHITE.	C. E. FISH, Principal.	O. FAULHABER.
W. R. MARSH.		H. C. JACKSON.
J. A. TUFTS.		A. J. DUDLEY.

the government. At the suggestion of Governor Wentworth, he formed a *corps d'élite* of Exeter men; this body was called the Exeter Cadets, and Phillips, its colonel, was justly proud of its admirable discipline and fine appearance in rich uniform of buff and scarlet. But on the morning after the great day of Concord and Lexington, a large number of these cadets, trained as a royal governor's escort, without waiting their colonel's orders, shouldered Governor Wentworth's fine muskets and marched off to join the colonial army.

At the beginning of the war, Phillips withdrew from business and devoted him self to the execution of his plans for the advancement of learning. He founded and endowed the Phillips Professorship of Theology at Dartmouth College, gave largely to Nassau Hall, now Princeton College, and, with his brother, founded the Academy at Andover; and for fourteen years he gave to his own special creation, the Exeter Academy, not only his wealth but his fostering care, solving by his ready wisdom the many difficult problems which arose, and establishing the school upon the sound basis which has supported it during its century of existence.

The formal dedication of the buildings and the installation of the first principal, William Woodbridge, took place in May, 1783. On this occasion an oration on the Advantages of Learning was delivered by David McClure; and Mr. Woodbridge, in a graceful address, accepted his trust. He congratulated the father of the institution, and expressed the wish, now long fulfilled, that unborn

G. A. WENTWORTH.

thousands of the rising empire should hail him as benefactor, and called upon all to cherish the institutions of knowledge, that "the science and virtue which have seated America in the throne of empires may be spread to form the minds and virtues of her illustrious sons, that so shall they be formed for usefulness and famed for wisdom, for virtue, and for glory."

"His appropriate monument are
        The institutions which bear
        his name,"

are the last words of the inscription upon John Phillips's monument in Exeter; and following this thought, we turn from the silent grave to the joyful, active life of the Academy which bears his name and continues his work. After a five years' charge of the school, Mr. Woodbridge was succeeded by Benjamin Abbot, a cultured scholar and a teacher "born, not made," who for fifty years exerted his marvellous influence for good upon hundreds of young, impetuous lives. He commanded the respect and

THE P. E. A. BASE-BALL TEAM.

the love of his pupils. Dignified and sweet in bearing, his very manners were a lesson. He understood boy nature, and the nagging process was no part of his discipline. As has been said, "his pupils got their ethics mainly by absorption." When there was cause for discipline, it was prompt and decisive, and there was no lingering remembrance of the sins to cloud subsequent intercourse.

Mr. Cunningham, in his delightful Sketches of Phillips Academy, relates many stories

THE NEW DORMITORY — SOULE HALL.

illustrative of Dr. Abbot's wise *régime*. One of his former pupils says: " I was once chairman of a board of inspection whose duty it was to report infraction of rules, among which was one against smoking. I was sent to ask the doctor if this applied to the Academy premises only. ' What,' said he, ' would you confine virtue to the Academy yard?'" Dr. Hoyt says: " He was a primate among teachers. He made the Academy the centre of his efforts and thoughts; he was a live man; his mind was a fountain, not a reservoir. He breathed his own spirit into the text-books of the schoolroom; modern literature, politics, and theology as well as the classics found place in his reading. Few men were so deeply versed as he in the most abstruse of all studies, the human nature of boys. His classes caught fire from him and glowed with the same enthusiasm; he was always fresh in his feelings; his heart was young to the last."

On his golden anniversary, after fifty years of happy union with the Academy, Master Abbot was visited by some four hundred of his children in learning. The Exeter elms which saw the sight still whisper the story of that day, and the " old Academy boys" never tire of telling of its glory. Dr. Abbot's boys, now

the famous men of the country, among them Judge Emery, Dr. Palfrey, John P. Hale, and Edward Everett with his silvery tongue of eloquence, gathered reverently about their master; and Daniel Webster, in behalf of the former pupils, presented Dr. Abbot with a massive silver vase, and spoke, as he alone could speak, in glowing eulogium upon the beloved master. Dr. Abbot rose to respond, but his voice failed. Then rose Edward Everett. " Brethren," said he, " the voice which never failed in fifty years' teaching, falters now," and taking the manuscript from Dr. Abbot's hand, he read it with graceful impressiveness to the assembly.

The third principal was Gideon Lane Soule, a descendant of the " Mayflower" pilgrim; Soule himself was a Phillips Academy boy and a graduate of Bowdoin College. He returned to Exeter as Professor of Ancient Languages, and his marked success as teacher and disciplinarian made him the man to whom all looked when Dr. Abbot laid down the burden of office; and from 1838 to 1873 Dr. Soule most wisely ruled the turbulent young life of the Academy. He was a man of great popularity among the boys, who scorned to deceive him; his trust in their honor made them worthy of that trust; he was

THE GYMNASIUM.

gentle and sympathetic, never suspicious, but always vigilant, kind but dignified, and exacting the deference due his office; he was calm, firm, and wise in judgment. During the Civil War, Phillips Academy knew no color line; and when four fiery students from Kentucky an-

is built from pressed brick and gray sandstone, and occupies the place of honor on the campus. Near it is old

P. E. A. STUDENTS.

nounced to Dr. Soule that if the one colored student of the school remained they must go, he replied promptly, "He will stay; you may do as you please."

In 1870, during the administration of Dr. Soule, the old Academy building was burned. An appeal to the alumni for $100,000 was immediately answered, and in 1872 was dedicated the new Academy Hall, a building harmonious in proportions and graceful in outlines. It

FROM AN OLD PORTRAIT.

WILLIAM ROBINSON.

FOUNDER OF ROBINSON SEMINARY.

Abbot Hall, and in the vicinity are the new physical and chemical laboratories, which have been constructed with the wisest thought, and are fitted for the most careful and delicate experiments of modern science. The gymnasium is equipped with the best apparatus, and contains all possible comforts and conveniences, including a boxing-room, running-track, bowling-alley, and room for base-ball practice. The school hall is made interesting by a collection of Academy portraits, the full-length picture of the founder with the head painted by Stuart, and portraits of Dr. Abbot, Dr. Soule, Bancroft, Benjamin Butler, Everett, and Webster, and many others of the Phillips men.

Dr. Soule closed his long service in 1873, and it was gracefully and truly said of him: "He entered into what was already a great office, and left it greater than he found it." In recent years, clear heads and steady hands have guided the rushing tide of youth in the Academy; and the principals, Dr. Perkins, Dr. Scott, and Mr. Fish, have found strong support in their assistant workers of the faculty, who have been the inspiration of their pupils. Many men of unusual ability have held the teacher's office in Phillips Academy. Among the honored names are Cleaveland, Bowen, Chadbourne, Ripley, Hale, Everett, and others of fame, who bring the list down to the day of Bradbury Cilley, who for more than thirty years has been Professor of Ancient Languages, and Professor Wentworth, who has since 1858, until his recent resignation, been the strong right hand of the Academy faculty, and who, in resigning, has still left the school a rich inheritance in his brilliant mathematical works. The present able faculty is faithfully working out the true Phillips Academy idea, with its principal, Professor Fish, and Professor Cilley of the ancient language department, and Professors Faulhaber and Tufts, who for nearly twenty years have been working in their respective departments, modern languages and English, and a company of younger teachers who are also scholars.

GEORGE N. CROSS.

PRINCIPAL OF ROBINSON SEMINARY.

The act of incorporation states the purpose of the school to be the promoting of piety and virtue, and the education of youth in the English, Latin, and Greek languages, and in writing, arithmetic, music, and the art of speaking, practical geometry, logic, and such other of the liberal arts and sciences and languages as opportunity may hereafter permit. Not every institution has thus in its beginning planned for days of wider knowledge and greater things.

The constitution is a document of wise and noble thoughtfulness. It declares that the school is established "to teach young men the great end and real business of living." It regards the finances, discipline, and study of the school. Since the trustees are custodians of a public fund, the founder declares

that the records of their meetings and the amount of all gifts and expenditures shall be "open for the perusal of all men." Every charge of nepotism is avoided, for "if a candidate for election is as closely related as first cousin to any member of the Board, such member is not to sit in the election." Among other acquirements it is declared that the principal shall have "good acquaintance with human nature." The institution shall ever give special attention to the health of the students and to encouraging habits of industry; but above all it is expected "that the attention of instructors to the disposition of the mind and morals of the youth under their charge will exceed every other care, well considering that though goodness without knowledge as it respects others is weak and feeble, yet knowledge without goodness is dangerous, and both united form the noblest character."

THE ROBINSON SEMINARY.

The object of the school has ever been to educate, and its discipline is not adapted to boys requiring severe restrictions; its methods assume that the pupils have a will to work, and are intended to cultivate self-control, a right sense of honor, and to produce a pure moral atmosphere. For boys whose influence is injurious to good scholarship or good morals there is no place at Phillips Academy.

cency and Order at Recitations and Prayers."

"They shall enter the Room without bold Forwardness and Noise."

A CLASS IN DOMESTIC SCIENCE, ROBINSON SEMINARY.

Among the interesting records of the school are the rules established by the first trustees, and probably written by the founder : —

"Diligence and Attention are required of all the Students of this Academy."

"As Idleness and Inattention will utterly defeat the End of this Institution, they are strictly forbidden."

"Students shall stand erect with De-

In their amusements they are not to exceed "the Bounds of Reason and the Rules of Virtue, Manliness, and Honor."

"On Sabbath Evening," it is recommended "that the students tarry at home or spend it regularly in Sacred Music, a noble and improving Amusement."

The course of study at Phillips Academy has always been liberal and progressive, fitting the students in the most complete way for Harvard and other colleges or for the work of the world. It is interesting to note the signs of the times in the changes of subjects and text-books, as shown in the published study courses.

In Dr. Abbot's day the boys were drilled in Adams's Latin Grammar and Murray's English Grammar, in Theology and Sacred Music. In 1850, Andrews and Stoddard's Latin Grammar had arisen in its glory, and Davies's Legendre

A ROOM IN THE JOTHAM LAWRENCE HOUSE.

and Paley's Evidences. Moreover, German and French were offered. Always with the best help of the time, Phillips Academy boys have plodded on, digging for Greek and Latin roots, hunting for the mysterious unknown — and sometimes utterly lost — quantity, and pursuing the heroic hexameter fortunes of the brave Achilles and the pious Æneas, till the happy youth of nowadays rejoice in learning made easy by the bright, inspiring text-books of to-day, many of them the work of their own Phillips Exeter men and scholars.

Athletic sports have received their due attention from the Academy students. One of the earliest recreations was the voluntary performance of military exercises; this was in the last century, and Lewis Cass was prominent in the movement. On the occasion of the obsequies of Gen. Washington, in 1799, the governor of New Hampshire, with his Council, the Senate, and House of Representa-

"The Washington Whites," and its uniform was a frock and trousers of white with a corresponding cockade and plume.

"UNDER THE ELM."

THE GOVERNOR BELL HOUSE.

When the Civil War broke out, the Phillips Academy boys formed themselves into drill clubs, and a goodly number marched away from school to join the Union Army.

Games of marbles, now long disappeared, were once in vogue, and the old-fashioned games of bat-and-ball have,

FRESH RIVER.

FROM A PHOTO BY FRANCES LAWRENCE BERNHARDT.

tives, marched in solemn procession to attend the religious services in Exeter. They were attended by a "military escort formed of the Phillips Academy students, with proper badges of mourning." This military corps was called

with time, developed into the modern base-ball, which, with foot-ball, has started the ambition and stirred the blood of the athletic men of the present generation and roused to wild excitement the quiet Academy town on those

THE GOVERNOR GILMAN HOUSE.

spring and autumn holidays when "fair women and brave men," seminary maidens, sedate scholars and serious-faced divines linger about the charmed scenes of the "game," and look with mournful mien at the brilliant plays of Harvard freshmen, or Andover boys, and, when the Exeter students win victory, make the welkin ring with jubilant yells of "P. E. A."

Boating was introduced in 1864, and rowing matches and regattas followed. Athletic tournaments, under the management of the Athletic Association, and hare-and-hound runs have held place among the Academy sports.

Societies have long flourished in the Academy; among them most prominent, The Christian Fraternity, The Golden Branch, and The Gideon Lane Soule Society. The Golden Branch, with its motto, F. S. T. (Friendship's Sacred Tie), and its classic name in memory of the Branch which conducted Æneas in safety through the world of spirits, was founded in 1818, and has numbered in its members many who are now famed men. Its aim is to give practice in extemporaneous speaking and parliamentary law; and one of its former members, long experienced in the excitement of the

political canvass, says he has never known one "equal to those held in the old room at the east end of the Academy." The Golden Branch has an interesting cabinet of valuable curiosities, and a fine library.

The G. L. Soule Society, with its motto, *Fortiter, Fideliter, Feliciter,* was organized in 1882, for the purpose of encouraging literary work among the students.

The *Exonian,* established in 1878, has been the chief newspaper organ of the school, and has met the usual vicissitudes of agony and glory which befall the "school paper."

The glory of a school lies in its children; and for a hundred years the sons of Phillips Academy, through the length and breadth of the great Union, have been gathering the laurels which crown their gentle mother's brows. On the Centennial Festival of the Academy, in 1883, it appeared that 5,278 pupils had been in the school. From these have been five ministers plenipotentiary to the courts of the most powerful nations, seven Cabinet ministers, eight senators and twenty representatives, twelve state governors, twenty-seven United States justices and assistant justices, nine college presidents, and a great number of professors,

ONE OF THE OLD FARMHOUSES.

attorneys, literary men, and army officers, most valuable in their respective fields of labor; and among the alumni of the Academy are the men whom the nation delights to honor, — the backwoods boy who became the American Demosthenes, Daniel Webster, and his brother in school, who has been called our Cicero, Edward Everett, and an honored list following these, — Cass, Saltonstall, Bancroft, the Gilmans, Sparks, Palfrey, Soule, A. P. Peabody, Bowen, Hale, Robert Lincoln, and the long-time librarian of Harvard University, John Langdon Sibley, who, with many another who has since worthily served his fellows, was a boy " on the foundation " at Phillips Academy, *i. e.*, was supported by the Phillips Charity Fund. Deeply grateful for the preparation for life which he received at Exeter, Mr. Sibley, from his hardly won savings, began in 1860 a series of noble gifts to the school for the support of needy and meritorious students. This bounty, with that of other friends of the Academy, forms a large fund, whose income is bestowed in generous and judicious gifts upon many faithful students. In the low tuition price of the school all the pupils have remitted an amount equal to half the cost of instruction.

The handsome modern buildings of the Academy stand conspicuous on Front Street, and copy, but " copy fair," the old buildings burned in 1870. Across the street and beyond the shaded common is the " Academy House," which has long been the residence of the masters; it is a properly dignified old mansion, and sits in quiet state beneath the branching trees, although, if on an early June day the wide hall doors at either end stand open, you may catch a glimpse of a fascinating garden with many a sweet-scented row of grandmother's flowers, a mass of delicious pinky-white apple-blossoms atilt in the summer breeze, and a swarm of sunbeams dancing and flickering as gayly and giddily as if this were not a house consecrated for many years to solemn wisdom and her representatives.

Near the Academy are the fine grounds and buildings of Robinson Seminary, a well-endowed institution for the general education and the " college fitting " of girls.

The founder, William Robinson, an Exeter and Phillips Academy boy, expressed plainly the purpose of the institution in these words of his will: he wished to give to girls " such instruction as shall fit them for the work of life and enable them to compete successfully with their brothers in that work." This school is a truly generous philanthropy, since, in accordance with the founder's will, it is forever free to the orphan and the poor girl. It is remarkably well equipped, with a valuable reference library, cabinets and laboratories well supplied with apparatus for use in various branches of natural science, and a fine collection of casts and photographs for the study of art history. Under the wise and watchful care of the principal, Professor Cross, faithful and progressive work is done in all the departments of the school, including, besides the preparatory, academic, and college fitting departments, a class in domestic science, in which cooking lessons are given by a graduate of the Boston Cooking School, and a post-graduate course of Normal instruction.

William Robinson, the founder of this school, took his New England thrift and New England education to the South, and in her rich industries reaped the fortune which he liberally scattered, with one hand, upon the home of his boyhood, and, with the other, upon the land of his adoption. Engraved upon the monument to his memory in Augusta, Ga., beneath the name and the date, are the words: " A Resident of Augusta and its vicinity for nearly fifty years, he was known as a courteous gentleman, an honorable Merchant and a Benefactor of the poor. His name will be held in grateful remembrance by the people of his birthplace and of his adopted home for the bounty which secured to their children and children's children the priceless benefits of Education."

The pilgrim who has wandered among the antiquities of Portsmouth and has revelled in her reminiscences should continue his pilgrimage to Exeter. He may choose from three routes, — he may spin prosaically over the railway in half an hour; or take a boat on the river which winds through salt meadows; or, best of all, may drive over the old highway on which, in former days, rolled the stage-coach with its six prancing horses and the merry sound of the horn.

This road runs through a good farming district, and if it is early June the fields are waving with golden buttercups and fragrant with clover; the great apple orchards are gardens in which hundreds of delicate pink nosegays delight the eye; large, comfortable farmhouses are seen on every side, and here and there is a neat schoolhouse. As we mount a rise of ground, we have a glimpse of the river and, far away, the hazy Deerfield hills and the blue waters of the Atlantic bordered by the white sands of Rye and Hampton Beaches and the rocks of Boar's Head. After we have climbed the last hill-slope, before us, in the river valley, is the town of Exeter. The wide streets are bordered by great elms, which throw feathery shadows upon the green yards lying between the highway and the large houses of wood and brick, which combine, with an air of stately old age, an expression of gracious hospitality shown in the wide doorways and the heavy knockers, which announce the arrival of a guest in hearty tones far different from the querulous peal of the modern door-bell. Among these old mansions the eye falls upon many a one with a name and history. Here is the low, gambrel-roofed house which was the earlier home of John Phillips; here is the former home of Major Cass and the birthplace of Lewis Cass; on the eastern bank of the Squamscott is the old Powder House, which was built about the year 1760, and was first used, probably, at the time of the French and Indian War, and later as a storehouse for the powder captured from Fort William and Mary; this quaint structure is built of brick, the walls being fourteen inches in thickness, and faces the cardinal points; the roof is pyramidal and is also of brick.

Opposite the county house, beneath a stately tree, is the historic mansion, "Under the Elm"; the gambrel roof preserves the antique appearance, and the large additions and verandas give an air of modern comfort. The main part was built before 1740 by Dr. Odlin; it was

conveyed to Col. Nicholas Gilman in 1782, and has since been in the possession of the Gilman family, and has seen, going in and out, the old-school gentlemen, the statesmen and the patriots of that family. The wide hall, with its broad panels and deep carved mouldings, has echoed the tread of many famous men, and the spacious library has been the silent witness of the growth of useful thought; the rare book treasures upon its shelves reveal the taste and scholarship of the old house's recent occupant, Ex-Governor Bell. Prominent among the imposing ancient mansions are the Gardner and Perry houses: the former was the girlhood home of Elizabeth Gardner, who has won many laurels by the brilliant results of her art work in Paris; and the latter, until recently, the residence of Dr. Perry, who was long known as the "oldest living graduate" of Harvard College, — a matter in which he took much pride as, indeed, he did in his great and honorable age, often saying as he met a stranger, "You never saw a man as old as I am." Dr. Perry belonged to the Harvard class of 1811, in which were also Professor Webster (who is unenviably famous as the murderer of Dr. Parkman) and Edward Everett; he died, in 1887, at the great age of ninety-eight years. The old doctor was a link between the past and present; and those may count themselves fortunate who have heard his vivid narrations of his early days, — perhaps of the trial trip of the "Katherine of Clermont," Fulton's first steamer, and the gaping crowds who lined the river-banks expecting to see the strange object explode, — or who have listened while the old man, with sturdy patriotism, discussed the questions of the day which bore upon his dearly loved country.

Perhaps the best preserved and most interesting relic of the past in Exeter is the "Old Governor Gilman House," a mansion of early colonial days. The huge chimneys, the curious roof, the massive walls of brick covered with wood, and the small-paned, deep-set windows have all an air of "ye olden time"; and when we step into the wide hall and shut out the nineteenth-century world, we find ourselves in the atmosphere of two hundred years ago. The rooms are spacious, though low; there are wood panels in walls and ceilings, uncovered oaken frames, windows in recesses so deep that the rooms are filled at high noon with twilight shadows, and great fireplaces with richly carved frames; there are closets in place and out of place, marvellous in design and mysterious in purpose, — closets that penetrate the walls, wander behind chimneys, turn right angles, describe triangles, and suggest geometry run mad. The kitchen has a huge fireplace where whole animals were roasted in the days of ancient state banquets. The house is now owned and occupied by John T. Perry, a descendant of Nicholas Gilman, the first of the family to dwell in it.

The "Old Curiosity Shop," near Great Bridge, has long been a joy to the modern dame with a taste for the antique. Here tall clocks look down upon ancient spinning-wheels restored to daylight after a Rip Van Winkle sleep in shadowy nooks; blue and brown platters dream of old-time Thanksgiving dinners, and willow-ware teacups cherish fragrant memories of long-ago tea parties; dusty shelves are piled high with leather-bound copies of old sermons as dead as the men who preached them, and with little New England primers rich in their wonderful treasures of literary and theological instruction.

At the remote end of Front Street is the old graveyard, beneath whose singing pines lie two early governors of New Hampshire, Jeremiah Smith and John Taylor Gilman; among the sunken stones, with winged death's-heads and moss-grown inscriptions, is a slab sacred to the memory of one "Rev. Mr. Rogers," who, as a preacher, followed in the footsteps of his famous ancestor, John, who was burnt at Smithfield, "in the presence of his wife and nine small children"; all of which and much more is related upon the Exeter tombstone.

Near the river and the railway station are carriage and cotton factories, foundry and machine shops, with their busy din and companies of operatives; for the old town does not scorn to lend a very active hand to the practical demands of the world.

Beyond the factories and the old residences are streets of modern cupola'd and bay-windowed villas, while, still farther out of town, fertile farms climb the gentle slopes of Kensington and Stratham Ridges.

The Squamscott River affords a fine practice-place for the Academy crews, and is the scene of many a moonlight row; and the pleasant country roads are excellent for driving and riding. About a mile from the Town Hall is the Eddy, a beautiful natural park which the young men and maidens of several generations have used as a trysting-place; various bridle and foot paths run under the tall pines; stray sunbeams flicker on the mossy banks and thickets of waving ferns, and the river ripples in blue waves at the Eddy, or bend in the banks. On pleasant afternoons the Eddy woods are gay with young persons enjoying a woodland ramble in summer, or plucking in autumn the wonderful white ferns which are bleached by the early frosts to a delicate ivory tint.

The manufacturing interests of Exeter, and its position as the commercial centre of a farming region, have saved it from the fatal stagnation of many of the older New England towns; and the fame of its schools brings a constant stream of young life and fresh thought to mingle in a wholesome way with the conservative elements of the place.

Exeter, the mother, sits serenely at the foot of her gray cathedral towers and no longer counts the passing hour, but recalls with pride the kings, and scholars, and saints, who have honored her walls, the raging battles, and the changing peoples of the days of old when as yet Columbus had not sat by the sea and dreamed that there lay beyond its flood a possible, nay, a certain, "undiscovered country." As the years roll on, Exeter, the daughter, fancies herself old, as children are wont to do, and narrates her brave deeds, and gleefully marks her birthdays, — two hundredth, two hundred and fiftieth; but though here and there she shows a weatherbeaten patch, like her own elm-trees, like them, also, she puts forth, year by year, delicate foliage, and is beautiful with the charm of new life and continuing growth.

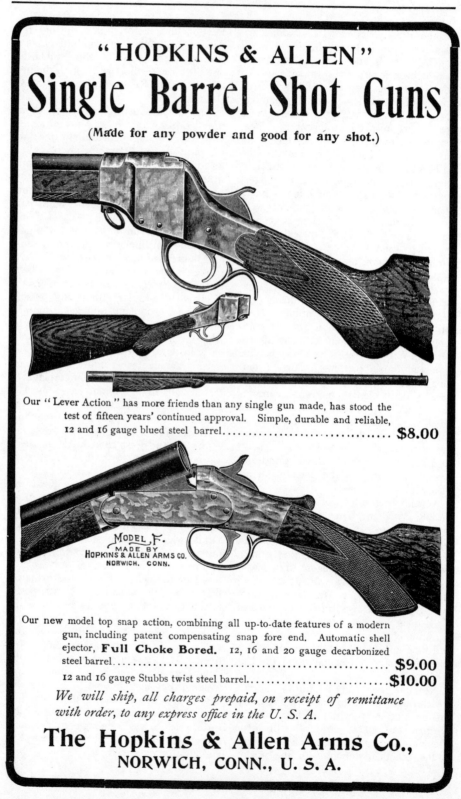

Old Marblehead
(1895)

THE HARBOR AND MARBLEHEAD NECK.

OLD MARBLEHEAD.

By John White Chadwick.

GIVE a title to this paper that is often found upon the lips of men and women born as I was in the ancient town of which I write. It is expressive of the tenderness which it inspires in those who have always clung to her maternal breast, or have yearned for it from afar. They bless their stars that they were born in such a town. Its natural beauty, its original quaintness, of which much survives, its traditions of sterling manhood and heroic independence, — all these things are so many hooks of steel that grapple to it the affections of its people. But the title of my paper suggests not only a sentiment which all decent Marbleheaders cherish for "the rock from which they were hewn," but also the limits within which I am determined to confine these divagations. Let those who choose to do so write of what the town has come to be in these last years. They will have plenty of material, — the smart new houses everywhere, the transformation of the Neck, the steam fire-engines, the electric lights, the trolley, and all that; yes, and those great white-winged creatures that come sailing in to comfort the harbor for its loneliness and to make the summer evenings beautiful with their "feast of lights." And then there are the great shoe manufactories which have twice gone up in smoke and flame, and now, instead of being aggregated as formerly about the railway station, are scattered far and wide, encroaching on the pastures which in the consulship of Plancus the boys and cows held in exclusive fee.

The trip from Boston to Marblehead is never pleasanter than in the late afternoon of a hot summer's day, so invigorating and so cool is the breath of the salt marshes and the sea beyond their scope. There are the great hay-cocks which the artists love, and the winding creeks that turn from blue to gold and crimson as the

405

LEE MANSION. BUILT 1768.

sun goes down behind the Saugus hills. Time was when our imaginary traveller went to Salem, — perhaps in June, when to right and left the pastures are "one laugh of color and embellishment" with Dyer's weed, — and then took the Marblehead Branch, skirting the head of Salem harbor and "The Pines," a sacred grove whose needles whisper of such things as *rixæ, pax et oscula;* for here the young people of the town were wont to hold their joyous festivals. Now there is a branch diverging at Swampscott, at first cutting through rocky hills, thick-grown with various tangle which should forever stay unspoiled, and then coming out into the open a few rods from the sea. Between it and the sea the summer cottages are getting numerous, where twenty years ago five or six farms divided the rich acres fertilized by the kelp and rock-weed heaped by the autumn gales along the

shore. Before the bequest of John Harvard, these acres had been selected as the site of a college by the General Court, and it is a great pity that the idea was not carried out. Our great seat of learning would have been much more "beautiful for situation" in that case than it is now on Cambridge's alluvial plain.

Devereux is the last of several stations between Swampscott and Marblehead. It gets its name from the Devereux farm, one of the oldest holdings in the town, where stood, and stands in melancholy degradation, the farmhouse in which Longfellow was staying when he wrote his lovely poem "The Fire of Driftwood," a bit of silver music with a golden ending : —

"O flames that glowed ! O hearts that yearned !
    They were indeed too much akin,
The driftwood fire without that burned,
    The thoughts that burned and glowed within."

It is at Devereux that passengers for the Neck leave the train. "The Neck" does not mean the narrow isthmus at the harbor's head, but the peninsula which that connects with the mainland. Time was when "the Neck" meant those parts which afterward were called "The Farms," at the base of the town peninsula, and what is now called "the Neck" was called "Great Neck."

"In my days of childhood, in my joyful school-days," this was nearly all one farm, except for the small government reservation for the lighthouse at its extremity ; and any one timely wise could have purchased it for as many thousand dollars as it has brought hundreds of thousands since. It was the

FRONT BEACH.

kingdom of Ephraim, a man of force and stature, whose endeavors to compel the town to build a good road across the isthmus to his farm made the town meeting lively off and on for many years. Fertile in resources, he gave the local economizers a great deal of trouble. Now, for some years, his farm has been for sale in lots to suit the purchasers; and it is no wonder they have come, so beautiful are the beaches and the cliffs, so magnificent the ocean's wide expanse, —

> "Eastward as far as the eye can see,
> Eastward, eastward, endlessly,
> The sparkle and tremor of purple sea."

and pleasant are some of the new cottages nested high among the rocks; but to have known and loved the beauty of the olden time is to be absolutely unreconciled to the new *régime*, save from the freeholder's or the tax-collector's point of view. Even Great Head (called also Castle Rock), a splendid jutting mass of rocks upon the ocean side, is not the place to grow Byronic with the ocean that it used to be when one could have it to himself or *solus cum solâ*, hour after happy hour. Further north there was a famous picnic and chowder-party ground, and the shore between that and Castle

BURIAL HILL.

Looking townward, too, across the harbor from the piazza of the Eastern Yacht Club house, or from any coign of vantage, the view is very picturesque, culminating in the tower of Abbot Hall. Many an etcher and painter has economized the beauty of the scene and transfigured the dominance of the modern building into that of some august and venerable church by the magic of his facile art.

A large hotel upon the Neck preserves the name of Nanepashemet, the great Indian sagamore of the whole region round about when the first English settlements began. In 1684 the widow of his son Winnepeeken formally deeded the Marblehead lands to the settlers on terms mutually satisfactory. Very picturesque

Rock was very rough, with stunted cedars twisting their roots among the rocks. Ah me! how good the resinous odor of those trees, and what invitation their seclusions were to those who had already learned that life is short and would improve its fleeting hours! Just off the Neck, at one extremity, is Tinker's Island, and through the channel between it and the shore I have seen vessels of good size sailing even at low tide. But my grandfather once beguiled me with a marvellous tale of his crossing the channel on horseback in his early prime. At the other extremity Marblehead Rock is separated from the Neck by a much narrower and deeper channel. For a long time its beacon was a pulpit from some Boston church, and it has seemed to me a kind of poetic justice that this "cave of the winds" should be subjected to the Atlantic's awful roar. Ships of the deepest hold can sail in to Marblehead, Salem and Beverly through the main channel, which is between Marblehead Rock and Cat Island; but an ancient mariner tells me he has seen it breaking from the bottom all the way across, and through

OLD POWDER-HOUSE.

the foamy crest went driving home in a most dangerous fashion.

Of all the ships that have come through this channel the most famous is the *Con-*

WASHINGTON STREET.

stitution. Chased for three days by the British frigates *Tenedos* and *Endymion*, she appeared off Marblehead on Sunday, April 3, 1814. Volunteers among her crew being called for to take her in, a score were ready, each to the manner born, and one Samuel Green had the great honor. The people of the town crowded to the headlands and their housetops and the steeples to see so brave a sight. The guns of Fort Sewall, or their ignorance of the channel, kept the British men-of-war at bay. Dr. William Bentley's sermon on the

text "There go the ships" has been ascribed to this incident; but it belongs to the raising of the embargo.

Why Cat Island was so called I do not know, unless it was that a smaller one close by suggested a kitten; but the smaller one was called Cat Island Rock, and I believe retains its name, while the larger one became Lowell Island when some Lowell people bought it and disfigured it with a big hotel, which never prospered much, perhaps because of the contracted range. It has lately been appropriated to the uses of some Children's Fresh Air Society; and where they could get fresher I cannot imagine. Long, long ago a small-pox hospital was built on the island, and one of the stories that pleased my boyhood most was the story of its destruction by a company of regulators variously disguised. Some progenitor or distant relative of mine was deep in the affair; and when my grandmother came to this part of the story her voice always sank lower as if the danger of detection were not wholly past.

Gerry's Island and Brown's are close up against the shore at the back of Fort Sewall. A pebbly bar connecting Gerry's

OLD TOWN HALL. BUILT 1727.

Island with the shore has been moved its entire width by the action of the sea within my recollection. One of the early ministers had this island for his glebe, and I suppose wrote his sermons at high tide when he was tolerably safe from intrusion. The whirligig of time brings its revenges, and now, where the Puritan clergyman forged terrible maledictions for the Scarlet Woman, there is a comfortable establishment belonging to a priest who ministers at her altars.

A co-operative enterprise in which I engaged about 1850 for the propagation of rabbits on Brown's Island was so successful that nothing I have read about the multiplication of these creatures in California and Australia has caused me the least surprise. Gerry's island was so named for Elbridge Gerry. The house in which he was born in 1744 is still in good preservation on Washington Street, the main street of the town, near the Old North Meeting-House. If I was not brought up at the feet of Elbridge Gerry, I was brought up at the foot of his garden, which is perhaps the next thing to it. It terminated in a head-way and fence impossible to climb, and beyond them were for me all the infinities and immensities. Some difference of opinion in a matter of fish or firewood or both had clouded Gerry's great reputation in my grandmother's estimation, who was moreover inoculated with the Federalist tradition.

Few that were active in the Revolutionary struggle were still lingering on the stage when I began to toddle over it; but I had the personal recollections of two generations well acquainted with many Revolutionary worthies to draw upon at will. It was a brave and generous part that the old town played in the Revolutionary struggle. Before that began, there had been no more

ST. MICHAEL'S CHURCH. BUILT 1714.

loyal town in the colony than Marblehead. When Sir William Pepperrell of Kittery would undertake the siege of Louisburg in 1745, the urgency that forced the General Court to come to his support was largely generated here, and here the fleet recruited many of the sailors and soldiers needed for the doubtful enterprise, which was destined to be crowned with memorable success. The Powder-House, still standing on the Ferry Road, is sacred to the memory of the French and Indian War. It was built in 1755, with a view

BILLOWS BOAT WHARF.

to storing ammunition against a possible invasion, which did not materialize, though the town suffered much in the properties and persons of its fishermen upon the banks and its merchantmen on the high seas. With all the more relish, therefore, it was in at the death in 1759, having a goodly representation on board

THE HARBOR.

the *Pembroke* and the *Squirrel* at the siege of Quebec.

The unwillingness to hold the king responsible for the abuses which led up to the war for independence was nowhere more strongly developed than in Marblehead; but the town could not resist the logic of events. Elbridge Gerry was the first to formulate the new conviction in town meeting, and, though at first shocking to his townsmen, it soon found lodgment in the popular heart and in the minds of many leading citizens, Colonel Azor Orne and Colonel John Glover being Gerry's right-hand men. Gerry, like Jefferson, his great chief, as time went on was a man of the pen, mighty in letters and in formulating resolutions, but not strong in speech. James Otis was that in Boston and Colonel Orne was that in Marblehead. Every fibre of the old Town Hall must bear some record of his stirring eloquence. The hall was built in 1727, and it is now a precious monument of the times when it was here what Faneuil Hall was in Boston, a cradle in which liberty was rocked *awake* with violent activity. Gerry, always in close political sympathy with Samuel Adams, was one of the most useful members of his "Committee of Correspondence," the most important agency developed by those trying times for the dissemination

EASTERN YACHT
CLUB HOUSE.

of revolutionary sentiments. These met with doughty opposition in the town from men of force and standing who were not wanting in the courage of their convictions. One of these was King Hooper, as he was called by the fishermen because he had a royal way of treating them, — his true name being Robert. When things were getting toward the worst he entertained Governor Hutchinson, greatly to the disgust of that fine gentleman's political enemies. Another conspicuous Tory was Ashley Bowen, the hero of the Quebec contingent, who on the way home had made the graves of its martyrs with his own faithful hands. But of all verbal protestations against the spirit of rebellion, that of Mrs. Thomas Robie was the most eloquent. Packed

CORINTHIAN YACHT CLUB HOUSE.

off to Nova Scotia with her husband and family, she said, as she stepped into the boat that was to take her to the ship, "I hope that I shall live to return, find this wicked rebellion crushed, and see the streets of Marblehead so deep with rebel blood that a long-boat can be rowed through them." Having so eased her mind, she must have felt much better.

When the obnoxious tea-tax was imposed, there was general agreement among the shopkeepers of the town not

boarding party lost his life in the desperate struggle, and "very like a whale," for he was struck with a harpoon.

It may be objected that this was a side issue, but it is certain that Marblehead and Salem came very near anticipating the distinction of Lexington and Concord on the twenty-sixth of February preceding the ever-glorious nineteenth of April. A dear old relative of mine, who was "in arms" that day, being a very little child, told me its story so

THE CHURN.

to import it; and when one of the recalcitrants sent for a chest, and it arrived, it went back quicker than it came, covered with emblems much easier for those who ran to read than the original Chinese.

So many cities did not claim to be the scene of Homer's birth as colonial towns have claimed to have anticipated the blood of Lexington and Concord. The claim of Marblehead is based on the heroic defence which for three hours the crew of a brig, homeward bound from Cadiz, made against the British sloop-of-war *Rose*, which attempted to impress some of their number into the British service. The lieutenant of the

many times that at last she quite fancied she was a witness to the lively scene. She had never read a word about it, but had been instructed by those who were present and saw Dr. Barnard, the hero of the day, with their own eyes. He was the minister of the North Church in Salem; and when Colonel Leslie, landing at Marblehead, marched to Salem to seize certain pieces of ordnance, it was he who persuaded him to return without them and not risk an outbreak of the people. As he marched his three hundred back through Marblehead, Colonel Glover's famous regiment was out, disposed to reckon with him if he had done anything amiss.

This regiment — the Twenty-First Provincial, Fourteenth Continental, and always the Marine — was recruited entirely from Marblehead men, whose descendants could probably furnish some thousands of members to the Sons and Daughters of the Revolution. In the spring of 1775 it was stationed at Beverly, and remained there until after the battle of Bunker Hill, when it went to Cambridge and was quartered in the Craigie house, a fact which enabled me to boast to Mr. Longfellow that an ancestor of mine had anticipated his occupancy of that lordly house. And what is more, I know the

Twice during the war Glover's regiment did service of such a peculiar character that it was pivotal to great events. It put Washington's army across East River on the doleful night of August 28, 1776, after the battle of Long Island, when without the skill of a body of good seamen it does not appear that the retreat could have been successfully accomplished. Nor does it appear how Washington could have crossed the Delaware with his army at that happy Christmas time, a few months later, without the same sturdy arms to row his boats and steer them through the blinding sleet.

THE OLD TOWN.

very room he occupied, from the testimony which he delivered to his son. Washington turned him out, the whole regiment in fact, and established himself and staff in the big handsome rooms. But this I trust had nothing to do with the quarrel of the Marblehead boys with the Virginian troops, whose regimentals impressed them as absurd. They derided them and, the legend says, snowballed them; but the snowballs melt away in the mid-summer weather. Washington had to interfere, and discovered even then that talent for strong language which afterward served him on some memorable occasions.

"To him that hath shall be given;" and this scripture was fulfilled when the same hardy fellows were called upon to lead the advance on Trenton with fixed bayonets, the locks of their muskets being clogged with ice. There seems to be no doubt that Captain William Blackler commanded the boat which carried Washington, and I have been assured that "Sir White," my ancestor aforesaid, was one of his rowers; but so many families in Marblehead cherish a similar tradition of some happy ancestor, that, if all the traditions were valid, the boat must certainly have been sunk. In deference therefore to the safety of Washington and the claims of history on his subsequent career, I have long since concluded to surrender any property I may rightfully inherit in the most signal honor of the illustrious event. Soon after, Glover was made a brigadier-general, and everywhere did himself credit ; nor can any deduction be made from this statement because it was his melancholy distinction to be on the court-martial which tried and condemned Major André, and officer of the day when he was executed for his complicity in Arnold's hideous crime. A statue of General Glover adorns, if it can be said to adorn, Commonwealth Avenue

its tragic close. Impressed on board the British frigate *Lively*, he was released upon the earnest representation of his wife that they had just been married. He had heard during his brief service that a "powder-ship" was expected by the British general, and applied for a commission to go out and meet her with a view to capturing her if possible. The commission hanging fire, he did not wait for it, and his haste was justified by the event (May 17, 1776). The whole business was of a piece with the most daring enterprises of Drake and Hawkins, and Froude would have celebrated

THE NEW TOWN.

in Boston, but his native town has been obliged to content itself with calling schools and fire-engines and militia companies by his honored name.

The work of Glover's regiment was only a part of the contribution made by the town to the Revolutionary struggle. An equal part was contributed by the amphibious patriots who took at once to the water when the war began. Mugford is not a euphonious name, but it is sweeter than honey to the citizen of Marblehead who loves her history and fame. A few rods from the railway station there is a simple monument which records the man's heroic adventure and

it with joyful heart if it had come within his scope. It was a prize well worth contending for, this good ship *Hope*, with fifteen hundred barrels of powder in her hold, one thousand carbines, with artillery carriages and implements galore. Captain Mugford's vessel was a fishing smack, but he captured the *Hope* in sight of the British squadron lying in Nantasket Roads and took her into Boston harbor through Pudding Point Gut, and by the same narrow passage he ventured out again after he had delivered the ship to Washington and, presumably, got his commission. By this time the British admiral was awake, and sent a dozen boats to dispute his passage. After a desperate struggle they were beaten off; but the *Franklin* did not go upon her way rejoicing, for Mugford was lying dead upon her deck, and it was imperfect consolation that his life had cost the enemy three score and ten. The next Sunday was a proud, sad day in Marblehead, Parson Story of the Second Church preaching the funeral sermon of the young hero, and the regiment in which he had been a captain following him to his grave on the Old Hill, where still the legend on the stone is plainly read.

The exploits of Manly and Tucker and Lee and Boden and Harris and Cowell were not unworthy of the fine beginning Mugford made. If they did not singe the beard of England's king as the English adventurers did King Philip's of Spain, it was because he was a smooth-faced gentleman. Privateering was the most attractive form of naval warfare; but the town furnished many captains and sea-

THE OLD NORTH CHURCH.

MUGFORD STREET, SHOWING SECOND CHURCH.

men to the regular service, and among these Captain Tucker of the frigate *Boston* attained to the rank of commodore. Thus dignified, he sailed from France with a distinguished passenger, John Adams, envoy to the court of France. Encountering a well-armed merchantman, the decks were cleared for action; and Adams had no idea of such good times and he not in them. Gun in hand he took his place with the marines; but Tucker ordered him to leave the deck. His disinclination being evident, Tucker with some physical energy and decisive language enforced his command. As Mr. Roads, the invaluable historian of these things, reports the commodore, his language is more respectful than in the tradition which I have received and less objectionable as a breach of the Mosaic law.

If Marblehead was eager for the struggle with King George, when it was over it was evident that it had cost her dear. Her shipping had fallen off from twelve thousand to fifteen hundred tons; her voters from twelve hundred to five hundred; she had five hundred widows and one thousand orphans in her charge. The fishing business revived at once, but the foreign trade rallied fitfully and slowly; and when Jefferson's embargo commanded it to commit *hara-kiri*, it had not the energy to resist. In the first years under the new constitution, which Gerry had refused to sign, Marblehead had been out of gear with the dominant politics of the nation; but when the Republicans came in with the new century, there was not a happier town than Marblehead in the whole country. The Louisiana purchase sorely tried its theoretic strict construction, and the embargo its commercial patience, but of weakening loyalty to the doctrine in which Gerry had instructed it there was little sign. Few towns had suffered more from the embargo, but no other was less influenced by the Federalist reaction which in 1812 cost Gerry the

SITE OF FOUNTAIN INN.

me of the hard necessity that was laid upon him — to have his own skull cleft with a boarding hatchet, or that of an opposing British tar. He never quite forgave himself for choosing as he did. Another of my annalists has often told me how she heard with maternal anxiety that " John " —

"SKIPPER IRESON'S" HOUSE.

gubernatorial election only to insure his vice-presidential nomination and election. Hartford convention politics were denounced in town meetings, and Madison and the Republicans in Congress were comforted by the spectacle of one historic town intensely loyal to the administration. Its reward was to be afterward identified with those aspects of the war which were its peculiar joy. Of one thousand men engaging in the war, more than seven hundred were privateersmen, and one hundred and twenty were in the regular navy, including eighty of the *Constitution*'s daring crew. When the *Constitution* had her famous duel with the *Guerrière*, it so happened that a Marblehead merchant captain was a prisoner on board the English vessel; and from him we have an inside view of the battle that is extremely interesting and dramatic.

Another duel, which had a very different result, was that of the *Chesapeake* and *Shannon* (June, 1813), in full view of the headlands of the Neck and town. Lawrence's bravery only in part atones for his sallying out to meet his enemy with his ship unfit for action and his crew wild with drink. One of the mildest-mannered men I ever knew has told

my father, then some four years old — was " down on the head with Charles [his brother] seein' the foight,"and how she took her arms out of the washtub and made haste to bring the little wanderer home. I must confess that it speaks ill for the fortunes of the Marblehead seamen that more than six hundred of them were in British prisons when the war was over, five hundred of them in Dartmoor. The most of these were privateersmen. Often from one whose name I bear — Captain John White — I heard the story of his fortunes and misfortunes, his imprisonment and release; and as I recall his words I see a face of perfect kindness, golden bronze, above a neck-cloth white as the driven snow, and below a crown of glory whiter yet. A kind of awe would fall upon him as he told me of a time when he saw Wellington's army of the Peninsula filing past a

THE TUCKER HOUSE.

GREGORY STREET.

whole day long, and then his face would brighten as he endeavored to impress me with the wonderful beauty and the more wonderful kindness of the Andalusian girls.

While I am on the war-path I must say a passing word about the way in which Marblehead did her duty in the late Civil War. Few towns were called upon to do so much when Lincoln issued his first call for troops; for she had three companies in the Eighth Regiment, and, as everybody knows, they were the first to reach the rendezvous at Faneuil Hall on the morning of April 16, 1861. That grand initiative was well followed up. The town's record for the war was not one of isolated distinction, but of the fidelity and courage of one thousand soldiers in the ranks and on the gunboat's or the frigate's polished deck. Nearly $250,000 was expended by the town in the course

PIRATE'S HOUSE AND OLD FISH WARE-HOUSES.

of four years to strengthen the sinews of war, — an amount phenomenal in its proportion to the modest wealth of the community.

The proportion of those who enlisted as seamen to those who enlisted in the army was two hundred and twenty-one to eight hundred and twenty-seven; and thereby evidently hangs a tale of changed conditions. In 1861 the fisheries and merchant marine of Marblehead had much declined from their estate in 1776 and 1812. The merchant marine was the first to show a falling off. Its development had begun in the second or third decade of the eighteenth century. John Barnard, minister of the First Church, had conceived its possibility, and stirred up a young man of the town to make a first experiment. This proving successful, others followed, and in 1740 the town had one hundred and fifty vessels engaged in fishing, and at least a third as many more in carrying the fish to Bilboa and other Spanish ports and bringing back the precious things of Spain. But the carrying trade was never the same after the Revolutionary War, and that of 1812, with the preceding embargo, had made bad matters worse. At last the foreign trade entirely ceased, and the appearance of any other vessels in the harbor except those of the fishing fleet, the ballast-lighters, and a few old "pinky sterns" and other coastwise craft, became the greatest rarity. Sometimes a great big ship would come laden with salt, and then the old Bilboa sailors would go down to the wharves and look at her with fond regret for glories past and gone, and many a yarn was spun of memory and imagination all compact, and the air grew heavy with the scent of Eastern spices and the threat of tropic storms. Once it was an African trader that arrived, the old *Chusan.* She was bound to Salem, but missed stays and came to Marblehead, landing on Jack's Rock, near the fort, and sticking there, for all that famous tug, the *R. B. Forbes,* could do to pull her off. Soon an easterly gale broke her in many pieces and scattered her cargo of gum-copal with fragments of her timbers all along the shore. Nothing but the craze

board and from the bow as well. The high tide flooded the wharves and lifted her great hull high in air, and I remember her straining in her toils like a great beast in chains with monstrous wail and groan.

And now the fishing business has followed the foreign trade into the country of things dead and done with. Twenty-five years ago there were some twenty vessels of the once numerous fleet, and now there is not one. Once the warehouses in which the fish were stored when cured and the fish-fences were thick and savory on hill and plain. Now the fish-fences are all pictures of memory, and such warehouses as re-

TUCKER'S WHARF.

for horse-hair rings was ever so prejudicial to the educational interests of the town as that gum-copal. Every boy had a piece which he shaped after the similitude of a heart for some beloved girl. If it had a fly in the middle, it was supposed to tell its story better to an imaginative mind.

In the dearth of foreign traders even the great coalers from Philadelphia were a welcome sight. One I remember in a fearful storm, — perhaps that which twisted Minot's Ledge Lighthouse from its base. She was caught in dock with half her cargo out; and the problem was to keep her from chafing against the sides of the dock. To this end hawsers were carried out to larboard and star-

main have suffered a land change into something poor and strange to their original use. Midway of the century there was a period of enterprise and resuscitation. A dozen or twenty new schooners were built in the town, larger than those of the old fleet, and five or six ships from eight hundred to a thousand tons burthen. What joy to see the beauteous creatures grow, to smell the sweet, clean smell of knees and timbers and the flying chips, and then to see the launch, and even, if it might be — delight unspeakable ! — to stand with the elect upon the towering deck and feel the first quivering start, — the poor creatures down below there shouting, "There

PEACH'S POINT.

the skippers were gracious and sailed round the harbor a good while with the invited guests and self-invited, and jugs and kegs were sampled with quite uniform approval; but the skipper I knew best was like Gallio, and "cared for none of these things," and would say, "Come, get ashore!" before the function had got fairly under way. Then followed anxious days for those who had been left, brightening a little when the *Hero* or the *Senator*, as the case might be, was "spoken," but with every storm that blew darkened with fear of what it might portend. And no wonder, for though the fleet had, before 1846, a long respite from any general disaster, there had been much diversity of individual mishap.

she goes!" — the gliding motion, the downward and then rising circumflex as she dipped into the sea and floated proudly on its breast. The *Emmeline* and *Ariel* were launched almost simultaneously. In the former I had the natural pride pertaining to the skipper's son; and when the two vessels sailed together, going to Boston for their salt, and the *Emmeline* distanced the *Ariel* handsomely, I felt that life had done its best for me, — the future being dark.

THE TOMB OF GENERAL GLOVER.

The old fishing-life of the town was full of poetry and beauty and romance. The home preparations for the voyage were fragrant with the "Harrison cake" and gingerbread that were seasoned possibly with "a few sad drops" that could not be repressed. All was stir and bustle at the stores where supplies and tackle were purchased. I see the groups about the door, the rough play hiding strange misgivings; and one who came not back takes me and carries me to "Aunt Charity Brimblecom's" or "Aunt Hannah Harris's" for such things as children like. I remember the oppressive silence of the breakfast on the morning of the start, the quiet uneffusive partings, the raising of the anchor and the bellying of the reluctant sails. Some of

"The September gale" has different meanings in different localities; in Marblehead it means the gale of September 19, 1846. On the Old Hill there is upon the topmost ledge a monument which tells the piteous tale. There were a dozen vessels lost, sixty-six men and boys. It was a bright day at home, and the good folk flocking to see Major Candler's funeral little imagined that the solemn dirge was

FORT SEWALL.

played for many, not for one alone. When the first news of the storm was brought, vague terror seized the town, and only very gradually the returning vessels gave to some assurance of surviving friends, to others sadder doubt or certain woe. One of these returns stands out from all the recollections of my boyhood clear and sharp. Hundreds of men and women packed the wharf, and there was none of the cheerful banter usually characteristic of the event as the crew came on shore. If anything was said, it was said very quietly. Each personal contingent followed this one of the crew or that to his own house to hear the fresh report. For myself, I walked beside the skipper, — I think it was his shoresman on the other side, — all the others making a kind of hollow square about us, the only sound, making the stillness audible, that made by my father's clumping fishing-boots, too heavy to be lifted from the ground. I remember the two words, " Jane ! " and " Father ! " that sufficed for greeting at the kitchen door, and the people swarming in all day with eager questionings, and my father almost wishing he had not survived for such a terrible ordeal. Many, many times since then I have begged him to repeat the story of that cruel storm. Then as never before the *Hero* made good her name, and my father speaks of her behavior as if her faithful timbers housed a conscious soul. The next morning proofs of the mischief wrought appeared and multiplied from hour to hour. For days they sailed through wreckage of all sorts strewing the bank from side to side, here some great schooner on her beam ends but not dismasted, lifting her masts high out of the water and then again submerging them with a most melancholy sound ; once the masts of two vessels keeping miserable company ; objects too easily identified as the belongings of old shipmates, relatives and friends. I can conceive of nothing more distressing than the things they saw. Stout-hearted men, the fishermen of '46, but tender too, as brave men always are ; and the September gale went far to spoil their pleasure in the treacherous sea, and gave the fisheries

of Marblehead a serious if not fatal shock.

Very different were the comings-home when all had prospered with the fleet. Whether the fish were " washed out " in a pound chained to the vessel's side or on the beach, the thing was good to see. Then the good housewife sinned the deadly sin of pride, resolving that the tin pails in which she sent her husband's dinner and a quart of tea should outshine all the rest. Small boys were in continual requisition, for there were things more or less palatable to be carried here and there for love and courtesy, and exquisite were the gradations which assigned here sea-crackers only and there added tongues and sounds, smoked halibut, and it might be a smoked hagdon, — gamiest bird that ever challenged mortal taste. All these things are so much a matter of the past that before long there will be none remembering them and loving, as I do, to dwell upon their works and days.

Meantime there is much consolation in the fact that Marblehead has become the yachting port *par excellence* of the New England coast. The Eastern Yacht Club has its club-house on the Neck, and almost any summer's day some of the largest yachts may be seen lying at anchor or tempting with their liberal sails the hesitating wind. Many of the summer cottages are occupied by yachting men rejoicing in the ownership of craft of more or less importance. Here Mr. Burgess, *ædificator navium,* — as President Eliot described him in the inadequate Latin of his A. M. degree, — found himself at home among the lovely creatures his genius had brought into being. It is when a race is imminent or over that the harbor makes the bravest show. You might think the lovely ghosts of all the fishing schooners and the Spanish traders were revisiting the scenes which formerly were all their own.

The transition from fishing to shoemaking was a gradual evolution. When the fishermen started on the first trip in March and returned from the last in December, the hibernation was but brief and generally inactive. But with a later start and earlier return, some intermediate employment became a necessity, enforced sometimes by miserable luck at sea. With some the winter work soon pushed the other from its seat, and the fisherman became a shoemaker the whole year round. The shoemakers' shops were small framed buildings some twelve or thirteen feet by ten, with room for eight workmen's benches. I have known shoe-makers who were as truly artists as Raphael or Mendelssohn, so beautiful they made their work. Loud the discussion raged above the hammers' beat in those far days when Squatter Sovereignty and " The Crime against Kansas " were the questions at the fore. We had our drowsy days, but there were others when the assistant sheriff, who had much leisure, would come in and, with the shop-tub for a seat, read Sumner's mighty speeches with impassioned declamation and sublime unconsciousness of any difficulty with the classical quotations. One could earn from $1.50 to $3.00 a day, according to his ability and diligence. Less wages might mean better luck. It did for me in 1857, when it seemed better economy to go to school again than to make good slick-bottomed ankle-ties for fifty cents a dozen; *i. e.*, a dozen pairs. The great manufactories have almost or entirely done away with the little shops, not without social loss together with the pecuniary gain.

If the æsthetic were everything, it would be necessary to regret that the summer-cottage, yachting life did not come immediately upon the heels of the marine decay without the intervention of shoemaking, which has made some things most unlovely in its time. But evidently the shoe business has done much more for the comfort of the people than the fisheries ever did. The facts in evidence are the scores and hundreds of neat little houses, generally owned by those who occupy them, and the general appearance of the town. Fifty years ago there were scores of unpainted ruinous houses, their broken windows stuffed with old hats and cast-off clothing, where now there is scarcely one. As are the houses, so are the clothes, the streets, the schools. An incipient socialism taxes the wealthy and the economical for the general good, those who contribute least into the com-mon treasury being often the more active in scattering its contents abroad. Hard times are not infrequent, but they are alleviated by visits of fire companies and militia from abroad, and there is always money enough in the old town for *panem et circences* — a band of music and a collation to sustain the hearts of the invaders, whoever they may be.

Many of the little workshops were high set upon the hills and headlands of the town. From one whose privilege I for some time enjoyed you could look across the town and Neck upon the open sea, where the coast-wise craft went to and fro, and the great ships sailed over the horizon's edge, coming and going. On Bailey's Fort there was another, which for situation could not be excelled, and there, aged ten, I made two pairs of " bats," for which a tin-pedler, incautiously or with deeper wisdom than appeared, allowed fifty cents upon a purchase from his cart. This shop was called " The Fountain ; " why, I did not then know, nor why the level space before my uncle's carpenter shop close by was called " the Fountain Yard ; " and, though I lived for a whole year upon an adjoining cliff which overhung the sea, that mystery was not made plain. But long since I learned that the yard was so called because there had stood the Fountain Inn, where Sir Harry Frankland found Agnes Surriage, her small feet bare and beautiful, washing the steps, with consequences too many times related for me to think of again telling the story, hard as it is to deny myself the most romantic legend of the town. But I must boast of having often seen the record of her baptism, where Parson Holyoke made it in the parish records in 1726, and of having seen a sumptuous quilt which was the ornament of her unlawful bed. When my interest in her career awoke, it was much discouraged by my grandmother, whose opinion was, " The less known of such the better."

The legend of Skipper Ireson is even better known than that of Agnes Surriage, and concerning that, too, I will be reticent ; and yet I can say *vidi tantum* of old Flood, whose right name was Benjamin, with a more personal accent than his poet, Whittier, or any of his historians, because in 1850 I "withstood him to the face, because he was to be blamed." Within a stone's throw of the Fountain Yard I had left my clothes and gone wading in in search of deeper water out beyond the flats. Returning, my new straw hat was missing, though I had ballasted it with proper care. We had seen Skipper Ireson coming that way as we went out, and now far up across the new-cut marshes we discerned his shape, and in his hand my hat. What possessed him to do so base a thing I do not know. We had not shouted after him derisively as many did. He was getting very old and feeble, and perhaps he thought my hat a vessel in distress, or a derelict that was his lawful spoil. There was no time to lose, and as it was, we did not overtake him, we "naked" and he "not ashamed," until he was near upon that precinct, "Oakum Bay," where still the curious go to see his house. Whittier's ballad is the best he ever wrote, and that is saying much. It contains hardly a particle of literal truth, but probably quite as much as any of the most famous ballads. It seems that Lowell bettered it by sending Whittier the dialect of the refrain.

The crooked streets of Marblehead have been a senseless wonder to the casual visitor and reporter. They originally followed the line of least resistance, winding between the ledges; that is all the mystery. The houses do not, like the inhabitants of Albany in Morse's venerable geography, "all present their gable ends to the street," but every conceivable elevation and perspective. Some of them are very old. The Tucker house on Front Street dates from 1640. Some of them were very lordly pleasure houses in their day, and are still so attractive and so venerable that it is difficult to comprehend the taste which now and then destroys one of the finest for some pretentious modern pile. The Lee mansion, which is now the Marblehead Bank, is a triumph of colonial architecture unexcelled. Its spacious hall and staircase are the joy of the colonial revivalists. Up and down these stairs and through this spacious hall have stepped Washing-

ton and Lafayette and Monroe and Andrew Jackson; and they should be forever sacred to their memory. Another noticeable mansion is that of "King Hooper," on Hooper Street; and yet others are Parson Barnard's on Franklin Street, and those of General Glover and his brother, Colonel Jonathan, on Glover Square; Gerry's birthplace; on Orne Street, the residence of Colonel Azor Orne, Gerry's excellent compatriot; near the Town House that of Dr. Elisha Story, the father of Judge Story, who was born under its roof, and just opposite the house built for himself by the Rev. Edward Holyoke of the Second Church. Here in 1728 was born Dr. Edward A. Holyoke, who lived till March 3, 1829, having entered on the practice of medicine in Salem in 1749. Around the Common, now the site of Abbot Hall, are several houses of interesting appearance and historic fame, and here and there about the town are many others murmurous for the ear attuned with old associations: in this Mugford "went to housekeeping," and to that nearly opposite they brought his lifeless body; close by, the "Committee of Safety" held its meetings, and of houses whose unblushing fronts masked many a Tory plot and counterplot there are not few.

The religious history of the town has many points of vital interest. The idea that New England was settled exclusively by saints gets little confirmation from this quarter. Rough and tough were the men, and the women were like unto them if Dr. Increase Mather deposeth truly in his contemporary letter of 1677, that when two Indian captives were brought into the town, the women, coming out of church, "fell on them in a tumultuous way and very barbarously murdered them." The heart of Rev. Samuel Avery of Newbury was stirred with pity for this people's wild and lawless state in 1635, and he set out with his family to settle amongst them, but was wrecked on Thatcher's Reef, as Whittier has sung in one of his most lovely poems. There was no ordained minister until 1686, but much trouble before that about building and enlarging the meeting-house and seating the people. The meeting-house stood on the Old Hill, and about it clustered the first grassy barrows of the dead. The headstones of the successive ministers of the church lean lovingly together, and the wild roses seem to get a deeper color from their manly blood. In 1714 some wanted the Rev. John Barnard, and some the Rev. Edward Holyoke. Barnard had the majority, but refused to come unless a second church were formed with his friend Holyoke for its minister; "and it was so" David and Jonathan were these; for when in 1737 Harvard College called Barnard to be its president, he declined, and told them Holyoke was their man. Whereupon Holyoke was called, but, hesitating, Barnard prayed so eloquently that he succumbed, and the verdict of the Second Church, which did not relish the loss of Mr. Holyoke, was, "Old Barnard prayed him away."

St. Michael's Episcopal Church also dates from 1714, — not only the organization, but the edifice, which has a "fine last-century face," and an interior that sets the worshipper a-dreaming of old English churches with immemorial yews about them and thick-leaved ivies climbing wall and tower. The Rev. George

Mossom of this church, who arrived in the "ded of winter," 1718, afterward went to Virginia, and there married George Washington to the widow Custis, a matter-of-fact conclusion to a romantic course of changeable desire. Parson Bartlett of the Second Church (1811–49) was equally a physician of bodies and of souls, and a most kind and generous benefactor and adviser of his people, especially in their distress. His contemporary, Parson Dana of the Old North, used to pray, as did all the ministers every Sunday, "for those who go down to the sea in ships and do business upon great waters," but he made an original addition, which, without correction, he went on repeating for some thirty years, "May they be blessed with a perpetual calm!" .

The most is still unsaid, but I must make an end. Strength and beauty are in the sanctuary of this dear old town, the beauty of sweet pastures and of rugged shores and the encircling sea; the strength of ocean storms and manly hearts and a great history that should bind the people who inherit it to every honest word and deed.

Fire Insurance in New England (1898)

FIRE INSURANCE IN NEW ENGLAND.

By Charles W. Burpee.

MAN'S personal endeavors may be crowned with success for a time, he may establish a business which gives him a satisfactory return, he may have mastered the problem of material existence; but fire may come, and in an hour his hard-earned savings, the source of his income, the proud result of his ingenuity and perseverance may vanish. Experience has taught this, and few are the men who have not learned the lesson. There must have been some form of insurance in the earliest history of commerce and industry. It is well established that in the old English guilds there was a common fund, maintained by fixed periodical payments, for security against "fire, water, robbery or other calamity."

After the days of William the Conqueror, it appears that in any great calamity in England an appeal was made to the whole nation through the clergy and the parish churches. The sovereign granted to individuals the right to collect for sufferers. The first definite form of insurance we have record of, is in the presentation by some unknown person to Count Anthony Gunther of Oldenburg of a plan, by which the count should take upon himself the losses of all who should pay him one dollar annually on each one hundred dollars valuation — either in his own or other countries. The count did not desire to mix up in such matters, fearing that if he did Providence might be tempted; and the man was sent on his way with a hint that this sort of business belonged to private persons.

The next record we have — though undoubtedly houses were individually insured much earlier — is when a petition for forming a fire insurance company was laid before Charles I., in 1635. Those were troublous times; life insurance might have proved a more absorbing topic for that unhappy monarch. Not till the Restoration is there further reference to the need which was demanding to be provided for as England's trade increased. Then a petition from "several persons of quality and eminent citizens of London" for forming a company was referred to Charles II.'s council. It was rejected on the ground, forsooth, that it was not reasonable that any but a city should reap profits of this kind.

Life insurance began to flourish, and there may have been fire insurance in other countries; but it can be asserted almost positively that there was none of the latter in England in 1662. It took the great fire of London, September 2, 1666, to arouse England to action. The following year Dr. Barton opened an office for assuming risks on the individual basis.

MARSHALL JEWELL.

The first office in France was not opened till 1745, and in Germany — Hanover — not till 1750. Deputy Newbold had a scheme for interesting the city of London in insurance, but though he pushed it with great perseverance he met with a cold reception. In 1680 Dr. Barton's "office" became a joint stock company, England's first. It took the name of "Insurance Office for Houses." This stirred Newbold to fresh activity; history shows that insurance rivalry is as old as organized insurance itself. Newbold finally succeeded in getting what we nowadays should call "a pull," and a city company was formed. The hints we get of the hot war of rates which followed have a somewhat familiar sound. Whatever the reasons may have been, Dr. Barton's company won, and the city company went to the

GEORGE L. CHASE.
President of the Hartford Fire Insurance Company.

wall in about a year. The "office" company now became known as the Phœnix, and soon as the "Old Phœnix," in distinction from others which selected this suggestive name. Its principle was the establishment of a fund of ground rents, to answer in case of loss.

Dr. Barton's earliest vigorous rivals

were the "Friendly Societies," whose tempting feature was that each subscriber should pay "toward building up the house of any contributor destroyed." All the societies learned in due season that an ounce of prevention is worth a pound of cure. Placing little dependence on the night watch, they engaged men whose duty it was to do all in their power to subdue flames wherever they started. Primitive as that may seem, in the days before firemen, it is remembered with credit that one of Hartford's largest companies, in this century, set aside a sum for the payment of men for fire service; that a similar idea is carried out in Providence, and that in general insurance people have done about as much to save communities from fire as they have to make losses good.

A company was organized in London in 1704 to insure household goods; and in 1710 the renowned Sun Insurance Company came into existence, illustrating the growth of the insurance idea. This company advertised to insure movable goods, merchandise and the like. It engaged skilled men in all crafts, whose business it was to hasten to any house that was threatened and remove the goods in it. If the house bore one of the signs of the Sun Insurance Company, the men received their pay from the company, the amount being deducted from the sum paid the insured. If it was any other house, the men were to look to the proprietors of that house for remuneration according to fixed rates. For a century this company did a large business, not only in London, but in many other cities on the island.

The English companies naturally established branches in America; one in Boston is mentioned in 1724. The honor of having the first purely American company belongs to Philadelphia, where the "Philadelphia Contributionship for the Insurance of Houses from Loss by Fire" was organized in 1752. Judging by the change it made in the conditions of its

THE HARTFORD FIRE INSURANCE COMPANY'S BUILDING, HARTFORD, CONN.

insurance in the course of years, this company had some remarkable experiences, from which it deduced a peculiar maxim: it refused to accept risks on houses where there were shade trees on the premises. Thereupon some of its members left it, to set up an independent company, which was dubbed the "green tree company." Its right name was the Mutual Association Company of Philadelphia. The original company, of which Franklin was a member, continues to-day, insuring brick buildings.

The first company in New York was a mutual — the Mutual Fire Insurance Company — founded in 1787. The Knickerbocker Company came next, in 1796. British offices began to push the agency business in New York and elsewhere in 1805. The first fire insurance lawsuit in this country was brought by one John L. Sullivan; that was in 1807, and the Massachusetts Mutual Fire Insurance Company was the defendant. Steam fire engines were first used in 1829. The National

Board of Fire Underwriters, which has done so much in the interests of honest insurance, came into existence in 1866.

After this preliminary history, we pass to show how the New England states, particularly Massachusetts, Rhode Island and Connecticut, have made so noteworthy a record for themselves in their achievements in fire insurance. We must understand the character of the native New Englander before we can appreciate the delay and then the comparatively slow growth at the outset. Puritan descendants of the English guildsmen had a wholesome fear of corporations; they were for independence in all things; they led isolated lives; there was small community of interests; and nothing brought them together till the Revolution came. In fire insurance they had to learn for themselves the lessons learned by people across the ocean. There were a few agencies of foreign companies, but for the most part business was done on the old individual basis, chiefly marine. It was not till after the new government had been formed that there was much indication of a tendency to organize companies; and in general the early history of fire insurance in New England is much like that in the mother country. The rapid strides in the present century prove a striking contrast with this early hesitation and delay.

John Marion was the agent for the London societies in Boston in 1724. When business took a fresh start under the state constitution, and as the number of fires increased, the important consideration of protection for invested capital was forced home. If profits were to accrue, there was no need that they should go across the seas; and that profits would accrue was evident, as also was the fact that individual underwriting did not meet the requirements. Moreover, a vital point in insurance is prompt settlement, which was made most difficult by the distance from the London companies. The people's dread of corporate greed was conquered.

In 1784 an invitation was extended to Providence people, who already were deeply interested in insurance, to attend a meeting at the tavern of John Marston on State street, Boston. Some enthusiasm was aroused; yet the petition of Boston men in 1785 for a fire office insurance company was refused as not "for the advantage of the town." The petitioners themselves approached the subject with fear and trembling, accompanying their arguments with excuses for their boldness. The names of these pioneers were William Shattuck, William Wetmore, Jesse Putnam, John Winthrop, Jonathan Harris, William Brown, Samuel Salisbury and John Andrews. They pointed out that neighborly charity, however generous, was inadequate and too precarious to bring relief to sufferers, whereas by paying a "very inconsiderable premium, they can secure a permanent resource competent to every possible loss."

But the times were ripening. Ten years later, June 25, 1795, the legislature granted a charter for the Massachusetts Fire Insurance Company, with a capital of $300,000 and not to exceed $600,000, in shares of $100 each. The stock was to be paid in in ten annual installments. If at any time the losses exceeded the capital so far received, assessments were to be levied and $10 extra was to be paid on each share, provided always that no proprietor should be liable for more than $100 on each share. No dividends were to be declared till the losses were all paid. The company was not to insure for an amount exceeding three-quarters of the value of the property. This would seem like reaching modern times with a jump, were it not that the old-time timidity was shown by limiting the existence of the company to twelve years. The company more than fulfilling expectations, it obtained a change of name to the Massachusetts Fire and Marine Insurance Company in 1799 and an extension of time for eight years. It was required to increase its capital stock by $300,000, of which $180,000 was to be paid in. Careful restrictions were made to protect the insured,

J. D. BROWNE.
President of the Connecticut Fire Insurance Company.

From a steel engraving by John A. Lowell.

THE CONNECTICUT FIRE INSURANCE COMPANY'S BUILDING, AT HARTFORD.

among them one that $300,000 should be held for fire risks only. Furthermore — and this is the first instance of state supervision — the company must make reports to the legislature whenever called upon to do so. Further extensions of time being granted, the company continued till 1848, when it retired by its own request.

Mutual fire insurance was the more popular form, perhaps we might say more in keeping with the sentiments of the people. No company was incorporated, however, till March 1, 1798, when a charter was given to the Massachusetts Fire Insurance Company. We get here a good idea of what it was then thought a "solid" mutual company should be. After $2,000,000 had been subscribed to be insured, the corporation might insure any building in the commonwealth for seven years; if any member's loss was more than the existing funds, the directors must make an assessment; no member to pay more than two dollars for each dollar advanced by him as premium deposit. The company had a prosperous career till the Boston fire wrecked it, and within a month after that event it reorganized and continued till 1894, when it reinsured its risks and retired.

According to Nathan Warren, who has made a careful study of the subject, the Newburyport Marine Insurance Company (1790), the Boston Fire Insurance Company, and one other, five in all, completed the list for Massachusetts up to 1800. With the opening of the new century, however, insurance asserted itself. Not only were companies permitted to organize; they were welcomed. Before 1830 there were twenty-seven companies. Not many of these lived till the Boston fire in 1872, and only two of them survived that.

The question now was, How shall insurance companies be controlled? rather than, Shall charters be granted?

THE NATIONAL FIRE INSURANCE COMPANY'S BUILDING, HARTFORD.

A new kind of laws was called for. Among the earliest of these laws was one, passed in 1807, requiring a statement of stock paid in, the character of investments and the amount of outstanding risks. Eleven years after that, the powers and duties of marine companies, with their restrictions, were defined by statute. It was decreed that not over ten per cent of the capital stock should be written on any one risk, and that annual statements should be made. Until 1820, right to insure against fire was delegated by special charter; in that year a law was passed giving all companies the authority to engage in this branch of the business. Dissatisfaction having made itself felt, it was, in 1827, forbidden that policies should be written with foreign companies with less than $2,000,000 capital, or ever for more than ten per cent of the capital.

Five years later a further restriction was made by requiring agents of foreign companies to give bonds of $5,000, to make returns of all business done, and to pay a tax of one and one-half per cent on premium receipts. Mutual companies were allowed in 1835 to issue policies in Massachusetts for seven years for three-quarters value, when the company had $50,000 subscribed to be insured, every policy to constitute a lien on property insured for the purpose of securing the deposit notes and any lawful assessment. In 1837 all companies were required to make annual returns to the secretary of state, instead of to the treasurer, as previously. The first official insurance report was issued by Secretary John P. Bigelow in 1838. It covered only the Massachusetts stock companies, of which there were forty-eight, including twenty-nine in

Boston. Ten companies failed to report. The aggregate capital was $9,415,000, and the outstanding risks amounted to $139,000,000.

The legislature of 1849 granted permission to the mutual companies to go into all New England states and New York. The year 1860 marked the inauguration of factory insurance in Massachusetts. The experiment first tried in Rhode Island in 1835 had proved eminently successful, and the only wonder is that the results had not been more quickly appreciated by manufacturing New England as a whole. In this year, 1860, the industrial concerns in Lowell were allowed to contract with each other for mutual protection against fire, and the Boston Manufacturers Fire Insurance Company was organized in Boston.

In 1852 the state secretary, treasurer and auditor were designated as the Board of Insurance Commissioners. The insurance department, bringing all the insurance business under the supervision of three commissioners, was established in 1855, being the first in the country, and a tremendous step forward it was. Of the 154 fire and marine insurance companies then doing business in the state, 113 were home companies, 41 came from other states, and 5 were foreign. Of the Massachusetts companies, 34 were stock companies, and Boston was the home of 19 of them. The aggregate paid up capital was $6,386,100, and the amount of outstanding risks was $185,000,000. Fifteen of the companies were mutual marine and mutual fire and marine, of which 7 were in Boston. The assets of all were $6,398,389, with outstanding risks of $130,000,000. Mutual fire companies numbered 69, including 11 in Boston, and the aggregate risks of all were $200,089,637. Not a few outside companies were utterly unreliable and depended on fraudulent methods. These the department quickly drove out. All companies seeking to do business in the state were obliged to show $1,000,000 in cash funds and

$1,000,000 in deposit notes, and new Massachusetts companies were prohibited from going outside the state. The insurance laws of Massachusetts are frequently taken as models by the legislatures of other states. The first codification of them is dated 1854.

Periodically since the days of Dr. Barton's "office" in London municipal control of insurance has been urged by this or that reformer. The stand taken by Massachusetts on the subject is worthy of study. The first serious agitation in this direction was in 1860. The insurance commissioners announced it as their opinion that good insurance companies were sufficient,

JAMES NICHOLS.
President of the National Fire Insurance Company.

though a system might be devised by which the companies should give a bonus (on a fixed ratio) to the firemen. Then the Virginia and Maine as well as the Massachusetts legislatures began to show a tendency to favor state insurance — not being so afraid of tempting Providence as was Count Anthony Gunther. In Massachusetts the subject was referred to the insurance commissioner, who reported emphatically that state insurance was not wise unless it should appear that regular fire offices lacked honor and

THE ÆTNA FIRE INSURANCE COMPANY'S BUILDING, HARTFORD.

integrity, which was not the case. The plan was opposed to the spirit of republican institutions and opened the doors for politicians and placemen. To quote from the report:— "The results of such loose and extra-hazardous method of underwriting as would be likely to follow are not difficult to predict. The state would thus hold out the strongest possible incentive to wholesale fraud and incendiarism. Moreover, these crimes would be encouraged, under such a system, by that lax sentiment of public morality which, as in the case of smuggling or false invoicing by respectable importers, does not scruple to defraud the government, so boundless in resources, of its dues; while the same persons, as a general rule, are strictly honorable in their private dealings and would shrink from dishonest action between man and man. Hence, in order to meet its inevitable losses on the score of incendiarism, bred and born of such a system, the state would either be compelled to raise its premium rates above the present standard of our private stock companies — thus exploding the delusive idea of state insurance — or it would have to meet this deficiency by falling back upon revenue from other sources. The manifest injustice to general taxpayers which the latter method would inaugurate would not long be tolerated, since the large class of heavy contributors to the state treasury either do not count among their possessions any insurable property, or that property (suburban residences and farmhouses, for instance) is so secure and isolated in its position that it would not be fair to tax it for the benefit of such as may be exposed to the dangers of a sweeping conflagration. The fundamental principle of reciprocity upon which all equitable insurance is based would be clearly violated by such an alternative." At the same time the commissioner pointed out evils in mutual insurance as conducted. As to municipal insurance, the law of 1872 — the year of the Boston fire — provided that there must be $50,000 in subscriptions before policies could be issued. The legislature of 1873 investigated this matter and the commissioner reported that the requisite amount of subscriptions should be $500,000, as with the mutual companies.

The Chicago fire in 1871 and the Boston fire in 1872 made an epoch in Massachusetts insurance, not only as to the companies themselves, but as to legislation. By the Chicago fire 106 companies doing business in Massachusetts lost $56,000,000, or about one-half of the total loss. Twenty-three Massachusetts companies lost $4,471,500; yet only 3 had to suspend, and the other 20 had a surplus of over $10,000,000 after losses were paid. And that was a bad year, too, for the marine insurers. The disaster of the Arctic whaling fleet, chiefly a Massachusetts enterprise, entailed a loss of $860,-000 on three New Bedford companies.

The flames in Boston in 1872 ate up $80,000,000 worth of property.

WILLIAM B. CLARK.
President of the Ætna Fire Insurance Company.

Of the $56,000,000 insurance, only $37,000,000 was paid by the 192 companies. No insurance man in Boston at that time will ever forget that day. The losses for the 52 Massachusetts companies footed up $35,500,000. Twenty-six of the 32 companies that went into insolvency were Massachusetts companies, four mutuals and 22 joint-stock companies. Of the latter,

one-half managed to pull through in time. Among those that failed were some of the oldest and most reliable in the land, paying magnificent dividends on the investments of hundreds of people who had no other dependence. Their combined capital was $6,000,000. The highest percentages of losses paid were as follows: the Massachusetts, 100; the Boot and Shoe Manufacturers Mutual, 90; the Bay State, 89.7; and the Mechanics, 85. The lowest percentage was 20, by the Franklin.

The legislature was called together in special session. A bill was put through immediately, allowing underwriting by companies without special charter, by mutual companies with a capital of from $100,000 to $300,000, and by mutual marine companies with a permanent fund of not less than $400,000. The mutual companies were required to have $500,000 subscribed.

Advocates of municipal insurance came to the front with renewed zeal, and a law was passed allowing towns and cities of less than 4,000 inhabitants to form themselves into insurance companies, while in towns and cities of over 4,000 population, fire insurance districts were authorized within the limits of the amount of insurance in each district. Courage revived when Deputy Stephen H. Rhodes, acting commissioner, secured statements from all the companies that carried the Boston insurance. Particularly gratifying was the good news from Connecticut.

Another result of the fire was the passage of a general law increasing the amount of paid-up capital re-

JOHN C. PAIGE.

THE JOHN C. PAIGE BUILDING, BOSTON.

quired. Dividends were limited, but
at the same time a capitalization of
surplus was allowed, in the interests
of both the stockholder and the policy-
holder. A new system was inaugurated also with the foreign companies,
the department taking full supervision
of all their business. This was an innovation for America.

With the companies themselves, it
had been demonstrated that premiums
were too low, and rates were increased
and revised. The variety in the forms
of policies caused trouble, so that in

1873 a standard form was prescribed by law. In 1881 this form was altered somewhat, to make it more elastic and also to provide for arbitration. This is the form in use at the present day, and it has been followed by several other states. Another act of that legislature was to remove the three-quarters restriction on mutual companies and to permit them to insure for full value, like the stock companies.

There have been times when it seemed as if incendiarism were the attendant curse of fire insurance. For years there has been constant work on the part of the companies to eradicate this evil — mostly due to over-insurance and competition in rates; and all sorts of methods have been resorted to, perhaps with too much timidity about contesting claims in court. The Massachusetts commissioners in 1862, Elizur Wright and George W. Sargent, called attention to the danger of too many companies and agents, and suggested consolidation as a remedy. In 1865 they declared that the public suffered more from fully insured men than from burglars. The stock companies, they held, suffered little, as fires raised rates "as surely as the moon does the tides." With mutual companies, they contended, over-insurance was prevented by statute, every proprietor being required to bear one-quarter of the risk of a total loss. Moreover, every one insured in a mutual is a co-proprietor and is on the watch.

Evidently in order to make good to the community the weak point with insurance companies as to prosecution in the courts, Massachu-

GEORGE P. FIELD.

setts in 1894 established the office of fire marshal, whose duty it should be to investigate all fires in the state, with power to arrest and also to attend to the matter of protection from fire. The state was divided into ten districts, and officers were detailed to hold inquests whenever necessary. The wisdom of this course was soon demonstrated. There had been an enormous amount of incendiarism, as is shown by the reports, mostly due to over-insurance.

There are now 203 companies doing business in Massachusetts, as follows: 6 state stock companies for fire only, 58 for fire and marine, 100 mutuals, and 39 foreign companies.

Rhode Island, which state in many ways has led in insurance, did not have a company till the close of the last century. Private underwriting was done in Providence by Stephen Hopkins, John Garnish, Joseph Lawrence and Thomas Manchester in 1756. Henry Paget was added to the number in 1762. In 1794 John Mason in Providence started a business "upon such principles and under such regulations as were established by the principle merchants of this town, at a regular meeting, which are nearly similar to those established in Boston." It was a typical "Lloyd" business and had its origin, like the Lloyd of London, in a coffee house. Each man put down his name with the amount to be insured by him at the end of a policy stating the conditions. Judging by the character of the business done in Rhode Island at that time, this probably was mostly marine insurance. Joseph Lawrence, Mason's competitor, put his

THE NEW HAMPSHIRE FIRE INSURANCE COMPANY'S BUILDING, MANCHESTER.

dred dollars. This was the first distinctive fire insurance work in the state; and the company has continued it with success to this day.

The Washington Fire Insurance Company, which was destined to consolidate with the Providence Fire Insurance Company in the well-known Providence Washington Company of to-day, dates from January, 1800, when its capital was $100,000, quickly increased by $10,000. E. L. Watson, who has delved in the old records of Rhode Island companies, noted a peculiar custom of the early directors of this company — early in a double sense. They held their meetings at six o'clock every Tuesday evening, and they were so annoyed by the tardiness of some of their number that

price for a policy at one dollar, with no other office fees, and guaranteed that in case of loss no deduction should be made from the sum insured.

Mason's company grew into the Providence Insurance Company, of which he was the first president, with William Hail Mason as secretary. The organization was on February 3, 1799, the capital was $150,000, and marine insurance was the only kind handled. The Newport Insurance Company was launched the same year, but soon found the seas too tempestuous. Though there had been a previous attempt, no mutual company was established till 1800, when the Providence Mutual Insurance Fire Company began to bid for business. Lawrence was back of this company. It sought subscriptions for insurance on one hundred houses with payment of twenty-five cents on every one hun-

JOHN C. FRENCH.
President of New Hampshire Fire Insurance Company.

they adopted a rule making tardiness punishable by the payment of a quart of porter. Richard Jackson was the first president and George Benson secretary. The company placed an agency in New London, allowing two and a half per cent commission. The Bristol Insurance Company, organized in Bristol in 1800, took slaveship risks, and ended its career in 1803.

Rhode Island suffered terribly by the war of 1812, and most of her insurance companies were forced to the wall. But as soon as peace was declared, more companies were formed, and nine more before 1821. The Providence and Washington consolidation took place in 1817, with a capital of $132,000, and a new charter was taken out in 1820. As the Providence Fire Insurance Company, chartered in 1818, never had organized, the directors of the consolidated company resolved to work the fire field. To-day the company has a fine building of its own and a name that is known far and wide.

The history of manufacturers' insurance in Rhode Island is full of interest. Zachariah Allen of Providence owned a cotton mill in Allensdale, which had been built as nearly fireproof as possible, even to laying the shingles in mortar. A heating apparatus was put in and the stoves removed, and finally the best known devices for extinguishing fire were provided. Then Mr. Allen confidently asked for a reduction in his rates. The only reply was that cotton mill rates would continue at two and a half per cent. "Then," said Mr. Allen, "cotton mills will insure themselves." He laid his methods before other manufacturers, and before long the Manufacturers Mutual was started, with Amasa Mason as president and John H. Ormsbee as secretary. When policies were written at a rate lower than the old companies could think of, there were many prophecies of failure, and even though the first year yielded a dividend of fifty per cent the wise ones shook their heads. There were

indeed losses and assessments in the second year, but the principle was accepted by manufacturers in other places, and eventually the great manufacturers' mutual system was the result. It is said that none of the companies in that system has had to levy an assessment since the second year of Mr. Allen's pioneer company. The reason is to be found in the strict requirements as to construction and fire apparatus. The original company was soon followed by the Firemen's Mutual, the State Mutual, the Blackstone, the Mechanics, the What Cheer, the Merchants, the Enterprise, the Hope, the American and the Mercantile, all of which are successful to-day.

The Rhode Island insurance commissioners office was established in 1859, with power to examine any company whose solvency was doubtful. At first there were three commissioners, but the number was reduced to one. The leading mutual companies formed were more successful than in some of the other states. The Union Mutual, which takes risks only on dwellings and contents, and the American Mutual Fire and Steam Boiler Insurance Company, which changed its name to the Providence Mutual and Steam Boiler, are good examples. The Insurance Association of Providence was organized by the underwriters in 1883, to prevent fraudulent practices. The Providence Protective Department is a voluntary association of underwriters for the maintenance of a salvage corps, and consists now of two companies, which are practically a portion of the regular municipal fire department, though supported by insurance funds. There are to-day 147 fire insurance companies doing business in Rhode Island, of which 30 are Rhode Island companies.

A group of men were engaged in fire insurance under a company name in Hartford before there was any chartered company in the state of Connecticut. The agents were Peleg Sanford and Daniel Wadsworth, and the name of the company which they signed for was the Hartford Fire Insurance Company. This was in 1794. The association proving successful, the group of private individuals was enlarged the following year by adding to the list the names of Colonel Jeremiah Wadsworth of Revolutionary fame, John Caldwell and John Morgan, and also Elias Shipman of New Haven. The new name was the Hartford and New Haven Insurance Company. Mr. Shipman not long afterward removed his interests to New Haven, where he set up the New Haven Insurance Company, which flourished from 1795 to 1833. Sanford and Wadsworth dissolved partnership in 1798, which ended the Hartford company.

Ezekiel Williams, Jr., had by this time built up considerable business in marine insurance, encouraged by the members of the other association. But as commerce increased it was found that there were serious disadvantages in the Lloyd system which was being followed, since subscribers developed a faculty of keeping out of sight except when dividends were due. Consequently, in October, 1803, the gentlemen interested secured a charter, and the Hartford Insurance Company was organized to do marine business. In 1825 it became the Protection Insurance Company. Marine companies were also established in New London, Norwich and Middletown. The war of 1812 wrecked marine business. The Norwich company went into fire insurance, the Hartford became the Protection as stated above, and the others that had been formed previous to the war gave up.

Mutual insurance in Connecticut has been exceptionally successful, largely because of conservative men and methods. The Mutual Association Company of the city of Norwich started in the untried field in May, 1795, and it is doing business to-day along the lines it then adopted. Each person joining was to pay on the sum insured by him a premium of one-half of one per cent the first year, one-third the second, and one-fourth the third and thereafter. When the profits had amounted to £2,000, the surplus was to be divided annually. If everything was swept away by a single loss, the members were to contribute not exceeding one per cent on the amounts insured by each. Growth was slow. It was almost twenty years before the first surplus was divided. But it was a sort of a family affair, every person insured being known to the officers of the company and to each other. The meetings were held in the court house, and partook of the nature of a town meeting. Policy number one is still in force. The assets to-day are $13,000; only dwelling houses are insured, and no risk of over $1,000 is taken, and there is no desire to extend business. A similar experiment in New Haven in 1801 failed miserably.

The first stock company to go outside of the state for risks was the Norwich Marine, which became the Norwich Fire in 1818. The Chicago fire destroyed it. This left the Hartford Insurance Company the oldest in the field, it having been incorporated in 1810, with a capital of $150,000, and with General Nathaniel Terry as its president. Its chief investment was in the stock of the Hartford Bank, which was established in 1792. As has been remarked by Secretary Woodward of the Hartford Board of Trade, one thing which has had much to do with making Hartford one of the foremost insurance centres in the world is the high character of the men who established its companies and who have maintained them. This company is an illustration. It took risks almost at the outset for one-third more than its entire assets, yet each risk was so carefully placed that there was no anxiety. The second year of its existence it tried placing agents in outlying towns, and ten years thereafter was encouraged to go still farther. The secretary, Walter Mitchell, in whose office the business was done, received a salary of $300, and $30 a year rent. The president had no salary till 1823, when he got $200. The company went on the principle that the secret of success in insurance is to insure; whenever there was a fire in which the losses were particularly heavy, the officers hurried to the place and let it be known that the Hartford stood ready to pay all claims. It was seldom that they went away from the place without taking more insurance. The Chicago fire loss, $1,968,225, was paid in full by the help of the company's old standby, the Hartford Bank, and of the Connecticut Mutual Life. The loss of $485,356 in the Boston fire was paid out of the current receipts. A stock dividend of twenty-five per cent was paid out of the profits in 1877, raising the capital to $1,250,000, at which figure it now stands. In 1870 the present handsome office building was erected, and enlarged in 1897.

The New Haven Fire Insurance Company, incorporated in 1813, was absorbed by the Hartford in 1819. The Middletown Fire, incorporated in 1813, was taken up by the Ætna of Hartford, which came into existence in May, 1819. The reason for starting the Ætna was peculiar. Secretary Mitchell of the Hartford lived in Wethersfield, and he was so erratic about his business hours that he exasperated the enterprising men of Hartford, till they resolved to have a fire insurance company of their own. The capital was $150,000. The company at an early date began to push its agencies. When the Protection Company gave up its business, it left an opening in the West, which the Ætna quickly filled; and since then it has continued to expand. In 1866 its capital was increased to $300,000. Full of ambition to be the largest company in the country, it issued 10,000 new shares at par in 1881, bringing its capital up to the present figure, $4,-000,000. Mr. Woodward says that to it belongs the credit of first using outline charts, out of which grew the invaluable system of Sanborn maps. To

meet its loss of $3,782,000 by the Chicago fire, it reduced its capital one-half, and at once built it up again by cash payments of $1,500,000. The Boston fire loss, $1,635,067, was met with a further contribution of $1,000,-000 from the shareholders. The City Fire Insurance Company of Hartford was destroyed by the Chicago fire.

The Connecticut Fire Insurance Company of Hartford is another company which has prospered by honest, conservative management. With a capital of $200,000 when it started in 1850, it now has a capital of $1,000,-000, assets of ever three and one-half millions, and one of the handsomest buildings in the city for its home. The Phœnix is still another of the same kind, founded by Henry Kellogg in 1854 with a capital of $100,000. Its advance has been remarkable. When the Chicago disaster brought it losses of $937,219.23, it had assets of $1,900,-000. Governor Marshall Jewell, who was connected with the company, appeared among the smoking ruins of the city, and in a short speech announced that the Phœnix was ready to give its check in full for every proved claim. The Boston fire caused no trouble whatever. The capital today is $2,000,000. Like the other companies, the Phœnix has an elegantly equipped building.

The Merchants Company having been ruined by the Chicago fire, the National Fire Insurance Company, just starting, decided to continue its business, and despite the sudden reverse by the Boston fire has taken its place among the first of Hartford companies. It has a beautiful building, erected in 1893. To complete the list of Hartford stock companies, mention is to be made of the Orient, succeeding the City in 1871, with a capital of $100,000.

To show that mutual insurance can be reliable and successful when properly conducted, reference may be made to the Hartford County Mutual Company, organized in May, 1831, modest and careful always, and with a name as good as gold. Further evidence is to be found in the Middlesex Mutual Association Company of Middletown, chartered in May, 1836, and a success from the first. The New London Company is still another mutual company which has had a long and honorable career, having been organized in 1840. The State Mutual of Hartford is the youngest, but gives excellent promise.

The office of the insurance commissioner in Connecticut was created by law in 1865, but the department was not established till 1871. Since then it has been foremost in promoting true insurance interests. Its report this year indicates the care that is always taken by the department. The national convention of Insurance Commissioners of the United States last year adopted a form for annual statements which the Connecticut department has accepted. It shows for each company, as the underwriting and investment exhibit, the net premiums received during the year, the interest earned, the net losses incurred, the expenses, the loss for the year, the amounts remitted to the home office, the surplus at the end of the year, the per cent of the total net losses incurred to the net premiums earned, and the per cent of the total expenses incurred to the total of the net premiums earned. This is followed by tables of statistics, which the Connecticut office has been publishing for some years. They cover: 1, capital, assets, liability, surplus and per cent of assets to amount at risk; 2, items composing assets; 3, items composing the liabilities; 4, income during the year; 5, items composing the expenditures; 6, income, expenditures, premiums received, commissions paid during the year; 7, fire risks, premiums, losses incurred and per cent thereof; 8, fire insurance transferred in Connecticut during the year; 9, fire risks written, premiums received and average premium per cent in last three years; 10, marine and inland business; 11, summary comparison of fire business

(including mutuals) in Connecticut for the past twenty years; 12, summary comparison of condition of fire insurance companies authorized in Connecticut from 1878 to 1898. And this gives but a feeble idea of the carefulness in detail essential for the insurer and the insured. The report just issued shows 142 companies doing business in the state. Of these the number of Connecticut stock companies is 9; mutuals, 17; outside stock companies, 75; outside mutuals, 6; foreign companies, 35.

Maine had little insurance of its own till 1868, although the laws had been favorable since 1821. After the state banks had been taxed out of existence, Governor Chamberlain in 1868 recommended the appointment of a bank and insurance examiner. Albert W. Paine was appointed. In the face of considerable opposition, he made two distinct departments of banking and insurance. In 1895 a law was passed requiring that fire inquests in every municipality should be reported, and a fire inspector was ordered in every town of more than 2,000 inhabitants to examine buildings in process of erection and to give directions as to precautions. A tax of two per cent is levied on all premiums received by foreign companies in excess of losses actually paid during the year. There are 145 companies doing business in the state, divided as follows: home mutuals, 48; Maine stock, 2; stock companies of other states, 64; mutuals of other states, 3; foreign companies, 28.

The first New Hampshire fire insurance companies were mutuals, and they proved very unsatisfactory. Three commissioners made the first report in 1852. The first regular company established, not chartered, was the New Hampshire Fire Insurance Company of Manchester, in 1869. Governor E. A. Straw was the president, Governor James A. Weston, vice-president, G. B. Chandler, treasurer. The success of the company has carried its name into almost every part of the country, and it has made an annual progressive growth for twenty-eight years.

In 1885 laws were passed forbidding the transfer of suits from the state to the United States courts, forbidding combinations of companies and the use of any but valued policies on buildings, and decreeing that wrong descriptions of warranties should not invalidate unless fraudulently given. Such legislation caused the out-of-state companies to withdraw at once. As a result of that, twelve mutuals were established, and the greatest precautions were taken against fire. At length the old companies went back, but declined to take farm buildings as risks. The failure of the People's Fire Insurance Company of Manchester in 1893 was a memorable event. The company was wrecked by the president and treasurer, and three hundred stockholders lost everything.

The total number of companies at work in the state is 94, of which 33 are mutuals and 6 are New Hampshire stock companies. The aggregate paid-up capital of the stock companies is $1,475,000.

What are known as the cash mutuals charge a full cash premium, and in addition insert a stipulation in the policy that once or twice the amount of the premium paid can be assessed on the policy-holders if necessary to pay losses. The county and town mutuals collect no premiums, but depend wholly on assessments to pay the losses as they occur.

The Grange Mutual, whose business is confined wholly to the members of that order, charge a cash premium of one-half of one per cent of the amount insured, and in addition a premium note of three per cent of the amount insured, upon which an assessment can be made when necessary.

Vermont people made good their fire losses in the last century by means of the lottery. Then companies were chartered and organized to extinguish fires. The Vermont Fire Insurance

Company was organized in 1827. Daniel Baldwin, long chief engineer of the Montpelier fire department, was the prime mover in this enterprise. Associated with him were Thomas Reed, Jr., James H. Langdon, Joshua Y. Vail and Chester Hubbard. The company was required to pay the state a tax of six per cent of its profits. Its first modest office cost $1,177.33; its present structure cost $48,000. Until recently representatives from each town in the state, when they went to attend the legislature, made it their first duty, says Joseph A. DeBoer, to carry into the treasurer of the company the assessments of the company from their towns, by them sent to pay their "insurance tax," a service gratuitously rendered by the representatives. The annual meeting was held early in the session; the representatives were also the representatives of the company. The insurance department was organized in 1852, and the first report was issued in 1869. In all 47 companies are placing insurance in Vermont. Of these all are from outside the state except three, and of these two are mutuals. The policies of the mutuals are mainly for five years.

The foreign fire insurance companies which do business in New England are so many in number, so great in influence and so large a factor in the making of New England insurance history, that an article on the fire insurance of New England without mention of them would be incomplete, indeed.

There are thirty-four foreign companies now regularly admitted to do business in some or all of the New England states. They include nearly all the great companies of the world. Until recently many companies contented themselves with having a representative in this country and received "surplus lines," but recent laws restricting the opportunities of the surplus line company, together with the great competition for business and, above all, the splendid future which far-seeing managers saw awaited this country, caused the strong companies who were on the outside to come properly into the fold, and quite recently half a dozen English and German companies have chosen United States trustees, deposited $300,000 or $500,000 with the treasurer of some leading state, and regularly applied for admission to the chief states of the Union.

Of the thirty-five companies doing business here, twenty-seven are British. They have assets of seventy-five millions of dollars and a surplus above all liabilities (including capital) of over thirty-two millions of dollars. These figures are constantly changing, and are greater now than when the records from which they were taken were made up, but this suffices to show the magnitude and strength of the foreign corporations.

In the year 1897 all the stock fire insurance companies doing business in the United States wrote risks with premiums amounting to $124,132,687, and of this the foreign companies obtained $42,494,120, or about 34 per cent of the whole. In New England the foreign companies wrote even a larger percentage of the business. All companies together took in New England premiums amounting to $12,928,406, and of this amount foreign companies captured $4,832,645, or about 37 per cent of the whole.

It is a matter of history that the foreign companies obtained their prestige through the magnificent manner in which those who were here in 1872 settled their losses at the great Boston fire. It is true that their losses were not as great as those of the Boston companies; but the princely way of dealing with the property owners impressed everyone, and the foreign corporations will never be forgotten by those who held their policies in 1872. To the Boston manager of the Royal of Liverpool at that time the English manager cabled: "Delighted to hear our loss is only a million; help the sufferers and push the business vigorously." Added to this, while financial

death and dismay met home companies at every turn, not a single foreign company of the first or second rank failed to pay one hundred cents on the dollar of every claim.

The first great English companies to enter the United States were the Liverpool and London and Globe and the Royal Insurance Company of Liverpool. They came in 1850 and 1851 respectively. They started in a small way, but to-day the Royal has funds in this country for the exclusive protection of American policy holders amounting to nearly eight millions of dollars, and if a succession of calamities should eat this up, as much of the fifty-one millions held on the other side would be sent over as may be needed.

The North British and Mercantile of Edinburgh is the next oldest foreign company here, coming in 1866, and two years later the great Imperial of London came. This company took a great impetus in New England when the late John C. Paige of Boston became United States manager, and the success it then had has been continued by his successors, who still represent it in Massachusetts. The Imperial has two millions of dollars here, and the millions in the company's vaults on the other side are ready when needed. In 1871 the Lancashire entered the United States; and in 1872 the London Assurance Corporation and the Commercial Union of London were admitted. Other companies followed quickly, and within the past three years seven or eight English and German companies have made their deposits and started in to do a regular agency business.

Here are a few figures which serve to show the part foreign fire companies play in the New England field. One hundred and twenty-four companies from all places took in New England in 1897 the following premiums:

Massachusetts $8,825,281
Maine 1,554,500
New Hampshire...... 974,246
Rhode Island........ 1,073,043
Vermont 501,336

Thirty-five foreign companies took in the same states as follows:

Massachusetts $3,105,839
Maine 417,879
New Hampshire...... 204,572
Vermont 116,062
Rhode Island........ 339,336
Connecticut 648,957

This amount of $4,832,645, being the New England premiums in 1897, is over one-third of all the premiums taken from New England by all classes of companies. Of this amount the Royal of Liverpool wrote about 12 per cent of all the business written in foreign companies.

The two houses in New England which have had the greatest influence on the business in New England, and which to-day do the largest business in these states are Field & Cowles and John C. Paige & Co. Both these houses are in Boston, and they do the largest business in the city.

The National Board of Fire Underwriters was established in 1866, at a time when the Portland fire had emphasized the need of controlling cutthroat competition. It was apparent that large companies were being undermined and becoming unreliable. This body has exercised a strong influence for good. Nearly every state and large city now has its board of fire underwriters to regulate rates and to attend to other matters of general interest. The New England Board of Fire Underwriters, with headquarters in Boston, is to New England what the national board is to the whole country. One of the beneficial results obtained is uniformity in policies. In special cases variations from the standard are printed separately and pasted upon the policy.

It is held that combinations as regards rating are to be commended when based on an analysis of the results of insurance. But there are limits to this, fixed always by the possibility that if the rates are unreasonably high, members of the combination will break away and adopt a schedule of their own. Much has been heard in recent years about combinations to rob the people. Color for such rumor should be studiously avoided. It had its origin, no doubt, in the attempt to get companies onto a better paying basis, it being a notorious fact that for some years insurance capital in general has brought poor return.

Perpetual fire insurance has never been popular in New England. The North America of Boston issued a few such policies, and some have been given by British underwriters. They are based usually on about ten annual premiums. It appears to New England people that deposits from perpetual insurance cannot be apportioned, but must go into convertible securities, where they may be returned on three days' notice; only the interest can be used for dividends, and there are likely to be sudden demands at any time, which may prove embarrassing.

Co-insurance has been adopted quite generally within the past few years as a means of protecting companies. In the beginning it developed considerable opposition, and is still a subject of legislative debate. By the conditions of this plan, the insured assumes part of the risk and in return gets a special rate.

It is clear that insurance in New England has been advanced steadily by the thoughtfulness and energy of the best class of men; and while there is more or less clashing as to details in the different states, the general insurance interest is on a sound and secure basis, affording the secure protection which business and society demand.

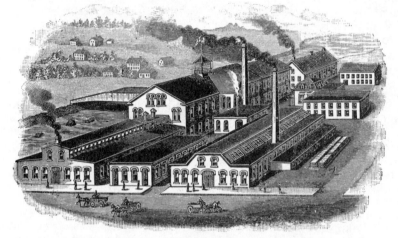

Great Industries
of New England
(1909)

Great Industries of New England

THE GREATEST MILL IN THE WORLD

By JOSEPH McCARTHY

AT Lawrence, Mass., a mill was started on its career of turning out finished worsted goods, in 1906, just eight months after ground was broken for its foundation, that is said by a great many expert mill men to be rightly entitled the greatest mill in the world.

It is such a mill as made many of the old-time mill men gasp when they first saw it in completed shape and in working order. They gasped with awe and astonishment not only at its tremendous proportions, its magnificent equipment of machinery, and its unparalleled capacity for turning raw wool into the finest finished suitings, but at the almost unheard of consideration given to the health and comfort of the six thousand men and women who were to work therein.

And when you think of how the average mill man, big hearted and big brained as he is, has been brought up in the old-time factories and under old-time conditions, it will not seem so strange that they were awestruck and dumfounded. For among other things in the new Wood mill at Lawrence, for that is the mill reputed to be the greatest in the world, was an escalator to be used by the mill help.

If you can fancy how an old-time Southern planter felt at the idea of the field hands in the days "before the war" coming in and sitting at the dining-table at the "great house," you can get an idea of how some of the old-time agents and superintendents of mills felt at the idea of providing a moving stairway for the mill help to reach their work on the third, fourth, fifth, or sixth story. But it was in the Wood mill, along with many another thing that showed that the directing mind which ordered that such a structure should rise on a tree-grown river bank really believed that mill operatives were his fellow-beings.

How Mr. Wood came to have the escalator installed in this big mill is characteristic of the man and his attitude towards the army of employees who work in the various mills controlled by him. While he was planning the mill he was in New York. After a trying day's work in the hot early summer he was preparing to go up town to his hotel. He was pretty well fagged when he reached the elevated station, and the thought of climbing the

WOOD WORSTED MILL

stairs was still more fatiguing. But he had reached an elevated station where there was an escalator, and he did not have to climb the stairs. The idea then came to his mind of how convenient an escalator would be for the hard-working men and women who would labor in the upper stories of his new six-story mill. He immediately decided to notify the architects to change their plan so that an escalator could be installed.

But that is only one of the many up to date and humane contrivances in this monster mill. It has recreation rooms for the help, waiting rooms, playrooms for the children who may bring dinners to their parents, a first-class restaurant where meals are served at cost to all

the employees who care to patronize it, and the airiest and brightest of working-rooms for all.

These evidences of his consideration for the men and women who do the laborious work in his mill has endeared him to all the farsighted people of Lawrence. They admire him for these revelations of his character as well as for the magical change that has come over the destiny of Lawrence since his advent.

From the stagnant mill town of 1885-1886 they acknowledge that Mr. Wood has been one of the main, if not the main, factors, in doubling its population in twenty years, and in giving the lie to these prophets of woe who were predicting that it would never grow any greater. Its

AT LAWRENCE, MASS.

industries have doubled their capacity for employing operatives since he went to Lawrence, and proved that here in old New England there are opportunities awaiting the coming of the right man which will show more golden returns than any of the glittering West can offer.

Of course no one recognizes better than Mr. Wood himself that others have done much to advance Lawrence, and no one would be quicker to disclaim any pretensions that all the wonderful growth of Lawrence in the past twenty years was due to him. Other enterprising mill men have done their share toward expanding the chances for gainful employment that has led to the doubling of the population in that time.

But it would be but simple justice to say that Mr. Wood has been in the van and has done more than any one other mill man to show that not in the West, not in the South, but here in New England where the water powers are, where the intelligent working people are, where in the energizing airs of our New England climate, lie the best opportunities for fame and fortune.

Figures are dull things. Statistics convey only a conception, a very faint one sometimes, of the thing they are trying to portray in the mind of the reader. But they serve like the lines jotted down in perspectiveless Chinese painting to give something on which a rightly imaginative person can get within seeing distance of what they are intended to convey. So for a few figures and statistics regarding this mill that is acknowledged to be the greatest along many lines.

Measure with your mind's eye a third of a mile of the earth's surface. That represents the extreme length of the Wood mill at a moderate estimate for taking in the building which is a component part of it, as it was designed to furnish power for it, and you will cover two thousand feet in length with any tape tried on the Wood mill.

Then for most of its length it is one hundred and twenty-three feet wide, in some places portions of it reaching the width of three hundred and thirty feet. It is six good stories above the high granite basement that bears the superstructure.

It has nearly thirty acres of floor space under one roof. It consumes seven hundred and fifty thousand pounds of wool a week when running to capacity. It covers 2,200,000 square feet. And for a few monetary statistics it might be added that the land, mill rights, buildings, machinery, new equipment, and working capital represent a working capital of an investment of ten million.

If the government at Washington should suddenly decide to order uniforms for one hundred thousand new troops the Wood mill could fill the order long before the government could get the troops. More than one hundred thousand sheep are sheared every week to supply the call of the Wood mill when running on full time.

Electricity generated by steam is the motive power employed. The boiler house contains a battery of forty horizontal boilers of the Robb-Mumford make. There are two steel smokestacks ten and one half feet in diameter and one hundred and twenty feet high. As in all other parts of the mill the boiler house is so arranged as to admit increasing the number of the boilers in case more power is needed.

In the engine room there is one double cylinder, non-condensing engine of eighteen hundred horsepower, on the shaft of which is a direct connected generator of fifteen hundred kilowatts, and a compound condensing engine with four cylinders, two vertical and two horizontal, on the shaft of which is a direct connected generator of four thousand kilowatts. Ample space is left in the engine house for more engines.

The main mill rests on a foundation as solid as a rock made of a reinforced concrete, and concrete columns were placed throughout the structure, so that a collapse of the mill is practically an impossibility. None of the six stories rest on the others, but on these concrete columns, so that it would be possible to remove one of the middle stories and yet not cause the building to collapse or even weaken it to any extent.

It is easy to get those kind of statistics and to put them down in type. But it is not so easy to get the statistics that will do anything toward representing the greatness of heart that made Mr. Wood so solicitous about the comfort of his operatives, and that the discriminating citizens of Lawrence are never tired of praising and holding up as an example. And it is an example that shines afar, as was shown when the commissioners from the Chinese government paid it a special visit last year because they had heard it was one of the wonders of industrial America. As such an example and emblem of America's supremacy in manufacturing it is one more illustration of the creative value of a poor boy's ideal.

Mr. Wood had the ideal with him when he was like dozens of other hustling young men in their twenties, in the employ of the Washington mill of Lawrence. Unlike most of them he lived to see his ideal realized, because he had that persistence that is so necessary to the carrying out of an ideal. And as mentioned previously he had that dash of adventurous experimenting which all great captains of whatever live line of human endeavor have. As an example, it is said that in the first years of his service with the reorganized and struggling Washington mills he was on the road trying to place their men's suitings and overcoats with the wholesale and jobbing houses.

Instead of starting out with the regular routine of fellow commercial travelers he had the best tailor in New York make for him six suits out of the kind of goods he was trying to place. When he was expatiating on his wares he simply drew attention to how the goods would look when made up. He is said to have made the most successful traveling representative the mills ever had on the road.

When young Wood went to Lawrence a little over twenty years ago he had all the energy and capacity for hard, creative work that is so typical of many New England raised boys. But he had in addition just a dash of the discoverer's imagination which could see the great possibilities in a mill city that was in the doldrums just then and of which many manufacturers were predicting that it had reached its limit of development and could not hope to do more than hold its own in the future.

With this equipment he went to work in the counting room of the Washington mills, which had practically failed a year or two before, and had been taken over by Mr. Ayer, of Lowell. Mr. Ayer was a shrewd and successful business man and he soon had the mill in successful running order again.

Young Mr. Wood, though, early proved to be the most efficient lieutenant Mr. Ayer had in his Lawrence enterprise, and it was not long before he was the mainspring and guiding force that was sending the Washington mills along to new and greater prosperity. To-day it employs on the average five thousand operatives.

His work with the Washington mills made it easy for him to gain the confidence and the backing of capitalists, and he put into successful operation a plan of his for the consolidation of the woolen mills of New England which resulted in the formation of the American woolen company, with Mr. Wood at the head of it.

This brilliant success at once placed him at the very forefront of the woolen manufacturers of America, and gave him a commanding position in the eyes of the wool gowers and the woolen manufacturers the world over.

His next step was made easier, and when he announced early in 1905 that he was going to build the most modern and best equipped worsted mill that money and skill could erect there were few to question that he would carry out his announcement successfully.

But few even then gave him credit for the ability and the intention to erect the largest worsted mill in the world as well as the one where the operatives would have the greatest opportunity to do their work under comfortable and healthful surroundings. There were not many either who would.

But he did, and in Lawrence in 1906, just twenty years after he first went there, a poor boy, he had the satisfaction of seeing in operation such a mill.

Around the great Wood mill and the Washington mill of Lawrence, prosaic and humdrum as they may seem, when humming with the energized workings of thousands of human bees, hangs the fragrance of that old idyll of humanity, that old yet ever new idyll that had its first recorded success in the dim dawn of history when Jacob married his employer's daughter after proving his worth by service. Mr. Wood married the daughter of Mr. Ayer just twenty years ago. Their married life has been ideally happy and four children have come to bless the union.

Mr. and Mrs. Wood have a most charmingly laid out and situated home in Andover, the academic suburb of Lawrence.

They have also a residence in Boston and a summer home on Buzzard's Bay, where they have had for neighbors ex-President Cleveland and the late Joseph Jefferson.

Mr. Wood is an enthusiastic yachtsman, as is his son, who has been taught to handle a boat with skill and safety. There is also no more ardent follower of automobiling than Mr. Wood, and his cars are generally able to keep in front of the dust raised by most other cars on the road, as well as being noted for their comfort.

When the romances of New England of the last quarter of a century are being written, the romances of great and creative work done by men who started life poor in purse but rich in mind and the blood that cleaves a way, the story of Mr. Wood and the great Wood mill will hold a leading place. As the Wood mill stands in its place in Lawrence and in the minds of every leading manufacturer of the country as the model of its kind, so will the career of Mr. Wood stand out as a beacon and an incentive to hundreds of New England born boys of what they can do here in the rugged old cradle of the American race.

But much as Mr. Wood has accomplished it is only a forerunner, those who know him best think, of what he will accomplish. For he is a young man yet, in the prime of life, being on the sunny side of fifty.

His fertile brain, his unconquerable perseverance, his resourceful mind and his clear-visioned view of the tremendous possibilities of this country make it more than likely that before his active career closes he will double the great mills his company now owns in Lawrence as well as the mills it controls in other cities.

ANOTHER VIEW OF W. M. WOOD'S HOME AT ANDOVER

The Lower Kennebec
(1895)

ICE HARVESTING.

KENNEBEC RIVER, MAINE.

INDEPENDENT ICE COMPANY'S HOUSES,

THE
NEW ENGLAND MAGAZINE.

NEW SERIES.   FEBRUARY, 1895.   VOL. XI.   No. 6.

PHOTOGRAPH BY EDWARD D. BAKER.

A WINTER SUNSET.

THE LOWER KENNEBEC.

By Winfield Thompson.

OUT of a great lake in the forest tumbles a bubbling stream, virile and eager, which gathers strength at every bound as it progresses noisily through the virgin woods to where farms border its shores and mill wheels are turned by its bridled force, — the upper Kennebec. Bearing on its broad bosom shipping from a dozen seas, its surface ruffled by the wake of pleasure steamers and fretting tugs, flows a noble river, a highway wide and smooth into the heart of the Pine Tree State, — the lower Kennebec. One courses over countless obstacles, with many a turn, through a good two hundred miles of wooded country. The other flows uninterrupted fifty miles to the sea. A dam at Augusta separates the domain of one from the other. So completely do the characteristics of the two parts differ, that they seem like two rivers, one coming up to receive the waters of the other; for the lower Kennebec responds to the promptings of the ocean, rising and falling with the same regularity as the tides along the coast.

Above Augusta the river is not different from other Maine rivers. The scenery along its banks is picturesque to a degree, and grows wilder as the stream grows smaller. Eighteen miles above Augusta is Waterville, the Elm city, and above that are Fairfield and Skowhegan and a number of smaller towns, where the water is shot through flumes and canals to turn the machinery of mills and factories. Charming at every turn and always mighty, the stream makes its way, now

LOADING ICE FOR BALTIMORE.

brawling over rocks, now purling past pebbly shores, lagging, hurrying, scolding, singing, all the way down from the lake in the wilderness. At the state capital it jumps its last barrier and turns its last wheel and, shaking itself free from obstructions, it broadens, stretches a bit, one might fancy, then becomes subservient to the ocean, doing its bidding whether it would or no.

In spite of its response to the ocean tides the water of the lower Kennebec is fresh to within about fifteen miles of the river's mouth, and so pure that the ice taken from it has become famous for its quality. In color, when held to the light in a glass, it is like rain water; and when cleft by the sharp prow of a steamboat, falling back to its level like outstretched wings, white-tipped and

transparent, it takes the hue of amber. In winter, seen through a hole in the ice from a distance, it seems at times almost black.

The river is always a source of pleasure or of profit to the people who live near it. In summer it is the royal road for traffic, as well as the excursion route of the people; and winter, when Jack Frost has closed its waters to navigation, brings its own sports and labors. Then the lovers of horses — and everybody in the Kennebec valley likes horses — find enjoyment in trotting matches held on the ice. Expert skaters are plenty in the towns along the river, and as long as the ice is in condition hosts of them indulge in the invigorating sport. Then comes the profit of the season, when the ice "crop" is harvested.

In the spring, when the ice has broken up and gone to sea, borne along by the early freshets that counteract for a time the force of tides, great vessels come up behind tugs to take the river's frigid product to ports south of New England. About one thousand five hundred vessels are required to move an average crop of ice, which when housed is about

BOUND FOR THE ICE-FIELDS. TEMPERATURE TEN BELOW ZERO.

one million tons. The waste in the houses is estimated to be from ten to thirty per cent of the amount stored. The freighting is done largely by three-masted and four-masted schooners, though recently barges, some of

A DOWN-RIVER STEAMER.

them old ships stripped of sails and rigging, have been pressed into the service, being towed from one port to another by ocean tugs.

Ice harvesting on the Kennebec gives employment to about four thousand five hundred men each winter. Four hundred horses are employed on the fields, scraping snow off the ice, dragging planers and groovers, and towing great rafts of square blocks down the canal. The

ports carry hundreds of people daily, and the smaller river steamers, swift, clean-cut craft, are never without crowds of passengers. The people of the Kennebec valley are in love with their river, and they spend as much time as they can spare each year enjoying the beauty of its scenery, which never seems to lose its charm for them. "Going down river" is one of the dearest pleasures of the Kennebecker, second only perhaps to the delight of cottage life on the islands of Boothbay Harbor, in which the climax of the journey is usually attained. At Capitol Island, thirteen miles below Bath, reached by the turbulent and crooked Sasanoa River, which is entered

SEGUIN.

FROM A PHOTOGRAPH BY N. L. STEBBINS.

workmen get from $1.25 to $1.75 a day; foremen from $2.00 to $2.50; and the owners of horses receive $1.25 to $1.50 for the labor of each animal. In summer about four hundred men find employment loading the vessels which take the ice away. There are now forty-eight groups of ice-houses along the Kennebec, twenty-four on the east bank, twenty-one on the west, and three on Swan Island.

With each passing summer the Kennebec is growing in favor as a resort of vacation people. The large steamboats which ply between Boston and the river

from the Kennebec at that point, is a group of cottages owned almost entirely by Gardiner people; while at Ocean Point across Boothbay Harbor, at Squirrel Island, Bayville and other points are to be found scores of other Kennebeckers, from Bath, Richmond and Augusta, and from the upper Kennebec, Vassalboro, Waterville, Fairfield and Skowhegan. The scenery of the Kennebec is of the kind to delight the lover of nature in modest garb. It is at its best, perhaps, in the rich warm days of early July, viewed from the deck of a steamer bound up stream. If the

"SHIPYARDS WHOSE PRODUCTS HAVE CARRIED BATH'S NAME INTO EVERY SEA."

craft be a friend's yacht, so much the better.

The object for which the pilot Kennebec-bound shapes his course is Seguin, lying about a mile from the river's mouth. Its shores are bold and ribboned with surf, and up its black rocky slopes, on a bit of level ground, are the lighthouse, fog-whistle station and keepers' houses. The sea is often in a turmoil around Seguin. Sailors call the neighborhood the roughest on the coast. The ebb tides from the river meet the rollers of the sea and, especially when the wind is from

"RICHMOND, NESTLING IN A BEND OF THE RIVER."

the south, a smart "chop" is created. Inside Pond Island, whose little lighthouse marks the way into the river, smooth water is found, and a panorama that has few equals begins. When the beach at Popham, with its life-saving station, hotels, cottages and old stone fort — a relic of the civil war — are left

behind, the shores become bold and rocky, rising into hills clothed in spruce and pine, with here and there the fresh green of maple or birch making a light patch in the sober foliage. Along the banks, half hidden among gnarled apple trees, with its bit of garden and field reclaimed from the woods and a tiny wharf in front, is seen at intervals a modest home. Villages there are also, Parker's Head and Phippsburgh, old and straggling, each with its little cove and wharves, quaint and pleasing to the eye. Opposite them on the east side of the river are the shores of Georgetown.

The tide is strong along here, and the water clear and as salt as where it churns around Seguin. Nine miles or so from the sands of Popham a sharp turn in the river to the west retards the vision; but once around a wooded point, a fine sweep of water five miles long and nearly a mile wide, with Bath, the city of ships, bordering its western shore, lies before the traveller's eye. The city's spires crown the slope on which the town is built, and all along the water front, fringed in places with masts, are the famous shipyards, whose products have carried Bath's name into every sea. The building of wooden ships has declined in Bath, until many of the yards are now idle; but a new industry is springing up in the construction of iron and steel craft. The Bath iron works have turned out three war vessels in the last three years, and several other craft, including the largest steam yacht ever built in the United States. A shipyard is also equipped in Bath where the experiment of building steel merchant ships has been tried by a firm whose name is widely known for its famous wooden clippers, of which it has turned out an even hundred.

Opposite Bath, in Arrowsic and Woolwich, two of the first stockades on the lower Kennebec were built. They were the scenes of a number of important councils and of several massacres in the long Indian wars. Above Bath the river turns again to the west a bit, between rocky points. The tide rushes fine and free, foam-flecked and dimpled, tossing and twisting around the shores of little islands. The weed along the rocks is here missed; the water changes in color and retains only a taint of salt; and the shores take on a richer cloak than farther down —maple, birch, beech and hazel being but sparsely sprinkled with needled pines. The channel lies again almost north and south. The broad sheet of Merrymeeting Bay, fully five miles long, receiving at its farther end the waters of the Androscoggin, spreads to the west. The waves splash merrily in the sun with the daintiest hint of yellow as they chase each other before a brisk southwest wind.

A little farther up the Kennebec, the Eastern River enters the larger stream between wide marshes. On the west side is the town of Bowdoinham; and here the sluggish Cathance yields itself to the keeping of the Kennebec. Swan Island, which constitutes the town of Perkins, a borough with nineteen voters, divides the current of the river a little farther up.

Along the shores of the island near the upper end are beaches; and here the cows on summer days may be seen standing in the water, some of them almost submerged, enjoying in quiet gratitude their cool immunity from the sting of flies. There is a good channel for navigation on both sides of the island. The west course is the one taken by passenger steamers; but up and down the east side go many tugs with their long "tows" of schooners. Opposite the head of Pond Island is Richmond, a quiet village nestling in a bend of the river. Shoe manufacturing has been the chief industry of the town for some years, but business changes have recently re-

"A FERRY, PRIMITIVE AND PICTURESQUE."

duced its importance. Ice cutting and the production of lumber furnish more labor for its residents than any other pursuits.

At this point is a ferry, primitive and picturesque, by which man and beast may cross the stream. The ferryman is old and gray, and lives in a tiny house near the water's edge on the Richmond side. For forty years he has plied the oar and managed the old gundelow back and forth across the stream; has seen commerce develop and landmarks disappear; and still he breasts the tide and wind day after day, placidly and slowly, apparently satisfied with his lot. He can remember when overland traffic to the east through Dresden to Wiscasset, when that place was important as a seaport, was of more

THE FERRY LANDING, RICHMOND SIDE.

recalls the appearance of the first train that ran from Portland to Augusta a few years earlier.

Above Richmond the country swells upward in rounded hillocks from the stream. The slopes are covered in June and July with waving grass and rich clover, which sends out an odor delicious beyond description. Tall, slender elms, shaped like long-stemmed sherry glasses, bend to the sweet breeze on the uplands, here and there one standing alone in a field. Down near the river willows are seen at intervals, and spreading poplars, the wind turning their leaves back and transforming them to silver in the sunlight. There is a pebbly beach between the foliage and the shore. As the steamer passes she seems to pull the water away from it, leaving a mark on the pebbles; then, when she has passed, the water rushes back again with a swish.

moment than it is now. People then rode in coaches or on horseback up and down the Kennebec roads, and the scream of locomotives and whir of long trains of palace cars along the glistening steel rails up there on the west bank of the stream did not disturb the quiet scene. He can remember when James Cheesman's first cargo of ice was shipped out of the Kennebec in 1860, leading the way for the endless procession of ice cargoes that have gone out of the river since, and he

The scene here on a clear summer day is idyllic. Ice-houses, great white broad-roofed, smooth-sided structures looking as clean as chalk, stand on the green river bank; big schooners swing at anchor in the stream, pointing their jib-booms now up the river and now down with the tide, or lie at wharves, the clear green ice-blocks disappearing down their hatchways. An ebon-faced steward smiles over a schooner's rail as the steamer goes by; and from the rigging of one high-sided craft a yellow-haired sailor, clad only in overalls, dives full twenty feet into the water, coming up alongside the steamer. All along the banks the story of peace, thrift and prosperity is told in the trim farms with well-kept buildings, the massive ice-wharves, small private landings, and at intervals a bit of road among the trees, with a sleek horse jogging along, the driver and his wife evidently having been to market with eggs and garden truck.

A GARDINER LOG-DRIVER.

Ancient Pownalborough, chartered as a township in 1760, now dwindled to Dresden, is passed on the right, the old court house of Revolutionary times, near the site of Fort Shirley, standing half hidden in the trees. On the west side of the stream the Dresden camp-meeting grove attracts the eye, then South Gardiner with its mills, and four miles farther up the city of Gardiner, where is met the first bridge that crosses the Kennebec. In response to a blast from the whistle a man will swing off the draw of the old wooden-covered structure, and the trip may be continued past Farmingdale and Hallowell to Augusta, "the head of the tide." The channel is narrow above the bridge, and only vessels and steamers of light draught can make the trip with certainty of not striking bottom. The stone piers of an old bridge which was long ago swept away stick out of the water at Hallowell. Along here great log booms are passed, with house-boats, in which the logging men live, lying beside them. Each boat has a cook who provides for the inner comforts of a gang of workers. The logs for all the big mills along the Kennebec are caught in the Hallowell booms, are sorted by aid of the private marks put on each one by the choppers in the woods, and are made into rafts to be towed by a little steamboat to their owners' private booms.

It is in this region that the tourist will find the essence of Kennebec life. Here is the natural centre of the valley. The climate is delightful and the people are typical New Englanders, who have maintained the tenets of their fathers and can trace their lineage in an unbroken line back to the state's pioneers. From this region many able men have gone forth to figure in affairs of state or achieve success in the world of commerce. James G. Blaine made his start in life in Augusta as a newspaper man. The city is now the residence of his widow, and the old office of the Kennebec *Journal* is pointed out to travellers as the spot where the great statesman first gave his ideas to the people.

One of the chief charms of life along the Kennebec, in Augusta, Hallowell and Gardiner especially, is afforded by the many ponds that dot the valley. Behind

PHOTOGRAPH BY EDWARD D. BAKER.

A FARM IDYL.

PHOTOGRAPH BY W. G. ELLIS.

THE BRIDGE AT GARDINER.

the hills that hedge the river lie in richly wooded vales scores of little lakes, placid and clear, connected in chains by vagrant brooks, a whole series yielding its waters to the river through some farm-bordered stream. There are no fewer than seventy-five named ponds set down in the atlas of Kennebec County, and this does not include all. One of the most important groups is that which has for its outlet Cobbosseecontee stream, abbreviated locally to "Cobbossee," which enters the river at Gardiner, tumbling in its last mile over eight dams and turning the wheels of a score of mills and shops.

The valley of the Cobbossee trends northwest and southeast, the chain of ponds and tributary streams being some

Cobbossee, — "Big Cobbossee" its lovers call it. The drive from Gardiner or Augusta to the outlet of the pond is about ten miles, and from Hallowell about six miles. The trip by canoe can be taken only from Gardiner, and is much longer, as it takes the excursionist through miles of winding stream and smaller ponds.

How dear to many Kennebec hearts is the trip "up stream!" Each little excursion brings some new pleasure. The scenery never palls on the fancy of the loyal Kennebecker. He may know the ripples of every eddy, the wash of every rapid, the shadow of every elm in the clear water, know just where to look for them, and be able to picture in his mind how they will appear long before they

"THE NATURAL CENTRE OF THE VALLEY."

VIEW FROM LOUDON HILL, HALLOWELL, LOOKING TOWARD AUGUSTA.

twenty miles in length, but affording at least seventy-five miles of waterways to the canoeist, with few carries. Lying back from five to ten miles from Gardiner, Hallowell and Augusta, these ponds have afforded the residents of those cities beautiful sites for rustic cottages, modestly called "camps," which are not only visited in the summer months, but in other seasons as well. The fishing at the ponds is always excellent. In summer, black bass, large, gamy and fat, bite freely, and perch, white and yellow, may be caught by the hundreds. In winter fishing for pickerel through the ice is a prime sport. The largest of this chain of ponds is

come in view; and yet the paddle is plunged into the stream, the canoe sent across the still places, disturbing the elm's straight reflection, and the light prow made to cut the quickening tide, with the same zest as if all were novel to the delighted senses of the canoeist.

A drive from the river to its limpid reservoirs behind the hills is scarcely less pleasing than the trip by water. It takes one upward over a rolling country from the river, past spreading farms, where the house dog basks in the sun before the door, and children pick daisies in the fields or climb the cherry trees by the roadside in quest of fruit. The road

ON THE ROAD TO COBBOSSEE POND.

dips at times into little intervales, the land clothed in tall grain; but the grade is up and up, until at last from the crest of a ridge above all the others the valley of the ponds is seen, with a bit of Cobbossee some miles off, shining under the sun's rays like quicksilver in its almost black setting of foliage. Far away in the northwest the mountains of the border counties loom purple in the warm air; and beyond them, sinking into the sky, is Mount Washington, white-capped and robed in blue. The way is then downward through shady dells. An old red schoolhouse is passed, its door-sill worn by many feet and its weather-beaten clapboards engraved with rude initials. A farmer raking his first cutting of hay stops in his work, leans on his rake, and greets you with a cheery "Howdy do, neighbor?" — his tone and attitude inviting conversation.

Thus lazily on, till a sudden turn in the road brings the pond into view. At the outlet you drive into the yard of a big bare-looking house, and a farm hand takes your horse. He will supply you with a boat if you desire to go fishing or to row to any of the many camps around the

pond; and he will tell you, if you invite his confidence, that he leads "a dorg's life." "This pond's a mighty lonesome place; git up at four o'clock in th' mornin', 'n' stay up harf th' night baitin' hosses; bin here forty year, 'n' never expect t' git ennywheres else; ain't never bin t' Boston; never bin out of Kennebec caounty." He does not see the poetry of the pond.

No writer ever more charmingly portrayed the beauties of the Kennebec valley than did Nathaniel Hawthorne in his "American Note-Book." In 1837, twelve years after his graduation from Bowdoin College in the class that also gave to the world Longfellow and many other men who became famous, Hawthorne paid a visit of a month to his college chum and classmate, Horatio Bridge.* It was probably the first visit of more than a day or two that Hawthorne

* Horatio Bridge was born in Augusta, April 8, 1806, and died at Athens, Pennsylvania, March 18, 1893. He was admitted to the bar of Kennebec County in 1828, and practised law in Augusta ten years. He entered the navy as paymaster in 1838. He made a three years' cruise in the Mediterranean in the *Cyane*, and one of two years off the coast of Africa in the *Saratoga*. He was stationed at Portsmouth navy yard, 1849–51; was chief of the Bureau of Provisions and Clothing of the Navy, 1854–69; Chief Inspector of Provisions and Clothing in 1867–73; and was then retired as Pay Director with the rank of Commodore. In 1845 he published the "Journal of an African Cruiser," edited by Nathaniel Hawthorne.

had then made outside of his own family circle. He was unknown in the world of letters. He had written much, but had found few publishers. Fixed upon him was what he styled "my cursed habit of solitude." He spent much time in strolling in the woods and along the river banks at Augusta, and in driving around the country with his friend Bridge, who lived a bachelor's life in his paternal mansion near the river. Hawthorne was

and a grassy track and gravel walk between. Beyond the road rolls the Kennebec, here two or three hundred yards wide. I can see it flowing steadily along, straightway between wooded banks; but arriving nearly opposite the house, there is a large and level island in the middle of the stream; and just below the island the current is further interrupted by the works of the mill-dam which is perhaps half finished." The dreamer sat at his window and wrote:

A CAMP ON "BIG COBBOSSEE."

"There is a sound of wind among the trees round the house; and, when that is silent, the calm, full, distant voice of the river becomes audible. Looking downward thither I see the rush of the current, and mark the different eddies, with here and there white specks or streaks of foam; and often a log comes floating on, glistening in the sun as it rolls over among the eddies, having voyaged,

in Augusta from July 5 to August 5. He wrote in his note-book a few days after his arrival: —

"I think I should become strongly attached to our way of life, so independent and untroubled by the forms and restrictions of society. The house is very pleasantly situated — half a mile distant from where the town begins to be thickly settled, and on a swell of land, with the road running at a distance of fifty yards,

for aught I know, hundreds of miles from the wild upper regions of the river, passing down, down, between lines of forest and sometimes a rough clearing, till here it floats by cultivated banks, and will soon pass by the village. Sometimes a long raft of boards comes along, requiring the nicest skill to navigate it through the narrow passage left by the mill-dam. Chaises and wagons go over the road, the riders all giving a passing glance at the

"UP STREAM."

OFF FOR A CAMPING TRIP.

dam, or perhaps alighting to examine it more fully, and at last departing with ominous shakes of the head as to the result of the enterprise."

The doubters were destined to say, " I told you so ; " for hardly was the dam finished when it was swept away, along with the Bridge mansion and grounds. Years after, when Horatio Bridge had made a place for himself in the naval service, Hawthorne visited him and his wife at their house in Portsmouth. One evening at twilight Mrs. Bridge asked Hawthorne to tell her a story. Mr. Bridge lay dozing on a sofa, being convalescent after an attack of malaria. " Looking at me," wrote Horatio Bridge of this incident, in his " Personal Recollections of Nathaniel Hawthorne," " he said : ' I will tell you one which I could write, making that gentleman one of the principal characters. I should begin with a description of his father — a dignified and conservative man — who, for many years, had lived in a great mansion, by the side of a noble river, and had daily enjoyed the sight of the beautiful stream flowing placidly by without a thought of disturbing its natural course. His children had played upon its banks, and the boys swam in the quiet stream or rowed their boats thereon. But after the father's decease, his sons, grown to manhood —

progressive in unison with the spirit of the age — conceived the project of utilizing the great body of water flowing idly by. So, calling in the aid of a famous engineer, they built a high and costly dam across the river, thus creating a great water power sufficient for the use of many prospective mills and factories. The river — biding its time — quietly allowed the obstruction to be finished, and then it rose in its wrath and swept away the expensive structure and the buildings connected with it, and took its course majestically to the sea. Nor did this satisfy the river gods, for they cut a new channel for the stream, and swallowed up the paternal mansion of the young men, and desolated its beautiful grounds, thus showing the superior power of nature whenever it chooses to assert itself.' "

A fine stone dam with a wide slippery " apron " of timber now stands on the site of the first structure ; and on the very spot where the old mansion stood is the gate house of a great cotton mill, where the water is let into the wheelboxes to set in motion hundreds of spindles and scores of looms.

Shortly after his arrival at Augusta, Hawthorne visited Gardiner and the famous Gardiner family estate, the " Oaklands." He wrote of the trip thus : " A drive with B— to Hallowell yesterday, where we dined, and afterward to Gardiner. The most curious object at the latter place was the elegant new mansion of ——. It stands on the site of his former dwelling, which was destroyed by fire. The new building was estimated to cost thirty thousand dollars; but twice as much has already been expended, and a great deal more will be required to complete it. It is certainly a splendid structure; the material, granite from the vicinity. At its angles it has small circular

ing and rippling stream, I saw a great fish, some six feet long and thick in proportion, suddenly emerge at whole length and turn a summerset and vanish in the water. It was of a glistening yellowish brown, with its fins all spread, and looking very strange and startling, darting so lifelike from the black water, throwing itself fully into the bright sunshine, and then lost to sight and to pursuit." At another time he wrote: "I saw also a long flat-bottomed boat go up the river, with a brisk wind and against a strong stream.

HELL GATE, FROM WHICH THE KENNEBEC TOOK ITS NAME.

towers; the portal is lofty and imposing. Relatively to the style of domestic architecture in our country, it well deserves the name of castle or palace. Its situation, too, is fine, far retired from the public road, and attainable by a winding carriage drive; standing amid fertile fields, and with large trees in the vicinity. There is also a beautiful view from the mansion down the Kennebec." *

Hawthorne in his notes spoke thus of his first glimpse of a sturgeon in the Kennebec: "While looking at the rush-

Its sails were of curious construction: a long mast with two sails, one on each side of the boat, and a broader one surmounting them. The sails were colored brown, and appeared like leather or skins, but were really cloth. At a distance the vessel looked like — or at least I compared it to — a monstrous water insect skimming along the river. If the sails had been crimson or yellow the resemblance would have been much closer. . . . It moved along lightly and disappeared between the woody banks. These boats . . .

* The founder of this estate was Dr. Sylvester Gardiner, who was born in Rhode Island in 1707. He settled in Boston, where as a physician and druggist he became rich. About 1754, as one of the proprietors of the Kennebec Purchase, he received from the General Court a grant of land at the mouth of Cobbosseecontee. He was very energetic in getting a thrifty class of settlers to go to the place, and more land was granted him, until in 1770 he owned twelve thousand acres in what is now Gardiner, including the water-power of the Cobbosseecontee, much of which is still owned by the Gardiner estate. Dr. Gardiner built a great house of wood south of the town, and on its site the present "Oaklands" stands. Dr. Gardiner's settlement was first called Gardinerston. In 1761 a grist mill was built on the Cobbosseecontee, and for many years this was the only place in the Kennebec valley where the settlers could get their corn ground. When the Revolutionary War broke out,

Dr. Gardiner's sympathies were with the Tories, and he went to join the British army. His real property at Gardiner was confiscated. He never returned to live in Gardiner, but practised his profession in Newport, Rhode Island, until his death in 1786. The greater part of his Gardiner estate was restored to his heir and grandson, Robert Hallowell, to whom the doctor willed the property on condition that he take the name of Gardiner, which he was allowed to do by the legislature in 1802. Gardiner was incorporated as a town in 1803. William Gardiner, son of Dr. Gardiner, continued to reside there after the departure of his father. He was a jolly fellow, fond of hunting and fishing. In 1785, General Henry Dearborn, charmed with what he had seen of the Kennebec valley in his eight years' service during the Revolution, bought land of William Gardiner, and made his home in the village until 1801, when he was made secretary of war.

trade to Waterville and thereabouts —
names, as *Paul Pry*, on their sails."
After seeing a raft of logs on the river,
guided by two men, Hawthorne wrote :
" It would be pleasant enough to float
down the Kennebec on one of these rafts,
letting the river conduct you onward at
its own pace, leisurely displaying to you
all the wild or ordered beauties along its
banks, and perhaps running you aground
in some peculiarly picturesque spot, for
your further enjoyment of it . . . Another
object seen on the river perhaps is a
solitary man paddling himself down the
river in a small canoe, the light, lonely
touch of its paddle in the water making
the silence seem deeper."

A fishing trip to one of Kennebec
County's famous ponds seems to have
given pleasure to Hawthorne. He wrote :
" A drive yesterday afternoon (July 19)
to a pond in the vicinity of Augusta,
about nine miles off, to fish for white
perch, . . . a beautiful, silvery, round-
backed fish, which bites eagerly, runs about
with the line while being pulled up, makes
good sport for the angler, and an admirable dish." After fishing some time, the
author and his friend went to a tavern

THE "OAKLANDS" FROM THE RIVER.

family written on a black tomb in an
engraving, where a father, mother and
child were represented in a graveyard
weeping over said tomb. . . . There was
also a wood engraving of the Declaration
of Independence with facsimiles of the
autographs ; a portrait of the Empress
Josephine, and another of Spring. In
the closets of this chamber were mine
hostess's cloak, best bonnet and go-to-
meeting apparel." What odors of lavender
and sweet clover probably came from that
closet ! Cannot each reader who has
been a " summer boarder " smell them?

THE "OAKLANDS."

where they supped and passed the night.
Hawthorne was evidently impressed with
the homely furnishings of the country
inn. " My own chamber, apparently the
best in the house, had its walls ornamented
with a small, gilt-framed, foot-square
looking-glass, with a hair brush hanging
beneath it ; a record of the deaths of the

To describe ade-
quately each city and
town along the Ken-
nebec, with its his-
tory, industry and
points of interest,
would require more
space than can be
allotted to a maga-
zine article. The
river is rich in his-
toric lore. At its
mouth Champlain
and De Monts
planted the cross and
banner of the Fleur-
de-lis, in May, 1605,
and took possession
in the name of the king of France.
The French had broken ground for
colonization at Passamaquoddy in the
fall of 1604. Englishmen followed at
the mouth of the Kennebec in 1607.
Neither colony was successful, but the
two began the history of New France
and New England, and the territory of

future Maine became the theatre of a series of conflicts which ended only when New France was expunged from the map of America by the fall of Quebec in 1759. Ancient Acadia passed nine times between

France and England in the period of one hundred and twenty-seven years. In this eventful conquest, the issue of which left North America to the English people, the Indians were important participants, and the valley of the Kennebec was the scene of many bloody affrays.

The Archangel, Captain George Weymouth's ship, cast anchor in the river opposite the site of Bath, early in June, 1605. She had been fitted out that spring by the Earl of Southampton, Lord Arundel and others, under the patronage of the crown, and sent to watch the French, rumors of their activity in the new country having reached England. The ship had cruised along the coast from Cape Cod to the Penobscot and back to Boothbay Harbor, where on June 3, off Damariscove Island, five Indian chiefs had been kidnapped. Captain Weymouth had found the " back way " (Sasanoa River) into the Kennebec, and through its troubled waters had towed his vessel. Weymouth and seventeen men rowed up the Kennebec in a boat to the mouth of the Androscoggin, and there planted a cross. Then, on June 16, 1605, Weymouth set sail for England, taking along the Indian captives, in spite of the entreaties of their people, who had followed him to the Kennebec in their canoes.

Weymouth's stories excited such interest in England that a company was formed to settle the country around the Sagadahock, as the Kennebec was then known by the English. The organization was called the Plymouth Company. James I. granted it all the territory between the 35th and 45th degrees of north latitude. Lord Popham and Sir Ferdinando Gorges were prominent members of the company. They fitted out a ship; and two of Weymouth's captives, Dehamaida and Assecomet, were taken along as guides. The ship sailed from Bristol in 1606, and was captured by the Spanish.

The next year two vessels were fitted out to go to the Sagadahock. One was *The Gift of God,* commanded by George Popham, a brother of Lord Popham; the other was *The Mary and John,* commanded by Raleigh Gilbert, a nephew of Popham. They took out one hundred and twenty " planters " and farming tools. The vessels sailed from Plymouth, May 31, 1607. They sighted Monhegan, July 31, and cruised in shore among the islands in and near Boothbay Harbor, anchoring at the mouth of the Kennebec, August 15. Wednesday, September 23, Captain Gilbert and nineteen men embarked in a shallop from the new fort at the mouth of the river, to " goe for the head of the river." William Strackey, the historian of the voyage, wrote that

THE LOCK IN THE DAM AT AUGUSTA.

" theye sailed all this daye and the 24th the like, until six of the clock in the afternoon, when they landed on the river side, where they found a champion land (camping ground), and very fertile, where they remayned all that night; in the morning they departed thence and sayled up the river and came to a flat low island, where ys a great cataract or downfall of water, which runneth by both sides of this island very shoald and swift. . . . They haled their boat with a strong rope through this downfall perforce, and when near a league further up, and here they lay all night; and in the first of the night there called certain savages on the further side of the river unto them in broken English." In the morning a sagamore came across in a canoe, and " called his name Sebenoa, and told us how he was lord of the river Sagadahock." " They entertained him friendly," the historian goes on; but in spite of this it seems that there was some misunderstanding on account of both sides wanting hostages. Captain Gilbert made a display of arms, and that quieted the savages. The party went up the river a few miles further the next day, and inland to a village where they traded with the natives. Then they went back to where they had spent the first night; and " here they sett up a crosse and then returned homeward."

This is the earliest record of a visit of white men above the region of Merrymeeting Bay. It was apparently copied with but few changes from Captain Gilbert's log book made by the scribe of the Popham colony, who was probably one of the party. Some historians have claimed that this trip was up the Androscoggin River, but this theory has been discredited. The plain where the village of Randolph now stands, opposite Gardiner, has been fixed upon as a camping ground most probably selected by the party on its second night. The " flatt lowe island in the midst of a great downfall of water" describes exactly the Kennebec at the place where the Augusta dam now stands, before the peculiar features of the spot were obliterated by the building of the dam. The camping place above was probably Gilley's Point, where many Indian relics have been found. The Indian

village was either in the present town of Sidney or Vassalboro.[*]

The story of Captain Popham's death, of the sickness that thinned the ranks of the colonists, and the departure of the survivors for England in the spring, is one of the familiar narratives of America's early history. Three years after the Popham colonists sailed dejectedly out of the river, Father Pierre Biard, a missionary of the Society of Jesus, visited the Kennebec with an expedition under De Biancourt, on a cruise from the eastward along the coast to the western boundary of Acadia, in quest of food for the French colony at Port Royal (now Annapolis, N. S.), founded by De Monts in 1604. He gives in his narrative of this trip a glimpse of scenes on the lower Kennebec two hundred and eighty-three years ago. The vessel came cautiously in by Seguin, and the party landed to inspect the abandoned fort of the English. They were delayed there three days by adverse winds; so, abandoning the purpose of sailing further westward, Biancourt went up the river. After sailing about nine miles they met a party of Indians, twenty-four warriors, in six canoes. " They went through a thousand antics before coming up to us," wrote Father Biard. " You would have likened them to a flock of birds which wishes to enter a hemp field, but fears the scarecrow." " All that night," the good father wrote, " there was nothing but haranguing, singing and dancing " among the Indians who were encamped on the opposite side of the river from where the ship cast anchor, probably on the Woolwich or Arrowsic shore, opposite Bath. " But since we presumed that probably their songs and dances were invocations to the devil," continues the priest, " and in order to thwart this accursed tyrant, I made our people sing a few church hymns, such as *Salve Regina* and *Ave Maria Stella* and others ; but being once in train and getting to the end of their spiritual songs, they fell to singing such others as they knew," and when these gave out they took to mimicking the dancing and singing of the Indians.[†]

* Blake's History of Kennebec County.

† " Pioneers of France in the New World," by Francis Parkman.

On the morning after the singing and dancing the Indians approached the ship, and made a bargain to conduct De Biancourt to a chief who had corn to trade. They guided him and a crew in a boat out of the Kennebec into the narrow river through which Weymouth had come from Boothbay Harbor five years before. When they came to the Hell Gates, the white men were afraid. Biard wrote: "We thought we should hardly ever escape alive; in fact in two places some of our people cried out piteously that we were all lost; but praise to God they cried too soon."

The party found the chief, whose name was Meteourmite; and while De Biancourt parleyed with him Father Biard said mass in a thicket, and later blessed the children of the savages. An Indian who had been brought from the St. John River by the party acted as interpreter. This was the first Catholic service in Maine, and so far as is known in New England. The spot where stood the rude altar which Father Biard reared is not known, but it was on one of the islands near the Sheepscot River.

The next well-identified visitor to the Kennebec was Captain John Smith, in 1614. He was cruising along the coast trading and fishing.

It was through the devious waterways that lie to the eastward of the lower Kennebec, where the rushing tides so frightened the French, that Samoset, the Indian whose "Welcome, Englishmen," spoken to the Pilgrim Fathers at Plymouth, has left his one of the dearest memories of his vanished people, plied the paddle in his birch canoe. He was a Wawenoc, it is thought, and is said to have been carried to England as a captive. He found his way back to his own woods and streams, as did likewise all but one of Weymouth's captives; and in 1623, two years after his famous greeting to the men of Plymouth, he was found at home, as much as wandering Indians can be, at Southport (ancient Cape Newagen), by Captain Christopher Leverett, an Englishman. Samoset showed such a liking for Leverett that he offered his newborn son as a perpetual brother in friendship to the Englishman. The last known of this noble savage is when he joined a brother chief in deeding to John Brown of New Harbor, afterward of the Kennebec, a tract of land at Pemaquid, July 25, 1625.

The Indians seem never to have given a name to the whole of a river. The portion of the Kennebec below Merrymeeting Bay at the confluence of the Androscoggin was known to the Indians as Sagadehoc. The people in that country were Wawenocs, and their chief was Sasanoa, whose name was given to the narrow river of troubled waters through which excursion steamers now pass daily in summer loaded with people who recite the legends of the place, some of them astonishingly transposed, as the boats pass through the boiling gates and across placid coves and bays.

To Champlain belongs the credit of having named the Kennebec. When he visited it with De Monts in 1605, he explored the river to the mouth of the Androscoggin. His quick ear caught from the Indians a word which he reduced to Quinibequi (or *Kinibeki*), which it seems the savages associated with the monsters they believed caused the waters in the Hell Gates to boil. The word comes from the Algonquin tongue, Kinaibik, meaning serpent.

After the closely grouped visits of the earliest voyagers to the Kennebec but little is heard of explorations there for a decade or more, when Edward Winslow and a few others from the colony at Plymouth went to the river to trade with the Indians. In 1628 they built a trading post at Cushnoc (Augusta), and obtained a deed from their English patrons to four hundred and fifty square miles of land in the Kennebec valley. Captain Charles E. Nash, a Kennebecker, writes of the Cushnoc trading house: "The illustrious men who founded the Plymouth colony came to this place every year for about a third of a century, bringing in their shallops a variety of commodities for the Indian market, and enjoying great profit so long as the supply of beaver skins continued good. Among these traders we discerned the conspicuous presence of Edward Winslow, the colony's resolute business leader. . . . Governor Bradford is recorded to have been on the river in 1634; and so are John Alden and John Howland. Captain Miles Standish was often here. . . . Governor Prince was also one of those early Kennebeckers; he was commissioned by the colony in 1654 to organize a local government for the pioneers whom the industries of fishing and trading had drawn to the shores of ancient Sagadahoc and Merrymeeting Bay."

The Pilgrims traded in friendship with the Indians for thirty-four years; but in that time the seeds of discord had been blown into the land on winds that favored adventurers, and had taken root. White settlers and traders began to push the savages to the wall; and before long a bloody warfare was begun. One conflict led to another. The French sent priests into the country, and the Indians affiliated with them. England sought to break this bond, and the colony in Massachusetts, growing yearly more powerful, at last offered large sums for the scalps of Indians. Through decades blood flowed along the Kennebec, until at last the original lords of the soil were reduced to a paltry handful of beggars, whose only friends were the Jesuits of Canada.

It was but natural that the persecuted savages should have looked to the black-robed fathers for comfort; for the first white man who had come among them to minister to their needs was a priest of the Jesuit order, Father Gabriel Druillettes, who came from Canada to the Kennebec in 1646. He was the first white man to enter the Kennebec valley from Canada. He reached the Cushnoc trading post in September of the year named, and was kindly received by John Winslow, with whom he tarried as a guest a few days. The father made a trip in a canoe along the coast of Castine, and returning established a mission house at Gilley's Point, a league above Cushnoc. Savages built him a chapel of planks, his record says, which he named "The Mission of the Assumption on the Kennebec." The story of the mission work of this priest is one of noble sacrifice. He was the physician of the sick, the friend of the outcast, the defender of the weak. The Indians loved and revered him, and he gave his whole strength to bettering their con-

dition. He made two journeys to Massachusetts to implore the colony to protect the Kennebec Indians from the incursions of the Mohawks and Iroquois from New York. Though these efforts failed, his work for the Indians redounded to his glory. He was recalled to Canada April 8, 1652, and his mission was abandoned.[*]

It was in time of war between France and England over the boundary of Acadia that a successor to Father Druillettes was sent to the Kennebec, in the person of Father Sebastian Rale (also spelled Rasle and Rallé). He was sent for reasons more political than religious; and the story of his patient labors and his massacre at Norridgewock, August 22, 1724, by a party of two hundred and eight men sent out by the colony of Massachusetts, headed by Captain John Harmon, is one of the conspicuous incidents in the history of New England. A price of $1,000 was paid by the colonial government for the scalp of Father Rale.

Trading on the Kennebec, which had been so profitable for the Plymouth settlers, declined to such an extent that in 1652 the right to trade on the river was leased for £50 a year, and in 1655 the lease was renewed for seven years at £35 a year. October 27, 1661, the patent was sold for £400 to Antipas Boyes, Edward Tyng, Thomas Brattle and John Winslow. From 1661 to 1749 no special efforts were made to settle lands on the Kennebec. In the latter year the heirs of the four purchasers of the patent claimed the Kennebec valley through the deed of 1661. A good part of their claim was legally confirmed. It was through the agency of the Plymouth Company that the valley was finally settled. The company built a fort about a mile above old Fort Richmond, which stood opposite the present site of Richmond village, and called it Fort Shirley, after Governor Shirley. They also built a fort on the site of the Cushnoc trading house at Augusta, which they called Fort Western.

---

[*] Father Druillettes was born in France in 1593. After his retirement from the Kennebec he labored among Canadian Indians, ascending the Saguenay in 1666 in an attempt to reach Hudson's Bay. He went west later in that year with the celebrated Marquette, and labored at Sault Ste. Marie until 1679, when he returned to Quebec and there died on April 8, 1681.

It stood near the spot where the passenger bridge over the river touches the east shore. Fort Shirley stood on what is now Dresden Neck. Here came a few German and French Huguenot families and formed a colony called Frankfort, afterward included in Pownalborough. Their descendants are still found in the old town of Dresden.

But the glory of the Kennebec is not in its past. Men came there seeking fortune, delved, and passed away. They were of hardy stock, and their children thrived in the land which their fathers had acquired. With the legacy of good blood and a promising country to live in, each generation broadened, until to-day the sons of the Kennebec, through their thrift in developing what was handed down to them, are possessed of a land which, though ice and lumber take the place of the Biblical milk and honey, is as smiling and prosperous a corner as can be found in the length and breadth of the land.

Trawling with Gloucester Fishermen (1894)

TRAWLING WITH GLOUCESTER FISHERMEN.

BY JOHN Z. ROGERS.

THE seventy-ton schooner *Annie T.*, Captain Tanner, was lying at her moorings. Mainsail, foresail and gaff-topsail were hoisted, and her jib ready to hoist as soon as the mooring was dropped. A young fisherman rowed me alongside, and in a moment I was on deck. I had known in a general way, from long residence on the coast, that there is no sea-fish in whose capture so many different methods are employed as the staple cod.

In Ipswich Bay, Mass., and in other places, cod, in the winter time, are caught in large grill nets made of coarse twine, and from twelve to thirty feet wide and often six hundred feet long; whilst on the Grand Banks hand-lines are used almost invariably, although during some portions of the year trawls are set. But trawling is by far the most popular method, and trawls are used by a great majority of the Gloucester fishermen, and by most of the schooners along the entire Massachusetts, New Hampshire and Maine coasts. Probably at least three-quarters of all the cod caught are taken by the trawls.

We were off trawling, and were soon gliding out of the harbor under all sail, bound for Richmond's Island for the purpose of buying bait. We reached the island at eleven o'clock, and dropped the anchor about a quarter of a mile from shore, close to the weir— a kind of circular fish-trap made by driving stakes into the bottom close together and weaving pieces of brush in and out between them to close up the interstices. The fish enter the weir through an opening at one end or side, and, once in, swim round and round, often passing close by the entrance, but not knowing enough to make their escape. One of the dories which were lying on deck, one within another, like a nest, was lowered over the side, and the captain and two of the crew got in and rowed to the cottage of the owner of the weir. He was at home, and a trade was soon made, the captain buying thirty bushels of bait at forty cents a bushel. The owner, taking two men with him in his boat, rowed to the weir, and, pulling up a large net which lay on the bottom, brought to the surface a great quantity of wriggling, flopping, half-sized herring, with a few small mackerel mixed in with them. The thirty bushels were taken out in dip nets and put into the boat, and then transferred to the schooner's dory, which was waiting outside the weir.

The herring were dipped into bushel baskets on reaching the schooner, then a ton of ice from the hold was chopped up fine and the herring were packed in it—a bushel of ice to a bushel of fish —and stowed below. This work had hardly been completed when the loud ringing of the cook's bell in the forecastle summoned all hands to dinner, and a rush was made for the draw-buckets, which were thrown over the side and filled with water. The washing-up process completed, twelve hungry

475

men gathered about the long, narrow table between the lockers and soon disposed of the fried beefsteak, potatoes, tea and coffee, hot biscuit and bread pudding which the cook had provided.

After dinner the anchor was heaved up and the course shaped south by east for Jeffrey's Banks, twenty-two miles away. The wind having shifted to the north and freshened, the captain concluded there would be sufficient time to set the trawls that night, and he gave orders at about two o'clock to bait up. The herring were passed up on deck, a bushel was given to each man, and all hands were soon busily at work. The *Annie T.* had five dories aboard, two men going in each boat, according to the custom of larger schooners. By this method the trawls could be set and hauled more quickly and in rougher weather than if but one man went in a dory, although many vessels, especially the smaller ones, carry a dory for each man.

The trawls were of cod-line, and tied to them at distances of six feet were smaller lines three feet in length, with a hook attached to the end. Each dory had six trawls, each one eighteen hundred feet long. The trawls were neatly coiled in tubs made by sawing flour barrels in two, and as fast as they were baited with pieces of herring they were carefully coiled into another tub, that they might run out quickly without snarling when being set.

The last trawl was finished just before supper, at five o'clock. After supper the men enjoyed a half-hour smoke, then preparations were made to set the gear, as the trawls are called. The schooner got well to windward of the place where the set was to be made, and the first dory was lowered by a block and tackle. One of the men jumped into it, and his partner handed him the tubs of gear and then jumped in himself. The dory was made fast to the schooner by her painter as she drifted astern, and the other dories were put over in the same manner. When all the dories were disposed of the first one was cast off. One of the men rowed the boat before the wind while the other ran out the gear. First he threw over a keg for a buoy, which could be seen from some distance. Fastened to the buoy-line at some sixty fathoms, or three hundred and sixty feet from the keg, was

the trawl with a small anchor attached to sink it to bottom. When this was dropped overboard the trawl was rapidly run out, and as fast as the end of one was reached it was tied to the next one, thus making a line of trawl ten thousand eight hundred feet long with eighteen hundred hooks attached. After the schooner had sailed on a straight course a few hundred yards, the captain cast off the second dory, then along a little farther the third one, and so on till the five boats were all setting gear in parallel lines to each other. When all set this gear practically represented a fishing-line over *ten miles* long with *nine thousand hooks* tied to it.

After the last dory had been cast loose the captain jogged about for half an hour, first on one tack, then on the other, always keeping near the boats to render assistance if needed. As dory after dory finished setting it was picked up and taken aboard by the schooner. When all were aboard the schooner beat back to the windward end of the first trawl and anchored a short distance from the buoy. The baiting tubs were washed out and packed away, the decks were deluged with water and scrubbed down, the vessel put to rights generally, and then the men sat about on deck for an hour, smoking, telling stories and watching and commenting on the passing vessels. At eight the white signal light was set on the fore peak halliards, and the watch was set for the night.

Most of the men turned in soon after the watch was set, as they had a hard morning's work before them, but a few quaint characters gathered in the cabin for a chat and a smoke. There was old Uncle Joe Bunker, who had followed the sea "man an' boy, nigh onter forty year;" Clem Reed, who was credited with consuming more tobacco than food, and Gus Baker, the wag of the crew. The conversation drifted from one subject to another, and Uncle Joe told of a place "down thar east'ard," which was so healthy that, after making a grave-yard and waiting in vain twenty years for the first occupant, the people were obliged to kill the oldest man in town (age one hundred and nineteen) to start it in good running order. Then Clem partially cleared his mouth and spun as follows:

"That was clost to ther place where Bug Christie an' some of ther boys what went in ther ole *Betsey* got their chowder 'bout five years back. They laid off shore 'bout a mile in a dead calm, an' Bug Christie, Si Jenkins an' Ben Field took a dory an' went ashore. A feller they met in a hay field told 'em they could get plenty er 'stuff' back a ways, an' off they started an' got two quarts. Well, when they got back to ther dory 'twas past dinner time an' they was powerful hungry. So Bug went up to a house clost by an' asked an ole lady what come to ther door to make 'em a clam chowder. Well, she'd had a chowder fer dinner, an' it was all eat up. 'Ye've got ther necks, ain't yer?' said Bug. 'Yes,' says she. 'Well,' says he, 'jes' make us one out'n ther necks.' Well Si was a-feelin' pretty stiff, he was far gone, an' Bug an' Ben had to 'mos carry him up to ther house, but ther ole lady didn't see 'em, an' didn't know how many ther was. She passed ther chowder in through ther door, but Si was fast asleep an' didn't eat none, but Bug an' Ben eat it all up clean, they was so hungry. An' when they got through what did they do but clear off ther table an' put pore Si on it, stretched out on his back. Then they crossed his hands on his chest, put a couple of cents on his eyes an' covered him up with ther table-cloth, an' sneaked out ther back door, after putting a dollar between Si's fingers ter pay fer ther chowder. When they got aboard they told us fellers Si had fell overboard an' got drownded. Long 'bout sun-set two men put him aboard on a dory an' he looked pretty sheepish, now I tell yer. Ther story never leaked out fer a long time, an' next Summer when we was down there ag'in, a man told us that when ther ole lady see Si a-lyin' on ther table she had nine fits one right after ther other."

It seemed I had hardly turned in to the vacant bunk in the cabin when I was awakened by the ringing of the cook's bell for breakfast. The breakfast was earlier than usual (five o'clock), as the men had a busy day before them, for the trawls were to be hauled in the morning and, if there was an opportunity, set again in the afternoon.

All the dories were made fast astern and left at the head of their respective trawls as the schooner sailed along. One of the men in each dory, after pulling up the anchor, put the trawl in the roller—a grooved wooden wheel eight inches in diameter. This was fastened to one side of the dory. The trawl was hauled in hand over hand, the heavy strain necessarily working the dory slowly along. The fish were taken off as fast as they appeared. A gaff—a stick about the size and length of a broom-handle with a large, sharp hook attached—lay near at hand, and was frequently used in landing a fish over the side. Occasionally a fish would free itself from the trawl hook as it reached the surface, but the fisherman, with remarkable dexterity, would grab the gaff, and hook the victim before it could swim out of reach. What would be on the next hook was always an interesting uncertainty, for it seemed that all kinds of fish were represented. Cod and haddock were, of course, numerous, but hake and pollock struggled on many a hook. Besides these, there was the brim, a small, red fish, which is excellent fried; the cat fish, also a good pan fish; the cusk, which is best baked; the whiting, the eel, the repulsive-looking skate, the monk, of which it can almost be said that his mouth is bigger than himself, and last, but not least, that ubiquitous fish, the curse of amateur harbor fishers, the much-abused sculpin. Nor were fish alone caught on the hooks, for stones were frequently pulled up, and one dory brought in a lobster, which had been hooked by his tail. Some of the captives showed where large chunks had been bitten out of them by larger fish, and sometimes, when a hook appeared above water, there would be nothing on it but a fish head. This was certainly a case of one fish taking a mean advantage of another.

While one fisherman attended to line and hooks, his comrade was busy amidships, pitchfork in hand, throwing the fish well into the stern, thus putting the boat in good trim and rendering the hauling more easy. When half the gear was hauled, the work was evenly divided by the men changing places.

On board the schooner, meanwhile, the cook was making pens for the fish by placing boards, about two feet wide, alongside the rail. There were ten of these, capable of holding about fifteen hundred-weight apiece.

At about ten o'clock the trawls were all hauled, and the dories were taken aboard again. The vessel sailed up to each one in turn and it was made fast alongside, while the fish were pitched by forks into a pen. As soon as unloaded the dory was hoisted aboard.

Dressing the fish was at once commenced and it was a lively scene. The crew were divided into two gangs, one chopping ice and stowing the dressed fish away below, well packed in it, while the other cleaned the fish. The livers, which are marketable on account of their oil, were saved and put into a hogshead. At eleven work was briefly suspended for an early dinner. At two o'clock the fish were all dressed and stowed below, and the men set to work baiting up again. This was difficult, as the head tide had snarled the trawls badly, many of them appearing to the novice to be in a hopeless tangle. There were many pieces of untouched old bait to be removed, and new hooks had to be put on in place of a number which had been carried away by big fish, or lost by fouling rocks and ledges.

The captain intended to set again after supper, but while the deck was being scrubbed down a fresh breeze sprang up from the southwest and prevented it. All hands were keen for the supper of fried haddock, baked beans, and the usual accessories, and all were tired enough to turn in when the watch was set.

The next morning there was no wind and, as the water was as smooth as the proverbial glass, the men were obliged to row to and from the schooner in setting their gear. They hauled in the afternoon, set again at night, and hauled for the third and last time the next morning.

In the middle of the afternoon all the fish were below, everything was trim and clean on deck, and we were bound for market with a fair wind. At seven o'clock the next morning (Friday) we were tied up at T wharf, Boston, and my cruise on the *Annie T.* was a thing of the past.

The captain made a good bargain for the fare at the following prices : steak fish, three dollars a hundred-weight ; market fish and haddock, two, and scrod one. The sale of the livers realized twelve dollars.

Steak fish are cod measuring twenty-two inches or more in length ; market fish are those measuring less, but weighing three pounds or more, and scrod are those weighing under the three pounds.

When all the fish had been passed on to the wharf and weighed, the result of the trip was as follows : thirteen thousand five hundred-weight of steak cod, five thousand-weight of market fish and haddock, and eighteen hundred-weight of scrod.

From the gross receipts the vessel took one-fifth as her share, the "grub bill " and cost of bait and ice was then deducted, and the balance was equally divided among the crew, making thirty-one dollars and fifteen cents to each man.

Most of the Maine vessels fit out as did the *Annie T.*, at the fifths, the men finding their gear, dories, etc., while many vessels and the majority of the Gloucester schooners fit at the halves. By this method the vessel owners furnish everything—food, bait, ice, gear and dories, and the gross receipts are equally divided between the vessel and crew.

It is the custom for the men to throw their fish together, but on some vessels, especially the hand liners that fish on the Grand Banks, the number of fish that each man catches is recorded by the captain, an average struck as to weight, and he is paid *pro rata.* Hence the origin of the expression "Going on his own hook."

The reader must not form too high an opinion of the lucrativeness of the fisherman's occupation, for the *Annie T.'s* trip was much better than the average. She had good weather, a quick trip, a large catch, and, reaching market on a Friday, obtained good prices.

Oftentimes a vessel will be out for a week, but will be unable to make a set on account of rough weather. The bait will spoil, the ice melt and her crew will return without having made a cent and in debt for what they have eaten. From the profits the cost of gear must be deducted, and this is not inconsiderable, as frequently a whole trawl is lost by the buoy lines parting in a storm, and the cost of hooks alone for a year's fishing is not a small item.

Then there is one great consideration : the hazardousness of the occupation, the vast number of lives lost each year, the wives left desolate and little children fatherless. In the year 1879, of the men who sailed from Gloucester alone, two hundred and fifty were never again heard from, and their remains, with those of thousands of other brave fellows, are strewn along our coast from Georges to the Grand Banks.

Seashore Lake and Mountain Resorts of

EASTERN & NORTHERN NEW ENGLAND and the MARITIME PROVINCES

Reached by the BOSTON AND MAINE RAILROAD

Illustrated descriptive pamphlets (containing complete maps) have been issued under the following titles, and will be mailed upon receipt of 2¢ in stamps for each book

ALL ALONG SHORE · AMONG THE MOUNTAINS
LAKES AND STREAMS · FISHING AND HUNTING
MERRIMACK VALLEY · LAKE SUNAPEE
SOUTHEAST NEW HAMPSHIRE
SOUTHWEST NEW HAMPSHIRE
THE HOOSAC COUNTRY AND DEERFIELD VALLEY
VALLEY OF THE CONNECTICUT
AND NORTHERN VERMONT
CENTRAL MASSACHUSETTS
THE MONADNOCK REGION
LAKE MEMPHREMAGOG

PORTFOLIOS

MOUNTAINS OF NEW ENGLAND
SEASHORE OF NEW ENGLAND
RIVERS OF NEW ENGLAND
LAKES OF NEW ENGLAND
PICTURESQUE NEW ENGLAND
HISTORIC — MISCELLANEOUS
THE CHARLES RIVER TO THE HUDSON
Will be sent upon receipt of 6 cents for each book

SUMMER TOURIST BOOK

Giving list of Tours and Rates,
Hotel and Boarding House list,
and other valuable information, free

COLORED BIRD'S EYE VIEW FROM MT. WASHINGTON
COLORED BIRD'S EYE VIEW OF LAKE WINNIPESAUKEE
Sent on receipt of 6¢ for each

For all Publications apply to Passenger Department, B. & M. R. R. Boston, Mass.
D. J. FLANDERS, GEN'L PASS'R & TICKET AGENT.